Financial Management

Core Concepts

Financial Management

Core Concepts

Raymond M. Brooks

Second Edition

PEARSON

Boston Columbus Indianapolis New York San Francisco Upper Saddle River
Amsterdam Cape Town Dubai London Madrid Milan Munich Paris Montréal Toronto
Delhi Mexico City São Paulo Sydney Hong Kong Seoul Singapore Taipei Tokyo

The Prentice Hall Series in Finance

Adelman/Marks
Entrepreneurial Finance

Andersen
Global Derivatives: A Strategic Risk Management Perspective

Bekaert/Hodrick
International Financial Management

Berk/DeMarzo
*Corporate Finance**

Berk/DeMarzo
*Corporate Finance: The Core**

Berk/DeMarzo/Harford
*Fundamentals of Corporate Finance**

Boakes
Reading and Understanding the Financial Times

Brooks
*Financial Management: Core Concepts**

Copeland/Weston/Shastri
Financial Theory and Corporate Policy

Dorfman/Cather
Introduction to Risk Management and Insurance

Eiteman/Stonehill/Moffett
Multinational Business Finance

Fabozzi
Bond Markets: Analysis and Strategies

Fabozzi/Modigliani
Capital Markets: Institutions and Instruments

Fabozzi/Modigliani/Jones/Ferri
Foundations of Financial Markets and Institutions

Finkler
Financial Management for Public, Health, and Not-for-Profit Organizations

Frasca
Personal Finance

Gitman/Joehnk/Smart
*Fundamentals of Investing**

Gitman/Zutter
*Principles of Managerial Finance**

Gitman/Zutter
*Principles of Managerial Finance—Brief Edition**

Goldsmith
Consumer Economics: Issues and Behaviors

Haugen
The Inefficient Stock Market: What Pays Off and Why

Haugen
The New Finance: Overreaction, Complexity, and Uniqueness

Holden
Excel Modeling in Corporate Finance

Holden
Excel Modeling in Investments

Hughes/MacDonald
International Banking: Text and Cases

Hull
Fundamentals of Futures and Options Markets

Hull
Options, Futures, and Other Derivatives

Hull
Risk Management and Financial Institutions

Keown
*Personal Finance: Turning Money into Wealth**

Keown/Martin/Petty
*Foundations of Finance: The Logic and Practice of Financial Management**

Kim/Nofsinger
Corporate Governance

Madura
*Personal Finance**

Marthinsen
Risk Takers: Uses and Abuses of Financial Derivatives

McDonald
Derivatives Markets

McDonald
Fundamentals of Derivatives Markets

Mishkin/Eakins
Financial Markets and Institutions

Moffett/Stonehill/Eiteman
Fundamentals of Multinational Finance

Nofsinger
Psychology of Investing

Ormiston/Fraser
Understanding Financial Statements

Pennacchi
Theory of Asset Pricing

Rejda
Principles of Risk Management and Insurance

Seiler
Performing Financial Studies: A Methodological Cookbook

Shapiro
Capital Budgeting and Investment Analysis

Sharpe/Alexander/Bailey
Investments

Solnik/McLeavey
Global Investments

Stretcher/Michael
Cases in Financial Management

Titman/Keown/Martin
*Financial Management: Principles and Applications**

Titman/Martin
Valuation: The Art and Science of Corporate Investment Decisions

Van Horne
Financial Management and Policy

Van Horne/Wachowicz
Fundamentals of Financial Management

Weston/Mitchel/Mulherin
Takeovers, Restructuring, and Corporate Governance

To Mom and Dad, Greta, Michael, and Tyler

Thanks for giving me such a rich and wonderful life.

Editorial Director: Sally Yagan
Editor-in-Chief: Donna Battista
Acquisitions Editor: Tessa O'Brien
Editorial Project Manager: Jill Kolongowski
Editorial Assistant: Elissa Senra-Sargent
Director of Marketing: Maggie Moylan
Marketing Assistant: Ian Gold
Senior Managing Editor: Nancy H. Fenton
Senior Production Project Manager: Meredith Gertz
Associate Production Project Manager: Alison Eusden
Permissions Project Supervisor: Estelle Simpson
Permissions Editor: Tracy Metivier
Art Director: Jonathan Boylan
Cover Designer: Gretchen Irmiger
Cover Images: Dreamstime/Alexey Bragin/Shutterstock
Image Manager/Image Asset Services: Rachel Youdelman
Photo Research: Integra
Senior Manufacturing Buyer: Carol Melville
Director of Media: Susan Schoenberg
MyFinanceLab Content Lead: Miguel Leonarte
Media Producer: Melissa Honig
Production Coordination, Composition, and Art Creation:
Cenveo Publisher Services/Nesbitt Graphics, Inc.

Credits and acknowledgments borrowed from other sources and reproduced, with permission, in this textbook appear on the appropriate page within the text or on p. 617.

Library of Congress Cataloging-in-Publication Data
Brooks, Raymond
Financial management : core concepts / Raymond M. Brooks. — 2nd ed.
p. cm. — (The Prentice Hall series in finance)
Includes index.
ISBN 978-0-13-267103-3
1. Business enterprises—Finance. 2. Corporations—Finance. I. Title.
HG4026.B686 2013
658.15–dc23
2011043153

10 9 8 7 6 5 4 3 2 1

PEARSON

www.pearsonhighered.com

ISBN-10: 0-13-267197-2
ISBN-13: 978-0-13-267197-2

About the Author

RAYMOND BROOKS is a Professor of Finance at Oregon State University. He has taught a variety of finance courses, including introduction to financial management, investments, advanced corporate finance, financial institutions, and risk management. Previously, he taught at Washington University in St. Louis, University of Missouri, and University of Southern Illinois, Edwardsville. Professor Brooks has authored a variety of articles on topics from dividends to when-issued trading. He has twice won best papers awards at financial conferences.

Professor Brooks was born in Portland, Oregon, is married, and has two sons. He is a former all-conference athlete for Oregon State and continues to enjoy swimming, biking, music, and watching OSU athletic teams.

The Student Front and Center

Designed for the nonfinance major, ***Financial Management: Core Concepts*** structures a student-centric learning environment built around three major competencies:

- Using tools
- Making connections
- Studying for success

Using the Power Tools of Finance

EXAMPLE 4.1 **Parent scholarships (future value of an annuity)**

Problem Kitty and Red put $1,500 into a college fund every year for their son, Eric, on his birthday, with the first deposit one year from his birth (at his very first birthday). The college fund has a guaranteed annual growth or interest rate of 7%. At his eighteenth birthday, they will pay the last $1,500 into the fund. How much will be in the college fund for Eric immediately following this last payment?

Solution For this problem, we are trying to determine the future value at the end of the eighteen annual payments of $1,500. Because the payments are the same amount each period at the end of a regular interval (one year apart), we are dealing with an ordinary annuity problem. The known variables are $r = 7\%$, $n = 18$, and $PMT = \$1{,}500$. We can solve for FV in three different ways.

METHOD 1 **Using the equation**

First, calculate the FVIFA value at $n = 18$ and $r = 7\%$:

$$FVIFA = \frac{(1 + r)^n - 1}{r}$$

$$= \frac{(1 + 0.07)^{18} - 1}{0.07} = \frac{(3.3799) - 1}{0.07} = \mathbf{33.9990}$$

Early TVM Tools. The author identifies the key concepts of finance as "tools." Students first need to learn how to use these tools of finance before they can apply them to larger problems. That's why the author drills down to basics quickly by developing time value of money (TVM) concepts and interest rates early in the course.

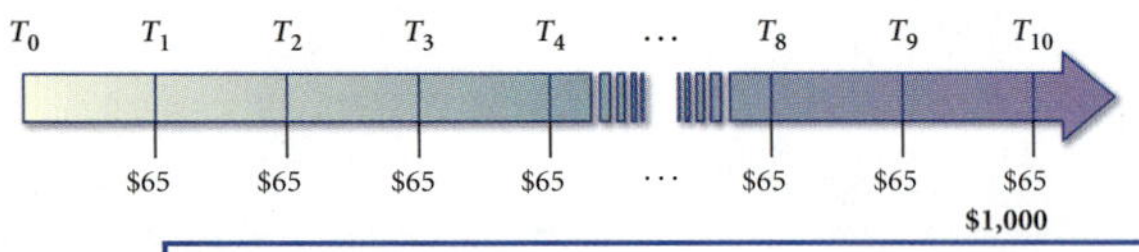

FIGURE 6.3 Future cash flow of a Merrill Lynch bond.

We can set out the future cash flow as Figure 6.3 shows. Note that in the time line, T_0 represents the original issue date of July 15, 2008, and T_1 is the first annual coupon payment date of July 15, 2009. The annual payments continue for ten years, with T_{10} being the last payment on July 15, 2018. This point is a moment of recognition in which we can apply previously learned concepts: the coupon pay-

Later Application and Visual Links. Students soon begin to see just how powerful these tools are. They learn to forge links between basic principles and new applications. A tool icon alerts students to the introduction of a new tool and when a tool can be applied in a new situation.

Problem Solving: Technology Tools and the Three-Methods Approach

The author helps students develop their skills in problem solving by using a three-pronged approach that shows there are several paths to the same destination.

EXAMPLE 3.3 **Saving for retirement (present value)**

Problem Your retirement goal is $2,000,000. The bank is offering you a certificate of deposit that is good for forty years at 6.0%. What initial deposit do you need to make today to reach your $2,000,000 goal at the end of forty years?

Solution The following time line illustrates the problem.

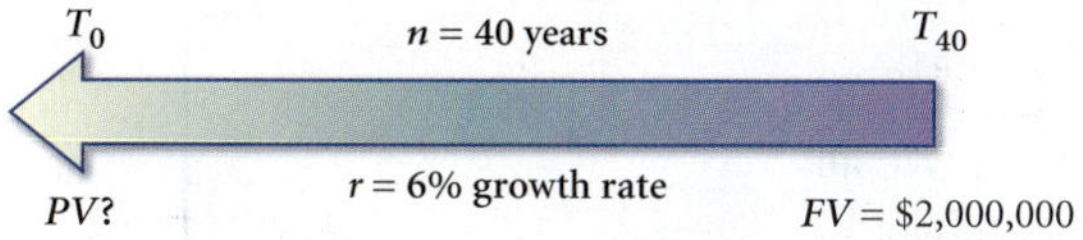

We designate today as T_0 and our future date forty years later as T_{40}.

Equation. He presents the equation and solves the problem mathematically.

METHOD 1 **Using the equation**

$$PV = \$2,000,000 \times \frac{1}{1.06^{40}} = \$2,000,000 \times 0.0972 = \mathbf{\$194,444.38}$$

Calculator. He then solves the problem using a calculator, explaining the key strokes. The answer is displayed in red on the appropriate calculator key.

METHOD 2 **Using the TVM keys**

Input	40	6.0	?	0	2,000,000
Key	N	I/Y	PV	PMT	FV
CPT			−194,444.38		

Spreadsheet. For some examples, an Excel® solution is added. The author explains the basic spreadsheet variables and how to set up the application.

METHOD 3 **Using a spreadsheet**

B6 | *fx* | =PV(B1,B2,B3,B4,B5)

Use the present value function to find the amount of dollars you need to invest today to reach $2,000,000 in 40 years.

	A	B	C	D	E
1	Rate	0.06			
2	Nper	40			
3	Pmt	0			
4	Fv	$2,000,000.00			
5	Type	0			
6	Pv	($ 194,444.38)			

The Overall Intent? To develop in the student an intuition about which problem-solving approach works best for a particular problem—in other words, to develop an informed "do-it-yourself" attitude toward the tools of technology.

The Student Front and Center

Finance Follies **boxes in *Financial Management***

Making Connections

With the Real World. "Finance Follies" capture some fascinating examples of current and historical scandals and manias and give the student context for the necessity of studying finance.

FINANCE FOLLIES

The Financial Meltdown of 2008

Between October 2007 and October 2008, financial markets in the United States lost more than 40% of their value, and several financial institutions collapsed or were swallowed up by healthier firms. This "perfect storm" of mortgage defaults, a housing market collapse, lack of appropriate regulation and oversight, and a major international credit freeze led to the worst financial meltdown since the Great Depression of the 1930s.

We can find the seeds of this financial debacle in the housing market, but the soil in which they were planted had been prepared for a long time. In the 1980s, a new philosophy that the capital markets worked best when regulations were removed became the prevailing paradigm. Over the next twenty years, a slow and deliberate dismantling of regulations surrounding the financial markets took place. The central ideas behind this deregulation were that government is the problem rather than the solution and that, if we remove the government from the market, free competition will efficiently allocate resources for a stronger economy.

A key catalyst for the meltdown was the dismantling of the Glass-Steagall Act (officially called the

Historically, commercial banks financed home mortgages with funds from their depositors—a limited supply of money. Banks rationed credit to customers with higher incomes and solid credit histories. Most individuals or couples who could qualify for a standard mortgage could get a conventional loan to buy a house, and defaults were low. With new competition and looser regulations, mortgage originators faced a choice: continue lending through conventional loans to qualified applicants or lower the qualifying standards with new, unconventional loans and risk higher defaults. Because mortgage originators could eliminate most risk by selling off the mortgages—which they repackaged and sold as securities—they naturally chose the latter course.

With relaxed loan qualifications, red-hot demand heated up the residential housing market. Many individuals found themselves in the middle of the American dream that they thought they might never realize—a new home—but the new home often brought with it an unconventional loan. The industry collectively called these unconventional loans "subprime" loans because the initial monthly payment on the loan in the first few

FINANCE FOLLIES

"Scam of the Century": Bernie Madoff and the $50 Billion Fraud

Toward the end of 2008, the last thing Wall Street wanted to hear was more bad news about financial management, but it came in spades with the SEC's announcement on December 11 that Bernard (known as Bernie) Madoff, head of Bernard L. Madoff Investment Securities LLC, had perpetrated a colossal fraud by setting up a so-called Ponzi scheme involving his clientele base. A slew of high-roller investors, as well as more ordinary ones, found that their investment money had evaporated. The scope of the damage was jaw-dropping: reputedly, the black hole Madoff dug could be responsible for $50 billion—and perhaps more—of investors' funds.

How could it happen? The irony is that a Ponzi scheme is a straightforward kind of fraud, and Madoff seemingly had nailed it for what may turn out to be the largest Ponzi scheme ever. Named after Charles Ponzi, who first hatched the swindle in Boston in 1919, a Ponzi scheme promises high rates of return with little risk, but it fraudulently uses the principal paid in by new investors to pay out to older investors. As money flows in from new clients, the scheme distributes it to old clients as returns. Because many long-term investors choose to reinvest the so-called returns in a "sure thing," the scam grinds on. Eventually, though, the edifice collapses in on itself because many of the earlier investors ultimately begin to withdraw their principal and earnings and the fund runs dry because it did not accumulate sufficient real earnings to make these payments.

Madoff launched his financial career in the 1960s with a mere $5,000 that he earned as a lifeguard. His investment firm rose to stellar success—thanks mostly

Spielberg and New York Mets owner Fred Wilpon, academic entities like Yeshiva University, high-profile financial institutions like the Royal Bank of Scotland, big retail brokers like Charles Schwab, and other wealthy individuals. To invest, Madoff "invited" clients into the company, thereby lending the whole enterprise a certain aura of exclusivity and glamour. Supposedly, not just *anybody* could get in. Over the years, his clients remained impressed with Madoff's Midas touch: reported returns ranged from about 10% to 15% a year, and according to others, from about 14% to 18%. In fact, in thirteen years, steady returns—even in down times—were the norm. Only five months showed any kind of downward movement. It was almost too good to be true.

Indeed, it was too good to be true. The worldwide financial crisis of 2008, like a string of dominoes, eventually caught up with Madoff when some clients wanted to pull out principal of about $7 billion. At this point, Madoff was forced to admit what no one could at first believe: that there were no investment gains and, indeed, no principal. The cupboard was bare. Madoff had evidently been paying returns to some investors from principal received from other investors, and now the firm was insolvent.

The Madoff parable illustrates one of the financial principles that we discuss in this chapter: returns are commensurate with risk. To earn higher returns, one must also take on more risk. Study of risk-return principles teaches us that there is no such thing as a free lunch. Although all investors want to maximize return and minimize risk, they still must make a trade-off between the two. Madoff handed investors a story that

With Careers. **"Putting Finance to Work"** answers a question students often ask: "Why do I need to take a finance course, anyway?" These snapshots of widely varied careers show that specific finance concepts are used in many different career paths.

Putting Finance to Work

Now Hiring

"Why do I need to take a finance course, anyway?" It is a fair question. To answer it, let's consider the following excerpts from recent job descriptions and qualifications on the leading Internet recruiting and placement service, Monster.com.

Job A

- Analyze financial results and take appropriate actions to ensure operational excellence and achieving annual goals. Develop and execute key financial and business targets/metrics.
- Track, analyze, and communicate key metrics.
- Qualifications: Advanced experience with Microsoft Office applications (Excel, Word, PowerPoint). Financial analysis, financial root cause investigation, and development of solutions/action plans to minimize risks and take advantage of opportunities.

Job B

- Prepare valuation models.
- Prepare analyses for asset management purposes focused on leasing and capital needs.
- Prepare investments memoranda.

Asset Management. Job C is from the IT section. The job title is IT (Information Technology) Finance Support. If you are not specializing in finance or accounting, and especially if you think of yourself as more conceptual and creative than quantitative, you may not immediately see the connection between a finance course and your career path. In real life, business careers—unlike college course requirements—are not divided into neatly separated subject matters that rarely seem to overlap or interact.

Consider the first job in marketing, for example. Marketing people rightly point out that nothing happens in business until it sells a product or service, but if sales do not result in an appropriate return on investment, the business does not have a very bright future. Two of marketing's most important "Ps" are product and price. A major section of the finance course deals with analyzing product and price decisions in terms of economic profit and whether such decisions will, in fact, increase or decrease the value of the business. Chapters 9 and 10, which deal with capital budgeting decisions, and Chapter 14, which deals with financial statement analysis, will be of particular interest to mar-

With Different Kinds of Businesses. **"Mini-Cases"** at the end of every chapter put abstract concepts to work in the types of organizations for which students will later work. The cases feature small businesses, large corporations, town organizations, and start-ups.

Mini-Case

General Energy Storage Systems: How Much Debt and How Much Equity?

This mini-case is available in MyFinanceLab.

General Energy Storage Systems (GESS) was founded in 2002 by Ian Redoks, a Ph.D. candidate in physics who was interested in "outside-the-box" solutions to the problem of storing electrical energy. Redoks had obtained several patents with potential applications for plug-in hybrid cars, off-grid home electrical systems, and large-scale storage of commercial electricity, produced by conventional means from excess capacity at off-peak hours or from non-fossil-fuel sources such as solar power and wind power.

The timeliness of Redoks's research has quickly attracted investors. For example, GESS has won contracts from an automobile company to manufacture batteries for a limited-production plug-in hybrid. It is also ready to begin commercial production of storage components for off-grid home electrical systems. More product means more storage space, however. To acquire the necessary manufacturing facilities, GESS needs to obtain additional financing.

Up to this point, GESS's primary source of funds has been from the sale of stock. The company is entirely equity-financed except for current liabilities incurred in the course of day-to-day operations. There are 200,000 shares outstanding, which are mostly owned by large, diverse technology companies that may wish to partner with or even acquire GESS at some point in the future. The shares trade occasionally in the NASDAQ over-the-counter market at an average price of $20.00.

The investment bankers who placed the stock have suggested that an all-debt plan would minimize taxes, but it would be risky and leave little room for future borrowing. Instead, they recommend staying close to the industry averages for debt-to-assets and debt-to-equity ratios. They have proposed two alternative plans:

a. plan A calls for $2,000,000 of new equity (100,000 new shares at the firm's current stock price of approximately $20.00) and $4,000,000 of privately placed debt at 9%

b. plan B calls for $4,000,000 of new equity (200,000 new shares at the current stock price of $20.00) and $2,000,000 of privately placed debt at 8%

Under either plan, GESS's combined state and federal marginal tax rate will be 40%.

Putting Finance to Work boxes in ***Financial Management***

CHAPTER 1
Now Hiring

CHAPTER 2
Look Before You Leap

CHAPTER 3
Sports Agent

CHAPTER 4
Modeling the Future with Actuarial Science

CHAPTER 6
Municipal Manager

CHAPTER 9
Marketing and Sales: Your Product = Your Customer's Capital Budgeting Decision

CHAPTER 12
Information Technology

CHAPTER 13
Operations Management

CHAPTER 15
Corporate Law

The Student Front and Center

For the Student On the Go. Tear-out Summary Cards for every chapter provide instantaneous mini-reviews. In addition to summarizing the main points of the chapter, these portable study aids include mathematical notation, calculator keys, and key equations, all great for right before an exam!

Chapter 3
The Time Value of Money (Part 1)
AT A GLANCE

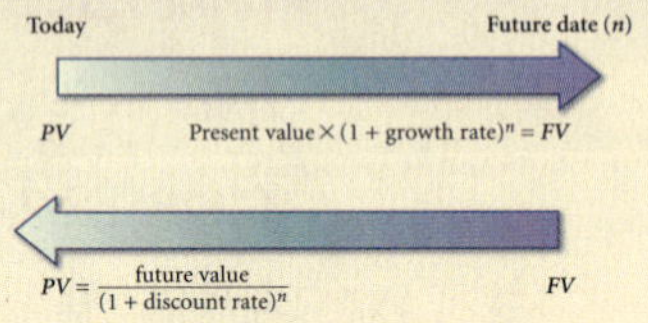

LO1 Calculate future values and understand compounding.

Future value is the value of an asset at a specific point in time in the future that is equivalent in value to a specific amount today. There is a direct relationship between the future value of an asset and the asset's present value, growth rate, and time to the future point. Future values grow faster and faster due to interest earning interest, a phenomenon called compounding of interest.

LO2 Calculate present values and understand discounting.

Present value is the value today of tomorrow's cash flow. You can determine the equivalent value of a future value in today's dollars by discounting the future value back to the present.

LO3 Calculate implied interest rates and waiting time from the time value of money equation.

For Students with Test Anxieties. "Prepping for Exams" is designed for those students who worry about how well they will do on the finance exam. To build confidence and expose students to the types of problems they will see on some exams, multiple-choice questions at the end of each chapter are pulled directly from the test bank. Answers are printed in the back of the book in Appendix 5.

Prepping for Exams

At the end of each chapter, you will find a list of ten multiple-choice questions that are quite similar, and in some cases identical to, multiple-choice questions that you might see on your mid-term and final exams.

1. The movement of money from lender to borrower and back again is known as ______________.
   a. the circle of life
   b. corporate finance
   c. the cycle of money
   d. money laundering

For the Student Who Wants Practice. The book features approximately 400 end-of-chapter problems and 180 conceptual questions to work. New to this edition, advanced spreadsheet problems appear at the end of each chapter for more flexibility in assigning problems for individuals or teams.

Key Terms

compounding, p. 62
compound interest, p. 56
discounting, p. 62
discount rate, p. 62
future value (FV), p. 56
future value interest fa
growth rate, p. 58
lump-sum payment, p. 56
present value (PV), p. 62
present value interest factor (PVIF), p. 62
rule of 72, p. 72

Questions

1. What are the four basic parts (variables) of the time value of money equation?
2. What does the term *compounding* mean?
3. Define a growth rate and a discount rate. What is the difference between them?

Problems

1. ***Future values.*** Fill in the future values for the following
   a. using the future value formula, $FV = PV \times (1 + r)^n$
   b. using the TVM keys or function from a calculator or

Advanced Problems for Spreadsheet Application

1. ***Future value of a portfolio.*** Rachel and Richard want to know when their current portfolio will be sufficient for them to retire. They have the following balances in their portfolio:
   Money market account: \$37,000
   Government bond mutual fund: \$140,000
   Large capital mutual fund: \$107,000
   Small capital mutual fund: \$71,000
   Real estate trust fund: \$87,000

For the Visual Student. **Illustrations with a Purpose** help students visualize important financial concepts. The time line is given special treatment in the all-important time value of money and capital budgeting chapters. To depict movement, present value is always in a lighter shade and future value in a darker shade, and PV is always on the left and FV always on the right. This setup makes it easier to see compounding from the present into the future and discounting "back from the future" to the present.

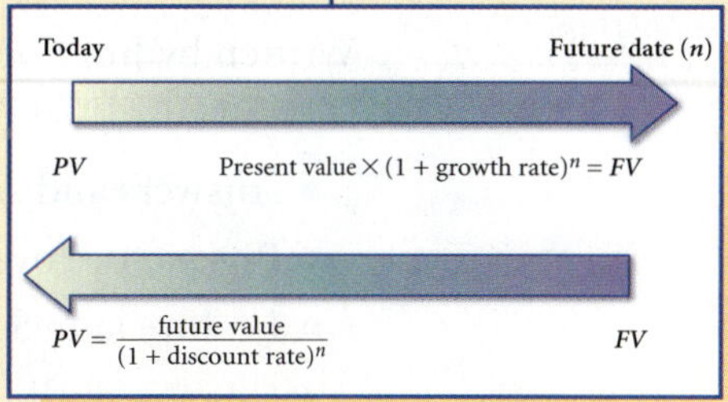

Graphic illustrations are occasionally presented as another way of "seeing" a concept. All illustrations say something about finance.

We can use the versatile time value of money equation to determine the amount of time it will take to reach a specific future value.

For All Students. **The Study Guide**, written by Vance Lesseig of Texas State University, provides a wealth of support material to help the student of finance master the material. Each chapter contains the following:

- Big-picture overviews of the main concepts
- Key idea(s) identified
- Additional worked examples to bolster the worked examples in the text
- Questions and problems for the student to work, approximately thirty-five per chapter, with answers and stepped solutions provided where appropriate

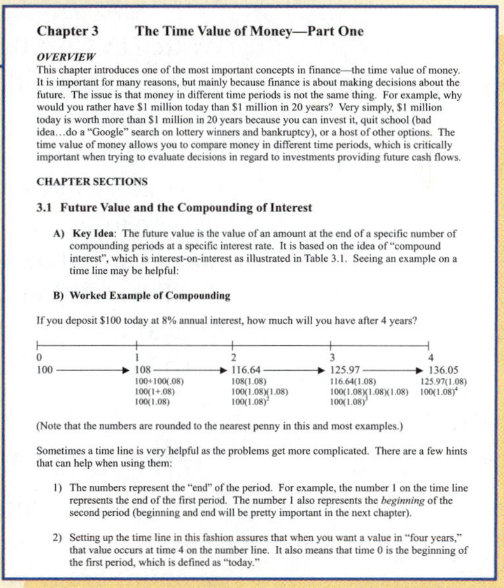

Chapter 3 The Time Value of Money—Part One

OVERVIEW

This chapter introduces one of the most important concepts in finance—the time value of money. It is important for many reasons, but mainly because finance is about making decisions about the future. The issue is that money in different time periods is not the same thing. For example, why would you rather have $1 million today than $1 million in 20 years? Very simply, $1 million today is worth more than $1 million in 20 years because you can invest it, quit school (bad idea…do a "Google" search on lottery winners and bankruptcy), or a host of other options. The time value of money allows you to compare money in different time periods, which is critically important when trying to evaluate decisions in regard to investments providing future cash flows.

CHAPTER SECTIONS

3.1 Future Value and the Compounding of Interest

A) **Key Idea**: The future value is the value of an amount at the end of a specific number of compounding periods at a specific interest rate. It is based on the idea of "compound interest", which is interest-on-interest as illustrated in Table 3.1. Seeing an example on a time line may be helpful:

B) **Worked Example of Compounding**

If you deposit $100 today at 8% annual interest, how much will you have after 4 years?

0	1	2	3	4
100 →	108 →	116.64 →	125.97 →	136.05
	100+100(.08)	108(1.08)	116.64(1.08)	125.97(1.08)
	100(1+.08)	100(1.08)(1.08)	100(1.08)(1.08)(1.08)	$100(1.08)^4$
	100(1.08)	$100(1.08)^2$	$100(1.08)^3$	

(Note that the numbers are rounded to the nearest penny in this and most examples.)

Sometimes a time line is very helpful as the problems get more complicated. There are a few hints that can help when using them:

1) The numbers represent the "end" of the period. For example, the number 1 on the time line represents the end of the first period. The number 1 also represents the *beginning* of the second period (beginning and end will be pretty important in the next chapter).

2) Setting up the time line in this fashion assures that when you want a value in "four years," that value occurs at time 4 on the number line. It also means that time 0 is the beginning of the first period, which is defined as "today."

For the Student Who Wants More Practice. **MyFinanceLab**, a fully integrated online home and tutorial system, enables students to complete problems and receive immediate feedback and help. **MyFinanceLab** also has a special section of spreadsheet problems for Chapters 2 through 18 that provide an opportunity to work more data-intensive problems with spreadsheet applications. See the inside front cover for more details on **MyFinanceLab**.

MyFinanceLab

Resources for the Instructor

Instructor's Manual

Written by Jim DeMello of Western Michigan University, the Instructor's Manual contains the following for each chapter:

- Answers and solutions to all end-of-chapter questions and problems
- Big-picture overviews
- Lecture launchers, often of real-world examples of the chapter concepts
- Chapter outlines, suitable as lecture notes, with appropriate PowerPoint slides referenced
- Trouble spots or pitfalls that students often encounter
- Additional examples and homework problems with worked-out solutions

PowerPoint Presentation

Prepared by Jim DeMello of Western Michigan University, the PowerPoint presentation includes lecture outlines, with equations and examples on separate slides; an assortment of new worked examples to provide fresh input on key points; and all chapter figures.

Computerized Test Bank

Written by Curt Bacon of Southern Oregon University and checked for accuracy by Joe Walker of the University of Alabama, Birmingham, the computerized test bank features approximately 1,800 questions and solutions broken down by chapter into multiple-choice questions of conceptual and numeric types, true or false questions, and short-essay questions. The test bank is written in the TestGen program, an easy-to-use testing software that allows instructors to view, edit, and add questions. The test bank has gone through two separate rounds of accuracy checking.

Ten questions are pulled from each test bank chapter and posted at the end of the text chapters to give students practice for exams. These questions are all identified by an asterisk in the test bank.

MyFinanceLab

MyFinanceLab offers assignable, algorithmically generated problems and special spreadsheet application problems that are automatically graded and recorded in an online grade book. See the inside front cover for details.

From the Author

NINE YEARS AGO, with the encouragement of Donna Battista, I started out on the journey of writing this textbook. We are now in the second edition of a process that has been a great adventure. The first edition was extremely successful, and our reviewers and adopters provided some suggestions for this second edition. So, what's new in this second edition?

First, we have strengthened the Chapter 2 material on the financial statements. We have added a connection between the Statement of Cash Flows and the other financial statements. Second, we have added a discussion on yield curves in Chapter 5 to help students understand the maturity premium on a macroeconomic scale. We have added advanced spreadsheet problems at the end of each chapter for more flexibility in assigning problems for individuals or teams. Of course, we have also updated the material that was time related and added some additional insights based on the feedback of students, reviewers, and adopters. But the general concepts and approach to the book have remained true to the original design we followed in the first edition.

I began with a simple concept. When a student takes an introductory finance class, he or she may encounter a wonderful instructor with great teaching talent and insight. But outside of class, it is the book and the student that form a partnership. *Therefore, the book needs to put the student front and center.* It needs to present the material in a way that encourages students' efforts to learn and connects directly to their experiences. So my goal in writing this book is to introduce the core concepts of finance in a way that reconnects students to their personal financial experiences and then uses such experiences as a springboard into the world of corporate finance.

The introductory finance class is the first and last class in finance for the vast majority of college students. The perspective of these students differs from that of a finance major. They need a book that shows why finance matters to all disciplines and that builds from the basics to more complex topics in an organic approach. So my purpose throughout has been to make the material as simple as possible, but not overly simplified. It is this balance that I hope creates a solid foundation for the fundamental concepts of finance for *all* students.

The evolution of technical support for finance has been amazing. Students now have advanced calculators or spreadsheet software that can provide solutions to many of the basic financial problems. However, understanding finance is more than just solving a financial problem with the aid of these technological tools. These different tools are all interconnected, and the student who can move seamlessly from one to another gains a better understanding of the basics behind the answer. So the book presents three methods to solve many financial problems: the equation approach, the calculator approach, and the spreadsheet approach. In this way, the student sees that there are different roads to the same destination.

The evolution of technical support has also been great for the instructor. MyFinanceLab has been developed to provide the extra support that time constraints often prevent an instructor from providing to the student. With every end-of-chapter problem formatted in MyFinanceLab, an instructor can assign a text-related problem that the students solve online with technical support.

The problem's solution is available to the student, and the marking of individual student homework assignments is completed by MyFinanceLab. In addition, MyFinanceLab has features such as "show me how to do this problem," which leads a student step by step through the problem with a different set of numbers.

The student is at the heart of this book. My hope is that I have made the path easier and finance more transparent.

Acknowledgments

I OWE A GREAT DEAL OF GRATITUDE to the many people who helped create this book.

First, I would like to thank the marvelous people at Pearson Education, especially the editors on the first edition on the text: development editor Mary Clare McEwing and editor-in-chief Donna Battista. Mary Clare and Donna were great supporters and contributors from the inception of the first edition to final production. For the second edition, I owe much gratitude to Tessa O'Brien, editor. All of these individuals have put as much love into the book as I have.

Meredith Gertz, Nancy Fenton, Alison Eusden, Mary Sanger, and the team at Nesbitt Graphics pulled off a superb production job. I also salute Arti Sharma, Miguel Leonarte, and Melissa Honig for the technological expertise they brought to the product, particularly in the development of MyFinanceLab and the Web site for the book. Editorial project manager Jill Kolongowski has been an invaluable contributor behind the scenes. A special thank you goes to Kathleen Abraham and Kelly Ross of Pearson Custom Publishing for their support of the two preliminary editions of this book used at Oregon State University. Sally Steele did a magnificent job on the interior design, and Jonathan Boylan gave us a splendid cover. My marketing manager, Maggie Moylan, spent productive time in talks with me, coaxing out the differential advantages of the book and putting all to use in a terrific marketing campaign.

I am particularly grateful to Robert Hartwig of Worcester State College for his creative work on the "Putting Finance to Work" boxes, the "Finance Follies" snapshots, and the "Mini-Cases" at the end of each chapter. Bob has been a great contributor to the project, although he did not know at the beginning how rich the source material would be for the "Finance Follies" boxes!

I have been most fortunate in having a talented team of supplement authors on this project. Curt Bacon of Southern Oregon University did an excellent job on the test bank, and Jim DeMello of Western Michigan University made great contributions with his authorship of the Instructor's Manual and PowerPoint slides. I would also like to single out Joe Walker of the University of Alabama at Birmingham, who did a meticulous job of checking the end-of-chapter solutions in the Instructor's Manual and the test bank for accuracy. Also, a special thank you to Kevin Thorpe, one of my teaching assistants, who helped with the solutions to the end-of-chapter questions and problems.

All the reviewers of the book—and there were many—provided exceptional insights for improving the various drafts, adding new dimensions to the chapters, and pointing out new directions to explore. I am most grateful to these instructors for lending their time and expertise to this project; their names appear on the following pages.

I cannot sufficiently thank those who inspired this book: my students at Oregon State University. Hundreds of them used the book in preliminary form and provided valuable feedback on all aspects of the presentation. I will forever be grateful for their patience and understanding.

Finally, I thank my family—my wife, Greta, and sons, Michael and Tyler—for their endless support and encouragement.

To all these people, my profound thanks. Your countless contributions have made for a better book and the writing of it all worthwhile.

Raymond M. Brooks

Reviewers

Arvi Arunachalam, *Salisbury University*
Tom Ashman, *Eckerd College*
Ted Azarmi, *University of Tuebingen, Germany*
Curtis Bacon, *Southern Oregon University*
John Banko, *University of Central Florida*
Robert Bartolacci, *Carnegie Mellon University*
Steve Bennett, *San Jose State University*
Karan Bhanot, *University of Texas, San Antonio*
Eugene Bland, *Texas A&M University, Corpus Christi*
Charles Blaylock, *Murray State University*
James Bohenick, *Pennsylvania State University*
Elizabeth Booth, *Michigan State University*
Lionel Booth, *Tulane University*
Patricia Born, *California State University, Northridge*
William Brunsen, *Eastern New Mexico University*
Alva Butcher, *University of Puget Sound*
Deanne Butchey, *Florida International University*
P. R. Chandy, *University of North Texas*
Yi-Kai Chen, *National University of Kaohsiung, Taiwan*
Darla Chisholm, *Sam Houston State University*
Cetin Ciner, *University of North Carolina, Wilmington*
William Compton, *University of North Carolina, Wilmington*
Anthony Daly-Leonard, *Delaware County Community College*
Jim DeMello, *Western Michigan University*
Philip DeMoss, *West Chester University*
Anand Desai, *Kansas State University*
John Dobson, *California Polytechnic State University*
Jocelyn Evans, *College of Charleston*
Eurico Ferreira, *Indiana State University*
Mary Filice, *Columbia College, Chicago*
Roger Fuhrman, *North Central College*
Scott Fullwiler, *Wartburg College*
Sharon Garrison, *University of Arizona*
Sudip Ghosh, *Penn State University*
Cathy Goldberg, *University of San Francisco*
Levon Goukasian, *Pepperdine University*
Lori Grady, *Bucks County Community College*
Ed Graham, *University of North Carolina, Wilmington*
Joe Greco, *California State University, Fullerton*
Terry Grieb, *University of Idaho*
Harry Griffin, *Sam Houston State University*
Wei Guan, *University of South Florida, St. Petersburg*
Manak Gupta, *Temple University*
Lester Hadsell, *College at Oneonta, State University of New York*
Joseph Haley, *St. Cloud State University*
Pamela Hall, *Western Washington University*
Thomas Hall, *Christopher Newport University*
Robert Hartwig, *Worcester State College*
Eric Hayden, *University of Massachusetts, Boston*
Vanessa Holmes, *Pennsylvania State University, Worthington Scranton*
Ping Hsiao, *San Francisco State University*
Stephen Huffman, *University of Wisconsin, Oshkosh*
Rob Hull, *Washburn University*
Nancy Jay, *Mercer University*
Tejendra Kalia, *Worcester State College*
James Kaney, *California Polytechnic State University*
Howard Keen, *Temple University*
Jim Keys, *Florida International University*
Daniel Klein, *Bowling Green State University*
Raj Kohli, *Indiana University, South Bend*
Samuel Kyle Jones, *Stephen F. Austin State University*
Mark Lane, *Hawaii Pacific University*
Dina Layish, *Binghamton University*
Vance Lesseig, *Texas State University*
Donglin Li, *San Francisco State University*
Huimin Li, *West Chester University*
Jo-Ann Li, *Towson University*
Ralph Lim, *Sacred Heart University*
Angelo Luciano, *Columbia College, Chicago*
Thomas Lyon, *Rockhurst University*
Yulong Ma, *California State University, Long Beach*
Anne Macy, *West Texas A&M University*
Inayat Mangla, *Western Michigan University*
Iqbal Mansur, *Widener University*
Jon Matthews, *Central Carolina Community College*
Stefano Mazzotta, *Kennesaw State University*
Lee McClain, *Western Washington University*
Ilhan Meric, *Rider University*
Cynthia Miglietti, *Bowling Green State University*
Richard Mikolajczak, *Tidewater Community College*
James A. Milanese, *University of North Carolina, Greensboro*
Lalatendu Misra, *University of Texas, San Antonio*
John Mitchell, *Central Michigan University*
William Mosher, *Clark University*
Tom Nelson, *University of Colorado*

William B. Nelson, *Indiana University Northwest*
Srinivas Nippani, *Texas A&M University, Commerce*
Rosilyn Overton, *New Jersey City University*
James Owens, *West Texas A&M University*
Warren Palmer, *Beloit College*
Coleen Pantalone, *Northeastern University*
Ohannes George Paskelian, *University of Houston, Downtown*
Tony Plath, *University of North Carolina, Charlotte*
Rose Prasad, *Central Michigan University*
Vijayan Ramachandran, *Oklahoma City Community College*
Rathin Rathinasamy, *Ball State University*
Mario Reyes, *University of Idaho*
Stanley Roesler, *Eastern Connecticut State University*
David Russell, *California State University, Northridge*
William Sawatski, *Southwestern College*
Atul Saxena, *Georgia Guinnett College*
Dennis Shannon, *Webster University*
Maneesh Sharma, *Indiana-Purdue University*
Kilman Shin, *Ferris State University*
David Suk, *Rider University*
Kenneth Surbrugg, *Labette Community College*
Michael Townsend, *Canyon College*
Victor Wakeling, *Kennesaw State University*
Joe Walker, *University of Alabama, Birmingham*
Sally Wells, *Columbia College of Missouri*
Susan White, *University of Maryland*
Alex Wilson, *University of Arizona*
Fred Yeager, *St. Louis University*
Emily Zietz, *Middle Tennessee State University*

Focus Group Participants

John Banko, *University of Central Florida*
Rafiqul Bhuyan, *California State University, San Bernardino*
George Chang, *Bradley University*
Chiaku Chukwuogor-Ndu, *Eastern Connecticut State University*
Cetin Ciner, *University of North Carolina, Wilmington*
Beverly Frickel, *University of Nebraska, Kearney*
Luis Garcia-Feijoo, *Creighton University*
Anne Gleason, *University of Central Oklahoma*
Terry Grieb, *University of Idaho*
Thomas Krissek, *Northeastern Illinois University*
Francis Laatsch, *Bowling Green State University*
Richard Levy, *Roosevelt University*
Piman Limpaphayom, *Chulalongkorn University, Thailand*
Angelo Luciano, *Columbia College, Chicago*
Elisa Muresan, *Long Island University, Brooklyn*
Prakash Pai, *University of Texas of the Permian Basin*
Debbie Psihountas, *Webster University*
Rasoul Rezvanian, *Northeastern Illinois University*
Jimmy Senteza, *Drake University*
Janikan Supanvanij, *St. Cloud State University*
Chu-Sheng Tai, *Texas Southern University*
Jill Wetmore, *Saginaw Valley State University*

Brief Contents

Detailed Contents

CHAPTERS 1–3

"*A very good job in making the concept of finance come alive for the student. I completely agree with the inclusion of TVM early in the text. The author has obviously taught this course many times.*" Emily Zietz, Middle Tennessee State University

"*The explanation of bond pricing and yield calculations is outstanding.*" Robert Hartwig, Worcester State College

"A terrific piece of work, perhaps the best description of risk and return I have ever seen in an introductory text."
Alex Wilson, University of Arizona

Risk and return: "A great job of explaining a lot of pretty sophisticated information very well."
Robert Bartolacci, Carnegie Mellon University

CHAPTER 9

Capital budgeting: "*Just exactly what I like to cover in an introductory course.*" Karen Hallows, George Mason University

CHAPTER 10

Cash flow estimation: "*Logical, easy to read, and covers all aspects well.*" Lalatendu Misra, University of Texas, San Antonio

Part 3

Capital Budgeting 255

CHAPTER 11

"*One of the best chapters on WACC I have come across in a text.*" Cathy Goldberg, University of San Francisco

CHAPTER 13

"*Excellent discussion of the cash conversion cycle . . . Outstanding in making accounts receivable management more real, more 'gritty' than the typical finance textbook.*" Warren Palmer, Beloit College

"*I, too, save financial statement material for later when it finally becomes relevant, especially after the students have a knowledge of cash flow and why financial statement analysis matters. Good idea! Bravo!*"

Joe Walker, University of Alabama, Birmingham

CHAPTER 16

“One of the best presentations of [Modigliani and Miller] for undergraduates that I have read.”

John Banko, University of Central Florida

"The presentation on foreign exchange is excellent." Eric Hayden, University of Massachusetts, Boston

Part 1

Fundamental Concepts and Basic Tools of Finance

Learning Objectives

LO1 Describe the cycle of money, the participants in the cycle, and the common objective of borrowing and lending.

LO2 Distinguish the four main areas of finance and briefly explain the financial activities that each encompasses.

LO3 Explain the different ways of classifying financial markets.

LO4 Discuss the three main categories of financial management.

LO5 Identify the main objective of the finance manager and how he or she might meet that objective.

LO6 Explain how the finance manager interacts with both internal and external players.

LO7 Delineate the three main legal categories of business organizations and their respective advantages and disadvantages.

LO8 Illustrate agency theory and the principal-agent problem.

LO9 Review issues in corporate governance and business ethics.

Chapter 1
Financial Management

In this text, we embark on a journey of the study of finance and financial management. It is probably your first trip through these uncharted waters, but you may already have an intuitive understanding of certain aspects of finance. If you have saved money, borrowed money, or loaned money, you have performed a fundamental activity of finance. Your intuition should serve you well as you develop your personal skill set for finance and financial management.

In this chapter, you will learn about finance activities, the main areas of finance, the key financial players, and the types of business organizations. Together, we'll examine the relationship of the officers of a company to its owners through a model called agency theory. Finally, we will touch on issues concerning how corporations govern their activities, and how the U.S. government attempts to regulate and monitor these activities.

Finance helps people and businesses make decisions about when to buy and when to sell, and what to buy and what to sell. Whether you are the manager of a small retail store or a senior officer in a large firm, the economic objective of your financial decision is the same: to make the enterprise and yourself better off.

Finance is not just about money and investing; it is much broader. Finance is the art and science of managing wealth. Generally defined, **financial management** includes many activities that create or preserve the economic value of the assets of an individual, small business, or corporation. The job of financial managers is to make, and help others to make, sound financial decisions. This book is designed to help you understand the processes used in making financial decisions and the effect these decisions have on the wealth of a company. Let's begin our journey here with an overview of the cycle of money.

1.1 The Cycle of Money

Say you borrow five dollars from a friend today and repay it a few days later. Your friend (the lender) is willing to forgo the use of the five dollars for a temporary period while you (the borrower) need the five dollars for a purchase today. You will be able to repay the five dollars a few days later and thereby repay the loan. Both parties benefit from the arrangement: the lender helps a friend in need, and you are able to spend five dollars at a time when you are short on cash.

The finance function of borrowing and lending is usually much more complicated than this scenario, but the objective of these types of transactions is always the same: to make both parties better off. The movement of money from lender to borrower and back again is called the **cycle of money**. In the business world, however, most lenders are not in direct contact with their borrowers. Most lenders invest their money with a financial institution such as a bank, which in turn loans these funds to another party. The bank in this instance is called a **financial intermediary**, an institution that acts as a "middleman" between borrowers and lenders. The borrower makes payments back to the bank, and the bank, in turn, pays back the lender. Figure 1.1 depicts these roles in the cycle of money.

FIGURE 1.1 The cycle of moving money from lender to borrower and back again is often accomplished through a financial intermediary like a bank.

Let's look at an example of the lending and investing activity of one individual and the borrowing activity of a second individual through a commercial bank. Paula decides to deposit \$500 in the bank by purchasing a certificate of deposit (CD). The CD is a promise by the bank that it will return the \$500 and pay Paula \$25 (5% interest) if she keeps the entire deposit in the bank for one year. Scott comes to the bank in need of \$500 for a tuition payment. The bank agrees to loan Scott \$500 if he will repay the loan principal of \$500 and an additional \$40 (8% interest) at the end of the year. These transactions benefit all three parties—Scott, the bank, and Paula. Scott is able to pay his tuition on time. If he then pays back \$540 to the bank, the bank can redeem Paula's certificate of deposit for \$525 and keeps \$15 for the services it provided: (1) matching the borrower and lender and (2) bearing the risk that Scott would not be able to pay back the loan with interest at the end of the year. And Paula has earned $25 interest on her money.

You might reasonably ask why Paula gave away a chance to earn an additional $15 of interest by not lending directly to Scott. One simple answer is that Paula would have risked losing the entire $500 had Scott not repaid the loan. But for now, let's just say that some additional complications underlie this set of transactions, and we will explore those in Chapter 15.

As noted at the beginning of this chapter, finance is about making decisions: when to buy and when to sell, and what to buy and what to sell. In our first example, it is fairly easy to see that Paula is buying a CD from the bank and the bank is selling the CD, but what is Scott buying or selling? Let's consider the cycle of money in this example in terms of buying and selling:

- Scott was selling a future stream of money ($540 a year from now) for $500 today.
- The bank was buying a promised future stream of money ($540 at the end of the year) for $500 today.
- The bank was selling a CD promising $525 at the end of the year for $500 today.
- Paula was buying a promised future stream of money (the CD with a payoff of $525) for $500 today.

So here we actually have two separate transactions at the start of the cycle of money. Scott is a seller and the bank a buyer in one transaction. The bank is the seller and Paula is the buyer in the other transaction. Note that all transactions always have a buyer and a seller. To Scott the transaction was a loan of $500. To Paula the $500 was an investment. Loans are from the perspective of the borrower, and investments are from the perspective of the lender, but lending and investing are buying and selling activities.

As you proceed through this book, the transactions may become more complex as they involve increasingly more players and ever more complicated contracts. Nevertheless, two things remain constant: (1) the cycle of money and (2) the economic objective of improving each participant's wealth.

1.2 Overview of Finance Areas

We often partition finance into four main areas:

1. Corporate finance
2. Investments
3. Financial institutions and markets
4. International finance

Corporate finance, as its name implies, is the set of financial activities that support the operations of a corporation or business, its use of money, and those decisions that affect the wealth of the owners. These activities can include borrowing funds to finance projects of the corporation, such as plant expansions, launching new products, or supplementing short-term cash needs. It also includes repayment of these borrowed funds through dividends, interest payments, and principal payments.

Investments are generally the activities centering on the buying and selling of assets, both real and financial. **Real assets** are physical assets such as property and buildings or commodities such as corn, oil, or gold. **Financial assets** are intangible assets such as stocks and bonds. This area of finance is concerned with accurate pricing of these assets, the process of buying and selling them, and the rules and regulations that govern the players and activities in these transactions.

Financial institutions and markets are the organized financial intermediaries and the forums that promote the cycle of money. The institutions take the form of commercial banks, investment banks, insurance companies, pension companies, and foreign exchanges. The activities of financial institutions range from matching lenders and borrowers in a simple transaction like Paula's in our example to managing large retirement portfolios for large classes of employees. The markets are the locations, both physical and virtual, where these activities take place. Some of these institutions and markets are icons of finance, such as the New York Stock Exchange (NYSE). Although the NYSE is a financial institution with a physical market, it operates mainly in the investments area, conducting activity in a sophisticated financial market.

International finance deals with the addition of multinational aspects of the finance activities outlined previously. Multinational corporations have operations in more than one country and must often finance these operations with local investors. Some of the decisions become more complicated because the rules and regulations for operating a business vary from country to country. In addition, economic conditions vary from country to country, making the process of assessing risk more difficult. Finally, most countries have their own currency, which adds another dimension—the converting of currency from one country to currency of another country—to international finance.

These four areas cover the main activities of finance, but they are not mutually exclusive. Rather, they are interconnected to establish a well-organized network for the cycle of money.

1.3 Financial Markets

Financial markets are the forums in which buyers and sellers of financial assets (such as stocks and bonds) and commodities (such as grains, oil, and gold) meet. Again, financial markets are the locations, both physical and virtual. The New York Stock Exchange has a physical trading floor at 11 Wall Street in New York City where buying and selling takes place. Other markets are virtual spaces where transactions occur over a network of computers, such as the National Association of Securities Dealers Automated Quotations (NASDAQ).

We can classify financial markets in a number of ways. Let's examine four: (1) by type of asset traded, (2) by the maturity of the assets, (3) by the owner of the assets, and (4) by the method of sale.

First, we can classify financial markets by the type of asset that sells in the market:

- *Equity markets*, where stocks are bought and sold
- *Debt markets*, where bonds are bought and sold
- *Derivatives markets*, where futures contracts on commodities are bought and sold (futures markets) or where options on equities, futures, or currencies are bought and sold (options markets)
- *Foreign exchange markets*, where currencies are bought and sold

Second, we can classify financial markets by the maturity of the assets. *Maturity* means the length of time the borrower has to pay back the borrowed funds. Investors buy and sell financial assets that will mature within the year in **money markets**. These assets are *short-term loans*, sometimes for as short as a day or two. Financial assets that have maturities over a year transact in the **capital markets**. These assets are *long-term loans* and may include bonds or stocks. Remember, loans are investments from the perspective of the lender who is buying a future cash flow from the borrower who is selling the future cash flow.

Third, we can categorize financial markets by who owns the assets. When a company offers stock for sale for the first time and the proceeds of the sale go to the company, the sale takes place in the **primary** (first) **market**. The Securities and Exchange Commission (SEC) regulates sales in the primary market.

After the initial public sale of stocks or bonds, the initial buyer of the stock or bond may choose to resell the asset to another party. When that happens, the sale takes place in the **secondary market**. Here the money for the sale goes to the initial buyer, with a notification to the original issuer (the company) that there is now a new owner of record. The Securities and Exchange Commission also regulates sales in the secondary markets.

A fourth classification of financial markets is by type of sale. Dealer markets and auction markets fall into this category. In a **dealer market**, an individual (or firm) buying and selling securities (stocks or bonds) does so out of his or her own inventory, much as in a used-car dealership. The dealer makes money by purchasing the asset at one price and then selling the same asset later at a higher price. In an **auction market** (such as the government bond market), many securities sell at the same time to many buyers. The various auctions for financial assets have specific procedures about who can bid, what type of bids are allowed, and how they distribute the financial assets to the winning bidders. The auctioneers, usually investment banks, receive a percentage of the sale as compensation for conducting the sale.

We will take a more detailed look at the financial markets in Chapters 7 and 15.

1.4 The Finance Manager and Financial Management

As noted, we generally define financial management activities as those that create or preserve the economic value of the assets of an individual, small business, or corporation. In a company, many different individuals perform these activities at many different levels. A **chief financial officer (CFO)** oversees all the company's financial activities, such as determining the best repayment structure for borrowed funds, which ensures that the company meets its debt obligations in a timely fashion and still has sufficient cash for its daily operations. Beyond the CFO, everyone in the corporation—from the person who decides where to advertise the company's products or services to the person who decides what type of copying machines will best meet the company's needs—faces similar challenges.

You make these same types of decisions everyday. You, too, must ensure that your monthly payments for a house or car are appropriate to your current income level so that you can meet your other daily obligations. You make many personal financial management decisions, some simple (Do I have enough money to have fries with my hamburger?) and some complex (How should I structure my retirement portfolio?). If managers of large companies fail to maintain the value of the company assets, the company may be forced into bankruptcy, losing millions of dollars for the owners. Similarly, if you fail to budget properly, you may lose many of your possessions. Because companies and individuals engage in parallel activities and make similar choices concerning financial matters, at times we use corporations in this book to illustrate different financial management activities and decisions. At other times, we use individuals and personal objectives to illustrate financial management issues.

We can divide financial management into three main categories:

1. **Capital budgeting**: the process of planning, evaluating, comparing, and selecting the long-term operating projects of the company. This answers the question, *What business should we be in over the long term?*

Capital budgeting requires a company to answer fundamental questions about its business focus. For Nike, that means making and selling athletic wear. For Coca-Cola, it is selling beverages. For Wal-Mart, it is the retail business of selling consumer products from multiple manufacturers. Each company picks its business based on its ability to generate a profit in its field over an extended period of time. This evaluation and selection of the products and services in which the company will invest its funds is called capital budgeting. In Chapter 9, we will study the various ways in which a company evaluates whether to invest in a product or service.

2. **Capital structure**: the means by which a company finances its business activities; for public companies, usually a mix of bonds (debt) and stocks (equity) sold to investors and owners. This answers the question, *Where do we raise the money to do our business activities?*

   Once we select the appropriate business area and product mix, it is usually necessary to raise funds to pursue our objectives. The sources and amounts of funding that individuals or companies raise to support the business activities is called capital structure of the company. In Chapters 15 and 16, we examine the different choices of how and where to raise funds as well as the availability of different types of funds.

3. **Working capital management**: the process of managing the day-to-day operating needs of the company through its current assets and current liabilities (we often refer to this as the short-term financing activities of the company). This answers the question, *How will we manage our day-to-day business needs?*

   Working capital management focuses on short-term operating needs and the company's day-to-day finance requirements. The company needs sufficient cash on hand to meet payments to employees, suppliers, and others. It also needs policies for collecting funds from its customers on a timely basis. Working capital management involves the selection of inventory levels, payment policies, and short-term cash holdings—all to enable the company to provide its products and services in a competitive marketplace and still meet current financial obligations. This financial management activity also includes efforts to seek short-term funding and to negotiate with creditors to restructure payments. We examine these topics in more depth in Chapters 12 and 13.

A finance manager is anyone who engages in any—or all three—of these financial management activities. Whether it is the top finance officer of a large company with the title of chief financial officer or the manager of a small business, finance managers help decide what new products or services the company should sell, how to finance these products or services, and the optimal level of product or services to have available for customers. The CFO of a large company may be faced with a capital budgeting decision about the number and types of trucks that will effectively and efficiently deliver the company's products to warehouses, which involves substantial costs. A business manager of a small plant nursery may need to select only one delivery truck rather than a fleet, yet both managers face the same challenge: making a prudent financial decision. Both individuals are making capital budgeting decisions, and both are performing financial management activities.

1.5 Objective of the Finance Manager

If the main objective of the finance manager is to create or preserve the economic value of the assets of the corporation, how should the manager accomplish this goal? Should the manager try to:

Maximize profits?
Keep all the company's customers happy?
Foster good relationships with the local community?
Maintain a safe and enjoyable workplace?
Attract and retain good employees?

All these and many more objectives may be desirable. However, managers must often decide between different strategies for pursuing a single objective. For example, should the company add a new product line to keep the customers happy even though it will cause problems with the local community? When some objectives conflict with others, how does a manager choose between or set priorities among them?

Profit Maximization

Let's consider two strategies that might maximize profit. First, a manager might decide to increase this year's profits at the expense of future years' profits by avoiding routine maintenance. Avoiding maintenance this year will decrease costs, which, in turn, will increase profits, but it will also potentially add greater costs to the future because postponed maintenance costs are often greater than current maintenance costs. Second, the manager might instead consider reducing inventories. By scaling down the inventories, the manager can avoid the restocking costs, but also runs the risk of losing sales (and profits) if the products are not available for future customers to purchase. Clearly, profit maximization can involve many trade-offs for a company's manager.

To home in on the primary objective of the finance manager, return for a moment to the original statement. Remember that financial management is about creating and maintaining wealth and ask yourself, "Whose wealth is a manager trying to increase or maintain?" It is a good question to ask because a manager ultimately manages the firm for a large set of individuals, from employees to suppliers to customers to owners. On reflection, you should conclude that it is the *owners* to whom a manager owes allegiance, and it is the owners whom a manager must satisfy. The owners' wealth in the company is the equity value of the company. For a publicly traded company, it is the stock value.

Maximizing Current Stock Price

For a public company, a rising stock price makes the owners better off, whereas a falling stock price makes them worse off. Therefore, in a publicly traded firm, *the primary objective of the finance manager is to maximize the current stock price of the firm*. Let's examine this objective more closely.

At first glance, maximizing the current stock price may seem to ignore many other desirable company objectives, such as maintaining a safe workplace or inducing some trade-offs, that would appear to harm other stakeholders such as employees, suppliers, or customers. However, maximizing the current stock price implies or embeds many of the other desirable objectives. To determine how this is true, let's take a closer look at what actions a company can perform to raise the price of its stock.

The ownership of stock entitles one to a proportional part of the future cash flow of the company. Later we will explore how to determine stock prices, but for now the key point is that stock prices reflect the company's future cash

The primary goal of the finance manager is to maximize the current stock price of the firm. This goal incorporates many other desirable goals that ultimately influence the value of the company's stock.

flow. The goal then becomes how to increase this future cash flow. One way is to maintain a safe and enjoyable workplace to attract and retain good employees. Good employees understand the business, are reliable, and add value to the products or services of the company. Another way is to work closely with customers to ensure that the products and services are meeting their needs. Another way is to establish good working relationships with suppliers so that the company receives quality materials in a timely fashion. Similarly, the firm must take into account the effect that the business has on the environment and the surrounding community. Failure to consider these issues may result in lawsuits and fines that could severely damage the future cash flow of the firm.

If all these factors are ingredients for increasing the firm's future cash flow, they also have an effect on its current stock price. Therefore, it bears repetition: the objective of the finance manager is to *maximize the current stock price of the company*. It is not a simple task to raise stock prices given competition, conflicts in some of the desired goals, and the uncertainty of the economy.

Maximizing Equity Value

What about companies that are not publicly traded and therefore do not have stock? We call the wealth of the owners in a privately held firm the **equity value**, the market value of the assets minus the claims against the company (the liabilities). A broader definition of the goal of the finance manager is to *maximize the current market value of equity of the company*. Whereas stock is the equity value of a publicly traded company, the equity value of a privately held company is the market value of the assets minus the claims against the company (the liabilities). Therefore, this broader goal includes within it maximizing the current stock price of the firm. Thus, the goal of the finance manager is to do those things that increase or maintain the wealth of the owners.

1.6 Internal and External Players

What is the relationship of the finance manager to the other functions, officers, and employees of a company? In other words, how does the finance manager interact with the other players in the company? An organizational chart, depicted in Figure 1.2, will help outline the functions and players.

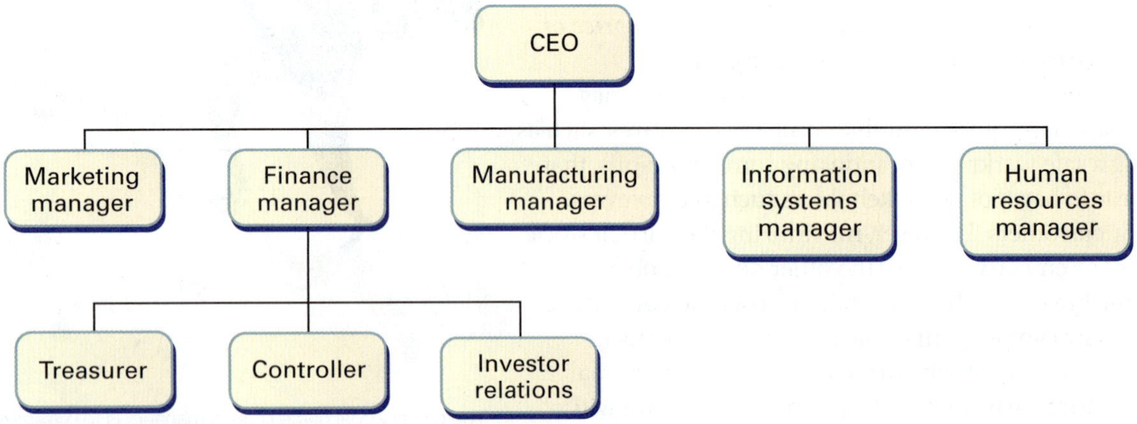

FIGURE 1.2 A basic organizational chart shows the formal reporting alignment of company managers, but the company also needs to maintain many informal relationships.

Figure 1.2 shows one example of a company's organization. The functions depicted include marketing, finance, manufacturing, information systems, and human resources. Some of these individuals may have different titles, such as vice president of manufacturing, vice president of finance, or manager of human resources, but the titles do not change the functions or general responsibilities assigned to each individual or area. The standard organizational chart shows a bottom-up reporting relationship, but in a successful business all functional areas are actually interconnected. The finance manager works with each of the other players in the firm to create and maintain the value of the company's assets.

For example, let's look at a standard company process, such as setting the company's annual sales target. Many players are involved in this process. The marketing manager might take the lead in setting the sales target, based on knowledge or information gathered about the product market and the competing firms. The manufacturing manager must deliver the product to the sales points and confirm that the sales target is reasonable given the current production and distribution facilities. The human resources manager must ensure that there is a sufficient number of trained workers to perform all the manufacturing and distribution duties and that the organization maintains all required safety standards for the employees. The information systems manager must work closely with the finance manager to guarantee that—given the level and location of the sales targets—the company can handle all data properly throughout the system for billing of customers, paying suppliers, producing reports to monitor quality of production, and keeping track of inventories. The finance manager, in turn, works with the marketing manager to set credit policies for targeted customers, appropriate prices of products, and budgets for required advertising to meet the sales target. The finance manager works closely with the manufacturing manager to cost the products properly and to budget the timing and amount of cash needed for the production schedule to meet the targeted sales. Across all the functions of a business, the players work together to deliver a quality product to their customer at a competitive price. All these individuals must work together to ensure that they meet the sales goal. If they don't, the company will eventually fail.

The company officers do not make up the entire list of players. The employees make up a much greater collection of players who are involved in creating and maintaining the wealth of the company. Together with the managers, we call this set of individuals the *internal players* of the company.

The *external players* are all the people outside the company who contribute to its success, such as customers and suppliers. The company needs to know what its customers want in terms of product design and quality, and it must maintain good relationships with external partners who provide vital products, materials, and services to the operations of the company. In addition, the company requires a number of services from its bank. This business relationship is the primary responsibility of the finance manager.

So, across both internal and external players, a finance manager has a variety of responsibilities and functions. It is imperative that the finance manager work with all players to create value for the firm.

In a successful business, the organizational chart is not only about levels of authority, but also about the connections and cooperation between different functional areas.

1.7 The Legal Forms of Business

We normally group business organizations into three legal categories: proprietorships, partnerships, and corporations. Over time, a business may change from one type of business organization to another. Some firms fail, some remain as small businesses, and some become large, multinational companies. Each form of business organization offers advantages and disadvantages.

Proprietorship

A **sole proprietorship** is a business owned entirely by an individual. This form of business means that a person does business in his or her own name. It is the simplest and least complicated business organization, with the least amount of formal documentation required. It is also the least regulated form of business. In the United States, it is the most popular form, and each year more new companies start up as sole proprietorships than any other form of business.

The financial advantage of the sole proprietorship is that the owner makes all the decisions and thus can act quickly without the need to consult or contact partners. In addition, the owner keeps all the profits. The financial disadvantage is that the owner pays all the company bills, even if it means selling off personal property to cover them. This form of business blends company assets and personal assets together so that there is no distinction between company property and personal property.

Another disadvantage of the sole proprietorship is that the business as a going concern or entity is limited to the life span of the owner. When the owner dies, so does the business. For the business to remain a going concern, the owner must sell the entire business to a new owner. Finally, the ability to raise capital for the business is limited to the owner's ability to do so. This limited supply of capital can impede the growth and development of the business.

Partnership

A **partnership** is a business owned jointly by two or more individuals. The partnership agreement spells out the percentage of ownership and level of participation. Partners can be **general partners**, who operate the daily business, **limited partners**, who participate only in certain aspects of the business, and **silent partners**, who participate in the business only as investors. Depending on the types and limitations of the different partners, the players can easily form the agreement or may require extensive legal documents. The agreement will also spell out how the business will distribute the profits and losses. For example, a general partner may be responsible for all outstanding debts of the business, a limited partner may be liable only up to a preset dollar amount, and a silent partner may have no liability above the initial contribution to the business.

The advantages of the partnership are that it involves more individuals in the business and that the business distributes all the profits only to this set of individuals. In addition, the larger number of owners usually increases the amount of capital available over that available to a sole proprietorship. The additional partners may also bring more talent and skills to the business. The main disadvantage is that the personal assets of the general partners are commingled with the business assets and could potentially be required to settle business debts. Typically, a limited partner or silent partner does not have his or her personal assets comingled with the business. The partnership treats profits as personal income; thus, the partners pay taxes on these earnings at personal income tax rates, which may be higher than corporate tax rates.

Other disadvantages of the partnership are the potential difficulty of transferring ownership from one partner to a new partner and the survival of the business when one partner dies. Legally, the partnership must develop a new agreement when a general partner sells to a new general partner or dies. Limited and silent partners can usually sell off their ownership rights to a new limited or silent partner without affecting the current partnership agreement. The difficult task may be finding a new partner willing to replace the retiring or deceased partner.

Both the sole proprietorship and the partnership have three things in common:

1. Unlimited liability of the owners
2. Limited life of the business
3. Potential difficulty in transferring the ownership of the business

Corporations

Unlike sole proprietorships and partnerships, the **corporation** is a legal, separate entity from its owners, meaning that it can enter into contracts, can sue or be sued, and pays taxes. To establish a business as a corporation, the business must file articles of incorporation and a set of bylaws in the state in which it resides. The corporation becomes a resident of the state and must pay taxes like any other citizen of the state. It is not uncommon for a business to incorporate in one state and have its operations in another state. Historically, many businesses choose to incorporate in Delaware because of its corporate-friendly regulations.

The articles of incorporation include the name of the business, the business intent of the corporation, the intended life of the corporation, and the number of shares the corporation can issue. These shares of common stock will be the ownership certificates of the newly formed corporation. Bylaws establish the operating procedures of the corporation and include such items as the specific procedures to elect the board of directors and how the corporation will conduct future changes of the bylaws.

The structure of a corporation separates the owners and managers of the firm. The owners are the shareholders, who elect the board of directors. The board selects the main corporate officers who manage the daily operations of the firm, such as the chairman of the board and chief executive officer (CEO) and the president and chief operations officer (COO). In principle, the owners control the company because they elect the board of directors. In practice, the CEO and COO manage the daily company operations under the rules and procedures set by the board of directors.

The key advantage of the corporate organization is that the shareholders or owners have **limited liability**. The corporation is a legal entity, distinct from the owners, so the personal assets of the owners are separate from those of the company. The owners can lose only what they paid for their shares and thus are limited in their exposure to the debts of the firm.

The corporation offers two additional advantages. First, the owners can easily transfer ownership by selling their shares to others without affecting the company. Second, the corporation can borrow money from banks and capital markets. As a separate entity, the corporation can contract with lenders and not affect the funds or borrowing ability of the owners of the company. A corporation can sell bonds to raise money while the owners remain removed from any liability on failure to repay the debt.

Inevitably, there are also major disadvantages to the corporate form of business organization. An important one is that the government taxes company profits prior to distribution to the owners and then the owners are taxed again on received distributions. We usually apply the term *double taxation* to this disadvantage. Other disadvantages include the legalities involved in forming a corporation, the reporting requirements of the corporation, and the many regulations that govern it. Public or publicly traded companies (for example, firms that sell shares at the NYSE or NASDAQ) must by law produce quarterly and annual reports and distribute these reports to current and prospective owners. An accounting firm must audit their financial statements and attest for them as meeting the requirements of generally accepted accounting principles (GAAP), which is a costly process for the company.

Hybrid Corporations

A business may elect yet other legal forms. Limited liability corporations (LLCs) are a hybrid of partnerships and corporations. One form of LLC is the popular **professional corporation (PC)**, which joins together licensed professionals such as doctors, lawyers, accountants, engineers, or architects. The main advantage of a PC is that the owners (licensed partners) in the PC are not personally liable for the malpractice of their partners. Incorporating as a PC requires that the name of the company contain the PC moniker. For example, an engineering company incorporated as a professional corporation such as Fox and Nelson must state its name as Fox and Nelson, P.C.

Another popular legal form is the subchapter S or **S corporation**, which is a small business corporate form with fewer than 100 shareholders. The income of the corporation passes directly to the owners, avoiding taxes at the corporate level. The government taxes owners on their distribution of profits as part of their annual personal tax filings in their Schedule E (gains and losses from personal business).

Not-for-Profit Corporations

Finally, some business-type activities form as not-for-profit corporations. Foundations, charities, trusts, and associations may incorporate and register through a state's Registry of Commerce. The organization's intent is usually charitable, educational, or professional development and therefore does not fall into our scope of study. The goal of such an organization is not to maximize shareholder wealth, but rather to provide for the social good of a community or development of a specific activity, profession, or affiliated group.

1.8 The Financial Management Setting: The Agency Model

The relationship between the owners and managers of a company is of critical importance to a company's success. The owners hire the managers to represent their interests and perform the daily tasks of operating the company in such a way as to benefit these interests. The managers have their own personal interests as well. Are these interests always aligned? In a sole proprietorship, the owner and the manager are one and the same, so there is no business decision that could directly benefit the manager at the expense of the owner. The same may hold true in partnerships in which the owners and the managers are the same. With corporations, however, conflicts can arise between the owners and managers over the appropriate decisions for the company. The owners' interests are to have the managers perform the daily tasks of operating the company in such a way as to benefit their wealth. Managers have their own personal interests and wealth as well. What happens if these interests are *not* aligned? Let's look at this situation a bit more closely.

The interests of owners and managers are not always perfectly aligned in a corporation, so conflict can ensue.

The owners of the business, or the **principals**, want the company managers to act in the owners' best interests and maximize the current stock price. The managers, or the **agents**, are hired to satisfy the owners' requests. At the same time, managers also want to earn high wages and receive benefits from the performance of their jobs. A natural conflict arises because the agents cannot always maximize their personal wages and benefits without reducing the wealth of the owners. The managers cannot maximize the current stock price without forgoing some of their personal compensation or bonus. This conflict raises a potential problem in the relationship between owners and managers. We call the problem of motivating one party (the agents, or managers in this setting) to act in the best interest of another party (the principals, or the owners in this setting) the **principal-agent problem**.

We can see the principal-agent relationship across a wide set of relationships, not just in the corporate workplace. Let's consider a simple contracting example to illustrate the costs in solving a principal-agent problem.

Let's assume you own a home in a very nice neighborhood and will be leaving for an extended twelve-week trip to Europe. You want to maintain the landscape of your home while you are away, so you hire a landscape company to mow the lawn weekly, trim the bushes and trees as needed, weed the gardens every other week, and apply fertilizer at specific times over the summer. This contract seems straightforward.

The landscape company prepares an estimate of the cost for all these services:

Weekly mowing and trimming of grass: \$50 per week × 12 weeks	\$600
Trimming of bushes and trees: \$30 per hour as needed (20 hours estimated)	\$600
Weeding of gardens: \$75 for each weeding × 6 weeks	\$450
Application and cost of fertilizers	\$250
Total	**\$1,900**

The \$1,900 contract is based on the effort the landscape company expects to extend and the frequency of performance you expect.

If you were home for the summer and contracted the landscape company to perform these services, you could observe the weekly mowing and trimming of the grass, see how many hours the company spent trimming the bushes and trees, and confirm that the firm applied fertilizer at the appropriate time and weeded the gardens every other week. Thus, the \$1,900 contract would be fair to you (the principal) and the landscape company (the agent). You would directly compensate the landscaping company for its effort as it would perform the services in accordance with your wishes.

This time, however, you will be away and cannot directly observe the effort or the decisions of the landscape company. When you return, you will be able to observe the landscape's current appearance, but you will not know if the firm truly maintained it over the summer or just spruced it up immediately before your return.

Let's look at the agency problems inherent in this contract, some of the choices of the landscaping company, and the resulting agency costs. Suppose the landscaping company has overbooked its services for the summer and is not able to mow and trim your grass weekly. Instead, it schedules and cuts the grass every ten days. Thus, over the summer, rather than providing twelve cuttings, it cuts the grass only eight times, but it accepts the total $600 cutting fee for this service. As owner of the home, you have overpaid for the mowing by $200. This $200 is an agency cost. Anytime you pay a cost to an agent acting on behalf of a principal for a service not rendered, it is an **agency cost**. In this instance, the landscape company (your agent) underperforms (versus the manner in which you would like it to perform), but still gets paid for a higher level of performance. You have incurred an agency cost. Here the first $400 dollars for the eight mowings (8 × $50 = $400) is the wage the agent earned, but the additional $200 is an agency cost because you did not receive that service.

Let's also assume that the landscape company does not fertilize the lawn and garden. Again, you cannot determine such a breach of contract from afar, but when you return, the current condition of the lawn and garden plants is not sufficient to verify that the firm completed the task. It will be months before you know the effects of applying or not applying the fertilizer. Again, you paid for this service and the fertilizer. If the company did not apply the fertilizer, you have an additional agency cost of $250.

All is not lost, however. If you can prove that the landscape company did not "live up" to the contract, you can reduce your payments to reflect compensation for only that work that the firm actually performed. How do you prove that the firm mowed the lawn every ten days, not weekly, and that they did not apply fertilizer? Or, how do you construct the contract payments so that you do not pay for unrendered services?

One way to determine how often the firm cut the grass during your absence is to ask your neighbor to keep track of the mowings, or to perform an audit function for you. If you need to compensate your neighbor for this task, that compensation is also an agency cost and increases the cost of the desired services. For example, let's assume the landscaping company performed as promised, and that your neighbor duly noted this fact, but you had to pay your neighbor $100 (you gave him two tickets to a fall football game in return). Therefore, the cost of the auditing increases the total cost for the summer to $2,000, not the $1,900 if you could have observed the effort yourself. That extra $100 to verify the work is an agency cost.

Another way to try to avoid overpaying for unrendered services is to delay payment to the landscape company until there is proof that it performed the service. For example, you could delay the fertilizer applications payment until the spring, when a healthy lawn and garden would demonstrate the benefits. Delaying the payment raises two problems for the landscape company, however. For one thing, it must carry the cost of the fertilizer and labor for six months. Rather than take a loss, the company increases the price of this service from $250 to $300. The additional $50 is an agency cost. In addition, what if the lawn and garden do not look healthy in the spring even though the landscaping company applied the fertilizer at the proper time? The landscape company suffers from a situation in which the outcome—the healthy lawn and garden—is not solely under its control. Other factors, such as the winter weather, may affect the health and appearance of the lawn in the spring. The landscaping company has no control over the winter weather, but that does affect the potential payoff. So, it raises the price it charges even more, to $400, to cover the chance that outside factors beyond its control will come into play. Again, this higher charge is an agency cost. By the time you add up all the contracting, recontracting, and auditing costs, the summer services exceed the original $1,900, and all costs above $1,900 are agency costs.

Let's apply these same concepts to a business setting. The principals (owners) of the company want the agents (managers) to make the right choice, that is, to choose those actions that most benefit the owners and are most consistent with their values. If the owner is present and can observe a manager's choice, the owner can then reward the right choice and punish the wrong one. However, shareholders (the owners) are spread out around the world, and cannot observe a manager's actions. They will need to hire auditors to confirm that they have made the right choice or construct compensation contracts that help managers make the right choice.

The best compensation contract from the perspective of the owner or principal is one that directly matches compensation with effort and performance, but it is often difficult to directly observe effort or measure the performance of managers. Thus, compensation contracts may need incentives that encourage an appropriate level and type of effort. How do shareholders provide incentives to a company's top managers to perform their tasks in the best interests of the shareholders? What is the appropriate goal for the managers of a company who are working on behalf of shareholders? To answer these questions, we return to the objective *to maximize the current stock price of a company*. Shareholders can provide the appropriate bonus incentive to top managers by fixing part of their compensation to the performance of the company's stock. The portion of the contract that provides this incentive is the stock options portion of the compensation contract.

A **stock option** is the right to buy the company stock at a preset price sometime in the future. Because the purchase price of the stock is preset, the value of the option increases when the stock price rises. Therefore, the manager has an incentive to increase the current share price of the firm and increase his or her personal compensation. We call a stock option an incentive-alignment contract because it aligns the incentives of the managers (agents) with those of the owners (principals). Every year, *Fortune* lists the highest paid executives in the United States and the different sources of their compensation packages. In a typical listing of the top ten executives, nearly 70 percent of their annual compensation comes in the form of bonuses for performances and, more specifically, stock options.

Agency theory is the processes surrounding recognition of principal-agent problems and ways to align the actions of agents with the interests of the principals. As with the simple contracting problem of a homeowner hiring a landscaping company to perform routine and standard tasks, agents do not always act in the best interests of the principals. Agents want to maximize their own compensation, which may be costly to the owners. The costs incurred to align agents' interests with those of the owners and the associated costs for which we pay, but for which agents do not always perform, are agency costs.

1.9 Corporate Governance and Business Ethics

How do the owners of a company support management activities that benefit the employees, suppliers, customers, or surrounding community of the firm and encourage management to act in an ethical manner? Such is the realm of **corporate governance**, an area that deals with how a company conducts its business and implements controls to ensure proper procedures and ethical behavior.

Although many companies and managers do operate with a fair and honest philosophy, others will try to exploit the temporary benefits of actions that fall outside ethical behavior. Companies do not always adhere to laws. In the news,

There is always a possibility that managers will act in their own self-interest and violate ethical practices.

you may have seen or read stories about false reporting of earnings, failure to reveal financial information, and payments of large bonuses to top executives shortly after filing for bankruptcy. In one infamous example, the insurance giant AIG paid for a lavish trip to California for top employees of the company immediately after declaring that the company was insolvent, asking for and receiving financial support from the U.S. government in the bailout of 2008. At other times, companies may cross the line between legal and illegal, temporarily violating a law to increase profits. Because of the potential for human self-interest and greed, governments have enacted laws and regulations that require specific actions or restrict activities of a company in an effort to ensure fair competition and ethical behavior.

Often, the U.S. Congress enacts laws and regulations in response to major economic or highly visible events. Following the stock market crash of 1929, the U.S. government created a new set of laws governing the issuing of securities (the Securities Act of 1933) and the selling of securities on stock exchanges (the Securities Exchange Act of 1934). The government also created the SEC to oversee these laws and regulations. The new laws required that firms make available specific financial information to current owners and prospective owners and that the SEC approve the initial sale of securities to the public.

More recently, following a series of major ethical lapses at some firms, the U.S. government enacted new legislation in 2002. One of the most sweeping acts is the Sarbanes-Oxley Act (known as SOX), which requires, among other things, the following:

1. That the CEO and CFO attest to the fairness of the financial report
2. That the company maintains an effective internal control structure around financial reporting
3. That the company and auditors assess the effectiveness of the controls over the most recent fiscal year

In addition, SOX created the Public Company Accounting Oversight Board, outlining prohibited activities of auditors. It also set a requirement that the SEC issue new rulings that establish compliance with the act.

SOX affects the procedures and documentation of those procedures within a company, particularly those dealing with financial reporting. With the role that technology plays in company documents, databases, and procedures, we will likely see the information system manager involved more and more in auditing and compliance.

Despite procedures and policies in place that aim at conducting the business in an ethical manner and in the interests of the shareholders, some managers need replacement, and there are a variety of ways to implement this step. The board of directors can vote out a CEO or CFO. Shareholders can vote out board members who do not use their position and power to discipline managers. Individuals or groups can file lawsuits to remove officers. Outside management teams can try to take over a company, effectively replacing its incumbent management team. All these procedures fall into the domain of *corporate control*, which is beyond the scope of this book. The important point is that the owners of a company choose the management team and can replace those managers who fail to serve the owners' interests.

Although the world of finance generally operates rationally with proven tools at the disposal of finance managers, things can go very wrong on occasion. In this book, we will from time to time offer some fascinating stories of "finance gone bad" in a feature called "Finance Follies." Among other topics, we will consider such fiascos as "cooking the books" at Enron, the bursting of the technology bubble, and, to kick us off, possibly the most spectacular folly of them all: the financial meltdown of 2008. There have been and will continue to be many explanations as to why this implosion occurred and what we should do about it. Here we will look at the broad outlines of the story, which is, in part, a lesson of failed corporate governance. As you read these boxes throughout the book, remember that there are many opinions about what went wrong in these various scenarios and that no one definitive answer can explain it all for each one. Instead, these features are designed to pique your curiosity about how things can go wrong in the world of finance and explore what alternative viewpoints exist about why they occurred and what we can do to correct them.

FINANCE FOLLIES

The Financial Meltdown of 2008

Between October 2007 and October 2008, financial markets in the United States lost more than 40% of their value, and several financial institutions collapsed or were swallowed up by healthier firms. This "perfect storm" of mortgage defaults, a housing market collapse, lack of appropriate regulation and oversight, and a major international credit freeze led to the worst financial meltdown since the Great Depression of the 1930s.

We can find the seeds of this financial debacle in the housing market, but the soil in which they were planted had been prepared for a long time. In the 1980s, a new philosophy that the capital markets worked best when regulations were removed became the prevailing paradigm. Over the next twenty years, a slow and deliberate dismantling of regulations surrounding the financial markets took place. The central ideas behind this deregulation were that government is the problem rather than the solution and that, if we remove the government from the market, free competition will efficiently allocate resources for a stronger economy.

A key catalyst for the meltdown was the dismantling of the Glass-Steagall Act (officially called the Banking Act of 1933). In 1999, the Gramm-Leach-Bliley Act overturned segments of Glass-Steagall that prevented investment banks from competing with commercial banks in areas like mortgage lending. Later, the SEC would relax requirements on investment banks regarding the amount of borrowing in which they could engage, and the race was on to sell more and more mortgages.

Historically, commercial banks financed home mortgages with funds from their depositors—a limited supply of money. Banks rationed credit to customers with higher incomes and solid credit histories. Most individuals or couples who could qualify for a standard mortgage could get a conventional loan to buy a house, and defaults were low. With new competition and looser regulations, mortgage originators faced a choice: continue lending through conventional loans to qualified applicants or lower the qualifying standards with new, unconventional loans and risk higher defaults. Because mortgage originators could eliminate most risk by selling off the mortgages—which they repackaged and sold as securities—they naturally chose the latter course.

With relaxed loan qualifications, red-hot demand heated up the residential housing market. Many individuals found themselves in the middle of the American dream that they thought they might never realize—a new home—but the new home often brought with it an unconventional loan. The industry collectively called these unconventional loans "subprime" loans because the initial monthly payment on the loan in the first few years was well below that of a conventional mortgage loan. The interest rate on subsequent payments, however, would increase well *above* that of a standard loan. So a new homeowner might enjoy relatively low mortgage payments in the first couple of years only to face a large increase when the financial institution reset the interest rate. In many of these loans, the monthly cost jumped by more than $500 per month.

Continued

Continued

When the loan payments jumped, many mortgage holders could no longer afford to stay in their homes. The default rate rose to over 20% on these loans, which is much higher than the typical 1% to 3% default rate on conventional loans. Normally, the bank would simply repossess the home, sell it, and recover the loan. But, with a glut of houses on the market, the housing market collapsed and prices fell. The banks could not sell these houses at any price near the value of the loan.

In addition, knowing that the potential for default was higher on these subprime loans, many banks participated in so-called collateral debt contracts, which were designed as insurance against falling housing prices and mortgage defaults. These contracts eventually wound up nearly worthless as insurance against the defaulting mortgages. In the end, banks ended up holding illiquid assets of diminishing value that dried up their ability to make loans, thus freezing the credit markets.

The collapse of the mortgage markets was the first in a set of dominoes that would eventually lead to a significant fall in the equity markets. Indexes like the Dow Jones Industrial Average fell from a high of 14,164 in October 2007 to a low of 6,726 in March 2009—a loss of more than 50%. This plummet in equity markets was worldwide due to the interconnected nature of the global financial markets. Large banks like Citigroup, mortgage brokers like Countywide Financial, and investment banks like Lehman Brothers and Bear Stearns either failed or were bailed out by the government because their failure posed unacceptable risks to the financial system. Both Main Street and Wall Street felt the sting of the massive losses.

In February 2009, Congress approved a $789 billion economic recovery package in a targeted effort to stimulate the bruised economy through tax cuts and other financial incentives. Three years later, the economy still struggles to recover. Although corporate profits have rebounded, unemployment hovers stubbornly around 9%. Many economists predict that the housing market will take a decade to recover fully. Individuals and businesses choose to pay off debt or horde cash rather than spend, adding to the problem of sluggish growth.

It is interesting that Alan Greenspan, former head of the Federal Reserve, has pointed to the failure of financial institutions to self-regulate as the primary factor in this collapse. Predictably, Congress passed reams of new legislation regulating financial institutions, including the 1,500-page Financial Regulation Bill in May 2010 and the Dodd-Frank Act a few months later. The latter bill regulates the risky behavior of institutions deemed "systemically important," or, in other words, "too big to fail." Just as predictable, the financial services industry claimed that the new regulations would stifle innovation and make U.S. institutions less competitive in world markets. Others attempted to shed assets in order to avoid the "systemically important" designation.

Carmen Rhinehart and Kenneth Rogoff recently published an important study of financial crises going back to the Middle Ages (*This Time Is Different: Eight Centuries of Financial Folly*, Princeton University Press, 2009). One of their principal conclusions is that recoveries from major financial crises are very slow and that although the wrong government actions can make things worse, we cannot do much to accelerate the recovery.

1.10 Why Study Finance?

By now, you should be convinced that studying finance is important. The study of finance can be invaluable, whether you plan to work in a small family business or a large corporation—or even if you only want to plan and invest in your own financial future. Finance can help you understand how large and small companies make financial decisions. Understanding how and why your employer makes decisions increases your ability to contribute to the company as well as your ability to increase your personal compensation. For your own future well-being, studying finance will help you understand the trade-offs you face in making personal financial choices and help you select the most appropriate action. Good economic sense and sound financial decision-making skills will help you gain more out of life in this global economy. To gain some more insight into how studying finance can help your professional development, see the "Putting Finance to Work" feature.

Putting Finance to Work

Now Hiring

"Why do I need to take a finance course, anyway?" It is a fair question. To answer it, let's consider the following excerpts from recent job descriptions and qualifications on the leading Internet recruiting and placement service, Monster.com.

Job A

- Analyze financial results and take appropriate actions to ensure operational excellence and achieving annual goals. Develop and execute key financial and business targets/metrics.
- Track, analyze, and communicate key metrics.
- Qualifications: Advanced experience with Microsoft Office applications (Excel, Word, PowerPoint). Financial analysis, financial root cause investigation, and development of solutions/action plans to minimize risks and take advantage of opportunities.

Job B

- Prepare valuation models.
- Prepare analyses for asset management purposes focused on leasing and capital needs.
- Prepare investments memoranda.
- Assist in the due diligence process.
- Assist in the financing of the acquired assets.

Job C

- Assist in creating and managing project budgets.
- Provide financial insights to Program Managers and Project Managers on an ongoing basis.
- Lead invoice review and payment process.
- Oversee the approval process for purchase requisitions for the program.
- Monitor capital allocation and spending for the e-commerce program.
- Consolidate and analyze financials-variance analysis.
- Qualifications: Degree in Accounting, Finance, MIS, or equivalent experience. Expert in Microsoft Excel. Proficient in Word, PowerPoint.

You may think that these openings are for entry-level or midlevel finance positions, but they are not. Job A comes from the marketing section. The job title is Product Manager: Portfolio Management and Marketing. Job B comes from the real estate section. The job title is Real Estate Analyst: Acquisitions and Asset Management. Job C is from the IT section. The job title is IT (Information Technology) Finance Support. If you are not specializing in finance or accounting, and especially if you think of yourself as more conceptual and creative than quantitative, you may not immediately see the connection between a finance course and your career path. In real life, business careers—unlike college course requirements—are not divided into neatly separated subject matters that rarely seem to overlap or interact.

Consider the first job in marketing, for example. Marketing people rightly point out that nothing happens in business until it sells a product or service, but if sales do not result in an appropriate return on investment, the business does not have a very bright future. Two of marketing's most important "Ps" are product and price. A major section of the finance course deals with analyzing product and price decisions in terms of economic profit and whether such decisions will, in fact, increase or decrease the value of the business. Chapters 9 and 10, which deal with capital budgeting decisions, and Chapter 14, which deals with financial statement analysis, will be of particular interest to marketing specialists.

Popular wisdom holds that the only important variables in real estate are location, location, and location, but professionals—especially in commercial real estate—know that they are really cash flow, cash flow, and cash flow. Real estate purchases involve major cash investments, often financed with large loans, and can succeed only if they produce cash flows large enough to provide an attractive return on investment. The principles of stock and bond valuation, which you will study in Chapters 6 and 7, and capital budgeting, which you will study in Chapters 9 and 10, all apply equally to real estate.

Many companies have IT positions like Job C, and many deal with financial data. In such a role, you will encounter enormous quantities of data that are most likely highly sensitive and confidential in nature. The continuous analysis of financial information, its timely distribution to those who need it in understandable formats, and the task of protecting it from prankster assaults or competitors are major challenges for information technology today.

In the following chapters, we explore the financial tools that enable professionals in every business to function. These tools help us define problems in ways that illuminate which solutions have a high likelihood of success and which we should abandon quickly. Once you master these tools, we put them to use in both personal finance and corporate settings. Like many tool sets, the more you use them, the easier they are to use and the more skillful you become. In finance, practice helps.

Throughout the book, we identify in the margin where these basic tools and their applications appear. Once you become proficient with them, you will be able to create and maintain the economic value of your company's assets—a core task for all managers. Just as important, with these tools you can create and maintain the value of your own personal assets.

To review this chapter, see the Summary Card at the end of the text.

Key Terms

agency cost, p. 16
agency theory, p. 17
agents, p. 15
auction market, p. 7
capital budgeting, p. 7
capital market, p. 6
capital structure, p. 8
chief financial officer (CFO), p. 7
corporate finance, p. 5
corporate governance, p. 17
corporation, p. 13
cycle of money, p. 4
dealer market, p. 7
equity value, p. 10
finance, p. 4
financial assets, p. 5
financial institutions and markets, p. 6
financial intermediary, p. 4
financial management, p. 4
general partners, p. 12
international finance, p. 6
investments, p. 5
limited liability, p. 13
limited partners, p. 12
money markets, p. 6
partnership, p. 12
primary market, p. 7
principal-agent problem, p. 15
principals, p. 15
professional corporation (PC), p. 14
real assets, p. 5
S corporation, p. 14
secondary market, p. 7
silent partners, p. 12
sole proprietorship, p. 12
stock option, p. 17
working capital management, p. 8

Questions

1. What is the cycle of money? Who participates in the cycle of money? What is the objective of a financial transaction?
2. Construct an example of the cycle of money, identify all the players involved, and identify their individual benefits from participating in the cycle of money.
3. What are the four areas of finance? Give an example of a financial activity that would fall into each area.
4. What is the difference between the primary market and the secondary market?
5. What is the general definition of the financial management function? Give an example of a financial management function that an individual might perform.
6. List a capital budgeting decision, a capital structure decision, and a working capital management decision that a business might make.

7. List the advantages and disadvantages of the three different types of business organizations.
8. What is the goal of the finance manager? How does the surrounding community where a business operates fit into this goal?
9. With what players in an organization does the finance manager work to ensure proper financial controls are in place? Can you give a real-world example of a situation in which this relationship was absent and ultimately brought down the company?
10. Name a natural conflict between a principal and an agent. How could this conflict be reduced?
11. Employees at the Jackson Hole Corporation typically take 45 minutes for lunch, although the allocated time is only 30 minutes. Employees are encouraged to eat in the company cafeteria located in the middle of the company facilities. Most employees choose to eat their lunch there. Is there an agency cost here? If so, how can management eliminate or reduce this agency cost?

Prepping for Exams

At the end of each chapter, you will find a list of ten multiple-choice questions that are quite similar, and in some cases identical to, multiple-choice questions that you might see on your mid-term and final exams.

1. The movement of money from lender to borrower and back again is known as ______________.

   a. the circle of life
   b. corporate finance
   c. the cycle of money
   d. money laundering

2. ______________ is the area of finance concerned with the activities of buying and selling financial assets such as stocks and bonds.

   a. Investments
   b. Corporate finance
   c. International finance
   d. Financial institutions and markets

3. Investors buy and sell stocks in ______________ markets.

   a. equity
   b. debt
   c. derivatives
   d. foreign exchange

4. The means by which a company is financed refers to the firm's ______________.

   a. capital budgeting
   b. capital structure
   c. accounts receivable management
   d. working capital management

5. Which of the following is *not* a capital budgeting question?
   a. the choice of which long-term assets to purchase to meet the firm's business goals
   b. the choice of what type of business a firm wants to operate
   c. the proper mix of stocks and bonds to hold for financing assets
   d. none of the above

6. A firm's stock price most closely reflects which of the following?
   a. current interest rates
   b. expected future cash flows of the firm
   c. the amount of debt held by the firm
   d. none of the above

7. Of the following activities, which is *not* likely to be an interaction between the financial manager and the marketing manager?
   a. costing products
   b. setting credit policies
   c. determining that there are a sufficient number of trained workers to develop the product
   d. setting advertising budgets

8. Which of the following is *not* an advantage of a sole proprietorship?
   a. the owner receiving all the after-tax profit
   b. limited liability
   c. quick decision making
   d. all of the above

9. Double taxation refers to which of the following scenarios?
   a. Both bondholders *and* shareholders of a corporation must pay taxes on proceeds received.
   b. The corporation pays taxes on its earnings, and creditors pay taxes on interest received.
   c. The corporation pays taxes on its earnings, and shareholders pay taxes on dividends received.
   d. All of the above statements are correct.

10. In agency theory, the owners of the business are ______________ and the managers are ______________.
    a. bondholders, principals
    b. stockholders, bondholders
    c. agents, principals
    d. principals, agents

MINI-CASE

Richards' Tree Farm Grows Up

This mini-case is available in MyFinanceLab.

Jake Richards is surprised to hear from Paul Augustus, his accountant for many years, that income from his tree farm is just more than $150,000 for the year and that his land and other assets are valued at almost $2,000,000. The $600,000 he owes to the bank is not a surprise.

Twenty years ago, Jake realized that with seven long days of back-breaking labor a week, his western Massachusetts dairy farm was just about breaking even. Without his wife's income as a high school science teacher and the health insurance that came with it, the young family would have been struggling.

Along the way, Jake sold the dairy herd, but he did want to keep the land that had been farmed by his family for three generations. At the time, his plan was to repurpose the farm and some of its equipment by boarding horses, selling hay bales to construction companies, starting a small landscaping business, and plowing snow in the winter. Almost on a whim, he planted a few acres with seedling-size blue spruces and Fraser firs, expecting to sell them as Christmas trees. He quickly found that he could use them more profitably in his landscaping business and that he could sell them to local nurseries and other landscapers. Gradually, he added plantings of other popular landscape trees: arborvitae, yew, dogwood, red maple, ornamental crabapple, pear, and cherry. Demand grew so rapidly that he gave up his other activities to concentrate on tree farming. He now has three full-time employees along with his wife, two college-age children, and several of their friends working for him in the summer. He also owns and leases some rather expensive specialized equipment for planting, digging, and preparing the trees for shipping.

Because the business has grown so rapidly and almost accidentally, Jake has not thought much about its organization. His accountant suggests that it is time to consider converting from an informal partnership with his wife and children to a more formal type of organization. Paul hands Jake some brochures on forming a regular corporation and two alternatives: subchapter S, or S corporations, and LLCs, or limited liability companies. He asks Jake to look them over and get back to him in a week or two.

Questions

1. Major financial management decisions involve capital budgeting, capital structure, and working capital management. Give an example of each that relates to Richards' Tree Farm.
2. Should the Richards form a regular corporation or choose one of the hybrid forms? Whichever form they use, they intend to distribute ownership equally among Jake, his wife, and their two children so that each party will own 25% of the shares. Consider the tax consequences of their decision.
3. How does incorporating affect the family's overall risk exposure?
4. How does incorporating affect the ability of the business to expand?
5. Jake is concerned that if the business gets much bigger or if he should just decide to slow down and enjoy life a little more, he will need to hire professional management and possibly lose control over key business decisions. Are his concerns justified?
6. Jake occasionally hires day workers, who may or may not be in the United States legally. What are his legal and ethical obligations with respect to this decision?
7. The Richards are deeply concerned with environmental issues and know that the best practices for pesticide and fertilizer usage increase production costs. Will incorporating affect their ability to give up a small amount of profit in exchange for protecting the environment?
8. How does incorporating affect the Richards' ability to transfer ownership of the tree farm to their children?
9. Suppose that at some point in the future, this business has an opportunity to become much larger. How might it obtain more equity funding and perhaps create considerable wealth for the Richards family in the process?

Learning Objectives

LO1 Explain the foundations of the balance sheet and income statement.

LO2 Use the cash flow identity to explain cash flow.

LO3 Provide some context for financial reporting.

LO4 Recognize and view Internet sites that provide financial information.

Chapter 2
Financial Statements

Before we can discuss how to make good financial decisions, we first need to understand how to interpret and use the information presented in the financial statements of a firm. The purpose here is not to assemble financial statements, but rather to assess those portions of the statements that help us to understand financial performance, which in turn informs our financial decision making.

Accounting and finance view the numbers in different ways. Accounting looks back to where a company has been, like looking through a rearview mirror. Finance, on the other hand, looks forward, like looking through the windshield, and has to do with deciding where to go and the best way to get there. Both perspectives are indispensable. The accountant provides the information and presents it from a historical viewpoint, and the financier uses it to project into the future and make sound financial decisions.

In addition to examining financial statements in this chapter, we'll take a special look at how to compute a firm's cash flow components, which will help you understand the amount of cash flow generated by the assets and the amount of cash flow returned to investors, both debt holders and equity holders. We'll end the chapter with a look at the rich stores of financial information available from sources on the Internet.

2.1 Financial Statements

We use four financial statements to measure and report the performance of a firm:

1. the balance sheet
2. the income statement
3. the statement of retained earnings
4. the statement of cash flows

Together, these four financial statements contain much of the essential historical information about a firm's performance and management choices. For the finance manager, the statements show where the money came from and where it went. Their format and interrelationships allow the finance manager to project future cash flow for projects of the firm, which is a key element in helping a manager decide whether to accept or reject projects.

Before managers can forecast future cash flow and make budgeting decisions, they must understand historical performance, which the financial statements provide. These financial statements show where the company *has been.* In finance, we want to determine where the company *should go.* From the information embedded in financial statements, we need to know where the firm generated cash and where the firm used cash during the recent time period. Understanding the sources and uses of cash in the recent past enables a manager to predict more accurately the potential cash flow for the company or a project and to recommend where the company should head.

In this chapter's opening section, we concentrate on the balance sheet and the income statement and touch briefly on the statement of retained earnings. Then, in the next section, we examine in detail the statement of cash flows. We first present the sources and uses of cash through the cash flow identity. Then we partition and combine these components of the cash flow identity into the statement of cash flows, which will help you understand why the statement of cash flows is so important in analyzing the performance of the firm and helping to predict the firm's future performance.

The Balance Sheet

The **balance sheet**—the first financial statement we consider—represents the set of assets owned by the company and all claims against these assets. Think of the words *own* and *owe.* The balance sheet states what the company owns and what it owes at a fixed point in time. Notice that fixed point. The balance sheet is like a snapshot of all the assets and claims to these assets at that particular point in time.

Assets are things of economic value that the company owns. They can be physical (such as buildings, equipment, and inventory), financial (such as accounts receivable), or intellectual (such as patents and trademarks), and include cash itself. **Liabilities** are the amounts of money that a company owes to others such as payroll, taxes, and borrowed money via loans. **Equity** is the third section of the balance sheet and is what the owners receive after they have satisfied their liabilities. In other words, it is what is left of the assets once the company has settled the liabilities. Thus, the owners of a company are sometimes called *residual claimants.* We typically call the liabilities the *debt* of the company. Equity represents ownership of the company.

The balance sheet reflects the fundamental starting point of all the financial statements: the basic accounting equation. This equation is actually an **accounting**

identity. An *identity* is a relationship that is always satisfied for all the variables in an equation and is noted by the symbol ≡. In other words,

$$\text{accounting identity: assets} \equiv \text{liabilities} + \text{owners' equity} \qquad \textbf{2.1}$$

The accounting identity is critical to the recording of financial information for a company. It requires that the company record a debit amount and equal credit amount each time it records an economic transaction. In accountancy, we call this system **double-entry bookkeeping** (or **double-entry accounting**). It is what ensures that the balance sheet balances.

Figure 2.1 shows a simplified balance sheet for the years ending 2010 and 2011 for a real company whose name we have changed to Battista Products. The balance sheet shows the change in each category or account over the year. Notice that the balance sheet in Figure 2.1 shows assets on the left and liabilities plus owners' equity on the right, in a graphic rendition of Equation 2.1.

From the finance perspective, the balance sheet has five principal sections of information:

1. cash account
2. working capital accounts
3. long-term capital assets accounts
4. long-term debt accounts
5. ownership accounts

We now look at these five principal sections of the balance sheet of Battista Products in a bit more detail.

Battista Products
Balance Sheet as of December 31, 2011, and December 31, 2010
($ in millions)

ASSETS	2011	2010	Change	LIABILITIES	2011	2010	Change
Current assets				**Current liabilities**			
Cash and equivalents	$ 1,651	$ 1,716	−$ 65	Accounts payable	$ 5,271	$ 5,357	−$ 86
Short-term investments	$ 1,171	$ 3,166	−$1,995	Short-term debt	$ 274	$ 2,889	−$2,615
				Other current liabilities	$ 1,315	$ 1,160	$ 155
Accounts receivable	$ 3,725	$ 3,261	$ 464	**Total current liabilities**	**$ 6,860**	**$ 9,406**	**− $2,546**
Inventories	$ 1,926	$ 1,693	$ 233	Long-term debt	$ 2,550	$ 2,313	$ 237
Other current assets	$ 657	$ 618	$ 39	Other long-term liabilities	$ 1,073	$ 1,688	−$ 615
				Total liabilities	**$10,483**	**$13,407**	**− $2,924**
Total current assets	**$ 9,130**	**$10,454**	**− $1,324**	**OWNERS' EQUITY**			
Net plant, property, and equipment	$ 9,687	$ 8,681	$1,006	Common stock	$ 2,614	$ 2,614	$ 0
				Retained earnings	$ 7,994	$ 5,221	$2,773
Other long-term assets	$ 2,274	$ 2,107	$ 167	**Total owners'equity**	**$10,608**	**$ 7,835**	**$2,773**
TOTAL ASSETS	**$21,091**	**$21,242**	**− $ 151**	**TOTAL LIABILITIES AND OWNERS' EQUITY**	**$21,091**	**$21,242**	**− $ 151**

FIGURE 2.1

Cash account The **cash account** is much like your individual checking account because it tells you how much money you currently have for paying bills or spending on new items. We can find the cash account for Battista Products in the cash and equivalents line under the current assets grouping. Note the change in the cash account from one period to the next. For Battista Products, the cash account decreased by $65 million from 2010 to 2011, which raises a primary question for us as we study financial statements: where did this reduction in cash come from? We will eventually answer this question when we break down some of the accounting information into the cash flow identity and its components in Section 2.2.

Working capital accounts The **working capital accounts** are the current assets and current liabilities of the company. We categorize and analyze these accounts together as those that directly support the daily operations of the firm. *Current assets* are accounts that will normally turn into cash over the course of the operating or business cycle of the firm. *Current liabilities* are accounts that will come due for payment over the operating or business cycle. For example, we expect to receive payment from our customers during the current operating period. On the Battista Products balance sheet, these expected payments are in the amount of $3,725 million (2011) on the accounts receivable line and are part of the company's current assets. On the flip side, Battista Products expects to pay its suppliers. The aggregate balance that Battista owes to the suppliers is in the amount of $5,271 million (2011) on the accounts payable line and is part of Battista's current liabilities. If a company has more current assets than current liabilities, it should be able to pay its bills as they come due over the next operating cycle. The measure of the relationship between current assets and current liabilities is **net working capital**:

$$\text{net working capital} = \text{current assets} - \text{current liabilities} \qquad \textbf{2.2}$$

Looking back at the Battista Products balance sheet, we see that for the two years, net working capital was positive:

$$2010 \text{ net working capital} = \$10{,}454 - \$9{,}406 = \$1{,}048 \text{ (millions)}$$

$$2011 \text{ net working capital} = \$9{,}130 - \$6{,}860 = \$2{,}270 \text{ (millions)}$$

Battista had more potential cash coming in than going out to suppliers, which is a good thing.

Long-term capital assets accounts The *long-term capital assets accounts* of the balance sheet represent the capital investment of the company in things such as land, building, and machinery. As such, they are assets that provide the basis for producing goods and services for sale to generate profit. Battista Products presents two categories in this area:

- Net plant, property, and equipment
- Other long-term assets

We calculate the net plant, property, and equipment category by taking the original value (purchase price) of the plant facility, properties, or equipment and subtracting the accumulated depreciation associated with these assets. Depreciation represents the annual reduction in assets, such as equipment, whose value diminishes over time. Thus, it is proper to call this line net plant, property, and equipment, which is the original cost of plant, property, and equipment minus the total accumulated depreciation that has occurred since the acquisition of the assets.

Other long-term assets include both tangible and intangible property of the company. For example, Battista Products owns patents and copyrights that have value but are not physical assets. These intangible assets are part of the company's value and are therefore listed on the balance sheet.

Long-term liabilities (debt) accounts Debts that a company must pay more than one year from now are *long-term liabilities*. These claims may be from banks and bondholders who have provided capital to a company but whose entire repayment is not due during the coming year or operating cycle. For example, Battista Products currently (2011) has a balance of $2,550 million in its long-term debt account. This account could represent a loan from a bank. Battista will not repay the outstanding balance on the loan this year, however, but over the next several years. Therefore, we do not carry it in a current liability account. Instead, we carry it in a long-term account that signifies a long-term repayment schedule for the loan.

Ownership accounts The final section of interest in the balance sheet is the ownership accounts or owners' equity section. As noted, **owners' equity** or **stockholders' equity** is the remaining or residual value of the company to the owners once the company has satisfied all liabilities. Typically, it is made up of common stock and retained earnings. The *common stock* account reflects the capital contributed to the firm by the stockholders: $2,614 million in the common stock account of Battista Products. *Retained earnings* are the earnings of the company that it reinvests in its core business or uses to pay off debt. The retained earnings of $7,994 million in 2011 represent the net income of Battista Products that the company has reinvested in its operations on behalf of the stockholders.

The Income Statement

The second financial statement, the **income statement**, measures a company's financial performance over a specific period of time. It summarizes and categorizes a company's revenues and the expenses associated with producing those revenues for that period, and it reports the profits of the company. Typically, companies prepare income statements quarterly and annually for outside distribution and usually monthly for internal managers. The bottom line of the income statement is net income, which is revenues minus expenses:

$$\text{net income} = \text{revenues} - \text{expenses} \qquad \textbf{2.3}$$

Figure 2.2 displays a simplified income statement for Battista Products for 2011. We will work our way down this income statement, stopping at key lines along the way to emphasize some of the information that is pertinent to the finance manager.

The income statement begins with revenue (sales) and subtracts various operating expenses until arriving at **earnings before interest and taxes (EBIT)**:

$$\begin{aligned}&\text{revenue} - \text{operating expenses}\\&\quad = \text{earnings before interest and taxes}\end{aligned} \qquad \textbf{2.4}$$

Battista Products Income Statement Year Ending December 31, 2011 ($ in millions)	
Revenue	$35,753
Cost of goods sold	$14,356
Depreciation	$ 1,406
Selling, general, and administrative expenses	$12,774
Other expenses	$ 162
Operating income	$ 7,055
Other income	$ 173
EBIT	$ 7,228
Interest expense	$ 239
Taxable income	$ 6,989
Taxes	$ 1,347
Net income	**$ 5,642**
EPS (diluted)	$ 3.73

FIGURE 2.2

This line is critical in understanding the operating income of a company, because it is an indicator of a company's profitability. Later, we will use EBIT as an important construct for projecting future cash flow for the company.

Next, we subtract interest expense to find the taxable income for the period. Then we calculate and subtract the appropriate taxes. The company must pay taxes at the federal, state, and local level, as well as any fees and licensing costs that are part of operating the business. We finally arrive at net income, the so-called bottom line of the income statement. The bottom line for Battista Products is the $5,642 million net income or profit for the year 2011.

The key issue regarding the income statement is that net income—here the bottom line of $5,642 million—is *not* cash flow. **Net income** is the accounting profit from the operations of the company during the period. **Cash flow** is the increase or decrease in cash for the period. Understanding the timing and amount of cash flow is a key component to making financial decisions. We, as financiers, want to know the cash flow from the business operations of Battista Products. So, how do we find it? We will use the framework of the income statement to find the operating income of the company (an accounting measure) and then make adjustments to it to find the cash flow from operations. To do so, we must first deal with three fundamental issues that separate net income and cash flow: (1) accrual-based accounting, (2) noncash expense items, and (3) interest expense.

Issue 1: Generally accepted accounting principles (GAAP) GAAP are the set of accounting standards, procedures, and principles that companies follow when assembling their financial statements. GAAP procedures allow the use of accrual-based accounting to record revenue. In **accrual-based accounting**, a company recognizes and records revenue at the time of sale, whether or not it has received the revenue in cash. Similarly, the company records expenses associated with the sale at the time of the sale, regardless of whether the company has paid out in cash the actual expenses. Notice the key point here. The company records sales and expenses at a given point in time, regardless of when cash transactions occur. For Battista Products, the revenue of $35,753 million from the income statement reflects both cash and credit sales, so the sales in a given year may not reflect the actual cash the company collected in that year. Because the company assembles the income statement at a specific point in time (at the end of a business quarter or business year), the company can make the sale in one period and receive the cash in another period. Similarly, the actual cash outflow to produce the product may have occurred in an earlier period. Thus, the bottom line—net income—may not reflect the actual cash flow during the period.

Issue 2: Noncash expense items The income statement contains the set of expenses associated with the products or services the company sells during the current operating period. However, we do not associate some of these expenses with current cash flow and label them *noncash expense items*. The primary example is **depreciation**. Depreciation is a current expense of a cash outflow in a previous period. Companies depreciate fixed assets (such as office furniture, equipment, machinery, and buildings) over an assigned time period, but the initial cash outlay for the fixed asset typically occurs at the time that the firm acquires the asset. Therefore, the annual depreciation expense on the income statement is not an actual cash outflow during the period. We adjust the accounting profits to reflect this and other noncash expense items.

Issue 3: Classifying interest expense as part of the financing decision We make a third adjustment to information from the income statement because

FIGURE 2.3

Battista Products Operating Cash Flow Year Ending December 31, 2011 ($ in millions)	
Net income	$ 5,642
Add back depreciation	$ 1,406
Add back interest expense	$ 239
Operating cash flow	**$ 7,287**

in finance, we prefer to classify interest expense as part of the financing decisions of the firm and not as part of its operating decisions. Thus, we distinguish between costs of raising of funds, such as securing and maintaining a loan from a bank, and costs of the normal running of the business, such as producing a product. So, when we measure the company's operating cash flow, we exclude interest expense from the operating expenses.

We are now ready to calculate the **operating cash flow (OCF)** for Battista Products (Figure 2.3). To arrive at the OCF, we start with the net income from the income statement and make adjustments for depreciation and interest expense.

Another way to find operating cash flow from the business for the year is to add depreciation expense to EBIT and then subtract the taxes:

$$\text{operating cash flow} = \text{earnings before interest and taxes} + \text{depreciation} - \text{taxes} \quad \textbf{2.5}$$

So, for Battista Products,

$$\text{operating cash flow} = \$7{,}228 + \$1{,}406 - \$1{,}347 = \$7{,}287 \text{ (million)}$$

The cash flow from operations is $7,287 million, which is considerably larger than the net income for the year of $5,642 million. OCF will become a very important measure later in the text when we apply many of the finance tools to decision making. For now, remember that the operating cash flow represents the funds that the company generates from its normal business operations. Battista requires these funds to maintain the business, grow the business, and pay back the creditors and owners of the company. Without good operating cash flow, a business will not survive.

Statement of Retained Earnings

One special financial statement is the **statement of retained earnings**, which shows the distribution of net income for the past period:

$$\text{change in retained earnings} = \text{net income} - \text{distributed earnings} \quad \textbf{2.6}$$

Each year, a company either reinvests net income in the company (retained earnings) or pays out dividends to owners (distributed earnings). The statement of retained earnings shows that Battista Products started with a beginning balance in retained earnings of $5,221 million from 2010 (from the balance sheet in Figure 2.1), added net income of $5,642 million (from the 2011 income statement in Figure 2.2), and subtracted the $2,689 million in dividends (see Figure 2.4) to owners during 2011. The ending balance is $7,994 million, as Figure 2.4 shows.

FIGURE 2.4

Battista Products Statement of Retained Earnings Year Ending December 31, 2011 ($ in millions)	
Beginning balance	$ 5,221
Add net income	$ 5,642
Subtract dividends	$ 2,869
Ending balance	**$ 7,994**

Please note that neither the balance sheet nor the income statement specifies dividends that Battista paid during the year, but they do appear on statement of retained earnings (Figure 2.4). We need the dividends information to calculate cash flow in Section 2.2.

2.2 Cash Flow Identity and the Statement of Cash Flows

Although financial statements present essential information about the performance of a company, they do not give us the information in a format that helps identify its cash flow. Armed with the accounting information they do provide, however, we can now examine cash flow. To gain insight into the operations and financing decisions of a company, we use the **cash flow identity**, which states that the cash flow from assets is equal to the cash flow to creditors and owners. In other words, it shows that the firm uses the cash that it generates from its operating decisions (money it takes in) to purchase additional assets or to pay creditors and the owners of the company (money it pays out):

$$\text{cash flow from assets} \equiv \text{cash flow to creditors} + \text{cash flow to owners} \qquad \textbf{2.7}$$

In this identity:

- *Cash flow from assets* shows the success or failure of how the company uses the assets (the operating and capital spending decisions) to generate cash inflow.
- *Cash flow to creditors* shows how the firm uses debt to finance the operations and its repayment of the debt.
- *Cash flow to owners* completes the overview of financing and shows any additional contributions by the owners and the return of capital to the owners.

Let's now show these financial cash flow relationships with Battista Products. We can build each of the three components and then put them together to verify that the identity holds. Figure 2.5 displays the set of cash flow equations that show how the individual components of cash flow add up to the cash flow identity, and we will examine each portion in turn. To keep the big picture in your mind, refer to this figure as you proceed through the discussion.

The First Component: Cash Flow from Assets

We start with the three components of the cash flow from assets: (1) operating cash flow, (2) capital spending, and (3) change in net working capital.

● **cash flow from assets** ≡ ● cash flow to creditors + ● cash flow to owners

● cash flow from assets

cash flow from assets = operating cash flow – net capital spending
– change in net working capital

operating cash flow = EBIT + depreciation – taxes

net capital spending = ending net fixed assets – beginning net fixed assets
+ depreciation

change in net working capital = ending net working capital
– beginning net working capital

net working capital = current assets – current liabilities

● cash flow to creditors

cash flow to creditors = interest expense – net new borrowing from creditors

net new borrowing = ending long-term liabilities – beginning long-term liabilities

● cash flow to owners

cash flow to owners = dividends – net new borrowing from owners

net new borrowing from owners = change in equity

change in equity = ending common stock and paid-in-surplus
– beginning common stock and paid-in-surplus

FIGURE 2.5 Cash flow identity and components.

Operating cash flow (*OCF*) is still the $7,287 million originally derived in Figure 2.3. It is the net income of the company, with depreciation and interest expenses added back in to show the operating cash flow.

Capital spending is the change in the long-term asset accounts from 2010 to 2011 (see Figure 2.1) plus the depreciation expense from the income statement. When we want to find the capital spending for the year, we look at the balance in the net long-term assets account at the end of the year (2011) and subtract the balance from the end of the preceding year (2010). Just as we removed the depreciation expense from the net income because it is not a cash flow, we also remove it from capital spending by adding it to the fixed assets at the beginning of the year. The income statement in Figure 2.2 indicates that depreciation expense for the year for Battista Products was $1,406 million.

So, taking the long-term assets accounts from the Battista Products balance sheet in Figure 2.1, we have the following information:

	2011	2010
Net plant, property, and equipment	$ 9,687	$ 8,681
Other long-term assets	$ 2,274	$ 2,107
Total long-term assets	**$11,961**	**$10,788**

$$\text{Capital spending} = (\text{ending long-term assets} - \text{beginning long-term assets}) + \text{depreciation}$$
$$= (\$11{,}961 - \$10{,}788) + \$1{,}406 = \$2{,}579 \text{ (million)}$$

On the balance sheet, the net plant, property, and equipment figure includes accumulated depreciation. So, as we add this year's depreciation expense from the income statement to the accumulated depreciation on the balance sheet, it will reduce the balance in the net plant, property, and equipment. We must account for the change in net plant, property, and equipment that comes from the increase in accumulated depreciation, as this is again not a cash flow. To get the true capital spending, we must add back the current year's depreciation expense. The previous equation reflects this. To verify this concept, ask yourself: what change would you see in total long-term assets if there were no capital spending for the year? You would see net plant, property, and equipment—and thus long-term assets—lower by the depreciation expense. This is why we add back the depreciation expense to get capital spending.

The *change in net working capital* looks at both current assets and current liabilities from the balance sheet (see Figure 2.1) and computes the change from 2010 to 2011. We have the following information for Battista Products:

ASSETS	2011	2010	LIABILITIES	2011	2010
Current assets			**Current liabilities**		
Cash and equivalents	$1,651	$ 1,716	Accounts payable	$5,271	$5,357
Short-term investments	$1,171	$ 3,166			
Accounts receivable	$3,725	$ 3,261	Short-term debt	$ 274	$2,889
Inventories	$1,926	$ 1,693			
Other current assets	$ 657	$ 618	Other current liabilities	$1,315	$1,160
Total current assets	**$9,130**	**$10,454**	**Total current liabilities**	**$6,860**	**$9,406**

Recall that net working capital equals current assets minus current liabilities. We therefore have

$$\text{net working capital for 2011} = \$9{,}130 - \$6{,}860 = \$2{,}270 \text{ (million)}$$

$$\text{net working capital for 2010} = \$10{,}454 - \$9{,}406 = \$1{,}048 \text{ (million)}$$

and the change is

$$\begin{aligned}\text{change in net working capital} &= \text{ending net working capital} \\ &\quad - \text{beginning net working capital} \\ &= \$2{,}270 - \$1{,}048 = \$1{,}222 \text{ (million)}\end{aligned}$$

Combining the three pieces gives us the cash flow from assets:

$$\begin{aligned}\text{cash flow from assets} &= \text{operating cash flow} - \text{capital spending} \\ &\quad - \text{change in net working capital} \\ &= \$7{,}287 - \$2{,}579 - \$1{,}222 = \$3{,}486 \text{ (million)}\end{aligned}$$

The cash flow from assets for Battista Products is therefore $3,486 million. Cash flow from assets thus provides a partial picture of the cash that the company generated, its operating cash flow, and how the company used some of the cash.

The Second Component: Cash Flow to Creditors

Now we look at the interest that a company pays and any new borrowing from creditors or repayments of principal to creditors. This information tells us if we borrowed new funds via debt or if we repaid some of the old debt as well as interest payments made to service the outstanding debt. These items come from the long-term liabilities section of the balance sheet (increase or decrease in borrowing) and the income statement (interest expense):

	2011	2010	Change
Long-term debt	$2,550	$2,313	$237
Other long-term liabilities	$1,073	$1,688	−$615
Total long-term liabilities	**$3,623**	**$4,001**	**−$378**

The creditors received a net of $378 million as the company paid down some of its outstanding debt (repaid principal). Adding the interest expense of $239 million (from the income statement), we have a total paid out to creditors of $617 million:

$$\text{cash flow to creditors} = \text{interest expense} - \text{net new borrowing from creditors}$$
$$= \$239 - (-\$378) = \$617 \text{ (million)}$$

The Third Component: Cash Flow to Owners

The final component is the cash that the company paid to owners (dividends) minus any new borrowing from owners through selling common stock or through any stock repurchased by the company. (Stock repurchases occur when a company buys back its own stock.) For Battista Products, dividends for the period (see Figure 2.4) were $2,869 million. For the past year, there was no change in common stock, no additional stock issued, and no repurchase of existing company stock, so

$$\text{cash flow to owners} = \text{dividends} - \text{net new borrowing from owners}$$
$$= \$2{,}869 - \$0 = \$2{,}869 \text{ (million)}$$

Putting It All Together: The Cash Flow Identity

We can now verify the cash flow identity for the past year for Battista Products:

$$\text{cash flow from assets} \equiv \text{cash flow to creditors} + \text{cash flow to owners}$$
$$\$3{,}486 \text{ (million)} \equiv \$617 \text{ (million)} + \$2{,}869 \text{ (million)}$$

By examining the components of the cash flow identity, we now know that Battista Products generated $7,287 million from operations (OCF) and used $2,579 million for new capital assets and $1,222 million to increase working capital. We also know that Battista Products paid out a total of $617 million to creditors and $2,869 million to owners through dividends. The cash flow identity has helped us see the year in terms of cash flow, which is the way a financier wants to see it.

The Statement of Cash Flows

Now that we have used the income statement accounts and the balance sheet accounts to partition the cash flow into (1) cash flow from assets, (2) cash flow to creditors, and (3) cash flow to owners, it is easy to show how these account for the change in cash for the year. We will now look at the fourth accounting statement, the **statement of cash flows**, and see how it ties back to the cash flow identity. We will convert the three sections of the cash flow identity into the three sections of the statement of cash flows:

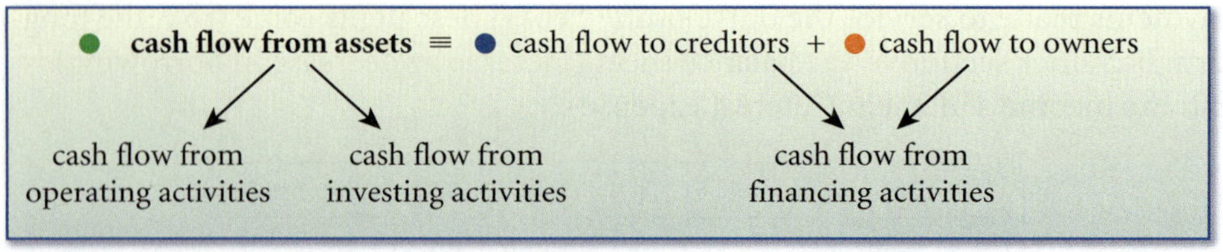

The statement of cash flows or the sources and uses of cash illuminates the impact of three areas for the year: (1) operating activities, (2) capital spending or investing activities, and (3) financing activities. The statement of cash flows also enables us to answer the question, "Where did Battista Products' $65 million decrease in cash come from?" On the statement of cash flows, sources signify cash inflows (positive amounts) and uses—in parentheses—signify cash outflows (negative amounts). The sources minus the uses equals the change in the cash account for the year. Figure 2.6 shows the statement of the sources and uses of cash for Battista Products.

The first section in the statement of cash flows displays the operating activities. It contains the $7,287 million that we calculated for the operating cash flow. It also contains the change in current assets and change in current liabilities. We had combined the current assets and current liabilities into net working capital for the cash flow identity, but now we separate the current assets and current liabilities. Using the balance sheet information from 2010 and 2011, we have the following changes for current assets:

$$\text{current assets in 2010 (minus cash)} = \$3{,}166 + \$3{,}261 + \$1{,}693 + \$618 = \$8{,}738$$

$$\text{current assets in 2011 (minus cash)} = \$1{,}171 + \$3{,}725 + \$1{,}926 + \$657 = \$7{,}479$$

and

$$\text{change in currents assets} = \$7{,}479 - \$8{,}738 = -\$1{,}259 \text{ (million)}$$

Battista Products **Sources and Uses of Cash** **Year Ending December 31, 2011** **($ in millions)**		
Sources and (uses): operating activities		
Operating cash flow	$ 7,287	
Decrease in current assets excluding cash	$ 1,259	
Increase in current liabilities	($ 2,546)	
Cash from operating activities		$ 6,000
Sources and (uses): investing activities		
Capital spending	($ 2,579)	
Cash from investing activities		($ 2,579)
Sources and (uses): financing activities		
Interest expense	($ 239)	
Dividends	($ 2,869)	
Decrease in long-term debt	($ 378)	
Increase in common stock	$ 0	
Cash from financing activities		($ 3,486)
Net sources and (uses) or change in cash account		($ 65)
Beginning balance in cash account		$ 1,716
Ending balance in cash account		**$ 1,651**

FIGURE 2.6

A reduction in current assets is a source of cash. An increase is a use of cash. Here we have a reduction that reflects a source of cash of $1,259 million for 2011. Next, we look at the change in current liabilities:

$$\text{current liabilities 2010} = \$9{,}406$$

$$\text{current liabilities 2011} = \$6{,}860$$

and

$$\text{change in current liabilities} = \$6{,}860 - \$9{,}406 = -\$2{,}546 \text{ (million)}$$

A reduction in current liabilities is a use of cash. An increase is a source of cash. Here we have a use of $2,546 million for 2011.

The second section presents capital spending, the change in the long-term asset accounts. We previously calculated the capital spending at $2,579 million. This increase is a use of cash.

The last section shows the financing activities of the firm for the year. From the cash flow identity, we can see that this section simply combines the cash flow to creditors and the cash flow to owners. Here, the payment of interest expense is a use of cash, so we report the $239 million from the income statement for interest expenses in this section. The payment of dividends from the statement of retained earnings is also a use of cash. Any additional borrowing from debt holders in the long-term liabilities section of the balance sheet is a source of cash; a reduction in the long-term liabilities accounts is a repayment of the borrowed funds, that is, a use of cash. As calculated earlier, the change in the long-term liabilities was a reduction of $378 million, a use of cash. The last part of this section is increases or decreases in borrowing from the owners. This year, we had no change in common stock, so there is neither an increase nor a decrease in cash from the sale or purchase of common stock.

The statement of cash flows for the year 2011 shows why the cash account decreased by $65 million. The operations generated $6,000 million, but the company spent $2,579 million on capital investments and another $3,486 million in repayments for borrowed funds. The repayment to shareholders was $2,869 million (via dividends) and to creditors $617 million (via repayment of loans and interest expense). Battista Products still has a healthy $1,651 million in cash as 2011 comes to a close, but now we know that operations provided a sufficient amount of cash to cover both the needed capital spending and payments to creditors and owners.

Free Cash Flow

We often associate the term **free cash flow** with valuing a firm based on the sources and uses of cash generated by a business. However, it is a misnomer, as nothing in business is free. Free cash flow generally refers to *cash flow from assets*: the cash available to pay back creditors and owners once the company has made the investments in working capital and capital assets necessary for growing and continuing the business. It is the remaining cash "free" to distribute to creditors and owners. Therefore, we will continue to use the term "cash flow from assets" instead of the term "free cash flow" to explain the cash that the company generates to operate the company. Regardless of which term we use, it is the timing and the amount of cash flow that is important when valuing a company or a future project of the company.

This concludes our review of the four accounting statements and our introduction to cash flow through the cash flow identity. We will reconnect with these topics and accounting statements throughout the book, especially in Chapter 14 when we break down the accounting numbers again into financial ratios to help you understand and evaluate firm performance.

2.3 Financial Performance Reporting

We have just examined some of the financial statements that public companies publish, but why do they report their performance? One reaction to the 1929 stock market crash was the creation of the SEC with the requirement that public companies report their financial performance. The annual report is now a regular activity of public firms. Companies send it to current owners (shareholders) and the SEC. They also make it available to prospective owners, financial analysts, and others interested in a company's performance. It usually contains a minimum of nine sections (with more components of the report available on the company's Web site):

1. Company highlights
2. President's letter to the shareholders
3. Description of the company's activities (usually with pictures and graphs)
4. Management's analysis of the company's performance
5. Financial statements
6. Notes to financial statements
7. Auditor's report
8. Financial ratios
9. Corporate information

We call the report, which companies must file annually with the SEC, the *10-K report*. It contains the annual report as well as additional information about company history, organizational structure, subsidiaries, and equity holdings. A company must file the 10-K within sixty days after the end of the company's fiscal year. Companies must also file quarterly reports, called *10-Q reports*, with the SEC.

Regulation Fair Disclosure

A problem in the world of finance can arise when some owners or potential owners have access to more information about a company than others do. For example, officers of a company or others who have financial responsibility to the owners cannot trade on their acquired private information about the company prior to making the information public, nor can they share their private information with a select group of investors. The SEC passed a regulation called **fair disclosure** (regulation fair disclosure, or Reg FD) that requires companies to release all material information to all investors at the same time. In the past, companies had released information in conference calls to select groups of analysts and had excluded many shareholders and the public. The release of company performance and the financial statements falls under this fair disclosure regulation.

Notes to the Financial Statements

Our examination of the financial statements in this chapter has concentrated on the accounts and their dollar balances. Some of the bases for these numbers may need more explanation. Notes to the financial statements help explain many details necessary to gain a more complete picture of a firm's performance. Some of the items that financial notes often disclose include:

- How a specific item was computed
- Additional information on a company's financial condition
  - Special issues concerning its debt or contingent accounts
  - Information on the potential effect of a pending lawsuit
  - Events regarding a loss or impairment
- Methods used to prepare the financial statements
- Difference between prior estimates and actual results

The notes are packed with information and round out the total picture of a firm.

2.4 Financial Statements on the Internet

Although companies print and mail the annual report to owners and the SEC, much of the financial statement information is available at various financial Web sites. The SEC has a site named EDGAR (for the Electronic Data Gathering, Analysis, and Retrieval system) that provides free access to the reports (www.sec.gov/edgar.shtml). An online tutorial at that site helps new viewers find a company and its financial statements.

Other sources specialize in presenting both the financial statements and financial data such as key statistics, recent news stories, analysts' coverage, price quotes, and historical stock prices and dividends. One of the most widely used is Yahoo! Finance (finance.yahoo.com). In addition to housing financial statements, profiles, and a rich array of additional information, Yahoo! Finance also links to market indexes, data sources, financial news sources, and many other helpful Web sites. If you submit a query about a company at the Yahoo! Finance site, you will see a menu of financial and company information that includes a section on financial statements and provides the past three years of each one. In addition, you can access the recent stock prices of the company and its dividend history. For example, a query of Minnesota Mining and Manufacturing Company, better known as 3M, under financial statements and then under income statements produced the income statement depicted in Figure 2.7.

Notice that we have *cost of revenue*, not cost of goods sold, in Figure 2.7. We do not specify depreciation expense because we have folded it into the cost of revenue section. To produce the operating cash flow, it is necessary to untangle the cost of revenue into the cost of goods sold and depreciation. We also have additional items such as minority interests, effect of accounting changes, and extraordinary items. All income statements at Yahoo! Finance include these line items, even though they may not be part of an individual company's income statement for that year.

All kinds of financial data are available at Web sites like Yahoo! Finance, including income statements, balance sheets, and statements of cash flow for publicly traded companies. As you proceed through this book, you will also find the Internet to be a rich resource for other financial data such as streaming stock quotes, interest rates, and exchange rates. The Internet is yet another tool in the arsenal of the finance manager.

FIGURE 2.7

Income Statement 3M Company ($ in thousands)			
Period ending	31 Dec 10	31 Dec 09	31 Dec 08
Total revenue	26,662,000	23,123,000	25,269,000
Cost of revenue	13,831,000	12,109,000	13,379,000
Gross profit	12,831,000	11,014,000	11,890,000
Operating expense			
Research and development	1,434,000	1,293,000	1,404,000
Selling, general, and administrative	5,479,000	4,907,000	5,245,000
Nonrecurring			23,000
Others			
Operating income	5,918,000	4,814,000	5,218,000
Total other income/expenses	38,000	37,000	105,000
EBIT	5,956,000	4,851,000	5,323,000
Interest expense	201,000	219,000	215,000
Income before taxes	5,755,000	4,632,000	5,108,000
Taxes	1,592,000	1,388,000	1,588,000
Minority interests	(78,000)	(51,000)	(60,000)
Net income continuing operations	4,085,000	3,193,000	3,460,000
Discontinued operations			
Extraordinary items			
Effect of accounting changes			
Net income	**4,085,000**	**3,193,000**	**3,460,000**

Figure 2.8 shows the balance sheet for 3M from Yahoo! Finance. Again, we see some line items that are new to our balance sheet, such as goodwill, deferred asset charges, and treasury stock. We will not go into additional detail on these balance sheet line items in this text.

In addition, a statement of cash flow for 3M at Yahoo! Finance provides information on where the company generated and used cash. Yahoo! Finance's chosen format is not consistent with the three-part examination that we went through in Section 2.2 to construct cash flows, and reconstructing it to fit our categories of cash flow is not a productive exercise for this book. Remember, though, that online cash flow statements show the depreciation expense for the period. If we want to break down the cost of revenue into its two major components—cost of goods sold and depreciation—we would need to look at the statement of cash flow to obtain the depreciation amount.

Financial data on the Internet or via company annual reports provide a wealth of knowledge about a firm's operations. Knowing the relationship of these financial statements and understanding how to use the data are important tools for all finance managers. Visit some of the Internet sites that provide financial information. As the "Putting Finance to Work" feature illustrates, it may be in your career interest to know as much as possible about a company's financial performance before you sign on as an employee or investor.

As we progress through the book, we will refer to financial statements, as well as the important concept of cash flow. These are fundamental tools of finance: work

FIGURE 2.8

3M Company Balance Sheet ($ in thousands)			
Period ending	31 Dec 10	31 Dec 09	31 Dec 08
ASSETS			
Current assets			
Cash and equivalent	3,377,000	3,040,000	1,849,000
Short-term investments	1,101,000	744,000	588,000
Net receivables	3,615,000	3,250,000	3,466,000
Inventory	3,155,000	2,639,000	3,013,000
Other	967,000	1,122,000	682,000
Total current assets	**12,215,000**	**10,795,000**	**9,598,000**
Long-term investments	686,000	928,000	430,000
Property, plant, and equipment	7,279,000	7,000,000	6,886,000
Goodwill	6,820,000	5,832,000	5,573,000
Intangible assets	1,820,000	1,342,000	1,398,000
Accumulated amortization			
Other assets	1,336,000	1,353,000	675,000
Deferred asset charges			807,000
TOTAL ASSETS	**30,156,000**	**27,250,000**	**25,547,000**
LIABILITIES			
Current liabilities			
Accounts payable	2,798,000	2,385,000	2,742,000
Short-term debt	1,269,000	613,000	1,755,000
Other	2,022,000	1,899,000	1,342,000
Total current liabilities	6,089,000	4,897,000	5,839,000
Long-term debt	4,183,000	5,097,000	5,224,000
Other liabilities	3,867,000	3,954,000	4,138,000
Deferred liability charges			43,000
Minority interest	354,000	538,000	424,000
Total liabilities	**14,493,000**	**14,486,000**	**15,668,000**
STOCKHOLDERS' EQUITY			
Common stock	9,000	9,000	9,000
Retained earnings	25,995,000	23,753,000	22,248,000
Treasury stock	(10,266,000)	(10,397,000)	(11,676,000)
Capital surplus	3,468,000	3,153,000	3,001,000
Other equity	(3,543,000)	(3,754,000)	(3,703,000)
Total stock equity	**15,663,000**	**12,764,000**	**9,879,000**
TOTAL LIABILITIES AND OWNERS' EQUITY	**30,156,000**	**27,250,000**	**25,547,000**

to master them. Keep in mind the difference between finance's perspective and accounting's perspective on the financial numbers of the company. The accounting perspective is a rearview mirror for constructing these historical financial statements (where we have been), whereas finance is a windshield view (where we are heading) for using and reformatting these financial statements.

Putting Finance to Work

Look Before You Leap

In 2008, the U.S. economy entered the deepest recession since the Great Depression of the 1930s. Three years later, in the summer of 2011, stock prices and corporate profits have rebounded, but unemployment remains close to 9%. Although the unemployment rate for college graduates is only half that for those with just a high school diploma (5% and 10%, respectively), many new graduates struggle to find employment and worry about their career prospects once they do.

Even in a sluggish economy, however, some industries grow as other shrink, and within industries, some companies thrive while others languish. Students in all majors would do well to spend some time studying the financial statements of companies for which they might be interested in working. Focusing your job search on growing industries and the fastest-growing companies within the industry is likely to produce more job offers and better opportunities for career advancement after employment.

Consider the restaurant industry and compare some key figures from the financial statements of Chipotle Mexican Grill and Denny's, for example. The two chains operate in the same industry—full-service restaurants—but their recent financial histories have been very different. These differences might have had important consequences for those who accepted entry-level management positions with these companies. While Chipotle Mexican Grill was rapidly opening new restaurants and recruiting new managers, Denny's was closing restaurants and announcing layoffs. How did financial statements reveal the differences between these two companies? Look at some key figures from the Denny's financial statements for the period 2008 through 2010:

Denny's ($ in millions)			
Year	**2010**	**2009**	**2008**
Sales revenue	$548	$608	$760
Operating income	$ 55	$ 72	$ 61
Net income	$ 23	$ 42	$ 15
Total assets	$311	$313	$347

For Denny's, every measure of size and profitability has decreased from 2008 to 2010. At best, companies with decreasing sales and assets will create fewer opportunities for professional growth and promotion. At worst, young managers and professionals may lose their jobs after a year or two, slowing their career momentum and forcing them to start over at another company. Companies may use downsizing as an opportunity to eliminate redundant or underperforming employees, but the default rule is last in, first out.

Chipotle Mexican Grill

Key figures from Chipotle tell a very different story. Although the company is not even 20 years old, it is now more than three times the size of Denny's. Sales revenue, operating income, net income, and total assets all indicate rapid growth. Chipotle's financial statements suggest a career environment that is both more dynamic and more stable than what might be expected at Denny's.

Chipotle Mexican Grill			
Year	**2010**	**2009**	**2008**
Sales revenue	$1,836	$1,518	$1,332
Operating income	$ 288	$ 204	$ 124
Net income	$ 179	$ 127	$ 78
Total assets	$1,122	$ 962	$ 825

Career advisors unanimously suggest that applicants for professional and managerial jobs learn all they can about a company before going to an interview. Studying the financial statements will help applicants in any business field—not just finance and accounting—ask intelligent and probing questions at the interview and also choose the company that offers the best opportunity for a stable and satisfying career.

To review this chapter, see the Summary Card at the end of the text.

Key Terms

accounting identity, p. 28
accrual-based accounting, p. 32
assets, p. 28
balance sheet, p. 28
cash account, p. 30
cash flow, p. 32
cash flow identity, p. 34
depreciation, p. 32
double-entry accounting, p. 29
double-entry bookkeeping, p. 29
earnings before interest and taxes (EBIT), p. 31
equity, p. 28
free cash flow, p. 39
generally accepted accounting principles (GAAP), p. 32
income statement, p. 31
liabilities, p. 28
net income, p. 32
net working capital, p. 30
operating cash flow (OCF), p. 33
owners' equity, p. 31
statement of cash flows, p. 37
statement of retained earnings, p. 33
stockholders' equity, p. 31
working capital accounts, p. 30

Questions

1. Debits always equal credits. What type of accounting system uses this requirement? What is the accounting identity? What is the connection between "debits always equal credits" and the accounting identity?
2. What is the difference between a current asset and a long-term asset? What is the difference between a current liability and a long-term liability? What is the difference between a debtor's claim and an owner's claim?
3. Why is the term *residual claimant* applied to a shareholder (owner) of a business?
4. What is the difference between net income and operating cash flow?
5. What is the purpose of the statement of retained earnings?
6. Why do financial notes accompany the annual report? Give an example of a financial note from an annual report. (Look up the annual report of a company on its Web site and read its financial notes.)
7. What are the three components of the cash flow from assets?
8. What does an increase in net working capital mean with regard to cash flow?
9. How does a company return money to debt lenders? How do you determine how much was returned over the past year?
10. Who receives the annual reports of a company? What effect does regulation fair disclosure have on the distribution of financial information?

Prepping for Exams

1. The purpose of studying financial statements is ____________.
   - **a.** to mechanically build portfolio analysis
   - **b.** to understand those portions of the statements that have relevance for financial decision making

c. to primarily investigate all portions of the statements that have relevance for dividend policy
d. to mechanically learn how to read and understand notes

2. Understanding the sources and uses of cash in the recent past will enable a manager to _______ the cash flow for a potential project of the firm.

a. determine with perfect precision
b. forecast with perfect precision
c. predict more accurately
d. know today

3. It is important to remember that the fundamental _________ of accounting is the debit and credit recording activity in which debits always equal credits.

a. effect
b. end product
c. outcome
d. identity

4. The income statement begins with revenue and subtracts various operating expenses until arriving at _____________.

a. earnings after taxes
b. net income
c. taxable income
d. earnings before interest and taxes (EBIT)

5. Which of the following statements is *true*?

a. The finance manager uses the framework of the income statement to find the operating income of the company (an accounting measure), which is also the true cash flow from operations.
b. In accrual-based accounting, a company records revenue at the time of sale if it has received the revenue in cash.
c. Three fundamental issues separate net income and cash flow: accrual accounting, noncash expense items, and interest expense.
d. Generally accepted accounting principles (GAAP) in the United States do not allow the use of accrual accounting to record revenue.

6. Which of the following equations is *true*?

a. operating cash flow = EBIT + depreciation − taxes
b. net capital spending = ending net fixed assets − depreciation
c. change in net working capital = current assets − current liabilities
d. cash flow from assets = operating cash flow + net capital spending

7. Cash and equivalents are $1,561; short-term investments are $1,052; accounts receivables are $3,616; accounts payable are $5,173; short-term debt is $288; inventories are $1,816; other current liabilities are $1,401; and other current assets are $707. What is the amount of total current liabilities?

a. $8,752
b. $6,974
c. $6,862
d. $6,574

8. Which of the following sections is *not* contained in the annual report?
   a. notes to financial statements
   b. management's analysis of the company's performance
   c. prediction of gross national product
   d. auditor's report

9. Which of the following items may be included on all balance sheets at Yahoo! Finance, even though they may not be part of an individual company's balance sheet for that year?
   a. effect of accounting changes, extraordinary items, and treasury stock
   b. deferred long-term asset charges, treasury stock, and extraordinary items
   c. goodwill, deferred long-term asset charges, and treasury stock
   d. cost of revenue, goodwill, and treasury stock

10. With regard to the cash flow statement, assume that we want to break down Yahoo! Finance's cost of revenue into its two major components: cost of goods sold and depreciation. To do so, we would need to look at _____________ for the depreciation amount.
   a. the statement of cash flow
   b. both the income statement and the statement of cash flow
   c. both the balance sheet and the statement of cash flow
   d. the income statement

Problems

These problems are available in MyFinanceLab.

1. ***Balance sheet.*** From the following balance sheet accounts,
   a. construct a balance sheet for 2010 and 2011.
   b. list all the working capital accounts.
   c. find the net working capital for the years ending 2010 and 2011.
   d. calculate the change in net working capital for the year 2011.

Balance Sheet Accounts of Roman Corporation

Account	Balance 12/31/2010	Balance 12/31/2011
Accumulated depreciation	$2,020	$2,670
Accounts payable	$1,800	$2,060
Accounts receivable	$2,480	$2,690
Cash	$1,300	$1,090
Common stock	$4,990	$4,990
Inventory	$5,800	$6,030
Long-term debt	$7,800	$8,200
Plant, property, and equipment	$8,400	$9,200
Retained earnings	$1,370	$1,090

2. ***Income statement.*** From the income statement accounts on the next page,
   a. produce the income statement for the year
   b. produce the operating cash flow for the year

Income Statement Accounts for the Year Ending 2011

Account	Balance
Cost of goods sold	$345,000
Interest expense	$ 82,000
Taxes	$ 2,000
Revenue	$744,000
Selling, general, and administrative expenses	$ 66,000
Depreciation	$112,000

3. ***Balance sheet.*** From the following balance sheet accounts,
   a. construct a balance sheet for 2010 and 2011
   b. list all the working capital accounts
   c. find the net working capital for the years ending 2010 and 2011
   d. calculate the change in net working capital for the year 2011

Balance Sheet Accounts of Athens Corporation

Account	Balance 12/31/2010	Balance 12/31/2011
Accumulated depreciation	$4,234	$4,866
Accounts payable	$2,900	$3,210
Accounts receivable	$3,160	$3,644
Cash	$1,210	$1,490
Common stock	$4,778	$7,278
Inventory	$4,347	$5,166
Long-term debt	$3,600	$2,430
Plant, property, and equipment	$8,675	$9,840
Retained earnings	$1,880	$2,356

4. ***Income statement.*** From the following income statement accounts,
   a. produce the income statement for the year
   b. produce the operating cash flow for the year

Income Statement Accounts for the Year Ending 2011

Account	Balance
Cost of goods sold	$1,419,000
Interest expense	$ 288,000
Taxes	$ 318,000
Revenue	$2,984,000
Selling, general, and administrative expenses	$ 454,000
Depreciation	$ 258,000

5. ***Operating cash flow.*** Find the operating cash flow for the year for Harper Brothers Inc. if it had sales revenue of $300,000,000, cost of goods sold of

$140,000,000, sales and administrative costs of $40,000,000, depreciation expense of $65,000,000, and a tax rate of 40%.

6. ***Operating cash flow.*** Find the operating cash flow for the year for Robinson and Sons if it had sales revenue of $80,000,000, cost of goods sold of $35,000,000, sales and administrative costs of $6,400,000, depreciation expense of $7,600,000, and a tax rate of 30%.

For problems 7 through 14, use the data from the following financial statements:

Partial Income Statement Year Ending 2011	
Sales revenue	$350,000
Cost of goods sold	$140,000
Fixed costs	$ 43,000
Selling, general, and administrative expenses	$ 28,000
Depreciation	$ 46,000

Partial Balance Sheet 12/31/2010			
ASSETS		**LIABILITIES**	
Cash	$ 16,000	Notes payable	$ 14,000
Accounts receivable	$ 28,000	Accounts payable	$ 19,000
Inventories	$ 48,000	Long-term debt	$190,000
Fixed assets	$368,000	**OWNERS' EQUITY**	
Accumulated depreciation	$142,000	Retained earnings	
Intangible assets	$ 82,000	Common stock	$130,000

Partial Balance Sheet 12/31/2011			
ASSETS		**LIABILITIES**	
Cash	$ 26,000	Notes payable	$ 12,000
Accounts receivable	$ 19,000	Accounts payable	$ 24,000
Inventories	$ 53,000	Long-term debt	$162,000
Fixed assets	$448,000	**OWNERS' EQUITY**	
Accumulated depreciation		Retained earnings	
Intangible assets	$ 82,000	Common stock	$180,000

7. ***Income statement.*** Complete the partial income statement if the company paid interest expense of $18,000 for 2011 and had an overall tax rate of 40% for 2011.

8. ***Balance sheet.*** Complete the balance sheet. *Hint:* Find the accumulated depreciation for 2011 first.

9. ***Statement of retained earnings.*** Complete the statement of retained earnings for 2011 and determine the dividends paid last year.

10. ***Fixed assets.*** What are the net fixed assets for the years 2010 and 2011?

11. ***Cash flow from assets.*** Find the cash flow from assets for 2011 and break it into its three parts: operating cash flow, capital spending, and change in net working capital.

12. ***Cash flow to creditors***. Find the cash flow to creditors for 2011 by parts and total, with the parts being interest expense and increases in borrowing.
13. ***Cash flow to owners***. Find the cash flow to owners for 2011 by parts and total, with the parts being dividends paid and increases in borrowing.
14. ***Cash flow identity***. Verify the cash flow identity: cash flow from assets = cash flow to creditors + cash flow to owners

For problems 15 through 17, obtain the balance sheet, income statement, and statement of cash flow for PepsiCo (ticker symbol PEP) for the most recent year from Yahoo! Finance and answer the following questions.

15. Provide the following amounts for PepsiCo:
    a. net income
    b. depreciation (see cash flow statement)
    c. cash flow from operating activities
    d. cash flow from investing activities
    e. cash flow from financing activities
    f. change in cash and equivalents
16. Explain the difference between net income and the change in cash and equivalents for PepsiCo. In other words, why is the profit or loss of PepsiCo different from the change in its cash and equivalents account?
17. Using the cash flow statement, find the dividends paid to PepsiCo owners in the most recent year.

For problems 18 through 20, obtain the balance sheet, income statement, and statement of cash flow for Pfizer (ticker symbol PFE) for the most recent year from Yahoo! Finance and answer the following questions.

18. Provide the following amounts for Pfizer:
    a. net income
    b. depreciation (see cash flow statement)
    c. cash flow from operating activities
    d. cash flow from investing activities
    e. cash flow from financing activities
    f. change in cash and equivalents
19. Explain the difference between net income and the change in cash and equivalents for Pfizer. In other words, why is the profit or loss of Pfizer different from the change in its cash and equivalents account?
20. Using the cash flow statement, find the dividends that Pfizer paid to its owners in the most recent year.

These problems are available in MyFinanceLab.

Advanced Problems for Spreadsheet Application

1. ***Income statement.***
    a. Company A and B have taken different approaches to selling glassware. Company A has decided to make glass stemware that sells for a premium at \$16.98 per glass. Company B has decided to make a less expensive glass (without stems) that sells for \$11.98 per glass. Last year, Company A sold 847,000 stemmed glasses. Company B sold 1,388,000 glasses. Given the following additional information about each firm, construct an income statement for the two companies and see which company had the highest gross margin (revenue minus cost of goods sold), highest EBIT (earnings before interest and taxes), highest taxable income, highest net income, and highest OCF (operating cash flow).

Information	Company A (stemware)	Company B (without stems)
Cost per unit of glassware	$ 8.17	$ 6.69
Fixed costs	$1,245,788	$1,354,218
Selling, general, and administrative expenses	$ 785,038	$ 584,431
Depreciation expense	$1,489,374	$ 1,137,890
Interest expense	$ 501,030	$ 698,540
Tax rate	37.5%	37.5%

b. Company B is thinking of upgrading the quality of its glassware. It believes it can raise its price by 25%, but doing so will cause its cost per unit to rise by 18%. Its sales volume will fall by 15% (85% of its current volume). However, letting the market know that it has a better quality glassware will require a doubling of the current selling, general, and administrative cost. Using a spreadsheet, redo the income statement for this scenario. Does it improve net income and operating cash flow for Company B? How does the company now compare to Company A?

Required: In the spreadsheet, use a separate cell for each piece of information and then construct the income statement by using a formula or cell reference for each individual line of the statement.

2. ***Balance sheet.*** Reach Manufacturing has lost their computer systems and must reconstruct the last two years of their balance sheet. They have been able to get the following information out of their crashed computer:

2010 Information

Cash	$ 23,000
Accounts receivable	$ 518,000
Inventory	$ 639,000
Total current assets	$1,242,000
Fixed assets	$ 4,387,000
Intangible assets	$ 465,000
Total assets	$5,085,000

Accounts payable	$ 419,000
Notes payable	$ 390,000
Long-term debt	$3,540,000
Common stock	$ 330,000

2011 Information

Cash	$ 26,000
Marketable securities	$ 58,000
Inventory	$ 910,000
Fixed assets	$4,975,000
Accumulated depreciation	$1,364,000
Intangible assets	$ 431,000

Notes payable	$ 210,000
Total current liabilities	$ 889,000
Common stock	$ 330,000
Retained earnings	$ 701,000
Total liabilities and owners' equity	$5,832,000

a. Reconstruct the balance sheet for 2010 and 2011 using a spreadsheet, and find the change in each account and each category balance (current assets, long-term assets, total assets, current liabilities, total liabilities, total owners' equity, and total liabilities and owners' equity) from 2010 to 2011. The balance sheet has the same accounts in both years. Verify that the changes in the total assets equal the changes in the total liabilities and owners' equity.

b. Find the cash from assets for the year 2010 if the OCF for 2010 is $389,000. *Note:* Treat intangible assets as a capital spending item.

MINI-CASE

Hudson Valley Realty

This mini-case is available in MyFinanceLab.

Hudson Valley Realty owns a number of commercial properties in suburban towns north and east of New York City. The firm previously rented one of them to an upscale department store renowned for jewelry and fine china, but that also sold everything from chandeliers to bed linens to lawn furniture. The building became vacant two years ago when the tenant broke a ten-year lease after only three years of occupancy and unexpectedly filed for bankruptcy. Hudson Valley considered any effort to recover early termination penalties a waste of time and money.

Interest expense, high real estate taxes, insurance, and security costs make it extremely expensive to hold vacant property in this area. Although Hudson Valley is obviously eager to find a new tenant, it does not want another unexpected vacancy to have a serious negative effect on its investment returns. Hudson Valley wants to be sure that the new tenant will be financially stable and will likely stay for at least the full term of the lease.

Vermont Heritage, a well-known furniture chain that targets affluent customers with traditional tastes, has expressed interest in the location. Peter Cortland, Hudson Valley's rental manager, wants to take a close look at the potential tenant's financial statements before entering into more serious negotiations. Vermont Heritage has submitted the following audited income statements and balance sheets for the last three years.

Vermont Heritage: Income Statement ($ in millions)

	2011	2010	2009
Sales	$ 949.00	$ 955.10	$ 907.30
Cost of goods sold	$ 466.60	$ 472.80	$ 436.60
Gross profit	$ 482.40	$ 482.30	$ 470.70
Selling and administrative expenses	$ 332.30	$ 320.80	$ 315.60
Depreciation	$ 21.30	$ 21.30	$ 21.30
Other income (expenses)	$ 1.40	($ 9.20)	($ 11.90)
EBIT	$ 130.20	$ 131.00	$ 121.90
Interest expense (net of interest income)	$ 0.80	$ 0.60	$ 0.60
Taxable income	$ 129.40	$ 130.40	$ 121.30
Taxes	$ 49.20	$ 50.10	$ 45.90
Net income	**$ 80.20**	**$ 80.30**	**$ 75.40**
Dividends	$ 24.06	$ 20.08	$ 18.85

Vermont Heritage: Balance Sheets ($ in millions)

ASSETS	2011	2010	2009	LIABILITIES	2011	2010	2009
Current assets				**Current liabilities**			
Cash and cash items	$ 57.40	$ 61.60	$ 81.90	Accounts payable	$ 20.40	$ 22.20	$ 26.10
				Short-term notes	$ 4.20	$ 4.70	$ 101.00
Accounts receivable	$ 28.02	$ 27.00	$ 26.40	Other current liabilities	$ 6.40	$ 7.37	$ 8.00
				Total current liabilities	**$ 31.00**	**$ 34.27**	**$ 135.10**
Inventory	$ 187.13	$ 186.90	$ 198.20	Long-term debt	$ 3.20	$ 4.50	$ 9.20
Other current assets	$ 56.52	$ 54.20	$ 53.80	Other long-term liabilities	$ 5.50	$ 52.40	$ 50.20
Total current assets	**$ 329.07**	**$ 329.70**	**$ 360.30**	**Total liabilities**	**$ 39.70**	**$ 91.17**	**$ 194.50**
				OWNERS' EQUITY			
Net fixed assets	$ 275.20	$ 277.00	$ 289.40	Common stock	$ 230.00	$ 230.00	$ 230.00
				Retained earnings	$ 423.37	$ 367.23	$ 307.00
Other assets	$ 88.80	$ 81.70	$ 81.80	**Total owners' equity**	**$ 653.37**	**$ 597.23**	**$ 537.00**
TOTAL ASSETS	**$ 693.07**	**$ 688.40**	**$ 731.50**	**TOTAL LIABILITIES AND OWNERS' EQUITY**	**$ 693.07**	**$ 688.40**	**$ 731.50**

Questions

1. Look at Vermont Heritage's sales revenue, EBIT, and net income over the three-year period. Would you classify it as a growing, diminishing, or stable company?
2. Look at Vermont Heritage's expense accounts, cost of goods sold, and selling and administrative expenses. Do they seem to be roughly proportional to sales? Do any of these categories seem to be growing out of control?
3. Depreciation expense is the same for all three years. What does that tell you about Vermont Heritage's growth?
4. Look at Vermont Heritage's EBIT, interest expense, and debt accounts (current liabilities, long-term debt, and other liabilities) over the three-year period. Comparing debt to equity, do you think the company seems to have excessive debt? Would you expect the company to have any problems meeting its interest payments?
5. Dividends have increased as a percentage of net income. Why do you think the company decided to pay out more of its earnings to shareholders?
6. Compare current assets with current liabilities. Would you expect Vermont Heritage to have any problems meeting its short-term obligations?
7. Overall, do you think Vermont Heritage will be a relatively safe tenant for Hudson Valley's building?

Learning Objectives

LO1 Calculate future values and understand compounding.

LO2 Calculate present values and understand discounting.

LO3 Calculate implied interest rates and waiting time from the time value of money equation.

LO4 Apply the time value of money equation using formula, calculator, and spreadsheet.

LO5 Explain the Rule of 72, a simple estimation of doubling values.

Chapter 3
The Time Value of Money (Part 1)

Suppose a relative opened a savings account on the day you were born in your name for a college education with a $15,000 deposit. The account was set to grow at 5% per year, and you were eligible to withdraw the money on your eighteenth birthday. While you were growing and maturing over the eighteen-year period, so was your account. On your eighteenth birthday, the account had about $36,000 in it, more than double the original amount. How did that happen?

In this chapter, we'll provide the answer to how the money in the college fund grew. You'll see that the interest rate you can earn means that time adds value to your invested money. The higher the interest rate or the longer you wait, the more money in your account.

The ability to calculate the value of money at different points in time is key to understanding the material ahead as well as making financial choices for your future.

3.1 Future Value and Compounding Interest

The **time value of money (TVM)** refers to a dollar in hand today being worth more than a dollar received in the future, because you can invest today's dollar in an interest-bearing account that grows in value over time. We call this the **future value (FV)**, the cash value of an asset (money, in this example) in the future that is equivalent in value to a specific amount today. In this chapter, we'll examine how interest accumulates (compounding) and how we discount future values to find present values. We'll look at the flexibility of the time value equation, how we can apply it, and one rule of thumb for estimating growth.

The Single-Period Scenario

We'll kick off with a simple one-period model. How much money will you have one year from today if you put $100 in a savings account that promises to pay you 5% over the coming year? The answer is $105. The additional $5 in the account is due to the earned interest. We can easily calculate this amount by multiplying the original deposit, or *principal* ($100), times the *interest rate* (5%):

$$\text{interest earned} = \$100 \times 0.05 = \$5.00$$

By adding the interest to the original deposit, you get the amount in the savings account at the end of the year: $105.00. Therefore, the $105 one year from now is equivalent to $100 today when you have a 5% earning rate. Although we will delve more deeply into interest rates later, for now you can think of the interest rate as a percentage of the principal that is earned by the lender or charged to the borrower. In this case, you are the lender and the bank is the borrower, and the bank pays you a fee for the use of your money.

This one-time payment of money at a future date is a **lump-sum payment**. In this example, the lump-sum payment comes at the end of one period (one year) and implies no additions or withdrawals along the way. The $105 at the end of the year represents the original principal of $100 and the earned interest of $5. This one-time lump-sum payment that you receive at the end of the year is a future value of the principal $100 invested for one year at 5% interest. In this chapter, we examine lump-sum payments only. In the next chapter, we study investments with multiple payments.

The Multiple-Period Scenario

What if you were willing to wait two years for your lump-sum payment? What will the future value of the deposit be after two years? To answer this question, it is important to realize that during the second year, you leave your principal ($100) and your earned interest ($5) in the account, thereby reinvesting the entire account balance for another year. The interest rate quoted at 5% reflects the interest you would receive each year, not over the entire two-year savings period. So, during the second year of savings, the $100 deposit and the $5 interest earned during the first year *both* earn 5%:

$$\$100 \times 0.05 + \$5.00 \times 0.05 = \$5.25$$

The additional 25 cents is interest on interest and reflects the *compounding of interest*. **Compound interest** is the interest you earn in subsequent periods on the earned interest in prior periods. Here, it is the 25 cents of earned interest in the second year on the $5.00 of earned interest in the first year. Therefore, at the end of two years, the account has $110.25:

- the original $100 (or principal)
- the $5.00 interest earned in year one
- the $5.25 interest earned in year two

The amount of $110.25 at the end of two years is the future value of $100 deposited today in an account earning 5% interest.

To calculate the future value of the savings account, we can multiply the deposit times 1 plus the interest rate for each year the money remains in the savings account:

$$\text{future value} = \text{deposit} \times (1 + r) \times (1 + r) \qquad \textbf{3.1}$$

where the number of times we use $(1 + r)$ in the equation reflects the number of years the money remains in the account prior to the one-time final lump-sum distribution of the account at the end of the chosen savings period. The 1 represents the principal amount in the account or the original deposit you get back at the end of the savings period. We can write Equation 3.1 in a more condensed mathematical form, using time value of money notation, as follows:

- FV = future value
- PV = present value
- r = interest rate
- n = the number of time periods

Using these inputs, we have

$$FV = PV \times (1 + r)^n \qquad \textbf{3.2}$$

With Equation 3.2, we can calculate the value of the savings account for any number of years. For example, suppose we are considering three, ten, and fifty years from the original deposit date at the annual 5% interest rate:

three years: $FV = \$100 \times (1.05)^3 = \$100 \times 1.1576 = \$115.76$

ten years: $FV = \$100 \times (1.05)^{10} = \$100 \times 1.6289 = \$162.89$

fifty years: $FV = \$100 \times (1.05)^{50} = \$100 \times 11.4674 = \$1{,}146.74$

How can the savings account be so large after fifty years? The answer: the compounding of interest. Each year, the earned interest in preceding years earns interest along with the initial deposit, which in turn accelerates the growth of the account. Table 3.1 illustrates the growing interest each year for $100 deposited with an interest rate of 10%. We can see from the table that the account balance doubles in a little more than seven years and that by the end of year eight (start of year nine) the accumulated interest in the account, $114.36, is greater than the initial $100 deposit. Such is the effect of the compounding of interest: money grows in larger and larger increments the longer you leave it in the savings account.

The compounding of interest over time accelerates the growth of money.

Methods of Solving Future Value Problems

Equation 3.2 is a basic tool for valuing all future lump-sum payments. All we need to

TABLE 3.1 Annual Interest Rates at 10% for $100 Initial Deposit (Rounded to Nearest Penny)

	Beginning Balance	Accumulated Interest	Interest on Principal	Interest on Interest	Ending Balance
Year 1	$100.00	—	$10.00	—	$110.00
Year 2	$110.00	$ 10.00	$10.00	$ 1.00	$121.00
Year 3	$121.00	$ 21.00	$10.00	$ 2.10	$133.10
Year 4	$133.10	$ 33.10	$10.00	$ 3.31	$146.41
Year 5	$146.41	$ 46.41	$10.00	$ 4.64	$161.05
Year 6	$161.05	$ 61.05	$10.00	$ 6.11	$177.16
Year 7	$177.16	$ 77.16	$10.00	$ 7.71	$194.87
Year 8	$194.87	$ 94.87	$10.00	$ 9.49	$214.36
Year 9	$214.36	$114.36	$10.00	$11.43	$235.79

know are the initial deposit or present value of the account (PV), the interest rate (r), and how long the money will remain in the account (n). The interest rate is the **growth rate**, or the annual percentage increase on an investment. The growth rate raised to the power of the number of periods, $(1 + r)^n$, is the **future value interest factor (FVIF)**: as n (time, or the number of periods) increases, the FVIF increases; and as r (the interest rate) increases, the FVIF increases. Thus, the future value is a function of both the interest rate and the time periods.

We can determine future values by using any of four methods: (1) equation, (2) financial functions on a calculator, (3) spreadsheets, and (4) FVIF tables. We've just looked at the equation method, which we will call Method 1. Now let's walk through the methods for calculating future value using the college fund account example from the chapter opener. The original deposit (birthday gift) is $15,000 (the present value, PV), and the annual interest rate is 5% (r) over the next eighteen years (n). How much will you have in your account at the end of eighteen years?

Method 1: The equation This method for calculating future values uses a standard calculator and the future value equation. We already know that we can find the solution by solving the equation

$$FV = PV(1 + r)^n$$
$$= \$15{,}000.00 \times (1.05)^{18}$$

Most standard calculators have a power function key (y^x) that allows us to raise 1.05 to the eighteenth power:

$$1.05 \; \boxed{y^x} \; 18 = 2.406619$$

We then multiply $15,000 by 2.406619, and the result is $36,099.29. This figure is slightly more than the $36,000 figure we used in the chapter introduction and is the actual value at the end of eighteen years.

Method 2: The TVM keys Many calculators also have financial functions and TVM keys. When you enter the variables directly into these keys, the calculator will display the answer. The row of keys or the functions with N, I/Y, PV, PMT, and FV are the time value of money keys, or variables.

Calculator Keys

N = number of periods

I/Y = interest rate per year

PV = present value

PMT = payment

FV = future value

Using the TVM keys, we enter 18 for N, 5.0 for I/Y, 15,000 for PV, and 0 for PMT. We will address PMT in Chapter 4 when we look at a series of deposits or payments. We then compute (CPT), and the calculator should display −36,099.29:

Input	18	5.0	15,000	0	?
Key	N	I/Y	PV	PMT	FV
CPT					**−36,099.29**

We will have more to say later in this chapter about the negative sign in front of the result. In the meantime, if you cannot reproduce this result with your calculator, do not worry. The calculator that we used here is a Texas Instrument BA II Plus. Other versions and brands have different setups and inputs, but all have instructions on how to use the TVM keys.

Method 3: The spreadsheet Another method for determining future value is to use a computer spreadsheet with financial functions. For example, Microsoft Excel® has a set of financial functions and calculates future values. If you open an Excel spreadsheet, look at the function input line above the spreadsheet (f_x), and click on the function sign (f_x), an equal sign (=) will appear in the cell input window and Excel will ask which function you want to use. In the set of financial functions will be a function labeled FV. When you call up the function, Excel will then ask for the variables to the problem.

Spreadsheet Variables for Future Value Function

Rate = interest rate

Nper = number of periods

Pmt = payment

Pv = present value

Type = type of payment stream (discussed in the next chapter)

We first enter 0.05 for the Rate, which represents our 5% annual interest rate. (Notice that the Excel default for interest rate is in the standard decimal format, whereas for many calculators the default is in percent form. You can reformat Excel to use the percent form if you prefer.) We enter 18 for Nper (the number of periods). Pmt stands for payments. We will look at this variable in Chapter 4 when we have a series of deposits to the account, but for now we leave it blank, or zero. We enter 15,000 for Pv, which is the initial deposit. Type refers to the timing of the deposit with respect to a series of deposits. We will address this variable later, but for now the zero default is proper. If you place the correct values in these variables, the Excel future value function will calculate the future value and display it in the cell. For our example, you will see −36,099.29 (again, note the negative sign, which we will explain shortly).

B6	*fx* =FV(B1,B2,B3,B4,B5)				
	Use the future value function to find the amount in the scholarship account after 15 years at 5% growth rate.				
	A	B	C	D	E
1	Rate	0.05			
2	Nper	18			
3	Pmt	$ –			
4	PV	$ 15,000.00			
5	Type	0			
6	Fv	($36,099.29)			

So, no matter what method you use—equation, TVM keys on a calculator, or spreadsheet—you get the same answer because they all use the same formula and concept to calculate future value. In other words, several roads can take you to the same destination.

Table 3.2 recaps the calculator and spreadsheet inputs and shows their correspondence.

We can also use a fourth method—the use of tables of future value interest factors—to find solutions to future value problems. Rather than directly calculating the FVIF, you would look up this value on a table and then multiply the present value by the FVIF to find the future value. Appendix 1 provides FVIF tables. To illustrate how these tables work, take a rate r of 5% and a time period n of 18. In the FVIF tables, find 18 in the n column and move across this row to the 5% column. There you will find the value 2.4066. By multiplying $15,000 by the FVIF of 2.4066, you will get a future value of $36,099. You can produce the FVIF yourself simply by calculating 1.05^{18} and getting the rounded 2.4066, as we did in Method 1. Tables usually display up to four decimal places, and the rounding of the FVIF to four decimal places will cause small differences in the table method versus the other three methods.

The table method provides a check for solving future value problems, but because it displays only a limited number of FVIFs, uses only a selected set of interest rates and periods, and rounds the results, it is a less desirable method. Given the speed and accuracy of today's calculators and spreadsheets, they are the preferred

TABLE 3.2 Variable Match for Calculator and Spreadsheet

Variable	TI Calculator TVM Keys	Excel Spreadsheet Variable Names
Number of periods	N	Nper
Interest rate	I/Y (annual rate)	Rate (periodic rate)
Present value	PV	Pv
Payment	PMT	Pmt
Future value	FV	Fv

methods. We will point out table methods for some other types of time value of money problems later, but we will rely on the equation, calculator (TVM keys), and spreadsheet methods for our solutions to time value of money problems.

If you used all three methods and compared the answers, you would notice one curious feature of the TVM keys and spreadsheet: the answer displayed would be *negative* $36,099.29 because the TVM keys and spreadsheet implicitly provide the *direction* of the cash flow. Usually, cash flow out is negative and cash flow in is positive. In this example, the proper way to view the initial deposit is as a cash flow out (from the investor to the bank) and the lump-sum payment at the end as a cash flow in (withdrawal from the bank to you). So, to get a positive $36,099.29 answer, you need to enter a negative value of $15,000 for the PV key or the Pv variable of the spreadsheet.

The future value of a savings deposit is a straightforward application of the equation, but the equation is much more versatile than that. It can also give you future values of all sorts of assets. Example 3.1 is one such application of the equation.

EXAMPLE 3.1 How much will that condo cost in six years? (future value)

Problem John and Jane Smith are in the market for a vacation place. They find a small but pleasant condo in Malibu listed at $400,000. They decide that now is not the right time to buy and that they will wait six years. The condos in Malibu appreciate each year at 3.5%, and the Smiths want to know what a similar condo will sell for in six years. Can you help them?

Solution The current price of the condo is the same as the present value of the condo, or $400,000. The number of years that the Smiths will wait is six, and the interest rate is the same as the appreciation rate, or 3.5%. Using the *FV* equation, in six years the condo will sell for

$$FV = \$400{,}000 \times (1.035)^6 = \$400{,}000 \times 1.2293 = \mathbf{\$491{,}702.13}$$

Can you verify this future value (future price) with the other two methods?

3.2 Present Value and Discounting

So far, you have learned how money grows over time, and it's a fairly straightforward concept. However, what if we are interested in the *current* value of something that we will receive in the future? This concept of present value is a bit trickier to understand, but it helps us put a price or value today on a future cash receipt.

The Single-Period Scenario

As with our future value calculations, let's start with a single-period case. Say you want to buy a new laptop next year, and the one you have in mind should be selling for $1,000 a year from now. How much do you need to put away today at 5% interest to have $1,000 a year from now? In essence, you are trying to determine how much $1,000 one year from now is worth today at 5% interest over the year.

You can use the present value formula to calculate how much money you need to invest today to finance future projects—such as retirement or a college education.

To find a present value, we reverse the growth concept and *discount* the future value back to the current period. The interest rate that we use to determine the present value of a future cash flow is the discount rate because it is bringing the money back in time. The **discount rate** is the annual reduction rate on a future value and is the inverse of the growth rate. Once we know this discount rate, we can solve for the **present value (PV)**, the value today of tomorrow's cash flow. Rearranging the *FV* equation, we turn $FV = PV \times (1 + r)^n$ into

$$PV = FV \times \frac{1}{(1 + r)^n} \qquad \textbf{3.3}$$

which is the present value equation. The fraction is the **present value interest factor (PVIF)**, and it is simply the reciprocal of the FVIF. Therefore, the amount you need to deposit today to reach \$1,000 in a year ($n = 1$) at 5% interest is

$$\$1{,}000 \times \frac{1}{(1.05)^1} = \$1{,}000 \times (0.95238) = \$952.38$$

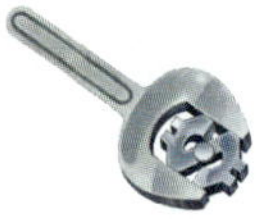

(Note: Appendix 2 displays various PVIFs for different periods and interest rates.)

The Multiple-Period Scenario

Many examples extend for more than one year. We can also use the present value formula to determine the value today of tomorrow's cash flows after multiple periods of time. Example 3.2 shows the present value equation at work in a multiple-period scenario.

EXAMPLE 3.2 How much does that savings bond cost? (present value)

Problem Donna wants to buy a savings bond for her newborn niece. The face value of the savings bond is \$500, the amount the niece would receive in twenty years (future value). The government is currently paying 4% per year on savings bonds. How much will it cost Donna today to buy this savings bond?

Solution The \$500 face value of the bond is the future value, and the number of years n that the owner of the savings bond must wait to get this face value is twenty years. The interest rate r is 4.0% and is the discount rate for the savings bond. Using the *PV* equation, the current price of this savings bond is

$$PV = \$500 \times \frac{1}{1.04^{20}} = \$500 \times (0.456387) = \mathbf{\$228.19}$$

Notice in Example 3.2 that we discounted the future value amount to its value today, which is the reverse of compounding interest. A simple rule to remember is that **compounding** takes present money into the future. **Discounting** brings future money back to the present.

In the previous section, we used three different methods to solve a future value problem. We can use these same methods to answer the question posed in Example 3.2 about the present value or cost of the savings bond.

Method 1, the equation method, is the style that we already used in Example 3.2. Method 2, the calculator method, uses the TVM keys. Here the inputs and result will be identical to the formula method.

Input	20	4.0	?	0	500
Key	N	I/Y	PV	PMT	FV
CPT			−228.19		

Method 3 is the spreadsheet function for present value. Rate is the interest rate. For this example, you would enter 0.04, which represents 4%. NPer is the number of periods. In this example, it is 20. Pmt is payments. Again, we will look at this variable later when we have a series of deposits to the account, but for now we will leave it blank, or 0. Fv is the face value, the maturity value, or the future value of the savings bond, which is $500. Excel will calculate the present value and display it in the cell. For this example, you will see −228.19. The equation method, the TVM keys, and the spreadsheet all give the same answer.

B6 | *fx* | =PV(B1,B2,B3,B4,B5)

Use the present value function to find the current price of a $500 face-value savings bond that matures in 20 years.

	A	B	C	D	E
1	Rate	0.04			
2	Nper	20			
3	Pmt	0			
4	Fv	$500.00			
5	Type	0			
6	Pv	($228.19)			

Again, we could use a fourth method and look up the PVIF in a table. According to Appendix 2, for $r = 4\%$ and $n = 20$, the PVIF is 0.4564. If we multiply this factor by the future value, we get

$$PV = \$500 \times 0.4564 = \$228.20$$

This answer is not exactly the same as the previous answer. Why? The one-cent difference in the answers results from rounding the values in the table to four decimal places. If you were to compute the factor and not round, you would get

$$PVIF = \frac{1}{1.04^{20}} = 0.456386946$$

Using this factor, you get the same answer as the one displayed in Example 3.2:

$$\$500 \times 0.456386946 = \$228.1934731$$

or, rounded to the nearest cent, $228.19.

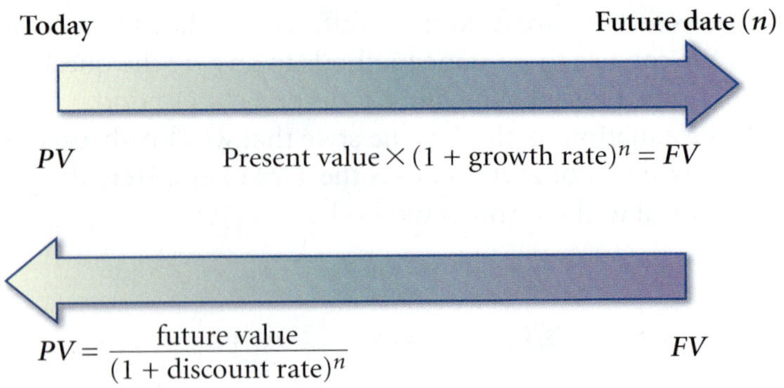

FIGURE 3.1 Time lines of growth rates (top) and discount rates (bottom) illustrate present value and future value.

The nice feature about using the equation with a calculator is that the calculator does not round the PVIF. As problems get more complicated, the rounding of PVIFs from a table becomes more problematic. Therefore, our choice to use the table method only as a check and not as a standard method to solve time value of money problems is appropriate.

The Use of Time Lines

Another useful tool for solving present value and future value problems is a **time line**, a linear representation of the timing of cash flows over a period of time. Figure 3.1 illustrates two time lines that can help us visualize the two key concepts of present value and future value.

Each time line shows today at the left, and the stopping, or future, point (maturity date) at the right. The time line displays the present value dollar amount at the left and the future dollar value at the right. The distance between the endpoints represents the total elapsed time and is reflected by n, the number of periods between PV and FV. The top time line depicts the growth rate. It gradates from lighter in the present to darker in the future, indicating an increase in value. The bottom time line depicts the discount rate. It gradates "back from the future," from darker to lighter.

Using a time line to lay out a time value of money problem will become more and more valuable as our problems become more complex. You should get into the habit of using a time line to set up these problems prior to using the equation, calculator, or spreadsheet to help minimize input errors. The time line can become one of your most useful tools.

3.3 One Equation and Four Variables

Our time value of money equation has considerable firepower in that each variable can answer different questions. By rearranging the equation, we can isolate the four different variables on the left side of the equation. Of course, we will need to know the values of the variables remaining on the right side of the equation before we can solve for the variable of concern.

The first form of the equation, $FV = PV \times (1 + r)^n$ (Eq. 3.2), isolates the variable FV at a specific future point in time. This form of the equation can answer a question such as, "How much money will I have in my account at a specific point in the future given a specific interest rate?"

The second form of the equation, $PV = FV \times \left[1/(1 + r)^n\right]$ (Eq. 3.3), isolates PV. Present value is the same as the current price of an asset, the current value of an asset, or the current purchasing power of cash. It answers questions such as, "What is the current value of an amount of cash that I will receive at a specific time in the future?"

The third form of the equation,

$$r = \left(\frac{FV}{PV}\right)^{1/n} - 1 \qquad \textbf{3.4}$$

isolates the variable r, which is the *interest rate*, *yield*, *discount rate*, or *growth rate*. It answers questions such as, "At what rate is my money growing over time?" and "What is the discount rate on my future cash?"

As we have seen, the discount rate is just the opposite of the growth rate. We use the discount rate when bringing a future value back to the present. We use the growth rate when taking a present value into the future.

For example, if you deposit \$250 in the bank today and in five years will get back \$400, what is your growth rate? From Equation 3.4, we have

$$r = \left(\frac{\$400}{\$250}\right)^{1/5} - 1 = 1.6^{0.2} - 1 = 1.09856 - 1 = 0.09856 \quad \text{or} \quad 9.856\%$$

Thus, the growth rate of the money going forward in time is 9.856%.

The fourth and last form of the equation,

$$n = \frac{\ln(FV/PV)}{\ln(1 + r)} \qquad \textbf{3.5}$$

isolates the variable n, or the time period between the present value and the future value. It answers the question, "How long will I have to wait to reach a certain future value?" We call this time period the *waiting time* for a present value to mature into a desired future value. We can use Equation 3.5 to find the waiting time, but it is much easier to compute with the TVM keys on a calculator or with a function in a spreadsheet. Consider a simple question such as, "How long will it take my \$500 savings bond to turn into its face value of \$1,000 if the government is now paying 3.5% on its savings bonds?"

Input	?	3.5	−500	0	1,000
Key	N	I/Y	PV	PMT	FV
CPT	20.15				

Again, one issue we deal with on a calculator is the direction of the cash flow. Here the present value is negative \$500, which reflects the purchase or cash outflow to buy the savings bond. The future value is positive \$1,000, which reflects the cash inflow that you receive when the government pays off the savings bond. So, using a calculator, you find that you will need to wait 20.15 years before you can cash in the savings bond for \$1,000.

Of course, if you are comfortable with natural logs and the formula, you can calculate this same waiting time of 20.15 years via Equation 3.5:

$$n = \frac{\ln(\$1{,}000/\$500)}{\ln(1 + 0.035)} = \frac{\ln(2)}{\ln(1.035)} = \frac{0.693147181}{0.034401427} \approx 20.15 \text{ years}$$

The natural logarithm function (ln) is on most calculators and is the logarithm to the base e, where e is equal to 2.718281828459. . . .

In conclusion, we have one equation with four variables that can answer a variety of questions. Always remember, though, that with only one equation you can solve for only one unknown at a time. To make use of this basic equation in any of the four forms, you must know the value of the other three variables before you can solve for the missing one.

3.4 Applications of the Time Value of Money Equation

As with any new tool, you get better at using it with practice. Let's now examine some typical questions that you can answer using the time value of money equation. We will use Methods 1, 2, and 3 to calculate our answers. Example 3.3 starts us off with a present value problem.

EXAMPLE 3.3 Saving for retirement (present value)

Problem Your retirement goal is $2,000,000. The bank is offering you a certificate of deposit that is good for forty years at 6.0%. What initial deposit do you need to make today to reach your $2,000,000 goal at the end of forty years?

Solution The following time line illustrates the problem.

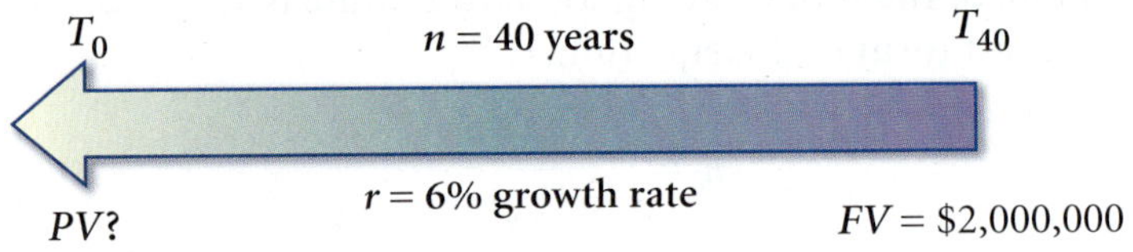

We designate today as T_0 and our future date forty years later as T_{40}.

METHOD 1 Using the equation

$$PV = \$2{,}000{,}000 \times \frac{1}{1.06^{40}} = \$2{,}000{,}000 \times 0.0972 = \mathbf{\$194{,}444.38}$$

METHOD 2 Using the TVM keys

Input	40	6.0	?	0	2,000,000
Key	N	I/Y	PV	PMT	FV
CPT			– 194,444.38		

METHOD 3 Using a spreadsheet

B6 | *fx* | =PV(B1,B2,B3,B4,B5)

Use the present value function to find the amount of dollars you need to invest today to reach $2,000,000 in 40 years.

	A	B	C	D	E
1	Rate	0.06			
2	Nper	40			
3	Pmt	0			
4	Fv	$2,000,000.00			
5	Type	0			
6	Pv	($ 194,444.38)			

Example 3.4 illustrates a future value problem that at first looks like a present value problem. It shows how important it is to understand where the unknown amount is in relation to time.

EXAMPLE 3.4 Let's make a deal! (future value)

Problem In 1867, Secretary of State William H. Seward purchased Alaska from Russia for the sum of \$7,200,000, or about two cents per acre. At the time, the deal was dubbed Seward's Folly, but from our vantage point today, did Seward get a bargain after all? What would it cost today if the land were in exactly the same condition as it was 140 years ago and the prevailing interest rate over this time were 4%?

Solution At first glance, it seems as if we have a present value problem, not a future value problem, but it all depends on where we are standing in reference to time. Phrasing this question another way, we could ask, "What will the value of \$7,200,000 be in 140 years at an annual interest rate of 4%?" Restated this way, we can more easily view the problem as a future value problem. A time line is particularly helpful in this instance. We can show the 140-year span from T_{-140} to T_0 or from T_0 to T_{140}.

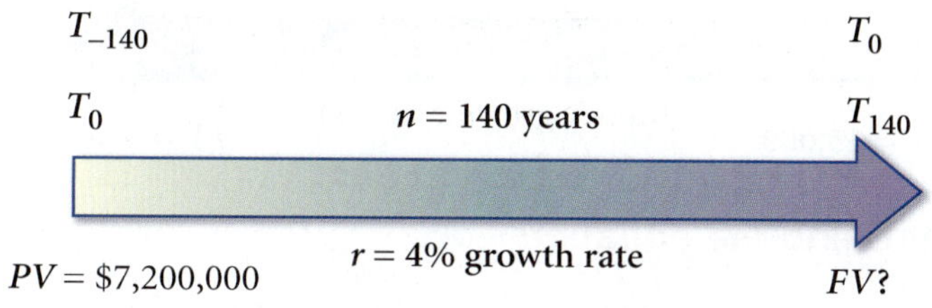

METHOD 1 Using the equation

$$FV = PV \times (1 + r)^n = \$7{,}200{,}000 \times 1.04^{140}$$
$$= \$7{,}200{,}000 \times 242.4753 = \mathbf{\$1{,}745{,}822{,}146}$$

METHOD 2 Using the TVM keys

Input	140	4.0	−7,200,000	0	?
Key	N	I/Y	PV	PMT	FV
CPT					1,745,822,146

METHOD 3 Using a spreadsheet

B6 | *fx* | =*FV*(*B1,B2,B3,B4,B5*)

Use the future value function to find the price of Alaska if purchased today instead of 140 years ago.

	A	B	C	D	E
1	Rate	0.04			
2	Nper	140			
3	Pmt	0			
4	Pv	(\$ 7,200,000.00)			
5	Type	0			
6	Fv	\$1,745,822,145.93			

This current price for Alaska is only \$4.78 per acre (approximately 365 million acres) and is still quite a bargain. Apparently, Seward was pretty shrewd after all!

Examples 3.5 and 3.6 illustrate the versatility of Equation 3.4 in determining r. Example 3.5 uses it for an interest rate Example 3.6 uses it for a growth rate.

EXAMPLE 3.5 What's the cost of that loan? (interest rate)

Problem John, a college student, needs to borrow \$5,000 today for his tuition bill. He agrees to pay back the loan in a lump-sum payment five years from now, after he is out of college. The bank states that the payment will need to be \$7,012.76. If John borrows the \$5,000 from the bank, what interest rate is he paying on his loan?

Solution A time line is helpful in this instance.

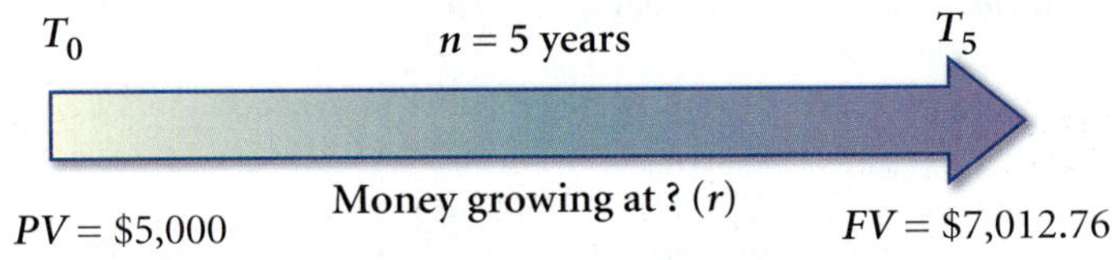

METHOD 1 Using the equation

$$r = \left(\frac{FV}{PV}\right)^{1/n} - 1 = \left(\frac{\$7{,}012.76}{\$5{,}000}\right)^{1/5} - 1$$

$$= 1.40255^{0.2} - 1 = \mathbf{0.07} \quad \text{or} \quad 7\%$$

METHOD 2 Using the TVM keys

Input	5	?	5,000	0	−7,012.76
Key	N	I/Y	PV	PMT	FV
CPT		7.00			

METHOD 3 Using a spreadsheet

B6 | *fx* | =RATE(B1,B2,B3,B4,B5)

Use the rate function to see the interest rate that a loan of \$5,000 is costing if it requires a payment of \$7,012.76 in 5 years.

	A	B	C	D	E
1	Nper	5			
2	Pmt	0			
3	Pv	\$ 5000			
4	Fv	(\$7012.76)			
5	Type	0			
6	Rate	7.0%			

Example 3.6 shows that the TVM equation is a tool that extends beyond financial problems. In this application, we use it to determine population growth.

EXAMPLE 3.6 Boomtown, USA (growth rate)

Problem You are the planning commissioner for Boomtown, a growing city in the Southwest. The city council has estimated that the city's population will increase very rapidly over the next twenty years, reaching an estimated 250,000. Today, the population is 94,222. What is the projected growth rate of this city?

Solution Here, the present value is the current population of Boomtown: 94,222. The future value is the projected 250,000 population. The period is twenty years. See the time line.

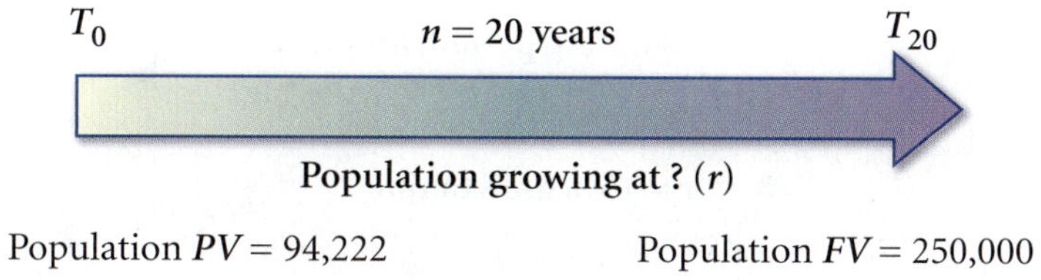

METHOD 1 Using the equation

$$r = \left(\frac{250{,}000}{94{,}222}\right)^{1/20} - 1 = 2.6533^{1/20} - 1 = 1.05 - 1 = \mathbf{0.05} \quad \text{or} \quad 5.0\%$$

METHOD 2 Using the TVM keys

Input	20	?	−94,222	0	250,000
Key	N	I/Y	PV	PMT	FV
CPT		5.0			

METHOD 3 Using a spreadsheet

B6 | *fx* | *=RATE(B1,B2,B3,B4,B5)*

Use the rate function to find the town's growth rate if its current population is 94,222 and it will be 250,000 in 20 years.

	A	B	C	D	E
1	Nper	20			
2	Pmt	0			
3	Pv	(94,222.00)			
4	Fv	250,000.00			
5	Type	0			
6	Rate	5%			

The logic we used here is the same as applying it to a more traditional finance problem. It is the same as asking, "If you deposit $94,222 today in a bank for a twenty-year period and withdraw $250,000 at the end of the period, what interest rate did you receive over that period?" The answer, as in Example 3.6, is 5.0%.

Example 3.7 illustrates an application for the waiting period between the present value and the future value. This time period is the n in Equation 3.5.

EXAMPLE 3.7 When will I be rich? (waiting time)

Problem Your goal in life is to be a millionaire. Today, your financial portfolio is worth \$3,733.24. Having studied this chapter carefully and as a shrewd investor, you determine that you can earn 15% every year on your portfolio. You do not plan to invest any additional money in this portfolio, nor will you withdraw any funds from it before it grows to \$1 million. Given your 15% interest rate, how long will you have to wait to become a millionaire if this investment represents all your wealth?

Solution See the time line.

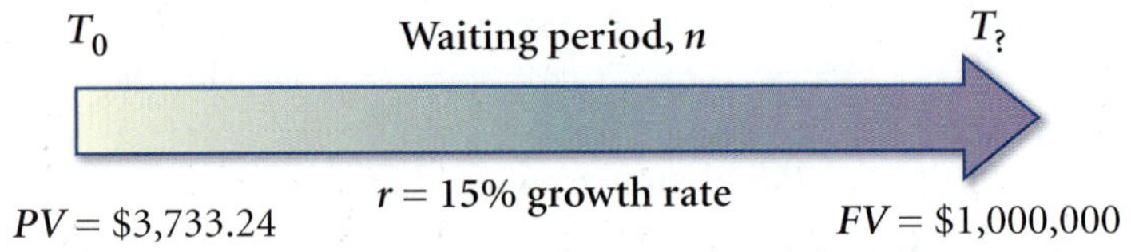

METHOD 1 Using the equation

$$n = \frac{\ln(\$1{,}000{,}000/\$3{,}733.24)}{\ln(1.15)} = \frac{\ln(267.8638)}{\ln(1.15)} = \frac{5.59}{0.1398} = \mathbf{40.00}$$

METHOD 2 Using the TVM keys

Input	?	15.0	−3,733.24	0	1,000,000
Key	N	I/Y	PV	PMT	FV
CPT	40.00				

METHOD 3 Using a spreadsheet

B6 | *fx* | =NPER(B1,B2,B3,B4,B5)

Use the number of periods function to find the years it will take to grow \$3,733.24 into \$1 million at 15% interest.

	A	B	C	D	E
1	Rate	0.15			
2	Pmt	0			
3	Pv	(\$ 3,733.24)			
4	Fv	\$1,000,000.00			
5	Type	0			
6	Nper	40.00			

From the examples in this section, you have seen how we can rearrange the single time value of money equation to isolate one of the four variables and use it to solve a variety of problems. This equation is so standard that it is programmed into financial functions on calculators and spreadsheets. Whatever method you choose will produce the same solution as any other method as long as you enter the data correctly and avoid mathematical errors. As we progress through the text, the calculator TVM keys and the spreadsheet will become even more useful.

We can use the time value of money concept and equations in many real-world applications. To see how you can use this tool in a career setting, see the "Putting Finance to Work" feature.

PUTTING FINANCE TO WORK

Sports Agent

Although the popular image of a sports agent is of a slick extrovert with cell phone glued to ear, many agents work under the radar and away from the camera's glare, negotiating contracts that are in the best interests of their clients. Often called athlete representation, this field can be extremely lucrative for those who establish and cultivate a strong client list. Some agents specialize in a particular sport, whereas others span a wide range. Leigh Steinberg, for instance—the agent on whom the movie *Jerry Maguire* was modeled—specialized in football but also had clients from six different sports areas. Sometimes sports agents work with large firms, and sometimes they work on their own. Some are lawyers. Some are former athletes.

Knowledge of finance—areas such as financial analysis and investment analysis—is as important to a sports agent career as deep knowledge of the particular sport. Whatever their background, sports agents need to be versed in financial matters. One particularly important task for the agent is negotiating a contract, which usually means getting the best salary for a player. The agent will analyze financial offers and advise the athlete as to what choices are best for his or her short-term and long-term financial position.

Here, we do something a little different and apply the principle of present value that you just studied to a hypothetical, but representative, situation. You can put these tools to work to form an analysis of a player's options.

Say that Reggie, a free agent, has three different contract offers. All three teams are desirable in terms of coaching, playoff possibilities, and teammates. The sports agent with whom Reggie works will put together a detailed analysis. The following table provides highlights. It lists the three contracts, the payment schedules, and the signing bonus. All three contracts are six-year, $7 million contracts. If Reggie uses a 6% discount rate on these future values, which contract is the most lucrative in terms of present value?

Contract Offers

Time of Payment	Northwest Team	Midwest Team	East Coast Team
Bonus	$1,000,000	$ 250,000	$1,750,000
Year 1	$1,000,000	$ 500,000	$ 250,000
Year 2	$1,000,000	$ 750,000	$ 500,000
Year 3	$1,000,000	$1,000,000	$ 750,000
Year 4	$1,000,000	$1,250,000	$1,000,000
Year 5	$1,000,000	$1,500,000	$1,250,000
Year 6	$1,000,000	$1,750,000	$1,500,000

Continued

To analyze this scenario, the sports agent will view each payment separately, find the present value of each payment, and add all the present values of the seven years. The first payment (signing bonus), at time 0, is already in present value form. To determine the present value of each contract, it is necessary to discount all future payments back to the present at the interest rate of 6%. The present value of the Northwest contract is

Year 0 = $1,000,000

Year 1 = $1,000,000 × $[1/(1.06)^1]$ = $943,396

Year 2 = $1,000,000 × $[1/(1.06)^2]$ = $889,996

Year 3 = $1,000,000 × $[1/(1.06)^3]$ = $839,619

Year 4 = $1,000,000 × $[1/(1.06)^4]$ = $792,094

Year 5 = $1,000,000 × $[1/(1.06)^5]$ = $747,258

Year 6 = $1,000,000 × $[1/(1.06)^6]$ = $704,961

Total **$5,917,324**

The present value of the Midwest contract is

Year 0 = $250,000

Year 1 = $500,000 × $[1/(1.06)^1]$ = $471,698

Year 2 = $750,000 × $[1/(1.06)^2]$ = $667,497

Year 3 = $1,000,000 × $[1/(1.06)^3]$ = $839,619

Year 4 = $1,250,000 × $[1/(1.06)^4]$ = $990,117

Continued

Year 5 = $1,500,000 × $[1/(1.06)^5]$ = $1,120,887

Year 6 = $1,750,000 × $[1/(1.06)^6]$ = $1,233,681

Total **5,573,500**

The present value of the East Coast contract is

Year 0 = $1,750,000

Year 1 = $250,000 × $[1/(1.06)^1]$ = $ 235,849

Year 2 = $500,000 × $[1/(1.06)^2]$ = $ 444,998

Year 3 = $750,000 × $[1/(1.06)^3]$ = $ 629,714

Year 4 = $1,000,000 × $[1/(1.06)^4]$ = $ 792,094

Year 5 = $1,250,000 × $[1/(1.06)^5]$ = $ 934,073

Year 6 = $1,500,000 × $[1/(1.06)^6]$ = $1,057,441

Total **$5,844,169**

The time value of money equation provides the present value of all three contracts. Although each contract pays $7,000,000 over the course of six years, the Northwest contract, with its steady payments each year, is the most lucrative contract in terms of present value.

Although this analysis cannot in itself determine the best team for Reggie, it does provide insight into the value of each of the offered contracts. The sports agent will consider many other factors in making a final recommendation and may shop the best contract to the other two teams. The choice may end up being which team is the best fit rather than which contract is best, but this tool helps prime the way.

3.5 Doubling of Money: The Rule of 72

Another application of the time value of money equation enables us to determine how long it takes your money to double at a certain growth or interest rate. We can easily adopt this equation to the required waiting period for money to double by realizing that it is a problem of scale for which we can select 1 as the present value and 2 as the future value. Substituting the growth rate or interest rate into the equation provides the solution of how long it takes money to double at a certain rate. For 8%,

Input	?	8.0	−1	0	2
Key	N	I/Y	PV	PMT	FV
CPT	9.01				

Thus, it takes about nine years for your money to double at 8%.

Prior to the use of calculators, this answer was not as easy to find, so financiers developed a simple rule of thumb, the **Rule of 72**, that still works quite well for interest rates between 4% and 30%. To find the length of time it takes to double your money, just divide 72 by the interest rate. So, in our example the answer is

TABLE 3.3 Doubling Time in Years for Given Interest Rates

Interest Rate	Doubling by Rule of 72	Doubling by Equation	Difference
2%	36.00	35.00	1.00
4%	18.00	17.67	0.33
6%	12.00	11.90	0.10
8%	9.00	9.01	0.01
10%	7.20	7.27	−0.07
12%	6.00	6.12	−0.12
14%	5.14	5.29	−0.15
16%	4.50	4.67	−0.17
18%	4.00	4.18	−0.18
20%	3.60	3.80	−0.20
24%	3.00	3.22	−0.22
30%	2.40	2.64	−0.24

$72/8 = 9$, or approximately nine years. Table 3.3 gives the doubling period using the equation and the Rule of 72. As Table 3.3 illustrates, the Rule of 72 is fairly accurate for the middle range of interest rates. It overestimates the time it takes to double below 8% and underestimates over 8%.

Another use for the Rule of 72 is to ask at what rate you will need to invest your money to have it double over a specific time period. To find this answer, just divide 72 by the time horizon. The answer is the interest rate. What rate is necessary to double your money in six years? The answer is $72/6 = 12$ or 12%.

To review this chapter, see the Summary Card at the end of the text.

Key Terms

compounding, p. 62
compound interest, p. 56
discounting, p. 62
discount rate, p. 62
future value (FV), p. 56
future value interest factor (FVIF), p. 58
growth rate, p. 58
lump-sum payment, p. 56
present value (PV), p. 62
present value interest factor (PVIF), p. 62
rule of 72, p. 72
time line, p. 64
time value of money (TVM), p. 56

Questions

1. What are the four basic parts (variables) of the time value of money equation?
2. What does the term *compounding* mean?
3. Define a growth rate and a discount rate. What is the difference between them?

4. What happens to a future value as you increase the interest (growth) rate?
5. What happens to a present value as you increase the discount rate?
6. What happens to a future value as you increase the time to the future date?
7. What happens to the present value as the time to the future value increases?
8. What is the Rule of 72?
9. Is the present value always less than the future value?
10. When a lottery prize is $10,000,000 but will pay out a series of $250,000 payments over forty years, is it really a $10,000,000 lottery prize?

Prepping for Exams

1. Which of the following will result in a future value of greater than $100?
   - **a.** $PV = \$50$, $r =$ an annual interest rate of 10%, and $n = 8$ years.
   - **b.** $PV = \$75$, $r =$ an annual interest rate of 12%, and $n = 3$ years.
   - **c.** $PV = \$90$, $r =$ an annual interest rate of 14%, and $n = 1$ year.
   - **d.** All the future values are greater than $100.

2. A home improvement firm has quoted a price of $9,800 to fix up John's back yard. Five years ago, John put $7,500 into a home improvement account that has earned an average of 5.25% per year. Does John have enough money in his account to pay for the back yard fix-up?
   - **a.** Yes. John now has exactly $9,800 in his home improvement account.
   - **b.** No. John has only $9,687 in his home improvement account.
   - **c.** Yes. John now has $10,519 in his home improvement account.
   - **d.** There is not enough information to answer this question.

3. You have purchased a savings bond that will pay $10,000 to your newborn child in fifteen years. If the bank discounts this bond at a rate of 3.875% per year, what is today's price (present value) for this bond?
   - **a.** $8,417
   - **b.** $8,500
   - **c.** $5,654
   - **d.** $10,000

4. To determine the present value of a future amount, one should ______________ the future cash flows.
   - **a.** annuitize
   - **b.** compound
   - **c.** discount
   - **d.** multiply

5. The question "What is the current value of an amount of cash that I will receive at a specific time in the future?" is best answered by which form of the TVM equation?
   - **a.** $PV = \dfrac{FV}{(1 + r)^n}$
   - **b.** $PV = PV \times (1 + r)^n$

c. $PV = \left(\frac{FV}{PV}\right)^{\frac{1}{n-1}}$

d. $PV = \frac{\ln(FV/PV)}{\ln(1 + r)}$

6. The Millville School District had 3,071 students enrolled five years ago. Today, the district enrollment is 2,418 students. What has been the annual rate of change of student enrollment in the Millville School District over this time period?

a. −5.40%
b. −4.25%
c. −4.67%
d. 4.25%

7. Average U.S. wages in 1990 were $28,960, far higher than the average wage in 1930 of $1,970. What was the average annual increase in wages over this sixty-year period?

a. 3.31%
b. 2.45%
c. 24.50%
d. 4.58%

8. For much of the twentieth century, new car prices rose at an annual rate of 5.73%. Given a beginning new car price of $600, how long did it take the average new car price to rise to $16,950? Round to the nearest year.

a. 40 years
b. 60 years
c. 70 years
d. 100 years

9. The dividends per share paid by Going Going Gone (GGG) doubled from a starting value of $1.50 in 2000 to a value of $3.00 in 2006 (a six-year period). What was the approximate average annual rate of growth of GGG's dividends per share? Use the Rule of 72 to determine your answer.

a. GGG's dividends grew at an annual rate of approximately 12% per year.
b. GGG's dividends grew at an annual rate of approximately 10% per year.
c. GGG's dividends grew at an annual rate of approximately 8% per year.
d. GGG's dividends grew at an annual rate of approximately 6% per year.

10. A manufacturer of LCD television sets has seen sales increase from 125,000 units per year to 500,000 units per year in eight years. What has been the firm's average annual rate of increase in the number of television sets sold? Use the Rule of 72 to determine your answer.

a. The average annual rate of change has been between 10% and 11%.
b. The average annual rate of change has been between 18% and 19%.
c. The average annual rate of change has been between 15% and 16%.
d. There is not enough information to answer this question.

These problems are available in MyFinanceLab.

Problems

1. ***Future values.*** Fill in the future values for the following table
   a. using the future value formula, $FV = PV \times (1 + r)^n$.
   b. using the TVM keys or function from a calculator or spreadsheet.

Present Value	Interest Rate	Number of Periods	Future Value
$ 400.00	5.0%	5	
$ 17,411.00	6.0%	30	
$35,000.00	10.0%	20	
$26,981.75	16.0%	15	

2. ***Future value (with changing years).*** Dixie Bank offers a certificate of deposit with an option to select your own investment period. Jonathan has $7,000 for his CD investment. If the bank is offering a 6% interest rate, how much will the CD be worth at maturity if Jonathan picks a
   a. two-year investment period?
   b. five-year investment period?
   c. eight-year investment period?
   d. fifteen-year investment period?
3. ***Future value (with changing interest rates).*** Jose has $4,000 to invest for a two-year period. He is looking at four different investment choices. What will be the value of his investment at the end of two years for each of the following potential investments?
   a. bank CD at 4%
   b. bond fund at 8%
   c. mutual stock fund at 12%
   d. new venture stock at 24%
4. ***Future value.*** Grand Opening Bank is offering a one-time investment opportunity for its new customers. A customer opening a new checking account can buy a special savings bond for $100 today, which the bank will compound at 7.5% for the next twenty years. You must hold the savings bond for at least five years but can then cash it in at the end of any year starting with year five. What is the value of the bond at each cash-in date up through twenty years? (Use an Excel spreadsheet to solve this problem.)
5. ***Future value.*** Jackson Enterprises has just purchased some land for $230,000. It purchased the land for a future beachfront property development project that will include rental cabins, lodge, and recreational facilities. Jackson Enterprises has not committed to the development project, but will decide in five years whether to go forward with it or sell off the land. Real estate values increase annually at 4.5% for unimproved property in this area. For how much can Jackson Enterprises expect to sell the property in five years if it chooses not to proceed with the beachfront development project? What if Jackson Enterprises holds the property for ten years and then sells?
6. ***Future value.*** The Portland Stallions professional football team is looking at its future revenue stream from ticket sales. Currently, a season package costs

$325 per seat. The Portland Stallions box office has promised season ticket holders this same rate for the next three years. Four years from now, the organization will raise season ticket prices based on the estimated inflation rate of 3.25%. What will the season tickets sell for in four years?

7. ***Future value***. Upstate University charges $16,000 a year in graduate tuition. Tuition rates are growing at 4.5% each year. You plan to enroll in graduate school in five years. What is your expected graduate tuition in five years?

8. ***Present values***. Fill in the present value for the following table
   a. using the present value formula, $PV = FV \times \left[1/(1 + r)^n\right]$.
   b. using the TVM keys or function from a calculator or spreadsheet.

Future Value	Interest Rate	Number of Periods	Present Value
$ 900.00	5%	5	
$ 80,000.00	6%	30	
$350,000.00	10%	20	
$ 26,981.75	16%	15	

9. ***Present value (with changing years)***. When they are first born, Grandma gives each of her grandchildren a $2,500 savings bond that matures in eighteen years. For each of the following grandchildren, what is the present value of each savings bond if the current discount rate is 4%?
   a. Seth turned sixteen years old today.
   b. Shawn turned thirteen years old today.
   c. Sherry turned nine years old today.
   d. Sheila turned four years old today.
   e. Shane was just born.

10. ***Present value (with changing interest rates)***. Marty received an offer for an injury settlement of $10,000 payable in three years. He wants to know what the present value of the injury settlement is if his opportunity cost is 5%. (The opportunity cost is the interest rate in this problem.) What if the opportunity cost is 8%? What if it is 12%?

11. ***Present value***. The State of Confusion wants to change the current retirement policy for state employees. To do so, however, the state must pay the current pension fund members the present value of their promised future payments. There are 240,000 current employees in the state pension fund. The average employee is twenty-two years away from retirement, and the average promised future retirement benefit is $400,000 per employee. If the state has a discount rate of 5% on all its funds, how much money will the state have to pay to the employees before it can start a new pension plan?

12. ***Present value***. Two rival football fans have made the following wager: if one fan's college football team wins the conference title outright, the other fan will donate $1,000 to the winning school. Both schools have had relatively unsuccessful teams but are improving each season. If the two fans must put up their potential donation today and the discount rate is 8% for the funds, what is the required upfront deposit if both expect a team to win the conference title in five years? Ten years? Twenty years?

13. ***Present value***. Prestigious University is offering a new admission and tuition payment plan for all alumni. On the birth of a child, parents can guarantee admission to Prestigious if they pay the first year's tuition. The university will pay an annual rate of return of 4.5% on the deposited tuition, and a full refund will be available if the child chooses another university. The tuition is $12,000 a year at Prestigious and is frozen at that level for the next eighteen years. What would parents pay today if they just gave birth to a new baby and the child will attend college in eighteen years? How much is the required payment to secure admission for their child if the interest rate falls to 2.5%?

14. ***Present value***. Standard Insurance is developing a long-life insurance policy for people who outlive their retirement nest egg. The policy will pay out $250,000 on your eighty-fifth birthday. You must buy the policy on your sixty-fifth birthday. The insurance company can earn 7% on the purchase price of your policy. What is the minimum purchase price the insurance company should charge for this policy?

15. ***Present value***. You are currently in the job market. Your dream is to earn a six-figure salary ($100,000). You hope to accomplish this goal within the next thirty years. In your field, salaries grow at 3.75% per year. What starting salary do you need to reach this goal?

16. ***Interest rate or discount rate***. Fill in the interest rate for the following table
    a. using the interest rate formula, $r = (FV/PV)^{1/n} - 1$.
    b. using the TVM keys or function from a calculator or spreadsheet.

Present Value	Future Value	Number of Periods	Interest Rate
$ 500.00	$ 1,998.00	18	
$ 17,335.36	$230,000.00	30	
$35,000.00	$ 63,214.00	20	
$ 27,651.26	$225,000.00	15	

17. ***Interest rate (with changing years)***. Keiko is looking at the following investment choices and wants to know what interest rate each choice produces.
    a. Invest $400 and receive $786.86 in ten years.
    b. Invest $3,000 and receive $10,927.45 in fifteen years.
    c. Invest $31,180.47 and receive $100,000 in twenty years.
    d. Invest $31,327.88 and receive $1,000,000 in forty-five years.

18. ***Interest rate***. Two mutual fund managers, Martha and David, have been bragging about whose fund is the top performer. Martha states that investors bought shares in her mutual fund ten years ago for $21.00, and those shares are now worth $65.00. David states that investors bought shares in his mutual fund for only $3.00 six years ago, and they are now worth $7.30. Which mutual fund manager has had the highest growth rate for the management period? Should this comparison be made over different management periods? Why or why not?

19. ***Interest rate***. In 1972, Bob purchased a new Datsun 240Z for $3,000. Datsun later changed its name to Nissan, and the 1972 Datsun 240Z became a classic. Bob kept his car in excellent condition and in 2002 could sell the car for six times what he originally paid. What was Bob's return on owning this car?

What if he keeps the car for another thirty years and earns the same rate? What could he sell the car for in 2032?

20. ***Interest rate.*** Upstate Bank is offering long-term certificates of deposit with a face value of $100,000 (future value). Bank customers can buy these CDs today for $67,000 and will receive the $100,000 in fifteen years. What interest rate is the bank paying on these CDs?

21. ***Discount rate.*** Future Bookstore sells books before they are published. Today, they are offering the book *Adventures in Finance* for $14.20, but the book will not be published for another two years. The retail price when the book is published will be $24.00 What is the discount rate Future Bookstore is offering its customers for this book?

22. ***Growth and future value.*** A famous disease control scientist is trying to determine the potential population infected by the new West Columbia flu. Two weeks ago, the first patient showed up with the disease. Four days later, the disease control center in Atlanta had six confirmed cases. The scientist estimates that it will be another two days before a cure will be ready, a total of sixteen days from the first confirmed case. How many patients will be infected two days from now?

23. ***Waiting period.*** Fill in the number of periods for the following table

a. using the waiting period formula, $n = \ln(FV/PV) \ / \ \ln(1 + r)$.

b. using the TVM keys or function from a calculator or spreadsheet.

Present Value	Future Value	Interest Rate	Number of Periods
$ 800.00	$ 1,609.76	6%	
$ 17,843.09	$ 100,000.00	9%	
$35,000.00	$3,256,783.97	12%	
$25,410.99	$ 300,000.00	28%	

24. ***Waiting period (with changing years).*** Jamal is waiting to be a millionaire. He wants to know how long he must wait if

a. he invests $24,465.28 at 16% today.

b. he invests $47,101.95 at 13% today.

c. he invests $115,967.84 at 9% today.

d. he invests $295,302.77 at 5% today.

25. ***Waiting period.*** Jeff, a local traffic engineer, has designed a new pedestrian footbridge. The bridge has been designed to handle 200 pedestrians daily. Once the bridge reaches 1,000 pedestrians daily, however, it will require a new bracing system. Jeff has estimated that traffic will increase annually at 5%. How long will the current bridge system work before a new bracing system is required? What if the annual traffic rate increases at 8% annually? At what traffic increase rate will the current system last only ten years?

26. ***Waiting period.*** Susan Norman seeks your financial advice. She wants to know how long it will take her to become a millionaire. She tells you that she has $1,330 today and wants to invest it in an aggressive stock portfolio. The historical return on this type of investment is 18% per year. How long will she have to wait if the $1,330 is the only amount she invests and she never withdraws from the market until she reaches her $1 million? (Assume no taxes on the earnings.) What if the rate of return is only 14% annually? What if the rate of return is only 10% annually?

27. ***Waiting period***. Upstate University currently has a 6,000-car parking capacity for faculty, staff, and students. This year, the university issued 4,356 parking passes. Parking passes have been growing at a rate of 6% per year. How long will it be before the university will need to add additional parking?

28. ***Double your money***. Approximately how long will it take to double your money if you get a 5.5%, 7.5%, or 9.5% annual return on your investment? Verify the approximate doubling period with the time value of money equation.

29. ***Double your wealth***. Kant Miss Company is promising its investors that it will double their money every three years. Is this promise too good to be true? What annual rate is Kant Miss promising? If you invested $250 now and Kant Miss were able to deliver on its promise, how long would it take before your investment reaches $32,000?

30. ***Challenge question***. In the chapter text, we dealt exclusively with a single lump sum, but often we may be looking at several lump-sum values simultaneously. Let's consider the retirement plan of a couple. Currently, the couple has four different investments: a 401(k) plan, two pension plans, and a personal portfolio. The couple is five years away from retirement. They believe they have sufficient money in their plans today so that they do not have to contribute to the plans over the next five years and will still meet their $2 million retirement goal. Here are the current values and the growth rate of each plan:

    401(k): $88,000 growing at 6.5%

    Pension plan 1: $304,000 growing at 7%

    Pension plan 2: $214,000 growing at 7.25%

    Personal portfolio: $149,000 growing at 8.5%

    Does the couple have enough already invested to make their goal in five years? *Hint:* View each payment as a separate problem and find the future value of each lump sum. Then add up what all the future values will be five years from now.

These problems are available in MyFinanceLab.

Advanced Problems for Spreadsheet Application

1. ***Future value of a portfolio***. Rachel and Richard want to know when their current portfolio will be sufficient for them to retire. They have the following balances in their portfolio:

    Money market account: $37,000
    Government bond mutual fund: $140,000
    Large capital mutual fund: $107,000
    Small capital mutual fund: $71,000
    Real estate trust fund: $87,000

    Rachel and Richard believe they need at least $2,000,000 to retire. The money market grows at 2.5% annually, the government bond mutual fund grows at 5.5% annually, the large capital mutual fund grows at 9.5% annually, the small capital mutual fund grows at 12.0% annually, and the real estate trust fund grows at 4.0% annually. Using a spreadsheet, calculate the end-of-year balance for the portfolio with the assumption that no more funds will be deposited into any of these accounts. How long until they reach the $2,000,000 goal?

2. ***Changing future value growth rates***. Sunshine Growers produces Christmas trees and is trying to determine the optimal harvest time for the trees. Trees sell for $5 per foot. The trees grow at the following rate after planted as seedlings that are one foot tall: first three years, 60% growth rate; second three years, 40% growth rate; all future years, 20% growth rate. The cost to maintain a tree increases each year. The first year, the maintenance cost is $3.00 per tree. The maintenance costs grow at a rate of 30% per year. When is the optimal time to harvest the trees? Use a spreadsheet and calculate the revenue each year if Sunshine Growers harvests the trees that year and subtract the accumulated costs of maintenance to find the gross profit for the year. At what height (year) do the trees produce the highest gross profit?

MINI-CASE

Richards' Tree Farm, Inc.: The Continuing Saga

This mini-case is available in MyFinanceLab.

Richards' Tree Farm, Inc. is doing well after its incorporation. Jake Richards, president, chief of operations, and majority shareholder, currently has a planting of 10,000 three-year-old Japanese dogwood trees in a recently introduced pink-flowered variety. Richards can sell this type of tree at a higher price than the more common white-flowered variety. The trees are now 6 feet tall on average and can command $24 each. At present, Richards has priced 8-foot trees at $34 and 10-foot trees at $40. Landscape contractors avoid trees larger than 10 feet tall because they are difficult to transplant successfully. With average weather, the 6-foot trees will be 8 feet tall in another three years and 10 feet tall in six more years.

Jake has to make financial decisions almost every day. Today's decision involves present value and future value computations, which Jake learned as a student at Oregon State University. He wants to know if he should sell the trees immediately at 6 feet tall, three years from now at 8 feet tall, or six years from now at 10 feet tall.

Size	Age	Current Market Value
6′	3 years	$24.00
8′	6 years	$34.00
10′	9 years	$40.00

Questions

1. Because of inflation, Jake expects the price at which he can sell the trees to increase by 3% per year. What price does he expect to receive if he keeps the trees until they reach 8 feet or 10 feet tall?
2. If Jake discounts the future price of the trees at 10% per year, what is the present value of their future prices?
3. Using the time value of money equation, compute the growth rate of the trees between the third year and the sixth year and between the sixth year and the ninth year.
4. When should Jake sell the trees?
5. **Challenge question**. A major landscape contractor who has bid successfully on a large-scale Boston beautification and urban greening project has offered to buy all 10,000 flowering dogwood trees at a price of $28,000, payable immediately. However, the contractor does not need the trees for three years. If Jake accepts, he will be obliged to deliver 10,000 trees three years from today. If anything should happen to his own crop, he would need to buy trees on the open market at the prevailing price, which might be higher or lower than the price estimated in Question 1. Should Jake accept the offer if his required rate of return is 10%? *Hint:* What is the present value of the price he expects to receive for the trees three years in the future? Discount the price at 10%.

Learning Objectives

LO1 Compute the future value of multiple cash flows.

LO2 Determine the future value of an annuity.

LO3 Determine the present value of an annuity.

LO4 Adjust the annuity formula for present value and future value for an annuity due and understand the concept of a perpetuity.

LO5 Distinguish between the different types of loan repayments: discount loans, interest-only loans, and amortized loans.

LO6 Build and analyze amortization schedules.

LO7 Calculate waiting time and interest rates for an annuity.

LO8 Apply the time value of money concepts to evaluate the lottery cash flow choice.

LO9 Summarize the ten essential points about the time value of money.

Chapter 4

The Time Value of Money (Part 2)

In Chapter 3, we examined lump-sum payments over both single and multiple time periods. Most investments, though, have multiple cash flows, and we now turn to the tools that will help us handle them efficiently. Many personal financial transactions feature equal cash amounts at regular, fixed intervals. For example, you may put away regular payments into a nest egg such as a 401(k) account for your retirement or a 529 college fund for your child's future tuition, or you may make regular payments to a landlord for apartment rental or to a bank for a home mortgage or car loan. We call these types of transactions *ordinary annuities* or *annuities due*. To learn how to determine their value, our basic tool remains the same: the time value of money equation. In this chapter, we will put the equation to somewhat more sophisticated use than we did in the previous chapter.

4.1 Future Value of Multiple Payment Streams

Suppose you plan to put away some money each year to build up a nest egg to use as a down payment on a house. You start off by putting away \$2,000 today, and over the next three years you are able to put away \$3,000 at the end of the first year, \$4,000 at the end of the second year, and \$5,000 at the end of the third year. How much will you have saved by the end of the third year if your investment rate is 5% per year?

The time line in Figure 4.1 will help us visualize these cash flows. As before, we will use T as the variable that indicates time and the subscript on T to identify the specific time period. So, T_0 will be today or time zero, T_1 will be at the end of the first period (in this example, the end of the first year), T_2 will be the end of the second period, and so on. Then we put the appropriate cash flow under the specific time period to visualize our multiple cash flows.

As in Chapter 3, we "grow" the cash deposit by the interest rate to the future date. The \$2,000, for example, will earn interest at 5% over the next three years and be worth \$2,315.25 at the end of the third year, T_3. To see the total amount at the end of T_3, we simply treat each annual deposit in the fund as a single lump-sum payment and then add the four different deposits (with their accumulated interest) at the end of the third year.

You can add money only if it is at the same point in time. In other words, it makes no economic sense to add the \$2,000 today to the \$3,000 a year from now, the \$4,000 two years from now, and the \$5,000 three years from now to get a total value of \$14,000. Rather, we should "bring" all the cash deposits to the same point in time and then add the value of the deposits and their accumulated interest to get the economic value of the cash deposits over time. So,

$$FV = PV \times (1 + r)^n$$

$$\begin{aligned}
&FV \text{ of cash flow at } T_0 = \$2{,}000 \times 1.05^3 = \$200 \times 1.157625 = \$2{,}315.25\\
&FV \text{ of cash flow at } T_1 = \$3{,}000 \times 1.05^2 = \$300 \times 1.1025 = \$3{,}307.50\\
&FV \text{ of cash flow at } T_2 = \$4{,}000 \times 1.05^1 = \$400 \times 1.0500 = \$4{,}200.00\\
&FV \text{ of cash flow at } T_3 = \$5{,}000 \times 1.05^0 = \$500 \times 1.0000 = \underline{\$5{,}000.00}\\
&\textbf{Total} \qquad \textbf{\$14,822.75}
\end{aligned}$$

The multiple payments require that we use the future value equation from Chapter 3 multiple times so that we can accurately state the value of the nest egg

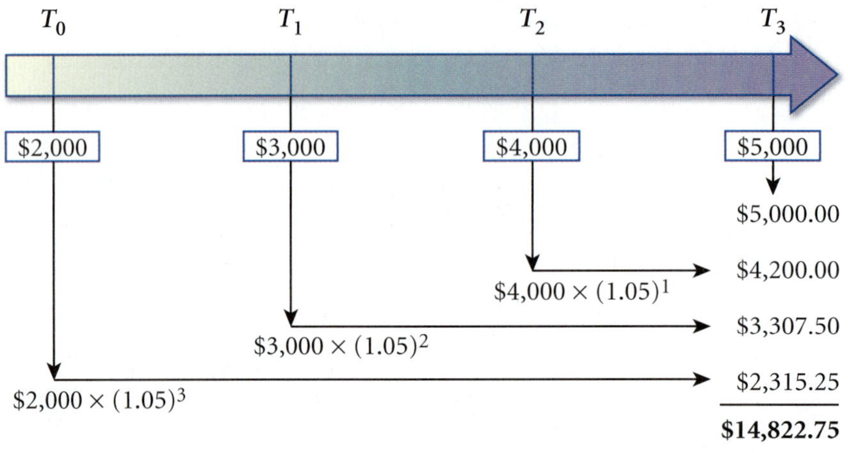

FIGURE 4.1 The time line of a nest egg.

at the end of the third year as $14,822.75. By examining the timeline closely, we can see that the first deposit earns interest over three years, the second deposit earns interest over two years, the third deposit earns interest over one year, and the final deposit does not earn any interest. We value all four deposits as future dollars at the end of year three, however, and can add at that single point in time.

The same issue exists for the present value of multiple cash flows. To find the present value of a series of future cash flows, you would need to use the Chapter 3 equation for present value multiple times and then sum those present values.

4.2 Future Value of an Annuity Stream

Let's vary the nest egg example with a different savings plan. Say you decide to put away $1,000 at the end of every year for the next five years. If you can earn 6% on the account, what is the value of the account at the end of the five years? Notice that unlike the previous problem, you do not put any money away *today.* The first deposit is at the end of the first year. To solve this problem with our current tools, we handle each payment separately and add the total value at the end of five years. See Figure 4.2.

$$
\begin{aligned}
FV \text{ of payment } 1 &= \$1{,}000 \times 1.06^4 = \$1{,}262.48 \\
FV \text{ of payment } 2 &= \$1{,}000 \times 1.06^3 = \$1{,}191.02 \\
FV \text{ of payment } 3 &= \$1{,}000 \times 1.06^2 = \$1{,}123.60 \\
FV \text{ of payment } 4 &= \$1{,}000 \times 1.06^1 = \$1{,}060.00 \\
FV \text{ of payment } 5 &= \$1{,}000 \times 1.06^0 = \$1{,}000.00 \\
\textbf{Total} & \qquad\qquad\qquad\quad\ \ \mathbf{\$5{,}637.10}
\end{aligned}
$$

This approach works but becomes cumbersome as we begin to lengthen the number of payments. However, if the payments are the same amount and at regular intervals across time, we can use a shortcut to solve this future value problem.

A series of equal cash flows at regular intervals across time is an **annuity**. This last example—putting away $1,000 at the end of every year for the next five years—is an annuity. It is the same amount of money that you deposit at regular intervals. On the other hand, your monthly electric bill is *not* an annuity because

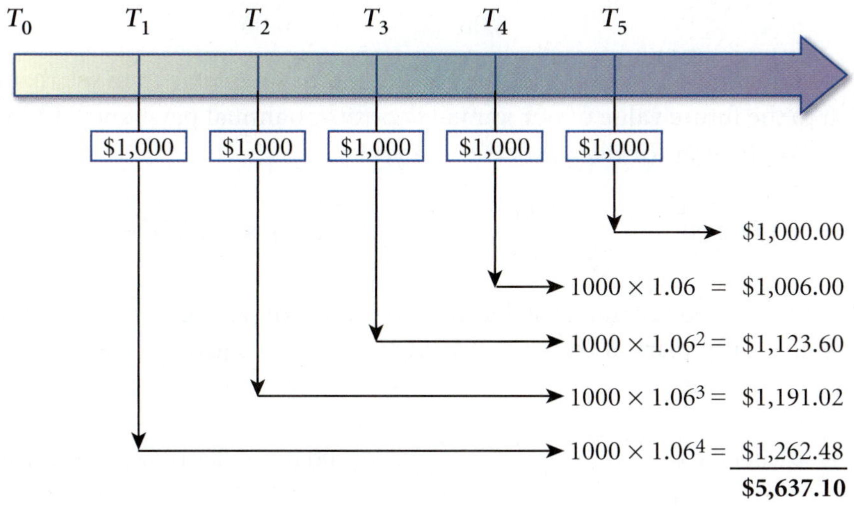

FIGURE 4.2 The time line of a $1,000-per-year nest egg.

even though the bill comes at regular intervals, the amount varies from month to month. Equal payments and regular intervals allow you to condense the set of future values into a single equation. Currently, the equation for this problem is rather lengthy:

$$FV = CF_1 \times (1 + r)^4 + CF_2 \times (1 + r)^3 + CF_3 \times (1 + r)^2 + CF_4 \times (1 + r)^1 + CF_5 \times (1 + r)^0$$

where CF is the same annual cash flow, r is the interest rate, and there are five payments, one at the end of each year.

Another way to write this equation is to note that the cash flow (CF_i) is the same amount every period. We can therefore collect these like payments and reduce the equation to

$$FV = CF \times \left[(1 + r)^4 + (1 + r)^3 + (1 + r)^2 + (1 + r)^1 + (1 + r)^0\right] \quad \textbf{4.1}$$

We can condense material in the brackets to $\left[(1 + r)^5 - 1)\right]/r$. Equation 4.1 now becomes

$$FV = CF \times \frac{(1 + r)^5 - 1}{r} \quad \textbf{4.2}$$

We often label the cash flow payments (PMT), so a more common form of this equation is

$$FV = PMT \times \frac{(1 + r)^n - 1}{r} \quad \textbf{4.3}$$

where n is the number of payments of the annuity. We use Equation 4.3 to determine the future value of an annuity, which is one of our basic finance tools. The last portion of the equation is the **future value interest factor of an annuity (FVIFA)**. So,

$$FVIFA = \frac{(1 + r)^n - 1}{r}$$

We multiply the annual payment by the FVIFA to calculate the future value. Appendix 3 provides FVIFAs for a set of payments (n) and interest rates (r). For our example, we see that the value of the FVIFA for $n = 5$ and $r = 6\%$ is

$$\frac{(1 + r)^n - 1}{r} = \frac{(1 + 0.06)^5 - 1}{0.06} = \frac{1.3382 - 1}{0.06} = 5.6371$$

Applying Equation 4.3, which uses the FVIFA and payment, we then see that the solution to the future value of our annual deposits or annual payments of \$1,000 at the end of the year for five years at 6% a year is

$$FV = \$1{,}000.00 \times \frac{(1 + 0.06)^5 - 1}{0.06} = \$1{,}000.00 \times 5.6371 = \$5{,}637.10$$

What would the account look like after ten years of payments? Twenty years of payments? Fifty years of payments? Using Equation 4.3 gives us the following answers:

$$FV_{10} = \$1{,}000.00 \times \frac{(1 + 0.06)^{10} - 1}{0.06} = \$1{,}000.00 \times 13.1808 = \$13{,}180.80$$

$$FV_{20} = \$1{,}000.00 \times \frac{(1 + 0.06)^{20} - 1}{0.06} = \$1{,}000.00 \times 36.7856 = \$36{,}785.60$$

$$FV_{50} = \$1{,}000.00 \times \frac{(1 + 0.06)^{50} - 1}{0.06} = \$1{,}000.00 \times 290.3359 = \$290{,}335.90$$

Notice the use of the subscript on the *FV* variable to signify the single point in time of the future value.

Thus, the condensed equation with FVIFAs helps minimize the calculation work for an annuity. Unfortunately, if the payments are *not* equal and are *not* at regular intervals, we cannot apply this shortcut to solving a future value problem. We are then back to handling each payment as a lump-sum payment and adding the values of the individual payments.

Equation 4.3 is set up to work with annuity payments at the *end* of each regular interval. We call this type of annuity, with payments occurring at the end of each period, an **ordinary annuity**. Common ordinary annuity payments are for mortgage payments, car loans, and corporate bond coupon payments. In Section 4.4, we will study an **annuity due**, in which we make the payment at the *beginning* of each period. Common annuity due payments are for rents for which the money is due at the first of each period and for insurance payments for which the money is due at the start of the policy period.

Future Value of an Annuity: An Application

Now let's look at an application of the FVIFA equation with the three different methods that Chapter 3 introduced (formula, calculator, and spreadsheet) for solving future value problems.

EXAMPLE 4.1 Parent scholarships (future value of an annuity)

Problem Kitty and Red put \$1,500 into a college fund every year for their son, Eric, on his birthday, with the first deposit one year from his birth (at his very first birthday). The college fund has a guaranteed annual growth or interest rate of 7%. At his eighteenth birthday, they will pay the last \$1,500 into the fund. How much will be in the college fund for Eric immediately following this last payment?

Solution For this problem, we are trying to determine the future value at the end of the eighteen annual payments of \$1,500. Because the payments are the same amount each period at the end of a regular interval (one year apart), we are dealing with an ordinary annuity problem. The known variables are $r = 7\%$, $n = 18$, and $PMT = \$1{,}500$. We can solve for FV in three different ways.

METHOD 1 Using the equation

First, calculate the FVIFA value at $n = 18$ and $r = 7\%$:

$$FVIFA = \frac{(1 + r)^n - 1}{r}$$

$$= \frac{(1 + 0.07)^{18} - 1}{0.07} = \frac{(3.3799) - 1}{0.07} = \mathbf{33.9990}$$

Then, multiply the annuity payment by this factor to get the future value in eighteen years:

$$\$1{,}500 \times 33.9990 = \$50{,}998.55$$

METHOD 2 Using the TVM keys

With this method, it is important to recognize that the calculator must be in END mode so that it treats the payments as an ordinary annuity. *Set the calculator to END mode.* (END and BGN modes are the second function above the PMT key on the TI BAII Plus calculator.) Then,

Mode = End					
Input	18	7.0	0	−1,500	?
Key	N	I/Y	PV	PMT	FV
CPT					**50,998.55**

METHOD 3 Using a spreadsheet

B6 | *fx* | *=FV(B1,B2,B3,B4,B5)*

Use the FV function to find the amount in the scholarship account at the end of eighteen years earning 7% on the initial deposit of $1,500.

	A	B	C	D	E
1	Rate	0.07			
2	Nper	18			
3	Pmt	($1,500.00)			
4	Pv	0			
5	Type	0			
6	Fv	$50,998.55			

All three methods produce the same future value because they all use the same equation (Equation 4.3). Eric can expect approximately $51,000 for college in eighteen years.

It is also interesting to see how changing the interest rate for the future changes the value of an ordinary annuity. What if the interest rate over the eighteen years in the preceding example were 3%, or 9%, or 12%?

$$\text{At } 3\%\text{: } FV_{18} = \$1{,}500.00 \times \frac{\left[(1 + 0.03)^{18} - 1\right]}{0.03} = \$1{,}500.00 \times 23.4144$$
$$= \$35{,}121.60$$

$$\text{At } 9\%\text{: } FV_{18} = \$1{,}500.00 \times \frac{\left[(1 + 0.09)^{18} - 1\right]}{0.09} = \$1{,}500.00 \times 41.3013$$
$$= \$61{,}951.95$$

$$\text{At } 12\%\text{: } FV_{18} = \$1{,}500.00 \times \frac{\left[(1 + 0.12)^{18} - 1\right]}{0.12} = \$1{,}500.00 \times 55.7497$$
$$= \$83{,}624.55$$

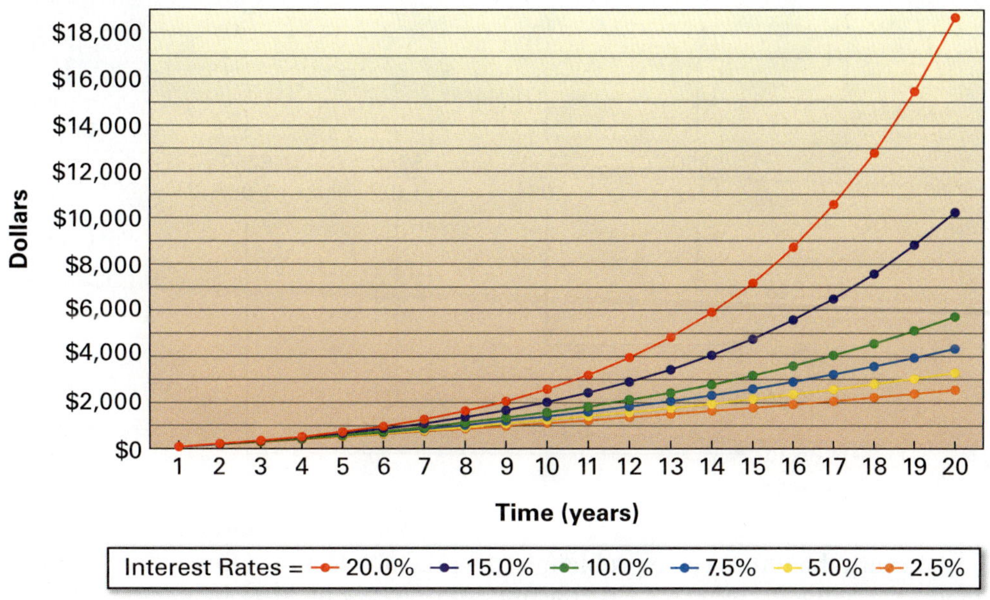

FIGURE 4.3 Interest and principal growth with different interest rates for $100 annual payments.

Figure 4.3 illustrates the different ending values of a series of deposits as the years extend and the interest rate increases. Notice that the longer the time, the more effect the higher interest rates have on the future value of the annuity. This is compounding of interest at work.

4.3 Present Value of an Annuity

Just as we found the present value of a lump sum in Chapter 3, we can also find the present value of an annuity stream. In fact, in finance we use the present value concept in a number of applications. When we determine the monthly payment on a mortgage or car payment, we are using a present value view, not a future value view. Here we are trying to determine the present value of a future cash flow that has annuity stream characteristics, equal amounts at regular intervals for a finite period.

Take the case of receiving four equal payments of $250 over the next four years (at the end of each year) with a discount rate of 8%. Using the separate lump-sum approach, the present value is

$$PV = FV_1 \times \frac{1}{(1+r)^1} = \$250 \times \frac{1}{(1+0.08)^1} = \$250 \times 0.9259 = \$231.48$$

$$PV = FV_2 \times \frac{1}{(1+r)^2} = \$250 \times \frac{1}{(1+0.08)^2} = \$250 \times 0.8573 = \$214.33$$

$$PV = FV_3 \times \frac{1}{(1+r)^3} = \$250 \times \frac{1}{(1+0.08)^3} = \$250 \times 0.7938 = \$198.46$$

$$PV = FV_4 \times \frac{1}{(1+r)^4} = \$250 \times \frac{1}{(1+0.08)^4} = \$250 \times 0.7350 = \underline{\$183.76}$$

$$\mathbf{\$828.03}$$

We can also see the solution with the use of a time line for the four future payments in Figure 4.4.

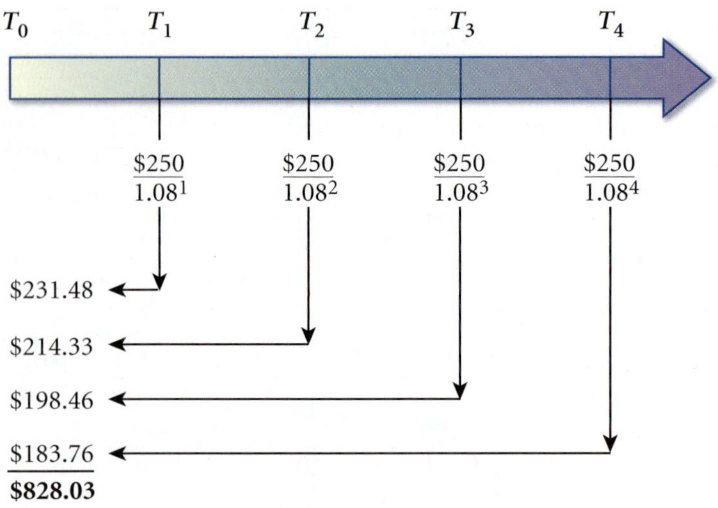

FIGURE 4.4 Time line of present value of annuity stream.

As with the future value problem in the previous section, after collecting the identical payments, we can write this present value problem as an equation. In general form, where *n* equals the number of payments or periods,

$$PV = PMT \times \frac{1 - [1/(1 + r)^n]}{r} \qquad \textbf{4.4}$$

The last portion of the equation is the **present value interest factor of an annuity (PVIFA)**. So,

$$PVIFA = \frac{1 - [1/(1 + r)^n]}{r}$$

Appendix 4 lists the values of various PVIFAs for different combinations of interest or discount rates (r) and number of payments (n).

The annuity equations for present value and future value are straightforward. Just as in Chapter 3, we have one equation and four variables, and to solve for any one of the four variables, we must know the other three. Example 4.2 shows a present value problem solved with the three methods that Chapter 3 introduced.

EXAMPLE 4.2 Making retirement golden (present value of an annuity)

Problem Ben and Donna determine that upon retirement, they will need to withdraw $50,000 annually at the end of each year for the next thirty years. They know that they can earn 4% each year on their investment. What is the present value of this annuity? In other words, how much will Ben and Donna need in their retirement account (at the beginning of their retirement) to generate this future cash flow?

Solution In this problem, we assume that Ben and Donna need to have the present value of the thirty-year annuity in their account at the start of their retirement, even though they will not make the first withdrawal of $50,000 until the end of the first year of retirement. They will make thirty withdrawals from this account during retirement. The investment rate is 4%. It is the same as the discount rate for the future payments of $50,000 that will come at the end of each year for the next thirty years. The known variables are $r = 4\%$, $n = 30$, and $PMT = \$50,000$. Solve for *PV*.

METHOD 1 Using the equation

First, calculate the PVIFA value for $n = 30$ and $r = 4\%$:

$$\frac{1 - [1/(1 + 0.04)^{30}]}{0.04} = \frac{[1 - (0.308319)]}{0.04} = 17.292033$$

Multiply the annuity payment by this factor:

$$PV = \$50{,}000 \times 17.292033 = \mathbf{\$864{,}601.67}$$

PUTTING FINANCE TO WORK

Modeling the Future with Actuarial Science

In the 2004 movie *Along Came Polly,* Reuben Feffer (played by Ben Stiller) wants to live life in complete safety, free from any unnecessary risk. He is an actuary who even tries to quantify personal choice as he feeds the advantages and disadvantages of two romantic interests in his life into his computer program, the Risk Master. By the end of the movie, Reuben has learned that to live life fully, he needs to take some risks in his own life.

There may not be a Risk Master machine in the real world, but there is a science that evaluates the likelihood of future events happening and that aims to decrease the effect of future undesirable events when they occur. The professionals who do such work and manage risk in its many forms are actuaries. Surveys in such publications as the *Wall Street Journal* and *U.S. News and World Report* have consistently ranked "actuary" near the top of lists of most desirable occupations, using criteria such as earnings, status, security, mobility, and happiness.

A majority of actuaries work for the insurance industry, although they also work for governments, large financial services firms, and firms that offer consulting services to businesses, governments, and pension funds. Actuaries play an important role in designing insurance plans and determining premiums, recommending corrective action to existing policies, and ensuring that there are enough funds set aside in the firms where they work in order to pay claims.

Some typical problems that actuaries might work on are determining the amount of reserves a company must have on hand to fund its liability for pension payments to retired employees and arriving at the appropriate premiums to charge for all sorts of insurance, from life insurance to property insurance to health insurance. Actuaries use statistical methods to estimate the timing and cost of future undesirable events. Alert students will recognize that these problems also involve the compounded and discounted cash flow patterns that you studied in Chapters 3 and 4. For example, the amount of assets required to fund a future liability is the present value of a future sum, annuity, or uneven cash flow, depending on the specific nature of the problem. The premiums paid for a life insurance policy are an annuity, and the policy's cash value is the annuity's future value.

Another issue important to actuarial science is the appropriate rate to use in compounding or discounting these cash flows. We will address this topic in future chapters dealing with interest rates, risk, and the cost of capital. Actuaries use their expertise in statistics and finance to develop new products for insurance and financial services industries. Some recent innovations based on actuarial principles include long-term care insurance, weather insurance, variable annuities, and reverse mortgages.

Although no specific major is required to become an actuary, the most typical backgrounds are mathematics, finance, economics, and accounting. Approved college-level courses in each of the first three areas are required, and each of these areas is covered in depth in the actuarial exams. All actuaries take one exam, regardless of their specialization, which is devoted exclusively to financial mathematics. Later exams reflect fields of specialization that relate to the various types of insurance, such as life, health, or property and casualty.

Sources: Bureau of Labor Statistics, www.bls.gov; Society of Actuaries, www.soa.org, www.beanactuary.org; American Academy of Actuaries, www.actuary.org.

METHOD 2 Using the TVM keys

Here again, it is important to recognize that the calculator must be in END mode so that you treat the payments as an ordinary annuity. Set the calculator for an ordinary annuity (END mode). Then,

Input	30	4.0	?	−50,000	0
Key	N	I/Y	PV	PMT	FV
CPT			**864,601.67**		

METHOD 3 Using a spreadsheet

B6	*fx* =*PV*(*B1,B2,B3,B4,B5*)				
Use the PV function to find out how much money is needed in the retirement account at the start of retirement to allow $50,000 withdrawal every year for the next thirty years if the account is earning 4% annually.					
	A	B	C	D	E
1	Rate	0.04			
2	Nper	30			
3	Pmt	($ 50,000.00)			
4	Fv	0			
5	Type	0			
6	Pv	$864,601.67			

Thus, all three methods produce the same present value. So, to receive $50,000 at the end of the year for the next thirty years, Ben and Donna must have $864,601.67 in their retirement account when they retire if they can earn 4% a year on the balance of their funds each year.

4.4 Annuity Due and Perpetuity

Not all annuities are ordinary (end-of-period) annuities. Some payments are due at the *beginning* of the time period. For example, when someone is paying rent on an apartment, the person applies the rent at the first or beginning of the month (a prepayment). Such payments differ from car payments or mortgage payments that the person applies at the end of a month (even though the due date is the first day of the month). The rental payment is an annuity due, whereas the car payment and mortgage payment are ordinary annuities. To make this distinction between the beginning of the month and the end of the month clearer, consider that making a rent payment allows you to use the apartment for the remainder of the month; that is, you are paying at the beginning of the period for the use of the apartment for that period. You are thus paying in advance. With a mortgage payment, you are paying down the principal and paying interest on the loan for the prior month. So in that case, the mortgage payment applies to the previous month or a payment at the end of the month. You are thus paying in arrears.

Does that mean that the annuity equations just presented for future value and present value calculations are good only with an ordinary annuity? No. You can adjust the equations for an annuity due. Before doing so, however, Figure 4.5 shows the necessary change, which compares an ordinary annuity with an annuity due, both with four equal payments of $100. For the ordinary annuity, the cash flow is at the end of the period, whereas the cash flow is at the beginning of the period for the annuity due.

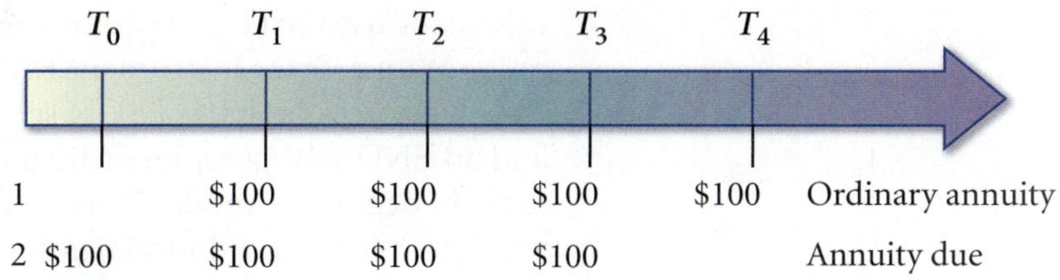

FIGURE 4.5 An ordinary annuity versus an annuity due.

Looking at Figure 4.5, we see that the annuity due has the same number of payments as those of the ordinary annuity, but it receives the payments one period earlier. So, if we want to calculate the present value of the annuity due, the payments would each receive one less period of discounting versus the ordinary annuity.

To solve for the present value of the annuity due problem, we need to remove the additional discount period for each payment of the ordinary annuity. We accomplish this by multiplying the present value of the ordinary annuity by 1 + r.

$$PV = PMT \times \frac{1 - [\,1/\,(1 + r)^n\,]}{r} \times (1 + r) \qquad \textbf{4.5}$$

or

$$PV \text{ annuity due} = PV \text{ ordinary annuity} \times (1 + r)$$

$$PV = \$100 \times \frac{1 - [1/(1 + 0.08)^4]}{0.08} \times (1 + 0.08) = \$357.71$$

What about a future value for an annuity due? Notice that each payment earns interest for one more period than the ordinary annuity. With the same $100 paid four times, but now at the *beginning* of the period, we have each payment with an extra year of interest. So, we again adjust the original future value equation by $(1 + r)$ for the annuity due:

$$FV = PMT \times \frac{(1 + r)^n - 1}{r} \times (1 + r) \qquad \textbf{4.6}$$

or

$$FV \text{ annuity due} = FV \text{ ordinary annuity} \times (1 + r)$$

Again, if we assume an 8% interest rate, we have

$$FV = \$100 \times \frac{(1 + 0.08)^4 - 1}{0.08} \times (1 + 0.08)$$

$$= \$100 \times 4.5061 \times 1.08 = \$486.66$$

You can also adjust a payment from an ordinary annuity to an annuity due using $(1 + r)$. Assume that you have the option to convert from an ordinary annuity to an annuity due for which the current payment is $100 per year. Let's use the same setup with an interest rate of 8%. To switch to an annuity due payment you simply divide the current ordinary annuity payment by 1 + 0.08, as in Equation 4.7.

$$\text{annuity due payment} = \text{ordinary annuity payment}\,/(1 + r) \qquad \textbf{4.7}$$

$$\text{annuity due payment} = \$100.00/1.08 = \$92.59259$$

The equations may seem a bit cumbersome to you, so you may want to use technology to calculate your answers. Both spreadsheets and TVM keys on a calculator use the $(1 + r)$ adjustment to properly account for the timing of an annuity. With a Texas Instrument BAII Plus calculator, a second function above the PMT key provides both a BGN setting for an annuity due (beginning of period) and an END setting for an ordinary annuity (end of period). When the calculator is in beginning mode, BGN displays in small letters at the top of the display window. When in end mode, however, nothing is displayed. The spreadsheet uses TYPE as the variable in the different equations, with Type set to 0 as the ordinary annuity and Type set to 1 as the annuity due.

Converting to BGN

2ND	PMT (BGN)	Display will have END.
2ND	ENTER	Display will change to BGN.

Converting back

2ND	ENTER	Display will return to END.

When you compare an ordinary annuity and an annuity due, the present or future value of an annuity due is always $(1 + r)$ greater than an ordinary annuity. However, you must assume the same number and size of payments. When computing an ordinary annuity payment or annuity due payment for the same future or present value, the ordinary annuity payment is always greater by $(1 + r)$.

Perpetuity

The annuity equations are nice shortcuts for payment streams that go on for a very long period. The longest possible period for an annuity is forever. We call this never-ending stream of cash flows a **perpetuity**. In England and Canada, the governments have issued bonds that, in effect, are perpetuities as part of the national debt. They pay interest forever, have no date of maturity, and make no promise to repay the principal. We call these bonds **consols**, which are priced as perpetual bonds.

Say you are shopping for a Canadian consol that pays \$30 a year in interest forever. What price will you pay if you want a 5% yield on this investment? The annuity stream equation is

$$PV = PMT \times \frac{1 - \left[1/(1 + r)^{\infty}\right]}{r}$$

where n is forever (∞ in the equation). At first glance, this present value factor of an annuity appears to be a very difficult equation, but fortunately it condenses quite nicely to 1/r. The solution is

$$PV = \$30 \times \frac{1 - \left[1/(1 + 0.05)^{\infty}\right]}{0.05} = \$30 \times \frac{1}{0.05} = \frac{\$30}{0.05} = \$600$$

The appropriate price for the Canadian consol paying \$30 per year in interest is \$600 for a 5% annual yield. The general equation for the present value of a perpetuity is

$$PV = \frac{PMT}{r} \qquad \textbf{4.8}$$

4.5 Three Loan Payment Methods

At this point, let's pause and synthesize some basic information on the time value of money. When you borrow money, there are three different ways to repay the loan:

1. With a **discount loan**, you can pay off the **principal** (the original loan amount that you borrowed) and all the **interest** (the amount that the lender charges you for borrowing the money) at one time at the maturity date of the loan. The discount loan is the payment method of the U.S. government on Treasury bills.
2. With an **interest-only loan**, you can make interest payments as you go and then pay the principal and final interest payment at the maturity date. The interest-only loan is the payment method of the bond market.
3. With an **amortized loan**, you can pay both principal and interest as you go by making equal payments each period. The amortized loan is the payment method of consumer loans.

Next, we'll use the time value of money tools you've learned to figure out the repayment schedule for $25,000 borrowed today (principal of the loan) for a period of six years with an annual interest rate of 8%. We'll examine this loan using each of the three common repayment possibilities.

Interest and Principal at the Maturity of Loan (Discount Loan)

If you agreed to pay back the principal and interest at the end of the six years, the total repayment at the end is simply the future value of the $25,000 over six years at the 8% loan rate. We will apply Equation 3.2:

$$FV = PV \times (1 + r)^n$$

$$FV_6 = \$25{,}000 \times (1 + 0.08)^6 = \$25{,}000 \times 1.5869 = \$39{,}671.86$$

The $39,671.86 total payment after six years reflects the repayment of the $25,000 principal plus interest of $14,671.86 on the borrowed principal at 8%.

Technically, a discount loan states the payoff amount as the size of the loan and then "deducts" or discounts the interest payment from the payoff or face value of the loan to arrive at the amount the lender is providing the borrower. For the borrower, in other words, the loan amount is the amount of money he or she receives at the start, and the final payment is both interest and principal combined. So, the term *discount loan* is accurate, but we state the loan value as the ending payment ($39,671.86) rather than the present value ($25,000). Compared with the other payment choices that use the present value of the loan to describe the amount, a discount loan can be confusing. The important point with a discount loan is that you receive a lump sum of money from the lender at the start of the period and pay back the entire interest and principal at the end.

Interest as You Go, Principal at Maturity of Loan (Interest-Only Loan)

Another acceptable repayment schedule is to pay the annual interest each year and then repay the principal at the maturity date with the last year's interest. Each year, the interest payment is the 8% loan rate times the principal:

$$\text{annual interest payment} = \$25{,}000 \times 0.08 = \$2{,}000$$

At the end of the sixth year, the final payment is $27,000, reflecting the $25,000 principal originally borrowed and the final $2,000 interest payment. Thus, the total outflow over the six years is six $2,000 interest payments, or $12,000 of interest, and the $25,000 principal repayment for a total of $37,000.

Interest and Principal as You Go (Amortized Loan)

The most common way for consumers to pay off a loan is to make equal payments each period, with a portion going to the interest for the period and the remainder applied against the outstanding principal. This common payment method is an application of an annuity, which you learned earlier in this chapter. If you were to make six equal annual payments to pay off this loan, how much would you pay each year?

This problem is a simple application of the present value annuity payment equation:

$$PMT = \frac{PV}{\dfrac{1 - [1/(1 + r)^n]}{r}} \qquad \textbf{4.9}$$

The known variables are the present value or principal, $25,000; the interest rate, 8%; and the number of payments, six. Using the TVM keys, we have

Mode = End

Input	6	8.0	25,000	?	0
Key	N	I/Y	PV	PMT	FV
CPT				**−5,407.88**	

Or, via the spreadsheet,

B6		*fx* =PMT(B1,B2,B3,B4,B5)			
	Use the PMT function to find the annual equal payments on a loan of $25,000 for six years at 8%.				
	A	B	C	D	E
1	Rate	0.08			
2	Nper	6			
3	Pv	$ 25,000.00			
4	Fv	0			
5	Type	0			
6	Pmt	($5,407.88)			

Or, via the equation,

$$PMT = \frac{\$25{,}000}{\dfrac{1 - [1/(1 + 0.08)^6]}{0.08}}$$

$$= \frac{\$25{,}000}{4.6229} = \$5{,}407.88$$

At the end of each year, you pay $5,407.88, and you pay the loan in full after the sixth payment. The total interest you paid over the six payments is $7,447.28, and

TABLE 4.1 Payment Plans and Total Interest on a Loan

Repayment Plan	Annual Payments	Total Interest	Principal Repayment	Total Repayment
Discount	$ 0	$ 14,671.86	$25,000.00	$39,671.86
Interest only	$2,000.00	$12,000.00	$25,000.00	$37,000.00
Amortized	$ 5,407.88	$ 7,447.28	$25,000.00	$32,447.28

you can determine it by multiplying the payment ($5,407.88) times the number of payments (six) and subtracting the original principal ($25,000):

$$\text{interest expense} = (\$5{,}407.88 \times 6) - \$25{,}000 = \$7{,}447.28$$

So, your total outlay for the loan has been $32,447.28 ($5,407.88 × 6).

Table 4.1 shows the three different payment plans and the total paid back on the loan. Why is the interest so different? With the first method of postponing the entire payment to the end, you are paying interest on the $25,000 and interest on the accumulated interest each year. With the second method, you are paying off the accumulated interest each year, so there is no compounding effect of the unpaid interest. With the third method, you are actually reducing the principal owed each year because the annual payment is for interest and principal, which lowers the annual interest expense in each consecutive year. So, what is the outstanding principal at the end of each year with the third method? We will answer that question in the next section.

4.6 Amortization Schedules

How do we find the remaining principal at the end of each year with an amortized loan repayment schedule? We need to determine how much of each annual payment is for interest and then apply the remaining amount against the principal. Each succeeding year starts with the new lower principal, and the interest owed for that year is simply the interest rate times this new lower principal amount. We call the listing of the annual interest expense, the reduction of principal each year, and the ending balance or remaining principal an **amortization schedule** of the payoff of the loan. A primary feature of an amortization schedule is that it shows the remaining principal after each payment.

Let's look at an amortization schedule for the $25,000 loan payoff at 8% annual interest expense with six equal annual payments. Recall that each year the payment is $5,407.88. What is the remaining principal of the loan at the end of the first year?

1. Determine the interest expense for one year when the principal is $25,000 and the interest rate is 8%:

$$\text{interest expense first year} = \$25{,}000 \times 0.08 = \$2{,}000$$

2. Determine the amount available for reducing the principal after you have subtracted the interest expense from the payment:

$$\text{available for principal reduction} = \$5{,}407.88 - \$2{,}000 = \$3{,}407.88$$

3. Determine the new lower principal at the end of the year:

$$\text{end-of-year remaining principal} = \$25{,}000 - \$3{,}407.88 = \$21{,}592.12$$

In the second year, the beginning outstanding principal is now $21,592.12, and it is this lower amount that is earning interest for the lender. This ending balance is also the present value of the remaining payments. So, for the second year, we have the following steps:

1. Determine the interest expense by multiplying the outstanding or remaining principal by the 8% interest rate:

$$\text{interest expense second year} = \$21{,}592.12 \times 0.08 = \$1{,}727.37$$

2. Determine the amount of the principal reduced in the second year by subtracting this year's interest expense from the annual payment:

$$\text{principal reduction second year} = \$5{,}407.88 - \$1{,}727.37 = \$3{,}680.51$$

3. Determine the new lower principal at the end of year two. It is the principal at the beginning of the year minus the principal reduction amount:

$$\text{remaining principal} = \$21{,}592.12 - \$3{,}680.51 = \$17{,}911.61$$

This process continues for the entire six years, and at the final payment of $5,407.88, the principal is entirely paid off. Table 4.2 presents the complete amortization schedule.

The last payment is four cents higher to make the remaining principal come out to exactly zero at the end of the six years because we rounded the interest calculations and the payments to the nearest whole cent. If you were to calculate the annual payment beyond two decimals, you would get $5,407.884656.

Amortization schedules are very common, and we use them on many loans, such as those for cars, mortgages, and consumer products. If you want to pay off a loan early, the present value of the remaining payments is the outstanding balance on the loan at the end of each period. Paying off a loan early is a common occurrence that you may encounter many times in your life. For example, many home loans are for thirty years, but the average time a person stays in the same home is around seven years. When individuals sell their current home to move to a new home, they must pay off their old loan from the proceeds of the sale of their current home. Just how much do they need to pay? The present value of the remaining payments determines that amount and is the current principal balance of the loan. You can easily find it by looking at the amortization schedule.

TABLE 4.2 Amortization Schedule for a $25,000 Loan at 8% with Six Annual Payments

Year	Beginning Principal	Annual Payment	Interest Expense	Principal Reduction	Remaining Principal
1	$25,000.00	$ 5407.88	$2,000.00	$ 3,407.88	$21,592.12
2	$21,592.12	$ 5407.88	$ 1,727.37	$ 3,680.51	$ 17,911.61
3	$ 17,911.61	$ 5407.88	$1,432.93	$ 3,974.95	$13,936.66
4	$13,936.66	$ 5407.88	$ 1,114.93	$ 4,292.95	$ 9,643.71
5	$ 9,643.71	$ 5407.88	$ 771.50	$ 4,636.38	$ 5,007.33
6	$ 5,007.33	$ 5407.92	$ 400.59	$ 5,007.33	$ 0
Total		$32,447.32	$ 7,447.32	$25,000.00	

4.7 Waiting Time and Interest Rates for Annuities

So far in this chapter, we have looked exclusively at three of the four variables from the time value of money equation: present value (*PV*), future value (*FV*), and payments (*PMT*). Now let's turn our attention to the time variable (n) in the equation and answer the question, "How long will it take to pay off the loan or build my nest egg?"

One common application of the equation is to determine the waiting time to reach a specific future value. In Example 4.3, we look at an annuity problem where the variable of concern is time.

We can use the versatile time value of money equation to determine the amount of time it will take to reach a specific future value.

EXAMPLE 4.3 So, you want to be a millionaire (finding the number of years)?

Problem Denise has her heart set on being a millionaire. She decides that at the end of every year, she will put away \$5,000 into her "I want to be a millionaire account" at her local bank. She expects to earn 6% annually on her account. How many years must Denise faithfully put away her money to succeed at becoming a millionaire?

Solution To set up the problem, we know that we have the following information or known variables: an annual payment stream or ordinary annuity of \$5,000 (*PMT*), interest rate of 6% (r), and a future value of \$1,000,000 (*FV*).

METHOD 1 Using the equation

We can use the future value equation for an annuity, Equation 4.3, to solve this problem:

$$FV = PMT \times \frac{(1 + r)^n - 1}{r}$$

$$\$1{,}000{,}000 = \$5{,}000 \times \frac{1 - \left[1/(1 + 0.06)^n\right]}{0.06}$$

We have to solve for n, the number of years or payments Denise will need to make. We can rewrite Equation 4.3 with n on the left-hand side to get

$$n = \frac{\ln\left(\dfrac{(FV \times r)}{PMT} + 1\right)}{\ln(1 + r)} \qquad \textbf{4.10}$$

Substituting in the known variables of $r = 0.06$, $FV = \$1{,}000{,}000$, and $PMT = \$5{,}000$, we can find the waiting time. Although we could use the formula, which involves logarithms, the TVM keys and spreadsheet methods are much faster and easier to use.

METHOD 2 Using the TVM keys

Mode = End

Input	?	6.0	0	−5,000	1,000,000
Key	N	I/Y	PV	PMT	FV
CPT	44.0192				

Denise will be a millionaire in approximately 44 years.

METHOD 3 Using a spreadsheet

B6	*fx* =NPER(B1,B2,B3,B4,B5)				
	Use the number of periods function, Nper, to find the waiting time to be a millionaire with an annual yearly savings of $5,000 earning 6% interest.				
	A	B	C	D	E
1	Rate	0.06			
2	Pmt	($ 5,000.00)			
3	Pv	0			
4	Fv	$1,000,000.00			
5	Type	0			
6	Nper	44.0192			

For those who like the equation approach (our Method 1), here is the solution to the waiting period.

METHOD 1 Using the equation

$$n = \frac{\ln\left(\frac{(\$1{,}000{,}000 \times 0.06)}{\$5{,}000} + 1\right)}{\ln(1 + 0.06)} = \frac{\ln(12 + 1)}{\ln 1.06} = \frac{2.5649}{0.0583} = 44.0192$$

Notice in Example 4.3 that on both the calculator and the spreadsheet, the $5,000 annual payment is negative and indicates a cash flow or payment *into* the account (from Denise to the bank), whereas the $1,000,000 is positive and represents the cash flow *out of* the account (from the bank to Denise) at the end. If you enter both the payment and future value as positive amounts, the calculator and spreadsheet will display an error in the calculation.

Now, what about our last variable, *r*, the interest rate? Unfortunately, we cannot isolate *r* on the left-hand side of the equation. Therefore, we must either estimate *r* using an iterative process or use the TVM keys of a calculator or a spreadsheet function. The iterative process requires plugging in different estimates of *r* until we narrow in on its correct value. Let's look at a special problem we would all like to have: the dilemma of what payment choice to elect after winning a lottery. We will illustrate the iterative process of finding an interest rate for a known annuity (*PMT*), time period (*n*), and present value (*PV*).

4.8 Solving a Lottery Problem

Jerry Berggren is not a famous financial expert, but on April 3, 2002, the self-employed appliance repairman did make the financial news. He was the sole winner of an advertised $48 million Powerball lottery game. He had a choice of one of two payoff options: either a lump-sum payment upfront or an annuity over twenty-five years. Berggren accepted a lump-sum payoff of $26,072,769 pretax ($17,729,483 after tax) in full settlement of the $48 million advertised pot. The annuity alternative was equal annual payments of $1,920,000 pretax, or

$1,305,600 after tax, over twenty-five years. Did Berggren make a sound financial decision as to how he should receive his winnings? Should he have taken the stream of annual payments instead of the lump sum?

The answer depends on Berggren's opportunity cost. If he could invest the lump-sum amount at 15%, perhaps the lump-sum distribution is the right choice, but how do we know that 15% is the key interest rate here? We can find the answer by determining the *indifference interest rate*, the interest rate that makes Berggren indifferent between the two payment choices. The question really becomes, "What is the implied interest rate at which the lump-sum choice is equal to the annuity choice?"

First, it is important to realize that the advertised $48 million was not a cash flow and was not part of the decision. Berggren did not have a choice of receiving $48 million at any one point in time. This sum represents the adding of the annual payment stream of $1,920,000 for twenty-five years ($1,920,000 × 25 = $48,000,000). As a budding financial expert, you probably realize that this advertised Powerball jackpot is not proper because *you can add only dollars that are at the same point in time to get the economic value of a cash flow.* The only items of interest to you (or Berggren) in this decision are the two sets of actual cash flow: the one-time lump-sum payment of $26,072,769 (pretax) or the annuity of $1,920,000 (pretax) for twenty-five years.

We can solve this question with our *PV* annuity equation. We will assume that Berggren receives the annual payments at the end of the year. We would like to isolate our variable of concern, *r*, on the left-hand side of the equation, but we cannot do so. So, we must start the iterative process to find *r*. We know the present value of the annuity, $PV = \$26{,}072{,}769$; the payment stream, $PMT = \$1{,}920{,}000$; and the number of payments, $n = 25$. Now we can get our starting point for *r* by using the PVIFA table (Appendix 4) and rearranging Equation 4.8, where *PVIFA* is isolated on the left-hand side:

$$PMT = \frac{PV}{\dfrac{1 - [1/(1+r)^n]}{r}}$$

$$\frac{1 - [1/(1+r)^n]}{r} = \frac{PV}{PMT}$$

$$\frac{1 - [1/(1+r)^n]}{r} = \frac{\$26{,}072{,}769}{\$1{,}920{,}000} = 13.5769$$

The PVIFA for $n = 25$ is 13.5769. If we look on the PVIFA table, we find 13.5796 between the 5% column (14.0939) and the 6% column (12.7834). Thus, we should select an *r* between 5% and 6% to start the process. If we select 5.5% for *r*, we have

$$\frac{1 - [1/(1+0.055)^{25}]}{0.055} = 13.4139 < 13.5796$$

This solution is close, but we need to find a smaller *r* for the solution to be acceptable. We try 5.25% (halfway between 5.5% and 5.0%). Now we have

$$\frac{1 - [1/(1+0.0525)^{25}]}{0.0525} = 13.7475 > 13.5796$$

This time, we are too low, so we try again, raising our estimate of *r*. We repeat this process, iterating between values, until we finally arrive at 5.3747%.

Unfortunately, getting to this point can be a very long process that illustrates why a calculator with TVM keys or a spreadsheet is the appropriate tool for finding *r*. With Method 2, we have

Mode = End					
Input	25	?	26,072,769	−1,920,000	0
Key	N	I/Y	PV	PMT	FV
CPT		5.3747			

With Method 3, the spreadsheet, we have the RATE function in the financial functions. The inputs are Nper 25, Pmt $1,920,000, PV −$26,072,769, Fv 0, and Type 0 (for ordinary annuity). The spreadsheet returns 5.3747% as the answer.

B6 | *fx* | *=RATE(B1,B2,B3,B4,B5)*

Use the rate function to find the interest rate that equates an annual payment over 25 years with a current lump sum.

	A	B	C	D	E
1	Nper	25			
2	Pmt	($ 1,920,000.00)			
3	Pv	$ 26,072,769.00			
4	Fv	0			
5	Type	0			
6	Rate	5.3747%			

What does the 5.3747% interest rate imply? It means that if Berggren could invest the lump-sum payment of $26,072,769 at 5.3747%, he can match the annuity and withdraw the $1,920,000 each year for the twenty-five years. To illustrate, find the payment stream for a present value of $26,072,769 at a rate higher than 5.374%. Let's see how much Berggren could withdraw each year from his account if he deposited the $26,072,769 at 6% interest:

$$PMT = \frac{\$26{,}072{,}769}{\dfrac{1 - \left[1/(1 + 0.06)^{25}\right]}{0.06}} = \$2{,}039{,}587$$

Therefore, if he can invest the lump-sum distribution at a 6% earnings rate, he can get more than $1,920,000 per year over the next twenty-five years. His opportunity cost is 5.374%, the interest rate at which he is indifferent between the lump-sum and the annuity choices. If he can invest at an interest rate higher than 5.3747% for the twenty-five-year period, he can withdraw more than the $1,920,000 annuity amount each year. If he receives an interest rate below 5.3747%, his annual withdrawals over the next twenty-five years will be lower than $1,920,000.

Looking back at our perpetuity stream, we see that if Berggren could invest the lump sum of $26,072,769 at 7.36%, he could receive $1,920,000 annually forever and never touch the principal. We can verify the infinite payment stream as

$$\$1{,}920{,}000 = \frac{\$26{,}072{,}769}{r}$$

or

$$r = \frac{\$1{,}920{,}000}{\$26{,}072{,}769} = 0.0736 \text{ or } 7.36\%$$

Although knowing the indifference or implied interest rate does provide more information for this decision, Berggren should consider other factors. First, Berggren could have access to the $26 million immediately and could spend some of it, invest some of it, or give some of it away. Second, he could also be financially foolish and lose it all, saving nothing for future years. What the financial tools allow us to do is quantify the difference between the two choices in terms of implied interest rates. The tools help us improve our information prior to decision making, but do not take all factors into account. We cannot determine whether the chosen lump-sum payment was the best choice for Berggren, but with the time value of money equation, we can better understand the implied trade-offs between the two choices.

4.9 Ten Important Points about the TVM Equation

This chapter has added the annuity equations to the tools that financial managers use. The use of annuities is quite common in many financial situations, from personal savings and retirement plans to repayment of loans. By now, you should have a fundamental understanding of the time value of money equation. Here are ten important points to remember:

1. You can add or subtract amounts of money only if they are at the same point in time.
2. The timing and the amount of the cash flow are what matters.
3. It is helpful to lay out the timing and amount of the cash flow with a time line.
4. Present value calculations discount all future cash flow back to current time.
5. Future value calculations value cash flow at a single point in time in the future.
6. An annuity is a series of equal cash payments at regular intervals across time.
7. The time value of money equation has four variables but only one basic equation, so you must know three of the four variables before you can solve for the missing or unknown variable.
8. There are three basic methods to solve for an unknown time value of money variable: (1) Method 1, using equations and calculating the answer; (2) Method 2, using the TVM keys on a calculator; and (3) Method 3, using financial functions from a spreadsheet. All three give the same answer because they all use the same time value of money equation.
9. There are three basic ways to repay a loan: (1) principal and interest at maturity, or discount loans; (2) interest as you go and principal at maturity, or interest-only loans; and (3) principal and interest as you go with equal and regular payments, or amortized loans.
10. Despite the seemingly accurate answers from the time value of money equation, in many situations we cannot classify all the important data into the variables of present value, time, interest rate, payment, and future value.

The principles presented in this chapter are featured prominently as we move through the following chapters and form the basis of many financial decisions.

In fact, the cornerstone of corporate financial decisions is the ability to properly estimate discounted cash flow. We will use these concepts to price financial and real assets, to determine whether we should accept or reject new projects, and to determine amounts for loan repayments or building nest eggs. The task now is to practice using these tools and perfect your individual financial skill set.

To review this chapter, see the Summary Card at the end of the text.

Key Terms

amortization schedule, p. 97
amortized loan, p. 95
annuity, p. 85
annuity due, p. 87
consol, p. 94
discount loan, p. 95
future value interest factor of an annuity (FVIFA), p. 86
interest, p. 95
interest-only loan, p. 95
ordinary annuity, p. 87
perpetuity, p. 94
present value interest factor of an annuity (PVIFA), p. 90
principal, p. 95

Questions

1. What is the difference between a series of payments and an annuity? What are the two specific characteristics of a series of payments that make them an annuity?
2. What effect on the future value of an annuity does increasing the interest rate have? Does a change from 4% to 6% have the same dollar effect as a change from 6% to 8%?
3. What effect on the present value of an annuity does increasing the interest rate have? Does a decrease from 7% to 5% have the same dollar effect as a decrease from 5% to 3%?
4. What is the difference between an ordinary annuity and an annuity due?
5. What is an iterative process?
6. What does the amortization schedule tell you about a loan repayment?
7. What does it mean that the current principal balance of a loan repaid as an amortized loan is the present value of the future payment stream?
8. If you increase the number of payments on an amortized loan, does the payment increase or decrease? Why or why not?
9. If you increase the interest rate on an amortized loan, does the payment increase or decrease? Why or why not?
10. If you won the lottery and had the choice of a lump-sum payoff or an annuity payoff, what factors would you consider besides the implied interest rate (indifference interest rate) in selecting the payoff style?

Prepping for Exams

1. Your company just sold a product with the following payment plan: $50,000 today, $25,000 next year, and $10,000 the following year. If your firm places the payments into an account earning 10% per year, how much money will be in the account after collecting the last payment?

a. $99,000
b. $98,000
c. $88,500
d. $85,000

2. Which of the following is *not* an example of annuity cash flows?

a. the university tuition bill you pay every month that is always the same
b. the grocery bill that changes every week
c. the $3.50 you pay every morning for a bagel and coffee as you run to your first morning class
d. All the examples above are annuity cash flows.

3. Which of the following choices will result in a greater future value at age 65? Choice 1 is to invest $3,000 per year from ages twenty through twenty-six (a total of seven investments) into an account and then leave it untouched until you are sixty-five years old, which is another 40 years. Choice 2 is to begin at age twenty-seven and make $3,000 deposits into an investment account every year until you are sixty-five years old (a total of thirty-nine investments). Each account earns an average of 10% per year.

a. Choice 1 is better than Choice 2 because it has a future value of $1,304,146.89, which is greater than the Choice 2 future value of $1,204,343.33.
b. Choice 2 is better than Choice 1 because it has a future value of $1,304,146.89, which is greater than the Choice 1 future value of $1,204,343.33.
c. Choice 2 is better than Choice 1 because it has a future value of $1,288,146.89, which is greater than the Choice 1 future value of $1,204,343.33.
d. Choice 1 is better than Choice 2 because it has a future value of $1,288,146.89, which is greater than the Choice 2 future value of $1,204,343.33.

4. You have an annuity of equal annual end-of-the-year cash flows of $500 that begin two years from today and last for a total of ten cash flows. Using a discount rate of 4%, what are those cash flows worth in today's dollars?

a. $3,899.47
b. $4,055.45
c. $4,380.24
d. $5,000.00

5. A wealthy woman just died and left her pet cats the following estate: $50,000 per year for the next fifteen years, with the first cash flow today. At a discount rate of 3.2%, what is the feline estate worth in today's dollars?

a. $588,352.84
b. $607,180.14
c. $750,000.00
d. $774,000.00

6. If you borrow $50,000 at an annual interest rate of 12% for six years, what is the annual payment (prior to maturity) on a discount loan?

a. $0
b. $6,000.00
c. $8,333.33
d. $12,161.29

7. Amortization tables are useful for each of the following reasons except:

   a. determining the principal balance due if you pay off the loan early.
   b. determining how much of a total payment is interest and how much is principal for tax purposes.
   c. determining the regular periodic total payment.
   d. All the reasons are useful purposes of an amortization table.

8. Marie has a $1,000,000 investment portfolio, and she wishes to spend $87,500 per year as an ordinary annuity. If the investment account earns 6% annually, how long will her portfolio last?

   a. 11.43 years
   b. 14.17 years
   c. 19.86 years
   d. 23.08 years

9. You currently have $67,000 in an interest-earning account. From this account, you wish to make twenty year-end payments of $5,000 each. What annual rate of return must you make on this account to meet your objective?

   a. 4.16%
   b. 5.03%
   c. 6.42%
   d. 7.32%

10. After winning the lottery, you state that you are indifferent between receiving twenty $500,000 end-of-the-year payments (first payment one year from today) or a lump-sum payment of $5,734,961 today. What interest rate are you using in your decision-making process such that you are indifferent between the two choices?

    a. 5.00%
    b. 6.00%
    c. 7.00%
    d. 8.00%

These problems are available in MyFinanceLab.

Problems

1. ***Different cash flow.*** Given the following cash inflow at the end of each year, what is the future value of this cash flow at 6%, 9%, and 15% interest rates at the end of the seventh year?

Year 1:	$15,000
Year 2:	$20,000
Year 3:	$30,000
Years 4 through 6:	$0
Year 7:	$150,000

2. ***Future value of an ordinary annuity.*** Fill in the missing future values in the following table for an ordinary annuity.

Number of Payments or Years	Annual Interest Rate	Present Value	Annuity	Future Value
10	6%	0	$ 250.00	
20	12%	0	$1,387.88	
25	4%	0	$ 600.00	
360	1%	0	$ 572.25	

3. ***Future value.*** A speculator has purchased land along the southern Oregon coast. He has taken out a ten-year loan with annual payments of $7,200. The loan rate is 6%. At the end of ten years, he believes he can sell the land for $100,000. If he is correct on the future price, did he make a wise investment?

4. ***Future value.*** Jack and Jill are saving for a rainy day and decide to put $50 away in their local bank every year for the next twenty-five years. The local Up-the-Hill Bank will pay them 7% on their account.

   a. If Jack and Jill put the money in the account faithfully at the end of every year, how much will they have in it at the end of twenty-five years?

   b. Unfortunately, Jack had an accident in which he sustained head injuries after only ten years of savings. The medical bill has come to $700. Is there enough in the rainy-day fund to cover it?

5. **Future value.** You are a new employee with the *Metro Daily Planet*. The *Planet* offers three different retirement plans. Plan 1 starts the first day of work and puts $1,000 away in your retirement account at the end of every year for forty years. Plan 2 starts after ten years and puts away $2,000 every year for thirty years. Plan 3 starts after twenty years and puts away $4,000 every year for the last twenty years of employment. All three plans guarantee an annual growth rate of 8%.

   a. Which plan should you choose if you plan to work at the *Planet* for forty years?

   b. Which plan should you choose if you plan to work at the *Planet* for only the next thirty years?

   c. Which plan should you choose if you plan to work at the *Planet* for only the next twenty years?

   d. Which plan should you choose if you plan to work at the *Planet* for only the next ten years?

   e. What do the answers in parts (a) through (d) imply about savings?

6. ***Different cash flow.*** Given the following cash inflow, what is the present value of this cash flow at 5%, 10%, and 25% discount rates?

Year 1:	$3,000
Year 2:	$5,000
Years 3 through 7:	$0
Year 8:	$25,000

7. ***Present value of an ordinary annuity.*** Fill in the missing present values in the following table for an ordinary annuity.

Number of Payments or Years	Annual Interest Rate	Future Value	Annuity	Present Value
10	6%	0	$ 250.00	
20	12%	0	$3,387.88	
25	4%	0	$ 600.00	
360	1%	0	$2,571.53	

8. ***Ordinary annuity payment.*** Fill in the missing annuity in the following table for an ordinary annuity stream.

Number of Payments or Years	Annual Interest Rate	Future Value	Annuity	Present Value
5	9%	0		$ 25,000.00
20	8%	$25,000.00		0
30	7%	0		$200,000.00
10	4%	$ 96,048.86		0

9. ***Present value.*** County Ranch Insurance Company wants to offer a guaranteed annuity in units of $500, payable at the end of each year for twenty-five years. The company has a strong investment record and can consistently earn 7% on its investments after taxes. If the company wants to make 1% on this contract, what price should it set on it? Use 6% as the discount rate. Assume that it is an ordinary annuity and the price is the same as present value.

10. ***Present value.*** A smooth used-car salesman who smiles considerably is offering you a great deal on a "preowned" car. He says, "For only six annual payments of $2,500, this beautiful 1998 Honda Civic can be yours." If you can borrow money at 8%, what is the price of this car?

11. ***Payments.*** Cooley Landscaping Company needs to borrow $30,000 for a new front-end dirt loader. The bank is willing to loan the funds at 8.5% interest with annual payments at the end of the year for the next ten years. What is the annual payment on this loan for Cooley Landscaping?

12. ***Payments.*** Sam Hinds, a local dentist, is going to remodel the dental reception area and two new workstations. He has contacted A-Dec, and the new equipment and cabinetry will cost $18,000. A-Dec will finance the equipment purchase at 7.5% over a six-year period. What will Hinds have to pay in annual payments for this equipment?

13. ***Annuity due.*** Reginald is about to lease an apartment for the year. The landlord wants the lease payments paid at the start of the month. The twelve monthly payments are $1,300 per month. The landlord says he will allow Reg to prepay the rent for the entire year with a discount. The one-time annual payment due at the beginning of the lease is $14,778. What is the implied monthly discount rate for the rent? If Reg is earning 1.5% on his savings monthly, should he pay by month or take the one annual payment?

14. ***Time line of cash flow and application of the time value of money.*** Mauer Mining Company leases a special drill press with annual payments of $150,000. The contract calls for rent payments at the beginning of each year for a minimum of six years. Mauer Mining can buy a similar drill for $750,000, but it will need to borrow the funds at 8%.

    a. Show the two choices on a time line with the cash flow.

    b. Determine the present value of the lease payments at 8%.

    c. Should Mauer Mining lease or buy this drill?

15. ***Perpetuities.*** The Canadian government has once again decided to issue a consol (a bond with a never-ending interest payment and no maturity date). The bond will pay $50 in interest each year (at the end of the year), but it

will never return the principal. The current discount rate for Canadian government bonds is 6.5%. What should this consol bond sell for in the market? What if the interest rate should fall to 4.5%? Rise to 8.5%? Why does the price go up when interest rates fall? Why does the price go down when interest rates rise?

16. ***Perpetuities.*** The Stack has just written and recorded the single greatest rock song ever made. The boys in the band believe that the royalties from this song will pay the band a handsome $200,000 every year forever. The record studio is also convinced that the song will be a smash hit and the royalty estimate is accurate. The record studio wants to pay the band up front and not make any more payments for the song. What should the record studio offer the band if it uses a 5% discount rate, a 7.5% discount rate, or a 10% discount rate?

17. ***Annuity due perpetuity.*** In Problem 16, the band agrees to the one-time payment at a 5% discount rate, but it wants to figure the royalty payments from the beginning of the year, not the end of the year. How much more will the band receive with annuity due payments on the royalty checks?

    Use the following information for Problems 18 through 21. Chuck Ponzi has talked an elderly woman into loaning him $25,000 for a new business venture. She has, however, successfully passed a finance class and requires Chuck to sign a binding contract on repayment of the $25,000 with an annual interest rate of 10% over the next ten years. She has left the method of repayment up to him.

18. ***Discount loan (interest and principal at maturity).*** Determine the cash flow to the woman under a discount loan, in which Ponzi will have a lump-sum payment at the end of the contract.

19. ***Interest-only loan (regular interest payments each year and principal at end).*** Determine the cash flow to the woman under an interest-only loan, in which Ponzi will pay the annual interest expense each year and pay the principal back at the end of the contract.

20. ***Fully amortized loan (annual payments for principal and interest with the same amount each year).*** Determine the cash flow to the woman under a fully amortized loan, in which Ponzi will make equal annual payments at the end of each year so that the final payment will completely retire the original $25,000 loan.

21. ***Amortization schedule.*** Ponzi may choose to pay off the loan early if interest rates change during the next ten years. Determine the ending balance of the loan each year under the three different payment plans.

22. ***Amortization.*** Loan Consolidated Incorporated (LCI) is offering a special one-time package to reduce Custom Autos' outstanding bills to one easy-to-handle payment plan. LCI will pay off the current outstanding bills of $242,000 for Custom Autos if Custom Autos will make an annual payment to LCI at a 10% interest rate over the next fifteen years. First, what are the annual payments and the remaining balance of the loan at the end of each year (should Custom Autos want to pay off the loan early)? Second, when will the balance be half paid off? Finally, what is the total interest expense on the loan over the fifteen years?

23. ***Waiting period with an ordinary annuity.*** Fill in the missing waiting periods (years) or number of payments in the table on the next page for an ordinary annuity stream.

Number of Payments or Years	Annual Interest Rate	Future Value	Annuity	Present Value
	6%	0	$250.00	$ 2,867.48
	8%	$ 5,794.62	$400.00	0
	10%	0	$636.48	$6,000.00
	4%	$100,000.00	$ 80.80	0

24. ***Number of payments.*** Tony is offering two repayment plans to Phil for a long overdue loan. Offer 1 is a visit from an enforcer and the debt due in full at once. Offer 2 is to pay back $3,900 per year at 20% interest rate until Tony pays off the loan principal. Phil owes Tony $15,000. How long will it take Phil to pay off the loan if he takes Offer 2?

25. ***Number of payments.*** Your grandfather will sell you a piece of beachfront property for $72,500. He says the price is firm whenever you can pay him cash. You know your finances will allow you to save only $5,000 a year and you can make 8% on your investment. If you invest faithfully every year at the end of the year, how long will it take you to accumulate the necessary $72,500 future cash for the beachfront property?

26. ***Estimating the annual interest rate with an ordinary annuity.*** Fill in the missing annual interest rates in the following table for an ordinary annuity stream.

Number of Payments or Years	Annual Interest Rate	Future Value	Annuity	Present Value
10		0	$ 500.00	$ 3,680.04
20		$ 25,000.00	$ 346.97	0
30		0	$1,946.73	$20,000.00
100		$1,044,010.06	$ 400.00	0

27. ***Estimating the annual interest rate with an annuity due.*** Fill in the missing annual interest rates in the following table for an annuity due stream.

Number of Payments or Years	Annual Interest Rate	Future Value	Annuity	Present Value
10		0	$ 500.00	$ 3,680.04
20		$ 25,000.00	$ 346.97	0
30		0	$1,946.73	$20,000.00
100		$1,044,010.06	$ 400.00	0

28. ***Interest rate with annuity.*** What are you getting in terms of interest rate if you are willing to pay $15,000 today for an annual stream of payments of $2,000 for the next twenty years? The next forty years? The next one hundred years? Forever?

29. ***Interest rate with annuity.*** A local government is about to run a lottery but does not want to be involved in the payoff if a winner picks an annuity payoff. The government contracts with a trust to pay the lump-sum payout to the trust and have the trust (probably a local bank) pay the annual payments. The first winner of the lottery chooses the annuity and will receive $150,000 a year for the next twenty-five years. The local government will give the trust $2,000,000 to pay for this annuity. What investment rate must the trust earn to break even on this arrangement?

30. ***Lottery.*** A lottery ticket states that you will receive $250 every year for the next ten years.

a. What is the value of the winning lottery ticket in present value if the discount rate is 6%, and it is an ordinary annuity?

b. What is the value of the winning lottery ticket in present value if the discount rate is 6%, and it is an annuity due?

c. What is the difference between the ordinary annuity and annuity due in parts (a) and (b)?

d. Verify that the difference in part (c) is the difference between the $250 first payment of the annuity due and the discounted final $250 payment of the ordinary annuity.

31. ***Lottery.*** Your dreams of becoming rich have just come true. You have won the State of Tranquility's lottery. The state offers you two payment plans for the $5,000,000 advertised jackpot. You can take annual payments of $250,000 for the next twenty years or $2,867,480 today.

a. If your investment rate over the next twenty years is 8%, which payoff will you choose?

b. If your investment rate over the next twenty years is 5%, which payoff will you choose?

c. At what investment rate will the annuity stream of $250,000 be the same as the lump-sum payment of $2,867,480?

32. ***Challenge problem.*** Each holiday season, Michael received a U.S. savings bond from his grandmother. Michael eventually received twelve savings bonds. The bonds vary in their rates of interest and their face value. Assume that today is December 31, 2011. What is the value of this portfolio of U.S. savings bonds? On what dates do each of the individual bonds reach their face value or maturity date (note that the price is half the face value)? Estimate to the nearest month and year for each bond. *Note:* The bonds continue earning interest past their maturity dates.

Issue Date	Price	Face Value	Interest Rate	Maturity Date
12/31/1990	$ 50	$100	6.0%	
12/31/1991	$ 50	$100	6.0%	
12/31/1992	$ 25	$ 50	5.0%	
12/31/1993	$ 25	$ 50	4.0%	
12/31/1994	$ 25	$ 50	4.0%	
12/31/1995	$ 50	$100	5.0%	
12/31/1996	$ 25	$ 50	5.0%	
12/31/1997	$ 25	$ 50	4.0%	
12/31/1998	$ 25	$ 50	4.0%	
12/31/1999	$ 50	$100	4.0%	
12/31/2000	$ 25	$ 50	4.0%	
12/31/2001	$ 25	$ 50	3.0%	
Total	$400			

These problems are available in MyFinanceLab.

Advanced Problems for Spreadsheet Application

1. ***Future value with an annuity.*** Thelma and Thomas want to retire with $2,000,000 in their portfolio. They plan on putting away $20,000 per year into five different accounts each year ($4,000 per account).They have set up the following accounts and will make their first contributions at the end of this year. They will make all contributions at the end of each year.

   Money market account

   Government bond mutual fund

   Large capital mutual fund

   Small capital mutual fund

   Real estate trust fund

   The money market grows at 2.5% annually, the government bond mutual fund grows at 5.5% annually, the large capital mutual fund grows at 9.5% annually, the small capital mutual fund grows at 12.0% annually, and the real estate trust fund grows at 4.0% annually.

   a. Using a spreadsheet, calculate the end-of-year balance for the portfolio with the assumption that Thelma and Thomas will not deposit any additional funds into any of these accounts above the $4,000 annual contributions to each account. How long until they reach the $2,000,000 goal?

   b. Thelma and Thomas decide that an equal split between the funds is not to their advantage. They decide to put only $2,000 annual in the mutual fund, $4,000 in government bonds, $5,000 in the large capital mutual fund, $6,000 in the small capital mutual fund, and $3,000 in the real estate trust fund. How much sooner will they reach their $2,000,000 goal compared to the strategy in part (a)? If they retire at the same time as in part (a), how much more will they have in their retirement account?

2. ***Amortization schedule.*** Sherry and Sam want to purchase a condo at the coast. They will spend $650,000 on the condo and are taking out a loan for the condo for twenty years at 7.0% interest. What is the annual payment on the mortgage? Construct the amortization of the loan for the twenty years in a spreadsheet to show the annual interest costs, the principal reduction, and the ending balance each year. Then change the amortization to reflect that after ten years, Sherry and Sam will increase their annual payment to $80,000 per year. When will they fully repay the mortgage with this increased payment if they apply all the extra dollars above the original payment to the principal?

MINI-CASE

Fitchminster Injection Molding, Inc.: Rose Climbs High

This mini-case is available in MyFinanceLab.

Rose Flamant, the plant manager of Fitchminster Injection Molding, Inc. (FIM), is pondering an interesting offer made by the president and majority shareholder, Sam Caldron. Sam recently turned sixty and is planning a gradual retirement. None of his children are interested in taking over the business and are currently pursuing careers unrelated to the plastics industry, so Sam has decided to offer his controlling share to Rose.

FIM began by manufacturing plastic lawn ornaments, including a colorful tropical bird that became a major fad in the 1980s. Pleased and amused by the success of his fanciful product, Sam added rabbits, skunks, trolls, angels, and garden fairies to the product line. Under Rose's leadership, FIM has also become an important secondary supplier of plastic housings for speakers, cell phones, calculators, and similar products.

Rose started working at FIM as a color technician shortly after graduating from the state university with a degree in chemical engineering. Within five years, she became the plant manager, a position she has held for the last eight years. Along the way, she has earned an MBA through the evening program of her alma mater.

Because FIM stock is publicly traded, we can confidently assign a value of $10,000,000 to Sam's shares. Sam has stated that he is open to any reasonable plan to finance the purchase.

Questions

1. Rose could probably borrow the money to purchase the shares outright because the shares would serve as collateral and dividends would cover a good part of the loan payments. The interest rate is 7%, and the lender will amortize the loan with a series of equal payments. What are the annual payments if the bank amortizes the loan over five, ten, or twenty years?
2. Repeat Question 1, but assume that Rose makes payments at the *beginning* of each year.
3. Complete the amortization schedule below for a $10,000,000 loan at 7% with five equal end-of-year payments.
4. Sam has offered to finance the purchase with a ten-year, interest-only loan. How much is Rose's annual payment? Describe the pattern of payments over the ten years.
5. Assume that Rose accepts Sam's offer to finance the purchase with a ten-year, interest-only loan. If Sam can reinvest the interest payments at a rate of 7% per year, how much money will he have at the end of the tenth year?

Year	Beginning Principal	Annual Payment	Interest Expense	Principal Reduction	Remaining Principal
1	$10,000,000.00				
2					
3					
4					
5					

Learning Objectives

LO1 Discuss how financial institutions quote interest rates and compute the effective annual rate on a loan or investment.

LO2 Apply the time value of money equation by accounting for the compounding periods per year.

LO3 Set up monthly amortization tables for consumer loans and illustrate the payment changes as the compounding or annuity period changes.

LO4 Explain the real rate of interest and the effect of inflation on nominal interest rates.

LO5 Summarize the two major premiums that differentiate interest rates: the default premium and the maturity premium.

LO6 Understand the implications of the yield curves.

LO7 Amaze your family and friends with your knowledge of interest rate history.

Chapter 5

Interest Rates

Borrowing money costs money. If you borrow money from a bank, it will charge you an amount over the initial loan (principal) in the form of interest. If you invest your money in a bond, the company issuing the bond is borrowing money from you. You will, in effect, charge the company an amount over the initial price of the bond in the form of coupon payments (interest). These interest rates fluctuate over time. Depending on your role—borrower or lender—interest rate changes can be good news or bad news. Rising interest rates are good for those lending money because they receive more interest on their principal, but they are not as good for those borrowing money because it costs more to borrow. Falling rates are good for borrowers because they pay less for the funds that they are borrowing, but they are not as good for lenders because they make less money on the loan.

Recall that the variables in the lump-sum time value of money equations are n (number of periods), r (interest rate), PV (present value), and FV (future value), with the additional variable in the annuity equations of PMT (payment). In this chapter, we take the time value of money equations for lump-sum payments and annuities and zoom in on r, the interest rate variable. We'll examine the actual borrowing rates for money, how financial institutions determine discount and investment rates, and how to apply the rates in the equation.

An understanding of interest rates is yet another key tool for the finance manager and the prudent investor or borrower. In future chapters, your understanding of how interest rates work will help you develop hurdle rates for company projects, the appropriate cost of capital for a firm, and the optimal capital structure for a firm. For now, we start with the basics.

5.1 How Financial Institutions Quote Interest Rates: Annual and Periodic Interest Rates

To begin our discussion of how financial institutions quote interest rates and why we sometimes refer to interest rates as the "price to rent money," let's look at a simple example. When you deposit money in a certificate of deposit (CD) at a bank, the bank is technically borrowing or renting money from you with a promise to repay that money with interest. Let's assume that you purchase a CD for $500 with a promised annual percentage rate (APR) of 5%. The **annual percentage rate (APR)** is the yearly rate that you earn by investing or charge for borrowing. Here it is 5%. Although the financial institution quotes the 5% interest rate on an annual basis, these institutions in fact often pay interest quarterly, monthly, or even daily. The period in which the financial institution applies interest or the frequency of times at which it adds interest to an account each year is the **compounding period** or **compounding periods per year (C/Y)**. To avoid some confusion and make the equations in this chapter more readable, we will let m represent the number of compounding periods per year ($C/Y = m$). For example, if the number of compounding periods per year is twelve (monthly compounding), we will have $m = 12$; if it is quarterly compounding, we will have $m = 4$; and so on.

So, what happens to the $500 CD with an annual percentage rate of 5% if we compound it on an annual, quarterly, monthly, or even daily basis? If an interest rate on a loan or investment compounds more than once a year, we must convert the annual percentage rate (APR) into a *periodic interest rate* so that we can account for compounding. To determine the interest that the financial institution pays each compounding period, we take the advertised annual percentage rate and divide it by the number of compounding periods per year to get the appropriate **periodic interest rate**. Table 5.1 illustrates the periodic rates for annual compounding, quarterly compounding, monthly compounding, and daily compounding. We derive the rates from the equation

$$\text{periodic interest rate, } r = \frac{APR}{m} \qquad \textbf{5.1}$$

We can now examine more closely the effect of compounding on our $500 investment on an annual, quarterly, monthly, or daily basis in terms of the annual interest at the end of the first year. With annual compounding, we know that we will receive $25.00 interest at the end of the year: $500 × 5% = $25.00. When compounding occurs on a more frequent basis, however, the bank applies the

TABLE 5.1 Periodic Interest Rates

Compounding Period	Annual Percentage Rate	$C/Y = m$	Periodic Rate (r)
Annually	5.0%	1	5.0%
Quarterly	5.0%	4	1.25%
Monthly	5.0%	12	0.4167%
Daily	5.0%	365	0.013699%

TABLE 5.2 $500 CD with 5% APR, Compounded Quarterly at 1.25%

Date	Beginning Balance	Interest Earned	Ending Balance
1/1–3/31	$500.00	$500.00 × 0.0125 = $6.25	$506.25
4/1–6/30	$506.25	$506.25 × 0.0125 = $6.33	$512.58
7/1–9/30	$512.58	$512.58 × 0.0125 = $6.41	$518.99
10/1–12/31	$518.99	$518.99 × 0.0125 = $6.48	$525.47

periodic interest rate each period to the balance in the account. The more compounding periods per year, the more interest you will earn or receive each year. For example, with quarterly compounding, you receive 1.25% interest on the new balance each quarter and over the year you will receive $25.47, as Table 5.2 illustrates.

The extra 47 cents is *interest on interest,* and so you have effectively earned 5.094% on your CD ($25.47/$500.00 = 0.05094). Whereas the 5.0% advertised interest on the account is the annual percentage rate (*APR*), the 5.094% is the effective annual rate. In other words, the **effective annual rate (EAR)** is the rate of interest that the financial institution actually pays or that you earn per year and depends on the number of compounding periods.

Some calculators will automatically calculate EARs from APRs as the compounding periods vary, but the conversion is quite straightforward to do yourself:

$$EAR = \left(1 + \frac{APR}{m}\right)^m - 1 \qquad 5.2$$

where m is the number of compounding periods per year. It is important to always convert APRs to EARs so that you know your true return or cost of money. Our CD example has four different compounding periods, so we have four different EARs:

$$\text{With annual compounding: } EAR = \left(1 + \frac{0.05}{1}\right)^1 - 1 = 5.00\%$$

$$\text{With quarterly compounding: } EAR = \left(1 + \frac{0.05}{4}\right)^4 - 1 = 5.094\%$$

$$\text{With monthly compounding: } EAR = \left(1 + \frac{0.05}{12}\right)^{12} - 1 = 5.1162\%$$

$$\text{With daily compounding: } EAR = \left(1 + \frac{0.05}{365}\right)^{365} - 1 = 5.12675\%$$

When the compounding is annual, the EAR and APR are the same, so on occasion, an APR is the actual cost of money. Now, with these different EARs, we can determine the ending balance of the $500 for each of the different compounding periods:

When borrowing or investing money, it is important to see the interest rate clearly, that is, to understand how it differs from the stated annual percentage rate (APR). The rate of interest that the financial institution actually paid or the amount that you earned per year is the effective annual rate (EAR) or the annual percentage yield (APY) and is usually higher than the APR because it involves compounding.

Quarterly compounding
$= \$500 \times (1 + 0.05094) = \$525.47$

Monthly compounding
$= \$500 \times (1 + 0.051162) = \$525.58$

Daily compounding
$= \$500 \times (1 + 0.0512675) = \$525.63$

Thus, the effective annual rate for a quarterly compounding investment with a stated APR of 5.0% is really 5.094%, 5.1162% for monthly compounding, and 5.12675% for daily compounding.

The Truth in Savings Act (1991) requires banks to advertise their rates on investments such as CDs and savings accounts as annual percentage yields (APY). The **annual percentage yield (APY)** and EAR are two different terms for the same quoting convention of interest rates: the rate of interest that the financial institution actually pays or what you earn per year. When quoting rates on loans, however, the Truth in Lending Act (1968) requires the bank to state the rate as an APR, effectively understating the true cost of the loan when the financial institution computes interest more often than once a year. So, when you go to a bank, the representative will quote the interest rate at the higher EAR when you are investing and at the lower APR when you are borrowing. Today, many banks state both the APR and the EAR on a loan. If, however, you are borrowing from a bank and you receive only an APR interest quote of 8% for your loan, but you must pay monthly, you can easily compute the true cost of borrowing the money as

$$EAR = \left(1 + \frac{APR}{m}\right)^m - 1 = \left(1 + \frac{0.08}{12}\right)^{12} - 1 = 8.30\%$$

How does this new understanding of compounding and interest rates fit into the time value of money equation from the previous chapters? The answer is straightforward: r, the interest rate in the equation, is a periodic rate ($r = APR/m$), which accounts for compounding; and n is the number of periods or the number of compounding periods per year times the number of years (n = years $\times$ m).

As we continue our discussion of interest rates, be aware of some technology issues. Some calculators and spreadsheets want the periodic rate; others want the annual rate. When you are using a calculator that has a TVM key of I/Y, for interest per year, it wants the annual percentage rate. Some calculators use the symbol *i*% for the interest rate and want the periodic interest rate. The Excel® spreadsheet wants the periodic rate. So, we will either enter APR for calculators with the I/Y notation or APR/m for calculators with the *i*% notation or our spreadsheet.

5.2 Effect of Compounding Periods on the Time Value of Money Equations

When a financial institution states or gives interest rates for loan repayments, we assume that they are annual percentage rates unless it specifically states otherwise. We must convert these APRs to the appropriate periodic rates when compounding is more frequent than once a year. Therefore, the tables of future value and present value interest factors in Appendices 1 through 4 provide answers for the *periodic rates* (annually, quarterly, monthly, daily, and so on) and the total number of periods over the length of the loan or investment. Let's look at the effect of the payments on a mortgage when we shift from annual payments to monthly payments and the application of our three different methods with the TVM equations.

EXAMPLE 5.1 Mortgage payments

Problem ABC Printing Company has just signed on the dotted line to buy a building worth \$200,000 to house its operations. ABC Printing paid \$10,000 down and must finance (borrow) the remaining \$190,000. The bank will loan the firm money at 8% APR, but ABC has an option to make annual payments or monthly payments on the loan. Both options have a thirty-year payment schedule. What are the mortgage payments under the two different plans?

Solution

METHOD 1: Using the equation

For the annual payment plan, apply Equation 4.9 and use the 8% APR as the interest rate, the \$190,000 as the present value of the loan, and thirty as the number of periods. The APR is the EAR because the compounding periods per year are 1. So,

$$PMT = \frac{\$190{,}000}{\dfrac{1 - \dfrac{1}{(1 + 0.08)^{30}}}{0.08}} = \frac{\$190{,}000}{11.2579} = \$16{,}877.21$$

(with the payment rounded to the nearest cent).

If ABC selects the monthly payment plan over the next thirty years, we must convert the 8.0% APR to the monthly interest rate:

$$r = \frac{APR}{m}$$

$$= \frac{0.08}{12} = 0.006666\overline{6} \text{ or } \frac{2}{3}\%$$

Also, the number of periods must reflect the number of payments that ABC will make on the loan over the next thirty years:

$$n = \text{number of years} \times m$$

$$= 30 \times 12 = 360$$

Using the payment form of the equations, we have

$$PMT = \frac{\$190{,}000}{\dfrac{1 - \left[\dfrac{1}{(1 + 0.00666\overline{6})^{360}}\right]}{0.00666\overline{6}}} = \frac{\$190{,}000}{136.2835} = \mathbf{\$1{,}394.15}$$

Notice that *the monthly payment is not one-twelfth of the annual payment* (12 × \$1394.15 = \$16,729.80 < \$16,877.21). By increasing the number of payments per year, we reduce the total cash outflow.

We can now see how the correct interest rate, r, in Equation 5.1 is the periodic rate. It's the APR of 8% for annual payments and the APR divided by m—8%/12, or $\frac{2}{3}$%—for the monthly payments. Let's look at the TVM keys in the calculator to incorporate this same adjustment. As we just noted, on many calculators the TVM key for interest is I/Y, which stands for interest per year, or the APR rate. Other calculators ask for *i*%, which is the periodic interest rate. For example, the Texas Instrument BAII Plus calculator requires you to set the number of compounding periods per year and automatically converts to the appropriate periodic rate during the calculation. The second function above I/Y is payments per year (P/Y). When we shift to monthly payments, enter the second function and set P/Y equal to 12. Then hit the down arrow key, and the C/Y variable (compounding periods per year) will display. Set this variable to 12. The calculator is now in a monthly mode for the problem.

Switch Periods per Year and Compounding per Year to Monthly

2ND	P/Y I/Y	Displays P/Y	12	ENTER
2ND	P/Y I/Y ↓	Displays C/Y.	12	ENTER

Notice that the N is no longer 30, but 360, reflecting the number of payments for the home loan ($N = 30 \times 12 = 360$). When the calculator performs the function of finding the monthly payment, it automatically takes the APR that you entered in the I/Y key and divides it by the C/Y value, thereby converting to the monthly rate before calculating the monthly payment.

Mode: P/Y = 12 and C/Y = 12

Input	360	8.0	−190,000	?	0
Key	N	I/Y	PV	PMT	FV
CPT				**1,394.15**	

You can also let the I/Y key be the periodic rate in the problem by leaving the P/Y and C/Y variables set at 1. If P/Y and C/Y are set to 1, the interest rate is the APR/m rate, or 8.0%/12 = 0.6667%. You must always be consistent (between the C/Y setting and the I/Y input).

Mode: P/Y = 1 and C/Y = 1

Input	360	$0.666\overline{6}$	−190,000	?	0
Key	N	I/Y	PV	PMT	FV
CPT				**1,394.15**	

Whether you use C/Y = 12 or C/Y = 1 is a personal choice, but it may depend on your calculator. Some calculators only allow the second style and use the symbol *i*% for the TVM interest key rate. This result is the periodic interest rate—the monthly rate of $P/Y = 12$ in this problem.

Of course, you can also use a spreadsheet. You will note that the spreadsheet uses the periodic interest rate, not the annual percentage rate:

B6		*fx* =PMT(B1,B2,B3,B4,B5)			
	Use the PMT function to find the monthly payment for a mortgage of $190,000 over thirty years with an annual interest rate of 8%.				
	A	B	C	D	E
1	Rate	0.00666666			
2	Nper	360			
3	Pv	($190,000.00)			
4	Fv	0			
5	Type	0			
6	Pmt	$ 1,394.15			

It is important to reiterate that the interest rate r that we used in the time value of money equations from Chapters 3 and 4 is the periodic interest rate. Advertised rates are annual percentage rates. Therefore, to use the equations or determine the actual cost to rent money, it is essential to know the number of compounding periods per year. *Remember that r and n must agree in terms of periods in the equation.* For example, if you are making monthly payments, you need a monthly periodic rate for r and the number of months over the life of the loan for n.

Our mortgage problem is very similar to a future value problem with an annuity. Again, we use the periodic rate, and the number of periods reflects the number of annuity payments. To illustrate how it works, let's return to the millionaire problem from Chapter 4, but we will now have Denise save money on a monthly basis in Example 5.2 instead of the annual savings plan.

EXAMPLE 5.2 Monthly versus annual savings for retirement

Problem How much does Denise need to save each period to become a millionaire by age sixty-five? Let's assume Denise is now thirty-five years old and has thirty years for saving toward her one-million-dollar goal. She anticipates an APR of 9% on her investments. How much does she need to save if she puts money away annually? How much does she need to save if she puts money away monthly?

Solution

METHOD 1: Using the equation

For the annual annuity payments, Denise will make thirty end-of-year payments at 9% APR. To reach $1,000,000, she will need to save

$$PMT = \frac{FV}{\frac{(1 + r)^n - 1}{r}} = \frac{\$1{,}000{,}000}{\frac{(1 + 0.09)^{30} - 1}{0.09}} = \frac{\$1{,}000{,}000}{136.3075} = \$7{,}336.35$$

If she puts money away monthly, we must convert the 9% APR to the monthly periodic rate of 0.0075 (0.09/12) and increase the number of payments to 360(30 × 12). The monthly savings requirement is

$$PMT = \frac{FV}{\frac{(1+r)^n - 1}{r}} = \frac{\$1{,}000{,}000}{\frac{(1+0.0075)^{360} - 1}{0.0075}} = \frac{\$1{,}000{,}000}{1830.7435} = \$546.23$$

Again, the monthly annuity is not one-twelfth of the annual annuity ($546.23 × 12 = $6,554.76 < $7,336.35). As we noted earlier, this example shows compounding interest at work for Denise when she increases the number of payments per year.

METHOD 2: Using a calculator

On the TVM keys for the monthly savings plan, we have

Mode: P/Y = 12 and C/Y = 12

Input	360	9.0	0	?	1,000,000
Key	N	I/Y	PV	PMT	FV
CPT				−546.23	

METHOD 3: Using the spreadsheet

B6 | *fx* | =PMT(B1,B2,B3,B4,B5)

Use the PMT function to find the required monthly savings to reach $1 million in thirty years at 9% earnings rate.

	A	B	C	D	E
1	Rate	0.0075			
2	Nper	360			
3	Pv	0			
4	Fv	$1,000,000.00			
5	Type	0			
6	Pmt	($546.23)			

5.3 Consumer Loans and Amortization Schedules

Twice so far in this chapter you have seen that the monthly payment is not one-twelfth of the annual payment. Why? The increasing of the compounding periods per year and the increasing of payments to more than once a year require us to revisit the typical consumer or business loan. By looking through the amortization window, you will also see what happens when you increase the number of payments during the year for a loan repayment.

Recall the example we used in Chapter 4 for paying off a business loan of $25,000 over a six-year period with an 8% annual percentage rate. The $5,407.88 ordinary annuity was an annual payment, but for most loans, payments are monthly. If we converted this loan to monthly payments and monthly compounding of interest, what would the monthly payments be and what would the amortization schedule look like?

The known variables are the present value of $25,000, the number of years at six, and the annual percentage rate of 8%. The compounding periods are twelve per year, so the two variables of change are r and n:

$$n = \text{number of years} \times \text{compounding periods per year} = 6 \times 12 = 72$$

$$APR = 0.08$$

$$m = 12$$

$$r = \frac{0.08}{12} = 0.00666\overline{6}$$

$$PMT = \frac{\$25{,}000}{\dfrac{1 - \left[\dfrac{1}{(1 + 0.00666\overline{6})^{72}}\right]}{0.00666\overline{6}}}$$

$$= \frac{\$25{,}000}{57.0345} = \$438.33$$

Solving for the payment variable, we get monthly payments of $438.33.

Table 5.3 shows an abbreviated amortization schedule that accounts for the switch to monthly payments. The borrower makes monthly payments at the end of each month, so the interest applies for the entire month on the outstanding balance. Monthly interest is equal to

$$\text{interest expense for the month} = \frac{\text{beginning principal balance} \times 0.08}{12}$$

The abbreviated amortization schedule illustrates that each month, the borrower applies less of the payment to interest and more to the principal. This schedule should make sense because each month we borrow less money (lower principal amount) than the month before, so the interest expense is lower with a constant APR of 8% on the loan. How does that compare with the annual annuity for this loan, in which the annual payment was $5,407.88?

The total interest for the first year on the monthly payment schedule is $1,877.77 (adding up the twelve months of interest), but under the annual payment, the first year's interest is $2,000 ($25,000 × 0.08). The average principal over the first year of the monthly loan repayment is $23,472.14 (using the monthly beginning balances) versus the $25,000 when paying off the loan with an annual payment. Therefore, the interest expense is lower for the monthly repayment plan ($23,472.14 × 0.08) versus the annual payment ($25,000 × 0.08). Over the life of the loan, the total interest expense for the monthly loan is $6,559.76, whereas the total interest payment for the annual loan is $7,447.28. The difference reflects the reduction of the principal each month versus the annual

TABLE 5.3 Abbreviated Monthly Amortization Schedule for $25,000 Loan, Six Years at 8% Annual Percentage Rate

Month	Beginning Principal	Payment	Interest Expense	Principal Reduction	Ending Principal
1	$25,000.00	$438.33	$166.67	$271.66	$24,728.34
2	$24,728.34	$438.33	$164.86	$273.47	$24,454.86
3	$24,454.86	$438.33	$163.03	$275.30	$24,179.56
4	$24,179.56	$438.33	$161.20	$277.13	$23,902.43
5	$23,902.43	$438.33	$159.35	$278.98	$23,623.45
6	$23,623.45	$438.33	$157.49	$280.84	$23,342.61
7	$23,342.61	$438.33	$155.62	$282.71	$23,059.90
8	$23,059.90	$438.33	$153.73	$284.60	$22,775.30
9	$22,775.30	$438.33	$151.84	$286.49	$22,488.81
10	$22,488.81	$438.33	$149.93	$288.40	$22,200.40
11	$22,200.40	$438.33	$148.00	$290.33	$21,910.07
12	$21,910.07	$438.33	$146.07	$292.26	$21,617.81
⋮					
23	$18,585.85	$438.33	$123.91	$314.42	$18,271.42
24	$18,271.42	$438.33	$121.81	$316.52	$17,954.90
⋮					
71	$ 868.06	$438.33	$ 5.79	$432.54	$ 435.52
72	$ 435.52	$438.42	$ 2.90	$435.52	$ 0.00

Note: Values have been rounded to the nearest cent. The last payment is $0.09 higher to cover the shortfall when the actual payments are rounded to the nearest cent.

reduction of the principal; hence, the monthly payment is not one-twelfth the annual payment. The average annual principal and the interest cost are lower the more frequent the payment. Reducing principal at a faster pace reduces the overall interest that the borrower pays on a loan.

An interesting side note to these increased payments per year is what happens when you pay more than the required annuity payment. For example, you may hear about making one extra payment a year (thirteen payments instead of twelve) on a home mortgage loan. The extra portion of the payment goes to the principal. The amazing thing with an extra payment above the required annuity is that it can significantly reduce the number of payments that you need to pay off the loan. Let's examine the case where you add "one extra payment" per year to a mortgage. For simplicity, we will add this extra payment equally across the twelve monthly payments.

EXAMPLE 5.3 Extra payment on a mortgage

Problem Assume you just bought a new home and now have a mortgage. The amount of the principal is $250,000, the loan is at 8% APR, and the monthly payments are spread out over thirty years. Your lender states that you may want to add an extra payment each year to the loan to reduce maturity of the loan and save money. First, what is the loan payment? Second, if you add an extra payment per year, how soon will you pay off the loan? What is the difference in the total cash payments?

Solution

METHOD 2: Using a calculator

The monthly payment is

Mode: P/Y = 12 and C/Y = 12

Input	360	8.0	250,000	?	0
Key	N	I/Y	PV	PMT	FV
CPT				**− 1,834.41**	

We will now add this extra annual payment of $1,834.41 by splitting it evenly across the twelve payments: $1,834.41/12. The result is $152.87, but we will add a slightly lesser amount of $149.22 each month to the current payment. (We have picked the amount of $149.22 so that the number of years is a whole number when we solve for how long it will take to pay off the loan at the higher payments.) We now make monthly payments of $1,983.63. We solve for the number of payments it will take to pay off the loan.

METHOD 2: Using a calculator

Mode: P/Y = 12 and C/Y = 12

Input	?	8.0	250,000	−1,983.63	0
Key	N	I/Y	PV	PMT	FV
CPT	**276.0**				

So, with an extra $149.22 in each payment, the borrower will pay off the loan in twenty-three years (276 months/12 = 23 years) instead of the contracted thirty years. This extra payment saves you the last seven years, or eighty-four payments at $1,834.41 (for a total of $154,090.44). The total extra cash upfront for the first 276 months is $41,184.72 (276 × $149.22), for a net savings of $112,905.72. The question then becomes whether you can afford an extra $149.22 per month over the first twenty-three years of the loan.

Another twist to interest rates that we hear about with consumer loans concerns car loans for zero interest rate for the first part of the loan. Have you ever seen a television ad that makes a big fuss about car loans for 0% financing or no payments for a full year? Are these commercials just hot air, or can you really borrow money for free? If you were to read the fine print, the 0% financing or the "no payments for a year" clause comes with a provision that you must pay off the loan within a specific period of time, say, the first two years for the 0% financing loan or one year for the "no payments for a year" loan. If you cannot fulfill these requirements, you will have to pay at the annual percentage rate stated for the entire loan period. Let's look at this scenario more closely.

EXAMPLE 5.4 Can you borrow money for free?

Problem Let's take a $25,000 loan over six years at 8% APR once again, but this time we'll assume it is for a car loan that offers 0% financing for the first two years of the loan or 8% financing over six years. What are your payment choices to ensure that you pay no interest on the loan?

Solution

Payment method 1

Make twenty-four equal monthly payments over the first two years so that the entire loan is paid in full at the end of the second year. With a 0% interest rate, you simply divide the car loan principal by the number of payments, twenty-four:

$$\text{payment} = \frac{\$25{,}000}{24} = \mathbf{\$1{,}041.67}$$

Payment method 2

A more likely scenario is that you will elect to make the payments over the first two years as though you were going to pay the loan off over the six-year period. Typically, a loan payment schedule is set with the assumption that you will pay off the loan over the entire six years. The car dealership uses the 8% APR to determine the monthly payments. The monthly payment will be $438.33 at the 8% APR.

Using a calculator:

Mode: P/Y = 12 and C/Y = 12

Input	72	8.0	25,000	?	0
Key	N	I/Y	PV	PMT	FV
CPT				438.33	

Then, at the end of the second year, you will pay a balloon payment on the remaining balance to pay off the car loan. How big a balloon payment will be necessary to pay off the loan so as to incur no interest?

One way to determine the final balloon payment is to realize that you can apply all your monthly payments to the original principal. You have paid twenty-four payments of $438.33, or a total so far of $10,519.92. Therefore, your balloon payment is

$$\text{balloon payment} = \$25{,}000.00 - \$10{,}519.92 = \$14{,}480.08$$

So, can you borrow money for free? In Example 5.4, the answer is yes *if* you are willing to make the loan period last just two years and can either pay off the balloon balance of $14,480.08 at the end of the second year following twenty-four equal payments of $438.33 or increase your monthly payments to $1,041.67. For many people, those are big *ifs*, and they usually end up making the $438.33 monthly payment for the six years.

5.4 Nominal and Real Interest Rates

We can also call the interest rates we are using in the introductory chapters **nominal interest rates**. As you shall see shortly, two primary components constitute nominal interest rates: inflation and the real interest rate. The **real interest rate** is the reward for waiting. We will talk more about it as we progress through this section. The nominal rate is the percentage change in the actual dollars that you receive on your investment. The real rate is the percentage change in the purchasing power of those dollars. With inflation, they buy less. Let's see how these rates work.

Assume that you are willing to postpone the consumption of \$500 today to buy a 7% certificate of deposit (CD) at your local bank. Holding the CD for one year provides you with a 7% return. This return for postponing consumption implies that at the end of the year you should be able to buy more goods or services than the \$500 would have purchased at the start of the year. You would have \$535 for spending. As we all know, however, the prices of goods and services tend to increase over time because of inflation. Inflation will eat away at some of the benefit of the extra \$35, so the 7% return should be sufficient both to cover inflation and provide some reward for waiting. Therefore, the first major component of the nominal rate is inflation, and the second is the *real rate* or **reward for waiting**, forgoing the use of the money today:

$$\text{nominal rate} = \text{real rate} + \text{expected inflation} \tag{5.3}$$

EXAMPLE 5.5 Nominal and real interest rates

Problem Marco Corso of Corso del Tempo Books is seeking to expand his rare book collection. He has \$1,000 to spend on these books today. Each year, rare books increase in price at a 4% rate (inflation). Marco believes that if he invests his money for two years, he should be able to buy twenty-one books for what twenty books would cost today. In other words, his reward for waiting two years should be the ability to buy one additional book for each twenty he could buy today.

What interest rate will Marco need to find in nominal terms to overcome the effects of inflation and still realize his reward for waiting?

Solution The real rate of interest or reward is the increase in the number of rare books Marco wants to purchase in two years:

$$\text{reward} = \left(\frac{FV}{PV}\right)^{1/n} - 1$$

where FV is the number of books he wants to purchase at the end of the second year, PV is the number of books he can currently purchase, and n is the waiting time between the two purchase options in years (and for this example is two years). So,

$$\text{real rate} = \left(\frac{21}{20}\right)^{1/2} - 1 = 0.024695$$

As discussed, the nominal interest rate is the real rate plus anticipated inflation. The assumed inflation rate is 4% on rare books, so the rate necessary to compensate for waiting and cover inflation is

$$\text{nominal interest rate} = 2.4695\% + 4\% = 6.4695\%$$

Marco will need to find a nominal interest rate of 6.4695% to meet his reward for waiting objective. We will see, however, that this simple addition of inflation and the real rate will leave him a little short in trying to buy the twenty-one books at the end of the second year. So, let's continue with the example and see why he comes up short.

What effect do inflation and the reward for waiting have on the price of books and Marco's choice to postpone buying rare books for two years? Assume the average rare book costs $50 today. With his current $1,000, Marco could buy twenty books today. If he waits two years, how much will he need to buy twenty-one books?

Each book will increase in price to $54.08 if we apply our anticipated inflation rate of 4%:

$$FV = PV \times (1 + r)^n$$

$$\text{price at the end of two years for a single book} = \$50 \times (1.04)^2 = \$54.08$$

To buy twenty-one books at the new price will cost $1,135.68 (21 × $54.08). Therefore, Marco must earn $135.68 on his invested $1,000 (investment earnings of 6.5683%) for the two years to cover both inflation and his required reward for waiting:

$$\text{nominal interest rate } r = \left(\frac{FV}{PV}\right)^{1/n} - 1 = \left(\frac{\$1{,}135.68}{\$1{,}000}\right)^{1/2} - 1 = 6.5683\%$$

One component of the nominal interest rate is the expected inflation rate. Inflation—the rate at which the general level of prices for goods and services is rising—takes a bite out of the purchasing power of money.

Notice that the required nominal rate is slightly greater than the simple addition of the expected inflation rate of 4% and the real rate of 2.4695%, and we are short by 0.0988% or about $2.10 for the twenty-one rare books if we invest at 6.4695% instead of the required 6.5683%.

We can write the true relationship between the nominal interest rate and the real rate and expected inflation as

$$(1 + r) = (1 + r^*) \times (1 + h) \qquad \textbf{5.4}$$

or

$$r = (1 + r^*) \times (1 + h) - 1 \qquad \textbf{5.5}$$

where r is the nominal interest rate, r^* is the real interest rate, and h is inflation. This relationship is called the **Fisher effect**, after economist Irving Fisher.

The Fisher effect is the relationship between three items: the nominal rate, the real rate, and inflation. We can restate Equation 5.5 as

$$r = r^* + h + (r^* \times h) \qquad \textbf{5.6}$$

This new equation tells us that the *true nominal rate* actually comprises three components: (1) the real rate, (2) the inflation rate, and (3) the product of the real rate and inflation. Looking back at Example 5.5, we find that the required nominal rate and the three components are

$$6.5683\% = 2.4695\% + 4\% + (2.4695\% \times 4\%)$$

We can think of the product of the real rate and the inflation rate as the additional compensation needed because the interest earned during the year is also subject to inflation or a loss of purchasing power at the end of the year. This product can be quite small—less than 0.1% in this problem (0.0988%). Therefore, it is very common to approximate the nominal rate as simply the real rate plus inflation:

$$\text{approximate nominal interest rate} = \text{real rate} + \text{inflation}$$

or

$$r = r^* + h \qquad \textbf{5.7}$$

To be accurate about the nominal rate, however, we need to use all three pieces:

$$\text{true nominal interest rate} = \text{real rate} + \text{inflation} + (\text{real rate} \times \text{inflation})$$

or

$$r = r^* + h + (r^* \times h)$$

Again, we want to emphasize that institutions quote almost all financial rates in nominal terms.

5.5 Risk-Free Rate and Premiums

We have looked at two important concepts in regard to interest rates: the concept of annual rates and periodic rates and the concept of real rates and nominal rates. When you visit any financial institution, however, you will see many different advertised rates. For example, a visit to the Web site of a local credit union revealed a number of borrowing rates and investing rates, as illustrated in Table 5.4.

Why are these nominal rates different? Why does the credit union charge you one rate when you borrow for a house and another rate when you borrow for a car or boat? When you get a credit card, why is the rate so much higher than the rate you get when you borrow for a house or car or boat? Also, why is the bank willing to pay you more the longer you leave your money in a certificate of deposit? Generally, we can explain these differences by two factors:

1. The level of risk of the investment or loan
2. The length of the investment or loan

TABLE 5.4 Advertised Borrowing and Investing Rates at a Credit Union, January 22, 2012

Type of Loan	Borrowing Rates	Certificates of Deposit	Investing Rates
Real estate 30-year fixed	6.50%	90 to 181 days	2.50%
Real estate 15-year fixed	6.02%	182 to 364 days	4.00%
New auto loan	7.14%	12 to 24 months	4.15%
Used auto loan	7.24%	24 to 36 months	4.20%
New boat or RV loan	7.50%	36 to 48 months	4.25%
Used boat or RV loan	8.50%	48 to 60 months	4.30%
Visa Rewards credit card	14.45%	Over 5 years	4.35%
Visa Value credit card	14.75%		

The two major components of the interest rate that cause rates to vary across different investment opportunities or loans relate to these two factors. They are, respectively, the *default premium* (which relates to risk) and the *maturity premium* (which relates to time).

Let's examine the default premium first. Looking back at the loan rates, we see that the house loan rate (thirty-year fixed loan) is 6.50%, the loan rate for a new car is 7.14%, and the borrowing rate for a Visa Rewards card is 14.45%. One reason that these rates vary is that the default rates or potential losses due to default are different for these different kinds of loans.

For the home loan, the collateral (the house) is an asset that will increase in value over time (in general); with a car loan, the collateral (the car) decreases in value over time. If the borrower cannot pay back the loan and must default, the lender can take the asset to cover the loan. With a house, the potential loss due to default is less because the growing value of the asset should be sufficient to cover the outstanding balance (principal) of the loan. For the car, however, the decreasing value of the collateral may not be sufficient to pay off the remaining balance of the loan with a default. A personal credit card essentially has no collateral, so the potential loss is even higher if the customer defaults on his or her credit card payments. The **default premium** is therefore that portion of a borrowing rate that compensates the lender for the higher risk associated with varying types of collateral and the probability that a borrower will default.

The second piece of the default premium has to do with the frequency of default by the borrower. Some investments or loans have a higher frequency of default than others. The frequency of default on a home loan is much lower than the frequency of default on a credit card. In the investment world, the frequency of bankruptcy (a default) for a high-tech start-up company is higher than for a blue-chip company, so we see higher borrowing rates for start-ups than for mature companies.

Is there a base rate that has no potential for default? The answer is yes, the risk-free rate. We will build the different rates for loans and investments from this rate. A **risk-free rate** is a theoretical interest rate at which an investor is guaranteed to earn the subscribed rate and at which the borrower will never default. In other words, it is the rate of return for an investment with zero risk. We typically think of the U.S. Treasury bill as a risk-free investment. That is, we assign a zero probability of default to the U.S. Treasury and assume that all U.S. Treasury bills will pay out in full at maturity and have a zero default premium ($dp = 0$):

$$\text{Treasury bill interest rate} = r_f \qquad \textbf{5.8}$$

Again, this stated risk-free rate comprises two pieces, the real rate plus inflation, so we can write the U.S. Treasury bill rate as

$$r_f = r^* + h \qquad \textbf{5.9}$$

where r_f is the risk-free interest rate, r^* is the real rate of interest, and h is the rate of inflation.

What happens when we add the element of default to an interest rate? Let's return to our rare book buyer, Marco Corso. We assumed that if he invested his $1,000 at 6.5683%, he was sure to receive a yield of 6.5683% compounded annually for two years. This guaranteed return by the bank would mean that Marco had assumed no default risk and thus was a risk-free nominal interest rate, but what if the bank were unable to pay the full 6.5683% at the end of each year? Then, Marco would be short of the needed funds to purchase his twenty-one rare books. Thus, Marco, like all investors, would also need to receive some extra compensation in the form of a higher yield or interest rate for this potential default on the part of the bank. The higher the potential default, the greater the risk assumed by the investor and hence the higher the required yield. In Marco's case, his default risk is based on the bank's financial stability of offering the 6.5683% interest rate. We add this default premium to determine the nominal interest rate for a specific investment or loan, so it now comprises the real rate, inflation, and a default premium (dp):

$$r = r^* + h + dp \qquad \textbf{5.10}$$

The default premium compensates the investor for the additional risk that the investor will not repay the loan in full.

We can now think of interest rates in two dimensions: an inflation dimension and a default dimension. Figure 5.1 illustrates these two dimensions.

Maturity Premiums

If you look back at the loan rates in Table 5.4 on a house for a fifteen-year loan versus a thirty-year loan (6.02% versus 6.50%) or the different rates on the available certificates of deposit (from 2.5% to 4.35%), you can see that the shorter the period, the lower the rate. That is, if you invest money for a short period—say you buy a six-month CD—you will not receive as high an interest rate as if you bought a CD with a longer maturity period. This difference in rates as the borrowing time or investment horizon increases is due to the *maturity premium* of the investments.

In the cases of the house mortgages and the CDs, remember that we are looking at different time horizons, with everything else held constant. In the case of the mortgage, it is the same house, the same lender, and the same borrower with the same capability for repaying the loan, but with two different choices: one loan for fifteen years and another for thirty years.

Real to nominal: add inflation →

	Real	Nominal
Risk-free	r^*	$r_f = r^* + inf$ (Treasury bill)
Risky		$r = r^* + inf + dp$ (Annual percentage rate)

Risk-free to risky: add default ↓

FIGURE 5.1 Interest rate dimensions.

In the case of the CD, it is the same credit union and the same investor, but seven different maturity dates for the different CDs.

How does extending the time horizon affect the interest rate? To answer this question, we need to ask two additional fundamental questions about borrowing and lending money:

1. When you borrow money, when is the optimal time for you to pay back the money?
2. When you loan money, how quickly do you want repayment?

When we borrow money, we would like to wait as long as possible to pay back the loan. When we loan money, we want repayment as quickly as possible. Therefore, borrowers want to borrow in the long term and lenders want to lend in the short term. In other words, we have different maturity preferences between borrowers and lenders.

How do these different time horizons play out in the real world? How does a lending institution encourage you to take a shorter period on your mortgage when your incentive might be to stretch it out to the full time horizon of the loan? It offers a lower rate on the shorter-period loan. How does the institution encourage you to invest your money in longer-term CDs when your incentive might be to cash in as soon as possible? It offers higher rates on longer-term CDs. By offering lower borrowing rates for shorter maturities, the lender (the institution) entices the borrower (you, the mortgagee) to shorten the loan period. Conversely, by offering higher investment rates for longer maturities, the borrower (the lending institution) entices the lender (you, the CD buyer) to lengthen the investment period.

The **maturity premium** (mp), then, represents that portion of the nominal interest rate that compensates the investor for the additional waiting time or the lender for the additional time it takes to receive repayment in full. In general, the longer the period of the investment, the greater the extra reward an investor demands. The longer the loan, the greater the risk of nonpayment and the higher the interest rate the lender demands.

We have now added another dimension to the nominal interest rate so that our nominal advertised interest rate reflects the real rate, inflation, the default premium, and the maturity premium:

$$r = r^* + h + dp + mp \tag{5.11}$$

Yield Curves

Interest rates vary based on the maturity date of a bond or loan. Typically, the longer a borrower wants for repayment of a loan and the longer the lender will accept repayment, the higher the interest rate. When we plot this concept on a graph with time to maturity on the x-axis and interest rates on the y-axis, we imply a **yield curve**. The relationship of the interest rate to the maturity date of a particular financial instrument is the yield curve of that financial instrument. We use the yield curve as a benchmark for debt in the market, such as mortgage rates or bank lending rates. Economists also use the curve to predict changes in economic output and growth.

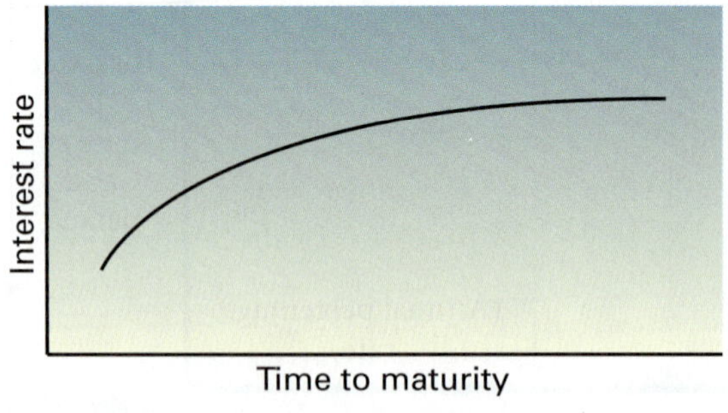

FIGURE 5.2 Upward-sloping yield curve.

The yield curve can take on various shapes over time. The most common "curve" is the upward-sloping curve illustrated in Figure 5.2. This upward-sloping yield curve is typically a function of the maturity premium. When the maturity of the loan grows, the lender receives additional compensation for the added waiting time to receive repayment of the loan. As we stated earlier in this section, the longer the loan, the greater the risk of nonpayment, thus the higher the interest rate on the loan. A positive maturity premium means an upward-sloping yield curve.

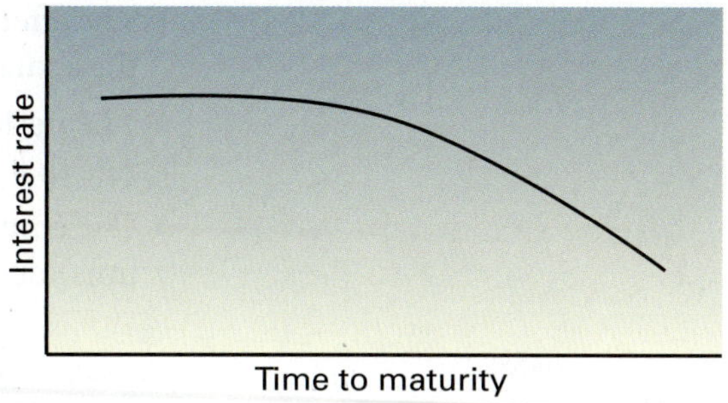

FIGURE 5.3 Downward-sloping yield curve.

The slope of the curve may be fairly flat or very steep. Economists explain a steep yield curve as an indication that the economy will be expanding. The steeper the curve, the greater and faster we anticipate economic expansion. Economists believe that a flat yield curve signals uncertainty about the future economy.

The yield curve can also become inverted. Figure 5.3 illustrates an inverted yield curve in which interest rates for longer maturities are less than interest rates for shorter maturities, which would imply a negative maturity premium. The inverted yield curve means that investors will settle for lower rates on long-term financial instruments, believing that the economy will slow or decline in the future. We can illustrate why an investor would take a lower rate on a bond with a longer maturity.

EXAMPLE 5.6 Inverted Yield Curve Investing

Problem Kevin wants to put away $10,000 today for his retirement in 20 years. The current interest rates on $10,000 zero-coupon government bonds are as follows (inverted yield curve):

Rate	6.50%	6.45%	6.35%	6.25%	6.15%	6.00%
Years to Maturity	1	2	5	10	15	20

However, if Kevin waits one year, the rates will fall to the following as the economy weakens:

Rate	5.50%	5.45%	5.35%	5.25%	5.15%	5.00%
Years to Maturity	1	2	5	10	15	20

Which current bond should Kevin select?

Solution By investing in the twenty-year government bond today at a lower rate than the one-year bond, Kevin will be able to lock in the 6.00% return for the next twenty years. If Kevin selects a one-year bond with the highest rate today, the bond will mature at the end of the year for $10,560, but Kevin will then need to select another bond and reinvest at an interest rate well below the 6.00% of the prior year's twenty-year bond. If Kevin is like many other investors and prefers the longer-term bond, then the investing community thinks the economy will weaken in the future, interest rates will fall, and the current yield curve will be inverted.

At this point, let's review the most important points about interest rates that you have learned so far in this chapter:

- It is standard to use the nominal annual percentage rate (APR) as the basic quoted rate for interest. The annual percentage rate remains the bellwether interest rate.

- The effective annual rate (EAR) is the rate that provides the best information on the actual cost of a loan for borrowers or yield on an investment for investors.
- The periodic interest rate (semiannual, quarterly, monthly, or daily rate) is the rate that we use in the time value of money equations.
- The components (real rate, inflation, default premiums, and maturity premiums) determine the nominal rate for individual loans or investments.

5.6 A Brief History of Interest Rates and Inflation in the United States

The four major components of interest rates vary over time. Thus, nominal interest rates vary across the same investment or loan over time. For example, interest rates change daily on mortgage and car loans, government bonds, corporate bonds, and other financial assets. During the early 1980s, interest rates on home mortgages were as high as 16%. Today, rates are around 5%, back near some of the all-time-low rates. How much do interest rates vary over time, and to what extent do the swings in the interest rate components of inflation, default premiums, and maturity premiums contribute to the variation in interest rates? By looking at historical interest rates, we can get a feel for the variation in the components (how much they move from period to period) and the range of the components (what the highest rates are and what the lowest rates are).

First and probably easiest to understand is that inflation varies over time. One year's inflation rate may be 3%; another year's inflation rate may be 15%. To appreciate the variation in inflation, we can look at historical U.S. inflation rates in Figure 5.4.

To illustrate how much a nominal rate composed of just inflation and the real rate can vary over time, we can examine the historical interest rates on the three-month U.S. Treasury bill from 1950 to 1999, as Figure 5.5 depicts. We assume that this investment instrument has a zero default premium and has the shortest maturity of the U.S. Treasury bills; thus, it has no maturity premium. We can attribute the year-to-year differences only to changes in the real rate and inflation.

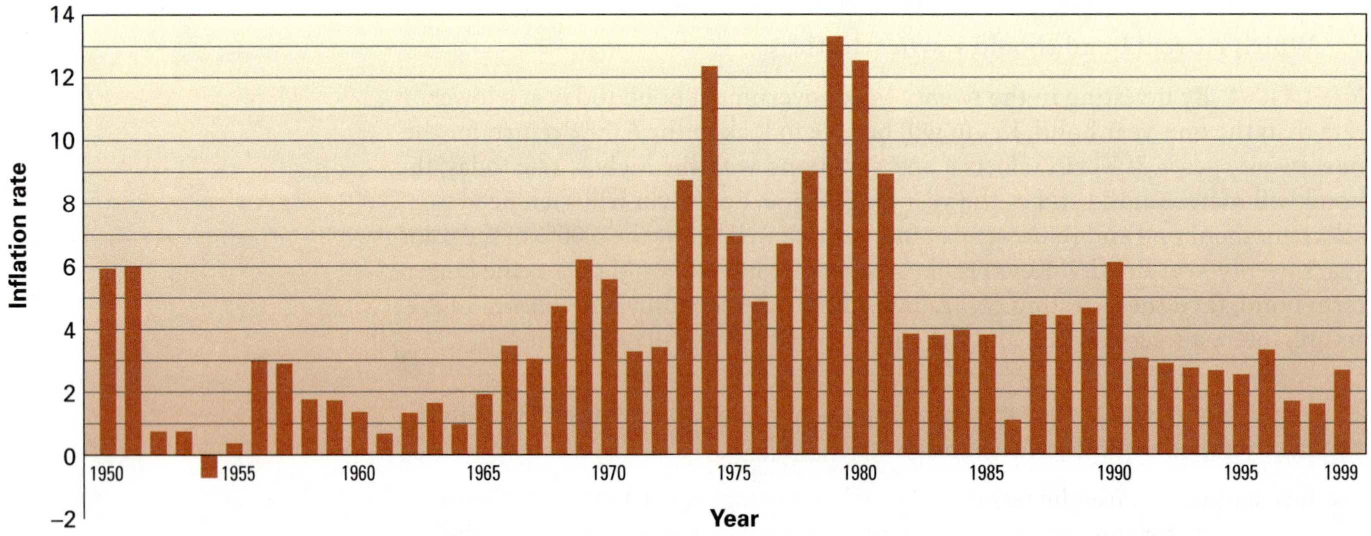

FIGURE 5.4 Inflation rates in the United States, 1950–1999.

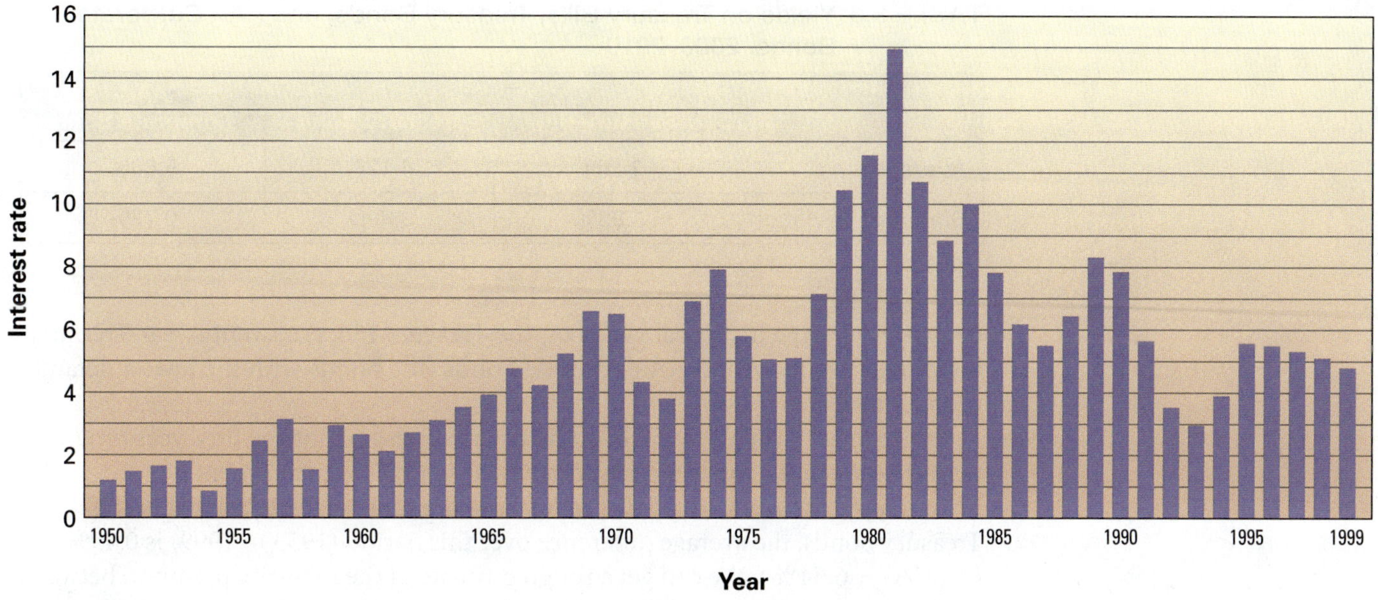

FIGURE 5.5 Interest rates for the three-month treasury bill, 1950–1999.

Because Figures 5.4 and Figure 5.5 present data over the same time period, from 1950 to 1999, can we combine the information in the two graphs to estimate the change in the real rate from year to year? There are a few problems with such a simple approach to estimating the real rate of interest. First, we base the yields on *expected* inflation, and Figure 5.4 shows *actual* inflation (historically measured). So, we actually have a nonsynchronous set of observations. We can get an average real rate if we assume that *expected* inflation and *actual* inflation are on average the same when we look over a relatively long period of time.

Figures 5.4 and 5.5 show that the risk-free rate (using the three-month U.S. Treasury bill) in the United States varied from slightly under 1% to a high of nearly 15% in the early 1980s. Inflation varied from a low of negative 1% to a high of slightly over 13%. The average rate for the three-month Treasury bill from 1950 to 1999 was 5.23%, and the average inflation rate during this same period was 4.05%. Using a simple approximation, we can say that the average real interest rate from 1950 to 1999 was 1.18%:

$$\text{nominal rate} = \text{real rate} + \text{inflation}$$

$$5.23\% = \text{real rate} + 4.05\%$$

$$\text{real rate} = 5.23\% - 4.05\% = 1.18\%$$

Other interest rate data provide insight into the magnitude of the default premium and the maturity premium. Table 5.5 shows the average and the standard

TABLE 5.5 Yields on Treasury Bills, Treasury Bonds, and AAA Corporate Bonds, 1950–1999

	Treasury Bill	Treasury Bond	AAA Corporate Bond
Average	5.23%	6.64%	7.13%
Standard deviation	2.98%	2.86%	2.95%

Source: St. Louis Federal Reserve.

TABLE 5.6 Yields on Treasury Bills, Treasury Bonds, and AAA Corporate Bonds, 2000–2010

	Treasury Bill	Treasury Bond	AAA Corporate Bond
Average	2.16%	4.12%	5.66%
Standard deviation	1.99%	0.80%	0.72%

Source: St. Louis Federal Reserve.

deviation of some historical yields on the Treasury bill, the twenty-year Treasury bond, and twenty-year AAA corporate bonds (the bonds with the lowest default probability).

We can get a rough estimate of the default premium for the fifty-year time period between the top-rated corporate bonds and U.S. government bonds. If we assume the AAA corporate bonds have the same maturity as that of the Treasury bonds, the average difference over this period (1953 to 1999) is 0.49% (7.13% − 6.64%). We can get a rough estimate of the maturity premium between the three-month Treasury bill and the twenty-year Treasury bond as well. The maturity premium is 1.41% when using the average yields (6.64% − 5.23%).

So, if we want an idea of the average size of the four components of the nominal interest rate in the market for a fifty-year period for twenty-year AAA corporate bonds, we have

Inflation at 4.05%
Real rate at 1.18%
Default premium of 0.49% (for AAA over government bonds)
Maturity premium at 1.28% (for twenty-year maturity differences)

Although this approach to estimating the size of the components is very simple, we do get an idea of their relative contribution. And, of course, the default premiums and maturity premiums will vary as we look at investments with more or less risk and longer or shorter maturities.

Interest rates dramatically fell from historical rates during the first years of the twenty-first century. Table 5.6 shows the average rates and standard deviations for the years 2000 to 2010. These latest rates are comparable to the rates during the 1950s.

To review this chapter, see the Summary Card at the end of the text.

Key Terms

annual percentage rate (APR), p. 116
annual percentage yield (APY), p. 118
compounding period, p. 116
compounding periods per year (C/Y), p. 116
default premium (dp), p. 130
effective annual rate (EAR), p. 117
Fisher effect, p. 128
maturity premium, p. 132
nominal interest rate, p. 127
periodic interest rate, p. 116
real interest rate, p. 127
reward for waiting, p. 127
risk-free rate, p. 130
yield curve, p. 132

Questions

1. Why does it make sense to say that the interest rate is the price to rent money?
2. Which of the following statements is *true*? Give all correct answers.
   a. effective annual rate > annual percentage rate
   b. effective annual rate = annual percentage rate
   c. effective annual rate < annual percentage rate
3. When you increase the number of payments per period, why does the total cash payments times the number of payments in the period not equal the original single payment for the period? (In other words, why does twelve times a monthly payment on a loan with a positive interest rate not equal the required annual payment on the same loan amount with the same interest rate?)
4. Explain why the real interest rate is the reward for saving.
5. What does the term *risk-free interest* mean, and why do we usually use the U.S. Treasury bill yield as the risk-free rate?
6. Why does a mortgage typically have a lower interest rate than a car loan?
7. On average, which factor do you think contributes more to the nominal risk-free rate, inflation or the real rate? How would you prove your opinion?
8. Since 1950, the interest rates for corporate bonds have averaged a higher interest rate than long-term government bonds. Why?
9. Since 1950, the interest rates for long-term government bonds have averaged a higher interest rate than short-term government bonds. Why?
10. During what decade from 1950 to 1999 did we see the highest interest rates in the United States?

Prepping for Exams

1. A company selling a bond is _____________ money.
   a. borrowing
   b. lending
   c. taking
   d. reinvesting

2. Suppose you deposit money in a certificate of deposit (CD) at a bank. Which of the following statements is *true*? Give all correct answers.
   a. The bank is borrowing money from you without a promise to repay that money with interest.
   b. The bank is lending money to you with a promise to repay that money with interest.
   c. The bank is technically renting money from you with a promise to repay that money with interest.
   d. The bank is renting money from you, but not borrowing money from you.

3. When a lender states or gives interest rates for loan repayments, we assume that they are _____________ unless specifically stated otherwise.
   a. daily rates
   b. annual percentage rates

c. effective annual rates
d. APYs

4. Which of the following statements is *true*? Give all correct answers.

a. By *decreasing* the number of payments per year, you *reduce* your total cash outflow but *increase* your effective borrowing rate.
b. By *increasing* the number of payments per year, you *boost* your total cash outflow but *increase* your effective borrowing rate.
c. By *increasing* the number of payments per year, you *reduce* your total cash outflow but *increase* your effective borrowing rate.
d. By *increasing* the number of payments per year, you *reduce* your total cash outflow but *decrease* your effective borrowing rate.

5. Monthly interest on a loan is equal to ______________.

a. the beginning balance times the APR.
b. the ending balance times the annual percentage rate.
c. the ending balance times the periodic interest rate.
d. the beginning balance times the periodic interest rate.

6. Suppose you postpone consumption so that by investing at 8% you will have an extra $800 to spend in one year. Suppose inflation is 4% during this time. What is the real increase in your purchasing power?

a. $800
b. $600
c. $400
d. $200

7. The Fisher effect tells us that the true nominal rate actually comprises three components. These three components are ______________.

a. the nominal rate, the real rate, and inflation
b. the real rate, inflation, and the product of the real rate and the nominal rate
c. the real rate, inflation, and the product of the real rate and inflation
d. the real rate and the product of the real rate and inflation

8. The two major components of the interest rate that cause rates to vary across different investment opportunities or loans are ______________.

a. the default premium and the bankruptcy premium
b. the liquidity premium and the maturity premium
c. the default premium and the maturity premium
d. the inflation premium and the maturity premium

9. Which of the following statements is *false*? Give all correct answers.

a. A part of the default premium has to do with the frequency of default by the borrower.
b. For the home loan, the collateral (the house) is an asset that will increase in value over time (in general), compared with a car loan in which the collateral (the car) decreases in value over time.
c. With a car, the potential loss due to default is less than a house because the growing value of the asset should be sufficient to cover the outstanding balance (principal) of the loan.

d. A personal credit card essentially has no collateral, so the potential loss is even higher if the customer defaults on his or her credit card payments.

10. Which of the four interest rate components had the greatest average percentage in the period from 1950–1999?

a. real rate
b. inflation premium
c. historical interest rates
d. default premium

Problems

These problems are available in MyFinanceLab.

1. *Periodic interest rates.* In the following table, fill in the periodic rates and the effective annual rates.

Period	APR	Compounding per Year	Periodic Rate	Effective Annual Rate
Semiannual	8%	2		
Quarterly	9%	4		
Monthly	7.5%	12		
Daily	4.25%	365		

2. *Periodic interest rates.* You have a savings account in which you leave the funds for one year without adding or withdrawing from the account. What would you rather have: a daily compounded rate of 0.045%, a weekly compounded rate of 0.305%, a monthly compounded rate of 1.35%, a quarterly compounded rate of 4.15%, a semiannually compounded rate of 8.5%, or an annually compounded rate of 17%?

3. *EAR.* What is the effective annual rate of a mortgage rate that is advertised at 7.75% (APR) over the next twenty years and paid with monthly payments?

4. *EAR.* What is the effective rate of a monthly car loan that is advertised at 9.5% (APR)?

5. *Present value with periodic rates.* Let's follow up with Sam Hinds, the dentist, from Chapter 4 and his remodeling project (Problem 12). The cost of the equipment for the project is $18,000, and he will finance the purchase with a 7.5% loan over six years. Originally, the loan called for annual payments. Redo the payments based on quarterly payments (four per year) and monthly payments (twelve per year). Compare the annual cash outflow of the two payments. Why does the monthly payment plan have less total cash outflow each year?

6. *Present value with periodic rates.* Cooley Landscaping needs to borrow $30,000 for a new front-end dirt loader. The bank is willing to loan the money at 8.5% interest for the next ten years with annual, semiannual, quarterly, or monthly payments. What are the different payments that Cooley Landscaping could choose for these different payment plans?

7. *Future value with periodic rates.* Matt Johnson delivers newspapers and is putting away $15.00 every month from his paper route collections. Matt is eight years old and will use the money when he goes to college in ten years. What will be the value of Matt's account in ten years with his monthly payments if he is earning 6% (APR), 8% (APR), or 12% (APR)?

8. ***Future value with periodic rates.*** We return to Denise, our hopeful millionaire from Chapter 4 (Example 4.3). In Chapter 4, Denise was putting away $5,000 per year at the end of each year at 6% interest, with the expectation that in forty-four years she would be a millionaire. If Denise switches to a monthly savings plan and puts one-twelfth of the $5,000 away each month ($416.66), how much will she have in forty-four years at the 6% APR? Why is it more than the $1,000,000 goal? In this chapter in Example 5.2, Denise was putting away $546.23 for thirty years at 9% to become a millionaire. Why does it take more per month when she is putting money away at 9% than when she was earning a lower rate of 6% over the forty-four years? *Hint:* What interest rate would Denise need for the thirty years putting away $546.23 to match the future value when she started fourteen years earlier (forty-four years) at 6%?

9. ***Payments with periodic rates.*** What payment does Denise (from Problem 8) need to make at the end of each month over the coming forty-four years at 6% to reach her retirement goal of $1,000,000?

10. ***Savings with periodic rates.*** What investment per month does Patrick need to make at the end of each month into his savings account over the coming twenty-eight months to reach his vacation goal of $5,000 if he is getting 8% APR on his account?

11. ***Amortization schedule with periodic payments.*** Moulton Motors is advertising the following deal on a new Honda Civic: "Monthly payments of $400.40 for the next 60 months and this beauty can be yours!" The sticker price of the car is $18,000. If you bought the car, what interest rate would you be paying in both APR and EAR terms? What is the amortization schedule of these sixty payments?

12. ***Amortization schedule with periodic payments.*** Moulton Motors is advertising the following deal on a used Honda Accord: "Monthly payments of $245.00 for the next 48 months and this beauty can be yours!" The sticker price of the car is $9,845.00. If you bought the car, what interest rate would you be paying in both APR and EAR terms? What is the amortization schedule of these forty-eight payments?

13. ***Inflation, nominal interest rates, and real rates.*** Given the following information, estimate the nominal rate with the approximate nominal interest rate equation and the true nominal interest rate equation.

Real Rate	Inflation Rate	Approximate Nominal Rate	True Nominal Rate
3.0%	5.0%		
8.0%	15.0%		
1.0%	4.0%		
2.5%	3.5%		

14. ***Inflation, nominal interest rates, and real rates.*** Given the information at the top of the next page, estimate the real rate with the approximate nominal interest rate equation and the true nominal interest rate equation (Fisher effect).

Nominal Rate	Inflation Rate	Approximate Real Rate	True Nominal Rate
13%	5%		
8%	2%		
21%	14%		
4%	7%		

15. ***Inflation, nominal interest rates, and real rates.*** Given the following information, estimate the inflation rate with the approximate nominal interest rate equation and the true nominal interest rate equation.

Nominal Rate	Real Rate	Approximate Inflation	True Inflation
11.00%	5.00%		
8.00%	2.00%		
21.00%	14.00%		
5.50%	1.25%		

16. ***Inflation, nominal interest rates, and real rates.*** From 1991 to 2000, the U.S. economy had an annual inflation rate of around 2.93%. The historical annual nominal risk-free rate for this same period was around 5.02%. What is the real interest rate using the approximate nominal interest rate equation and the true nominal interest rate equation for that decade?

17. ***Inflation, nominal interest rates, and real rates.*** The minister of finance for the State of Tranquility has just estimated the expected inflation rate for the coming year at 6.75%. If the real rate for the coming year is 3%, what should the nominal interest rates at the central bank of the State of Tranquility be for the coming year?

18. ***Inflation, nominal interest rates, and real rates.*** The Republic of New South Brazillia, a small developing island country in South Central America, is experiencing a very high inflation rate at this time. The annual inflation rate is 40%. If the real rate of interest is 2%, what nominal interest rates must the residents of New South Brazillia get to stay ahead of inflation and still have a reward for waiting?

19. ***Negative inflation (deflation), nominal interest rates, and real rates.*** The Republic of Northern Lights, a small stable country in the North Atlantic, is experiencing a negative inflation rate (deflation) at this time. The annual inflation rate is −4%. If the nominal rate of interest is 6%, what is the real interest rate that the Northern Lightians are getting as a reward for waiting?

20. ***Negative interest rates.*** Is it possible to have promised negative nominal interest rates? Why?

21. ***Interest premium.*** The U.S. government offers two bonds: one selling to yield 6.5% and the other to yield 8.5%. Why would one bond sell for a lower yield if the originator is the same on both bonds?

22. **Interest premium.** Shaky Company has just issued a five-year bond with a yield of 9%; Stable Company has issued an identical five-year bond but with a yield of 7%. Why did the market demand a higher return from Shaky?

23. ***Interest premium.*** Ben has just purchased a long-term government bond and expects to make a 7% return. Donna has just purchased a stock in a new start-up company but expects to make a 20% return. Why is Donna expecting a higher return?

24. ***Interest premium.*** Estimate the default premium and the maturity premium given the following three investment opportunities: a Treasury bill with a current interest rate of 3.5%; a Treasury bond with a twenty-year maturity and a current interest rate of 5.5%; and an AAA, twenty-year corporate bond with an interest rate of 7.0%.

25. ***Historical interest rates.*** Refer to Figure 5.5 in the text. For the risk-free rate, what decade experienced the highest interest rate? The lowest?

26. ***Historical interest rates.*** Refer to Figure 5.4 in the text. What decade experienced the highest inflation rates? The lowest?

27. ***Historical interest rates.*** Refer to Table 5.6 for the average interest rates for the 2000 to 2010 period and estimate the default premium using the average Treasury Bond rate and the AAA corporate bond rate.

28. ***Historical interest rates.*** Refer to Table 5.6 for the average interest rates for the 2000 to 2010 period and estimate the maturity premium using the average Treasury Bond rate and the Treasury Bill rate.

29. ***Challenge question I.*** Michael is shopping for a special automobile. He finds the exact car he wants, a 1966 dark-blue Pontiac GTO. This car is currently the property of a neighbor, so to buy it for the agreed-upon price of $35,000, Michael must secure his own financing. He visits four different financial institutions and gets the following available loans:

    Bank 1: 60 monthly payments of $726.54
    Bank 2: 48 monthly payments of $870.97
    Bank 3: 156 weekly payments of $256.20
    Bank 4: 24 quarterly payments of $1,115.81

    Which loan should Michael take? *Hint:* Which loan has the lowest EAR?

30. ***Challenge question II.*** Tyler wants to buy a beach house as part of his investment portfolio. After searching the coast for a nice home, he finds a house with a great view and a hefty price of $4,500,000. Tyler will need to borrow from the bank to pay for this house. Mortgage rates are based on the length of the loan, and a local bank is advertising fifteen-year loans with monthly payments at 7.125%, twenty-year loans with monthly payments at 7.25%, and thirty-year loans with monthly payments at 7.375%. What is the monthly payment of principal and interest for each loan? Tyler believes that the property will be worth $5,500,000 in five years. Ignoring taxes and real estate commissions, if Tyler sells the house after five years, what will be the difference in the selling price and the remaining principal on the loan for each of the three loans?

These problems are available in MyFinanceLab.

Advanced Problems for Spreadsheet Application

1. ***Monthly amortization schedule.*** Sherry and Sam want to purchase a condo at the coast. They will spend $650,000 on the condo and are taking out a loan for the condo for twenty years at 7.0% interest.

a. What is the monthly payment on the mortgage? Construct the amortization of the loan for the twenty years in a spreadsheet to show the monthly interest costs, the principal reduction, and the ending balance each month.

b. Then change the amortization to reflect that after ten years, Sherry and Sam will increase their monthly payment to $7,500 per month. When will they fully repay the mortgage with this increased payment if they apply all the extra dollars above the original payment to the principal?

2. ***Inflation's impact on price of an asset.*** Tyler is working on his pilot's license and dreams of one day owning his own personal aircraft. Tyler is putting away $1,250 per month in an account earning 9.25% annually. The plane he would like to buy currently costs $430,000 and is expected to increase in price at an annual inflation rate of 3.25%. How long will it take Tyler to "save up" the funds to buy this plane? Tyler also wants to know what monthly savings it would take to buy the plane at the end of each year. For example, if he wanted to buy the plane in one year, what would the monthly savings need to be for the next twelve months? If he wanted to buy the plane in two years, what would the monthly savings need to be for the 24 months? Do this for every year up to twenty years. In the spreadsheet, estimate the future price of the plane at the end of each year and then, based on this future value, find the monthly savings that equals this future value at an earnings rate of 9.25%.

MINI-CASE

Sweetening the Deal: Povero Construction Company

This mini-case is available in MyFinanceLab.

Povero Construction is a large company listed on the New York Stock Exchange that specializes in the construction, marketing, and financing of detached homes and condominium units throughout the South and Midwest. Regional marketing and finance executives are concerned with fifty undeveloped parcels in a condominium development near Orlando, Florida. One hundred units were completed in 2005 and early 2006. Prices ranged from $290,000 to $350,000, depending on location within the development, number of bedrooms, and optional upgrades selected by customers. The first units sold quickly, but by the end of the year, agents noticed that the inventory of unsold units had started to climb alarmingly and that some of the first units sold were now back on the market.

Povero executives decided to suspend construction of additional units until they sold most of the excess inventory and the market started to recover. Five years later, the market was still soft; the undeveloped parcels, some with slab foundations in place, had become unsightly patches of sand, concrete, and weeds. Povero's agreement with the local planning authorities called for the completion of all units by the end of 2011; otherwise, the company would have to default on a $2,000,000 performance bond. At this point, the company just wanted to avoid the default and recover its original investment. Executives decided to construct and sell fifty new units at a base price of $261,000 and ran a full page ad in the *Orlando Sentinel.* Within days, a group of original buyers threatened to sue Povero because the lower prices of the new units made it impossible for them to recover their investment and therefore put them in a "negative equity" position.

Povero decided that, win or lose, a lawsuit would be a public relations disaster and chose instead to pursue other options to move the properties. One possibility the company explored was to maintain the original price but offer subsidized low-interest rates that would keep mortgage payments affordable for their typical customers.

Questions

1. Povero believes that interest rates are a major factor in the real estate market. What are the implications of rising, falling, and steady interest rates for future real estate prices?
2. If the risk-free interest rate is 3.86% and the inflation rate is 2.2%, what is the real rate of interest? Compute the rate with and without the Fisher effect.

Continued

Continued

3. Interest on a conventional thirty-year fixed-rate mortgage at the time of the case was 4.75%. At that rate, what is the monthly payment on a $290,000 mortgage? What is the monthly payment on a $261,000 mortgage?
4. At what interest rate would the monthly payments on a "pseudo-$290,000 mortgage" be the same as the monthly payments on the $261,000 loan at 4.75%? *Hint:* Use the monthly payment rate for the $261,000 loan at 4.75% and then compute the rate if Povero used these same payments to pay off a loan of $290,000 over thirty years.
5. What is the EAR equivalent to an APR of 3.86% compounded monthly? Could Povero offer an even lower APR to customers who agreed to make two payments per month?
6. Would it make much difference to either the buyer or the seller whether the price of the same unit were $261,000 financed at 4.75% or $290,000 financed at 3.86%?
7. Do you think Povero could use subsidized interest rates to make its condominium units more marketable while avoiding a dispute with owners of the previously sold units?

Part 2

Valuing Stocks and Bonds and Understanding Risk and Return

Learning Objectives

LO1 Understand basic bond terminology and apply the time value of money equation in pricing bonds.

LO2 Understand the difference between annual and semiannual bonds and note the key features of zero-coupon bonds.

LO3 Explain the relationship between the coupon rate and the yield to maturity.

LO4 Delineate bond ratings and why ratings affect bond prices.

LO5 Appreciate bond history and understand the rights and obligations of buyers and sellers of bonds.

LO6 Price government bonds, notes, and bills.

Chapter 6
Bonds and Bond Valuation

We are now ready to put to work the remarkable tools of the financial analyst from Part 1. We'll start in this chapter by using the time value of money equation to price bonds, one of the most basic of all financial assets.

When you buy a bond, you are, in effect, loaning money to a company or government. In turn, the company or government promises to repay the loan with something extra for your "trouble," in the form of interest. This loan is an agreement between a lender (the bond buyer) and the borrower (the bond seller) in which the borrower receives cash today and the lender receives a stream of cash flows in subsequent years.

As you sharpen your time value of money tools, we will also add the vocabulary of the bond world to your financial management arsenal. Keep in mind that we are dealing with financial assets: assets that derive their value from their claim to future cash flow. Bonds are one of the most basic of financial assets, and we will use our time value of money equation from Chapters 3 and 4 to price them.

6.1 Application of the Time Value of Money Tool: Bond Pricing

When companies or governments (federal, state, or local) need to borrow money, they often sell bonds. A **bond** is a long-term debt instrument by which a borrower of funds agrees to pay back the funds (the principal) with interest on specific dates in the future. If you buy one of these bonds, you are buying a promised future cash flow. We sometimes call bonds "fixed-income" securities because they pay a set amount (fixed cash flow) on specific future dates. Thus, the future cash flow is fixed at the time of initial sale of the bond.

Key Components of a Bond

Although bonds are fairly straightforward financial agreements, bond terminology is quite extensive. Part of the reason for the special vocabulary around bonds is that it makes clear that a loan is like any other kind of security in that we can buy and sell it. We will deal with much of the terminology later in the chapter, but for now we set out the nuts and bolts. To illustrate the terms, let's say that you buy a $1,000 bond that Hewlett-Packard issues at 7% interest for thirty years. Here, you are the lender, and Hewlett-Packard, the corporation, is the borrower.

We need the following basic bond terms and pricing for the time value of money equation:

Par value: The bond states its face or par value as the principal amount that the corporation repays at the bond's maturity. In our example, the $1,000 is the par value.

Coupon rate: This is the interest rate for the coupons, which we express in annual terms. It normally remains the same throughout the life of the bond. In our example, it is the 7% interest rate.

Coupon: This is the bond's regular interest payment. We determine it by multiplying the coupon rate times the par value of the bond for a bond paying interest annually. Here, it is $\$1{,}000 \times 0.07 = \$70$. You may notice that because these payments are the same amount at regular intervals, they constitute an annuity stream.

Maturity date: This is the bond's expiration date, on which the corporation makes the final interest payment and repays the principal. In our example, it is thirty years.

Yield or yield to maturity (YTM): This is the bond's discount rate or the return the bondholder receives if he or she holds it to maturity. You can think of it as an interest rate that summarizes a bond's overall investment value. We will learn how to compute this rate later in the chapter.

Most bonds trade in a dealership market. Bond dealers, usually in money center banks, quote buying and selling prices for daily transactions in bonds. Table 6.1 displays a selected listing of bonds available for purchase or sale. Let's go across the columns so you can learn how to read this table.

Column 1: Issuer. The first column shows the company, state, or country issuing the bond. The bonds have both a state issuer (the State of Kentucky) and several corporate issuers.

Column 2: Price. The second column shows the price as a percent of par value. It is the price someone is willing to pay for the bond in today's market. We quote the price in relation to $100. For example, the Goodyear bond is selling for

TABLE 6.1 **Bond Information, August 1, 2008**

Company or Government Agency	Price	Coupon Rate	Maturity Date	Yield to Maturity	Current Yield	Rating
Kentucky (State)	43.18	0.00%	10-1-2027	4.410%	0.000%	AAA
Merrill Lynch	109.13	6.50%	7-15-2018	5.300%	5.960%	AA
Coca-Cola	128.63	8.50%	2-1-2022	5.473%	6.548%	A
H.J. Heinz	103.19	6.375%	7-15-2028	6.100%	6.139%	BBB
Dillard Stores	99.50	7.75%	7-15-2026	7.799%	7.789%	BB
MGM Mirage	102.00	7.50%	6-1-2016	7.184%	7.353%	BB
Goodyear	90.50	7.00%	3-1-2028	7.321%	7.305%	B
Toys R Us	91.75	7.625%	8-1-2011	10.248%	8.311%	CCC

90.50% of its par value, or $90.50 per $100 of par value. If this bond has a $1,000 par value, it would sell for $905.00 ($1,000 × 90.50%). Throughout this chapter, we use $1,000 as the par value of a bond because it is the most common par value for corporate bonds.

Column 3: Coupon Rate. The third column states the coupon rate—the annual interest rate—of each bond.

Column 4: Maturity Date. The fourth column shows the maturity date of the issue, the date on which the corporation pays the final interest installment and repays the principal.

Column 5: Yield to Maturity. The fifth column indicates the bonds' yield to maturity: the yield or investment return that you would receive if you purchased the bond today at the price listed in Column 2 and if you held the bond to maturity. For us, it will be the discount rate in the bond pricing formula.

Column 6: Current Yield. The sixth column lists the bonds' current yields. The **current yield** is the annual coupon payment divided by the current price. Because current yield is not always an accurate indicator in all cases, we will not explore it in this chapter.

Column 7: Rating. The seventh column gives the bond rating, a grade indicating credit quality.

As we progress through this chapter, we will examine the price, coupon rate, yield, and bond ratings in more detail. First, we will put the time value of money tools to work as we examine how to calculate the value of a bond's promised future cash flows.

Pricing a Bond in Steps

Why do we want to learn how to price a bond? The answer really goes to the heart of finance: the valuation of assets. We need to ascertain what a given bond is worth to a willing buyer and a willing seller. What is its value to these interested parties? Remember that a bond is a financial asset that a company sells to raise money from willing investors. Whether you are the company selling the bond or the investor buying the bond, you want to make sure that you are selling or buying at the best available price.

FIGURE 6.1 Merrill Lynch corporate bond.

Merrill Lynch As of 15-Jul-2008

OVERVIEW

Price (% of par):	109.13
Coupon rate:	6.50%
Maturity date:	15-Jul-2018
Yield to maturity:	5.30%
Current yield:	5.96%
Fitch ratings:	AA
Coupon payment frequency:	Annual
First coupon date:	15-Jul-2009
Type:	Corporate
Callable:	No

Let's begin our pricing with the Merrill Lynch corporate bond listing in Table 6.1. Figure 6.1 shows the facts concerning this bond. What does this information tell us? First, it tells us that Merrill Lynch issued a corporate bond that promised to pay a coupon annually on July 15 and pay back the principal or par value on the maturity date, July 15, 2018. This particular bond was a ten-year corporate bond, so it was issued on July 15, 2008. Second, it provides the annual coupon rate of 6.5%, which indicates the annual interest payment on the bond. The discount rate on these future payments is the yield to bond maturity, 5.30%. Finally, it tells us some of the bond's features. For example Fitch, Inc.—an international ratings agency—rates Merrill Lynch AA (very high credit quality), and the bonds are not callable, meaning that the issuer cannot redeem the bond before its maturity date.

We can price a bond using the same methods from earlier chapters: using an equation, a calculator, and a spreadsheet. Let's start with the equation method.

Method 1: Using an equation Let's now proceed through the four main steps in pricing a bond. You may want to refer to Figure 6.2 as you read through the discussion.

Step 1 is to *lay out the timing and amount of the future cash flows.* The first future cash flow we need to determine is the annual interest payment. Here it is the coupon rate of 6.5% times the par value of the bond. We will use $1,000 as the par value of this bond:

$$\text{annual coupon or interest payment} = \$1{,}000 \times 0.065 = \$65.00$$

FIGURE 6.2 How to price a bond.

1. Lay out the timing and amount of future cash flow promised.
2. Determine the appropriate discount rate for the cash flow.
3. Find the present value of the lump-sum principal and the annuity stream of coupons.
4. Add the present value of the lump-sum principal and the present value of the coupons.

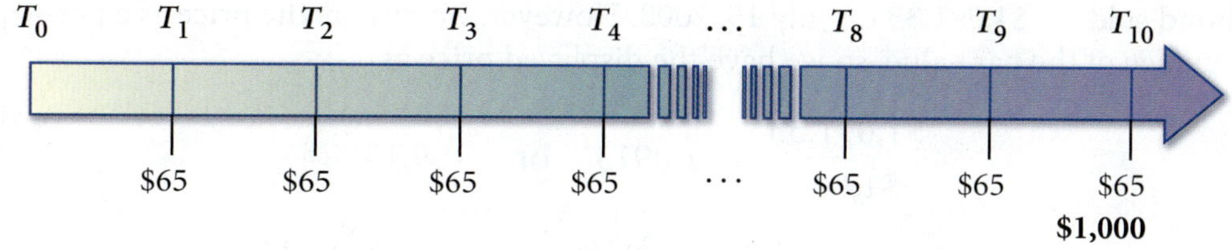

FIGURE 6.3 Future cash flow of a Merrill Lynch bond.

The second future cash flow that we need is the payment of the par value or principal—in this case, the $1,000 par value of the bond—at the maturity date of July 15, 2018. Recall from Chapter 4 that this payment is one method of paying back a loan: interest as you go and principal repaid at maturity.

We can set out the future cash flow as Figure 6.3 shows. Note that in the time line, T_0 represents the original issue date of July 15, 2008, and T_1 is the first annual coupon payment date of July 15, 2009. The annual payments continue for ten years, with T_{10} being the last payment on July 15, 2018. This point is a moment of recognition in which we can apply previously learned concepts: the coupon payments constitute an annuity stream, the same amount at regular intervals. The principal or par value of $1,000 also pays out at maturity. Here we recognize another key concept: the final amount is a lump-sum payment. So, we now have the promised set of future cash flows for the Merrill Lynch bond.

Step 2 is to *determine the appropriate discount rate for this cash flow.* We will jump to the answer now and use the yield of 5.30% from the bond data in Table 6.1. Later, we will develop the concepts behind an appropriate discount rate.

For Step 3, we now apply two of the time value of money equations to *find the present value of the cash flow.* Because we know that the coupon payments constitute an annuity stream, we can use the equation for the present value of an annuity from Chapter 4. To value the par value, we use the equation for the present value of a lump sum payment from Chapter 3. So,

$$\text{Present value of coupon stream} = PMT \times \frac{1 - \dfrac{1}{(1 + r)^n}}{r}$$

$$\text{Present value of this coupon stream} = \$65 \times \frac{1 - \dfrac{1}{(1 + 0.053)^{10}}}{0.053}$$

$$\text{Present value of this coupon stream} = \$65 \times 7.6105 = \$494.68$$

$$\text{Present value of par value} = FV \times \frac{1}{(1 + r)^n}$$

$$\text{Present value of this par value} = \$1{,}000 \times \frac{1}{(1 + 0.053)^{10}}$$

$$\text{Present value of this par value} = \$1{,}000 \times 0.5966 = \$596.65$$

Step 4 is to *add these two present values to get the price or value of the bond:*

$$\text{bond price} = \$494.68 + \$596.65 = \$1{,}091.33$$

This bond price is the value of the financial asset to a willing buyer and willing seller. In this example, the willing seller is Merrill Lynch. The willing buyer is an investor who is demanding a 5.30% yield on the investment. The Merrill Lynch bond sold for $1,091.33 on July 15, 2008. However, we display the price as a percentage of the par value, so we have the displayed price as

$$\frac{\$1{,}091.33}{\$1{,}000} = 1.0913 \quad \text{or} \quad 109.13\%$$

Because we round the percent of par to the nearest one hundredth, we do not see the cents digit in the quoted price.

In general, the price of a bond is the two cash flow components (the annuity coupon payments and the par value) discounted at

$$\text{bond price} = \text{par value} \times \frac{1}{(1+r)^n} + \text{coupon} \times \frac{1 - \frac{1}{(1+r)^n}}{r} \qquad \textbf{6.1}$$

Of course, we can also use a spreadsheet or calculator to find the bond's price.

Method 2: Using a calculator

Mode: P/Y = 1 and C/Y = 1

Input	10	5.3	?	65.00	1,000
Key	N	I/Y	PV	PMT	FV
CPT			−1,091.33		

Method 3: Using a spreadsheet This method requires you to use the PV function to calculate the present value of the annuity stream and par value (like Method 2 on the calculator). The spreadsheet input for annuity stream and principal is as follows:

B6 | *fx* =PV(B1,B2,B3,B4,B5)

Use the present value function for pricing a bond.

	A	B	C	D	E
1	Rate	0.053			
2	Nper	10.00			
3	Pmt	$ 65.00			
4	Fv	$ 1,000.00			
5	Type	0			
6	Pv	($1,091.33)			

Again, the negative price for the calculator and spreadsheet implies an initial cash outflow for the buyer, with cash inflow in the future.

All three methods lead to the same price if you use the appropriate inputs and settings. The key is that you need to calculate the coupon payment properly, use the correct number of coupon payments, and include the appropriate discount rate in all three methods. Thus, the bond's price is its discounted promised future cash flows.

6.2 Semiannual Bonds and Zero-Coupon Bonds

Our first pricing example had annual coupon payments, but that is rarely the case. Nearly all corporate and government bonds pay coupons on a semiannual basis. Let's look now at the Coca-Cola bond in Figure 6.4 and see how the semiannual feature affects the cash flows, the values that we use in the bond pricing equation, and thus the bond's price.

Coca-Cola Enterprises — As of 1-Aug-2008

OVERVIEW

Price (% of par):	128.63
Coupon rate:	8.50%
Maturity date:	1-Feb-2022
Yield to maturity:	5.473%
Current yield:	6.548%
Fitch ratings:	A
Coupon payment frequency:	Semiannual
First coupon date:	1-Aug-1992
Type:	Corporate
Callable:	No

FIGURE 6.4 Coca-Cola semiannual corporate bond.

Unlike the Merrill Lynch bond, Coca-Cola issued its bond many years ago. The price of 128.63% reflects the 2008 trading price of the Coca-Cola bond. We will go back to the original issue date of the Coca-Cola bond, which was February 1, 1992 (six months prior to the first coupon date of August 1, 1992), to find the original issue price. We will use some of the data from the current bond description, but will have to pick the appropriate yield to maturity at the original issue date. Again we start with the coupon payments. The coupon rate for Coca-Cola's bond is 8.5%, but coupon payments are semiannual, or two payments per year. To calculate the coupon payments, take the par value multiplied by the coupon rate and then divided by the number of payments per year:

$$\frac{\$1{,}000 \times 0.085}{2} = \$42.50$$

So we have two payments every six months of \$42.50 or an annual total of \$85.00 for the Coca-Cola bond.

Again, with a par value of \$1,000, we can display the cash flow on a time line as Figure 6.5 depicts.

Here, T_0 is the original issue date of February 1, 1992, and T_1 is the first semiannual coupon payment date of August 1, 1992. The second coupon payment is T_2 on February 1, 1993. Coupon payments will occur every August 1 and February 1 over the thirty years, with the last payment at maturity on February 1, 2022, T_{60}. The bond pays out the principal or par value of \$1,000 at maturity. We now have the promised set of future cash flows for the Coca-Cola bond.

Recall that we worked with periodic interest rates and payment periods of less than one year apart (semiannual, quarterly, monthly, and daily) in Chapter 5. We can now use this concept to price the future cash flow of this semiannual bond accurately. When this bond first sold, it had a yield to maturity of 8.8% stated on an annual basis. We will use this yield to maturity for pricing the bond. The coupon payments are every six months, however, so we need a six-month interest

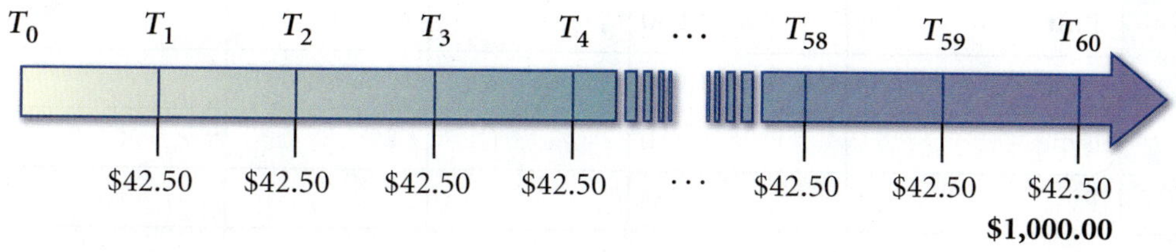

FIGURE 6.5 Future cash flow of the Coca-Cola bond.

or discount rate to price these semiannual cash flows. The bond pricing equation uses the six-month rate for discounting the cash flows of the bond:

$$\frac{0.088}{2} = 0.044 \quad \text{or} \quad 4.4\%$$

This 4.4% is the discount rate r in the equation. In addition, we must count the total number of payments: the number of payments per year times the number of years is 2 × 30, or sixty payments for n in the equation. So, when we look at the bond pricing equation (Eq. 6.1), we use 4.4% for r and 60 for n to price the Coca-Cola semiannual bond at original issue:

$$\text{bond price} = \text{par value} \times \frac{1}{(1+r)^n} + \text{coupon} \times \frac{1 - \frac{1}{(1+r)^n}}{r}$$

$$= \$1{,}000 \times \frac{1}{(1+0.044)^{60}} + \$42.50 \times \frac{1 - \frac{1}{(1+0.044)^{60}}}{0.044}$$

$$= \$1{,}000 \times 0.0755 + \$42.50 \times 21.0113$$

$$= \$75.50 + \$892.98 = \$968.48$$

At original issue, the Coca-Cola bond sold for $968.48, or 96.85% of par value. We can also use a spreadsheet or calculator to find the price of this bond.

Method 2: Using a calculator Again, we must set the calculator to the proper payment periods by setting P/Y and C/Y to 2 for the semiannual payments. The interest rate is the annual rate of 8.8%.

Mode: P/Y = 2 and C/Y = 2

Input	60	8.8	?	42.50	1,000
Key	N	I/Y	PV	PMT	FV
CPT			−968.48		

Method 3: Using a spreadsheet We note again that the spreadsheet wants the periodic rate of 4.4%, not the annual yield to maturity rate of 8.8%.

B6 | *fx* =PV(B1,B2,B3,B4,B5)

Use the present value function for pricing a bond with the rate set at the semiannual interest rate.

	A	B	C	D	E
1	Rate	0.044			
2	Nper	60			
3	Pmt	$ 42.50			
4	Fv	$ 1,000			
5	Type	0			
6	Pv	($968.48)			

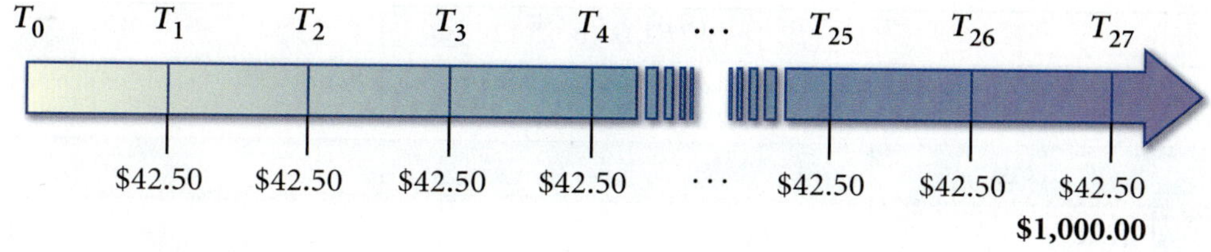

FIGURE 6.6 Remaining cash flow of the Coca-Cola bond.

Pricing Bonds after Original Issue

The price displayed in the Coca-Cola bond data is 128.63%, but this price reflects the price on August 1, 2008. Bond owners can sell their bonds prior to maturity dates to a willing buyer. The new owner will receive the remaining coupon payments and the final principal payment. If we stop in time at August 1, 2008, for the Coca-Cola bond, we can price the remaining coupons and principal using the yield to maturity on August 1, 2008, for the bond as the annual discount rate. Looking back at the data on Coca-Cola, we see a yield to maturity of 5.473% on August 1, 2008. We determine the remaining coupon payments (assume that the issuer has just paid the current bond owner the August 1, 2008, payment, so the first coupon payment to the new owner will be in six months). Therefore, there are twenty-seven coupon payments between now and February 1, 2022. With T_0 as August 1, 2008, and T_{27} as February 1, 2022, the time line in Figure 6.6 shows the remaining cash flows.

Method 1: Using an equation The semiannual discount rate for the bond pricing equation is the current yield divided by 2, or $0.05473/2 = 0.027365$. Therefore, using Equation 6.1, the current bond price is

$$\text{bond price} = \$1{,}000 \times \frac{1}{(1 + 0.027365)^{27}} + \$42.50 \times \frac{1 - \dfrac{1}{(1 + 0.027365)^{27}}}{0.027365}$$

$$= \$1{,}000 \times 0.48243 + \$42.50 \times 18.91369$$

$$= \$482.43 + \$803.83 = \mathbf{\$1{,}286.26}$$

We can also use a spreadsheet or calculator to find the price of a bond quickly and efficiently.

Method 2: Using a calculator

Mode: P/Y = 2 and C/Y = 2

Input	27	5.473	?	42.50	1,000
Key	N	I/Y	PV	PMT	FV
CPT			−1,286.26		

Method 3: Using a spreadsheet This method requires you to use the PV function to calculate the present value of the annuity stream and par value (like Method 2 on the calculator). The spreadsheet input for annuity stream and principal is

B6		*fx* =PV(B1,B2,B3,B4,B5)			
	Use the present value function for pricing a bond with the rate set at the semiannual interest rate.				
	A	B	C	D	E
1	Rate	0.027364			
2	Nper	27			
3	Pmt	$ 42.50			
4	Fv	$ 1,000			
5	Type	0			
6	Pv	($1,286.26)			

We can now see that a bond price is simply the present value of the promised or remaining future cash flows discounted at the yield to maturity.

Zero-Coupon Bonds

In 1981, PepsiCo introduced the first **zero-coupon bond,** and it was exactly as the name indicates: a bond that paid zero coupons. The only payment that bondholders would receive would be the par value at the maturity date. So, why buy these bonds? The answer is that issuers price zero-coupon bonds at a deep discount; therefore, the rise in price over time provides an appropriate return on the bond.

How do we price such bonds? The convention is to use the semiannual pricing formula and calculate the present value of the principal or par value, a lump-sum payment:

$$\text{zero-coupon bond price} = \text{par value} \times \frac{1}{(1 + r)^n} \qquad \textbf{6.2}$$

where n is the number of six-month periods until maturity (n = years to maturity × 2) and r is the six-month discount rate or yield on the bond divided by 2 (r = yield/2). After PepsiCo introduced this type of bond, many other companies followed its example, and now there are many firms with zero-coupon bonds. Probably more interesting, though, is that as investors, we may purchase many U.S. government bonds as zero-coupon bonds. These bonds are U.S. Government **STRIPS** (*S*eparate *T*rading of *R*egistered *I*nterest and *P*rincipal), which are fixed-income securities that sell at a significant discount to face value and offer no interest payments because they mature at par. The lowest coupon rate a firm or government can assign to a bond is zero.

EXAMPLE 6.1 Zero-coupon bond

Problem The State of Kentucky issued a zero-coupon bond with a par value of $1,000 that matures on October 1, 2027. Let's assume that it is now October 1, 2007, the original issue date of this zero-coupon bond. We will assume that the original issue of the bond had a yield to maturity of 4.3% stated annually. What was the bond's original issue price?

Solution Remember that it is customary to price these bonds as semiannual bonds. So, we will count the number of periods as the number of six-month periods to maturity. Here we have twenty years or forty six-month periods until maturity.

METHOD 1 Using an equation

The yield is 4.3%, so the semiannual discount rate is $0.043/2 = 0.0215$ or 2.15%:

$$\text{bond price} = \$1{,}000 \times \frac{1}{(1 + 0.0215)^{40}} = \$1{,}000 \times 0.4270 = \mathbf{\$427.04}$$

When we look at Table 6.1, we see that the price of the State of Kentucky bond is 43.18%, or $431.80. If we use the stated yield of 4.410% and price it from August 1, 2008, the current date of the table, we have 38.5 semiannual periods left for the bond. We would therefore have

$$\text{bond price} = \$1{,}000 \times \frac{1}{(1 + 0.02205)^{38.5}} = \$1{,}000 \times 0.43184 = \mathbf{\$431.84}$$

We can also use a calculator or spreadsheet to find the price of this bond.

METHOD 2: Using a calculator

Mode: P/Y = 2 and C/Y = 2

Input	38.5	4.410	?	0.00	1,000
Key	N	I/Y	PV	PMT	FV
CPT			−431.84		

METHOD 3: Using a spreadsheet

B6 | *fx* | =PV(B1,B2,B3,B4,B5)

Use the present value function for pricing a bond with the Rate set at the semiannual interest rate and with Nper as the number of semiannual periods.

	A	B	C	D	E
1	Rate	0.02205			
2	Nper	38.5			
3	Pmt	0			
4	Fv	$1,000.00			
5	Type	0			
6	Pv	($ 431.84)			

In Example 6.1, the price of this zero-coupon bond reflects a deep discount from its face value. The difference between the issue price, $427.04, and the par value repayment to the bondholder at maturity, $1,000, reflects the accumulated interest of $572.96 over the twenty years. The current bond owner receives $572.96 interest at maturity, but it is annually accrued interest on a zero-coupon bond for tax purposes. So, how much interest do you earn each year? We can use an amortization schedule to determine the amount.

Amortization of a Zero-Coupon Bond

First, let's look at a short-term zero-coupon bond to minimize the exercise. Assume that we have a three-year zero-coupon bond that has a yield of 8% and a par value of $1,000. We first need to find its price at issue and then to determine the price every six months. We will use the semiannual convention here. The difference in price each period is the implied interest each six months. We will use Method 2 and will start with N = 6 in the calculator for the six remaining time periods until maturity; then we will just change N by one each period (5, 4, 3, 2, 1, 0) to find the next prices:

Mode: P/Y = 2 and C/Y = 2

Input	6	8.0	?	0.00	1,000
Key	N	I/Y	PV	PMT	FV
CPT			**−790.31**		

The difference in the price at issue ($790.31) and the par value ($1,000) is the total interest earned over the three years, $209.69. Now, input the following with $N = 5$ for the next price after six months:

Input	5	8.0	?	0.00	1,000
Key	N	I/Y	PV	PMT	FV
CPT			**−821.93**		

Table 6.2 shows the answers. We first calculate the price for each period as we reduce N (remaining time periods). In addition, we will amortize the bond each period by multiplying the price at the beginning of the period times the periodic interest rate (8%/2, or 4%) and adding the interest to the price to get the price at the end of the period. You can think of the beginning price as the price at the start of the period and the price at the end of the period as the beginning price plus earned interest for that period. So, for Period 1, we have the price at the beginning of period one (price at issue) as $790.31 and the interest earned for the period as $31.62. Thus, the price at the end of the period is $821.93. The change in price

TABLE 6.2 Amortized Interest on a Zero-Coupon Bond

T (Periods)	Calculator Price	Change in Price	Beginning Price	Interest Earned	Ending Price
0	$ 790.31				
1	$ 821.93	$ 31.62	$790.31	$790.31 × 0.04 = $31.62	$ 821.93
2	$ 854.80	$ 32.88	$821.93	$821.93 × 0.04 = $32.88	$ 854.80
3	$ 889.00	$ 34.19	$854.80	$854.80 × 0.04 = $34.19	$ 889.00
4	$ 924.56	$ 35.56	$889.00	$889.00 × 0.04 = $35.56	$ 924.56
5	$ 961.54	$ 36.98	$924.56	$924.56 × 0.04 = $36.98	$ 961.54
6	$1,000.00	$ 38.46	$961.54	$961.54 × 0.04 = $38.46	$1,000.00
Total		$209.69			

Note: Prices and interest rounded to nearest whole cent.

each period is the implied or earned interest, but it does not pay until maturity. So, we amortize the interest each period.

The change in price each period reflects the earned interest on the zero-coupon bond. You should also notice that the earned interest grows each period, another example of the compounding of interest over time. Why is it important to understand this implied earned interest each period? If you buy a zero-coupon bond, the government will tax you on the earned interest even though you did not receive an actual coupon payment.

6.3 Yields and Coupon Rates

The two "interest rates" that we associate with a bond are often confusing to students when they first begin to work with bonds. The coupon rate is the interest rate printed on the bond; we use it only to determine the coupon payments. The yield to maturity is an interest rate that we use to discount the bond's future cash flow. We derived it from the marketplace, based on the riskiness of the cash flow. As we have seen when pricing bonds, the bond's yield is the rate of return that the bondholder will receive at the current price if the investor holds the bond to maturity. The common name for this rate is **yield to maturity**.

The First Interest Rate: Yield to Maturity

As just noted, the market sets this discount rate, the yield to maturity. The yield reflects the going rate in the bond market for this type of bond and the bond issuer's perceived ability to make these future payments. Hence, we base the yield on a mutually agreeable price between seller and buyer. The bond market determines the yield and the available supply of competing financial assets. By competing against other available financial assets, the rate or yield reflects the risk-free rate and inflation, plus such premiums as maturity and default specific to the issued bond. The yield is the expected return rate on the bond held to maturity.

How do we determine the bond's yield? We can use our same three methods.

Method 1: Using an equation The solution, as in Chapter 4 when solving for discount rates, requires us to revisit the bond pricing formula, Equation 6.1:

$$\text{bond price} = \text{par value} \times \frac{1}{(1+r)^n} + \text{coupon} \times \frac{1 - \dfrac{1}{(1+r)^n}}{r}$$

Of course, with one equation we can solve for only one unknown, and here the variable of concern is r. Unfortunately, we cannot isolate r on the left-hand side of the equation. Therefore, we return to a calculator or spreadsheet to solve the bond's yield to maturity.

Let's take another bond—the Goodyear bond—from Table 6.1 and again back up our time to the original issue date of March 1, 2008. The bond is a twenty-year semiannual bond with a coupon rate of 7.0% and an original price of \$905.00 at issue (Fig. 6.7). What was the bond's yield to maturity at its issue date?

We'll start by filling in the values we have on this bond: \$1,000 par value, forty payments (n = twenty years × two payments per year), and \$35 coupon per period (coupon = \$1,000 × 0.07/2 = \$35). If the bond's selling price was \$905 at issue, what was the bond's yield to maturity at issue?

Method 2: Using a calculator

Mode: P/Y = 2 and C/Y = 2

Input	40	?	−905	35	1,000
Key	N	I/Y	PV	PMT	FV
CPT		7.96			

Method 3: Using a spreadsheet Now the 0.0398 is the six-month periodic rate, so we need to annualize this rate by multiplying it by the compounding periods (2) to get the yield to maturity of 7.96% at issue.

B6 | *fx* | =RATE(B1,B2,B3,B4,B5)

Use the rate function to find the periodic interest rate on semiannual yield for the bond.

	A	B	C	D	E
1	Nper	40			
2	Pmt	$ 35.00			
3	Pv	($ 905)			
4	Fv	$1,000.00			
5	Type	0			
6	Rate	3.98%			

Using the calculator is fast and accurate for finding bond yields. The spreadsheet approach uses the Rate function and gives the six-month rate as well. Thus, if you know the bond's current price and the future cash flow, you can find the yield to maturity or the return rate that the bond buyer is receiving on the loaned funds to the bond issuer.

FIGURE 6.7 Goodyear semiannual corporate bond.

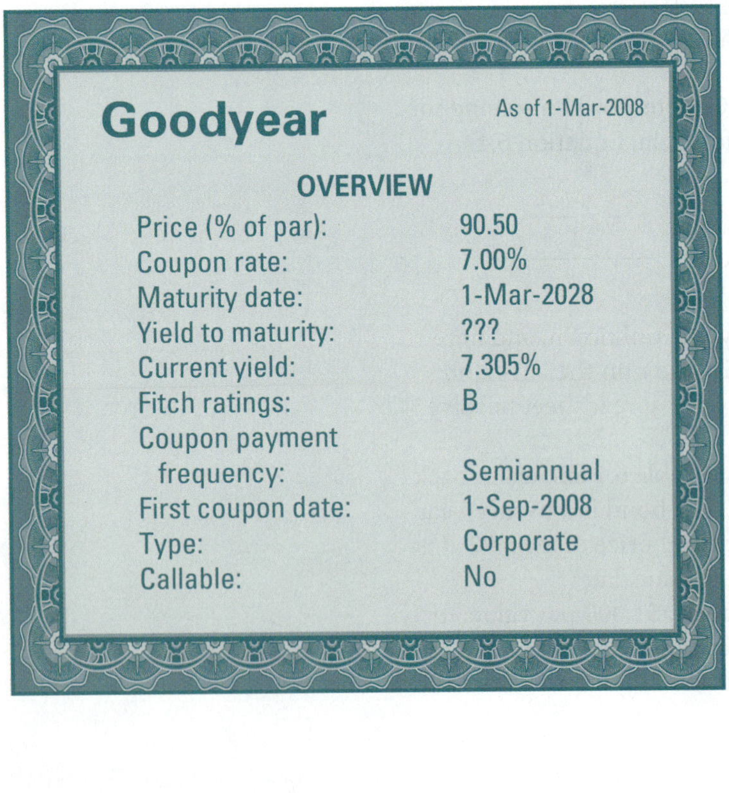

The "Other" Interest Rate: Coupon Rate

The coupon rate is the rate that we use to determine the coupon payments. The issuer states the rate as an annual rate, even though payments may be more frequent. Thus, for semiannual bonds, the most common type of corporate and government bond, the coupon payment is the par value of the bond multiplied by the annual coupon rate and then divided by the number of payments per year, or 2.

We have already seen the coupon rate. The first bond we looked at, the Merrill Lynch bond, was an annual coupon bond with a coupon rate of 6.5%.

Using a par value of $1,000, we determined that the coupon payments would be

$$\text{annual coupon payment} = \$1{,}000 \times 0.065 = \$65.00$$

For the Coca-Cola bond, we noted that it had a coupon rate of 8.5% but it paid semiannually. Using a par value of $1,000, we determined that the coupon payments would be

$$\text{semiannual coupon payment} = \frac{\$1{,}000 \times 0.085}{2} = \$42.50$$

Relationship of Yield to Maturity and Coupon Rate

The price of the bond has a direct relationship with these two interest rates:

1. When the coupon rate is less than the yield to maturity, the bond sells for a discount against its par value. That is, the price of the bond is less than the par value. We call this kind of bond a **discount bond.**
2. When the coupon rate is more than the yield to maturity, the bond sells for a premium above its par value. We call this kind of bond a **premium bond**.
3. When the yield to maturity and coupon rate are the same, the bond sells for its par value. We call this kind of bond a **par value bond.**

Table 6.3 summarizes these relationships.

Why does the relationship that Table 6.3 shows between the yield to maturity and coupon rate produce a bond selling at a premium or a discount? The coupon rate establishes the size of the interest payment on the bond. If the bond market currently requires a rate (yield) less than the coupon rate, bidders will pay a premium to get a bond with a high coupon rate, upping the price above the par value. However, when the market demands a higher yield than the coupon rate, the market will discount the bond price below the par value, thereby raising the yield above the coupon rate.

This relationship is helpful when we realize that interest rates change over time and the prices of bonds change in response to interest rates. When interest rates go up, bond prices fall. When interest rates go down, bond prices rise. Figure 6.8 shows this relationship. So, bond investors are not always thrilled by good economic news. They know that when interest rates are rising, signaling inflation, their bond investments are worth less. We label bonds with very low coupon rates as deep-discount bonds. Of course, the bond that has the greatest discount is the

TABLE 6.3 Premium Bonds, Discount Bonds, and Par Value Bonds

Type of Bond	Coupon Rate versus Yield to Maturity	Price Relationship to Par Value
Premium bond	Coupon rate > yield to maturity	Price > par value
Par value bond	Coupon rate = yield to maturity	Price = par value
Discount bond	Coupon rate < yield to maturity	Price < par value

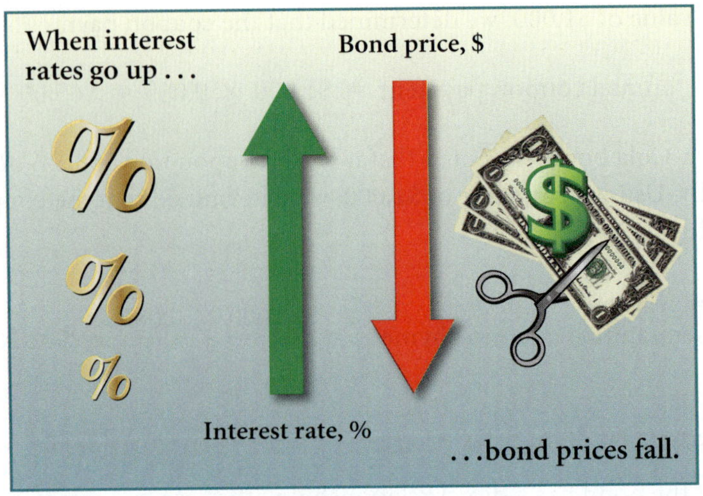

FIGURE 6.8 Bond prices and interest rates move in opposite directions.

zero-coupon bond, with a coupon rate of zero. The smaller the coupon rate, the greater we will see a change in price when interest rates move.

6.4 Bond Ratings

Suppose we want to know the appropriate discount rate or yield for a bond. The yield to maturity of one bond may be quite different from the yield to maturity of another, much like the different rates of return that we examined in Chapter 5 for different financial assets such as Treasury bills, government bonds, and corporate bonds. As we can see from Table 6.1, bonds have different yields based on different issuers. How can we be sure that we have the right yield for each issuer? We turn to bond rating agencies for their expertise.

Bond rating agencies help assess the default premium for an individual bond issue and hence establish a yield for the bond. The most famous rating agencies are Moody's, Standard & Poor's, and Fitch. These agencies produce bond ratings that help investors assess the likelihood of default. Table 6.4 lists the categories and rating classifications. The top rating is Aaa or AAA, which signifies that the company or government issuing the bond should have no trouble making the promised bond payments. As you move down the chart to each new rating category, the probability of default increases. Standard & Poor's places a D rating on a bond that has missed a scheduled payment, implying that the bond is technically in default.

We call speculative bonds with a rating below Baa3 or BBB– **junk bonds**. These bonds have a perceived higher default risk. Today, though, the term *speculative grade* seems more appropriate because issuers pay off many of these bonds on schedule.

Why have these ratings? There are two main reasons. First, many investors do not have the resources, time, talent, or access to information to assess the creditworthiness of a new bond issue properly. These agencies provide potential investors with reliable information about potential default. Second, each company issuing a new bond usually seeks a credit rating to signal to the market that it has the financial stability to meet the bond payment obligations. The rating agencies help the company market the bond by providing a rating so that potential investors can establish a reasonable yield for the new bond.

Recall that in Chapter 5 we introduced the default premium as one of the components of the nominal interest rate. Table 6.5 shows the nominal interest

TABLE 6.4 Bond Ratings

	Rating Company		
Credit Description	**Fitch**	**Moody's**	**Standard & Poor's**
Investment Grade Bonds			
Highest Credit Rating	AAA	Aaa	AAA
	AA+	Aa1	AA+
High Credit	AA	Aa2	AA
	AA−	Aa3	AA−
	A+	A1	A+
Upper Medium Credit	A	A2	A
	A−	A3	A−
	BBB+	Baa1	BBB+
Lower Medium Credit	BBB	Baa2	BBB
	BBB−	Baa3	BBB−
Speculative-Grade Bonds (Junk Bonds)			
Low Credit	BB+	Ba1	BB+
	BB	Ba2	BB
	BB−	Ba3	BB−
Very Low Credit	B+	B1	B+
	B	B2	B
	B−	B3	B−
Extremely Speculative Bonds			
Extremely Low Credit	CCC+	Caa	CCC+
	CCC		CCC
	CCC−		CCC−
Extremely Speculative	CC	Ca	CC
	C	C	C
Bonds in Default			D

rates for twenty-year bonds from 1980 to 2006 based on their bond rating. The difference between the ratings is the additional default premium. The highest rated bonds, AAA bonds, have the lowest probability of default and therefore the lowest yields. As the ratings go down, the yield goes up, reflecting a higher probability of default. For example, on average, the Aa bond is 31 basis points higher than the Aaa bond. A **basis point** is one-hundredth of a percentage point, or we can say that 100 basis points equal 1% (1 basis point = 0.01%, 100 basis points = 1.0%). In Table 6.5, the spread between the Aa and A is 33 basis points, and the average spread between the A and Baa is 46 basis points.

TABLE 6.5 Annual Interest Rates on Corporate Bonds Rated Aaa to Baa, 1980 to 2006

Year	Aaa	Aa	A	Baa
1980	11.9%	12.5%	12.9%	13.7%
1981	14.2%	14.7%	15.3%	16.0%
1982	13.8%	14.4%	15.4%	16.1%
1983	12.0%	12.4%	13.1%	13.6%
1984	12.7%	13.3%	13.7%	14.2%
1985	11.4%	11.8%	12.3%	12.7%
1986	9.0%	9.5%	9.9%	10.4%
1987	9.4%	9.7%	10.0%	10.6%
1988	9.7%	9.9%	10.2%	10.8%
1989	9.3%	9.5%	9.7%	10.2%
1990	9.3%	9.6%	9.8%	10.4%
1991	8.8%	9.1%	9.3%	9.8%
1992	8.1%	8.5%	8.8%	9.0%
1993	7.2%	7.4%	7.6%	7.9%
1994	8.0%	8.1%	8.3%	8.6%
1995	7.6%	7.7%	7.8%	8.2%
1996	7.4%	7.5%	7.7%	8.1%
1997	7.3%	7.5%	7.5%	7.9%
1998	6.5%	6.8%	6.9%	7.2%
1999	7.0%	7.3%	7.5%	7.9%
2000	7.6%	7.8%	8.1%	8.4%
2001	7.1%	7.3%	7.7%	8.0%
2002	6.5%	6.9%	7.2%	7.8%
2003	5.7%	6.1%	6.4%	6.8%
2004	5.6%	5.9%	6.1%	6.4%
2005	5.2%	5.4%	5.6%	6.1%
2006	5.7%	5.9%	6.1%	6.5%
Average	**8.67%**	**8.98%**	**9.29%**	**9.75%**
Highest	14.2%	14.7%	15.4%	16.1%
Lowest	5.2%	5.4%	5.6%	6.1%

Source: Moody's Corporate Bond Yields (www.sifma.net).

As you look through Table 6.5, you will see that in 1992 that an A-rated bond would have had a yield to maturity of around 8.8%. We used this rate when we priced the A-rated Coca-Cola bond at its original issue in the first part of this chapter.

Each new issue receives a bond rating. Therefore, companies with multiple bond issues can have different ratings on each individual issue.

Bond ratings on a particular issue can change through time if a company's financial conditions change. For example, bonds that were originally issued at investment grade (rating of Baa3/BBB– or better) but analysts have subsequently downgraded to speculative bonds are known as **fallen angels**. It is not unusual for ratings to change in response not only to financial conditions within the company issuing the bond but also to the financial conditions within the company's industry. Moody's, for example, will "rerate" between 300 and 400 bonds per year if economic conditions change or if industries experience large economic changes. Downgrades are more common, but upgrades also happen.

Notice in Table 6.1 and the eight bonds listed there that, in general, the higher the rating, the lower the bonds' yield to maturity. Only the Dillard Store bond is out of line. It has a yield to maturity of nearly 7.8% and a rating of BB, whereas the other BB bond, MGM Mirage, is at 7.2% and the B-rated Goodyear bond is at 7.3%. So, Dillard Stores may be a candidate for a reduction in its rating. Although there will always be exceptions to the ratings and the corresponding yields, a higher bond rating usually means a lower yield.

6.5 Some Bond History and More Bond Features

Institutions originally issued bonds as **bearer bonds,** meaning that Whoever held the bond was entitled to the interest payments and the principal repayment. The bondholder would "clip" a coupon as the interest payment date arrived and present the coupon to the bond's trustee for payment. The trustee was typically a bank. After clipping the coupons, only the **corpus**, or body of the bond, remained. The bondholder presented the corpus to the trustee at maturity for repayment of the principal. Whenever one owner sold the bond to the next, the price was a reflection of the current yield and the remaining or unclipped coupons and bond principal. When the owner wished to sell the bond prior to maturity, the new potential owner could verify all remaining coupon payments and principal by examining the attached coupons and the corpus. As a result, these bonds earned the name *coupon bonds*.

One problem with bearer bonds is there is no registered owner's name printed on the bond, therefore a financial institution could pay interest and principal to anyone tendering a bond certificate, regardless of the true owner. To avoid problems with stolen bonds, companies started registering the owners and making coupon payments and principal repayment based on the list of registered owners. If an owner wanted to sell his or her bond before maturity, the holder would need to notify the company of the change in ownership for future coupon payments.

A second problem with bearer bonds is that the company might not be able to notify the bondholder of a significant event, such as calling in the bond prior to its maturity. With registered bonds, the company can communicate with bondholders because the company has the official list of owners.

Today, an **indenture** or **deed of trust**—a written contract between the bond issuer and the bondholder—specifies bond agreement details. Among other things, it spells out the terms of the bond, the number of bonds for issuance, a description of any collateral supporting the bond, any special repayment provisions or call options, and details of protective covenants. We now turn to a brief consideration of some of these important terms.

Collateral or **security of a bond** refers to the assets that support the bond, should the bond issuer fail to make the obligated coupon payments or principal repayment. Collateral can be physical assets such as company inventories, equipment, or real property. Collateral can also be financial assets such as common stock in the company. The use of physical assets to back loans is very common. For example, if you purchase a car and secure a loan through a bank to purchase the car, the bank requires that you place the car (title to the car) as collateral against the loan. The bank secures a lien against the title and retains this lien until you fully repay the loan. If you fail to make your monthly car payments, the bank can "repossess" the car as payment against the loan. If you faithfully make your car payments, however, the bank cannot "repossess" the car. The same is true of corporate bonds with assets pledged as security for the payment of interest and principal. As long as the company faithfully pays the coupon payments and principal on time, the bondholder has no entitlement to the collateral. If the company should default—that is, fail on its promised payments—the bondholder is entitled to possess the pledged collateral as payment for the bond. When you use real property as collateral, we call it a **mortgaged security**.

We call unsecured bonds **debentures**, which simply means that the bondholder has no recourse against specific assets of the issuing company, should the company fail on its promised payments. The majority of bonds issued in the United States today are debenture bonds.

When a company gets into financial difficulty and cannot pay its creditors, creditors line up in a predetermined order for repayment of their claims. Creditors at the front of the line are senior to creditors behind them in line. It is also true that companies can issue more than one set of bonds at different points in time. The oldest bonds are **senior debt** over the more recently issued **junior debt**, with the older bondholders entitled to coupon payments and principal repayment ahead of the younger bondholders.

The final principal payment of a bond issue can be a substantial cash outflow for a company. To meet this obligation, a company may have to build a fund over time to aid in the principal payment. We call this **sinking funds**. The company makes annual payments into the sinking fund, usually managed by a trustee, to ensure that the company can retire the bonds at maturity. A company can use sinking funds to buy back some of the bonds over time or to call in bonds early, or it can hold them until bond maturity. The specific details of the sinking fund are detailed in the indenture.

Within the indenture of the bond is a set of **protective covenants**. The covenants spell out both required and prohibited actions of the bond issuer. The covenants usually protect the bondholder against actions that the company might take that would diminish the value of the bond. For example, the indenture might state that the company may not sell or lease back assets that it uses as collateral for a bond. A sale and leaseback would effectively remove the collateral from the bond because the title for the collateral would transfer to a new owner, leaving the bondholder with no recourse to the promised collateral in case of default. In general, protective covenants protect the bondholder and enhance the value of the bond, thus helping the company sell the bond at a higher price.

Issuers may sell bonds with attached options. These options entitle either the bondholder or the company to specific future actions. One of the most common options is a call option. A **callable bond**, as we briefly mentioned earlier, allows the bond issuer to "call in" the bond prior to maturity at a predetermined price. A bond issuer exercises this option when interest rates are falling so that the institution can reissue the debt at a lower cost. Typically, the issuer cannot exercise the "call" in the first few years of the bond, and the call price is usually a premium over the par value. The size of the premium falls as the bond approaches its natural maturity date.

Let's look at a current callable bond for Pacific Bell (Fig. 6.9), which the company originally issued on October 15, 1993, as a callable bond with a forty-one-year maturity.

After twenty years, Pacific Bell can call the bond. In this instance, the bondholder must sell the bond to Pacific Bell at a preset price. The preset price at the first call date might be the principal of the bond plus one extra coupon payment. The bond could be called as early as October 15, 2013. How does one price this callable bond?

Pacific Bell As of 1-Aug-2008

OVERVIEW

Price (% of par):	103.96
Coupon rate:	6.625%
Maturity date:	15-Oct-2034
Yield to call:	6.277%
Current yield:	6.340%
Fitch ratings:	B
Coupon payment frequency:	Semiannual
First coupon date:	15-Apr-1994
Type:	Corporate
Callable:	Yes

FIGURE 6.9 Pacific Bell semiannual callable corporate bond.

The **yield to call** now replaces the yield to maturity as the discount rate for the bond. In Pacific Bell's case, it is 6.277%. The cash flow is the promised cash flow at the first call date. If Pacific Bell calls the bond on October 15, 2013, and pays the par value plus one extra interest payment, we can determine the cash flows, which the time line in Figure 6.10 illustrates. Again, the coupon payment is the coupon rate times the par value divided by 2 to reflect the semiannual payment of coupons:

$$\text{coupon} = \frac{\$1{,}000 \times 0.06625}{2} = \$33.125$$

As of today, August 1, 2008, there are eleven coupon payments and a final payment of the par value plus an extra interest payment. The bond is priced to this call date of October 15, 2013, and has a yield to call of 6.277%. We will use the calculator and spreadsheet methods to price this bond on October 15, 2013:

Mode: P/Y = 2 and C/Y = 2

Input	11	6.277	?	33.125	1,033.125
Key	N	I/Y	PV	PMT	FV
CPT			**−1,039.56**		

B6	*fx*	*=PV(B1,B2,B3,B4,B5)*			
Use the present value function to find the price of the bond.					
	A	B	C	D	E
1	Rate	0.031385			
2	Nper	11			
3	Pmt	$ 33.125			
4	Fv	$1,033.125			
5	Type	0			
6	Pv	($1,039.56)			

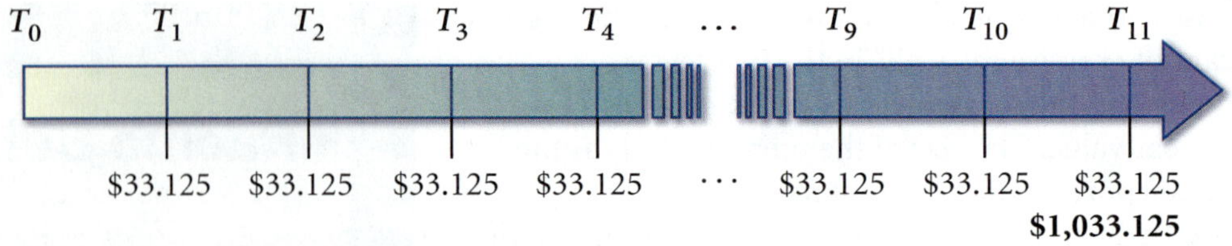

FIGURE 6.10 Pacific Bell callable bond cash flows.

The preset call price on a bond erodes as the callable bond approaches its maturity date. The extra premium for the early call will eventually fall to zero on October 15, 2034. So, pricing a callable bond is more difficult than pricing other bonds because the owner is not sure exactly when the issuer might call the bond, if at all. It is prudent to assume that the issuer will call the bond at the first available date and the bond's price will be the price at the first call date.

Two other options that the issuer might attach for the bondholder are put and conversion options. A **putable bond** gives the bondholder the right to sell the bond back to the company at a predetermined price prior to maturity. In effect, it is the reverse of a callable bond, and the bondholder would choose to exercise this right to sell when interest rates are rising. A **convertible bond** gives the bondholder the right to swap the bond for another asset. Common stock in the company is typical. A preset conversion ratio exists for the bond such that the bondholder will receive a stated number of shares of common stock for each bond one redeems.

These options are valuable and have an effect on the bond's price. If the company holds the option—a callable bond—the bond's price is lower than an otherwise equal bond without this call option attached. If the bondholder holds the option—a putable bond—the bond's price is higher than an otherwise equal bond without this option. Pricing putable or convertible bonds is beyond the scope of this textbook, but note that we add the put's price or conversion option to the straight bond price. An issuer cannot take away options from the option holder, but the bond issuer could force the bondholder to exercise the outstanding option. For example, if a bond is both callable by the bond issuer and convertible by the bondholder, the issuer could call in the bond and force the bondholder to either sell the bond at the call price or convert to common shares.

Although we have dealt only with fixed coupon rates, one feature that can change is the bond's coupon rate. If we allow this rate to change over time, the bond becomes a **floating-rate bond**. A floating-rate bond's annual interest rate adjusts based on a benchmark rate such as the **prime rate**. The prime rate is the rate at which banks charge their best customers for money. When the prime rate increases, the bond's coupon rate and payment also increase. When the prime rate falls, the coupon rate and the bond's coupon payment also fall.

We can also tie the payment schedule and coupon amount to a company's income. We call these types of bonds **income bonds**. Income bonds pay coupons based on the company's income. During periods of low income, the company reduces or eliminates coupon payments, which reduces the probability of default on an income bond, but also reduces its attractiveness.

The more creative the issuer gets with the bond's features, the more exotic the bond. In general, **exotic bonds** are bonds with special features distinct to that particular bond. As the issuer gets more creative, however, the more difficult it is to price the bond and the harder it is to sell it. With these special features, the bond attracts fewer potential buyers and is less liquid. For example, you could buy a bond in one currency, U.S. dollars, but receive your coupons and principal in euros.

You may not be an expert in bonds yet, but you should now be proficient at pricing standard bonds with their promised set of future cash payments. We will leave these creative features of bonds for another finance class.

PUTTING FINANCE TO WORK

Municipal Manager

Whether you hail from a big city or a small town, you know that the financing of large capital projects is important to the smooth running of the community. There are schools, police stations, and libraries to renovate or build. The upkeep of water supplies and sewer systems and road paving and repair can carry steep price tags. Current tax revenues cannot finance these items, and the availability of grants from state or federal governments is unpredictable.

Enter the municipal manager, whose job is not unlike that of a corporate CFO. Among their many financial responsibilities, these managers need to raise funds, and one of the chief ways they do it is to sell bonds.

Fortunately, municipalities have relatively easy access to capital markets. They cannot sell stock, of course, but even small and medium-size communities have better access to the bond markets than similar-sized corporations. High-income investors like to purchase municipal bonds and notes because the interest is often—but not always—exempt from federal, state, and city income taxes. The tax exemption means that the community can issue municipal bonds at lower coupon rates, yet still offer a higher after-tax yield than corporate bonds.

When they need to issue bonds, municipal managers face the same rating system that corporations face. To be marketable, one or more of the major rating agencies—Standard & Poor's, Moody's, or Fitch—must rate the bonds. To obtain a good rating, communities must have their fiscal house in order, which means adequate capacity to raise revenues through taxes, balanced budgets, manageable existing debt, stable population, and a qualified financial team. In addition, like corporations, agencies can downgrade municipal bonds in status. For example, in 2009, in the face of a declining local economy and a $300 million budget deficit, Moody's and Standard & Poor's lowered Detroit's rating to junk bond status.

Municipal managers must decide whether to issue *general obligation bonds*, backed only by tax revenues; *revenue bonds*, which pay interest from some revenue source such as water and sewer fees; or *mortgage bonds*, secured by buildings or other assets. Then there is the marketing challenge: sewers and city streets are not as glamorous compared with most corporate assets.

A good understanding of bonds and debt markets is a must to become a municipal manager, whether in a big city or a small town. Salaries for municipal managers may not equal those in much of the corporate world, but most have comfortable incomes and excellent benefit packages. The knowledge, experience, and political contacts that these managers acquire in their positions can result in lucrative opportunities to move to the private sector, especially to banks, insurance companies, construction companies, and consulting firms that do business with municipal governments.

6.6 U.S. Government Bonds

Both Treasury notes and Treasury bonds are semiannual bonds. Their only difference is the maturity or age of the financial asset. The government issues **Treasury notes** with maturities of between two years and ten years. It issues **Treasury bonds** with maturities of more than ten years. The **Treasury bill** is a short-term borrowing instrument with a maturity of less than one year. The Treasury issues

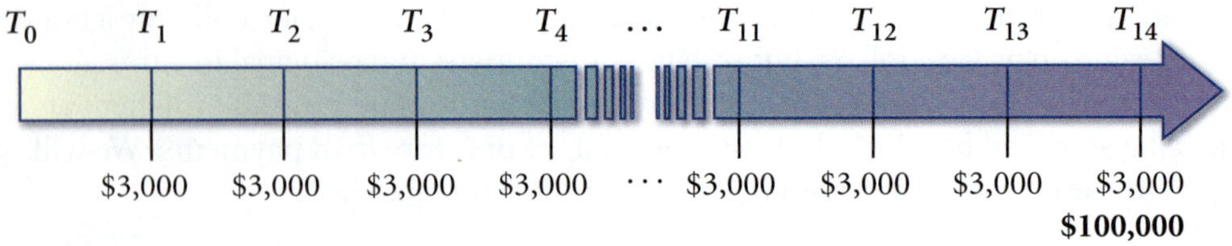

FIGURE 6.11 U.S. Government Treasury note cash flows.

one-month (four-week), three-month (thirteen-week), six-month (twenty-six-week), and one-year (fifty-two-week) Treasury bills. In addition to shorter maturities than the notes and bonds, the Treasury bills are zero-coupon instruments in that they pay both the principal and interest at maturity only.

There are also **state bonds**, issued by individual state governments, and **municipal bonds** (sometimes called **munis**), issued by county, city, or local government agencies. To see municipal bonds at work in a job setting, read the "Putting Finance to Work" feature earlier in this chapter. In addition, foreign corporations or governments issue **foreign bonds**.

Pricing a U.S. Government Note or Bond

Suppose the U.S. government has announced that it intends to raise funds by selling a seven-year Treasury note with a 6% coupon rate with a par value of $100,000. Let's assume that you want to buy one of these notes and want to earn 8% on it over the coming seven years. What price should you pay?

The same process applies here as with a corporate bond. The first step is to set up the cash flow from the note and then discount the future cash flow at the appropriate discount rate. The semiannual coupon payments are

$$\text{coupon payments} = \frac{\$100{,}000 \times 0.06}{2} = \$3{,}000$$

Figure 6.11 depicts the timing of the cash flow.

Using a calculator:

Mode: P/Y = 2 and C/Y = 2

Input	14	8.0	?	3,000	100,000
Key	N	I/Y	PV	PMT	FV
CPT			−89,436.88		

Using a spreadsheet:

B6 | *fx* | *=PV(B1,B2,B3,B4,B5)*

Use the present value function to find the price of the bond.

	A	B	C	D	E
1	Rate	0.04			
2	Nper	14			
3	Pmt	$ 3,000.00			
4	Fv	$100,000.00			
5	Type	0			
6	Pv	($89,436.88)			

TABLE 6.6 Government Notes and Bonds, Prices as of April 8, 2008

Type	Issue Date	Price	Coupon Rate	Maturity Date	Yield to Maturity	Current Yield	Rating
Note	Feb 2000	105.84	6.50%	2-15-2010	3.952%	6.142%	AAA
Note	May 2005	99.19	4.125%	5-15-2013	4.248%	4.158%	AAA
Bond	Aug 1994	117.09	6.25%	8-15-2023	4.711%	5.337%	AAA
Bond	Feb 1985	144.17	11.25%	2-15-2015	4.250%	7.803%	AAA

Table 6.6 provides an abbreviated list of government notes and bonds.

Pricing a Treasury Bill

Treasury notes and bonds follow our standard bond pricing conventions using the time value of money equation from Chapters 3 and 4. Pricing Treasury bills is different. We price Treasury bills using a bank discount basis. We discount the Treasury bill price from its par value based on the discount rate and the days to maturity. This pricing technique ignores compounding and conventional return calculation methods, so it is important to review it.

Table 6.7 lists selected Treasury bills and their bank discount rates. We have selected these bank discount rates from the U.S. Treasury Web site's historical records. These reflect the rates during the first week of April for the year selected. (We have not included the 52-week Treasury bill because the government recently reinstated it as part of the Treasury bill offerings, and we therefore do not have yields for the period 2005 to 2008.)

The bank discount rate is a special rate for Treasury bills. To find the price of the Treasury bill, you must discount its face value and adjust for the days to maturity with the bank discount rate. If we use \$10,000 as its face value, we can calculate the price of any of the twelve Treasury bills from Table 6.7. For example, let's look at the 2005 row and find the price of the four-week Treasury bill. The formula for the price is

$$\text{price} = \text{face value} \times \left[1 - \left(\text{discount rate} \times \frac{\text{days to maturity}}{360}\right)\right] \qquad \textbf{6.3}$$

For the four-week Treasury bill (at issue), the days to maturity would be twenty-eight and the discount rate is 0.0261 (2.61%):

$$\text{price} = \$10{,}000 \times \left[1 - \left(0.0261 \times \frac{28}{360}\right)\right] = \$9{,}979.70$$

or

$$\text{discount} = \text{face value} \times \text{discount rate} \times \frac{\text{days to maturity}}{360} \qquad \textbf{6.4}$$

$$= \$10{,}000 \times 0.0261 \times \frac{28}{360} = \$20.30$$

$$\text{price} = \$10{,}000 - \$20.30 = \$9{,}979.70$$

The bank discount rates are not consistent with our earlier treatment of interest rates. So, let's find the rate that would be similar to our earlier treatment

TABLE 6.7 Selected Historical Treasury Bill Bank Discount Rates

Year	4-Week Treasury Bill	13-Week Treasury Bill	26-Week Treasury Bill
2005	2.61%	2.74%	3.04%
2006	4.58%	4.55%	4.68%
2007	5.03%	4.91%	4.88%
2008	1.53%	1.38%	1.50%

of yields and find the **bond equivalent yield** (BEY) of this Treasury bill. We will make two adjustments to the discount process. First, we will use the price instead of the par value as the initial investment (cost of the bond). Second, we will use 365 days for the year instead of 360.

Using the initial bond cost and the earned interest we find the holding period return (HPR) of the investment:

$$HPR = \frac{\$10{,}000 - \$9{,}979.70}{\$9{,}979.70} = 0.002034129$$

Then, using the simple interest approach, we annualize the result:

$$\text{bond equivalent yield} = 0.002034129 \times \frac{365}{28} = 0.026516328 \text{ or } \approx 2.65\%$$

Another way to find the bond equivalent yield is to use the formula

$$BEY = \frac{365 \times \text{discount yield}}{360 - \text{days to maturity} \times \text{discount yield}} \qquad \textbf{6.5}$$

$$= \frac{365 \times 0.0261}{360 - 28 \times 0.0261} = 0.026516328 \approx 2.65\%$$

We have another name for the bond equivalent yield, one we have met earlier in the text. It is the annual percentage rate (APR).

Why pay so much attention to the Treasury bill? The yield on the Treasury bill is a nominal risk-free rate. The U.S. government guarantees it. It has an essentially zero-default premium, and we determine its interest at purchase as a discount bond. Thus, we know at purchase the guaranteed or risk-free return for buying a Treasury bill. In future chapters, when we need a risk-free rate, we will often use the yield on a Treasury bill.

For an interesting look at the amount of money that the U.S. government has borrowed, you can visit the Debt Clock Web site at www.brillig.com/debt_clock. You can also see, given the current population of the United States, your prorated share of the debt. Be forewarned, though. Venture to this site only if you are not intimidated by huge numbers!

To review this chapter, see the Summary Card at the end of the text.

Key Terms

basis point, p. 163
bearer bond, p. 165
bond, p. 148
bond equivalent yield (BEY), p. 172
callable bond, p. 167
collateral, p. 166
convertible bond, p. 168
corpus, p. 165
coupon, p. 148
coupon rate, p. 148
current yield, p. 149
debentures, p. 166
deed of trust, p. 166
discount bond, p. 161
exotic bond, p. 169
fallen angel, p. 165
floating rate bond, p. 168
foreign bond, p. 170
income bond, p. 168
indenture, p. 166
junior debt, p. 166
junk bond, p. 162
maturity date, p. 148
mortgaged security, p. 166
municipal bond (munis), p. 170
par value, p. 148
par value bond, p. 161
premium bond, p. 161
prime rate, p. 168
protective covenant, p. 166
putable bond, p. 168
security of a bond, p. 166
senior debt, p. 166
sinking fund, p. 166
state bond, p. 170
STRIPS, p. 156
Treasury bill, p. 169
Treasury bond, p. 169
Treasury note, p. 169
yield to call, p. 167
yield to maturity, p. 159
zero-coupon bond, p. 156

Questions

1. What is a bond? What determines the price of this financial asset?
2. What is the primary difference between an annual bond and a semiannual bond? What changes do you need to make in finding the price of a semiannual bond versus an annual bond?
3. When we talk about the yield of a bond, we usually mean the yield to maturity of the bond. Why?
4. Does a zero-coupon bond pay interest?
5. If a zero-coupon bond does not pay coupons each year, why buy it?
6. How does the potential for default of a bond affect the yield of the bond?
7. Why are some bonds sold with a premium, some at par value, and some at a discount?
8. How does collateral impact the price of a bond?
9. What role do Moody's, Standard & Poor's, or Fitch's bond ratings play in the pricing of a bond?
10. What must happen for us to call a bond a "fallen angel"?

Prepping for Exams

1. Five years ago, Thompson Tarps Inc. issued twenty-five-year 10% annual coupon bonds with a $1,000 face value each. Since then, interest rates in general have risen, and the yield to maturity on the Thompson Tarps bonds is now 12%. Given this information, what is the price today for a Thompson Tarps bond?

a. $843.14
b. $850.61
c. $1,181.54
d. $1,170.27

2. Endicott Enterprises Inc. has issued thirty-year semiannual coupon bonds with a face value of $1,000. If the annual coupon rate is 14% and the current yield to maturity is 8%, what is the firm's current price per bond?

a. $578.82
b. $579.84
c. $1,675.47
d. $1,678.70

3. Benson Biometrics Inc. has outstanding $1,000 face value 8% coupon bonds that make semiannual payments and have fourteen years remaining to maturity. If the current price for these bonds is $1,118.74, what is the annualized yield to maturity?

a. 6.68%
b. 6.67%
c. 6.12%
d. 6.00%

4. Delagold Corporation is issuing a zero-coupon bond that will have a maturity of fifty years. The bond's par value is $1,000, and the current yield on similar bonds is 7.5%. What is the expected price of this bond using the semiannual convention?

a. $25.19
b. $250.19
c. $750.00
d. $1,000.00

5. From 1980 to 2006, the default risk premium differential between Aaa-rated bonds and Aa-rated bonds has averaged between _______________.

a. 5 to 10 basis points
b. 11 to 23 basis points
c. 24 to 35 basis points
d. 36 to 50 basis points

6. Which of the following bond types may the issuer buy back before maturity?

a. callable bond
b. putable bond
c. convertible bond
d. zero-coupon bond

7. Bonds that pay interest tied to a company's earnings are ______________ bonds.

a. income
b. exotic
c. floating rate
d. variable earnings

8. The U.S. Treasury bill is currently selling at a discount basis of 4.25%. The par value of the bill is $100,000, and it will mature in ninety days. What is the price of this Treasury bill?

a. $95,750.00
b. $98,937.50
c. $98,952.05
d. $99,952.78

Problems

These problems are available in MyFinanceLab.

Bond prices: For Problems 1 through 4, use the information in the following table.

Par Value	Coupon Rate	Years to Maturity	Yield to Maturity	Price
$1,000.00	8%	10	6%	?
$1,000.00	6%	10	8%	?
$5,000.00	9%	20	7%	?
$5,000.00	12%	30	5%	?

1. Price the bonds from the table with annual coupon payments.

2. Price the bonds from the table with semiannual coupon payments.

3. Price the bonds from the table with quarterly coupon payments.

4. Price the bonds from the table with monthly coupon payments.

Yield to maturity: For Problems 5 through 8, use the information in the following table.

Par Value	Coupon Rate	Years to Maturity	Yield to Maturity	Price
$1,000.00	8%	10	?	$1,000.00
$1,000.00	6%	10	?	$ 850.00
$5,000.00	9%	20	?	$5,400.00
$5,000.00	12%	30	?	$4,300.00

5. What is the yield of the above bonds if interest (coupon) is paid annually?

6. What is the yield of the above bonds if interest (coupon) is paid semiannually?

7. What is the yield of the above bonds if interest (coupon) is paid quarterly?

8. What is the yield of the above bonds if interest (coupon) is paid monthly?

9. How long to maturity for the following bonds?

Par Value	Coupon Rate	Years to Maturity	Yield to Maturity	Price	Coupon Frequency
$1,000.00	8%	?	8.7713%	$ 950.00	Annual
$1,000.00	6%	?	7.7038%	$ 850.00	Semiannual
$5,000.00	9%	?	8.1838%	$5,400.00	Quarterly
$5,000.00	12%	?	16.0938%	$4,300.00	Monthly

10. ***Coupon rates.*** What are the coupon rates for the following bonds?

Par Value	Coupon Rate	Years to Maturity	Yield to Maturity	Price	Coupon Frequency
$1,000.00	?	30	6.0%	$1,412.94	Annual
$1,000.00	?	25	10.0%	$1,182.56	Semiannual
$1,000.00	?	20	9.0%	$ 907.63	Quarterly
$1,000.00	?	10	8.0%	$ 862.63	Monthly

11. ***Bond prices and maturity dates.*** Moore Company is about to issue a bond with semiannual coupon payments, a coupon rate of 8%, and par value of $1,000. The yield to maturity for this bond is 10%.

a. What is the bond price if it matures in five, ten, fifteen, or twenty years?
b. What do you notice about the bond price in relationship to the bond's maturity?

12. ***Bond prices and maturity dates.*** Les Company is about to issue a bond with semiannual coupon payments, a coupon rate of 10%, and par value of $1,000. The yield to maturity for this bond is 8%.

a. What is the bond price if it matures in five, ten, fifteen, or twenty years?
b. What do you notice about the bond price in relationship to the bond's maturity?

13. ***Zero-coupon bond.*** Addison Company will issue a zero-coupon bond this coming month. The bond's projected yield is 7%. If the par value is $1,000, what is the bond's price using a semiannual convention if

a. the maturity is 20 years?
b. the maturity is 30 years?
c. the maturity is 50 years?
d. the maturity is 100 years?

14. ***Zero-coupon bond.*** Wesley Company will issue a zero-coupon bond this coming month. The projected bond yield is 5%. If the par value is $1,000, what is the bond's price using a semiannual convention if

a. the maturity is 20 years?
b. the maturity is 30 years?
c. the maturity is 50 years?
d. the maturity is 100 years?

15. ***Zero-coupon bond.*** What is the annual implied interest of a five-year zero-coupon bond (using the semiannual pricing convention) with a current yield of 12% and a par value of $1,000.00?

16. ***Callable bond.*** Corso Books has just sold a callable bond. It is a thirty-year semiannual bond with a coupon rate of 6%. Investors, however, can call the bond starting at the end of ten years. If the yield to call on this bond is 8% and the call requires Corso Books to pay one year of additional interest at the call (two coupon payments), what is the bond price if priced with the assumption that the call will be on the first available call date?

17. ***Callable bond.*** McCarty Manufacturing Company makes baseball equipment. The company decides to issue a callable bond that it expects to sell for $840 per bond. If the bond is a twenty-year semiannual bond with a 6% coupon rate and a current yield to maturity of 7%, what is the option cost attached to the bond? Assume $1000 par value. *Hint:* Find the price of an equivalent bond without the call option.

18. ***Missing information on a bond.*** Your broker faxed to you the following information about two semiannual coupon bonds that you are considering as a potential investment. Unfortunately, your fax machine is blurring some of the items, and all you can read from the fax on the two different bonds is the following:

Features	IBM Coupon Bond	AOL Coupon Bond
Face value (par)	$1,000	$1,000
Coupon rate	9.5%	
Yield to maturity	7.5%	9.5%
Years to maturity	10	20
Price		$ 689.15

Fill in the missing data from the information that the broker sent.

Treasury notes and bonds. For Problems 19 through 23, use the information in the following table.

Today Is February 15, 2008

Type	Issue Date	Price	Coupon Rate	Maturity Date	YTM	Current Yield	Rating
Note	Feb 2000	—	6.50%	2-15-2010	3.952%	6.199%	AAA
Bond	Aug 2005	100.00	4.25%	8-15-2018	—	4.250%	AAA
Bond	Aug 2003	—	7.25%	8-15-2023	4.830%	5.745%	AAA
Bond	Feb 1995	126.19	8.50%	2-15-2015	—	6.736%	AAA

19. What is the price in dollars of the February 2000 Treasury note if its par value is $100,000? Verify the current yield of this note.

20. What is the yield to maturity of the August 2005 Treasury bond? Compare the yield to maturity and the current yield. How do you explain this relationship?

21. What is the price of the August 2003 Treasury bond (assume a $100,000 par value) with the yield to maturity from the table? Verify the current yield. Why is the current yield higher than the yield to maturity?

22. What is the yield to maturity of the February 1995 Treasury bond based on the price in the table? Verify the current yield. Why is the current yield higher than the yield to maturity?

23. What pattern do you see in the yield to maturity of these Treasury notes and bonds?

Treasury bills. For Problems 24 through 28, use the information in the following table. A face value of $10,000 is assumed for these Treasury bills.

Maturity	Days to Maturity	Bank Discount
Mar 30	28	1.20
Apr 30	59	2.00
Jun 30	120	2.45
Aug 30	181	?

24. What is the price for the March 30 Treasury bill?

25. What is the price for the April 30 Treasury bill?

26. What is the price for the June 30 Treasury bill?

27. Determine the bank discount rate of the August 30 Treasury bill if it is currently selling for $9,841.625. What is the bond equivalent yield?

28. What are the bond equivalent yields of the March 30, April 30, and June 30 Treasury bills?

These problems are available in MyFinanceLab.

Advanced Problems for Spreadsheet Application

1. ***Bond ladder.*** Mathew and Anna are setting up a retirement pay-out account for the next twenty years. They have decided to buy government bonds that have various coupon rates. The following table gives the yield to maturity and the coupon rate on each bond for each maturity date.

Maturity	YTM	Coupon	Maturity	YTM	Coupon
1	3.2500%	5.50%	11	4.8750%	5.25%
2	3.5000%	6.25%	12	5.0000%	4.75%
3	3.7500%	4.75%	13	5.0625%	4.00%
4	4.0000%	7.00%	14	5.1250%	4.50%
5	4.1250%	6.50%	15	5.1875%	5.25%
6	4.2500%	8.25%	16	5.2500%	6.00%
7	4.3750%	8.00%	17	5.3125%	6.50%
8	4.5000%	7.25%	18	5.3750%	6.75%
9	4.6250%	6.50%	19	5.4375%	7.50%
10	4.7500%	5.50%	20	5.5000%	8.00%

They decide to buy ten bonds of each maturity (par value of $1,000). Using a spreadsheet, determine the cost of this bond portfolio and the payment of the bond portfolio each year and at the six-month intervals. (Assume that all bonds have June and December coupon dates.)

2. ***Callable bond and call premium.*** Edward has just purchased a callable bond and wants to set up the bond's potential pay-off price if it is called at any time during its callable life. The callable bond is a twenty-year semiannual bond that an investor can call starting at year ten. It is callable every six months on the coupon payment date. The call price is declining and starts out as one extra year's coupon (a full annual coupon payment). It reduces each period (every six months by 1/20th the annual coupon payment) until—at the bond's maturity—there is no call premium price. If the original bond is an 8% semiannual coupon bond with a par value of $1,000 and an original yield to maturity of 6.5%, what is the bond price today at each potential callable date (coupon payment date), given no change in its original yield to maturity? Compare the callable bond price at each callable date with that of a noncallable bond that is identical in every way other than the call feature (same yield to maturity, same coupon rate, and same maturity date). The difference between the callable bond price and the noncallable bond price is the call premium if called on that date. Find the call premium for each potential call date.

MINI-CASE

Bay Path Cranberry Products

This mini-case is available in MyFinanceLab.

Bay Path Cranberry Products is a leading producer of cranberry juice, canned cranberry sauce, fresh berries, and sweetened dried cranberries, with production and processing facilities in Massachusetts and Wisconsin. Sales of traditional products such as fresh berries and canned cranberry sauce have been declining for a long time; the fastest-growing products have been juices and dried fruit, especially "light" and sugar-free juices. Industry-sponsored advertising has highlighted research showing that cranberries are rich in antioxidants and other phytonutrients that may protect against heart disease, cancer, stomach ulcers, gum and urinary tract infections, and even such age-related afflictions as loss of coordination and memory.

These trends confirm the marketing department's belief that Bay Path should aggressively pursue the same health-conscious consumers who purchase certified organic products. Despite the growing popularity of organic food products and the demonstrated willingness of affluent consumers to pay a premium price for them, the cranberry industry has been slow to enter the field. Bay Path executives have now decided to introduce an organic line of products, starting with juice and blended juice. This new line will become their highest strategic priority for the next two years.

The introduction of certified organic products will be expensive. Preliminary estimates indicate that Bay Path will need to invest $80 million in production and processing facilities. The company hopes to finance the expansion by using $30 million of its own liquid assets and $50 million in new debt in the form of bonds with a maturity of 20 years. Bay Path expects the bonds to receive a rating of Aa1 or better from Moody's.

Questions

For all questions, assume par value is $1,000 and semiannual bond interest payment.

1. A company in a line of business similar to Bay Path's recently issued at par noncallable bonds with a coupon rate of 5.8% and a maturity of 20 years. Moody's rated the bonds Aa1 and Standard & Poor awarded them AA. What rate of return (yield to maturity) did investors require on these bonds if the bonds sold at par value?
2. Bay Path has one outstanding bond issue with a coupon of 8% that will mature in five years. The bonds now sell for $1,141.69. What is the yield to maturity on these bonds? You may want to use a calculator or spreadsheet in determining your answer.
3. Based on your answers to Questions 1 and 2, what coupon rate should Bay Path offer if it wants to realize $50 million from the bond issue and sell the bonds as close to par value as possible? (Ignore the cost of selling the bonds.)
4. Suppose Bay Path actually offers a coupon rate of 6% on its twenty-year bonds, expecting to sell the bonds at par. What will happen to the price of a single bond with a par value of $1,000 if the required bond yield unexpectedly falls to 5% or rises to 7%?
5. How much money will Bay Path realize from its $50 million bond issue if the actual yield is either 5% or 7%? *Hint:* Refer to your answers to Question 4 and ignore selling costs.
6. How would the following affect the yield on Bay Path's newly issued bonds?
   a. The bonds are callable.
   b. The bonds are subordinated to Bay Path's existing bond issue.
   c. The bond rating is better or worse than the Moody's Aa1 that Bay Path anticipates.

Learning Objectives

LO1 Explain the basic characteristics of common stock.

LO2 Define the primary market and the secondary market.

LO3 Calculate the value of a stock given a history of dividend payments.

LO4 Explain the shortcomings of the dividend pricing models.

LO5 Calculate the price of preferred stock.

LO6 Understand the concept of efficient markets.

Chapter 7
Stocks and Stock Valuation

In Chapter 6, we showed how companies raise money by issuing bonds. We now consider another major source of funding for the corporation: issuing stocks. Stocks are different from bonds in several ways. Perhaps most notable is that they represent ownership in the company. With stocks, you actually have a piece of the company pie. Some stockholders have larger slices than others and thus have a bigger say in the management of the company.

In this chapter, we'll look at the basics of stocks—both common stocks and preferred stocks—and how they are traded. We'll pay considerable attention to the pricing of stocks and how future dividends help determine a stock's value. We'll look at some famous dividend models, and as we consider some of their shortcomings, you'll see that nothing is perfect. Finally, we'll touch briefly on the role that information plays in the pricing of stocks.

7.1 Characteristics of Common Stock

Common stock, a financial asset, signifies ownership in a company. Besides selling bonds to raise funds for operations, expansion, or other business needs, selling stock is a major financing source for public companies. Like a bond, common stock entitles the owner to some of the company's cash flow. Unlike a bond, there is no specific promise of how much you will receive and when you will receive it. With stocks, there is no maturity date, and the asset does not state the promised cash flow; instead, the board of directors determines the dividend payments at a later date. Let us first look at the basic characteristics of common stock, which will help you in understanding the valuation models that follow. As we proceed through the discussion, we will contrast the features of common stock with those of bonds to show you how the two securities differ.

Ownership

Common stock represents part ownership in a company. Ownership is an **equity claim**, that is, a claim to all the company's assets and cash flow once it has paid debt claimants. As an owner, the common stockholder is entitled to a share of the company's profits. These profits, of course, come after payment to the employees, suppliers, government (taxes), and creditors.

Ownership via common stock gives the shareholder the right to participate in the management of the company. Shareholders elect the board of directors, which ultimately selects the management team that runs the company's day-to-day operations. The size of your voice in the company depends on the percentage of common shares you own. If you own more than one-half the outstanding shares, you have a majority and a very powerful voice in the company operations. If you have just a few out of millions of shares, your voice is quite small and is often muted amid the roar of business operations.

Claim on Assets and Cash Flow (Residual Claim)

We often refer to common stock's ownership claim on the company's assets and cash flow as a **residual claim**. This claim begins after the company satisfies (pays) its liabilities and shareholders now have claim to all the remaining assets, "the residual." In contrast, debt holders (bondholders) have a specific claim to a fixed amount (listed as a liability), and that amount is the maximum that they will receive from the company. For example, if a company fails, it will sell off all its assets and pay the debt holders first, according to their fixed claims. Only after the company satisfies these claims will the remaining, or *residual*, money go to the common stockholders. This arrangement places them as the lowest priority, or last claimant. The upside of common stock ownership is that there is no limit on the potential return on the investment, unlike bonds, for which the return is fixed.

Vote (Voice in Management)

Common stock usually carries the right to participate in the management of the firm through the right to vote for the members of the board of directors and for changes to the company's charter and bylaws. Although the standard is one vote for each share of owned stock, companies can alter this standard. Some firms issue several classes of common stock, and these classes may have unequal voting rights. There are two typical ways to alter the one vote–one share standard. One way is for companies to issue nonvoting common stock. Often, these nonvoting rights are temporary, and these shares turn into fully participating shares after a period of time. Another method is to issue classes of stock whereby one or more classes have *super* voting rights. Shareholders of super voting right shares have multiple votes per share, which increases their influence and control over the company. Bondholders typically do not participate in the management of the company through voting rights.

No Maturity Date

We consider common stock permanent funding for the company. Unlike bondholders, shareholders do not have a promised future date when they will receive their investment back. Bonds have a specific maturity date when the company repays the bond's par value in full. Bonds are therefore temporary financing, even though this temporary condition may last for thirty or more years.

Dividends and Their Tax Effect

Typically, many companies distribute part of the earnings to shareholders through cash dividends, with each share receiving an equal amount. Many companies pay their dividends quarterly.

The payment of cash dividends to shareholders is not a deductible expense for the company. Unlike coupon payments on bonds, which we treat as an interest expense on the firm's income statement, we do not treat dividends as an expense. For the shareholder, though, the receipt of dividends *is* a taxable event. Each year, shareholders must declare their ordinary dividend income on their tax returns and pay a tax on this distribution. We will explore dividends and dividend policies in more detail in Chapter 17.

Authorized, Issued, and Outstanding Shares

The company's charter specifies the number of common shares that it may sell. This charter can subsequently change to increase the maximum number of shares the firm can issue—the **authorized shares**—but current shareholders must ratify by vote such a policy change. Even though a company sets a limit on the number of shares it will sell, the company must—before selling any of them—receive authorization to market the shares from the **Securities and Exchange Commission** (SEC). The SEC authorizes the public sale of a specific number of shares. A company may, however, choose to issue to the public only a certain percentage of these authorized shares. The shares available for public purchase and subsequent trading in a secondary market such as the NYSE or NASDAQ are the company's **issued shares.** Not all issued shares are available for public trading. Shares that sell and remain in the "public domain" are **outstanding shares**. Shares that the company holds for future sales or compensation to managers or employees comprise the other portion of the issued shares. Shares that the company holds are treasury stocks.

There is an exception to requesting approval from the SEC for selling stock. If the issue is for less than $5 million, the SEC does not require firms to file. This exception is **Regulation A**, but we informally refer to it as the small business exception rule.

Treasury Stock

A company can keep shares, which we call treasury shares or **treasury stock**, in its own treasury. Often, a company creates treasury stock when it first issues stock and keeps some shares for future needs, or they may be shares that the company repurchased. Unlike outstanding shares, treasury shares have no voting rights or claims to declared dividends. It makes sense that treasury stock should not have the same rights as outstanding shares because a company cannot own itself. If that were so and we took it to the extreme, a company could buy up all its outstanding shares. All dividend distributions would accrue to the company, and the company would vote on all its own initiatives, with no opportunity for healthy disagreement. Thus, a company cannot have voting rights or participate in the distribution of dividends in and of itself.

Preemptive Rights

A final item of importance in understanding common stock is that of preemptive rights. As we have seen, common shares represent an ownership claim in the company. If an investor purchases 10% of the initial issue, the investor then owns 10% of the company, but the company can sell more shares to the public at a later date. If the investor who originally purchased 10% does not purchase 10% of the subsequent issue, his or her ownership is diluted and falls below 10%. Thus, to be able to maintain this level of ownership, the initial investor must have "first access" to all subsequent shares at his or her ownership level. This access constitutes a so-called **preemptive right**, a privilege that allows current shareholders to buy a fixed percentage of all future issues before the company offers them to the general public, and thus maintains the same percentage ownership in the firm. Although this right might not be particularly valuable to shareholders with very small ownership percentages, it may be critical to an owner with a large or controlling interest in the company.

7.2 Stock Markets

There are two major markets for the sale of stock: the **primary market** and the **secondary market**. The primary market is the market of *first* sale, where companies first sell their shares to the public. The secondary market comprises the aftersale markets of the existing outstanding shares. Here, individual or institutional stock owners sell their shares to other investors. You can think of the secondary market as the "used stock" market, much as you can think of the secondary market for cars as the "used car" market.

Primary Markets

Although we discuss much of the detailed information about the primary market in Chapter 15, we present some basic information here to provide a foundation about issuing shares. First, selling of shares is the selling of ownership in the company. A company will "go public" when it opens its ownership structure to the general public through the sale of common stock. Companies choose to sell stock to attract permanent financing through equity ownership in the company. So, a major company benefit from issuing stock is this direct infusion of cash into the business.

The process of selling common stock begins with the current owners' decision to go public. The owners must seek SEC permission to conduct a public sale of common stock. Most companies do not have the resident expertise to complete an **initial public offering (IPO)**, or first public equity issue, so they hire an investment banker to help accomplish the sale. The investment banker becomes a partner in the IPO. The investment banker will use the talent and expertise of the bank's management to structure the sale and comply with all SEC regulations. Among the more important investment banker functions is working with the owners to prepare the **prospectus**, a document that provides potential buyers with information about the company and the impending sale. As part of this preparation, the investment banker must perform **due diligence**, that is, ensure the disclosure of all relevant information prior to the sale. Nondisclosure of material information prior to the sale can make both the issuing company and the investment banker liable to a lawsuit brought on by those who buy the newly issued shares.

The hiring process for an investment banker can happen in one of two ways. A company can simply pick a desirable investment banking firm, usually basing the choice on the reputation and history of the banker in its particular industry. Alternatively, the company can solicit bids from many investment bankers. The most common practice for corporations selling common stock is the hand-picked selection process, and the most common for government agencies selling bonds is the multiple bidder process.

Part of the negotiation with the investment banker during the selection process revolves around compensation, and bankers usually use two standard compensation packages. The first is a **firm commitment** approach. With firm commitment, the investment banker essentially buys the entire stock issue from the company at one price and then sells the issue for a higher price. The investment banker makes money only if the sale to the public brings in more funds than the promised or committed funds to the company. In effect, the investment banker is guaranteeing a fixed amount of funding to the company.

A second compensation package is a **best efforts** sale by the investment banker. Here, the investment banker pledges to give his or her best in trying to sell the shares and will take a small percentage of the sale of each stock. This pledge, however, does not guarantee the firm a specific amount from the sale. It receives only the proceeds of the sale minus the commission to the investment banker on a per-share basis. Of course, the investment banker wants to sell as many shares as possible because the more the banker sells, the greater his or her commission-driven compensation.

Immediately after this initial sale of stock in the primary market, the stock begins trading in the secondary market.

Secondary Markets: How Stocks Trade

The secondary market, or "used stock" market, provides a place for current common stockholders to sell their stock or acquire more stock or for new stockholders to acquire stock for the first time. In the United States, there are three well-known secondary stock markets:

1. The **New York Stock Exchange (NYSE)**
2. The **American Stock Exchange (AMEX)**
3. The **National Association of Securities Dealers (NASD)** and its trading system, the **National Association of Securities Dealers Automated Quotation System (NASDAQ)**

Both the NYSE and AMEX are physical trading locations with trading floors. To complete a trade (the selling or buying of shares), dealers must process orders at trading posts on the exchange's floor. Each stock listed on the exchange trades at only one post. The exchange assigns each stock to one **specialist**, whose job is to maintain an orderly market for the stock. The specialist has many tasks, including keeping a record of orders awaiting execution (called the "limit order book"), standing ready to buy and sell shares at stated prices, and auctioning orders to market makers gathered around the trading post.

Connected by a computer network, registered NASDAQ traders accomplish everything "virtually." Each authorized dealer posts an **ask price** (a price at which he or she is willing to sell) and a **bid price** (a price at which he or she is willing to buy) along with the number of shares that they will buy or sell at the respective prices. Individuals wishing to buy or sell shares then submit orders to the dealer with the lowest ask (if they are buying) or the highest bid (if they are selling). The dealers make money on the difference between the stock purchase and sale prices, much as a car dealer makes money by buying a used car at one price and then selling the car later at a higher or marked-up price. The difference between the asking price and the bidding price is the **spread** or the **bid-ask spread**. The NYSE and AMEX also use the bid and ask prices for buying and selling the stock because the specialists must post bid and ask prices for individuals seeking to buy or sell shares at the exchange.

Bull Markets and Bear Markets

Two descriptive terms are associated with secondary markets: bull markets and bear markets. A **bull market** is a prolonged rising market, one in which stock prices in general are increasing. A **bear market** is a prolonged declining market, one in which stock prices in general are decreasing. A variety of stories try to explain the origin of these two general market descriptors. Perhaps the best description of the origin of a bear market stems from the practice of preselling bearskins before hunters actually caught the bear. Jobbers (middlemen) would take orders from customers at a preset price for bearskins before they acquired them from trappers. They hoped that the trappers would have an abundant season (increase in supply) and prices would fall by the time they needed to acquire and deliver the bearskins. This practice is known as short selling and requires prices to fall for the jobber to make a profit. The jobber makes a profit by acquiring the bearskin at the lower market price after a plentiful hunt and delivering the bearskin to the contracted buyer at the agreed-to higher price prior to the hunt. The jobber would engage in this practice only if he or she thought that there would be a prolonged fall in prices (plentiful hunt) and hence a bear market.

Bull markets and bear markets are terms used to describe the financial markets for stocks. Bull markets are going up: prices are rising or are expected to rise. Bear markets are going down: prices are falling or are expected to fall. Bullish investors are confident and optimistic; bearish investors are wary and pessimistic.

Unfortunately, we don't have as colorful a tale or story about the origin of a bull market. Today, we draw an analogy from the attacking style of bulls and bears to signify the rising or declining markets. A bull attacks with its horns from bottom up, and a bear swipes with its paw from top down. Therefore, a bull market rises and a bear market declines. There is no accepted definition of an actual bull market or bear market in terms of how low or how high stocks must go or how long the rally (upswing) or sell-off (downswing) lasts. So, when describing rising or falling prices, we use these terms very loosely.

7.3 Stock Valuation

The value, or price, of a financial asset is the present value of the expected future cash flow you will receive while you maintain ownership of the asset. For example, with a stock, you may receive cash dividends from the company, and when you decide to relinquish your ownership rights—that is, you decide to sell the stock—you will receive your final cash payment, the sales price, from the new owner. Let's look at a simple illustration of the price of a single share of common stock when we know the future dividends and final selling price.

EXAMPLE 7.1 Stock price with known dividends and sale price

Problem Steve wants to purchase shares of Old Peak Construction Company and hold these common shares for five years. The company has stated the following dividend policy: $5.00 annual cash dividend per share for the next five years. At the end of the five years, Steve will sell the stock. He believes that he will be able to sell the stock for $25.00. If Steve wants to earn 10% on this investment, what price should he pay today for this stock?

Solution The current price of the stock is the discounted cash flow that Steve will receive over the next five years while holding the stock. If we let the final price represent a lump sum future value and the dividend payments an annuity stream over the next five years, we can apply the time value of money concepts from Chapters 3 and 4.

METHOD 1: Using an equation

$$\text{price} = \text{future price} \times \frac{1}{(1+r)^n} + \text{dividend stream} \times \frac{1 - \dfrac{1}{(1+r)^n}}{r} \qquad \textbf{7.1}$$

$$= \$25.00 \times \frac{1}{(1+0.10)^5} + \$5.00 \times \frac{1 - \dfrac{1}{(1+0.10)^5}}{0.10}$$

$$= \$25.00 \times 0.6209 + \$5.00 \times 3.7908$$

$$= \$15.52 + \$18.95 = \mathbf{\$34.47}$$

We can also use a calculator or spreadsheet to find the price of the stock.

METHOD 2: Using the TVM keys

Mode: P/Y = 1 and C/Y = 1

Input	5	10.0	?	5.00	25.00
Key	N	I/Y	PV	PMT	FV
CPT			–34.47		

Do you recognize Equation 7.1? It looks just like the bond pricing formula from Chapter 6. There, we found the present value of a coupon stream and the present value of the par value. Here, we find the present value of a dividend stream and the present value of the lump-sum future price. So, if we know the dividend stream, the future price of the stock, the future selling date of the stock, and the required return, we can price stocks just as we priced bonds.

TABLE 7.1 Differences between Bonds and Stocks

	Bonds	Stocks
Cash flows	Certain; amounts known and guaranteed	Uncertain; amounts unknown and not guaranteed
Number of payments	Known	Unknown
Maturity	Specific known date	Time of final sale unknown
End value	Known: par value of principal	Unknown
Rate of return	Known if held to maturity	Unknown until it is sold

Unfortunately, the pricing of stocks is not that easy. Table 7.1 summarizes those differences between stocks and bonds that make stock valuation more challenging than bond valuation. As you can see from the table, with stocks, we do not know or cannot guarantee future cash flow. Cash dividends are not always the same year after year as are coupons for bonds. We do not know a final stock price, unlike the par value of a bond, which is set. Because of the stock's unknown maturity date, we do not know when the final sale will take place. Therefore, we must make some adjustments to the pricing of stocks. We begin with the dividend pricing models.

We start the valuation process with a dividend pricing model that looks much like the bond pricing model. We will use four variations, each of which makes a different assumption about the dividend stream and the maturity of the stock, whether the dividends are constant or growing, and whether we hold the stock forever or up to a point at which we sell it. The variations are:

1. The constant dividend model with an infinite horizon
2. The constant dividend model with a finite horizon
3. The constant growth dividend model with an infinite horizon
4. The constant growth dividend model with a finite horizon

We must heed two cautions as we move to the dividend models and stock pricing. First, our objective is to determine how a stock's projected cash flow affects its current price. The actual stock price, however, reflects the general consensus of investors on the expected future cash flow from owning the stock and their consensus on the appropriate discount rate for this expected future cash flow. Just as with bond pricing, we are interested in how this price can change over time, so we want to understand the underlying process. We can find the price of any publicly traded stock by looking up the current price using the company's ticker symbol at many financial Web sites.

Second, this market consensus changes moment by moment. Witness the constant fluctuation of individual stock prices. So, as we move into different models and exercises with the dividend model, we are not trying to find the most accurate model for predicting stock prices but rather to connect with the idea that what matters is the timing and amount of cash flow in pricing stocks. Because the dividend models use expected future cash flow and required return rates (appropriate discount rates), they help us develop an understanding of stock prices. Despite the seeming accuracy of the prices that we get from the dividend model applications, real prices are in constant motion, and the best we can expect to do with any one of these dividend models is establish a foundation for understanding why investors are buying and selling the stock at the prices we can see.

The Constant Dividend Model with an Infinite Horizon

Let's start with the first model, a constant dividend with an infinite horizon. We apply the term **constant annual dividend** to a dividend payment that is the same year after year. Note that there is no growth in payments:

$$\text{Div}_1 = \text{Div}_2 = \text{Div}_3 = \text{Div}_4 = \text{Div}_5 = \text{Div}_6 = \text{Div}_7 = \text{Div}_8 = \cdots = \text{Div}_\infty$$

If we believe a company is following a constant dividend policy, we can use the *current* dividend to predict all *future* dividends because they are the same. If we assume the company will be in business forever, we have a perpetual dividend stream. In Chapter 4, we first introduced this concept of a never-ending annuity as a perpetuity. Recall Equation 4.8, the formula for a perpetuity:

$$PV = PMT \times \frac{1}{r}$$

So, we can price a share of stock that pays the same dividend (*PMT*) forever by dividing the dividend by the required rate of return:

$$\text{price} = \frac{\text{dividend}}{r} \qquad \mathbf{7.2}$$

Depending on the return we require for our stock investment, we have the following returns and implied prices for a stock with a constant $1 annual dividend:

Required Return	$1 Dividend Forever/Required Return	Price
5%	$1/0.05 =	$20.00
10%	$1/0.10 =	$10.00
25%	$1/0.25 =	$ 4.00

Notice that as we increase the desired or required return on a stock with a constant future payment stream, we lower the price that we are willing to pay for it. The lower the price we are willing to pay for a fixed payment stream, the greater the return. As with bonds, the price moves in the opposite direction of the return or yield on a financial asset.

Do not confuse this concept with the notion that higher returns mean higher *future prices*. In this example, the future amount was fixed (a set payment stream for the dividends), so the higher the required return, the lower the price an investor is willing to pay for the stock. If, however, we fix the current price—say, $20.00—and want to know the future value of the stock at different returns, the higher the return, the higher the *future price*. Our objective now, though, is to find the *current price* given the expected future cash flow from owning the stock.

We again note that the required return is stated on an annual basis. If the company pays a constant dividend each quarter, we need to adjust the required return to a quarterly required return. Let's look more closely at this situation.

EXAMPLE 7.2 Quarterly dividends forever

Problem Four Seasons Resorts pays a $0.25 dividend every quarter and will maintain this policy forever. What price should you pay for one share of common stock if you want an annual return of 10% on your investment?

Solution You can restate your annual required rate of 10% as a quarterly rate of 2.5% (10%/4). Apply Equation 7.2 with the quarterly dividend amount and the quarterly rate of return to determine the price:

$$\text{price} = \frac{\text{dividend}}{r}$$

$$\text{price} = \frac{\$0.25}{0.025} = \mathbf{\$10.00}$$

Even though we anticipate that companies will be in business "forever," we are not going to own the stock forever. Therefore, the dividend stream to which we would have legal claim is only for that period of the company's life when we own the stock. We need to modify the dividend model to account for a finite period when we will sell the stock at some future time. This modification brings us from an infinite to a *finite* dividend pricing model. We will maintain a constant dividend assumption.

The Constant Dividend Model with a Finite Horizon

Although the company is an ongoing concern and we "expect" it to live forever, an investor does not anticipate holding the stock forever. Therefore, as in Example 7.1, we modify the dividend model to price a finite amount of dividends and the future selling price of the stock. Let's assume we will hold a share in a $1 dividend-paying company for twenty years and then sell the stock.

Method 1: Using an equation The dividend pricing model under a finite horizon is a tool that we have met before. It is a simple present value annuity stream application:

$$\text{value of future dividends for specific period} = \text{dividend} \times \text{PVIFA} \qquad \textbf{7.3}$$

$$\text{dividend stream} \times \frac{1 - \dfrac{1}{(1+r)^n}}{r} = \$1.00 \times \frac{1 - \dfrac{1}{(1+0.10)^{20}}}{0.10}$$

$$= \$1.00 \times 8.5136 = \$8.51$$

We now need to determine the selling price that we would get in twenty years if we sell the stock to someone else. What would a willing buyer give us for the stock twenty years from now? This price is difficult to estimate, so, for the sake of this exercise, we will assume that the price in twenty years is $30. So, what is the present value of the price in twenty years with a 10% discount rate? Again, this is just a simple application of Equation 3.3, the *PV* formula:

$$PV = \frac{\text{price}_{20}}{(1+r)^{20}} = \frac{\$30}{(1.10)^{20}} = \$4.46$$

We can now price the stock just like a bond with a dividend stream of twenty years, a sales price in twenty years, and a required return of 10%:

- The dividend stream matches the coupon payments.
- The sales price matches the bond's principal.
- The twenty-year investment horizon matches the bond's maturity date.
- The required return matches the bond's yield.

We are now back at Equation 7.1. So,

$$\text{price} = \$30 \times \frac{1}{(1 + 0.10)^{20}} + \$1.00 \times \frac{1 - \dfrac{1}{(1 + 0.10)^{20}}}{0.10}$$

$$= \$4.46 + \$8.51 = \$12.97$$

We can also find the answer with a calculator.

Method 2: Using the TVM keys

Mode: P/Y = 1 and C/Y = 1

Input	20	10.0	?	1.00	30.00
Key	N	I/Y	PV	PMT	FV
CPT			−12.97		

Before proceeding, we need to inject a dose of reality. First, we have looked at the simplest possible dividend pattern, a constant dividend stream. Unfortunately, we rarely see such a pattern in the real world. Instead, dividend patterns tend to grow over time. Second, we needed to predict a price twenty years forward when we were trying to find the price of the stock today, which seems like nonsense. We do, however, need to understand that we base the current stock price on two different pieces: the expected finite dividend stream one receives while holding the stock and the expected future selling price. So, let's now look at a model that relaxes the constant dividend assumption and allows the dividends to change over time.

One common dividend pattern is to raise or grow dividends by a fixed amount or percentage each year. Table 7.2 shows annual cash dividends and the increase in the dividend from the prior year for Coca-Cola over a ten-year span from 2001 to 2010. What dividend would you predict for the year 2011? The most recent dividend raise has been 12 cents over the last two years, so your guess might be \$1.88 for 2011. The average increase has been just under 12 cents, so again another guess might be slightly less than \$1.88. A third way to estimate the next dividend is to calculate the annual growth rate of this dividend stream.

Table 7.3 shows that the average growth rate for a dividend increase each year is approximately 10.44%. Therefore, we have a third guess for the 2011 dividend: 0.1044 × \$1.76, for an 18-cent increase and a dividend estimate of \$1.94. So, which guess for the 2011 dividend—\$1.88, or \$1.94—is best? There is no sure way to predict it.

It is easy to see that the Coca-Cola dividend pattern is not a constant growth dividend pattern. The term *constant growth* can be misleading, so we need to define it carefully. **Constant growth** means that the percentage increase in the dividend is the same each year. The Coca-Cola dividend growth pattern is not constant from year to year, but over this ten-year period, the average growth rate is 10.44%. So, can we use this average growth in dividends? The answer is yes, because what we really want to estimate is a *series* of future dividends, not just the very next dividend. We can use the average growth rate as an approximation of a

TABLE 7.2 Coca-Cola Annual Dividends

	2001	2002	2003	2004	2005	2006	2007	2008	2009	2010
Dividend	\$0.72	\$0.80	\$0.88	\$1.00	\$1.12	\$1.24	\$1.36	\$1.52	\$1.64	\$1.76
Change		\$0.08	\$0.08	\$0.12	\$0.12	\$0.12	\$0.12	\$0.16	\$0.12	\$0.12

TABLE 7.3 Annual Dividend Growth for Coca-Cola

Year	Dividend	Prior Dividend	Change	% Growth
2001	$0.72			
2002	$0.80	$0.72	$0.08	$0.08/$0.72 = 0.1111
2003	$0.88	$0.80	$0.08	$0.08/$0.80 = 0.1000
2004	$1.00	$0.88	$0.12	$0.12/$0.88 = 0.1364
2005	$1.12	$1.00	$0.12	$0.12/$1.00 = 0.1200
2006	$1.24	$1.12	$0.12	$0.12/$1.12 = 0.1071
2007	$1.36	$1.24	$0.12	$0.12/$1.24 = 0.0968
2008	$1.52	$1.36	$0.16	$0.16/$1.36 = 0.1176
2009	$1.64	$1.52	$0.12	$0.12/$1.52 = 0.0789
2010	$1.76	$1.64	$0.12	$0.12/$1.64 = 0.0732
Average			$0.1156	0.1044 or 10.44%

constant growth rate, so we can use the constant growth dividend model. In reality, using this method overestimates some years and underestimates others, but in general, we will be close to the future dividend pattern.

The Constant Growth Dividend Model with an Infinite Horizon

Let's look again at Coca-Cola and estimate the current stock price given the 10.44% constant growth rate of dividends forever and a desired return on the stock of 13.5%. Let g be the growth rate on the dividend stream and r be the rate of return required by the potential stock purchaser. Also, we will assume that the current stock owner has just received the most recent dividend, Div_0, and the new buyer will receive all future cash dividends, beginning with Div_1. This part of the setup of the model is important because the price reflects all future dividends, starting with Div_1, discounted back to today. (Price_0 refers to the price at time zero or today.) The first dividend you would receive is one full period away. Using the discounted cash flow approach, we have

$$\text{price}_0 = \frac{\text{Div}_0 \times (1+g)^1}{(1+r)^1} + \frac{\text{Div}_0(1+g)^2}{(1+r)^2} + \frac{\text{Div}_0(1+g)^3}{(1+r)^3} + \cdots + \frac{\text{Div}_0(1+g)^\infty}{(1+r)^\infty} \qquad \textbf{7.4}$$

where g is the annual growth rate in the dividends and r is the required rate of return on the stock.

We can simplify Equation 7.4 to:

$$\text{price}_0 = \frac{\text{Div}_0 \times (1+g)}{r-g} \qquad \textbf{7.5}$$

and

$$\text{Div}_1 = \text{Div}_0 \times (1+g)$$

so

$$\text{price}_0 = \frac{\text{Div}_1}{r - g} \quad \textbf{7.6}$$

This classic constant growth dividend model, or the Gordon model, is a fundamental stock pricing model. The **Gordon model** determines a stock's value based on a future stream of dividends that grows at a constant rate. Again, we assume that this constant growing dividend stream will pay forever.

To see how the constant growth model works, let's use Coca-Cola once again as a test case. The last dividend (Div_0) is \$1.76, the growth rate (g) is 10.44%, and the required rate of return (r) is 13.5%, so, applying Equation 7.5,

$$\text{price}_0 = \frac{\$1.76 \times (1 + 0.1044)}{0.135 - 0.1044} = \frac{\$1.943774}{0.0306} = \$63.52$$

Our estimated price for Coca-Cola with a 13.5% required return is \$63.52. The price was \$62.40 at the end of the year 2010.

Notice that the formula requires the return rate r to be greater than the growth rate g of the dividend stream. If g is greater than r, we are dividing by a negative number and producing a negative price, a price that is meaningless.

Let's pick another company and see if we can apply the dividend growth model and price the company's stock with a different dividend history. In addition, Example 7.3 will provide a shortcut method to estimate g, although you could still calculate each year's percentage change and then average the changes over the ten years.

EXAMPLE 7.3 Estimating a stock price from a past dividend pattern

Problem Johnson & Johnson paid the following dividends per share from 2001 to 2010:

Johnson & Johnson Annual Dividends

2001	2002	2003	2004	2005	2006	2007	2008	2009	2010
\$0.70	\$0.80	\$0.925	\$1.095	\$1.275	\$1.455	\$1.59	\$1.795	\$1.93	\$2.11

If you believe Johnson & Johnson will continue this dividend pattern forever and you want to earn 17% on your investment, what would you be willing to pay for the company's stock as of January 1, 2011?

Solution First, we need to estimate the annual growth rate of this dividend stream. We can use a shortcut to determining the average growth rate by using the first and last dividends in the stream and the time value of money equation. (You have already seen this method in Chapter 3 when we solved for the interest rate or growth rate.) We want to find the average growth rate given an initial dividend (present value) of \$0.70, the most recent dividend (future value) of \$2.11, and the number of years between the two dividends (n) of 9, or the number of dividend changes. So,

$$g = \left(\frac{FV}{PV}\right)^{1/n} - 1 \quad \textbf{7.7}$$

$$= \left(\frac{\$2.11}{\$0.70}\right)^{1/9} - 1 = 3.0142857^{1/9} - 1 = 0.1304 \quad \text{or} \quad 13.04\%$$

A calculator makes short work of obtaining the average growth rate:

Input	9	?	−0.70	0	2.11
Key	N	I/Y	PV	PMT	FV
CPT		**13.04**			

Now, if the growth rate g equals 13.04% and the required rate of return r equals 17.00%, the price you should be willing to pay for Johnson & Johnson, according to Equation 7.5, is

$$\text{price}_0 = \frac{\$2.11 \times (1 + 0.1304)}{0.1700 - 0.1304} = \frac{\$2.3852}{0.0396} = \mathbf{\$60.23}$$

At the beginning of January 2011, Johnson & Johnson sold for around $61.00 per share. Truth be told, we selected the 17% return for Johnson & Johnson in Example 7.3 so that the price would be consistent with the actual trading price as of January 1, 2011. In reality, though, it is not an unreasonable return for that company.

We now have two methods to estimate g, the growth rate of the dividends. The first method of calculating the change in dividend each year and then averaging these changes is the arithmetic approach. The second method of using the first and last dividends only is the geometric approach. The arithmetic approach is equivalent to a simple interest approach, and the geometric approach is equivalent to a compounded interest approach.

The Constant Growth Dividend Model with a Finite Horizon

To apply Equation 7.6, we had to assume that the company would pay dividends forever and that we would hold onto our stock forever. If we assume that we will sell the stock at some point in the future, however, can we use this formula to estimate the stock's value held for a finite period of time? The answer is a qualified yes. We can adjust this model for a finite horizon to estimate the present value of the dividend stream that we will receive while holding the stock. We still have a problem in estimating the stock's selling price at the end of this finite dividend stream, and we will address this issue shortly. For the finite growing dividend stream, we adjust the infinite stream in Equation 7.5 to

$$\text{price}_0 = \frac{\text{Div}_0 \times (1 + g)}{r - g} \times \left[1 - \left(\frac{1 + g}{1 + r}\right)^n\right] \qquad \textbf{7.8}$$

where n is the number of future dividends. Equation 7.8 may look very complicated, but just focus on the far right part of the model. This part calculates the percentage of the finite dividend stream that you will receive if you sell the stock at the end of the nth year. Say you will sell Johnson & Johnson after ten years. What percentage of the $60.23 (the finite dividend stream) will you get? Begin with:

$$\text{10 years: percent} = 1 - \left(\frac{1 + 0.1304}{1 + 0.170}\right)^{10}$$

$$= 1 - 0.966154^{10} = 1 - 0.7087 = 0.2913$$

Now multiply the result by the price for your portion of the infinite stream:

$$\text{price} = \$60.23 \times 0.2913 = \$17.55$$

The next step is to discount the selling price of Johnson & Johnson in ten years at 17% and then add the two pieces for the stock's price. So, how do we estimate the stock's price at the end of ten years? If we elect to sell the stock after ten years and the company will continue to pay dividends at the same growth rate, what would a buyer be willing to pay? How could we estimate the selling price (value) of the stock at that time?

1. We need to estimate the dividend in ten years and assume a growth rate and required return of the new owner at that point in time. Let's assume that the new owner also wants 17% return and that the dividend growth rate will remain at 13.04%. We calculate the dividend in ten years by taking the *current growth rate* plus one raised to the tenth power times the current dividend:

$$\text{Div}_{10} = \$2.11 \times (1.1304)^{10} = \$2.11 \times 3.4066 = \$7.1879$$

2. We then use the dividend growth model with infinite horizon, Equation 7.5, to determine the price in ten years:

$$\text{price}_{10} = \frac{\$7.1879 \times (1 + 0.1304)}{0.1700 - 0.1304} = \frac{\$8.1252}{0.0396} = \$205.1828$$

Your value for the stock today—given that you will receive the growing dividend stream for ten years and sell for $258.10 in ten years, and also given that you want a 17% return over the ten years—is:

$$\text{price} = \frac{\$205.18}{(1.1700)^{10}} + \frac{\$2.11 \times (1 + 0.1304)}{0.1700 - 0.1304} \times \left[1 - \left(\frac{1 + 0.1304}{1 + 0.1700}\right)^{10}\right]$$

$$= \$42.68 + \$17.55 = \$60.23$$

Why did you get this same $60.23 for your stock (the infinite horizon price) with the finite model? The reason is that the required rate of return of the stock remained at 17% (your rate) and the growth rate for the dividends remained at 13.04%. The infinite growth model gives the same price as the finite model with a future selling price as long as the required return and the growth rate are the same for all future sales of the stock.

Although this point may be subtle, what we have just shown is that the stock's price is its future dividend stream. When you sell the stock, the buyer purchases the remaining dividend stream. If that individual should sell the stock in the future, the new owner would buy the remaining dividends. That will always be the case: a buyer is buying the future dividend stream.

For a fascinating case of mispricing an asset, see the nearby "Finance Follies" feature.

Nonconstant Growth Dividends

One final issue to address in this section is how we price a stock when the dividend pattern is not constant or constant growth. Let's go back to Chapter 4, where we first introduced the annuity stream concept. When a future pattern is not an annuity or the modified annuity stream of a constant growth, there is no shortcut. You would have to estimate every future dividend and then discount each individual dividend back to the present. All is not lost, however. Sometimes you can see patterns in the dividends. For example, a firm might shift into a dividend stream pattern in which you can use one of the dividend models to take a shortcut for pricing the stock. Let's look at an example.

FINANCE FOLLIES

Irrational Expectations: Bulbs and Bubbles

Why do investors behave the way they do? Can we assume they act rationally by considering all available information before making buy or sell decisions?

Consider the phenomenon of *herding*, the tendency to assume the crowd has superior knowledge. When a particular stock or group of stocks rises remarkably in price over a period of time, investors sometimes "pile on," buying the stocks and driving their prices up even further. Just as with a herd, large numbers of investors head in the same direction at the same time. At some point, however, the herd switches direction and all exit at the same time, driving the price below fundamental values. Eventually, these trends reverse yet again and the prices reflect more reasonable expectations about future economic performance.

The most notorious case of herding and speculation in financial history was the tulip bulb mania that spread throughout Holland in the 1630s. Imported from Turkey at the turn of the sixteenth century, tulip bulbs eventually developed a benign virus that resulted in beautiful streaks of color on the petals and all sorts of unusual color combinations. Soon, the normally sane Dutch middle class bid up prices, and it became all the rage to collect bulbs. In one month, the price of a bulb increased twentyfold. (Put in other terms, it was as if you had invested $1,000 and then one month later returned to find your investment yielding $20,000.) At the peak of the speculation, a single bulb could be traded for an entire estate! Then, suddenly, wiser investors began to sell their bulbs for cold cash, and soon the market plummeted. Fortunes were lost, panic ensued. The bulb that had been able to buy an estate was now worth the price of an onion.

Such a heightened state of speculative fervor has been dubbed "irrational exuberance," a phrase coined by Alan Greenspan in 1996. It can be used to describe any overvalued market such as the Dutch tulip craze. Could such mania strike again?

It did in a partial sense not too long ago. From 1997 through 2000, many Internet stocks—the so-called glamour stocks of the time—rose to values that seemed completely disconnected from their future earnings potential. Investors believed that Internet companies, many of them in start-up phase, would revolutionize commerce and become extremely profitable. These investors seemed to forget their history lessons. Many Internet companies did, in fact, fail in 2000 and 2001. As with the Dutch tulip case, irrational exuberance was a contributing factor in the bursting of the technology bubble.

Such speculative fervor (or speculative mania, depending on one's point of view) can cause stocks to be mispriced for fairly long periods, but investors eventually get it right and the price approaches levels consistent with the valuation models. All speculative crazes and stampeding herds eventually subside.

EXAMPLE 7.4 Nonconstant dividend pattern

Problem DiSante and Company is a small start-up firm that will institute a dividend payment—a $0.25 dividend—for the first time at the end of this year. The company expects rapid growth over the next four years and will increase its dividend to $0.50, then to $1.50, and then to $3.00 before settling into a constant growth dividend pattern with dividends growing at 5% every year. If you believe that DiSante and Company will deliver this dividend pattern and you desire a 13% return on your investment, what price should you pay for this stock?

Solution First, let's look at a time line of the dividends of DiSante and Company.

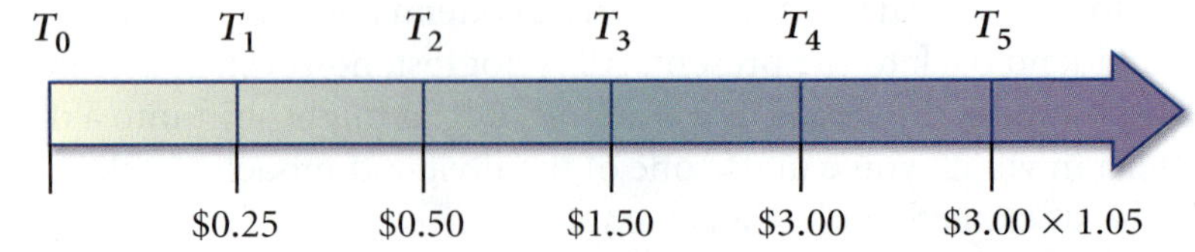

To price this stock, we will need to discount the first four dividends at 13% and then discount the constant growth portion of the dividends where the purchaser would receive the first dividend at the end of period five. Let's calculate the first four dividends:

$$PV = \frac{\$0.25}{(1.13)^1} + \frac{\$0.50}{(1.13)^2} + \frac{\$1.50}{(1.13)^3} + \frac{\$3.00}{(1.13)^4}$$
$$= \$0.22 + \$0.39 + \$1.04 + \$1.84 = \$3.49$$

We now turn to the constant growth dividend pattern, where we can use our infinite horizon constant growth model:

$$\text{price}_4 = \frac{\$3.00 \times (1 + 0.05)}{0.13 - 0.05} = \frac{\$3.15}{0.08} = \$39.375$$

This figure is the price of the constant growth portion at the end of the fourth period, so we still need to discount it back to the present at the 13% required rate of return:

$$\text{price}_0 = \frac{\$39.375}{(1.13)^4} = \$24.15$$

So, the price of this stock with the nonconstant dividend pattern is

$$\text{price} = \$3.49 + \$24.15 = \mathbf{\$27.64}$$

7.4 Dividend Model Shortcomings

The dividend models (constant growth and constant dividend) appeal to the fundamental concepts of asset pricing: (1) the future cash flow to which the owner is entitled while holding the asset and (2) the required rate of return for the cash flow determines the value of a financial asset. A problem arises, however, in that future cash flow may be difficult to predict as to timing and amount. To illustrate this failure, let's look first at five different companies in which the dividend growth model appears to work well with their recent dividend histories. We will then look at five other companies in which the model does not provide us with a reasonable estimate and is out of line with our understanding of a reasonable return when investing in these companies.

First, let's look at the companies in Table 7.4 in which the dividend model works well. Rather than assign an expected return, we will let the dividend pattern and current price solve for the return. We'll use the recent dividend pattern to calculate the growth rate, and, using the current price, we'll determine the required return for the stock using the dividend growth model.

We have provided the growth rates in Table 7.4, but let's look at one company to see how we derived the rate. For Coca-Cola,

$$g = \left(\frac{FV}{PV}\right)^{1/n} - 1$$

$$\text{Coca-Cola's } g = \left(\frac{\$1.76}{\$0.72}\right)^{1/9} - 1 = 0.1044 \quad \text{or} \quad 10.44\%$$

TABLE 7.4 Recent Dividend History of Five Firms

	Annual Dividends				
Year	Coca-Cola	J & J	Wal-Mart	3M	Intel
2001	$ 0.720	$ 0.700	$ 0.280	$ 1.200	$ 0.080
2002	$ 0.800	$ 0.800	$ 0.300	$ 1.240	$ 0.080
2003	$ 0.880	$ 0.925	$ 0.360	$ 1.320	$ 0.080
2004	$ 1.000	$ 1.095	$ 0.520	$ 1.440	$ 0.160
2005	$ 1.120	$ 1.275	$ 0.600	$ 1.680	$ 0.320
2006	$ 1.240	$ 1.455	$ 0.672	$ 1.840	$ 0.400
2007	$ 1.360	$ 1.590	$ 0.880	$ 1.920	$ 0.452
2008	$ 1.520	$ 1.795	$ 0.952	$ 2.000	$ 0.548
2009	$ 1.640	$ 1.930	$ 1.092	$ 2.040	$ 0.560
2010	$ 1.760	$ 2.110	$ 1.212	$ 2.100	$ 0.632
Price	$ 62.40	$ 58.72	$55.31	$ 86.88	$ 21.11
Growth	10.44%	13.04%	17.68%	6.42%	25.82%

You can confirm the growth rates for the other four companies using this same approach.

Again, the calculator makes short work of obtaining the average growth rate, but we need to remember that N is the number of changes, not the number of dividends in the pattern. So, for a ten-year string of dividends, N is 9 because there are nine dividend changes.

Input	9	?	−0.72	0	1.76
Key	N	I/Y	PV	PMT	FV
CPT		10.44			

Now, if we take the current price and use the dividend growth formula, we have the following expected returns (assuming the past dividend stream is a good predictor of future dividend streams):

$$r = \frac{\text{Div}_0 \times (1 + g)}{\text{price}} + g \tag{7.9}$$

$$\text{Coca-Cola's } r = \left(\frac{\$1.76 \times (1 + 0.1044)}{\$62.40}\right) + 0.1044 = 0.1356 \quad \text{or} \quad 13.56\%$$

$$\text{Johnson \& Johnson's } r = \left(\frac{\$2.11 \times (1 + 0.1304)}{\$58.72}\right) + 0.1304 = 0.1710 \quad \text{or} \quad 17.10\%$$

$$\text{Wal-Mart's } r = \left(\frac{\$1.212 \times (1 + 0.1768)}{\$55.31}\right) + 0.1768 = 0.2026 \quad \text{or} \quad 20.26\%$$

$$3M\text{'s } r = \left(\frac{\$2.10 \times (1 + 0.0642)}{\$86.88}\right) + 0.0642 = 0.0899 \quad \text{or} \quad 8.99\%$$

$$\text{Intel's } r = \left(\frac{\$0.632 \times (1 + 0.2582)}{\$21.11}\right) + 0.2582 = 0.2958 \quad \text{or} \quad 29.58\%$$

Although these returns may look reasonable, there may be a problem brewing here. Recall from Chapter 5 that we require a higher return for riskier investments. If we rank these five stocks based on the lowest to highest required return using the dividend model, we should also be ranking these stocks based on the lowest to highest risk (see Table 7.5).

Most analysts would not have a problem with the order of risk for these firms, but the spread between the returns may be much too large over the long run. In Chapter 8 we look at the risk and return relationship that gives rise to our concern over these results.

Now let's look at five companies in which the dividend growth model provides no answer or answers that seem way out of line for long-run expected returns. See Table 7.6. The first problem we see is that the dividend growth

TABLE 7.5 Ranking of Stock Risk Levels Based on Expected Returns

Company	Return	Risk Rank
3M	8.99%	Lowest (1)
Coca Cola	13.56%	Low (2)
Johnson & Johnson	17.10%	Middle (3)
Wal-Mart	20.56%	High (4)
Intel	29.58%	Highest (5)

TABLE 7.6 Recent Annual Dividends of Five Other Firms

Year	Exxon	GM	Ford	Google	Amazon
2001	$ 0.900	$ 2.00	$ 1.05	$ —	$ —
2002	$ 0.920	$ 2.00	$ 0.40	$ —	$ —
2003	$ 0.980	$ 2.00	$ 0.40	$ —	$ —
2004	$ 1.060	$ 2.00	$ 0.40	$ —	$ —
2005	$ 1.140	$ 2.00	$ 0.40	$ —	$ —
2006	$ 1.280	$ 1.00	$ 0.25	$ —	$ —
2007	$ 1.370	$ —	$ —	$ —	$ —
2008	$ 1.550	$ —	$ —	$ —	$ —
2009	$ 1.660	$ —	$ —	$ —	$ —
2010	$ 1.740	$ —	$ —	$ —	$ —
Price	$79.80	$36.49	$15.95	$600.36	$169.64
Growth	7.60%	−100.00%	−100.00%		

model appears to underestimate the expected return for some stocks. Look at ExxonMobil, with steady and increasing dividends from year to year, but low growth rates in the dividend stream. The model produces a very low expected return. Applying Equation 7.9, we have

$$\text{ExxonMobil's } r = \left(\frac{\$1.74 \times (1 + 0.076)}{\$79.80}\right)^{1/9} + 0.076 = 0.0995 \quad \text{or} \quad 9.95\%$$

ExxonMobil, with its strong and steady dividend policy, fits in well with the first five firms, but we may be seeing the first signs of analysts underestimating some firms with this method (ExxonMobil and 3M) and overestimating others (Wal-Mart and Intel). The second problem with the dividend growth model relates to situations in which firms have a dividend reduction or suspension. The next two firms, General Motors (GM) and Ford, paid fairly large dividends over the first part of the ten-year period, but the firms suspended their dividends in 2007. Therefore, the estimated growth rate and expected return is a negative 100%.

$$\text{General Motor's } r = \frac{\$0 \times (1 - 1)}{\$38.49} - 1.00 = -1.00 \quad \text{or} \quad -100\%$$

$$\text{Ford's } r = \frac{\$0 \times (1 - 1)}{\$15.95} - 1.00 = -1.00 \quad \text{or} \quad -100\%$$

This second set of data shows that the dividend growth model will produce a negative expected return of 100% whenever a firm suspends dividends. If a firm simply reduces dividends, the model produces a negative return. A negative expected return implies that stock prices will fall. Why would anyone want to buy a stock whose value is expected to fall?

On the other hand, the cutting of dividends and the negative growth rate may just foreshadow a fall in stock prices. With rising gasoline prices in 2008 and the financial meltdown in the fall of 2008, General Motors' and Ford's prices plummeted to $0.75 and $1.58, respectively, by the spring of 2009. General Motors filed for bankruptcy and emerged with a new stock offering on November 18, 2010. General Motors' new stock was trading at $36.49 at the end of 2010, and Ford was trading at $15.95 at year's end 2010.

The final two firms, Google and Amazon.com, have yet to pay a cash dividend. This lack of a dividend pattern means that we cannot use historical dividend changes to estimate the growth of future dividends or when the companies will pay dividends, if ever. We will need to either estimate the future dividend stream from some other source or model or abandon the dividend models for estimating the current prices of non-dividend-paying stocks.

Apparently, what we need is a pricing model that is more inclusive than the dividend model, one that can estimate expected returns for stocks without the need for a stable dividend history. Enter the capital asset pricing model, which we address in Chapter 8. We will introduce an application of this model called the security market line that will be more inclusive and will provide expected returns for companies based on their risk, the premium for taking on risk, the reward for waiting and not on their historical dividend patterns.

7.5 Preferred Stock

A rather unique stock sold by companies is **preferred stock**, an ownership class of stock that has preferential claims. It generally features a dividend that the company must pay out before dividends to common stockholders, and in case of bankruptcy and liquidation, it has priority claim to assets before common stockholders. The preferred stock holder is entitled to a set (or constant) dividend every period. The preferred stock usually has a stated or par value, but—unlike bonds—the company does not repay this par value at maturity because preferred stocks do not have a maturity date. The only time the company would pay this par value to the shareholder is if the company ceases operations or retires the preferred stock. Some preferred stocks are **cumulative** in dividends, meaning that if a company skips a cash dividend, it must pay it at some point in the future. Skipped dividends become a company liability. Other preferred stocks are **noncumulative**, in which case if the company skips dividends, they are forever lost to the shareholder.

The term *preferred* comes from preferred shareholders receiving all past (if cumulative) and present dividends before common shareholders can receive any cash dividends. In other words, preferred shareholders' dividend claims are preferred over common shareholders' dividend claims. Preferred stock is usually permanent funding, but there are circumstances or covenants that could alter the payoff stream. For example, the company can convert preferred stock into common stock at a preset point in the future. In fact, it is not uncommon for companies to issue preferred stock with the right to convert to common shares after a specific waiting period.

It is this constant and preferred dividend stream that makes preferred stock look more like debt than like stock. In addition, the constant dividend stream leads nicely to the pricing of preferred stock with the four dividend models that we presented in this chapter. To price preferred stock, we use the following process:

1. We first determine the annual dividend by multiplying the stated dividend rate by the par value of the stock.
2. We then use the constant dividend model with infinite horizon (Eq. 7.2) because we have g equal to zero and n equal to infinity. We can also rearrange Equation 7.2 to determine the required return on this stock given its annual dividend and current price:

$$r = \frac{\text{dividend}}{\text{price}} \tag{7.10}$$

EXAMPLE 7.5 Return on preferred stock

Problem Foster Trucking Incorporated has just issued preferred stock (cumulative) with a par value of \$100 and an annual dividend rate of 7%. The preferred stock is currently selling for \$35 per share. What is the yield or return on this preferred stock?

Solution The first step is to determine the annual dividend by multiplying the dividend rate by the par value: $\$100 \times 0.07 = \$7.00$. Now, using this \$7 annual dividend, the \$35 current price, and Equation 7.10, we have

$$r = \frac{\$7.00}{\$35.00} = \mathbf{0.20} \quad \text{or} \quad \mathbf{20\%}$$

We have introduced the concept of *return* here, which you should think of as both the anticipated return for the preferred stockholder and the cost of borrowing money for this particular type of capital. We will examine what we call the cost of capital more closely in later chapters. It will become very apparent that the cost of capital is directly related to yields for bonds, which we introduced in Chapter 6, and the returns for stock from this chapter.

7.6 Efficient Markets

For the public, the real concern in the buying and selling of stock through the stock market is the question, "How do I know if I'm getting the best available price for my transaction?" We might ask an even broader question: "Do these markets provide the best prices and the quickest possible execution of a trade?" In other words, we want to know whether markets are efficient. By **efficient markets**, we mean that these stocks trade in a market in which costs are minimal and prices are current and fair to all traders. To answer our questions, we will look at two forms of efficiency: operational efficiency and informational efficiency.

Operational Efficiency

Operational efficiency concerns the speed and accuracy of processing a buy or sell order at the best available price. Through the years, the competitive nature of the market has promoted operational efficiency. For example, today the NYSE uses a designated-order turnaround computer system (SuperDOT) to manage orders. SuperDOT executes more than a billion shares of trading every day. The system matches buyers and sellers within seconds and executes trades with confirmation to both parties in a matter of seconds, with buyers and sellers getting the best available prices.

NASDAQ uses a small-order execution system (SOES) to process orders. Current practice with registered dealers is for SOES to display all limit orders (orders awaiting execution at specified price), public display of the best dealer quotes, and public display of the best customer limit order sizes. Public access to the best available prices promotes operational efficiency.

This speed at matching buyers and sellers at the best available price is strong evidence that the stock markets are operationally efficient.

Informational Efficiency

A second measure of efficiency is **informational efficiency**, or how quickly a source reflects comprehensive information in the available trading prices. A price is efficient if the market has used all available information to set it, which implies that stocks always trade at their fair value. If an investor does not receive the most current information, the prices are "stale"; therefore, the investor is at a trading disadvantage. Financial economists have devised three versions of efficient markets from an information perspective: weak form, semi-strong form, and strong form. These three forms constitute the efficient market hypothesis. Believers in these three forms of efficient markets maintain, in varying degrees, that it is pointless to search for undervalued stocks, sell stocks at inflated prices, or predict market trends.

In **weak-form efficient markets**, current prices reflect the stock's price history and trading volume. It is useless to chart historical stock prices to predict future stock prices such that you can identify mispriced stocks and routinely outperform the market. In other words, technical analysis cannot beat the market. The market itself is the best technical analyst.

In **semi-strong-form efficient markets**, current prices already reflect the stock's price history and volume, as well as all available public information. It is useless to try to exploit publicly available news or financial statement information to routinely outperform the market. The semi-strong form incorporates the assumptions of weak form and adds public information.

In **strong-form efficient markets**, current prices reflect the stock's price and volume history, all publicly available information, and even all private information. All information is already embedded in the price, and there is no advantage to using insider information to routinely outperform the market. This form incorporates the assumptions of weak form, semi-strong form, and private information.

Efficient market beliefs, in their various forms, can be controversial. For example, it is probably incorrect to assume that insiders—especially company officers—do not have access to information that they could use to routinely profit on the stock. This version is usually not supported in belief or research. It is probably correct to believe that insider information exists and that one can use it to beat the market.

The question then becomes, "Are markets efficient at the weak or semi-strong versions?" Most academic research supports markets as semi-strong efficient. In fact, research has demonstrated that markets fully reflect public information within minutes, leaving little opportunity for exploiting this information into sizable gains.

Stock markets are essentially efficient markets because, in the Internet age, all public information is fully available within minutes and fully reflected in stocks' prices. In efficient markets, it is difficult to exploit information for personal gain because all parties have access to the same history and information.

The equity markets are quite dynamic in terms of processing trades and incorporating information in prices, and therefore are very efficient markets. Most traders believe that the market treats their orders fairly and that they are receiving the best available price, yet there is always room for the diligent trader to try to capture valuable information for trading. As in many areas, there are the lucky investors who see their investments rise without any specific trading knowledge or company information.

To review this chapter, see the Summary Card at the end of the text.

Key Terms

American Stock Exchange (AMEX), p. 185
ask price, p. 186
authorized shares, p. 183
bear market, p. 186
best efforts, p. 185
bid price, p. 186
bid-ask spread, p. 186
bull market, p. 186
common stock, p.182
constant annual dividend, p. 189
constant growth, p. 191
cumulative (dividends), p. 201
due diligence, p. 185
efficient markets, p. 202
equity claim, p. 182
firm commitment, p. 185
Gordon model, p. 193
informational efficiency, p. 202
initial public offering (IPO), p. 185

issued shares, p. 183
National Association of Securities Dealers (NASD), p. 185
National Association of Securities Dealers Automated Quotation System (NASDAQ), p. 185
New York Stock Exchange (NYSE), p. 185
noncumulative (dividends), p. 201
operational efficiency, p. 202
outstanding shares, p. 183
preemptive rights, p. 184
preferred stock, p. 201
primary markets, p. 184
prospectus, p. 185
Regulation A, p. 183
residual claim, p. 182
secondary markets, p. 184
Securities Exchange Commission, p.183
semi-strong-form efficient markets, p. 203
specialist, p. 185
spread, p. 186
strong-form efficient markets, p. 203
treasury stock, p. 184
weak-form efficient markets, p. 202

Questions

1. What are three key features of common stock?
2. What are the differences between authorized, issued, and outstanding shares?
3. What is the role of the investment banker in the primary sale of common stock?
4. What are the potential repercussions if the investment banker does not perform the due diligence task?
5. What is the function of a specialist in the secondary market?
6. What is a bid price, and what is an ask price?
7. What is the difference between preferred stock and common stock?
8. How is operational efficiency different from informational efficiency?
9. What are SuperDOT and SOES, and what do they do?
10. What does a semi-strong-form efficient market require?

Prepping for Exams

1. Stocks are different from bonds because _______________.
   - **a.** stocks, unlike bonds, are major sources of funds
   - **b.** stocks, unlike bonds, represent residual ownership
   - **c.** stocks, unlike bonds, give owners legal claims to payments
   - **d.** bonds, unlike stocks, represent voting ownership

2. A typical practice of many companies is to distribute part of the earnings to shareholders through _______________.
   - **a.** quarterly stock splits
   - **b.** quarterly cash dividends
   - **c.** semiannual cash dividends
   - **d.** annual stock dividends

3. Which of the following statements is *false*?
   - **a.** Selling of shares is the selling of ownership in the company.
   - **b.** A company is said to go "public" when it opens up its ownership structure to the general public through the sale of common stock.

c. Private companies choose to sell stock to attract permanent financing through equity ownership of the company.
d. Most companies have the resident expertise to complete an initial public offering or first public equity issue.

4. You want to invest in a stock that pays $6.00 annual cash dividends for the next five years. At the end of the five years, you will sell the stock for $30.00. If you want to earn 10% on this investment, what is a fair price for this stock if you buy it today?
   a. $41.37
   b. $40.37
   c. $22.75
   d. $18.63

5. Kwak Motors Inc. pays a $1.77 preferred dividend every quarter and will maintain this policy forever. What price should you pay for one share of preferred stock if you want an annual return of 9.25% on your investment?
   a. $66.54
   b. $70.54
   c. $74.54
   d. $76.54

6. The last dividend (Div_0) is $1.80, the growth rate (*g*) is 6%, and the required rate of return (*r*) is 12%. What is the stock price according to the constant growth dividend model?
   a. $31.80
   b. $30.80
   c. $30.00
   d. $15.00

7. Sedgwick Inc. has a 12% required rate of return. It does not expect to initiate dividends for fifteen years, at which time it will pay $2.00 per share in dividends. At that time, Sedgwick expects its dividends to grow at 7% forever. If you currently own the stock and will sell it following the first dividend, what is your estimated selling price at P_{15}?
   a. $42.80
   b. $33.40
   c. $31.20
   d. $30.00

8. Which of the following statements is *true*?
   a. Preferred stock usually has a stated or par value, and, like bonds, the company does not repay this par value at maturity because preferred stocks do not have a maturity date.
   b. The company repays the par value for preferred stock at maturity, like bonds.
   c. A company bases a preferred stock's cash dividend due each year on the stated dividend rate times the stock's market value.
   d. Some preferred stocks are cumulative in dividends, meaning that if a company skips a cash dividend, it must pay it at some point in the future.

9. Dividend models suggest that _______________ determine the value of a financial asset to which the owner is entitled while holding the asset.

a. present cash flows
b. past cash flows
c. future cash flows
d. past and present cash flows

10. Which of the following statements is *true*?
a. Stock dealers are not allowed to make money on the difference between stock purchase prices and stock sale prices.
b. A bear market is a prolonged rising market, one in which stock prices in general are increasing.
c. The ask price is the price at which a dealer is willing to sell, and the bid price is the price at which a dealer is willing to buy.
d. A bull market is a prolonged declining market, one in which stock prices in general are decreasing.

These problems are available in MyFinanceLab.

Problems

1. Anderson Motors Inc. has just set the company dividend policy at $0.50 per year. The company plans to be in business forever. What is the price of this stock if
a. an investor wants a 5% return?
b. an investor wants an 8% return?
c. an investor wants a 10% return?
d. an investor wants a 13% return?
e. an investor wants a 20% return?

2. Dietterich Electronics wants its shareholders to earn a 15% return on their investment in the company. At what price would the stock need to be priced today if Dietterich Electronics had a
a. $0.25 constant annual dividend forever?
b. $1.00 constant annual dividend forever?
c. $1.75 constant annual dividend forever?
d. $2.50 constant annual dividend forever?

3. Singing Fish Fine Foods has a current annual cash dividend policy of $2.25. The price of the stock is set to yield a 12% return. What is the price of this stock if the dividend will be paid
a. for 10 years?
b. for 15 years?
c. for 40 years?
d. for 60 years?
e. for 100 years?
f. forever?

4. Pfender Guitars has a current annual cash dividend policy of $4.00. The price of the stock is set to yield an 8% return. What is the price of this stock if the dividend will be paid
a. for 10 years and then a liquidating or final dividend of $25.00?
b. for 15 years and then a liquidating or final dividend of $25.00?
c. for 40 years and then a liquidating or final dividend of $25.00?
d. for 60 years and then a liquidating or final dividend of $25.00?

e. for 100 years and then a liquidating or final dividend of $25.00?

f. forever with no liquidating dividend?

5. King Waterbeds has an annual cash dividend policy that raises the dividend each year by 4%. Last year's dividend was $0.40 per share. What is the stock's price if

a. an investor wants a 5% return?

b. an investor wants an 8% return?

c. an investor wants a 10% return?

d. an investor wants a 13% return?

e. an investor wants a 20% return?

6. Seitz Glassware is trying to determine its growth rate for an annual cash dividend. Last year's dividend was $0.25 per share. The stock's target return rate is 10%. What is the stock's price if

a. the annual growth rate is 1%?

b. the annual growth rate is 3%?

c. the annual growth rate is 5%?

d. the annual growth rate is 7%?

e. the annual growth rate is 9%?

7. Miles Hardware has an annual cash dividend policy that raises the dividend each year by 3%. Last year's dividend was $1.00 per share. Investors want a 15% return on this stock. What is the stock's price if

a. the company will be in business for five years and not have a liquidating dividend?

b. the company will be in business for fifteen years and not have a liquidating dividend?

c. the company will be in business for twenty-five years and not have a liquidating dividend?

d. the company will be in business for thirty-five years and not have a liquidating dividend?

e. the company will be in business for seventy-five years and not have a liquidating dividend?

f. the company will be in business forever?

8. Sia Dance Studios has an annual cash dividend policy that raises the dividend each year by 2%. Last year's dividend was $3.00 per share. The company will be in business for forty years with no liquidating dividend. What is the price of this stock if

a. an investor wants a 9% return?

b. an investor wants an 11% return?

c. an investor wants a 13% return?

d. an investor wants a 15% return?

e. an investor wants a 17% return?

9. Fey Fashions expects the following dividend pattern over the next seven years:

Year 1	Year 2	Year 3	Year 4	Year 5	Year 6	Year 7
$1.00	$1.10	$1.21	$1.33	$1.46	$1.61	$1.77

The company will then have a constant dividend of $2.00 forever. What is the stock's price today if an investor wants to earn

a. 15%?

b. 20%?

10. Staton-Smith Software is a new start-up company and will not pay dividends for the first five years of operation. It will then institute an annual cash dividend policy of $2.50 with a constant growth rate of 5% with the first dividend at the end of year six. The company will be in business for twenty-five years total. What is the stock's price if an investor wants

a. a 10% return?

b. a 15% return?

c. a 20% return?

d. a 40% return?

11. Fenway Athletic Club plans to offer its members preferred stock with a par value of $100 and a 6% annual dividend rate. If a member wants the following returns, what price should he or she be willing to pay?

a. Theo wants a 10% return.

b. Jonathan wants a 12% return.

c. Josh wants a 15% return.

d. Terry wants an 18% return.

12. Yankee Athletic Club has preferred stock with a par value of $50 and an annual 6% cumulative dividend. Given the following market prices for the preferred stock, what is each investor seeking for his or her return?

a. Alexis is willing to pay $40.00.

b. Derek is willing to pay $30.00.

c. Marcia is willing to pay $20.00.

d. Johnny is willing to pay $15.00.

13. Villalpondo Winery wants to raise $10 million from the sale of preferred stock. If the winery wants to sell one million shares of preferred stock, what annual dividend will it have to promise if investors demand

a. a 12% return?

b. an 18% return?

c. an 8% return?

d. a 6% return?

e. a 9% return?

f. a 7% return?

14. Find the annual dividend growth rate for each firm listed in the following table.

Dividend Payment per Year

Firm	2006	2007	2008	2009	2010	2011
Loewen	$1.00	$1.05	$1.10	$1.16	$1.22	$1.28
Morse	$1.00	$0.90	$0.81	$0.73	$0.66	$0.59
Huddleston	$1.00	$1.00	$1.00	$2.00	$2.00	$2.00
Meyer	$0.00	$0.00	$0.25	$0.50	$0.75	$1.00

15. Using Yahoo! Finance (http://finance.yahoo.com) and ticker symbol PEP, find PepsiCo's most recent dividend payments and current price. Historical dividends are available in the historical price section. Use these payments to find the annual dividend growth rate. (If you have a quarterly pattern, be sure to annualize this quarterly growth rate.) Now, find the required rate of return for this stock, assuming the future dividend growth rate will remain the same and the company has an infinite horizon. Does this return seem reasonable for PepsiCo?
16. Using Yahoo! Finance (http://finance.yahoo.com) and ticker symbol HPQ, find Hewlett-Packard's most recent dividend payments and current price. Historical dividends are available in the historical price section. Use these payments to find the annual dividend growth rate. (If you have a quarterly pattern, be sure to annualize this quarterly growth rate.) Now, find the required rate of return for this stock, assuming the future dividend growth rate will remain the same and the company has an infinite horizon. Does this return seem reasonable for Hewlett-Packard?
17. Using Yahoo! Finance, update the dividends for Coca-Cola for the last ten years. Find both the arithmetic growth rate and the geometric growth rate of the dividends.
18. Using Yahoo! Finance, update the dividends for Johnson & Johnson for the last ten years. Find both the arithmetic growth rate and the geometric growth rate of the dividends.
19. Using Yahoo! Finance, update the dividends of Wal-Mart for the last ten years. Find the arithmetic growth rate and the geometric growth rate of the dividends.
20. Using Yahoo! Finance, update the dividends of Intel for only the last six years. Find the arithmetic growth rate and the geometric growth rate of the dividends.
21. Using the answer to Problem 17 on Coca-Cola's growth rates and the current trading price, determine the current required rate of return for the company.
22. Using the answer to Problem 18 on Johnson & Johnson's growth rates and the current trading price, determine the current required rate of return for the company.
23. Using the answer to Problem 19 on Wal-Mart's growth rates and the current trading price, determine the current required rate of return for the company.
24. Using the answer to Problem 20 on Intel's growth rates and the current trading price, determine the current required rate of return for the company.
25. Given the growth rates for Coca-Cola, Johnson & Johnson, Wal-Mart, and Intel from the dividend history in Problems 21 through 24, what price would you predict for each stock if each had a required return of 18%? Why are Wal-Mart and Intel prices troublesome?
26. Assume ExxonMobil's price dropped to $30 overnight. Given the dividend growth rate of ExxonMobil of 5.07% and the last annual dividend of $1.28, what is the implied required rate of return necessary to justify the new lower market price of $30.00?
27. Peterson Packaging Inc. does not currently pay dividends. The company will start with a $0.50 dividend at the end of year three and grow it by 10% for each of the next six years until it nearly reaches $1.00. After six years of growth, it will fix its dividend at $1.00 forever. If you want a 15% return on this stock, what should you pay today given this future dividend stream?

These problems are available in MyFinanceLab.

Advanced Problems for Spreadsheet Application

1. ***Dividend history and dividend growth rates.*** Following is a recent twenty-year period in the history of Chevron. Given these data, construct the average dividend growth rate of Chevron quarter by quarter. Restate the quarterly rate as an annual rate. Find the growth rate using the formula $g = (FV/PV)^{1/n} - 1$ where FV is the last dividend in the dividend history, PV is the first dividend in the dividend history, and n is the number of dividend changes (the number of dividends minus 1). Find both the quarterly change and the annual dividend change. Restate the quarterly average as an annual average using both the simple and compounding approach.

Date	Dividend	Date	Dividend	Date	Dividend	Date	Dividend
2-7-90	$0.175	2-10-95	$0.231	2-16-00	$0.325	2-14-05	$0.40
5-1-90	$0.175	5-11-95	$0.231	5-17-00	$0.325	5-17-05	$0.45
7-31-90	$0.19375	8-15-95	$0.25	8-16-00	$0.325	8-17-05	$0.45
11-6-90	$0.19375	11-15-95	$0.25	11-15-00	$0.325	11-16-05	$0.45
2-5-91	$0.19375	2-13-96	$0.25	2-14-01	$0.325	2-14-06	$0.45
4-30-91	$0.20625	5-14-96	$0.25	5-16-01	$0.325	5-17-06	$0.52
8-6-91	$0.20625	8-13-96	$0.27	8-15-01	$0.325	8-16-06	$0.52
11-5-91	$0.20625	11-13-96	$0.27	11-14-01	$0.35	11-15-06	$0.52
2-4-92	$0.20625	2-18-97	$0.29	2-13-02	$0.35	2-14-07	$0.52
5-5-92	$0.20625	5-16-97	$0.29	5-15-02	$0.35	5-16-07	$0.58
8-4-92	$0.20625	8-18-97	$0.29	8-15-02	$0.35	8-15-07	$0.58
11-3-92	$0.20625	11-18-97	$0.29	11-14-02	$0.35	11-14-07	$0.58
2-4-93	$0.21875	2-16-98	$0.305	2-12-03	$0.35	2-13-08	$0.58
5-4-93	$0.21875	5-18-98	$0.305	5-15-03	$0.35	5-15-08	$0.65
8-3-93	$0.21875	8-18-98	$0.305	8-15-03	$0.365	8-15-08	$0.65
11-4-93	$0.21875	11-18-98	$0.305	11-14-03	$0.365	11-14-08	$0.65
2-4-94	$0.23125	2-17-99	$0.305	2-13-04	$0.365	2-12-09	$0.65
5-4-94	$0.23125	5-18-99	$0.305	5-17-04	$0.365	5-15-09	$0.65
8-4-94	$0.231	8-18-99	$0.305	8-17-04	$0.40	8-17-09	$0.68
11-4-94	$0.231	11-17-99	$0.325	11-16-04	$0.40	11-16-09	$0.68

2. ***Changing stock price year by year.*** The price of a stock can vary from year to year. Using the dividend model and the information on the next page, calculate the dividend price each year and then graph the changing price of the stock.

Current dividend is $2.80, dividend growth rate is 4.0%, and required return is:

Year	Return	Year	Return	Year	Return	Year	Return	Year	Return
1	11.20%	4	11.45%	7	11.55%	10	11.73%	13	10.96%
2	12.15%	5	12.06%	8	10.83%	11	11.98%	14	12.15%
3	10.98%	6	12.98%	9	10.22%	12	11.42%	15	11.55%

MINI-CASE

Lawrence's Legacy: Part 1

This mini-case is available in MyFinanceLab.

Don Kraska, a senior stockbroker and certified financial analyst with a well-known, full-service brokerage, was studying the list of questions that were to form the basis of his presentation before a committee of officials from the town of Webley. Two days ago, he received a call from Webley's finance director. She informed him that the town had received a pleasant but challenging surprise in the form of a bequest from the estate of a successful local businessman, James Lawrence. Lawrence had left the town 2,000 shares of Google stock, currently valued at approximately $1,250,000.

Lawrence had purchased the shares in 2004 at the subscription price of $100 per share. When the stock's value increased tremendously, Lawrence decided that rather than sell it and pay capital gains taxes, he would donate the shares to a good cause upon his death. The terms of the legacy required the town to set up a trust fund, which they would name the Virginia Lawrence Memorial Trust, in honor of James Lawrence's wife, who had been active in youth-oriented community groups. The trust was to distribute 5% of the trust's value in the form of grants each year to community groups involved with youth activities.

The will specifically stated that the trust should sell the Google shares as soon as possible and use the proceeds to create a diversified stock portfolio. Over the long term, Lawrence expected the portfolio's value to increase by 8% to 12% a year, thus allowing the grants to grow at the rate of inflation or better.

Assume that you are in Kraska's position, preparing to answer the committee's questions. The committee members are educated, intelligent people with no specialized training in investments. Kraska realizes that for some of the questions, he will inevitably have to "do the math." He originally intended to use his laptop, a projector, and a computer program that emulates a financial calculator, but when he learned that the committee included a high school math teacher and a civil engineer, he decided to use basic formulas in his presentation as well. Following are some of the questions that committee members asked at the meeting.

Questions

1. Why do you think that Lawrence specified to invest the money in stocks rather than bonds or certificates of deposit?
2. How will the trust obtain the cash to make the grants if the dividends do not amount to 5% of the portfolio's value?
3. What is the difference between common stock and preferred stock?
4. How do we know if we are paying a fair price for the stock that we purchase?
5. For what are we actually paying when we buy a share of stock?

   Kraska intends to use the following examples to answer this question.

   a. ABC Inc. preferred stock pays a constant dividend of $5.00 per year. Assume that investors require a 9% rate of return.
   b. DEF Inc. common stock recently paid a dividend of $1.50. The estimated growth rate of dividends is 6% per year, and the required rate of return is 11%.
   c. GBH Inc. pays no dividend and reinvests all its earnings into rapid growth, but it is expected to begin paying dividends in five years. The first dividend will be $5.00, dividends will grow at 5% per year, and the required rate of return throughout the period is 15%.
6. Why do stock prices change so quickly and by so much?

Learning Objectives

LO1 Calculate profits and returns on an investment and convert holding period returns to annual returns.

LO2 Define risk and explain how uncertainty relates to risk.

LO3 Appreciate the historical returns of various investment choices.

LO4 Calculate standard deviations and variances with historical data.

LO5 Calculate expected returns and variances with conditional returns and probabilities.

LO6 Interpret the trade-off between risk and return.

LO7 Understand when and why diversification works at minimizing risk, and understand the difference between systematic and unsystematic risk.

LO8 Explain beta as a measure of risk in a well-diversified portfolio.

LO9 Illustrate how the security market line and the capital asset pricing model represent the two-parameter world of risk and return.

Chapter 8
Risk and Return

"Nothing ventured, nothing gained." This old proverb packs tremendous financial sense. One of the fundamental lessons of finance is that there is seldom a reward without some measure of risk. Investors understandably want to maximize return and minimize risk. Can they do so? Yes, if they follow another proverb: "Don't put all your eggs in one basket." By spreading investments across a number of different assets, a portfolio can absorb some bad performances. In other words, if a few eggs break, it is not a total disaster.

In Chapter 7, we priced stocks based on the future anticipated dividend stream. We used the dividend models with both a growth variable on the anticipated dividend stream and a required rate of return for the stock. What, though, *is* the required rate of return on a stock? Even more to the point, what is the *appropriate* required rate of return on a stock? In this chapter, we will refine our view of return and tie it to its very important partner, risk. In fact, we will only consider a world with these two concepts together. We will explore ways of avoiding some risk through *diversification*—the financial term for not putting all your eggs in one basket. Finally, we will look at ways to measure risk.

8.1 Returns

The world of finance functions in a two-parameter world of risk and return. Together, these concepts provide the formal environment for selecting investments and evaluating performance. All investors want to **maximize return** (get the most out of their investment) while at the same time **minimize risk** (eliminate their potential for loss). This risk-and-return trade-off is the "ability-to-sleep-at-night test" because it is concerned with what level of risk one can bear while remaining comfortable with one's return on an investment. In general, if your investments keep you up at night worrying about their performance, you are probably bearing too much risk.

Although return and risk are joined at the hip, so to speak, return often receives all the attention in casual conversation, whereas we relegate risk to silent-partner status. However, we must always account for risk when considering return. Making a choice based on return alone is like buying a coat for a person you have never met, with the only information available that the person weighs 150 pounds. Without knowing the person's height, you will probably find it difficult to select a coat that will be a good fit. Both pieces of information, height and weight, are critical in selecting the optimal coat size. The same is true for investment choices. You must consider both risk and return when selecting the investment that best fits the investor. We start here with an examination of return.

Dollar Profits and Percentage Returns

The measure of an asset's performance in the finance world is its profit or return. We often ask questions such as, "How much did you make on your investment?" or "How much did you lose?" There are two standard replies. You might state the answer in a dollar amount: "I made $25 on my investment," or you might state it as a percentage: "I lost 5% on my investment." We can state investment gain or loss in either dollars or percentages.

The **profit** (or loss) on an investment is the dollars that you gained (or lost) measured as the difference between the original cost of an investment and its ending value, plus any distributions that you received over the life of the investment:

$$\text{profit} = \text{ending value} + \text{distributions} - \text{original cost} \qquad \textbf{8.1}$$

Another common way to report performance is **return**, the measure of the percentage of change or the ratio of the gain (or loss) to the cost of the investment:

$$\text{return} = \frac{\text{profit}}{\text{original cost}} \quad \text{or} \quad \text{return} = \frac{\text{loss}}{\text{original cost}} \qquad \textbf{8.2}$$

Let's look at how it works.

EXAMPLE 8.1 Profit and return with and without distributions

Problem Kevin made two investments over the past two years. His first investment was a baseball card that cost $50.00, which he sold three months later for $55.00. The second was a share of stock in a start-up company. The stock cost $42.00. He held the stock for two years, received a cash dividend of $0.90, and then sold the stock for $47.82. What were his profit and return for these two investments? Which was the better investment?

Solution For the baseball card, Kevin's profit was $5.00, the difference between his selling and buying prices: $55.00 − $50.00. His return was

$$r = \frac{\$5.00}{\$50.00} = \mathbf{10\%}$$

For the start-up company stock, his profit was $6.72, the $0.90 cash dividend and the $5.82 difference between his selling and buying prices: $47.82 − $42.00. His return was

$$r = \frac{\$6.72}{\$42.00} = \mathbf{16.0\%}$$

Which was the better investment? Based on the dollar profit or percentage return, most would say that the stock was a better investment because it had a higher profit and higher rate of return. However, we have some issues to handle concerning these two investments before we can conclude which actually was better.

These numbers are not really comparable because the investment periods are different. The first investment choice is for a three-month period, whereas the second is for two years. Investment choices often span periods that are shorter or longer than a year. To compare investment performances, however, it is necessary to view them over a similar period of time. Recall in Chapter 5 that we normally state interest rates on an annual basis. The same holds true for investment returns. Above we have calculated a **holding period return (HPR)**, which is the return that we measured from the initial purchase to the final sale of the investment without regard to the length of time the individual holds the investment.

We can state the holding period return in a variety of ways, three of which are:

$$HPR = \frac{\text{profit}}{\text{cost}} \qquad \textbf{8.3a}$$

$$HPR = \frac{\text{ending price} + \text{distributions} - \text{beginning price}}{\text{beginning price}} \qquad \textbf{8.3b}$$

$$HPR = \frac{\text{ending price} + \text{distributions}}{\text{beginning price}} - 1 \qquad \textbf{8.3c}$$

Converting Holding Period Returns to Annual Returns

To compare investments based on returns, we need to state them in annual terms. So, we need to restate the 10% holding period return on the baseball card and the 16% return on the start-up company stock in annual terms before we can compare them. There are two ways to convert a holding period return to an annual return. One method uses the concept of simple interest, and the other uses the concept of compounding interest. Simple interest is akin to the annual percentage rate (APR), and compounded interest is akin to the effective annual rate (EAR).

Let's look at the 10% and the 16% returns from both perspectives.

1. In the simple interest perspective, we divide the holding period rate by the number of years (n). For the 10% return, we need to remember that it is for one-fourth or 0.25 of a year, and for the 16%, it is for two years. So,

$$\text{simple annual return} = \frac{HPR}{n} \qquad \textbf{8.4}$$

$$APR \text{ baseball card} = \frac{0.10}{0.25} = \mathbf{0.40} \text{ or } \mathbf{40\%}$$

$$APR \text{ start-up company stock} = \frac{0.16}{2} = \mathbf{0.08} \text{ or } \mathbf{8\%}$$

2. Now let's see what we get from the compounding perspective. The effective annual return (or investment return) when we use compounding interest is

$$EAR = (1 + HPR)^{1/n} - 1 \qquad \textbf{8.5}$$

where n is the number of years. Again, in our first case, the three-month holding period n is 0.25 year, and in the second case, it is two years:

$$EAR \text{ baseball card} = (1 + 0.10)^{1/0.25} - 1 = \mathbf{0.4641} \text{ or } \mathbf{46.41\%}$$

$$EAR \text{ start-up company} = (1 + 0.16)^{1/2} - 1 = \mathbf{0.0770} \text{ or } \mathbf{7.70\%}$$

Method 2: Using the TVM keys We could also compute these two EARs via a calculator using the dollar returns.

For the baseball card EAR:

Mode: P/Y = 1 and C/Y = 1

Input	0.25	?	−50	0	55
Key	N	I/Y	PV	PMT	FV
CPT		**46.41**			

For the start-up company stock EAR (note that the future value is the ending price of $47.82 plus the $0.90 dividend):

Mode: P/Y = 1 and C/Y = 1

Input	2.0	?	−42	0	48.72
Key	N	I/Y	PV	PMT	FV
CPT		**7.70**			

We now compare these two investments by looking at their returns stated on an annual basis. We have eliminated the issue that the two investments have different time periods by annualizing the holding period returns. Using either the APR or the EAR as the basis for comparison, we can see that Kevin received a much higher annualized return for the baseball card. Which method is best, the APR or the EAR? We will not debate this issue here, but we fall into the camp that prefers to use the EAR. Before we can compare the two returns, however, we have some other items to consider. The first is that we must be careful when we annualize investments that are held for relatively short periods of time, an issue we explore now.

Extrapolating Holding Period Returns

When extrapolating a holding period return of less than one year to the annualized return, it is important to remember that you must be able to continue to make that same rate on the investment over the remainder of the year. In our baseball card case, Kevin earned 10% over the first three months of the year, which converts into an annual rate (EAR) of 46.41%. To reach this level of investment return for the entire year, Kevin must be able to reinvest his entire proceeds at the end of the first three months ($55.00) at a 10% holding period return for each of the following three-month periods of the year. So,

Period one: $\$50.00 \times 1.10 = \$55.00$
Period two: $\$55.00 \times 1.10 = \$60.50$
Period three: $\$60.50 \times 1.10 = \$66.55$
Period four: $\$66.55 \times 1.10 = \$73.205$

$$\text{Total return: } \frac{\$73.205 - \$50.00}{\$50.00} = 0.4641 \quad \text{or} \quad 46.41\%$$

We can see this result mathematically by compounding the interest using the original three-month investment period and then reinvesting each of the next three quarters (through the end of the year) at the same holding period return of 10%:

$$EAR = (1.10 \times 1.10 \times 1.10 \times 1.10) - 1 = 1.10^4 - 1 = 0.4641 \quad \text{or} \quad 46.41\%$$

Such a situation may not always be possible, though, so take care when you use extrapolated returns for investments of less than one year. This step becomes more important when you consider investments for even shorter time periods. For example, if you loan $5.00 to a friend who pays you back a week later with an extra $0.25 for your trouble (interest of $0.25), the holding period and annualized returns are:

$$HPR = \frac{\$5.25}{\$5.00} - 1 = 0.0500 = 5.00\%$$

$$EAR = (1.05)^{52} - 1 = 11.6428 = 1{,}164.28\%$$

So, it may be a rare opportunity to earn a 5% holding period return over one week and then consistently reinvest every week for the next fifty-one weeks at this same rate. In fact, most of us would consider it a good loan just to get the $5.00 back within the week!

It still seems as if Kevin's better investment was the baseball card. Again, though, we are missing a key element before we can make a meaningful comparison. The other issue to consider is how much *risk* Kevin assumed with each of these investment choices. Again, always remember that risk and return define the finance world, and both have an important effect on how we evaluate investments.

8.2 Risk (Certainty and Uncertainty)

We can define risk in terms of uncertainty. Certainty is knowing what is going to happen before it happens. **Uncertainty** is the absence of knowledge of the actual outcome of an event before it happens. For example, in a horse race with ten horses in the field, we cannot know the winner for certain before the race takes place. Although one horse might be a heavy favorite, there is the real possibility that another horse could pull an upset and win the race. There are ten potential winners for the race, and we cannot predict for certain which horse will win. When there is more than one potential outcome of an event, there is uncertainty, and if we pick the wrong horse, we lose our bet. You may wonder if gambling is much like investing. To see an evaluation of how gamblers and investors approach risk and return, see the "Finance Follies" feature on the next page.

FINANCE FOLLIES

"Dangerous to Your Wealth": Is Investing Just Gambling?

In the classic 1994 film *Forrest Gump*, the intellectually challenged hero becomes fabulously rich after making early investments in "some fruit company" that turns out to be Apple. As you read this chapter, many of you may wonder whether careful calculations of risk and return are any more likely to lead to successful investments than mere instinct and hunches. Isn't investing just a form of gambling anyway?

Investors and gamblers approach risk and return in fundamentally different ways:

1. *In gambling, the odds are against you; in investing, they are in your favor.* Except for blackjack and poker, the gambler plays against the house. If you sit at the casino table long enough, you are guaranteed to lose money. If you invest long enough in the stock markets, however, you can earn (historically speaking) roughly 6% to 10% a year.

   Even if you're clever enough to get to the point that you can count the cards and start to win more consistently in gambling, you'll find yourself banned from the casino. The house wants only players who are willing to go up against the mathematical odds, not players with skill. Vegas wasn't built on winners!
2. *Gamblers seek fast gains; investors are (usually) patient.* Gamblers want instant gratification and hope for a high return in a short time, which is a possible but unlikely outcome. Investors realize that investing is a long-term effort that allows for time to grow money and make adjustments along the way. In general, gamblers want to double or triple their money quickly, but that rarely happens. It *can* happen with a slower investment process in which time builds value. Although some investors do treat the market like a casino through speculative investments, most do not and choose the duller but safer route of long-term investing.
3. *In gambling, if you lose, your money is gone; in investing, when share prices fall, you still own the stock.* Games of chance are all or nothing. If you lose, you lose 100% of what you bet. Investments losses are usually partial and often temporary. Unless every company in your portfolio goes bankrupt, you will not lose all your money.

In a nutshell, investing is a matter of skill, and gambling is a matter of luck. Therefore, no rational person will use gambling as more than entertainment. The risk-and-return models that you will study in this chapter really do make sense. In the final analysis, gambling can be dangerous to your wealth, but prudent investing can enhance it.

Risk is a measure of the uncertainty in a set of potential outcomes for an event in which there is a chance of some loss. If there is no uncertainty, there is no risk and we can say that the event is risk-free. Consider a three-month U.S. Treasury bill. When an investor buys a Treasury bill at a discount (pays less than the payoff at maturity) with a face value of $10,000, we know the future payoff for certain: in three months, the investor will receive $10,000. This investment is risk-free because the investor always makes the difference between the $10,000 and the lower purchase price as the U.S. government backs its promise and historically has never failed to pay its debt on time. On the other hand, consider a single stock. Although we may have a reasonable estimate of what the stock will do over the next three months, there is still uncertainty about what direction it will move (up or down) and the magnitude of the change (large or small). Throughout this book, we associate risk with uncertainty.

Whenever we are faced with an investment choice, we must understand that some choices have greater risk than others. Our objective is not to avoid risk but rather to measure and understand the acceptable level of risk for our investment choices.

Let's look again at the baseball card scenario, but let's play out a different ending for the investment at the end of three months. Although one always hopes that investments will make money, some lose it; however, even if we have a losing investment, the holding period return formula still provides the appropriate measure of performance on the investment. For example, let's assume that Kevin bought the pristine baseball card at \$50.00 and held it for three months. At some point during the three months, however, the card was accidentally damaged. Because it is now flawed, Kevin can only get \$41.50 for the card. What is the return in this case? Using Equation 8.3, we have

$$HPR = \frac{\$41.50 - \$50.00}{\$50.00} = -17\%$$

Kevin lost 17% on this investment over the three-month holding period and thus has an annualized return of

$$EAR = (1 - 0.17)^4 - 1 = -0.5254 \quad \text{or} \quad -52.54\%$$

So, the baseball card investment can have both a "good" investment ending and a "bad" one. Kevin does not know which scenario will play out when he buys the baseball card, so he assumes the risk or uncertainty of its future price.

Kevin also assumed risk with the start-up company stock. He did not know whether the company would be successful and the stock would go up in price or the company would struggle and the stock price would fall. Which of the two investments had a higher risk? Can we even measure risk? If so, how? We will address the last question first as we revisit some typical investment choices and their returns and risk over time.

8.3 Historical Returns

Does market history reveal any insights about different investment choices and their risk over time? In Chapter 5, we looked at returns for Treasury bills and Treasury bonds. We now look at some of the historical rates for these two investment types and add large-cap and small-cap stocks. "Cap" refers to a company's capitalization: it is the price of the company stock times the outstanding shares, or, in other words, the company's net worth. Large-cap stocks are stocks that have a net worth of more than \$5 billion. Small-cap stocks are stocks that have a net worth of less than \$1 billion. Table 8.1 displays annual returns for three-month U.S. Treasury bills, long-term government bonds, large-cap stocks, and small-cap stocks over the fifty-year period from 1950 to 1999.

What does Table 8.1 tell us? First, we can see that small-company stocks had the highest average return over the fifty years, but also had the widest swings from year to year. Although, on average, small-company stocks provided the best return, you could still lose considerable money if you happened to have picked the wrong time. At the other end of the spectrum are the dependable three-month U.S. Treasury bill returns. This investment type has the lowest average return, but it is always positive and, as a result, risk-free. You would never have lost money by investing in a three-month U.S. Treasury bill, regardless of the time period that you selected for your investment.

Another way to view Table 8.1 is to look at the tendency of the returns with a histogram. What are the most common occurrences of the investment in terms of their annual returns?

TABLE 8.1 Year-by-Year Returns and Decade Averages, 1950–1999

Year	Three-Month U.S. Treasury Bills	Long-Term Government Bonds	Large Company Stocks	Small Company Stocks
1950	1.20%	−0.96%	32.68%	48.45%
1951	1.49%	−1.95%	23.47%	9.41%
1952	1.66%	1.93%	18.91%	6.36%
1953	1.82%	3.83%	−1.74%	−5.66%
1954	0.86%	4.88%	52.55%	65.13%
1955	1.57%	−1.34%	31.44%	21.84%
1956	2.46%	−5.12%	6.45%	3.82%
1957	3.14%	9.46%	−11.14%	−15.03%
1958	1.54%	−3.71%	43.78%	70.63%
1959	2.95%	−3.55%	12.95%	17.82%
1950s average return	1.87%	0.35%	20.94%	22.28%
1960	2.66%	13.78%	0.19%	−5.16%
1961	2.13%	0.19%	27.63%	30.48%
1962	2.72%	6.81%	−8.79%	−16.41%
1963	3.12%	−0.49%	22.63%	12.20%
1964	3.54%	4.51%	16.67%	18.75%
1965	3.94%	−0.27%	12.50%	37.67%
1966	4.77%	3.70%	−10.25%	−8.08%
1967	4.24%	−7.41%	24.11%	103.39%
1968	5.24%	−1.20%	11.00%	50.61%
1969	6.59%	−6.52%	−8.33%	−32.27%
1960s average return	3.90%	1.31%	8.74%	19.12%
1970	6.50%	12.69%	4.10%	−16.54%
1971	4.34%	17.47%	14.17%	18.44%
1972	3.81%	5.55%	19.14%	−0.62%
1973	6.91%	1.40%	−14.75%	−40.54%
1974	7.93%	5.53%	−26.40%	-29.74%
1975	5.80%	8.50%	37.26%	69.54%
1976	5.06%	11.07%	23.98%	54.81%
1977	5.10%	0.90%	−7.26%	22.02%
1978	7.15%	−4.16%	6.50%	22.29%

Year	Three-Month U.S. Treasury Bills	Long-Term Government Bonds	Large Company Stocks	Small Company Stocks
1979	10.45%	9.02%	18.77%	43.99%
1970s average return	6.31%	6.80%	7.55%	14.37%
1980	11.57%	13.17%	32.48%	35.34%
1981	14.95%	3.61%	−4.98%	7.79%
1982	10.71%	6.52%	22.09%	27.44%
1983	8.85%	−0.53%	22.37%	34.49%
1984	10.02%	15.29%	6.46%	−14.02%
1985	7.83%	32.68%	32.00%	28.21%
1986	6.18%	23.96%	18.40%	3.40%
1987	5.50%	−2.65%	5.34%	−13.95%
1988	6.44%	8.40%	16.86%	21.72%
1989	8.32%	19.49%	31.34%	8.37%
1980s average return	9.04%	11.99%	18.24%	13.88%
1990	7.86%	7.13%	−3.20%	−27.08%
1991	5.65%	18.39%	30.66%	50.24%
1992	3.54%	7.79%	7.71%	27.84%
1993	2.97%	15.48%	9.87%	20.30%
1994	3.91%	−7.18%	1.29%	−3.34%
1995	5.58%	31.67%	37.71%	33.21%
1996	5.50%	−0.81%	23.07%	16.50%
1997	5.32%	15.08%	33.17%	22.36%
1998	5.11%	13.52%	28.58%	−2.55%
1999	4.80%	−8.74%	21.04%	21.26%
1990s average return	5.02%	9.23%	18.99%	15.87%
50-year average	5.23%	5.94%	14.89%	17.10%
Standard deviation	2.98%	9.49%	16.70%	29.04%

Note: Sources for annual returns are the Center for Research on Security Prices, Standard & Poor's 500 index, the Russell 2000 index, and the Salomon Smith Barney U.S. Treasury bill index.

Figure 8.1 gives us our first look at a potential measure of risk. These four histograms plot fifty years of returns in terms of the number of occurrences within specific spans of rates of return for stocks and interest rates for bonds. In Figure 8.1a, the returns are bunched together more than the other assets. The most

FIGURE 8.1 Histograms of (A) U.S. Treasury bills from 1950 to 1999, (B) long-term government bonds from 1950 to 1999, (C) large company stocks from 1950 to 1999, and (D) small company stocks from 1950 to 1999.

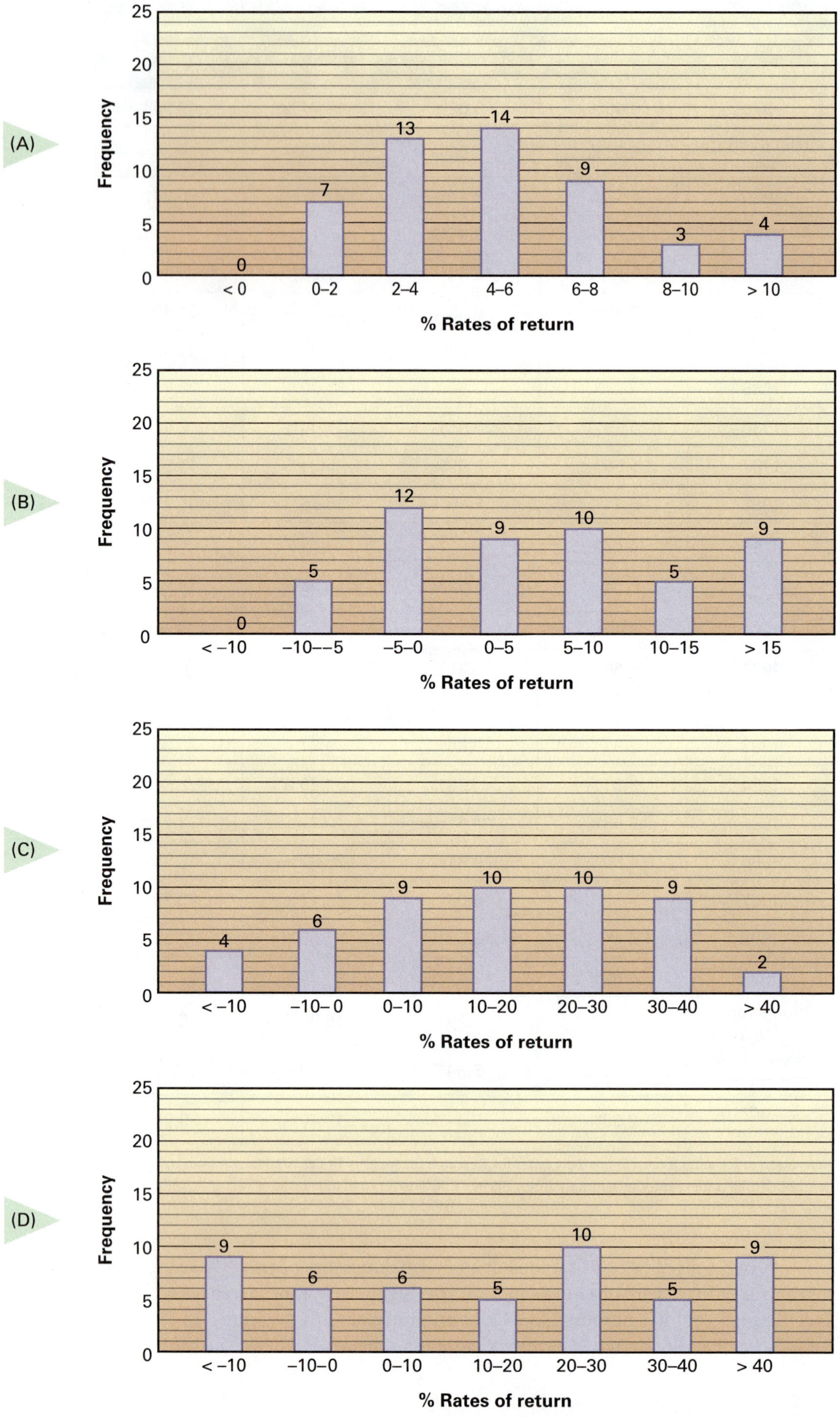

common outcome was a return in the 4% to 6% region (fourteen observations), and more than half the observations were between 0% and 6% (thirty-four out of fifty). On the other hand, Figure 8.1d shows that the small-company stocks are spread out more than any other investment. We can conclude that returns are tightly bunched for the U.S. Treasury bill and increasingly spread out as we move from long-term bonds to large-company stocks to small-company stocks.

Another way to think about risk is to consider just the potential range of outcomes. Again looking at Table 8.1, there was a high of 14.95% in 1981 and a low of 0.86% in 1954 for Treasury bills, compared with a high of 103.39% in 1967 and a low of negative 40.54% in 1973 for small-company stocks (Table 8.1). If we were to predict the returns for the coming year, we would have more confidence in trying to predict the Treasury bill return compared with the small-company stock return.

So, we have two factors that affect risk:

1. The range of possible outcomes
2. The tendency or lack of tendency of the returns to bunch together near the mean or average

In statistics, we use these two factors to calculate a variance or standard deviation, one of the tools for measuring risk.

8.4 Variance and Standard Deviation as a Measure of Risk

Put simply, the *variance* is a way of describing how spread out a set of numbers or values is around its mean or average. The mean is a simple concept. For example, what is the average height of all the students in your finance class? To find the mean, you add all the heights of all the students and then divide by the number of students. Knowing the mean, however, doesn't tell you how spread out the different individual student heights are. Is there an exceptionally tall person in the class? How many students in the class are close to the average height? How many students are taller than the mean? How many are shorter than the mean?

To give us more information about the heights of the students in the class, we can figure out the variance, which—as its name implies—indicates how dispersed the set of observations (the students' heights) is around the mean. Put simply, it is the variability from the average. In statistical terms, the **variance** measures the statistical dispersion by finding the average squared difference between the *actual observations* (individual heights of the students in this case) and the *average observation* (average class height). The larger the variance, the greater the dispersion. Using the data from Table 8.1, let's compute the variance of the small-company stock returns from 1990 to 1999.

EXAMPLE 8.2 Calculating the variance of returns for small-company stocks

Problem Calculate the variance of the small-company returns for 1990 to 1999.

Solution We will solve for the statistical dispersion of the ten individual returns.

1. Determine the average return for the ten-year period. Even though Table 8.1 gives us the average return, let's see how we calculate it. Add all the individual

year returns for the small-company stocks and divide by the number of years or observations (n):

$$-27.08 + 50.24 + 27.84 + 20.30 - 3.34 + 33.21 + 16.50 + 22.36$$
$$-2.55 + 21.26 = 158.74$$

$$\text{average} = \frac{158.74\%}{10} = 15.87\%$$

For steps 2 through 5, you can follow the calculations in the variance calculation table.

2. Subtract the average return from each year's individual return to find the difference between the individual return and the average return (column 4).
3. Square these differences (column 5).
4. Add up these squared differences (bottom of column 5).
5. Divide the sum of the squared differences by $n - 1$. We divided the sum by one less than the number of observations. In our example, n is ten observations, so $n - 1$ is therefore nine. Subtracting 1 from the number of observations is an adjustment for degrees of freedom. If needed, you can refresh your knowledge about degrees of freedom with any introductory statistics textbook.

Variance Calculation

Year	Observation (Actual Return) a	Average Return b	Difference $a - b$	Squared Difference $(a - b)^2$
1990	−27.08	15.87	$-27.08 - 15.87 = -42.95$	$(-42.95)^2 = 1{,}844.70$
1991	50.24	15.87	$50.24 - 15.87 = 34.37$	$(34.37)^2 = 1{,}181.29$
1992	27.84	15.87	$27.84 - 15.87 = 11.97$	$(11.97)^2 = 143.28$
1993	20.30	15.87	$20.30 - 15.87 = 4.43$	$(4.43)^2 = 19.62$
1994	−3.34	15.87	$-3.34 - 15.87 = -19.21$	$(19.21)^2 = 369.02$
1995	33.21	15.87	$33.21 - 15.87 = 17.34$	$(17.34)^2 = 300.68$
1996	16.50	15.87	$16.50 - 15.87 = 0.63$	$(0.63)^2 = 0.40$
1997	22.36	15.87	$22.36 - 15.87 = 6.49$	$(6.49)^2 = 42.12$
1998	−2.55	15.87	$-2.55 - 15.87 = -18.42$	$(-18.42)^2 = 339.30$
1999	21.26	15.87	$21.26 - 15.87 = 5.39$	$(5.39)^2 = 29.05$
Total	158.74			$\Sigma = 4{,}269.46$

$$\text{Variance} = \frac{\text{sum of the squared differences}}{10 - 1} = \frac{4{,}269.46}{9} = 474.38$$

The variance is represented by the Greek letter sigma squared, σ^2, or Var(X), where X is the variable of interest. In this case, X stands for the annual returns of the small-company stocks. The **standard deviation** is the square root of the variance of the actual returns and is represented by sigma, σ, or STD(X):

$$\text{variance }(X) = \frac{\sum (X_i - \text{average})^2}{n - 1} = \sigma^2 \qquad \textbf{8.6}$$

$$\text{standard deviation} = \sqrt{\text{variance}} = \sqrt{\sigma^2} = \sigma \qquad \textbf{8.7}$$

Therefore, the standard deviation for the small-stock returns from 1990 to 1999 is

$$\sigma = \sqrt{474.38} = 21.78$$

Do not let the statistical formula intimidate you because the concept behind it is actually simple. In short, it measures the volatility of an investment. The higher a security's volatility, the more its return fluctuates over time. Let's take a look at a common distribution and review how we interpret the standard deviation.

Normal Distributions

How do we interpret the 21.78% standard deviation of the small-company stock returns from 1990 to 1999? To find out, we turn to the concept of the normal distribution, which is one of the most common probability distributions. Its shape resembles a bell. This familiar bell-shaped curve varies in height and width according to the mean and standard deviation of the particular data. The mean is at the center and highest point of the bell-shaped curve, and the standard deviation tells us the curve's width. For data with a large standard deviation, the curve is wide and flat with a small peak at the mean. For data with a small standard deviation, the curve is narrow with a very high peak at the center.

Figure 8.2 is a standard normal bell-shaped curve with a mean of zero and a standard deviation of 1. This particular bell-shaped curve tells us the following:

1. About 68% of all observations of the data fall within one standard deviation of the average: the mean plus one or minus one standard deviation (add the 34% on the right of the mean with a corresponding 34% on the left of the mean).
2. About 95% of all observations of the data fall within two standard deviations of the mean: the mean plus two or minus two standard deviations.
3. About 99% of all observations of the data fall within three standard deviations of the mean: the mean plus three or minus three standard deviations.

If we look back at the returns for small-company stocks for the fifty-year period from 1950 to 1999 (Table 8.1), we see in the bottom two rows that we have a mean of 17.10% and a standard deviation of 29.04%. Therefore, we should see about thirty-four of the fifty years (approximately two-thirds or 68%) falling between −11.94% (17.10% minus one standard deviation of

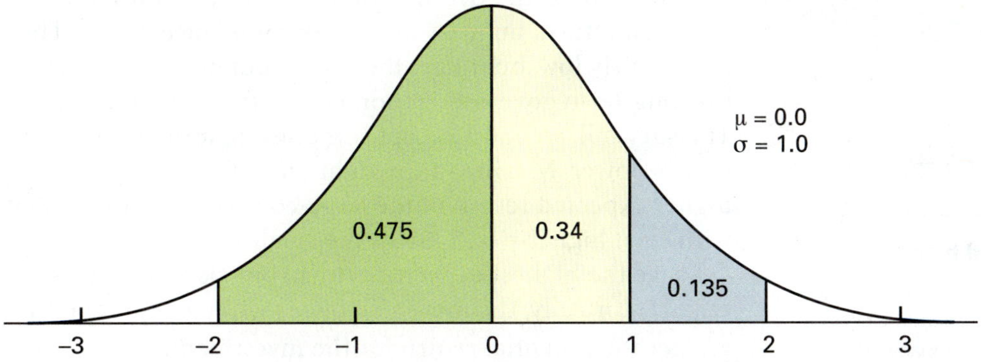

FIGURE 8.2 Standard normal distribution.

TABLE 8.2 Returns, Variances, and Standard Deviations of Investment Choices, 1950–1999

	Three-Month U.S. Treasury Bills	Long-Term Government Bonds	Large Company Stocks	Small Company Stocks
Average return	5.23%	5.94%	14.89%	17.10%
Variance	0.0888%	0.9006%	2.7889%	8.4332%
Standard deviation	2.98%	9.49%	16.70%	29.04%
Number of negative returns	0	17	9	14
Number of positive returns	50	33	41	36

29.04%) and 46.14% (17.10% plus one standard deviation of 29.04%). In fact, we can count thirty-five annual returns within this range. To be accurate, however, the principle that two-thirds of the observations fall within one standard deviation of the mean is for a very large number of observations. So, we again return to the question, "What does this mean when we want to compare different investment choices?"

One way to think of variances or standard deviations is as measures of the uncertainty of the outcome. The greater the standard deviation, the greater the uncertainty. As we look at the returns for small-company stocks and the U.S. Treasury bill, we can clearly see that the swing from year to year is much greater for small-company stocks. As noted, if we tried to predict the next year's return for these two investment choices, we would be more certain about the U.S. Treasury bill return next year than we would be about the small-company stock return.

Let's now return to our four investment choices and their respective levels of uncertainty or risk as measured by standard deviation. Table 8.2 presents the average return, variance of the return, and standard deviation of the return for the four investment types over our fifty-year period and provides us with some indication of the trade-off between risk and return.

Let's plot the information from Table 8.2 on a standard two-dimensional graph and see what we can deduce about the relationship between historical returns and historical standard deviations. Figure 8.3 illustrates the trade-off between risk and return across the four assets. At the very left of the graph are the three-month U.S. Treasury bills (T), which have no risk. We know for *certain* that if we invest in this security, we will get the promised return. Moving to the right, we see that the long-term government bonds (B) provide a higher expected return, but they also carry some uncertainty. The risk is fairly low, but to get the higher potential return of the long-term government bonds over the three-month Treasury bill, we must accept some risk that the return may be lower. Moving to the right once more, we see the higher expected return of the large-company stocks (L), but with even higher risk. Finally, the small-company stocks (S) have the highest expected return, but also the highest risk. Historically, the more risk one is willing to accept, the greater the potential return for the investment.

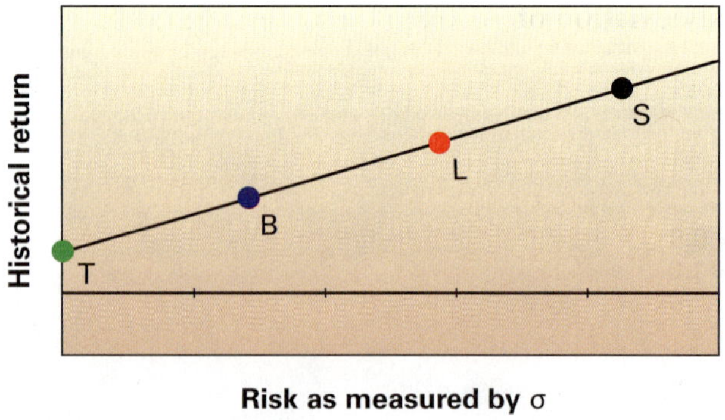

FIGURE 8.3 Historical returns and standard deviations of bonds and stocks. T = Treasury bills, B = government bonds, L = large-company stocks, and S = small-company stocks.

8.5 Returns in an Uncertain World (Expectations and Probabilities)

As you have just seen, when looking at events that have already happened, we can summarize them with statistics such as average or mean, variance, and standard deviation. These statistical tools help us understand the history of certain investment choices.

When we are making an investment choice, we do not know our return. It lies in the future. When we are looking at history, or looking back at events, we are taking an **ex-post** view (after the fact). When we are looking at future outcomes or investment possibilities, we are taking an **ex-ante** view (before the fact). The statistics of looking forward, which we will consider in this section, are different from the statistics of looking backward. For the ex-ante view, we need to estimate the chances or probabilities of different outcomes as part of the information that we require to make an investment decision, but the two parameters of an investment—risk and return—still apply.

Let's start with a relatively simple investment opportunity. You intend to buy shares in a company that makes ice cream, and you plan on holding the investment for one year. What are the potential outcomes? That will depend on how much ice cream the company can sell. If the summer is hotter than usual, the company will probably sell more ice cream than usual. If the summer is colder than usual, the company will probably sell less ice cream than usual. The current stock price is $25, and the price will rise to $30 if the summer is hotter than usual or fall to $20 if colder than usual. Therefore, you could make $5 or lose $5.

So, what is the average or expected return of this potential investment? To find the expected payoff, we take the probability of each possible return outcome (probability_i) and multiply it by the payoff outcome itself (payoff_i), or

$$\text{expected payoff} = \sum \text{payoff}_i \times \text{probability}_i \qquad \textbf{8.8}$$

where the subscript i on each payoff and probability is the individual potential outcome and the matching probability that we associate with that particular outcome. If we assign a 60% chance of hotter weather and a 40% chance of colder weather, we have

$$\text{expected payoff} = 0.60 \times \$5.00 + 0.40 \times -\$5.00 = \$1.00$$

and

$$\text{expected return} = \frac{\$1.00}{\$25.00} = 4.00\%$$

Notice that *expected* return does not mean *guaranteed* return.

Again, return and risk travel together, so we also need to calculate the risk of this investment:

$$\sigma^2 = \sum (\text{payoff}_i - \text{expected payoff})^2 \times \text{probability}_i \qquad \textbf{8.9}$$

where i is again the individual payoff and matching probability of that particular outcome. The variance and standard deviation of the payoff are

$$\begin{aligned}
\sigma^2 &= (\$5.00 - \$1.00)^2 \times 0.60 + (-\$5.00 - \$1.00)^2 \times 0.40 \\
&= (\$4.00)^2 \times 0.60 + (-\$6.00)^2 \times 0.40 \\
&= \$9.60 + \$14.40 = \$24.00 \\
\sigma &= (\$24.00)^{1/2} = \$4.90
\end{aligned}$$

We now have both a forward-looking measure of return (the expected return of $1) and of risk (the standard deviation of $4.90). Whether you choose to buy shares in the ice-cream company is your choice, depending on whether you think that the potential rewards of the investment outweigh the risk. That is the key question for all financial investments: Given the level of risk, is the potential reward acceptable? For an implausible interpretation of the risk-reward trade-off, see the "Finance Follies" feature.

Finance Follies

"Scam of the Century": Bernie Madoff and the $50 Billion Fraud

Toward the end of 2008, the last thing Wall Street wanted to hear was more bad news about financial management, but it came in spades with the SEC's announcement on December 11 that Bernard (known as Bernie) Madoff, head of Bernard L. Madoff Investment Securities LLC, had perpetrated a colossal fraud by setting up a so-called Ponzi scheme involving his clientele base. A slew of high-roller investors, as well as more ordinary ones, found that their investment money had evaporated. The scope of the damage was jaw-dropping: reputedly, the black hole Madoff dug could be responsible for $50 billion—and perhaps more—of investors' funds.

How could it happen? The irony is that a Ponzi scheme is a straightforward kind of fraud, and Madoff seemingly had nailed it for what may turn out to be the largest Ponzi scheme ever. Named after Charles Ponzi, who first hatched the swindle in Boston in 1919, a Ponzi scheme promises high rates of return with little risk, but it fraudulently uses the principal paid in by new investors to pay out to older investors. As money flows in from new clients, the scheme distributes it to old clients as returns. Because many long-term investors choose to reinvest the so-called returns in a "sure thing," the scam grinds on. Eventually, though, the edifice collapses in on itself because many of the earlier investors ultimately begin to withdraw their principal and earnings and the fund runs dry because it did not accumulate sufficient real earnings to make these payments.

Madoff launched his financial career in the 1960s with a mere $5,000 that he earned as a lifeguard. His investment firm rose to stellar success—thanks mostly to Madoff's uncanny ability to generate double-digit returns for his investor base—and became the envy of much of Wall Street. Along the way, Madoff became chair of NASDAQ for a while, sat on an SEC advisory board, and was generally regarded with awe on Wall Street. Hundreds of wealthy individuals, banks, and hedge funds parked their money with him. Among Madoff's many clients were famous players like director Steven Spielberg and New York Mets owner Fred Wilpon, academic entities like Yeshiva University, high-profile financial institutions like the Royal Bank of Scotland, big retail brokers like Charles Schwab, and other wealthy individuals. To invest, Madoff "invited" clients into the company, thereby lending the whole enterprise a certain aura of exclusivity and glamour. Supposedly, not just *anybody* could get in. Over the years, his clients remained impressed with Madoff's Midas touch: reported returns ranged from about 10% to 15% a year, and according to others, from about 14% to 18%. In fact, in thirteen years, steady returns—even in down times—were the norm. Only five months showed any kind of downward movement. It was almost too good to be true.

Indeed, it was too good to be true. The worldwide financial crisis of 2008, like a string of dominoes, eventually caught up with Madoff when some clients wanted to pull out principal of about $7 billion. At this point, Madoff was forced to admit what no one could at first believe: that there were no investment gains and, indeed, no principal. The cupboard was bare. Madoff had evidently been paying returns to some investors from principal received from other investors, and now the firm was insolvent.

The Madoff parable illustrates one of the financial principles that we discuss in this chapter: returns are commensurate with risk. To earn higher returns, one must also take on more risk. Study of risk-return principles teaches us that there is no such thing as a free lunch. Although all investors want to maximize return and minimize risk, they still must make a trade-off between the two. Madoff handed investors a story that they would enjoy returns well above average for practically no risk.

Finance follies like this one also have an underlying psychological component, just as many scams do. Human nature is remarkably consistent. It is human to want easy money. It is human to think that because someone is famous, he or she must be smart. It is human to think that if an operation is hard to get into, it's because it's better than most. It is human to think that if we do get in, *we* must be smart, and the aura of prosperity becomes ours by association.

What is amazing in the Madoff saga is the lack of what we call due diligence: the care a reasonable person or company should take before entering into a financial agreement or transaction. Many investors chose not to ask questions, but to trust Bernie, in many cases because their parents had trusted him with their cash. Proper due diligence would have revealed that Madoff himself was the only person in the firm to have full access to the accounts and that the company auditors were a small accounting firm. Although the consistency of the bullish returns did spark suspicion with some, most did not question it. Red flags did, however, go up for some. Among them was independent fraud investigator Harry Markopolos, who on several occasions warned the SEC that Madoff was a fraud, but his whistle-blowing had no effect.

In 2009, Congress started to repair many of the dysfunctional parts of the U.S. financial regulation system. New rules are working their way through the long and tedious process of regulation reform and should affect the financial industry and investors going forward. In the meantime, Web sites started popping up that advertised litigation services for those duped by Madoff. Madoff himself pled guilty and later received a 150-year prison term. He left in his wake depleted investors, some of whom had lost millions of dollars. The "scam of the century," as CNBC dubbed it, was one of the saddest chapters in investment history.

Determining the Probabilities of All Potential Outcomes

Assigning the appropriate or correct probability to each outcome can be an easy, straightforward task or a difficult one, but you should always keep in mind two important points:

1. The sum of the probabilities always adds to 1 (as in our 60%–40% example).
2. Each individual probability is positive. We cannot have a negative probability.

These points ensure that we account for all outcomes when calculating expected returns and the variance or standard deviation of the outcomes.

In our ice-cream company example, we considered only two potential outcomes. For most events, though, the number of potential outcomes is large, and assigning probabilities to each potential outcome may not be straightforward. Let's return to the horse race example. In a horse race, one horse may be the clear favorite, which would translate into a higher probability of winning for the favorite than for any other horse in the field. Does that mean that the favorite should win 60% of the time, 50% of the time, 40% of the time, or even less than 40% of the time? We base assigning odds (probabilities) and payoffs to each horse in the race on our perceived abilities of the individual horses and the condition of the track. The past history of an individual horse's performances may be our best indicator of future performance and the basis for assigning a probability for winning the race. But when we add up all the probabilities of winning across the ten horses, the probabilities must add to 1. Keep in mind that the historical performance of an investment is often an important ingredient in trying to determine its future performance.

In our ice-cream company example of uncertainty, we had two states of the world, or two possible outcomes: a hot summer or a cold summer. As with the horse race, though, there are often more than two states of the world or possible outcomes. We will now look at a slightly more complicated setting in which there are three potential outcomes: a boom economy, a steady economy, and an economy in recession.

EXAMPLE 8.3 Expected return and risk

Problem Tim has been studying the government bond market and has made the following observations. When the economy is booming, the long-term bond return is 2%. When the economy is in a steady period, the return is 5%. When the economy is in a recession, the return is 10%. Tim believes that there is a 25% chance of an economic boom next year, a 55% chance of a steady period, and a 20% chance of a recession next year (25% + 55% + 20% = 100% or 1). He is trying to determine the expected return for next year on government bonds and also wants to know what kind of variance he can expect for the coming year. Using the ex-ante statistics for expected return and variance, can you help Tim find the expected risk and return for the long-term government bond for this next year?

Solution Step 1: Find the expected return. The expected return is the sum of the probabilities times the return:

$$E(r) = 0.25 \times 0.02 + 0.55 \times 0.05 + 0.20 \times 0.10 = \mathbf{0.0525} \text{ or } \mathbf{5.25\%}$$

Notice that we use the notation $E(r)$ for expected return.

Expected Return of Long-Term Bond

State of the Economy	Probability of Economic State (*a*)	Return in Economic State (*b*)	Probability × Return (*a*) × (*b*)	Result (*c*) = (*a*) × (*b*)
Boom	25%	2%	25% × 2%	0.50%
Steady	55%	5%	55% × 5%	2.75%
Recession	20%	10%	20% × 10%	2.00%
expected return = 0.50% + 2.75% + 2.00% = 5.25%				

Step 2: Find the variance of the expected return, which is the sum of the probability of each outcome times the squared difference between the outcome and the expected return. Subtract the expected return from the outcome of each individual state and square the result. Then multiply this result by that state's probability of occurrence. Add these results to find the variance:

$$\text{variance} = (0.02 - 0.0525)^2 \times 0.25 + (0.05 - 0.0525)^2 \times 0.55$$
$$+ (0.10 - 0.525)^2 \times 0.20$$
$$= 0.000264063 + 0.000003438 + 0.00045125 = 0.00071875$$

The standard deviation is the square root of the variance.

$$\text{standard deviation} = (0.00071875)^{1/2} = \mathbf{0.026809513} \approx \mathbf{2.68\%}$$

Variance of Long-Term Bond

State of the Economy	Probability of Economic State (*a*)	Return in Economic State r_j	Difference Squared (r_j – expected return)^2 (*b*)	Probability × Difference^2 (*a*) × (*b*)
Boom	0.25	0.02	$(0.02 - .0525)^2 = 0.00105625$	0.000264
Steady	0.55	0.05	$(0.05 - .0525)^2 = 0.00000625$	0.000003
Recession	0.20	0.10	$(0.10 - .0525)^2 = 0.00225625$	0.000451
variance = sum of squared differences times probability of that outcome = 0.00071875				

With Tim's assessment of outcomes and probabilities, he believes the bond has an expected return of 5.25% and his investment would require him to bear a risk of 2.68% standard deviation. If he believes the 5.25% return is acceptable given the level of risk, he will consider this bond as one of his investment possibilities. Otherwise, he will not consider buying government bonds at this time.

8.6 The Risk-and-Return Trade-off

Now that we know the risk and expected return for an individual investment, how do we use this information to make a financial decision? With an expected return of 5.25% and a standard deviation of 2.68%, should Tim invest in long-term government bonds for the coming year? Just as with our earlier horse race example in which we would like to know the odds of all the horses before placing a bet, we also need to know the risk and expected return for all our potential investments. Only then can we make a prudent financial decision about which investment we will select. We need to know how much additional expected return an investment carries before we accept the additional risk that comes with it compared with other available investment opportunities.

Let's look at four investment opportunities facing another investor, George. Like most investors, George has the option of investing in Treasury bills, government bonds, large-cap stocks, or small-cap stocks. We've just seen the outcomes for the long-term government bonds. Using the same data from Example 8.3 on the three potential states of the economy and the probability of each economy, we have to determine the outcome in each state for the other three investment choices. Table 8.3 shows the predicted outcomes for the other three choices. The different expected returns for each asset in each economic state are *conditional* returns. They are dependent on that particular state or condition of the economy for that asset. Here we have provided the numbers for the predicted outcomes, but in reality, you need to determine each asset's expected return in each state prior to calculating each asset's expected return. In Example 8.3, we calculated the government bond's expected return to be 5.25%. The expected return for each of these other assets is, then,

$$E(r) \text{ Treasury bill} = 0.25 \times 4\% + 0.55 \times 4\% + 0.20 \times 4\% = 4.0\%$$

$$E(r) \text{ large-company} = 0.25 \times 22\% + 0.55 \times 16\% + 0.20 \times -8\% = 12.7\%$$

$$E(r) \text{ small-company} = 0.25 \times 36\% + 0.55 \times 20\% + 0.20 \times -18\% = 16.4\%$$

Using the expected return should remind us that we are estimating a future outcome or expected outcome given the probabilities of different states of the economy and the conditional returns in each of the states of the economy.

TABLE 8.3 Conditional Returns of Investment Choices

States of the Economy	Probability of the State	Three-Month Treasury Bill	Large-Company Stock	Small-Company Stock
Boom	25%	4%	22%	36%
Steady	55%	4%	16%	20%
Recession	20%	4%	−8%	−18%

The government bond's standard deviation in Example 8.3 was 2.68%. The standard deviations for the other three assets for the coming year are as follows:

σ for Treasury bill

$$[0.25 \times (4.0\% - 4.0\%)^2 + 0.55 \times (4.0\% - 4.0\%)^2 + 0.20 \times (4.0\% - 4.0\%)^2]^{1/2} = 0\%$$

σ for large-company stock

$$[0.25 \times (22.0\% - 12.7\%)^2 + 0.55 \times (16.0\% - 12.7\%)^2 + 0.20 \times (-8.0\% - 12.7\%)^2]^{1/2} = 10.64\%$$

σ for small-company stock

$$[0.25 \times (36.0\% - 16.4\%)^2 + 0.55 \times (20.0\% - 16.4\%)^2 + 0.20 \times (-18.0\% - 16.4\%)^2]^{1/2} = 18.43\%$$

George can now choose any of the four investments available to him for the coming year with knowledge of each investment's expected return and standard deviation.

Investment Rules

Despite different levels of risk tolerance between individuals, we can state some simple rules that all should follow.

Investment rule number 1: If two investments have the same expected return and different levels of risk, the investment with the lower risk is preferred.

Investment rule number 2: If two investments have the same level of risk and different expected returns, the investment with the higher expected return is preferred.

Figures 8.4 and 8.5 depict these rules. The *x*-axis travels from zero risk at the point of origin to increasing amounts of risk.

We can summarize the two rules as follows: investors aim to maximize return and minimize risk. Using either rule, we can easily see that an investor prefers an investment with both a higher expected return and lower level of risk over another asset. What about two investments in which one investment has a higher expected return and a higher level of risk? Is there a rule that tells us which asset to choose? For example, which is the preferred asset in Figure 8.6, Asset L or Asset S?

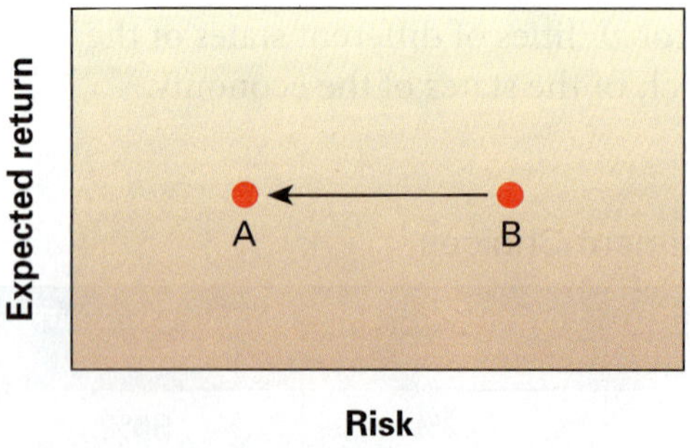

FIGURE 8.4 Minimizing risk: Rule 1. Asset A is preferred to asset B because, for the same return, there is less risk.

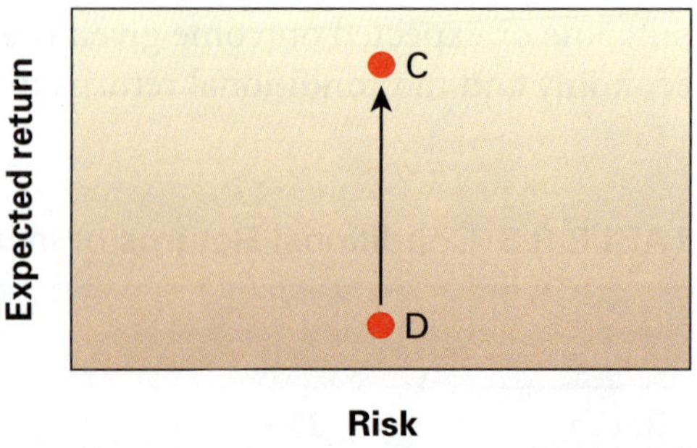

FIGURE 8.5 Maximizing return: Rule 2. Asset C is preferred to asset D because of higher expected return with the same risk.

Asset L has a lower expected return and lower risk, and Asset S has a higher expected return and higher risk.

As you have probably guessed, there is no rule that tells us whether investment L or S is the wiser choice. Here, an individual must assess whether the additional reward of Asset S—the greater expected return—is worth the extra risk. So, George can view his choice as a trade-off between the amount of risk and the potential reward for his investment. With the potential four assets facing George, we cannot advise him as to which is the best investment using investment rules 1 and 2 as our only guides.

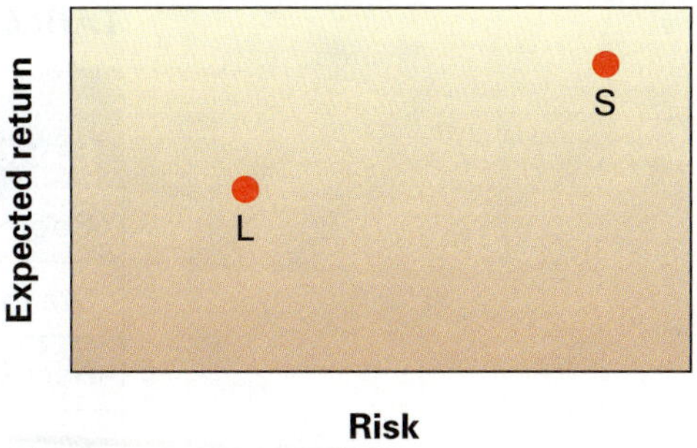

FIGURE 8.6 Which asset, L or S?

One choice that George can make is to divide his money into more than one investment. We call this strategy diversification, and we will discover some interesting things about it next.

8.7 Diversification: Minimizing Risk or Uncertainty

We have learned that risk is a measure of the uncertainty about future events in which one or more of the potential outcomes results in a loss. Is there a way to lower or minimize risk without giving up return potential? As you saw at the beginning of this chapter, the old adage "Don't put all your eggs in one basket" is one possible answer. If eggs are dollars for investment and baskets are investment opportunities, the proverb means that you should put your investment dollars into different assets, so that if one should fail, the others remain intact, preventing disaster. The modern-day equivalent of this proverb is "Diversify your investments."

What does it mean to diversify one's investments or assets? **Diversification** is the spreading of wealth over a variety of investment opportunities so as to eliminate some risk. When we think about investing in the stock market, diversification means selecting a variety of stocks from different companies across a variety of industries. When we think about investing in bonds, diversification means selecting a variety of bonds such as corporate, municipal, state, and federal bonds. We refer to one's total investment as a **financial portfolio**.

What are the benefits of diversifying one's portfolio? Let's look at two investment opportunities for Jane: she can purchase shares in Zig Company or Zag Company, or she can split her money between both. Her portfolio choice is to split her money 50/50 between the two companies. The portfolio return in each state of the economy is simply 50% of the expected return on Zig plus 50% of the return on Zag.

$$\text{expected portfolio return} = 50\% \times \text{Zig return}$$
$$+ 50\% \times \text{Zag return}$$

Table 8.4 shows that the 50/50 portfolio conditional expected returns are all 15%, regardless of the state of the economy. Let's verify this outcome:

In a diversified portfolio, the money invested is spread across a variety of assets, companies, and industries. Dividing up the wealth decreases some of the risk, in that a low outcome for one asset can be offset by a higher outcome of another asset.

TABLE 8.4 Returns of Zig, Zag, and a 50/50 Portfolio of Zig and Zag

State of Economy	Probability of State	Return of Zig Company	Return of Zag Company	Return of 50/50 Portfolio
Boom	0.20	25%	5%	15%
Steady	0.50	17%	13%	15%
Recession	0.30	5%	25%	15%
E(*r*)		15%	15%	15%

$$\text{expected portfolio return in boom state} = 0.5 \times 0.25 + 0.5 \times 0.05 = 0.15$$

$$\text{expected portfolio return in steady state} = 0.5 \times 0.17 + 0.5 \times 0.13 = 0.15$$

$$\text{expected portfolio return in recession state} = 0.5 \times 0.05 + 0.5 \times 0.25 = 0.15$$

If the 50/50 portfolio has the same outcome in all states of the economy, Jane knows her exact return regardless of the ups and downs of the economy. What is the risk? The standard deviation is zero:

$$\sigma = \left[(0.15 - 0.15)^2 \times 0.20 + (0.15 - 0.15)^2 \times 0.50 + (0.15 - 0.15)^2 \times 0.30\right]^{1/2}$$

$$= \left[(0.00)^2 \times 0.20 + (0.00)^2 \times 0.50 + (0.00)^2 \times 0.30\right]^{1/2} = 0.00 \quad \text{or} \quad 0\%$$

Should Jane take the 50/50 portfolio, or should she select one of the individual stocks? The portfolio choice that diversifies her investments is better than putting all her money in either Zig or Zag according to investment rule 1. She can eliminate all uncertainty by taking the 50/50 portfolio and getting the same expected return as either Zig or Zag Company. She could get a higher actual return if she invested in Zag Company and the economy went into a recession or if she invested in Zig Company and the economy was steady or turned into a boom. She could, however, also get a lower return by investing all her money in only one of the stocks. Clearly, if minimizing risk is important to Jane, she is better off picking the 50/50 portfolio rather than bearing the risk of either Zig or Zag Company. Diversification is beneficial to Jane.

When Diversification Works

Jane's scenario is an extreme example of risk reduction across a two-asset portfolio. We do not always get such dramatic levels of reduction whereby we can remove all the risk. When does diversification work, and when is it of no benefit? The level of benefit will depend on the relative performance of stocks across changing economic conditions.

Underlying the principle of diversification is the idea of **correlation**, a measure of how stocks perform relative to one another in different states of the economy. One statistical measure of correlation is the correlation coefficient. Perhaps you are familiar with it. The **correlation coefficient** is a measurement of the co-movement between two variables that ranges from +1 to −1. **Positive correlation** means that two different asset returns move in the same direction over time. **Negative correlation** means that two different asset returns move in different directions over time. Two assets that have a correlation coefficient of +1 will move in the same direction. They also have the same magnitude. These are

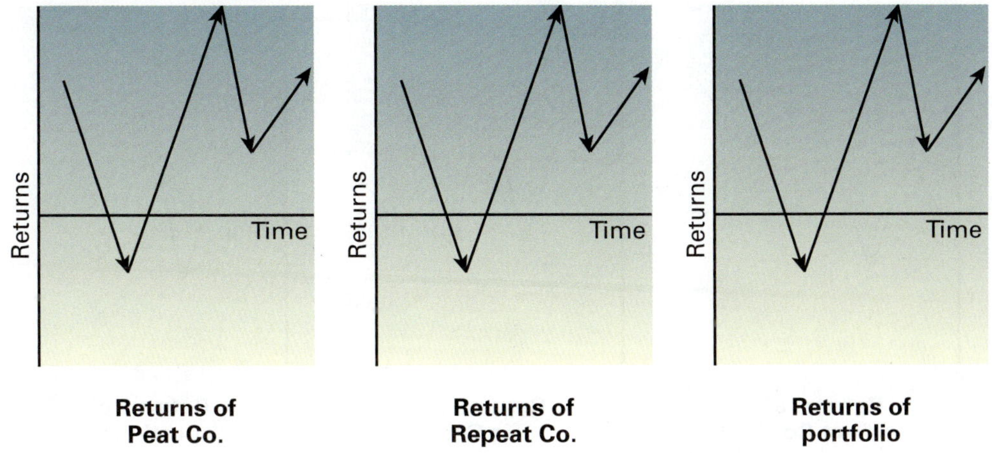

FIGURE 8.7 Perfectly positive correlation of two assets' returns.

perfectly positively correlated. Two assets that have a correlation coefficient of −1 will move in the opposite direction. They also have the same magnitude. These are perfectly negatively correlated.

Let's look at Peat and Repeat Companies, two stocks that have a +1 correlation coefficient, and see the effect of combining these two assets.

Figure 8.7 shows that these companies have the same returns year after year. When Peat goes up, so does Repeat. When Peat goes down, so does Repeat. If we split our investment between these two stocks in a portfolio, the portfolio has the same return as the two individual companies. In addition to the same return, though, the portfolio has the same standard deviation as the two individual assets. Therefore, there is no diversification benefit with stocks that are perfectly positively correlated.

Now, let's look again at Zig and Zag, two stocks that have a −1 correlation coefficient. Figure 8.8 shows that when Zig has a good year, Zag has an off-setting bad year, and when Zig has a bad year, Zag has an off-setting good year. With this perfectly negative correlation, we see that the portfolio's performance is constant. It never varies. The benefit of combining Zig and Zag in a portfolio is to offset the bad performance of one company with the good performance of the other company. We can eliminate all risk if we pick the right percentage in Zig and Zag.

For most stocks, the correlation coefficient with other stocks is positive, but not +1 (perfectly positively correlated). Let's look at Peat and Zig (Fig. 8.9), two stocks with a positive correlation coefficient less than +1 and greater than zero.

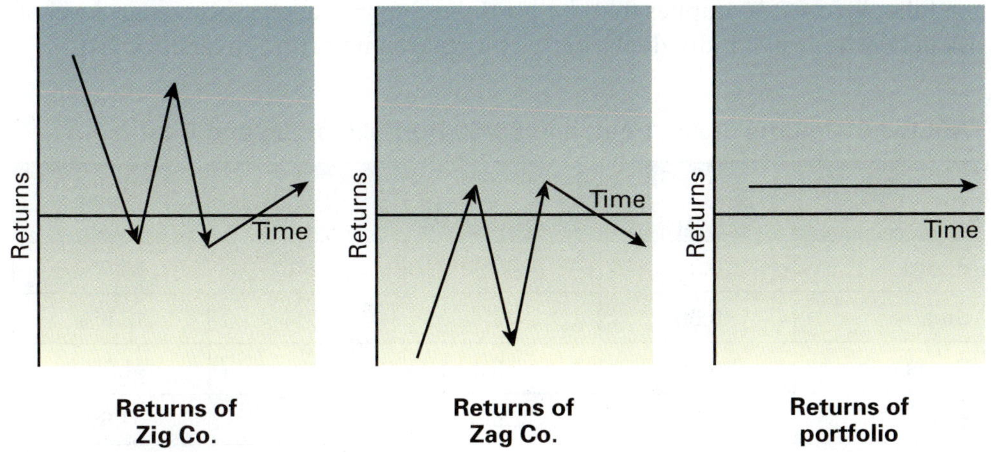

FIGURE 8.8 Perfectly negative correlation of two assets' returns.

FIGURE 8.9 Positive correlation of two assets' returns.

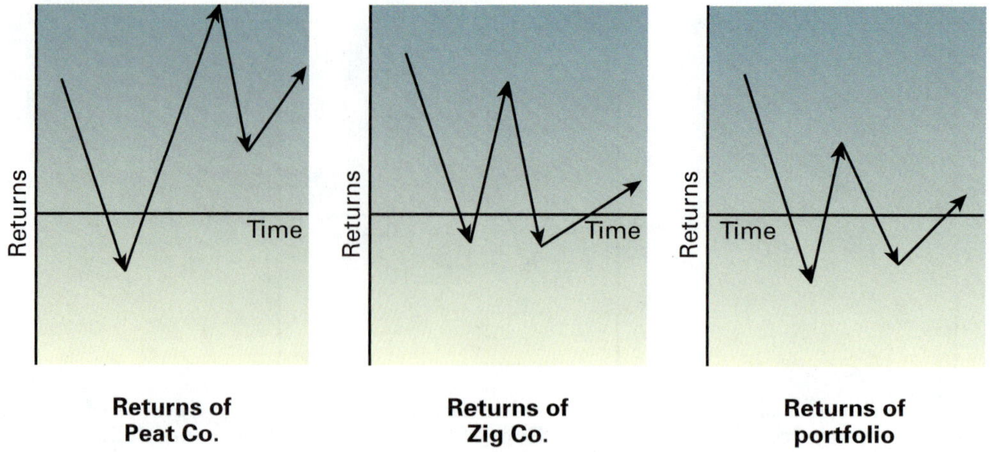

A 50/50 portfolio of Peat and Zig has an expected return of 11.60% (Table 8.5) and a standard deviation of 12.44%.

$$\text{expected return 50/50 portfolio of Zig and Peat} = 0.5 \times 0.125 + 0.5 \times 0.107$$
$$= 0.1160$$

$$\sigma = \left[(0.31 - 0.116)^2 \times 0.20 + (0.135 - 0.116)^2 \times 0.50 + (-0.045 - 0.116)^2 \times 0.30\right]^{1/2}$$
$$= \left[(0.007527) + (0.000181) + (0.007776)\right]^{1/2}$$
$$= \left[0.015484\right]^{1/2} = 0.1244 \quad \text{or} \quad 12.44\%$$

If we were to calculate the standard deviation of Zig and Peat, we would get 15.6% for Zig and 10.0% for Peat. If we now graph the three choices—all our money in Zig, all our money in Peat, or a portfolio of half our money in Zig and the other half in Peat—we would see a slight improvement in the expected return with respect to the level of risk as measured by the standard deviation for the portfolio. If there were no benefit to diversification, the portfolio would plot on the line between Peat and Zig. Instead, as Figure 8.10 shows, it plots above the line, signifying that the portfolio's return is higher than we would expect for the given level of risk. This is the benefit of diversification.

If we step back and look at the different two-asset combinations (Zig and Zag, Peat and Repeat, and Peat and Zig), we can infer that the closer the correlation coefficient is to -1 (coming from $+1$), the greater the effect of diversification on the portfolio. Figure 8.10 implies that the portfolio return is above the average level of risk between the two individual assets, a positive benefit from diversification.

TABLE 8.5 Returns of Zig, Peat, and 50/50 Portfolio of Zig and Peat

State of Economy	Probability of State	Return of Zig Company	Return of Peat Company	Return of Portfolio
Boom	0.20	40%	22%	31.0%
Steady	0.50	12%	15%	13.5%
Recession	0.30	−5%	−4%	−4.5%
E(*r*)		12.5%	10.7%	11.6%

Adding More Stocks to the Portfolio: Systematic and Unsystematic Risk

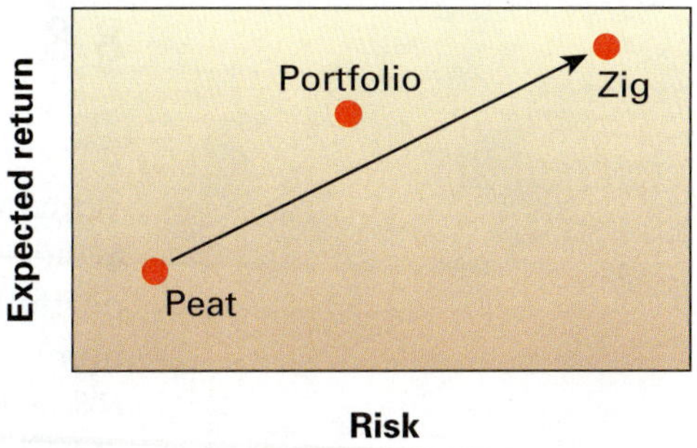

FIGURE 8.10 Diversification benefit for combining Zig and Peat into a 50/50 portfolio.

If diversifying with two assets is good, is diversifying with three better? Most equity assets in the economy are positively correlated in returns. When the economy is doing well, most stocks rise in value, and when the economy is doing poorly, most stocks fall in value. When we combine two positively correlated stocks, we see only a little risk reduction. Therefore, if we use more stocks in a portfolio, will we be able to eliminate more risk? The answer is yes, but only up to a point. To see how that works, we must understand two new components of risk: risk that we can eliminate through diversification and risk that we cannot eliminate through diversification.

Unsystematic risk is firm-specific or industry-specific risk. For example, if a manufacturing company has a labor strike, the strike affects the company's operations, but may have little, if any, effect on other companies. Conversely, **systematic risk** is marketwide risk, affected by the uncertainty of future economic conditions that affect all stocks (companies) that operate in the economy. For example, rising interest rates have an effect on the operations of many companies.

Unsystematic risk is **diversifiable risk**. We can eliminate it when we spread our investments over different stocks. Systematic risk is **nondiversifiable risk**. We cannot eliminate it as we spread our investments.

As we add more assets to a portfolio, we eliminate more unsystematic risk. If we add enough stocks to the portfolio, we eventually end up with only systematic risk. Figure 8.11 represents the benefit of adding more stocks. It shows that unsystematic risk falls as we add more stocks, but systematic risk is the lower boundary and we cannot eliminate it, no matter how many stocks we add to our portfolio.

Estimates of the number of stocks necessary to eliminate nearly all unsystematic risk range from twenty to thirty. Beyond that, the effect seems negligible. We will use the term **well-diversified portfolio** to proxy for the portfolio that has essentially eliminated all unsystematic risk.

Because we now know that we have a tool to minimize unsystematic risk, you might ask if there is a way to measure the systematic risk of an asset or portfolio. The answer is yes. This measure of systematic risk of an individual asset is beta, and we cover it next.

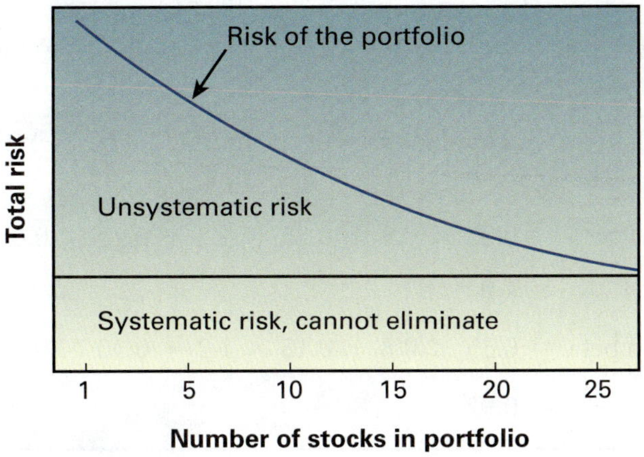

FIGURE 8.11 Portfolio diversification and the elimination of unsystematic risk.

8.8 Beta: The Measure of Risk in a Well-Diversified Portfolio

When we examine nondiversifiable or systematic risk—risk that you cannot avoid—we are actually measuring the co-movement of an individual asset or portfolio with the market. We associate this systematic risk with the general economic and political forces that move the economy up or down. We quantify such risk with the measure beta. **Beta** is a statistical measure of the volatility of an individual security compared with the market as a whole. It is the relative tendency of a security's returns to respond to overall market fluctuations.

The average beta is 1.0, and a stock with a beta of 1.0 has the same level of risk as that of the market in general. Securities with a beta less than 1.0 are less risky than the average stock and the market in general. Securities with a beta greater than 1.0 are more risky than the average stock and the market in general. You will often find technology stocks with a beta greater than 1 and utilities with a beta less than 1. A zero beta means that an asset has no co-movement with the market. Such is the case with the U.S. Treasury bill, whose payoff at maturity is not altered by the ups and downs of the economy.

The nice thing about beta is that we can use a weighted average of the betas of the securities in a portfolio to find the portfolio's beta (Eq. 8.10):

$$\beta_p = \sum_{i=1}^{n} w_i \times \beta_i \qquad \textbf{8.10}$$

where w_i is the percentage weight of the individual asset in the portfolio and β_i is the beta of the individual stock. When you sum the percentage weights, they equal 1. When you sum the weights times the betas, you have the portfolio's beta.

EXAMPLE 8.4 What's your beta?

Problem Jack and Liz are forming individual portfolios from the four following assets:

Peat Company with a beta of 0.8
Repeat Company with a beta of 1.2
Zig Company with a beta of 0.6
Zag Company with a beta of 1.4

Jack has chosen to put 25% of his investment in each of the four assets. Liz, on the other hand, has decided to put 35% in Peat Company, 15% in Repeat Company, 30% in Zig Company, and 20% in Zag Company. What are the betas of their portfolios?

Solution We use a weighted average of the individual betas in the portfolio to find the portfolio's beta. So,

$$\text{Jack's portfolio beta} = 0.25 \times 0.8 + 0.25 \times 1.2 + 0.25 \times 0.6 + 0.25 \times 1.4$$
$$= \mathbf{1.0}$$

$$\text{Liz's portfolio beta} = 0.35 \times 0.8 + 0.15 \times 1.2 + 0.30 \times 0.6 + 0.20 \times 1.4$$
$$= \mathbf{0.92}$$

Liz chooses a more conservative portfolio than Jack by allocating more of her investment to the less risky stocks—those stocks with lower betas. It's your allocation choice across a set of stocks that determines the beta or systematic risk of your portfolio.

We have introduced two different measures of risk in the finance world, standard deviation (or variance) and beta. The standard deviation is a measure of the asset's total risk, both systematic and unsystematic. Beta is a measure of an asset's systematic risk. When we view any one of our assets as part of a well-diversified portfolio, it is proper to use beta as the measure of risk. If we do not have a well-diversified portfolio, it is more prudent to use standard deviation as the measure of risk for our asset.

8.9 The Capital Asset Pricing Model and the Security Market Line

At this point, we can visualize the special relationship between the expected return of any asset or portfolio and its beta, the current risk-free rate, and the market risk premium, a term that you will meet shortly. We will first consider three fundamental assumptions to building this relationship, which will end up as a positively sloped line with risk on the *x*-axis and expected return on the *y*-axis. This special line is the **security market line (SML)**. Let's explore the three assumptions behind it:

1. There is a basic reward for waiting: the risk-free rate.
2. The greater the risk, the greater the expected reward.
3. There is a consistent trade-off between risk and reward at all levels of risk.

Assumption 1: There is a basic reward for waiting. If you choose not to spend your money today, but save it for a "rainy day," you want to be able to buy just as much and a little bit more on that rainy day as you could buy right now. Earlier, we introduced this concept in Chapter 5 when we talked about the cost of inflation and a reward for waiting—the real rate—when postponing spending. We again use this same idea and state that any investment that is riskless will have a return equal to the risk-free rate, a rate sufficient to cover the cost of inflation and compensate for waiting. This will become the *y*-intercept on the SML: the point of zero risk.

Assumption 2: The greater the risk, the greater the expected reward. If you are willing to take on risk, you want compensation for this choice. Failure to reward you for extra risk means that you would be better off with a lower-risk investment that has the same payoff. We are expanding on an earlier conclusion from this chapter (our investment rules 1 and 2) and stating that more risk requires more potential reward. To increase your potential reward when investing, you have to assume additional risk, which translates to a positive slope for the SML.

Assumption 3: There is a consistent trade-off between risk and reward at all levels of risk. This assumption simply means that if a person takes on twice as much risk as someone else, he or she should expect twice as much additional reward above the risk-free rate. Thus, every additional increase in risk provides a proportional additional unit of reward, which translates to a straight line for the SML.

Figure 8.12 shows the SML based on these three assumptions. We can also define **market risk premium** as the slope of the SML, yet another term for taking on more risk. It is the difference between the expected return on a market portfolio (a theoretical portfolio of all the assets in the market) and the risk-free rate.

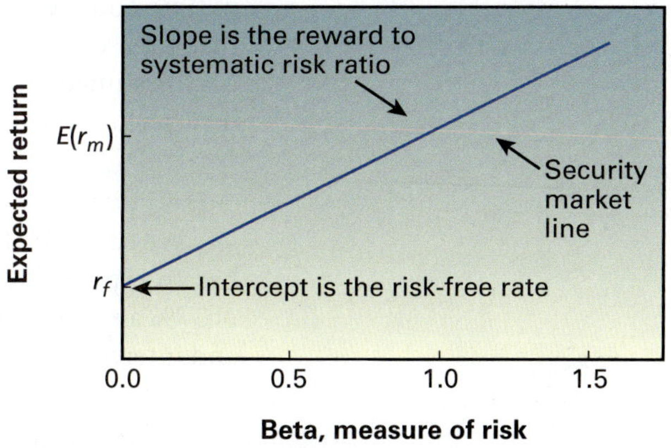

FIGURE 8.12 Security market line.

The Capital Asset Pricing Model (CAPM)

The compilation of these three assumptions in a two-parameter world of risk on the x-axis and return on the y-axis is the foundation of the **capital asset pricing model (CAPM)**, which is the equation form of the SML. We use this to explain the behavior of security prices. The CAPM states that the expected return of an investment is a function of

1. The time value of money (the reward for waiting)
2. A reward for taking on risk
3. The amount of risk

Full disclosure requires a statement that the CAPM is more complicated than what we present here. At this stage, however, a basic application of the CAPM via the SML is a solid foundation for understanding the special relationship between risk and expected return.

Recall from geometry that we typically write the equation for a line as

$$y = a + b \times x$$

where y is the value of the function, a is the y-intercept of the function, b is the slope of the line, and x is the value of the random variable on the x-axis. By substituting expected return $E(r_i)$ for the y variable, the risk-free rate r_f for the intercept a, the market risk premium $E(r_m) - r_f$ for the slope b, and the random variable β_i for the random variable on the x-axis, we have the formal equation for the SML. It bears repeating that the **slope of the security market line** is the market risk premium, or the **reward-to-risk ratio** for taking on units of systematic risk.

We can now write the relationship of the asset's expected return with respect to the market as a linear function:

$$E(r_i) = r_f + \left[E(r_m) - r_f\right] \times \beta_i \qquad \textbf{8.11}$$

Equation 8.11 is the CAPM, in which $E(r_i)$ is the expected rate of return of an individual investment. We can determine it if we know the current risk-free rate, the current market risk premium, and the risk of the individual asset as measured by beta.

Once we understand how the SML represents our risk-and-return world, we can plot different investment choices. If we know the risk-free rate and the expected return on the market, we can construct the line. We know that the risk-free rate is the intercept, and the difference between the expected return on the market and the risk-free rate is the slope of the line. For example, if we look back in time and see that the Treasury bill usually returned 3% (the risk-free rate) and that large-cap stocks (a proxy for the market in general) usually returned 13%, we could estimate the SML if we believe that these historical returns represent the future performance of the market. Our SML would be

$$E(r_i) = 3\% + (13\% - 3\%) \times \beta_i$$

We can also construct the SML from two risky assets. Let's assume Asset A has an expected return of 8% and a beta of 0.5 and Asset B has an expected return of 17% and a beta of 1.4. If we know two points on a line, we can find the slope and intercept of the line. The slope of the SML with these two risky assets is

$$\text{slope of line} = \frac{\Delta Y}{\Delta X} = \frac{17\% - 8\%}{1.4 - 0.5} = \frac{9\%}{0.9} = 10\%$$

Now that we have the slope of the SML, or market risk premium, we need to find the intercept of the line. We start with the general equation for the SML:

$$E(r_a) = r_f + \left[E(r_m) - r_f\right] \beta_a$$

We then plug in our known values for one of our assets, say Asset A: $E(r_a)$ = the expected return of Asset A at 0.08, β_a = the beta of Asset A at 0.5 and $E(r_m) - r_f$ = the slope of the SML or market risk premium at 10% (calculated previously). So,

$$0.08 = r_f + 0.10 \times 0.5$$

Then, rearranging the equation, we find the risk-free rate, the intercept for the SML:

$$r_f = 0.08 - 0.05 = 0.03$$

We can now write the equation for the SML in the economy with the slope and intercept determined from the two known assets, A and B, that plot on the SML:

$$\text{SML: } E(r_i) = 3\% + (10\%)\beta_i$$

What does an average risk taker expect for return in this market? Again, the average risk is a beta of 1 and reflects both the average expected return and the expected return on the market, $E(r_m)$. With a beta of 1, the expected return on the market in this setup is 13%. It is the reward for taking on one full unit of risk.

$$\begin{aligned}\text{market risk premium} &= \text{expected return on the market} - \text{risk-free rate}\\ &= E(r_m) - r_f\end{aligned}$$

EXAMPLE 8.5 Finding expected returns for a company with known systematic risk

Problem If Portland General Electric has a beta of 0.75 and Ford Motor Company has a beta of 1.2, what is the expected return of these two companies if the current market risk premium (slope of the SML) is 10% and the current risk-free rate is 3%?

Solution The first step is to write out the SML in equation form with the known economic information:

$$\text{SML: } E(r_i) = 3\% + (10\%)\beta_i$$

Now, we simply substitute the beta of the two companies into the equation to find their respective expected returns:

$$E(r_{\text{PGE}}) = 3\% + 10\% \times 0.75 = \mathbf{10.5\%}$$

$$E(r_{\text{Ford}}) = 3\% + 10\% \times 1.2 = \mathbf{15.0\%}$$

If we know the SML (the current risk-free rate and the expected return on the market or market risk premium), we can determine the expected return for any asset or portfolio that falls on the line, given that we know the beta of the asset or portfolio. In addition, if we know our risk tolerance—that is, the level of risk that we are willing to bear as measured by beta—we can determine our expected return in the current economy. To test your understanding of this relationship and the concepts in Chapter 8, and to exploit the power of the SML, work through the following application.

Application of the SML

If both assets R and S plot on the SML, Asset R has a beta of 0.60 and an expected return of 8.9%, and Asset S has a beta of 1.20 and an expected return of 14.3%, then find the slope of the SML or market risk premium, the risk-free rate, and the expected return on the market.

Solution Step 1 is to find the slope of the SML given that the two assets, R and S, plot on the line:

$$\text{slope of line} = \frac{\Delta Y}{\Delta X} = \frac{14.3\% - 8.9\%}{1.2 - 0.6} = \frac{5.4\%}{0.6} = 9\%$$

Step 2 is to find the risk-free rate by substituting either Asset R or Asset S into the SML. Substituting with Asset R:

$$E(r_R) = r_f + \left[E(r_m) - r_f\right] \times \beta_R$$

$$0.089 = r_f + 0.09 \times 0.6$$

$$r_f = 0.089 - 0.054 = 0.035$$

Substituting with Asset S:

$$E(r_S) = r_f + \left[E(r_m) - r_f\right] \times \beta_S$$

$$0.143 = r_f + 0.09 \times 1.2$$

$$r_f = 0.143 - 0.108 = 0.035$$

So, the risk-free rate is 3.5% and the SML is

$$\text{SML: } E(r_i) = 3.5\% + (9\%)\beta_i$$

Step 3 is to find the expected return on the market. The expected return on the market is the solution to the SML with a beta of 1, so we find

$$E(r_m) = 3.5\% + 9\% \times 1.0 = 12.5\%$$

Notice that we can always find the expected return on the market if we know the slope and the risk-free rate because

$$\text{market risk premium} = \text{slope} = E(r_m) - r_f$$

$$E(r_m) = \text{slope} + r_f$$

$$= 9\% + 3.5\% = 12.5\%$$

The next question is a little more complicated because it deals with an asset that is currently plotting off the SML. Here we are trying to determine whether we should buy or sell assets plotting above or below the SML. To start, suppose that there is an asset T with an expected return of 20.5% and a beta of 1.80. What *should* you expect for Asset T in terms of return if the beta of the stock is correctly measured at 1.80? What would a typical asset with a beta of 1.80 provide in an expected return? Let's plug the beta into the SML:

$$\text{SML: } E(r_T) = 3.5\% + 9\% \times 1.80 = 19.7\%$$

If assets with a beta of 1.80 should be returning 19.7% (those assets are plotting on the line) and Asset T is promising 20.5%, Asset T is plotting above the SML.

Therefore, you should buy this asset (according to investment rule number 2). It is offering a greater reward for the same level of risk for assets plotting on the SML with a beta of 1.80. By the same logic, if you find an asset plotting below the SML, you should sell that asset. We buy assets that plot above the SML and sell assets that plot below the SML.

Finally, what if you are willing to take only an 0.8 unit of risk (you desire a beta of 0.8 for your portfolio because you are a conservative investor)? What combination of Assets R and S will give you a portfolio with a beta of 0.8, and what is the expected return of your portfolio? This question is typical because it asks an investor to determine the allocation of a portfolio—for instance, between stocks and bonds—and hearkens back to the admonition of not putting all your eggs in one basket. In general, the positive performance of some assets (bonds) will neutralize the negative performance of others (stocks), and vice versa.

If you want a portfolio with a beta of 0.8 and you can use only Assets R and S, you must invest the following percentages in Assets R and S, where w is the percent of your wealth in Asset R and $1 - w$ is the percent of your wealth in Asset S:

$$0.8 = w \times 0.6 + (1 - w) \times 1.2$$

$$w = \tfrac{2}{3} \text{ and } 1 - w = \tfrac{1}{3}$$

To get a beta of 0.8, put two-thirds of your investment in Asset R and one-third of your investment in Asset S. You can find the expected return of this portfolio—we'll call it Portfolio P—either by taking the beta of the portfolio and plugging it into the equation for the SML or by using the weights with the expected return of the two assets. So,

$$\text{SML: } E(r_P) = 3.5\% + 9\% \times 0.8 = 10.7\%$$

or

$$E(r_P) = \tfrac{2}{3} \times 8.9\% + \tfrac{1}{3} \times 14.3\% = 10.7\%$$

Figure 8.13 shows Assets R and S plotting on the SML; asset T plotting above the SML; and Portfolio P, the combination of R and S with its beta of 0.8, plotting on the SML between Assets R and S.

As we move to the corporate world, we will take the portfolio concept forward. In the next part of this book, we view a company as a portfolio of products or projects, each with its own level of risk.

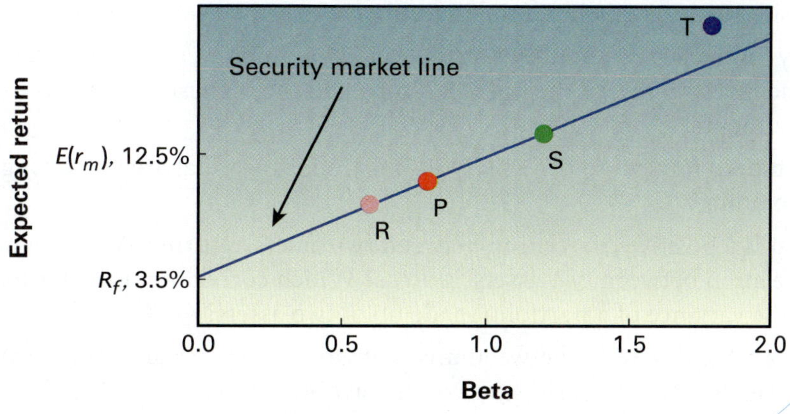

FIGURE 8.13 Security market line with individual assets.

To review this chapter, see the Summary Card at the end of the text.

Key Terms

beta, p. 238
capital asset pricing model (CAPM), p. 340
correlation, p. 234
correlation coefficient, p. 234
diversifiable risk, p. 237
diversification, p. 233
ex-ante, p. 227
ex-post, p. 227
financial portfolio, p. 233
holding period return (HPR), p. 215
Investment rule number 1, p. 232
Investment rule number 2, p. 232
market risk premium, p. 239
maximize return, p. 214
minimize risk, p. 214
negative correlation, p. 234
nondiversifiable risk, p. 237
positive correlation, p. 234
profit, p. 214
return, p. 214
reward-to-risk ratio, p. 240
risk, p. 218
security market line (SML), p. 239
slope of the security market line, p. 240
standard deviation, p. 224
systematic risk, p. 237
uncertainty, p. 217
unsystematic risk, p. 237
variance, p. 223
well-diversified portfolio, p. 237

Questions

1. What are the two parameters for selecting investments in the finance world? How do investors try to get the most out of their investment with regard to these two parameters?
2. What are the two ways to measure performance in the finance world?
3. Why is it not practical to convert holding period returns from very short periods to annual returns?
4. How do we define risk?
5. What type of investment had the highest return on average and the largest variance from 1950 to 1999? How much has this investment varied over that fifty-year period?
6. What is one of the problems of dealing with an event that has a large number of potential outcomes?
7. What are the two investment rules, and how do they influence choices when considering a pair of potential investments?
8. Why might two different investors select two different potential investments if one investment had the highest return and the highest risk over the other investment?
9. What does it mean to diversify your portfolio, and what are you trying to gain by so doing?
10. What is a positive correlation between two assets' returns? What is a negative correlation between two assets' returns? Which correlation is better for reducing the variance of a portfolio made up of two assets?
11. What is the difference between unsystematic and systematic risk? Which risk can you avoid? Which risk can you not avoid?

12. What is beta in the financial world? What is standard deviation in the financial world? What type of risk does each measure? What assumption do you make about the stock when you use beta as a measure of its risk?

Prepping for Exams

1. Travis bought a share of stock for $31.50 that paid a dividend of $0.85 and sold six months later for $27.65. What was his dollar profit or loss and holding period return?

   a. −$3.00, −9.52%
   b. −$3.85, −12.22%
   c. −$0.85, −2.70%
   d. −$3.85, −9.52%

2. ______________ is a measure of uncertainty in a set of potential outcomes for an event in which there is a chance for some loss.

   a. Diversification
   b. Risk
   c. Uncertainty
   d. Collaboration

3. Which of the following classifications of securities had the smallest range of annual returns over the period 1950–1999?

   a. large-company stocks
   b. long-term government bonds
   c. small-company stocks
   d. three-month U.S. Treasury bills

4. You are considering buying a share of stock in a firm that has the following two possible payoffs with the corresponding probability of occurrence. The stock has a purchase price of $15.00. You forecast that there is a 30% chance that the stock will sell for $30.00 at the end of one year. The alternative expectation is that there is a 70% chance the stock will sell for $10.00 at the end of one year. What is the expected percentage return on this stock, and what is the return variance?

   a. 6.67%, 9.17%
   b. 1.00%, 93.50%
   c. 6.67%, 37.33%
   d. 10.00%, 84.00%

5. George is considering an investment in Vandelay Inc. and has gathered the following information:

State of the Economy	Probability of the State	Conditional Expected Return Vandelay Inc.
Recession	0.25	−20%
Normal	0.60	10%
Boom	0.15	35%

What is the expected return for a share of the firm's stock?

a. 5.00%
b. 6.25%
c. 8.33%
d. 10.00%

6. When considering expected returns, what is true about the states of the world?

a. They must have probabilities that sum to 100%.
b. They represent all possible outcomes.
c. They are sometimes simplified into outcomes such as boom, bust, and normal.
d. Statements (a) through (c) are all true.

7. The correlation coefficient, a measurement of the co-movement between two variables, has what range?

a. From 0.0 to +10.0
b. From 0.0 to +1.0
c. From −1.0 to +10.0
d. From −1.0 to +1.0

8. The type of risk that can diversify away is ______________.

a. unsystematic risk
b. systematic risk
c. nondiversifiable risk
d. systemwide risk

9. Joel owns the following portfolio of securities:

Company	Beta	Percent of Portfolio
ExxonMobil	0.95	40%
Pacific Industries	1.20	35%
Payson Restaurants	1.35	25%

What is the beta for the portfolio?

a. 0.9500
b. 1.0000
c. 1.1375
d. 1.1705

10. Both Assets A and B plot on the SML. Asset A has an expected return of 15% and a beta of 1.7, and Asset B has an expected return of 12% and a beta of 1.1. What is the risk-free rate of return?

a. 5.0%
b. 6.5%
c. 11.5%
d. It cannot be determined from this information.

Problems

These problems are available in MyFinanceLab.

1. ***Profits.*** What are the profits on the following investments?

Investment	Original Cost of Investment	Selling Price of Investment	Distributions Received	Dollar Profit
CD	$ 500.00	$540.00	$ 0.00	
Stock	$ 23.00	$ 34.00	$ 2.00	
Bond	$1,040.00	$980.00	$80.00	
Bicycle	$ 400.00	$220.00	$ 0.00	

2. ***Profits.*** What are the profits on the following investments?

Investment	Original Cost of Investment	Selling Price of Investment	Distributions Received	Dollar Profits
CD	$ 500.00	$ 525.00	$ 0.00	
Stock	$ 34.00	$ 26.00	$ 2.00	
Bond	$ 955.00	$1,000.00	$240.00	
Car	$42,000.00	$3,220.00	$ 0.00	

3. ***Returns.*** What are the returns on the following investments?

Investment	Original Cost of Investment	Selling Price of Investment	Distributions Received	Percent Return
CD	$ 500.00	$540.00	$ 0.00	
Stock	$ 23.00	$ 34.00	$ 2.00	
Bond	$1,040.00	$980.00	$80.00	
Bicycle	$ 400.00	$220.00	$ 0.00	

4. ***Returns.*** What are the returns on the following investments?

Investment	Original Cost of Investment	Selling Price of Investment	Distributions Received	Percent Return
CD	$ 500.00	$ 525.00	$ 0.00	
Stock	$ 34.00	$ 26.00	$ 2.00	
Bond	$ 955.00	$1,000.00	$240.00	
Car	$42,000.00	$3,220.00	$ 0.00	

5. ***Holding period and annual (investment) returns.*** Baker Baseball Cards Inc. originally purchased the rookie card of Hammerin' Hank Aaron for $35.00. After holding the card for five years, Baker Baseball Cards auctioned the card for $180.00. What are the holding period return and the annual return on this investment?

6. ***Holding period and annual (investment) returns.*** Bohenick Classic Automobiles restores and rebuilds old classic cars. The company purchased and restored a classic 1957 Thunderbird convertible six years ago for $8,500. Today at auction, the car sold for $50,000. What are the holding period return and the annual return on this investment?

7. ***Comparison of returns.*** Looking back at Problems 5 and 6, which investment had the higher holding period return? Which had the higher annual return?
8. ***Comparison of returns.*** WG Investors is looking at three different investment opportunities. Investment one is a five-year investment with a cost of $125 and a promised payout of $250 at maturity. Investment two is a seven-year investment with a cost of $125 and a promised payout of $350. Investment three is a ten-year investment with a cost of $125 and a promised payout of $550. WG Investors can take on only one of the three investments. Assuming that all three investment opportunities have the same level of risk, calculate the annual return for each investment and select the best investment choice.
9. ***Historical returns.*** Calculate the average return of U.S. Treasury bills, long-term government bonds, and large-company stocks for 1990 to 1999 from Table 8.1. Which had the highest return? Which had the lowest return?
10. ***Historical returns.*** Calculate the average return of U.S. Treasury bills, long-term government bonds, and large-company stocks for 1950 to 1959, 1960 to 1969, 1970 to 1979, and 1980 to 1989 from Table 8.1. Which had the highest return? Which had the lowest return?
11. ***Standard deviation.*** Calculate the standard deviation of U.S. Treasury bills, long-term government bonds, and large-company stocks for 1990 to 1999 from Table 8.1. Which had the highest variance? Which had the lowest variance?
12. ***Variance and standard deviation***. Calculate the variance and the standard deviation of U.S. Treasury bills, long-term government bonds, and small-company stocks for 1950 to 1959, 1960 to 1969, 1970 to 1979, and 1980 to 1989 from Table 8.1. Which had the highest variance? Which had the lowest variance? *Hint:* Use a spreadsheet.
13. ***Internet exercise.*** Find the thirteen-week Treasury bill rates for 2000 to the present. Go to Treasury Direct (www.treasurydirect.gov) and in the "Institutions" section, click "Find Historical Auction Data." Select the thirteen-week Treasury bill historical data from January 1, 2000, to the present. Record the first auction of each year from 2000 to the present using the investment rate. What was the average from 2000 to the present? What was the standard deviation of this sample of auction rates? How does it compare with the data in Table 8.1?
14. ***Internet exercise.*** Find the Standard & Poor's 500 annual returns for 2000 to the present. Go to Yahoo! Finance (www.finance.yahoo.com), and in the "Get Quotes" search field, enter SPY (the ticker symbol for the Standard & Poor's 500 electronically traded fund). Select historical prices and find the year-end prices for the fund and all dividends from 2000 through the end of the most recent year. Find each year's return (remember to add in the dividend distributions for the year). What was the average annual return? What was the standard deviation? How does the standard deviation compare with the data in Table 8.1?
15. ***Expected return.*** Hull Consultants, a famous think tank in the Midwest, has provided probability estimates for the four potential economic states for the coming year. The probability of a boom economy is 10%, the probability of a stable growth economy is 15%, the probability of a stagnant economy is 50%, and the probability of a recession is 25%. Estimate the expected returns on the following individual investments for the coming year.

Investment	Forecasted Returns for Each Economy			
	Boom	Stable Growth	Stagnant	Recession
Stock	25%	12%	4%	−12%
Corporate bond	9%	7%	5%	3%
Government bond	8%	6%	4%	2%

16. *Variance and standard deviation (expected).* Using the data from Problem 15, calculate the variance and the standard deviation of the three investments: stock, corporate bond, and government bond. If the estimates for both the probabilities of the economy and the returns in each state of the economy are correct, which investment would you choose, considering both risk and return? Why?

17. *Expected return.* Bacon and Associates, a famous Northwest think tank, has provided probability estimates for the four potential economic states for the coming year. The probability of a boom economy is 20%, the probability of a stable growth economy is 45%, the probability of a stagnant economy is 20%, and the probability of a recession is 15%. Estimate the expected return on the following individual investments for the coming year.

Investment	Forecasted Returns for Each Economy			
	Boom	Stable Growth	Stagnant	Recession
Stock	25%	12%	4%	−12%
Corporate bond	9%	7%	5%	3%
Government bond	8%	6%	4%	2%

18. *Variance and standard deviation (expected).* Using the data from Problem 17, calculate the variance and the standard deviation of the three investments: stock, corporate bond, and government bond. If the estimates for both the probabilities of the economy and the returns in each state of the economy are correct, which investment would you choose, considering both risk and return? Why?

19. *Expected return and standard deviation.* Use the following information to answer the questions.

State of Economy	Probability of State	Return on Asset A in State	Return on Asset B in State	Return on Asset C in State
Boom	0.35	0.040	0.210	0.300
Normal	0.50	0.040	0.080	0.200
Recession	0.15	0.040	−0.010	−0.260

a. What is the expected return of each asset?

b. What is the variance of each asset?

c. What is the standard deviation of each asset?

20. *Expected return and standard deviation.* Use the information on the following page to answer the questions.

State of Economy	Probability of State	Return on Asset D in State	Return on Asset E in State	Return on Asset F in State
Boom	0.35	0.060	0.310	0.150
Normal	0.50	0.060	0.180	0.120
Recession	0.15	0.060	−0.210	−0.060

a. What is the expected return of each asset?

b. What is the variance of each asset?

c. What is the standard deviation of each asset?

21. ***Expected return and standard deviation.*** Use the following information to answer the questions.

State of Economy	Probability of State	Return on Asset J in State	Return on Asset K in State	Return on Asset L in State
Boom	0.30	0.050	0.240	0.300
Growth	0.40	0.050	0.120	0.200
Stagnant	0.20	0.050	0.040	0.060
Recession	0.10	0.050	−0.100	−0.200

a. What is the expected return of each asset?

b. What are the variance and the standard deviation of each asset?

c. What is the expected return of a portfolio with 10% in Asset J, 50% in Asset K, and 40% in Asset L?

d. What are the portfolio's variance and standard deviation using the same asset weights from part (c)?

22. ***Expected return and standard deviation.*** Use the following information to answer the questions.

State of Economy	Probability of State	Return on Asset R in State	Return on Asset S in State	Return on Asset T in State
Boom	0.15	0.040	0.280	0.450
Growth	0.25	0.040	0.140	0.275
Stagnant	0.35	0.040	0.070	0.025
Recession	0.25	0.040	−0.035	−0.175

a. What is the expected return of each asset?

b. What are the variances and standard deviations of each asset?

c. What is the expected return of a portfolio with equal investment in all three assets?

d. What are the portfolio's variance and standard deviation using the same asset weights as in part (c)?

23. ***Benefits of diversification.*** Sally Rogers has decided to invest her wealth equally across the three assets on the following page. What are her expected returns and the risk by investing in the three assets? How do they compare with investing in Asset M alone? *Hint:* Find the standard deviation of Asset M and of the portfolio equally invested in Assets M, N, and O.

States	Probability	Asset M Return	Asset N Return	Asset O Return
Boom	30%	12%	19%	2%
Normal	50%	8%	11%	8%
Recession	20%	2%	−2%	12%

24. ***Benefits of diversification.*** Use the same assets as Problem 23. Could Sally reduce her total risk even more by using Assets M and N only, Assets M and O only, or Assets N and O only? Use a 50/50 split between the asset pairs and find the standard deviation of the asset pairs.

25. ***Beta of a portfolio.*** The betas of four stocks—G, H, I, and J—are 0.45, 0.8, 1.15, and 1.6, respectively. What is the beta of a portfolio with the following weights in each asset?

	Weight in Stock G	Weight in Stock H	Weight in Stock I	Weight in Stock J
Portfolio 1	25%	25%	25%	25%
Portfolio 2	30%	40%	20%	10%
Portfolio 3	10%	20%	40%	30%

26. ***Expected return of a portfolio using beta.*** Use the same four assets from Problem 25 in the same three portfolios. What are the expected returns of each of the four individual assets and the three portfolios if the current SML is plotting with an intercept of 4% (risk-free rate) and a market premium of 10% (slope of the line)?

27. ***Beta of a portfolio.*** The betas of four stocks—P, Q, R, and S—are 0.6, 0.85, 1.2, and 1.35, respectively. What is the beta of a portfolio with the following weights in each asset?

	Weight in Stock P	Weight in Stock Q	Weight in Stock R	Weight in Stock S
Portfolio 1	25%	25%	25%	25%
Portfolio 2	30%	40%	20%	10%
Portfolio 3	10%	20%	40%	30%

28. ***Expected return of a portfolio using beta.*** Use the same four assets from Problem 27 in the same three portfolios. What are the expected returns of each of the four individual assets and the three portfolios if the current SML is plotting with an intercept of 3% (risk-free rate) and a market premium of 11% (slope of the line)?

29. ***Changing risk level.*** Mr. Malone wants to change the overall risk of his portfolio. Currently, his portfolio is a combination of risky assets with a beta of 1.25 and an expected return of 14%. He will add a risk-free asset (U.S. Treasury bill) to his portfolio. If he wants a beta of 1.0, what percent of his wealth should be in the risky portfolio and what percent should be in the risk-free asset? If he wants a beta of 0.75? If he wants a beta of 0.50? If he wants a beta of 0.25? Is there a pattern here?

30. ***Changing risk level.*** Ms. Chambers wants to change the expected return of her portfolio. Currently, she has all her money in U.S. Treasury bills with a return of 3%. She can switch some of her money into a risky portfolio with an expected return of 15%. What percent of her wealth will she need to invest in the risky portfolio to get an expected return of 5%? Of 7%? Of 9%? Of 11%? Of 13%? Of 15%? Is there a pattern here?

31. ***Reward-to-risk ratio.*** Royal Seattle Investment Club has $100,000 to invest in the equity market. Frasier advocates investing the funds in KSEA Radio with a beta of 1.3 and an expected return of 16%. Niles advocates investing the funds in Northwest Medical with a beta of 1.1 and an expected return of 14%. The club is split 50/50 on the two stocks. You are the deciding vote, and you cannot pick a split of $50,000 for each stock. Before you vote, you look up the current risk-free rate (the one-year U.S. Treasury bill with a yield of 3.75%). Which stock do you select?

32. ***Reward-to-risk ratio.*** Uptown Investment Club has $50,000 to invest in the equity market. Chandler advocates investing the funds in Monica's Restaurant with a beta of 1.8 and an expected return of 22%. Ross advocates investing the funds in Rachel's Clothing Store with a beta of 0.9 and an expected return of 11%. The club is split 50/50 on the two stocks. You are the deciding vote, and you cannot pick a split of $25,000 for each stock. Before you vote, you look up the current risk-free rate (the one-year U.S. Treasury bill with a yield of 2.45%). Which stock do you select?

33. ***Different investor weights.*** Two risky portfolios exist for investing: one is a bond portfolio with a beta of 0.5 and an expected return of 8%, and the other is an equity portfolio with a beta of 1.2 and an expected return of 15%. If these portfolios are the only two available assets for investing, what combination of these two assets will give the following investors their desired level of expected return? What are the betas of each investor's combination of the bond and equity portfolio?

a. Bart: desired expected return 14%

b. Lisa: desired expected return 12%

c. Maggie: desired expected return 10%

34. ***Different investor weights.*** Two risky portfolios exist for investing: one is a bond portfolio with a beta of 0.7 and an expected return of 9%, and another is an equity portfolio with a beta of 1.5 and an expected return of 17%. If these portfolios are the only two available assets for investing, what combination of these two assets will give the following investors their desired level of expected return? What are the betas of each investor's combination of the bond and equity portfolio?

a. Jerry: desired expected return 16%

b. Elaine: desired expected return 13%

c. Cosmo: desired expected return 10%

These problems are available in MyFinanceLab.

Advanced Problems for Spreadsheet Application

1. ***Returns and variances in the period 2000 to 2009.*** The text presents the return rates for Treasury bills, Treasury bonds, large-cap stocks, and small-cap stocks from 1950 to 1999 in Table 8.1. The returns and prices are for the period 2000 to 2009 in the table at the top of the next page. Find the average return for each investment for the decade, and the variance and standard deviation of the returns. The data for S&P 500 Index and Russell Index are the end of the year values (prices). Convert this information to returns. The 13-week Treasury bill and 10-year Treasury note are the yields of the auctions.

Year	13-Week Treasury Bills	10-Year Treasury Notes	Standard and Poor's 500 Index	Russell 2000 Index (Small-Cap)
1999			146.88	504.75
2000	0.05864	0.05865	131.19	483.53
2001	0.01740	0.04220	114.30	488.50
2002	0.01207	0.04095	88.23	383.09
2003	0.00884	0.04365	111.28	556.91
2004	0.02269	0.04150	120.87	651.57
2005	0.03999	0.04490	124.51	673.22
2006	0.05004	0.04580	141.62	787.66
2007	0.0363	0.04164	146.21	766.03
2008	0.00041	0.0267	90.24	499.45
2009	0.00112	0.03448	111.44	625.39

2. ***Portfolio of assets with expected returns.*** There are four potential states of the economy for the coming year and there are five potential assets for investing. First, find the expected return and the expected standard deviation of the five assets. Next, construct a set of portfolios with the different weights listed in the second following table for the assets in each portfolio. Find each portfolio's expected return and standard deviation. Determine the reduction in the standard deviation of the portfolio by comparing the weighted average standard deviation of the assets in the portfolio to the standard deviation of the portfolio.

States	Probability	Asset A Return	Asset B Return	Asset C Return	Asset D Return	Asset E Return
Boom	0.25	0.30	0.24	0.15	0.05	−0.20
Normal	0.45	0.15	0.12	0.12	0.09	0.02
Recession	0.20	0.05	0.00	0.06	0.14	0.10
Bust	0.10	−0.35	−0.20	0.02	0.20	0.30

Weights in the Various Portfolios

Portfolio	Percent in A	Percent in B	Percent in C	Percent in D	Percent in E
1	0.20	0.20	0.20	0.20	0.20
2	0.35	0.30	0.20	0.10	0.05
3	0.20	0.30	0.30	0.10	0.10
4	0.10	0.15	0.25	0.35	0.15

MINI-CASE

Lawrence's Legacy: Part 2

This mini-case is available in MyFinanceLab.

In Chapter 7, we saw stockbroker Don Kraska, CFA, preparing to answer a list of questions concerning stock valuation. These questions and answers were to serve as the outline for a presentation before a committee of officials from the Town of Webley. The committee needed advice on how best to follow

Continued

Continued

instructions in the will of James Lawrence, who had left the town 2,000 shares of Google stock, currently valued at approximately $1,250,000. Lawrence's will instructed the town to sell the Google shares and set up a diversified stock portfolio that would fund annual grants for youth groups in the town.

During the course of Kraska's first presentation, Webley officials expressed a great deal of concern about the risks of the stock market, yet Lawrence's instructions were quite clear. The town was to invest the money in stocks, not bonds or certificates of deposit, and it could retain only limited amounts of cash for grant-making purposes.

Kraska has set up a second meeting to discuss risk. He really wants this account, so he will try to strike the right tone and behave reassuringly but still be realistic. He has been in the business since 1985, so he knows very well that the market has its ups and downs.

Assume once again that you are Kraska preparing to answer a set of return- and risk-oriented questions that have surfaced as a result of the first presentation.

Questions

1. How do we measure the returns on our portfolio?

   Kraska will answer this question by assuming that a $1,000,000 portfolio in a given year earns $30,000 in dividends and either gains or loses $100,000 in market value. Show his computations. Be prepared to answer a follow-up question about the value of the portfolio after a 5% grant distribution. Kraska will also compute Lawrence's EAR on his investment in Google to illustrate a multiyear perspective. Lawrence purchased the Google stock for $200,000 and held it for three years before he died.

2. How can we assess the risk of an individual stock?

   a. Kraska will first address this question by looking at recent returns on Amazon.com and on Coca-Cola. Compute the mean and standard deviation for each and explain their meaning. He has collected the return data at the top of the page:

Year	Amazon.com	Coca-Cola
2007	134.77%	33.35%
2006	−16.31%	26.35%
2005	6.46%	2.24%
2004	−15.83%	13.93%
2003	178.56%	21.94%

   b. Kraska will also suggest that it is good to assess risk by looking forward to how we expect stocks to react to a particular set of circumstances or "states of nature." Use the following set of assumptions for the coming year to compute the expected rate of return and the standard deviation for Amazon.com, Coca-Cola, and a portfolio with equal dollar amounts invested in Amazon.com and Coca-Cola (see table at the bottom of the page).

3. What kinds of investments are safe and earn a high rate of return?

4. Google seems to be a great company. Why did Lawrence require the town to sell the Google stocks and reinvest the money in a diversified portfolio?

5. How many stocks should we have in our portfolio?

6. How much risk will the portfolio carry?

   a. Kraska will answer this question by explaining the capital asset pricing model in the most straightforward terms possible.

   b. He will illustrate how we use CAPM to compute the expected rate of return on a stock. Use an expected market return of 12%, a risk-free rate of 5%, and the betas for Amazon.com (3.02), Coca-Cola (0.62), and Merck Pharmaceuticals (1.11) to compute the expected rate of return on these stocks.

   c. He will illustrate the concept of portfolio beta using the same three stocks. Compute the beta for a portfolio composed of $20,000 invested in Amazon.com, $50,000 in Coca-Cola, and $35,000 in Merck Pharmaceuticals.

State of Economy	Probability of State	Amazon.com Conditional Return	Coca-Cola Conditional Return	50/50 Portfolio Conditional Return
Recession	30.00%	−25.00%	5.00%	−10.00%
Average	50.00%	30.00%	12.00%	21.00%
Boom	20.00%	50.00%	20.00%	32.50%

Part 3

Capital Budgeting

Learning Objectives

LO1 Explain capital budgeting and differentiate between short-term and long-term budgeting decisions.

LO2 Explain the payback period model and its two significant weaknesses and how the discounted payback period model addresses one of the problems.

LO3 Understand the net present value (NPV) decision model and appreciate why it is the preferred criterion for evaluating proposed investments.

LO4 Calculate the most popular capital budgeting alternative to the NPV, the internal rate of return (IRR); explain how the modified internal rate of return (MIRR) model attempts to address the IRR's problems.

LO5 Understand the profitability index (PI) as a modification of the NPV model.

LO6 Compare and contrast the strengths and weaknesses of each decision model in a holistic way.

Chapter 9

Capital Budgeting Decision Models

Is it worthwhile? That is the question the capital budgeting decision process considers. Because money is not limitless, companies must be careful to choose projects that are feasible and profitable. They use the cash flow to "water" only those ideas that they deem most likely to grow into money-making or money-saving projects. If there are alternatives, the companies must identify and accept the most beneficial over other projects.

Capital budgeting is concerned with making the best investment choices, and is the heart of corporate finance. In this chapter, we will study several different models that can help a company determine whether it should accept or reject a project. A "project" can be anything from a new copy machine to a new factory. Whatever it is, we still must apply decision-making criteria to answer the question, "Is it worthwhile?" Here, we will "evaluate the valuation techniques" by considering each decision model's advantages and disadvantages, and we will determine that one method—the net present value model—trumps all others.

9.1 Short-Term and Long-Term Decisions

What is the difference between a short-term decision and a long-term decision? The obvious answer is the time frame that the decision affects.

As an illustration of a short-term decision, you will decide today what to eat for your next meal. This decision may involve a set of choices with varying costs. The choice affects you for only a short period of time, and the difference in cost of the different menu options is relatively small. In addition, you will face the same decision again in a few hours and can make a different choice for the next meal selection.

Then there are long-term decisions. Recall for a moment your decision concerning which college to attend. This decision affects you for a number of years and carries with it significant financial costs. Moreover, this choice may well have been a once-in-a-lifetime decision. Although you can change schools after your initial choice, you cannot pick a different school to attend every few hours as you can with your menu choice.

In general, we can separate short-term and long-term decisions into three dimensions:

1. Length of effect
2. Cost
3. Degree of information gathering prior to the decision

The longer the effect and the higher the associated cost of a decision, the greater the time and degree allotted to gathering information on choices and the more sophisticated or complex the decision model.

Businesses use these dimensions when making choices about how to allocate money to products, services, and activities.We call long-term decisions **capital budgeting** decisions and typically view them as having long-term effects that we cannot easily reverse or that we can change only at great cost. An example of a long-term decision is determining the number of manufacturing facilities that the firm should operate. For a decision that had massive long-term repercussions, see the nearby "Finance Follies" feature.

On the other hand, we view short-term decisions as those that have short-term effects and that we can change or modify at relatively low costs. For example, one short-term decision is determining the appropriate level of inventories a firm should maintain. A firm can change the inventory amount with the next order if a product's sales are faster or slower than originally anticipated. It is much easier to adjust or change inventory levels than it is to open or close a manufacturing facility.

By its nature, capital budgeting is concerned with long-term decision making. We can define it as the planning, appraising, comparing, and selecting of a firm's long-term projects. Long-term projects are those with lives that extend over a year, or longer than the normal business operating cycle. As we noted at the opening of the chapter, capital budgeting is the process that answers the question, "Is this project worthwhile financially to the firm?"

We can make three key observations about the capital budgeting decision:

1. A capital budgeting decision is typically a go or no-go decision on a product, service, facility, or activity of the firm. We either accept the business proposal or we reject it.
2. A capital budgeting decision will require sound estimates of the timing and amount of cash flow for the proposal.
3. The capital budgeting model has a predetermined accept or reject criterion.

FINANCE FOLLIES

IBM Exits the Consumer Software Market: Misreading Future Cash Flows

According to legend, the original inhabitants of Manhattan sold the island in 1625 to Dutch Colonial Governor Peter Minuit for $24. The story is an example of an exceptionally good or bad capital budgeting decision, depending on whether one looks at it from the buyer's or the seller's point of view. In one of the many variations on the story, Minuit was actually the dupe because the tribe sold him land it didn't own. Another interpretation claims that if Minuit could have invested the $24 in an average index fund, it would have grown to several trillion dollars by now, so the sellers actually received a fair price. There seems to be only one opinion, however, concerning IBM's decision to outsource the operating system for its personal computers (PCs) to the fledgling software firm Microsoft. It was one of the greatest financial bloopers in history.

To understand how it happened, today's students have to imagine a technology world that was—somewhat like seventeenth-century Manhattan—ripe for development. Such was the tech world of the early 1980s, when the only computer games were primitive versions of Pong and Pac-Man. There was no Outlook®, no Word®, no Excel®, no PowerPoint®, and no Internet. Personal computers had no internal storage, and we had to connect most to television sets that served as monitors.

In 1980, IBM was eager to compete with Commodore, Tandy, and especially Apple in the emerging small-computer market. IBM formed a special division in Boca Raton, Florida, staffed with top-level managers and scientists. The task of some of the scientists, now software engineers, was to adapt IBM's operating systems for large computers to the desktop computer. Others were to tackle a similar project for processors.

To accelerate the introduction of a competitive home computer, IBM made the fateful decision to purchase an operating system from Microsoft rather than proceed with in-house development. Microsoft's programmers had never created an operating system, so, for $50,000, they purchased a simple, but surprisingly effective system written by Tim Paterson of Seattle Computer Systems. Microsoft renamed Paterson's Q-DOS (quick and dirty operating system) "MS-DOS" and sold it with IBM PCs. Perceiving that he could easily clone the IBM PC, Microsoft's shrewd wonder boy, Bill Gates, managed to retain the rights to market MS-DOS independently. Non-IBM computers running on MS-DOS were then known as IBM-compatibles, but the revenues from their operating systems went to Microsoft. Microsoft's early dominance in operating systems easily transitioned to Windows and then to the popular Microsoft Office Suite and other consumer software written to run on Windows. Microsoft made a fortune.

Even though IBM had built its dominant position in large computers by vertically integrating hardware and software, it completely missed the opportunity to do the same with small computers. IBM executives believed that the future of small computers was in home entertainment, and they projected robust cash flows from this channel. They were taken aback when PC sales to businesses quickly surpassed the home market. They began to perceive the PC as a threat to IBM's large business computers, so they eliminated the PC division in Boca Raton and brought the company's operations under central corporate control.

MS-DOS and all its later permutations and related products such as Windows and Office would never have achieved a dominant market share had Microsoft not packaged them with IBM computers. By allowing an outside firm to own and sell its operating system, IBM gave away all the value that Microsoft eventually created—and probably a good part of the value that companies such as Dell, Compaq, and Intel developed—for something that cost Bill Gates and his partners only $50,000. In capital budgeting, technique is important, but inaccurate estimates of future cash flows from a project can lead to extremely bad decisions. We look at cash flow in more detail in the next chapter.

What about Tim Paterson? Had he invested the $50,000 that he received for Q-DOS in Microsoft stock at the initial public offering price of $21 per share in 1986, he would have bought 2,381 shares. Microsoft stock has since split nine times, so each original share is now 288 shares. As of late June 2011, at $26 per share, Paterson's 685,728 shares would be worth $17,821,440. At the current annual dividend rate of $0.64 per share, Paterson's stock would also provide him with an annual income of $438,857.

First, capital budgeting is about making decisions. The choice of accepting or rejecting a proposed project is the cornerstone of financial management at all levels of a business. Second, the appropriate future cash flow is a necessary input into all capital budgeting decisions. We explore how to estimate the cash flow in the following chapters. For now, we assume that we have the appropriate estimate of future cash flow

Capital budgeting is about making decisions about what projects are worthwhile for a firm to fund. If the project that the company is considering does not meet a predetermined criterion ("go" or "no-go"), the company should reject it.

so that we can examine the various decision making models. Finally, all capital budgeting models have a predetermined criterion for accepting or rejecting proposed projects. We will examine the validity of these criteria within each decision model.

In this chapter, we introduce three standard models and three modified models for capital budgeting decisions:

1. Payback period (standard)
2. Discounted payback period (modified from payback period)
3. Net present value (NPV) (standard)
4. Internal rate of return (IRR) (standard)
5. Modified internal rate of return (MIRR) (modified from the IRR)
6. Profitability index (PI) (modified from the NPV)

Throughout the chapter, we use simple examples such as copy machines and popcorn production machines for projects so that you can see the various techniques at work in uncomplicated settings. You can, however, extrapolate the principles of capital budgeting, and apply them to complex projects such as whether to build a new plant or whether to develop an oil field. That is not to say that we can rely exclusively on a formula to decide whether to fund large ventures. Large ventures will also require involvement of far-reaching strategic considerations. At the heart of the investment analysis process, though, the same tools are at work—regardless of the project's scope.

9.2 Payback Period

By far, the easiest decision model to administer is **payback period**. This model answers one basic question: How soon will I recover my initial investment? The model assumes that there is an outflow of cash at the beginning of the project and a series of cash inflows during future periods. It simply calculates at what point in time the company recovers its cash outflow or payback with corresponding future cash inflow.

EXAMPLE 9.1 Payback period of a new copier: to buy or not to buy?

Problem Clinko Copiers wants to buy a new color copier with scanner. The initial cost of the copier is $5,000. The store manager estimates that the new copier will be functional for five years and will produce the following net cash inflow (the time line shows the future anticipated cash inflow minus the initial cost). What is the payback period for the copier?

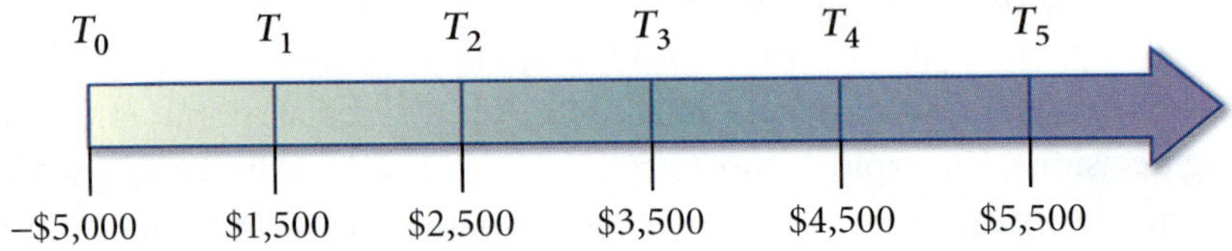

Solution The initial outlay or cost is $5,000 for the copier. In year one, the copier returns $1,500 of its initial cost or outlay, and the project still needs to recover an additional $3,500. In year two, it recovers $2,500 and is left with only $1,000 to recover. In year three, it recovers the final $1,000, but the recovery does not take the whole year because the year in total brings in $3,500; rather, it only takes 29% of the third year ($1,000/$3,500). So, the company recovers the initial cost of $5,000 in a little more than two years; more formally, this project has a payback period of 2.29 years. Notice that we use negative dollars to reflect cash outflow such as the initial cost of the copier and we use positive dollars to reflect cash inflow. When the positive dollars are sufficient to fully recover the cash outflow, we are at the payback period.

Payback Period for Copier

Year	Cash Flow	Yet to Be Recovered	Percent of Year Recovered/Inflow
0	−$5,000	Initial cash outflow at start	
1	$1,500	−$5,000 + $1,500 =−$3,500	
2	$2,500	−$3,500 + $2,500 =−$1,000	
3	$3,500	−$1,000 + $3,500 = $0 (recovered)	$1,000/$3,500 = 29%
4	$4,500	Not used in decision	
5	$5,500	Not used in decision	

We now know how long it will take to recover the initial cost of the copier. If the company's required recovery period is less than three years, Clinko Copiers will buy the new copier. If the required payback period is less than two years, then Clinko Copiers will not buy it.

We base our payback period example on two important assumptions. First, we assume that the cash inflow is constant and steady throughout each year. That is, the $3,500 in year three comes in increments of $292 each month ($3,500/12), or approximately $67.31 each week ($3,500/52), or $9.59 per day ($3,500/365). Actual cash inflow, however, may or may not be steady. If you can estimate the actual cash inflow, you can estimate the payback period better. Second, the appropriate cutoff time for the payback period is a decision specific to the company. If the company chooses three years as the appropriate cutoff time, it may be a well-reasoned decision, but it is not based on economic theory.

Although the payback period method is used widely, it has two significant weaknesses:

1. It ignores all cash flow after the company has recovered initial cash outflow.
2. It ignores the time value of money.

So, if this model is biased against projects with late-term payouts and does not discount future cash flow, why do companies use it? Many companies use the payback period for small-dollar decisions. For example, a large company may have a policy that all capital expenditures under $10,000 must have a payback period of three years or less. Although $10,000 may be considerable money to us, a large company may have many potential projects of $10,000 or less. In addition, the company

FIGURE 9.1 Initial cash outflow and future cash inflow of Copiers A and B.

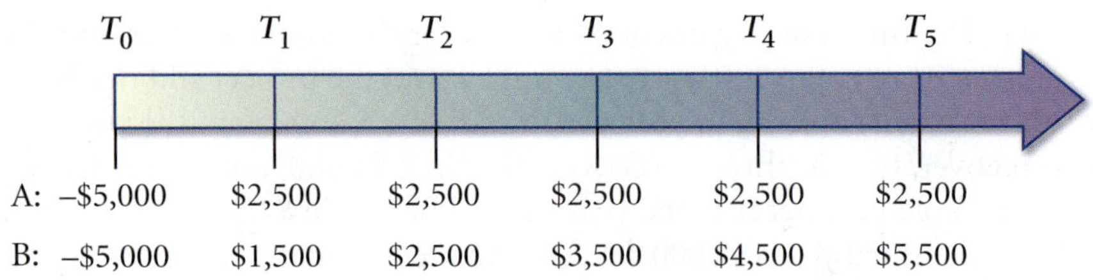

can lower the time spent estimating cash inflows substantially if it requires only the first three years. The accuracy of future cash flow projections on these smaller projects may be quite difficult to estimate far into the future. Therefore, the company establishes a short, arbitrary cutoff date for handling the initial screening of many small-dollar opportunities. Finally, it does prevent a serious error when the future cash flow is never sufficient to recover the initial cash outlay.

Even if we accept the short-term focus of the model, the payback period still has a fundamental flaw from a finance perspective: it fails to account for the time value of money. We can easily correct this problem by adjusting to a payback period model with discounting, which we turn to now.

Discounted Payback Period

To account for the time value of money with the payback period model, we need to restate the future cash flow in current dollars. It is fairly easy to do if you have an appropriate discount rate for the future cash flows and the proper timing of the cash flows. We just apply the time value of money concept from Chapters 3 and 4. This modified version of the payback period model, the **discounted payback period** method, considers the time it takes to recover the initial investment *in current dollars.*

Let's return to the copier problem for Clinko Copiers and add a second type of copier to the decision mix to see what effect the discounted payback period model has on the decision. To illustrate, let's use a 6% discount rate on the future cash flow.

Clinko can purchase either Copier A or Copier B but needs only one, so it must choose either A or B. The initial cost of each copier is $5,000. Figure 9.1 shows the cash inflows of each copier.

As before, Clinko Copiers requires a three-year payback period for any new copier. Based on the payback period, which copier should Clinko's buy?

Table 9.1 shows the calculations of the present value of each of the future cash flows discounted at 6%. We can now determine how long it will take to recover the initial investment for the two copy machines in current dollars.

TABLE 9.1 Discounted Cash Flow of Copiers A and B

Year	Copier A Cash Flow	Copier A Discounted Cash Flow	Copier B Cash Flow	Copier B Discounted Cash Flow
1	$2,500	$ 2,500/1.06 = $2,358.49	$1,500	$ 1,500/1.06 = $1,415.09
2	$2,500	$2,500/(1.06^2) = $2,224.99	$2,500	$2,500/(1.06^2) = $2,224.99
3	$2,500	$2,500/(1.06^3) = $2,099.05	$3,500	$3,500/(1.06^3) = $2,938.67
4	$2,500	$2,500/(1.06^4) = $1,980.23	$4,500	$4,500/(1.06^4) = $3,564.42
5	$2,500	$2,500/(1.06^5) = $1,868.15	$5,500	$5,500/(1.06^5) = $4,109.92

For Copier A,

Year 1: −$5,000.00 + $2,358.49 = −$2,641.51 remaining cost to recover
Year 2: −$2,641.51 + $2,224.99 = −$416.52 remaining cost to recover
Year 3: −$416.52 + $2,099.05 = $1,682.53; the cost is fully recovered by the end of year 3.

For Copier B,

Year 1: −$5,000.00 + $1,415.09 = −$3,584.91 remaining cost to recover
Year 2: −$3,584.91 + $2,224.99 = −$1,359.92 remaining cost to recover
Year 3: −$1,359.92 + $2,938.67 = $1,578.75; the cost is fully recovered by the end of year 3.

Using the discounted payback period method, we can see that both copiers have a three-year payback period. Why did we use all year three's cash inflows when we did not need the full-year amount to recover the final part of the initial investment? The reason is one of consistency. When we discounted the future cash flow using 6% with our standard time value of money concepts, we inherently assumed that the company received the entire cash flow at the end of the year. We could assume monthly cash flow and discount each monthly cash flow by the periodic monthly interest rate of 0.5% (6%/12) and then see how many months it takes to recover the $5,000 investment. If we did so, we would see that Copier A takes twenty-six months and Copier B takes twenty-nine months. Both are within the thirty-six-month cutoff date. The decision rule does not distinguish between these two copiers, however, even though it takes slightly less time for Copier A to pay back the $5,000.

By switching to monthly cash flow, we get a more accurate estimate of the discounted payback period, but at a higher computational cost. We must be sure that our future cash flow estimates are accurate in each month, and this requirement may necessitate more review of the seasonality of cash flow. Of course, with spreadsheets, the marginal cost of the extra calculations may be small once we have the monthly cash flow forecasts.

Although we have corrected for one of the problems in the payback period model for capital budgeting, we still have not corrected for ignoring the cash flow after the recovery of the initial outflow. How do we correct for this flaw? The answer is a discounted cash flow model that includes all future cash flow, net present value.

9.3 Net Present Value

The capital budgeting decision model that uses all the discounted cash flows of a project is **net present value (NPV)**, one of the single most important models in finance. The NPV of an investment is the present value of all benefits (cash inflows) minus the present value of all costs (cash outflows) of the project.

The NPV model states all cash flow in present value or current dollars, and we "net" the inflow against the outflow to see if the net amount is positive or negative. If the net amount is positive (benefits exceed costs), the project or choice is a "go." If the net amount is negative (costs exceed benefits), the project is a "no-go." If we are comparing two projects, we select the one with the highest positive net present value. We discount the future cash flow at the rate *r*, the cost of capital. In Chapter 11, we address how to determine the cost of capital, but for now we assume that we have an appropriate discount rate for each cash flow (CF). The NPV decision model is

$$NPV = -CF_0 + \frac{CF_1}{(1 + r)^1} + \frac{CF_2}{(1 + r)^2} + \frac{CF_3}{(1 + r)^3} + \cdots + \frac{CF_n}{(1 + r)^n} \quad \textbf{9.1}$$

accept if $NPV > 0$ reject if $NPV < 0$

Let's return to Clinko Copiers and look again at Copiers A and B to determine their respective NPVs. Again, for Copier A we have the following information. Notice that the company typically pays for the cost of the copier at time of purchase, which is a cash outflow. Negative dollars represent outflow. So,

CF_0 = \$5,000 (the cost of the copier)
CF_1 = \$2,500 (cash inflow from copier at end of year one)
CF_2 = \$2,500 (cash inflow from copier at end of year two)
CF_3 = \$2,500 (cash inflow from copier at end of year three)
CF_4 = \$2,500 (cash inflow from copier at end of year four)
CF_5 = \$2,500 (cash inflow from copier at end of year five)
r = 6% (the appropriate discount rate for this project)

$$\begin{aligned} NPV &= -\$5{,}000 + \frac{\$2{,}500}{(1 + 0.06)^1} + \frac{\$2{,}500}{(1 + 0.06)^2} + \frac{\$2{,}500}{(1 + 0.06)^3} \\ &\quad + \frac{\$2{,}500}{(1 + 0.06)^4} + \frac{\$2{,}500}{(1 + 0.06)^5} \\ &= -\$5{,}000 + \$2{,}358.49 + \$2{,}224.99 + \$2{,}099.05 + \$1{,}980.23 \\ &\quad + \$1{,}868.15 \\ &= \$5{,}530.91 \text{ (positive)} \end{aligned}$$

Therefore, we may buy Copier A.

Now, for Copier B,

CF_0 = \$5,000 (the cost of the copier)
CF_1 = \$1,500 (cash inflow from copier at end of year one)
CF_2 = \$2,500 (cash inflow from copier at end of year two)
CF_3 = \$3,500 (cash inflow from copier at end of year three)
CF_4 = \$4,500 (cash inflow from copier at end of year four)
CF_5 = \$5,500 (cash inflow from copier at end of year five)
r = 6% (the appropriate discount rate for this project)

$$\begin{aligned} NPV &= -\$5{,}000 + \frac{\$1{,}500}{(1 + 0.06)^1} + \frac{\$2{,}500}{(1 + 0.06)^2} + \frac{\$3{,}500}{(1 + 0.06)^3} \\ &\quad + \frac{\$4{,}500}{(1 + 0.06)^4} + \frac{\$5{,}500}{(1 + 0.06)^5} \\ &= -\$5{,}000 + \$1{,}415.09 + \$2{,}224.99 + \$2{,}938.67 \\ &\quad + \$3{,}564.42 + \$4{,}109.92 \\ &= \$9{,}253.09 \text{ (positive)} \end{aligned}$$

Therefore, we may buy Copier B.

The NPV calculation indicates that it is acceptable for Clinko Copiers to buy either copier. Both copiers make money for the company. If Clinko needs only one new copier this year, however, which copier should it select? If the need is for a single new copier this year, the correct choice is Copier B with the highest NPV. Intuitively, it is a rather simple choice between the two copiers. By calculating the present value of all future cash flows, the options are one "bag of money" at \$9,253.09 or a second "bag of money" at \$5,530.91. Which would you rather have, \$9,253.09 or \$5,530.91? The choice is obvious.

What if Clinko Copiers could spend \$10,000 on new copiers this year and needed *two* additional copiers? What business choice would you advise the company to make? Again, the answer is obvious: buy two Copier Bs. Of course, we are assuming that the cash flow for a second Copier B is the same as the cash flow for the first Copier B, and we assume that the supplier has two Copier Bs available for delivery.

Mutually Exclusive versus Independent Projects

At this time, let's address an important issue when comparing projects using the NPV decision model. The decision criterion tells us to take all positive NPV projects. That is true when all projects are independent and the company has a sufficient source of funds to accept all positive NPV projects. Two projects are independent if the acceptance of one project has no bearing on the acceptance or rejection of the other project.

Some projects, however, are mutually exclusive. With **mutually exclusive projects**, picking one project eliminates the possibility of picking the other project. This situation can arise for two reasons:

1. There is a need for only one project, and both projects can fulfill that need.
2. There is a scarce resource that both projects need, and by using it in one project, it is not available for the second.

An example of the first case is the copier decision for Clinko Copiers, in which the company needs just one new copier for the coming year. The standard example for the second case is a situation in which two projects under consideration would both use the same parcel of land. By using the land in one project, the other project is no longer viable because it is missing a necessary component, the land.

Even if we are not considering mutually exclusive projects, all companies—even the largest and most successful—have constraints on their capital and can take on only a limited number of projects. The NPV model is an economically sound model when comparing different projects across a wide variety of products, services, and activities under capital constraint. Projects are ranked from most desirable to least desirable, based solely on their respective NPVs. The greater a project's NPV, the greater the profit for taking the project. Because more money is better, we choose the largest "bag of money."

Two projects are considered independent if the acceptance of one has no bearing on the acceptance or rejection of the other.

One important aspect of the NPV model is that it is consistent with the concepts of the time value of money. Recall from Chapters 3 and 4 that we can only add or subtract money streams if they are at the same point in time. By discounting all future cash flow to the present, adding up all inflow, and subtracting all outflow, we are determining the current value of the project. That is what we did in Chapter 4 when we used discounted cash flow analysis to find the present value of an annuity. In Example 9.2, we again put former tools to work as we look at a capital constraint problem and simplify the cash inflow for each project as an annuity stream. We will adapt Equation 4.4 for the present value of an annuity stream:

$$PV = PMT \times \frac{1 - [1/(1 + r)^n]}{r}$$

EXAMPLE 9.2 NPV model: which project do you accept?

Problem Pop's Popcorn has three project choices for the coming year, but only $9,000 in its budget for new projects.

Project 1 is a new corn seed separator that identifies "grannies" (seeds that do not pop when making popcorn in a microwave) and will separate them from good popcorn seeds prior to packaging. The ability to advertise "no grannies" in the popping process is worth $3,000 per year in additional net sales and should be good for five years. Project 1 is an average-risk project, so the company has assigned a 10% discount rate to it.

Project 2 is a new product: kettle corn. To make microwave kettle corn packages, the company needs a new processing machine. Adding kettle corn to the lineup will increase net sales by $3,500 over the next four years. Project 2 is a high-risk project, so the company has assigned a 15% discount rate to it.

Project 3 is a more efficient packaging machine. This new packaging machine requires less maintenance and runs on less electricity than the current machine. The projected annual cost savings is $2,000 over the next eight years. Project 3 is a low-risk project, so the company has assigned an 8.5% discount rate to it.

All three machines cost $9,000 and will exhaust all the capital budgeting dollars for the year. Which machine do you buy?

Solution Find the NPV of each machine and pick the highest positive NPV.

Granny detector machine:

$$NPV_1 = -\$9{,}000 + \$3{,}000 \times \frac{1 - [1/(1 + 0.10)^5]}{0.10}$$
$$= -\$9{,}000 + \$3{,}000 \times 3.7908 = -\$9{,}000 + \$11{,}372.36$$
$$= \$2{,}372.36$$

Kettle corn machine:

$$NPV_2 = -\$9{,}000 + \$3{,}500 \times \frac{1 - [1/(1 + 0.15)^4]}{0.15}$$
$$= -\$9{,}000 + \$3{,}500 \times 2.8550 = -\$9{,}000 + \$9{,}992$$
$$= \$992$$

Packaging machine:

$$NPV_3 = -\$9{,}000 + \$2{,}000 \times \frac{1 - [1/(1 + 0.085)^8]}{0.085}$$

$$= -\$9{,}000 + \$2{,}000 \times 5.6392 = -\$9{,}000 + \$11{,}278.37$$
$$= \$2{,}278.37$$

The choice is the highest NPV. In this case, it is the granny detector machine for this year's capital budget expenditure with its NPV of $2,372.

Later in the chapter, we demonstrate how you can find these same solutions with a calculator that has the financial function NPV. We also show the spreadsheet solution, but it requires one additional step.

Unequal Lives of Projects

Although on the surface it seems as if we have found a model that is consistent with our time value of money concepts and includes all the cash flow of the projects in the analysis, another problem may arise with mutually exclusive projects. It is possible that projects cover different periods of time—a situation we call "unequal lives"—and we may need to correct for this disparity. Let's assume that our popcorn company must purchase a new packaging machine. We looked at the first choice in Example 9.2. What if there is the possibility of a second machine that is less expensive, but has a shorter life span?

Let's look at this situation in more detail. We'll assume that the second machine is a low-tech packaging machine with a price tag of $5,250 and will save costs over the coming three years at $2,700 first year, $2,500 the second year, and $2,300 the last year. At the end of three years, however, we will need to replace this machine. Using the same 8.5% discount rate that we used in Example 9.2, we see in Figure 9.2 that the NPV of the low-tech machine is $1,162.81. If we look only at the NPV, we will pick the high-tech, eight-year machine. By doing so, however, we will lose the potential for a positive cash flow from purchasing another low-tech machine during the extra five years after the first one expires.

When using the NPV approach, there are two ways to correct for mutually exclusive projects with unequal lives. One is to find a "common life" by extending the projects to the least common multiple of their lives. We then calculate the NPV for the same time periods by repeating the cash flows (repeating the projects). For the two packaging machine choices, we derive the least common life by multiplying the eight-year packaging machine life and the three-year packaging machine life for a twenty-four-year common life. The end of twenty-four years is the first point in time when the company needs to replace both machines at the same time. We would then proceed by repeating the high-tech cash flows three times and the low-tech cash flows eight times, therefore ending at twenty-four years with equal lives. As you probably suspect, extending the cash flows to twenty-four years on a packaging machine is unreasonable and will present some significant issues concerning the accuracy of the future cash flows, technology changes, interest rate changes, and other factors.

A second way to deal with unequal lives is to find the **equivalent annual annuity (EAA)** for the project's NPV over its life. To do so, we

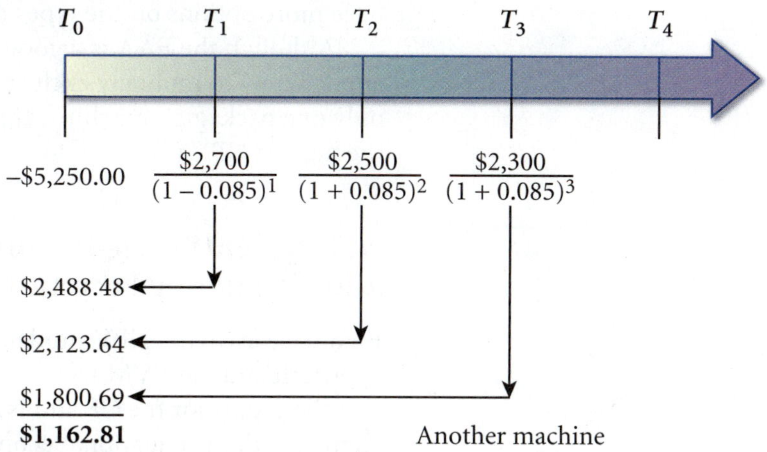

FIGURE 9.2 Net present value of a low-tech packaging machine.

take the project's NPV and, using the appropriate discount rate for the project and life of the project, we find the annuity stream that equates to the NPV. The EAA is our payment solution in the time value of money equation from Chapter 4 (Eq. 4.8), in which we find the payment stream that equates to a present value. We adapt it here by substituting the project's NPV for the present value (PV) in the annuity equation. We then divide the NPV by the present value interest factor of an annuity (PVIFA) to find the EAA. Recall that the PVIFA is the present value interest factor of an annuity with discount rate (r) and life of the project (n):

$$PVIFA = \frac{1 - [1/(1 + r)^n]}{r}$$

So,

$$EAA = \frac{NPV}{PVIFA} \qquad \textbf{9.2}$$

For these two projects, we can find the EAA with our standard calculator TVM keys as follows.

The EAA for the low-tech packaging machine:

NPV = \$1,162.81, discount rate 8.5%, and life three years

Input	3	8.5	−1,162.81	?	0
Key	N	I/Y	PV	PMT	FV
CPT				**445.29**	

The EAA for the high-tech packaging machine:

NPV = \$2,278.33, discount rate 8.5%, and life eight years

Input	8	8.5	−2,278.33	?	0
Key	N	I/Y	PV	PMT	FV
CPT				**404.02**	

The project with the higher EAA is the best choice. So, now that we have corrected for unequal lives, our decision is the reverse of the earlier one: we decide to buy the low-tech machine, not the high-tech machine with the higher NPV. We will still face another decision in three years on replacing the expiring low-tech machine with another packaging machine, but when we reach that date, we may have more options on the types of machines available.

Although the EAA is a good way to correct for unequal lives, you should apply it only to mutually exclusive projects. In this example, the company can use only one packaging machine. If projects are independent, choose the projects with the highest NPVs.

Net Present Value Example: Equation and Calculator Function

Before we leave the NPV model, let's work an example using both the equation approach and the TVM keys. We do so for two reasons. First, it will make clear that the inputs for the CF and NPV functions on the calculator are directly aligned with the equation. Second, it will reinforce the point that the NPV is the best model for capital budgeting decisions.

A ceramic manufacturing company is thinking about expanding its product line to coffee mugs with athletic team logos. The initial cost is the licensing to print the team logos on the mugs for $750,000. The license is good for only five years. At that time, the company will reassess its success in the logo coffee mug business before purchasing a new license. The anticipated annual cash flows for the new line are as follows:

Year 1: $125,000
Year 2: $175,000
Year 3: $200,000
Year 4: $225,000
Year 5: $250,000

The company will discount these future cash flows at 12%, the required rate of return on this project.

The equation setup for the project is

$$NPV = -\$750{,}000 + \frac{\$125{,}000}{(1+0.12)^1} + \frac{\$175{,}000}{(1+0.12)^2} + \frac{\$200{,}000}{(1+0.12)^3} + \frac{\$225{,}000}{(1+0.12)^4} + \frac{\$250{,}000}{(1+0.12)^5}$$

If we calculate the present values of the individual future cash flows, we have

$$\begin{aligned} NPV &= -\$750{,}000 + \$111{,}607 + \$139{,}509 + \$142{,}356 + \$142{,}992 \\ &\quad + \$141{,}857 \\ &= -\$71{,}679 \end{aligned}$$

Now, let's turn to a calculator solution. With the CF function, the first input is for CF0, the cash flow at time 0 (the beginning of the project). That is the cost of the licensing ($750,000) and is a negative cash flow. The next inputs are for C01 through C05—the cash flows at the end of each year. The final input is the discount rate of 12% for the variable *I*, which appears when you access the NPV function. So,

CF

CF0 = −750,000
C01 = 125,000 (F01 = 1)
C02 = 175,000 (F02 = 1)
C03 = 200,000 (F03 = 1)
C04 = 225,000 (F04 = 1)
C05 = 250,000 (F05 = 1)

NPV

I = 12.0

↓ (NPV appears)

CPT = −$71,679

This computed negative NPV of $71,679 says that the company should not purchase the license to sell team logo coffee mugs. As you can see, the values in the equation correspond directly to the CF and NPV functions on a calculator. As the time horizon and number of cash flows increase, you will find it much more efficient to find NPVs with a calculator.

9.4 Internal Rate of Return

The most popular alternative to the NPV for capital budgeting decisions is the **internal rate of return (IRR)**. This is the discount rate that produces a zero NPV, or the specific discount rate at which the present value of the cost (the investment or cash outflows) equals the present value of the future benefits (cash inflows).

The IRR rule prescribes that we should accept those investments in which the internal rate of return exceeds the required rate of return. If the IRR is less than the required rate of return, we should reject the project. The required rate of return on a project is the appropriate cost of capital for the project, a topic we visit in Chapter 11. For now, we provide the required rate of return for the IRR decision. Notice that the IRR criterion is a rate rather than a dollar amount as in the NPV. That may account somewhat for its popularity, because we are often prone to speak of returns in terms of percentages rather than dollars, such as, "I made 20% on my $100 investment" rather than "I made $20."

If we look at the NPV model and set the NPV equal to zero, we can find a discount rate (the IRR) specific to these sets of cash flows that makes the NPV zero:

$$\$0 = CF_0 + \frac{CF_1}{(1+r)^1} + \frac{CF_2}{(1+r)^2} + \frac{CF_3}{(1+r)^3} + \cdots + \frac{CF_n}{(1+r)^n} \qquad \textbf{9.3}$$

Let's look back at our two copiers, A and B, to see if we can find their respective IRRs. Finding the discount rate for each set of cash flows may be tedious because it is an iterative process:

$$\text{Copier A: } \$0 = -\$5{,}000 + \frac{\$2{,}500}{(1+r)^1} + \frac{\$2{,}500}{(1+r)^2} + \frac{\$2{,}500}{(1+r)^3} + \frac{\$2{,}500}{(1+r)^4} + \frac{\$2{,}500}{(1+r)^5}$$

$$\text{Copier B: } \$0 = -\$5{,}000 + \frac{\$1{,}500}{(1+r)^1} + \frac{\$2{,}500}{(1+r)^2} + \frac{\$3{,}500}{(1+r)^3} + \frac{\$4{,}500}{(1+r)^4} + \frac{\$5{,}500}{(1+r)^5}$$

We must now solve each equation in terms of r, the specific discount rate at which the NPV is zero. We can use an iterative process to find the actual IRR of the project. We substitute different interest rates in the equation until we find one that works. We would continue bouncing around the discount rate until we finally found 41.04% for Copier A and 47.45% for Copier B to make the NPV equal zero.

Once you find the IRR, it is then a simple case of applying the decision criterion for accepting or rejecting a project. As noted, the decision criterion is to accept a project if the IRR exceeds the desired or required rate of return and to reject it if the IRR is less than the desired or required rate of return. Because of this decision rule, we often call the required rate of return the **hurdle rate**. If the IRR can clear the hurdle rate, the project is a go. If the IRR cannot clear the hurdle rate, the company rejects the project:

$$\text{accept if IRR} > \text{hurdle rate; reject if IRR} < \text{hurdle rate}$$

You should always set the hurdle rate so that it reflects the proper risk level for the project. Many companies routinely post such rates, which a project must clear before funding can go forward. If we have to choose between two projects with similar risk and similar hurdle rates, we would select the one that has a higher IRR. In this case, we would choose Copier B over Copier A. You can think of it as the investment return on the project, and here the higher IRR is the better choice.

If this process is so cumbersome, though, why is IRR so popular? With the advent of calculators and spreadsheets, the cumbersome calculation (our iterative process with Copiers A and B) became a thing of the past. Calculators with NPV and IRR functions can help us find both NPV and IRR solutions quickly and accurately. Spreadsheets also have these functions. Example 9.3 calculates NPVs and IRRs for the three popcorn machines in Example 9.2 using a calculator.

EXAMPLE 9.3 Calculating IRRs with a standard financial calculator

Problem Find the IRR of each popcorn machine from Example 9.2 and verify the NPV of each, using a standard financial calculator with IRR and NPV keys.

Solution Using a Texas Instrument BA II Plus calculator, we see the following keys above the TVM keys:

2ND CF NPV IRR →

The CF key is the input for the project's cash flow. If you press the CF key, the display shows CF0 and asks for the initial cash flow at time 0. For the granny selection machine, we enter −9000 for the initial cash outlay. (You press 9000 and then the +/− key to make the cash flow −9000, then press the Enter key and see the display with $CF_0 = -9000$.) Now, press the down arrow key above the IRR key, and the display switches to C01. Enter the cash flow for period one (we are using years, so it is year one, but it could be month one, week one, or even day one). For the granny selection machine, enter 3000. Again, make sure you hit "Enter" after 3000 so that the display shows C01 = 3000. Again, press the down arrow key, and the display shows F01. The calculator asks how many periods in a row we will have the same cash inflow. Because this project has five years of $3,000 cash inflow, we could enter 5 at this time, but let's reserve this shortcut for later. For now, we'll follow a pattern of entering each year's cash flow separately. We now enter 1 for F01. We then press the down arrow key again and see C02 displayed. We will continue to cycle through the cash flow entries until we are at C05 and F05. Once we enter all the cash flows, we press IRR and then the CPT key (compute key). The calculator now proceeds through the iterative process until it arrives at the IRR of 19.8577%.

Now, press the NPV key. The display shows I and asks for the discount (interest) rate for this particular set of cash flows. Enter 10.0 for a 10% discount factor for this project. Press the down arrow key again, and NPV will appear in the display. Press CPT, and the NPV of the cash flow will appear. For the granny selection machine, you should see $2,372.36, which is our previously calculated NPV in Example 9.2. To complete the other two machines' IRRs and NPVs, press CF again, then clear all the prior information from the calculator by pressing 2nd and CLR Work. CLR Work is the bottom left key on the key pad and is the second function of the CE/C key. Now, all the values are reset to zero, and you can start the next IRR calculation.

Input and Results of NPV and IRR Calculations on Calculator

Input Keys	Grannies	Kettle	Packaging
CF0	−$9,000	−$9,000	−$9,000
C01	$3,000	$3,500	$2,000
C02	$3,000	$3,500	$2,000
C03	$3,000	$3,500	$2,000
C04	$3,000	$3,500	$2,000
C05	$3,000		$2,000
C06			$2,000
C07			$2,000
C08			$2,000
IRR CPT	**19.86%**	**20.35%**	**14.91%**
I	10.0	15.0	8.5
NPV CPT	**$2,372**	**$992**	**$2,278**

Appropriate Discount Rate or Hurdle Rate

We slipped right by a critical assumption in the initial calculations of NPV and IRR decision criteria. From where do the discount rates or the hurdle rates for the future cash flows of the copiers come, and from where did the discount rates for the various popcorn machine projects of Example 9.2 come? We will explore this question in more detail in later chapters, but for now, the discount rate (I) represents the appropriate risk-adjusted required rate of return for an individual project. The discount rate is a reflection of the riskiness of the future cash flow.

What if we are not sure about the project's appropriate discount rate? We can select a series of discount rates as in Table 9.2 and then plot the corresponding NPVs at these discount rates in a graph. The result is the project's **NPV profile**, as Figure 9.3

TABLE 9.2 NPVs for Copier A with Varying Risk Levels

Risk Level	Discount Rate	NPV Copier A
Zero	0.00%	$7,500.00
Low	5.00%	$5,823.69
Average	10.00%	$4,476.96
Moderately high	15.00%	$3,380.39
High	20.00%	$2,476.53
Extremely high	40.00%	$ 87.91
IRR	41.04%	$ 0.00
Ridiculously high	50.00%	−$ 658.44
Unbelievably high	100.00%	−$2,578.13

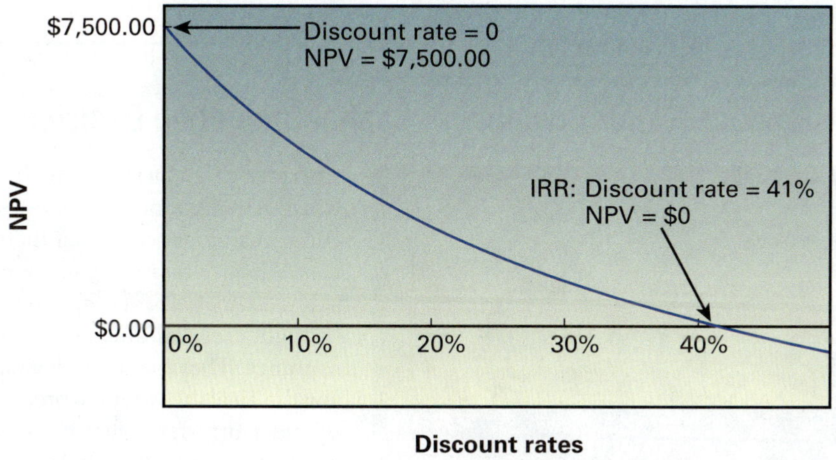

FIGURE 9.3 Net present value profile of Copier A.

shows. The NPV profile is the project's NPV at different interest rates. It shows the range of interest rates where the project is acceptable and the range of interest rates where the project is not acceptable. The *x*-axis is discount rates, and the *y*-axis is the NPV in dollars. The intercept on the *x*-axis is the discount rate where the present value of the cash inflow (benefits of the project) exactly equals the present value of the cash outflow (costs of the project), our IRR. The intercept on the *y*-axis is the NPV at which the discount rate is zero. We can find every point on the NPV profile line simply by substituting a discount rate into the NPV model and solving for the NPV.

For an example of how we can apply an understanding of capital budgeting strategically in a sales and marketing situation, see the nearby "Putting Finance to Work" feature.

Problems with the Internal Rate of Return

Technology has solved the cumbersome calculation part of the IRR, but it still remains somewhat of a mystery why firms continue to use it as a capital budgeting decision model. It has some inherent problems. Looking at Example 9.3 and the IRRs and NPVs of the popcorn machines, we can see the rankings for project choice according to the IRR and the NPV as expressed in Table 9.3.

If we use the IRR as our decision model and pick the highest IRR among projects, we select the kettle corn machine, but if we use NPV and select the highest NPV, we select the granny machine. Why do these two decision models produce different answers? The answer is that the internal rate of return suffers from two potential problems:

1. There is a potential for multiple IRRs.
2. We make an erroneous assumption about the reinvestment rate for IRRs.

We will look at both problems and offer a potential solution for the second.

TABLE 9.3 Project Rankings Based on the Internal Rate of Return and the Net Present Value

	Granny Machine	Kettle Corn Machine	Packaging Machine
IRR	19.86%	20.35%	14.91%
IRR ranking	2	1	3
NPV	$2,372.36	$992.42	$2,278.37
NPV ranking	1	3	2

Putting Finance to Work

Marketing and Sales: Your Product = Your Customer's Capital Budgeting Decision

Students interested in marketing and sales may instinctively think in terms of familiar consumer products, but the highest salaries for sales and marketing executives go to those responsible for selling capital equipment. In this field, annual incomes of $250,000 and more are not uncommon. Capital equipment includes those physical assets that a firm needs to conduct business operations, and they can carry major price tags. Whether you are selling enterprise software, dump trucks, copying machines, or airplanes, it is important to recognize that your product is your customer's capital budgeting decision. The more you understand the parameters of this decision, the more you will be able to provide informed customer service.

Take the airline industry, for instance. The Airbus A380 features a wingspan nearly the length of a football field, seats 525 passengers in a typical three-class configuration or as many as 800 in an all-coach configuration, and carries a list price of $300 million (more or less, depending on exchange rates and the customer's bargaining power). In September 2007, British Airways ordered a dozen of them from Airbus, reportedly at a considerable discount from the list price.

From British Airways' point of view, the decision to purchase the state-of-the-art superjumbo jets was extremely complex. Among the variables that they had to consider included future fuel costs, occupancy rates, and the number of major airports that could now, or would in the future, accommodate the world's largest airplane. The decision also had to consider the economics of the new superjumbo jets versus updated versions of Boeing's time-tested 747, now the most popular airplane in everyday use, and Boeing's new, smaller 787 Dreamliner. British Airways was considering three mutually exclusive projects if it limited its order to a single aircraft type.

Despite the complexity, however, the capital budgeting basics remain the same as those in this chapter. The seller of capital equipment will not be able to complete a sale unless the buyer expects a positive net present value. Airbus's marketing and sales managers had to have a good idea of the price at which British Airways and other potential customers could sell their seats. Airbus's finance managers had to estimate fixed costs such as the flight crew, landing fees, and insurance. They had to understand how the airplane would depreciate under British accounting rules and the tax consequences. Finally, they had to have a good estimate of the customer's cost of capital (which we study in more detail in Chapter 11). Recall from Chapter 1 the discussion of the interaction of various functional areas to project sales numbers. We see that collaborative process at work here.

If marketing and sales managers of capital equipment firms can accurately estimate their customers' revenues, expenses, and tax obligations, they will have a good idea of the effect of the investment decision on their customers' operating cash flows. With a reasonable estimate of the customers' cost of capital, they can compute the present value of those cash flows. Sellers of capital goods may have little or no control over their customers' cash flows or cost of capital, but they do have some control over a key variable in the decision: the price of the equipment. If the manufacturer or vendor can keep the price of the equipment below the present value of the cash flows that the purchaser expects, the NPV will be positive, the IRR will exceed the cost of capital, and a sale is likely to happen. If, however, manufacturers cannot sell at that price and make a reasonable profit, they may very well decide not to manufacture the equipment at all.

As in the case of the Airbus A380, competition alters the problem. British Airways could have decided to purchase more 747s or the new 787 from Boeing. In capital budgeting terms, these alternatives make the decision mutually exclusive. One choice eliminates the other. For Airbus, it meant that its equipment had to result not only in a positive NPV, but the highest NPV. As it turned out, British Airways ended decades of loyalty to the Boeing 747 jumbo and ordered a dozen of Airbus's superjumbos at a reputed cost of nearly $4 billion. That's a sale price on which any salesperson would love to receive a commission.

Multiple Internal Rates of Return

The first potential problem with the IRR as a decision rule is that if cash flow is not standard, there is a possibility of multiple IRRs for a single project. When we talk about standard cash flow for a project, we assume an initial cash outflow at the beginning of the project and positive cash flow in the future. Some projects, however, may have negative cash flow in future years. Take the example of a restaurant that requires a large initial outlay of cash to get operations going, has positive cash flow for a few years, and then expands or updates facilities during a particular future year, thereby causing a negative net cash flow for that year. The following years return to positive cash flow. When we apply the IRR to nonstandard cash flow, we have the potential for more than one IRR solution. For every period that the cash flow has a change of sign (negative to positive or positive to negative), the NPV profile could cross the x-axis, generating an IRR. If the profile crosses the x-axis more than once, we have an IRR for each time it does so. Unfortunately, there is no economic basis for picking one of the IRRs over the others. Example 9.4 illustrates this result and the problem with multiple IRRs.

EXAMPLE 9.4 Multiple IRRs

Problem Pay Me Later Franchise Company offers you a project with the following cash flows: an initial outlay of \$11,000 for licensing and franchising fees at the start of the project, \$7,500 cash inflow for the next four years (at the end of each year), and a balloon payment to Pay Me Later of \$20,000 at the end of year five. What are the project's IRRs? If you were to rank this project against other projects using IRR as the ranking, which IRR would you use?

Solution The IRRs that solve

$$\$0 = -\$11{,}000 + \frac{\$7{,}500}{(1+r)^1} + \frac{\$7{,}500}{(1+r)^2} + \frac{\$7{,}500}{(1+r)^3} + \frac{\$7{,}500}{(1+r)^4} - \frac{\$20{,}000}{(1+r)^5}$$

are 5.62% and 27.78%. See Figure 9.4. Which one is correct? Which one do you use for ranking against other projects? They both are IRRs, but we have no economic basis for selecting one over the other when ranking this project against other projects.

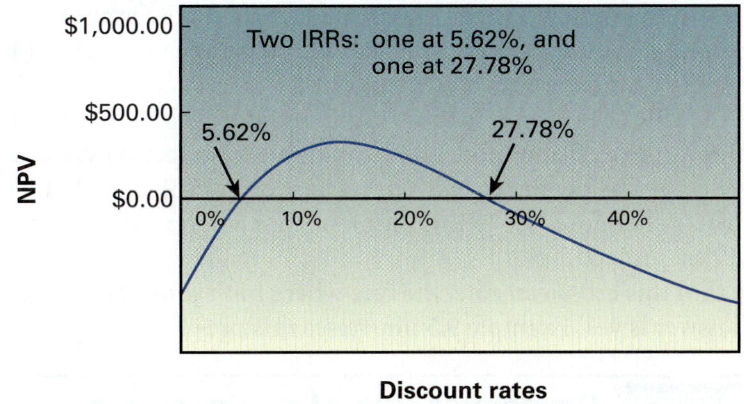

FIGURE 9.4 Pay Me Later Franchise Company multiple internal rates of return.

Now, think again about our decision rule for the IRR. If the IRR is greater than the hurdle rate, accept the project. In this franchise example, if you looked only at the single IRR at the 5.62% plot point on the graph and could borrow at 5%, you should reject the project because it would have a negative NPV. The NPV profile is negative in the range of 0% to 5.62%. If you used only the IRR as your decision criterion without viewing the NPV profile, you would accept the project because the IRR is greater

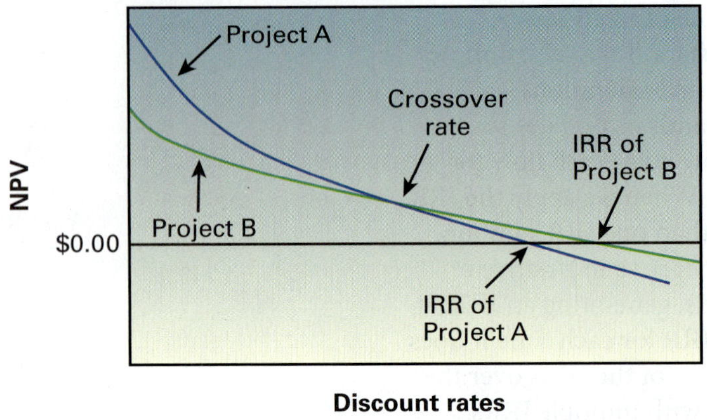

FIGURE 9.5 Mutually exclusive projects and their crossover rates.

than the hurdle rate (5.62% > 5.0%). If you could borrow above 5.62% (but below 27.78%), you would have a positive NPV project, but you would reject with a 5.62% IRR because the IRR is less than the hurdle rate. The IRR decision rule logic breaks down because of the $20,000 future cash outflow. As the borrowing rate increases, the present value of this future payment decreases.

Using technology for the IRR calculation presents another wrinkle: it will display only one of the two IRRs. In the Example 9.4 franchise problem, it displays only 5.62%. You must find the second IRR using an iterative process. So, when you have sign changes in your yearly cash flow, you must plot the NPV profile to interpret the IRR of the project properly.

Reinvestment and Crossover Rates

The second problem with the IRR calculation is its reinvestment rate assumption, which is a little more subtle than the multiple IRR problem. To illustrate, let's again compare two mutually exclusive projects. Projects are mutually exclusive if the selection of one prohibits the selection of the other. The question that we must answer with mutually exclusive projects is, "Which one is better using IRR?"

If we plot the NPV profiles of two mutually exclusive projects on the same graph, we see that the problem is with the IRR's selection criterion. Figure 9.5 shows that Project A has a higher *y*-axis intercept for its NPV profile than Project B. Thus, Project A has a higher NPV than Project B when the discount rate is zero. As long as the profile of Project A is above the profile of Project B, Project A will have a higher NPV value for that particular discount rate. The NPV profile of Project A, however, has a much steeper decline as we increase discount rates. The two projects intersect in terms of the NPV at the **crossover rate**, which is the discount rate at which both projects have the same NPV. Past this crossover point, as we proceed to the right along the *x*-axis, Project B's profile is above Project A's profile. So, for all discount rates greater than the crossover rate, Project B will have a higher NPV.

Finally, the IRR of Project B is to the right of the IRR for Project A. If we were to use the IRR as the decision model, we would select Project B over Project A. For borrowing rates below the crossover rate, however, Project A should be the selected project. Therefore, the IRR value alone may not be a sufficient criterion to select the best project.

Can we find this crossover rate, the rate where both projects have the same NPV? The answer is yes. Example 9.5 illustrates this process.

EXAMPLE 9.5 Crossover rate of two projects

Problem Pop's Popcorn Company wants to determine the crossover rate for the kettle corn machine and a new pollution control device that will cost $7,000 but save the company $2,750 each year over the next four years. Recall that the company projects that the kettle corn machine will increase net sales by $3,500 over the next four years and costs $9,000.

Solution The crossover rate is the discount rate at which the two projects have the same NPV. Therefore, we can set the discounted cash flow of the two projects

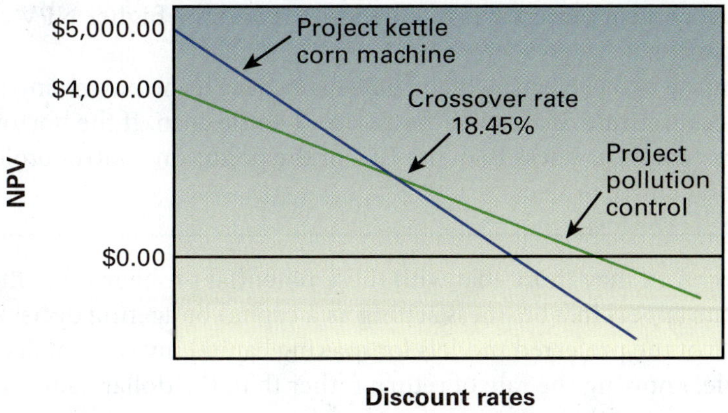

FIGURE 9.6 Crossover rate for two projects.

equal to each other and then solve for the discount rate. We actually subtract the cash flow of the pollution control device from the kettle corn machine to get the difference in cash flow for each period.

Kettle corn machine:

$$\$0 = -\$9{,}000 + \frac{\$3{,}500}{(1+r)^1} + \frac{\$3{,}500}{(1+r)^2} + \frac{\$3{,}500}{(1+r)^3} + \frac{\$3{,}500}{(1+r)^4}$$

$$IRR = 20.35\%$$

Pollution control device:

$$\$0 = -\$7{,}000 + \frac{\$2{,}750}{(1+r)^1} + \frac{\$2{,}750}{(1+r)^2} + \frac{\$2{,}750}{(1+r)^3} + \frac{\$2{,}750}{(1+r)^4}$$

$$IRR = 20.89\%$$

So,

$$-\$9{,}000 + \frac{\$3{,}500}{(1+r)^1} + \frac{\$3{,}500}{(1+r)^2} + \frac{\$3{,}500}{(1+r)^3} + \frac{\$3{,}500}{(1+r)^4}$$

$$= -\$7{,}000 + \frac{\$2{,}750}{(1+r)^1} + \frac{\$2{,}750}{(1+r)^2} + \frac{\$2{,}750}{(1+r)^3} + \frac{\$2{,}750}{(1+r)^4}$$

We can now "rearrange" the values so that all the cash flow is on one side of the equation and the difference in cash flow for each period is set to equal zero on the other side of the equation:

$$\$0 = -\$2{,}000 + \frac{\$750}{(1+r)^1} + \frac{\$750}{(1+r)^2} + \frac{\$750}{(1+r)^3} + \frac{\$750}{(1+r)^4}$$

By examining this net cash flow, we are looking at an IRR calculation for the difference between the two cash flows of the two projects. Now, using a calculator, we can put the difference between the cash flows in the cash flow keys and solve for the IRR of these cash flows. We find the interest rate at which the difference between the NPV of the two projects is zero and at which both projects have the same NPV:

CF CF0 = −$2,000, C01 = $750, C02 = $750, C03 = $750, C04 = $750

IRR **CPT = 18.45%**

Figure 9.6 shows the plotted NPV profile of the mutually exclusive projects. The kettle corn project has the higher NPV at the lower discount rates, and the pollution control project has the higher IRR and the higher NPV above the crossover rate.

Given these two projects, which choice is better? If the borrowing rate is less than the crossover rate of 18.45%, the choice is kettle corn. If the borrowing rate is greater than 18.45% and less than the IRR of the pollution control project, select the pollution control project.

Although you may think that with these potential problems that the IRR would lose its appeal in a business setting as a capital budgeting decision model, it remains one of the preferred models for making capital investment decisions. For many people, knowing the rate of return rather than the dollar value via the NPV seems more comfortable.

Is there a way to modify the IRR to eliminate some of its inherent problems in order to be more consistent with the NPV approach? The answer is a qualified yes. We can adjust the IRR to add a realistic reinvestment rate for the cash flows.

Modified Internal Rate of Return

An underlying assumption of the IRR model is that we can reinvest all cash inflow at the individual project's internal rate of return over the project's remaining life. Therefore, some NPV profiles have steeper slopes than others and cause profiles to cross. For the kettle corn project with a 20.35% IRR, the company could reinvest the $3,500 at the end of each year at 20.35% until the end of the project. For the pollution control project, it could reinvest at 20.85%. What is probably more appropriate for cash inflow is that we can reinvest it at a different rate, at the cost of capital for the company. That is the underlying assumption of the **modified internal rate of return (MIRR)**: the firm reinvests all cash flows at its cost of capital. What exactly does that mean in terms of how we view the cash flow within the IRR decision model? Let's look at a simple example.

Suppose you have an investment that costs $1,500,000 at the beginning of the project and generates $700,000 in year one, $600,000 in year two, $500,000 in year three, $400,000 in year four, and $300,000 in the last year, year five. The project's IRR is 23.57%. The IRR model assumes that you can invest the cash flow at the end of the first year at 23.57% for the remaining years of the project, and we apply this same assumption for each subsequent year. However, investing the project's cash inflow at the IRR may not be feasible. For instance, if a company has a project with a 40% IRR, that 40% is a function of an opportunity unique to the company. After this unique project generates positive cash flows, there may not be another opportunity that will allow the company to invest at the same 40% rate. Therefore, the company will reinvest the positive cash flow at a lower, more reasonable rate (and compute the project's MIRR).

We can verify this reinvestment assumption by first determining the IRR via a calculator and then, by steps, for each year-end cash flow to the end of the project to find the future value of the cash flow:

CF0 = −1,500,000
C01 = 700,000 (and F01 = 1)
C02 = 600,000 (and F02 = 1)
C03 = 500,000 (and F03 = 1)
C04 = 400,000 (and F04 = 1)
C05 = 300,000 (and F05 = 1)
IRR **CPT** = 23.5734%

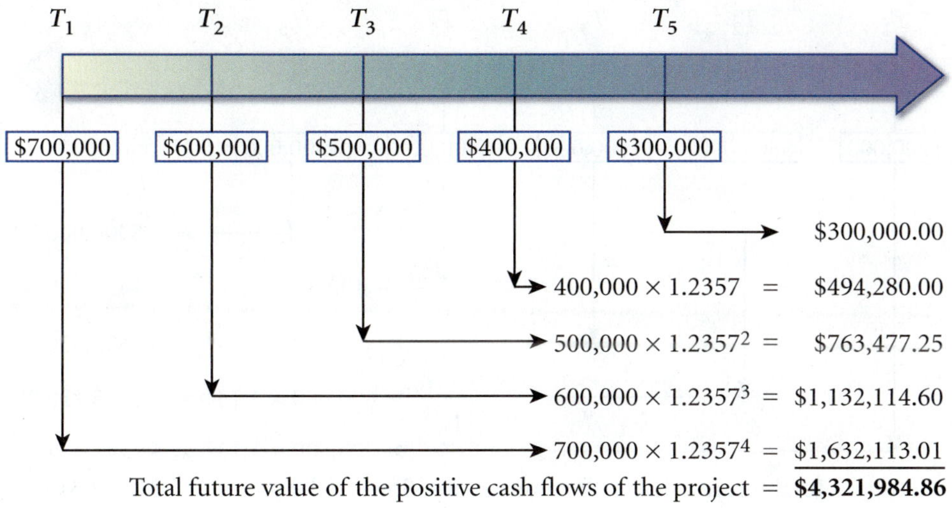

FIGURE 9.7 Future value of cash inflows reinvested at the internal rate of return.

We can also use a time line to visualize the cash flows. Figure 9.7 shows the cash inflows and their growing future value at the end of the project. Notice that the future positive cash flow, if reinvested at the IRR, grows to $4,321,948.86 at the end of the project.

We now take the formula for finding the implied interest rate of a future value, given a present value and the five years for the project for *n*, and verify the original IRR and the reinvestment rate assumption:

$$IRR = \left(\frac{FV}{PV}\right)^{1/n} - 1 = \left(\frac{\$4{,}321{,}984.86}{\$1{,}500{,}000.00}\right)^{1/5} - 1 = 2.8831^{0.2} - 1$$
$$= 1.2357 - 1 = 0.2357 = 23.57\%$$

Reinvesting at this high rate seems inappropriate. Instead, we could reinvest the funds at a lower, more appropriate rate and then see what type of MIRR the new reinvestment rate produces. We will correct for the reinvestment rate that the IRR calculation implies. If we look at the terminal value of the cash inflows (their future values based on the company's average earnings rate), we can then find an MIRR that gives the answer in terms of returns generally consistent with the NPV's dollar amounts.

So, we will now use the same cash flows for the project, but with a more reasonable reinvestment rate of 13%, and then solve for the MIRR, as Figure 9.8 shows. As before, we take the formula for finding the implied interest rate of *FV*, given *PV* and *n*:

$$MIRR = \left(\frac{FV}{PV}\right)^{1/n} - 1 = \left(\frac{\$3{,}397{,}519.73}{\$1{,}500{,}000.00}\right)^{1/5} - 1 = 2.2650^{0.2} - 1$$
$$= 1.1776 - 1 = 0.1776 = 17.76\%$$

Is the MIRR a better way to accept or reject projects than the IRR? There are two thoughts concerning this question. Although some believe that the MIRR is an improvement to the IRR because the reinvestment rate is more appropriate, others contend that it is not a true IRR for the project and that the MIRR depends on the selected reinvestment rate. The IRR depends only on the cash flows. Some will argue that how a company reinvests cash flows is irrelevant and that it is important only that you know the timing and the amount of the cash flow. A company can use the future cash flow for many different

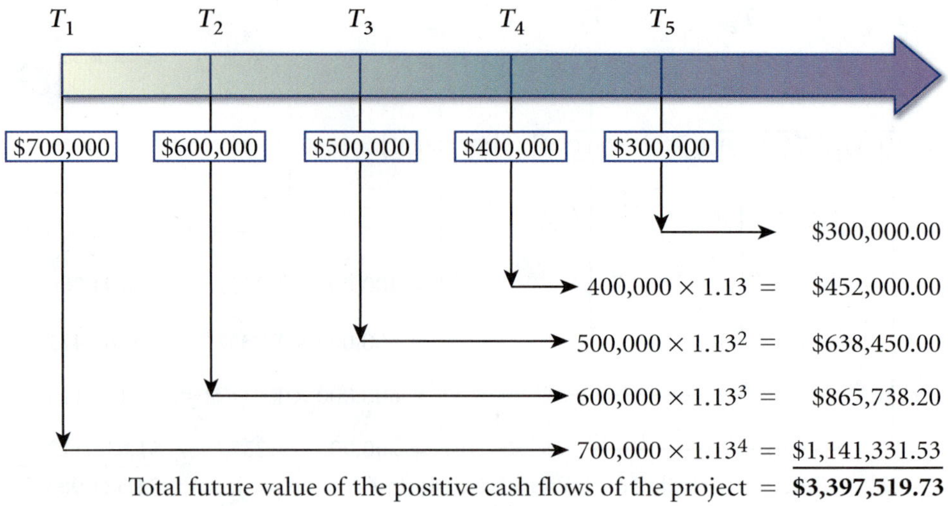

FIGURE 9.8 Future value of cash inflows reinvested at 13%.

reasons, so reinvestment is irrelevant. Given all the debates and the necessity to use an appropriate discount rate, then, why not just calculate the NPV and use the project's NPV as the decision rule for accepting or rejecting? We support using the NPV model.

9.5 Profitability Index

If people have a natural affinity for rate of return rather than current dollars for a project, is there a way to adjust the preferred NPV model and still have the ability to assign the appropriate level of risk for the project (the discount rate or hurdle rate)? The answer again is a qualified yes, and the decision model to achieve this goal is the profitability index.

The **profitability index (PI)** is a modification of the NPV to produce the ratio of the present value of the benefits (future cash inflow) to the present value of the costs (initial investment):

$$\text{profitability index} = \frac{\text{present value of benefits}}{\text{present value of costs}} \qquad \textbf{9.4}$$

The decision criterion is very straightforward: if $PI > 1.0$, accept the project. If $PI < 1.0$, reject the project. Therefore, when the PI is greater than 1, the benefits exceed the costs.

If you already have the project's NPV and it has a standard cash flow setup of all cash outflow at the beginning and cash inflow at a later period, you can quickly calculate the project's PI. If we realize that the NPV is the present value of the benefits minus the present value of the costs, we simply need to add back the costs to the NPV to get the present value of the benefits. Let's once again look at Copiers A and B at the 6% discount rate and find their PIs, knowing that they fit the standard cash flow setup:

$$PI \text{ with standard cash flow} = \frac{NPV + \text{cost}}{\text{cost}}$$

$$PI \text{ Copier A} = \frac{\$5{,}530.91 + \$5{,}000}{\$5{,}000} = 2.11$$

$$PI \text{ Copier B} = \frac{\$9{,}253.09 + \$5{,}000}{\$5{,}000} = 2.85$$

Both are acceptable projects, but how do we interpret the numbers 2.11 and 2.85? Are they returns? They are not, but they are not too far off! We can interpret the 2.11 and 2.85 as the dollar amount of return for every $1.00 invested in the project in terms of current dollars. So, Copier A returns $2.11 current dollars for every invested dollar and Copier B returns $2.85 current dollars for every invested dollar. If we use a standard return model, we have $2.11/$1.00 − 1 = 1.11 or 111% return on investment for Copier A and $2.85/$1.00 − 1 = 1.85 or 185% return on investment for Copier B. In much the same way as our NPV decision model, if we had to choose between these two copiers using the PI, we would choose the highest index number, 2.85, and therefore Copier B. What is probably more important than trying to decide which copier to pick based on its PI, however, is to make sure we have the correct discount rate (level of risk) for each project. Let's take one more look at these two copiers with different discount rates based on the two projects' cash flow risks.

EXAMPLE 9.6 PI for a high-risk copier and a low-risk copier

Problem You have decided that the technology in Copier B is much riskier than that in Copier A and that the downtime and maintenance of Copier B could be much higher than for Copier A. Therefore, you have decided to increase the discount rate on Copier B to 16%. Copier A has an assigned discount rate of 10%. What are the PIs with this newly assigned risk level? Which copier is the wiser choice now?

Solution Find Copier B's NPV, add back the costs to find the PV of the benefits, and divide by the PV of the costs.

For Copier B:

$$NPV = -\$5{,}000 + \frac{\$1{,}500}{(1 + 0.16)^1} + \frac{\$2{,}500}{(1 + 0.16)^2} + \frac{\$3{,}500}{(1 + 0.16)^3} + \frac{\$4{,}500}{(1 + 0.16)^4} + \frac{\$5{,}500}{(1 + 0.16)^5} = \$5{,}497.24$$

$$PI \text{ copier B} = \frac{\$5{,}000 + \$5{,}497.24}{\$5{,}000} = \mathbf{2.10}$$

For Copier A (no change from earlier calculations):

$$NPV = -\$5{,}000 + \frac{\$2{,}500}{(1 + 0.06)^1} + \frac{\$2{,}500}{(1 + 0.06)^2} + \frac{\$2{,}500}{(1 + 0.06)^3} + \frac{\$2{,}500}{(1 + 0.06)^4} + \frac{\$2{,}500}{(1 + 0.06)^5} = \$5{,}530.91$$

$$PI \text{ copier A} = \frac{\$5{,}000 + \$5{,}530.91}{\$5{,}000} = \mathbf{2.11}$$

We now have almost identical PIs for the two copiers, but Copier A has a slightly higher NPV ($5,530.91 versus $5,497.24) and is therefore the best choice. The PIs will be consistent with NPV, so it's probably best just to compute the NPV for the copiers and all other business decisions.

9.6 Overview of Six Decision Models

In this chapter, we considered six different models for making capital investment decisions: (1) payback period, (2) discounted payback period, (3) net present value (NPV), (4) internal rate of return (IRR), (5) modified internal rate of return (MIRR), and (6) profitability index (PI). Let's look at the strengths and weaknesses of each model:

1. Payback period is simple and fast, but economically unsound. It ignores all cash flow after the cutoff date and ignores the time value of money.
2. Discounted payback period incorporates the time value of money, but still ignores cash flow after the cutoff date.
3. Net present value (NPV) is economically sound and properly ranks projects across various sizes, time horizons, and levels of risk, without exception, for all independent projects.
4. Internal rate of return (IRR) provides a single measure (return), but has the potential for errors in ranking projects. It can also lead to an incorrect selection when there are two mutually exclusive projects or incorrect acceptance or rejection of a project with more than a single IRR.
5. Modified internal rate of return (MIRR), in general, corrects for most of—but not all—the problems of IRR and gives the solution in terms of a return. However, the reinvestment rate may or may not be appropriate for the future cash flows.
6. Profitability index (PI) incorporates risk and return, but the benefits-to-cost ratio is actually just another way of expressing the NPV.

Table 9.4 compares these strengths and weaknesses.

Having gone through all six capital budgeting decision models, you may wonder whether corporations actually use them. Table 9.5 displays a sampling of companies and their response to the question, "How frequently does your firm use the following techniques when deciding which projects or acquisitions to pursue?" The first column of the table shows the decision models under consideration. (The survey did not ask about the MIRR or discounted payback period.) Respondents answered on a scale of 0 (never) to 4 (always). The percent column shows the number of companies that responded with either a 3 or 4. The ranking is based on the average score. As you can see, NPV and IRR are essentially tied in usage, and the payback period model—the easiest method to apply but, as we have learned, a flawed one—came in third.

Capital Budgeting Using a Spreadsheet

We can easily apply capital budgeting on a spreadsheet, but we require an extra step when using the NPV decision model. Here is an example using a spreadsheet to solve for a project's IRR, MIRR, and NPV.

TABLE 9.4 Summary of Six Decision Models

	Models					
Issues	Payback Period	Discounted Payback Period	Net Present Value	Internal Rate of Return	Modified Internal Rate of Return	Profitability Index
Decision criterion	Recover investment before a set period	Recover investment before a set period	NPV is positive	IRR rate is greater than hurdle rate	MIRR rate is greater than hurdle rate	PI is greater than 1
Complexity of application	Easiest to apply	Easy to apply	Time-consuming without a calculator or spreadsheet	Time-consuming without a calculator or spreadsheet	Time-consuming without a calculator or spreadsheet	Time-consuming without a calculator or spreadsheet
Time value of money	Ignored	Consistent with time value of money	Consistent with time value of money	Consistent with time value of money	Consistent with time value of money	Consistent with time value of money
Risk	Ignores cash flow after cutoff date	Ignores cash flow after cutoff date	Applies appropriate level of risk to cash flow	Risk level applied by selected hurdle rate	Risk level applied by selected hurdle rate	Applies appropriate level of risk to cash flow
Economic basis and evaluation	Too simple	Too simple	Economically sound application in risk and return. **Best decision model**	Potential for multiple IRRs and picking wrong project	Potential for multiple IRRs	Economically sound application in risk and return

TABLE 9.5 Corporate Use of Different Decision Models: What Capital Budgeting Decision Models Do You Use?

Capital Budget Model	Overall Use	Small Firms Ranking	Large Firms Ranking
Payback	56.74%	3	3
Net present value	74.93%	2	1
Internal rate of return	75.61%	1	2
Profitability index	11.87%	4	4

Source: Based on John R. Graham and Campbell R. Harvey, "The Theory and Practice of Corporate Finance: Evidence from the Field," *Journal of Financial Economics* 60, May–June 2001, pp. 187–244.

Trout Pro Shops is considering adding a new line of fishing gear to its current product set. The initial investment is $2,000,000 for the manufacturing equipment. The additional cash flow to the company is estimated at $40,000 the first year, $130,000 the second year, $320,000 the third year, and then $500,000 for each of the next six years. The cost of capital for Trout Pro Shops is 9%. What are the IRR, MIRR, and NPV of this new product line of fishing gear? Titles for the cash flow, discount rate, and reinvestment rate are in Column A of the spreadsheet. Cash flow, discount rate, and reinvestment rate are in Column B. The solution for the IRR is in cell C1. The solution for the MIRR is in Cell D1. The solution for the NPV is in Cell E2.

The data in the spreadsheet are as follows:

C1		*fx* =IRR(B1:B10)			
Use the different functions to solve for IRR, MIRR, and NPV.					
	A	B	C	D	E
1	Initial investment	(2,000,000)	10.20%		
2	Cash flow year 1	40,000			
3	Cash flow year 2	130,000			
4	Cash flow year 3	320,000			
5	Cash flow year 4	500,000			
6	Cash flow year 5	500,000			
7	Cash flow year 6	500,000			
8	Cash flow year 7	500,000			
9	Cash flow year 8	500,000			
10	Cash flow year 9	500,000			
11	Discount rate	0.09			
12	Reinvestment rate	0.09			

Now, calculate the project's IRR. In Cell C1, enter the IRR function from the list of functions. It will request the range of cash flows. Enter B1.B10 for the range, and the IRR displays in Cell C1. The function returns the value of 10.20% for the IRR.

Next, calculate the project's MIRR. In Cell D1, enter the MIRR function from the list of functions (*fx* = *MIRR*). The function will request the range values (B1.B10), the finance rate (discount rate, B11), and the reinvestment rate (B12). The answer will display the MIRR of 9.74% for this project:

D1		*fx* =MIRR(B1:B10,B11,B12)			
	A	B	C	D	E
1	Initial investment	(2,000,000)	10.20%	9.74%	

In this example, we have set both the cost of capital and the reinvestment rate at 9%, but they could be different values. The spreadsheet discounts all future cash flow back to the present at the cost of capital and then grows this present value of the future cash flow at the reinvestment rate. It is one way to incorporate the cash flow risks inside the MIRR model. Therefore, we can assign different projects different borrowing costs.

Finally, calculate the project's NPV. In Cell E1, enter the NPV function from the list of functions (*fx* = *NPV*). The function will request the discount rate (B11). It will request the annual cash flow values, but in this spreadsheet application, the values are only the future cash flow from the end of period one to the end of period nine (B2.B10). The Excel NPV function assumes that the first cash flow is one period away. So, if you list B1 (the initial investment at time 0), the function assigns it to the *end* of period one, not the *start*. It is a conceptual error in the NPV function by Excel. The project's initial investment of $2,000,000 is not in the set of cash flows to discount back to the present. The value return is the present value of all cash flows from the end of period one to the end of the project (B2 through B10). To get the NPV, you must then subtract the initial cash outflow ($2,000,000 in Cell B1) from the result in Cell E1, which is not a complicated adjustment. In Cell E2, enter = E1 + B1 to find the project's NPV. We add B1 to E1 because we entered the initial cost in Cell B1 as negative dollars.

E1		fx =NPV(0.09,B2:B10)			
	A	B	C	D	E
1	Initial investment	(2,000,000)	10.20%	9.74%	2,125,190.47

E2		fx =E1+B1			
	A	B	C	D	E
1	Initial investment	(2,000,000)	10.20%	9.74%	2,125,190.47
2	Cash flow year 1	40,000			125,190.47

Calculating the IRR, NPV, or MIRR is easy and efficient using a spreadsheet once you know the relevant cash flow, the timing of the cash flow, and the reinvestment rate.

To review this chapter, see the Summary Card at the end of the text.

Key Terms

capital budgeting, p. 258
crossover rate, p. 276
discounted payback period, p. 262
equivalent annual annuity (EAA), p. 267
hurdle rate, p. 270
internal rate of return (IRR), p. 270
modified internal rate of return (MIRR), p. 278
mutually exclusive projects, p. 265
net present value (NPV), p. 263
NPV profile of a project, p. 292
payback period, p. 260
profitability index (PI), p. 280

Questions

1. How does a business determine whether a project (new product or service) is worthwhile?
2. What is the difference between a short-term decision and a long-term decision?
3. What question is the payback period model answering? What are the two major drawbacks of the payback period model? In what situations do businesses still use it?
4. If you switch to the discounted payback period from the payback period, what assumption are you making about the timing of the cash flow?
5. What drawback of the discounted payback period does the net present value overcome?
6. Why is it straightforward to compare one project's NPV with that of another project's NPV? Why does ranking projects based on the greatest to least NPV make sound financial sense?

7. Why do different projects have different discount rates in the NPV model?

8. When does the internal rate of return model give an inappropriate decision when comparing two mutually exclusive projects?

9. If you switch from the internal rate of return to the modified internal rate of return model, what assumption changes with respect to the cash flow of the project?

10. The profitability index produces a ratio between the project's present value of the benefits and the present value of the costs. Is there a time when the PI and the NPV do not agree on the ranking of projects? If so, under what circumstances would they have different project rankings?

Prepping for Exams

1. __________ is at the heart of corporate finance because it is concerned with making the best choices about project selection.

a. Capital budgeting
b. Capital structure
c. Payback period
d. Short-term budgeting

2. Consider the following four-year project. The initial after-tax outlay or after-tax cost is $1,000,000. The future after-tax cash inflows for years one, two, three, and four are $400,000, $300,000, $200,000, and $200,000, respectively. What is the payback period without discounting cash flows?

a. 2.5 years
b. 3.0 years
c. 3.5 years
d. 4.0 years

3. Which of the statements below is *false*?

a. To account for the time value of money with the payback period model, you need to restate the future cash flow in current dollars.
b. The discounted payback period method is the time it takes to recover the initial investment in future dollars.
c. When we discount a future cash flow with our standard time value of money concepts, we inherently assume that the company received the entire cash flow at the end of the year.
d. The discounted payback period method does not correct for the cash flow after the recovery of the initial outflow.

4. Projects are mutually exclusive if picking one project eliminates the ability to pick the other project. This mutually exclusive situation can arise for different reasons. Which of the following is *not* one of these reasons?

a. One project will always have a negative NPV.
b. There is a scarce resource that both projects would need.
c. There is need for only one project, and both projects can fulfill that current need.
d. By using funds for one project, there are not enough funds available for the other project.

5. Dweller Inc. is considering a four-year project that has an initial after-tax outlay or after-tax cost of $80,000. The future after-tax cash inflows from its project are $40,000, $40,000, $30,000, and $30,000 for years one, two, three, and four, respectively. Dweller uses the NPV method and has a discount rate of 12%. Will Dweller accept the project?

a. Dweller accepts the project because the NPV is greater than $30,000.
b. Dweller rejects the project because the NPV is less than −$4,000.
c. Dweller rejects the project because the NPV is −$3,021.
d. Dweller accepts the project because the NPV is greater than $28,000.

6. Flynn Inc. is considering a four-year project that has an initial after-tax outlay or after-tax cost of $80,000. The future after-tax cash inflows from its project for years one, two, three, and four are $40,000, $40,000, $30,000, and $30,000, respectively. Flynn uses the internal rate of return method to evaluate projects. What is the approximate IRR for this project?

a. The IRR is less than 12%.
b. The IRR is between 12% and 20%.
c. The IRR is about 24.55%.
d. The IRR is about 28.89%.

7. The IRR model suffers from three problems. Which of the following is *not* one of these problems?

a. comparing mutually exclusive projects
b. cumbersome computations not resolvable by the latest technology
c. incorporates the IRR as the reinvestment rate for the future cash flows
d. multiple IRRs

8. Corbett and Sullivan Enterprises (CSE) use the MIRR when evaluating projects. CSE's cost of capital is 9.5%. What is the project's MIRR if the initial costs are $10,200,000 and the project lasts seven years, with each year producing the same after-tax cash inflows of $1,900,000?

a. about 7.95%
b. about 8.01%
c. about 8.24%
d. about 8.88%

9. The __________ is a modification of the NPV to produce the ratio of the present value of the benefits (future cash inflow) to the present value of the costs (initial investment).

a. modified internal rate of return method
b. profitability index
c. payback period method
d. discounted cash flow method

10. The __________ method is economically sound and properly ranks projects across various sizes, time horizons, and levels of risk, without exception, for all independent projects.

a. NPV
b. discounted payback period
c. profitability index
d. modified IRR

These problems are available in MyFinanceLab.

Problems

1. ***Payback period.*** Given the cash flow of four projects, A, B, C, and D, and using the payback period decision model, which projects do you accept and which projects do you reject with a three-year cutoff period for recapturing the initial cash outflow? For payback period calculations, assume that the cash flow is equally distributed over the year.

Cash Flow	A	B	C	D
Cost	$10,000	$25,000	$45,000	$100,000
Cash flow year 1	$ 4,000	$ 2,000	$10,000	$ 40,000
Cash flow year 2	$ 4,000	$ 8,000	$15,000	$ 30,000
Cash flow year 3	$ 4,000	$14,000	$20,000	$ 20,000
Cash flow year 4	$ 4,000	$20,000	$20,000	$ 10,000
Cash flow year 5	$ 4,000	$26,000	$15,000	$ 0
Cash flow year 6	$ 4,000	$32,000	$10,000	$ 0

2. ***Payback period.*** What are the payback periods of Projects E, F, G, and H? Assume all the cash flow is evenly spread throughout the year. If the cutoff period is three years, which projects do you accept?

Cash Flow	E	F	G	H
Cost	$40,000	$250,000	$75,000	$100,000
Cash flow year 1	$10,000	$ 40,000	$20,000	$ 30,000
Cash flow year 2	$10,000	$120,000	$35,000	$ 30,000
Cash flow year 3	$10,000	$200,000	$40,000	$ 30,000
Cash flow year 4	$10,000	$200,000	$40,000	$ 20,000
Cash flow year 5	$10,000	$200,000	$35,000	$ 10,000
Cash flow year 6	$10,000	$200,000	$20,000	$ 0

3. ***Discounted payback period.*** Given the following four projects and their cash flow, calculate the discounted payback period with a 5% discount rate, 10% discount rate, and 20% discount rate. What do you notice about the payback period as the discount rate rises? Explain this relationship.

Cash Flow	A	B	C	D
Cost	$10,000	$25,000	$45,000	$100,000
Cash flow year 1	$ 4,000	$ 2,000	$10,000	$ 40,000
Cash flow year 2	$ 4,000	$ 8,000	$15,000	$ 30,000
Cash flow year 3	$ 4,000	$14,000	$20,000	$ 20,000
Cash flow year 4	$ 4,000	$20,000	$20,000	$ 10,000
Cash flow year 5	$ 4,000	$26,000	$15,000	$ 10,000
Cash flow year 6	$ 4,000	$32,000	$10,000	$ 0

4. ***Discounted payback period.*** Becker Inc. uses the discounted payback period for projects less than $25,000 and has a cutoff period of four years for these small-value projects. Two projects, R and S, are under consideration. Their anticipated cash flow is listed in the following table. If Becker uses an 8% discount rate on these projects, are they accepted or rejected? If it uses a 12% discount rate? A 16% discount rate? Why is it necessary to look at only the first four years of the projects' cash flow?

Cash Flow	Project R	Project S
Initial cost	$24,000	$18,000
Cash flow year 1	$ 6,000	$ 9,000
Cash flow year 2	$ 8,000	$ 6,000
Cash flow year 3	$10,000	$ 6,000
Cash flow year 4	$12,000	$ 3,000

5. ***Comparing payback period and discounted payback period.*** Mathew Inc. is debating using the payback period versus the discounted payback period for small-dollar projects. The company's information officer has submitted a new computer project with a $15,000 cost. The cash flow will be $5,000 each year for the next five years. The cutoff period used by the company is three years. The information officer states that it doesn't matter which model the company uses for the decision; the project is clearly acceptable. Demonstrate for the information officer that the selection of the model does matter.

6. ***Comparing payback period and discounted payback period.*** Nielsen Inc. is switching from the payback period to the discounted payback period for small-dollar projects. The cutoff period will remain at three years. Given the following four projects' cash flows and using a 10% discount rate, determine which projects it would have accepted under the payback period and which it will now reject under the discounted payback period.

Cash Flow	Project 1	Project 2	Project 3	Project 4
Initial cost	$10,000	$15,000	$8,000	$18,000
Year 1	$ 4,000	$ 7,000	$3,000	$10,000
Year 2	$ 4,000	$ 5,500	$3,500	$11,000
Year 3	$ 4,000	$ 4,000	$4,000	$ 0

7. ***Net present value.*** Quark Industries has a project with the following projected cash flows:

Initial cost: $240,000
Cash flow year one: $25,000
Cash flow year two: $75,000
Cash flow year three: $150,000
Cash flow year four: $150,000

a. Using a 10% discount rate for this project and the NPV model, determine whether the company should accept or reject this project.
b. Should the company accept or reject it using a 15% discount rate?
c. Should the company accept or reject it using a 20% discount rate?

8. ***Net present value.*** Lepton Industries has a project with the following projected cash flow:

Initial cost: $468,000
Cash flow year one: $135,000
Cash flow year two: $240,000
Cash flow year three: $185,000
Cash flow year four: $135,000

a. Using an 8% discount rate for this project and the NPV model, determine whether the company should accept or reject it.
b. Should the company accept or reject it using a 14% discount rate?
c. Should the company accept or reject it using a 20% discount rate?

9. ***Net present value.*** Quark Industries has four potential projects, all with an initial cost of $2,000,000. The capital budget for the year will allow Quark to accept only one of the four projects. Given the discount rates and the future cash flow of each project, determine which project Quark should accept.

Cash Flow	Project M	Project N	Project O	Project P
Year 1	$500,000	$600,000	$1,000,000	$ 300,000
Year 2	$500,000	$600,000	$ 800,000	$ 500,000
Year 3	$500,000	$600,000	$ 600,000	$ 700,000
Year 4	$500,000	$600,000	$ 400,000	$ 900,000
Year 5	$500,000	$600,000	$ 200,000	$ 1,100,000
Discount rate	6%	9%	15%	22%

10. ***Net present value.*** Lepton Industries has four potential projects, all with an initial cost of $1,500,000. The capital budget for the year will allow Lepton to accept only one of the four projects. Given the discount rates and the future cash flow of each project, determine which project Lepton should accept.

Cash Flow	Project Q	Project R	Project S	Project T
Year 1	$350,000	$400,000	$700,000	$ 200,000
Year 2	$350,000	$400,000	$600,000	$ 400,000
Year 3	$350,000	$400,000	$500,000	$ 600,000
Year 4	$350,000	$400,000	$400,000	$ 800,000
Year 5	$350,000	$400,000	$300,000	$1,000,000
Discount rate	4%	8%	13%	18%

11. ***NPV unequal lives.*** Grady Enterprises is looking at two project opportunities for a parcel of land that the company currently owns. The first project is a restaurant, and the second project is a sports facility. The restaurant's

projected cash flow is an initial cost of $1,500,000 with cash flows over the next six years of $200,000 (year one), $250,000 (year two), $300,000 (years three through five), and $1,750,000 in year six, when Grady plans to sell the restaurant. The sports facility has the following cash outflow: initial cost of $2,400,000 with cash flows over the next four years of $400,000 (years one through three) and $3,000,000 in year four, when Grady plans to sell the facility. If the appropriate discount rate for the restaurant is 11% and the appropriate discount rate for the sports facility is 13%, use the NPV to determine which project Grady should choose for the parcel of land. Adjust the NPV for unequal lives with the equivalent annual annuity. Does the decision change?

12. ***NPV unequal lives.*** Singing Fish Fine Foods has $2,000,000 for capital investments this year and is considering two potential projects for the funds. Project One is updating the store's deli section for additional food service. The estimated after-tax cash flow of this project is $600,000 per year for the next five years. Project Two is updating the store's wine section. The estimated annual after-tax cash flow for this project is $530,000 for the next six years. If the appropriate discount rate for the deli expansion is 9.5% and the appropriate discount rate for the wine section is 9.0%, use the NPV to determine which project Singing Fish should choose for the store. Adjust the NPV for unequal lives with the equivalent annual annuity. Does the decision change?
13. ***Internal rate of return and modified internal rate of return.*** What are the IRRs and MIRRs of the four projects for Quark Industries in Problem 9?
14. ***Internal rate of return and modified internal rate of return.*** What are the IRRs and MIRRs of the four projects for Lepton Industries in Problem 10?
15. ***MIRR unequal lives.*** What is the MIRR for Grady Enterprises in Problem 11? What is the MIRR when you adjust for the unequal lives? Does the adjusted MIRR for unequal lives change the decision based on the MIRR? *Hint:* Take all cash flows to the same ending period as the longest project.
16. ***MIRR unequal lives.*** What is the MIRR for Singing Fish Fine Foods in Problem 12? What is the MIRR when you adjust for the unequal lives? Does the adjusted MIRR for unequal lives change the decision based on MIRR? *Hint:* Take all cash flows to the same ending period as the longest project.
17. ***Comparing NPV and IRR.*** Chandler and Joey are having a discussion about which financial model to use for their new business. Chandler supports the NPV, and Joey supports the IRR. The discussion starts to intensify when Ross steps in and states, "Gentlemen, it doesn't matter which method you choose. They give the same answer on all projects." Is Ross correct? Under what conditions will IRR and NPV be consistent when accepting or rejecting projects?
18. ***Comparing NPV and IRR.*** Monica and Rachel are having a discussion about the IRR and the NPV as decision models for Monica's new restaurant. Monica wants to use the IRR because it gives a very simple and intuitive answer. Rachel states that IRR can cause errors, unlike NPV. Is Rachel correct? Show one type of error with the IRR and not with the NPV.
19. ***Profitability index.*** Given the discount rates and the future cash flow of each project listed on the next page, use the PI to determine which projects the company should accept.

Cash Flow	Project U	Project V	Project W	Project X
Year 0	−$2,000,000	−$2,500,000	−$2,400,000	−$1,750,000
Year 1	$ 500,000	$ 600,000	$1,000,000	$ 300,000
Year 2	$ 500,000	$ 600,000	$ 800,000	$ 500,000
Year 3	$ 500,000	$ 600,000	$ 600,000	$ 700,000
Year 4	$ 500,000	$ 600,000	$ 400,000	$ 900,000
Year 5	$ 500,000	$ 600,000	$ 200,000	$1,100,000
Discount rate	6%	9%	15%	22%

20. ***Profitability index.*** Given the discount rates and the future cash flow of each project listed, use the PI to determine which projects the company should accept.

Cash Flow	Project A	Project B	Project C	Project D
Year 0	−$1,500,000	−$1,500,000	−$2,000,000	−$2,000,000
Year 1	$ 350,000	$ 400,000	$ 700,000	$ 200,000
Year 2	$ 350,000	$ 400,000	$ 600,000	$ 400,000
Year 3	$ 350,000	$ 400,000	$ 500,000	$ 600,000
Year 4	$ 350,000	$ 400,000	$ 400,000	$ 800,000
Year 5	$ 350,000	$ 400,000	$ 300,000	$1,000,000
Discount rate	4%	8%	13%	18%

21. ***Comparing all methods.*** Given the following after-tax cash flows on a new toy for Tyler's Toys, find the project's payback period, NPV, and IRR. The appropriate discount rate for the project is 12%. If the cutoff period is six years for major projects, determine whether management will accept or reject the project under the three different decision models.

Initial cash outflow: $10,400,000
Years one through four cash inflow: $2,600,000 each year
Year five cash outflow: $1,200,000
Years six through eight cash inflow: $750,000 each year

22. ***Comparing all methods.*** Risky Business is looking at a project with the estimated cash flow as follows:

Initial investment at start of project: $3,600,000
Cash flow at end of year one: $500,000
Cash flow at end of years two through six: $625,000 each year
Cash flow at end of years seven through nine: $530,000 each year
Cash flow at end of year ten: $385,000

Risky Business wants to know the payback period, NPV, IRR, MIRR, and PI of this project. The appropriate discount rate for the project is 14%. If the cutoff period is six years for major projects, determine whether the management at Risky Business will accept or reject the project under the five different decision models.

23. ***NPV profile of a project.*** Given the following cash flow of Project L-2, draw the NPV profile. *Hint:* Be sure to use a discount rate of zero for one intercept (*y*-axis) and solve for the IRR for the other intercept (*x*-axis).

Year 0 = −$250,000
Year 1 = $45,000
Year 2 = $75,000
Year 3 = $115,000
Year 4 = $135,000

24. ***NPV profile of two mutually exclusive projects.*** Moulton Industries has two potential projects for the coming year, Project B-12 and Project F-4. The two projects are mutually exclusive. The cash flow is listed in the table on the next page. Draw the NPV profile of each project and determine their crossover rate. If the appropriate hurdle rate is 10% for both projects, which project does Moulton Industries choose?

Cash Flow	Project B-12	Project F-4
Year 0	−$4,250,000	−$3,800,000
Year 1	$2,000,000	$ 0
Year 2	$2,000,000	$1,000,000
Year 3	$2,000,000	$1,500,000
Year 4	$ 0	$2,000,000
Year 5	$ 0	$2,500,000

Advanced Problems for Spreadsheet Application

These problems are available in MyFinanceLab.

1. ***NPV profile.*** Siesta Incorporated is looking at a project and has the appropriate cash flow. However, there is much disagreement on the appropriate discount rate to use with the project. Aracely, the CFO, has requested that you provide the NPV at various interest rates between 0% and 40% at 2% intervals. That way, when Siesta is able to access the proper discount rate for this project, it will know if the project is a go. In addition, graph your NPV results at each interest rate to show the project's NPV profile.

The cash flow for the project is listed here in millions of dollars:

Year	0	1	2	3	4	5	6	7	8
CF	–35.05	3.44	5.79	9.23	14.68	18.39	21.07	16.42	11.68

2. ***IRR and MIRR.*** Using the same cash flows from Problem 1 for Siesta Incorporated, confirm that the IRR intersects the horizontal axis at the $0 NPV for the project. Then, calculate the project's MIRR at different discount and reinvestment rates. Assume that the discount rate and the reinvestment rate are the same for MIRR (use 2% and 2%, 4% and 4%, and so on). Find the MIRR for all reinvestment rates from 0% to 30% by increments of 2%.

MINI-CASE

BioCom, Inc.: Part 1

This mini-case is available in MyFinanceLab.

BioCom was founded in 1993, when several scientists and engineers at a large fiber-optic-cable company began to see that optical fiber for the telecommunications industry was becoming a cheap commodity. They decided to start their own firm, which would specialize in cutting-edge applications for research in the life sciences and medical instruments. BioCom is now one of the leading firms in its niche field. BioCom's management attributes the firm's success to its ability to stay one step ahead of the market's fast-changing technological needs. Almost as important is BioCom's ability to select high-value-added projects and avoid commercial disasters.

Over lunch, BioCom's director of research and development (R&D) mentioned to the CFO that one of his best young scientists had recently left the company because his line manager had rejected his project. Although not a pattern, R&D had experienced similar losses in the past. The two executives discussed the problem and agreed that if the R&D people understood the selection process better, they might come up with more commercially viable projects and understand the project's financial implications. The CFO has asked his assistant, Jane Donato, to prepare a retreat for the R&D department to explain the company's project selection procedures. Jane is encouraged by the thought that this group will have no trouble in following the math!

BioCom's standard capital request form includes a narrative description of the project and the customer need that the company must fulfill. If the request originates with R&D, it then goes to the marketing department for a preliminary sales forecast and then to the production manager and cost analysts for cost estimates. If a proposal shows promise after these steps, it goes to the CFO, who has a staff member enter the data into a spreadsheet template. The template computes payback, discounted payback, net present value, internal rate of return, and modified internal rate of return. BioCom uses net present value as its primary decision criterion, but company executives believe that the other statistics provide some useful additional perspectives.

To explain BioCom's capital budgeting techniques, Jane has decided to present the cash flows from two recent proposals: the nano test tube project and the microsurgery kit project. All figures are in thousands of dollars:

Time of Cash Flow	Nano Test Tubes	Microsurgery Kit
Investment	−$11,000	−$11,000
Year 1	2,000	4,000
Year 2	3,000	4,000
Year 3	4,000	4,000
Year 4	5,000	4,000
Year 5	7,000	4,000

Help Jane answer the following questions.

Questions

1. Compute the payback period for each project.
   a. Explain the rationale behind the payback method.
   b. State and explain the decision rule for the payback method.
   c. Explain how the company would use the payback method to rank mutually exclusive projects.
   d. Comment on the advantages and shortcomings of this method.
2. Compute the discounted payback period for each project using a discount rate of 10%.
   a. Explain the rationale behind the discounted payback method.
   b. Comment on the advantages and shortcomings of this method.
3. Compute the net present value (NPV) for each project. BioCom uses a discount rate of 9% for projects of average risk.
   a. Explain the rationale behind the NPV method.
   b. State and explain the decision rule behind the NPV method.
   c. Explain how the company would use the NPV method to rank mutually exclusive projects.
   d. Comment on the advantages and shortcomings of this method.
   e. Without performing any calculations, explain what happens to the NPV if the company adjusts the discount rate upward for projects of higher risk or downward for projects of lower risk.
4. Compute the internal rate of return (IRR) for each project.
   a. Explain the rationale behind the IRR method.
   b. State and explain the decision rule behind the IRR method. Assume a hurdle rate of 9%.

c. Explain how the company would use the IRR method to rank mutually exclusive projects.
d. Comment on the advantages and shortcomings of this method.

5. Compute the modified internal rate of return (MIRR) for each project.
   a. Explain the rationale behind the MIRR method.
   b. State and explain the decision rule behind the MIRR method. Assume a hurdle rate of 9%.
   c. Explain how the company would use the MIRR method to choose between mutually exclusive projects.
   d. Explain how this method corrects for some of the problems inherent in the IRR method.
6. Explain to the R&D staff why BioCom uses the NPV method as its primary project selection criterion.
7. **Challenge question**. Construct NPV profiles for both projects using discount rates of 1% through 15% at intervals of one percentage point. At approximately what discount rate does the nano test tube project become superior to the microsurgery kits? You are better off solving this problem using an electronic spreadsheet.

Learning Objectives

LO1 Understand the importance of cash flow and the distinction between cash flow and profits.

LO2 Identify incremental cash flow.

LO3 Calculate depreciation and cost recovery.

LO4 Understand the cash flow associated with the disposal of depreciable assets.

LO5 Estimate incremental cash flow for capital budgeting decisions.

Chapter 10
Cash Flow Estimation

A major metric of a company's health and its prospects for a long life is how much cash flow it can generate. Most businesses fail because their cash flow dries up. Managing the streams of money in and out of a business enterprise is critical to its success. It doesn't necessarily matter how much profit you may have projected on paper because you cannot spend profits. You can only spend cash. It is the same as looking at your income tax filings at the end of a year. You may have made considerable money during the year and have a very high adjusted gross income line, but you can currently spend only what's in your checking account.

In this chapter, we examine how to measure and predict cash flow as we continue our quest to build a solid tool kit for the financial manager. We will see that the timing and amount of cash flow are critical to business decisions, business growth, and ultimately business success. Without an understanding of a project's cash flow, the potential for poor decisions and failure is high. Good business decisions start with understanding how the timing and amount of cash flow—not just estimating or measuring profit—affect the viability of a project.

10.1 The Importance of Cash Flow

What is the distinction between profits and cash flow? **Profits** are an accounting measure of performance during a specific period of time. **Cash flow** is the actual inflow or outflow of money. One way to think about cash flow is to match it to your checking account. When you write a check or use your debit card for payments, money flows out of your account. When you deposit funds in your checking account, money flows into your account. As we all know, the balance in your checking account is not your profit or earnings. It is just the cash available to spend.

So, can you spend profits? The answer is no. As stated in the chapter opening, you can only spend cash. Consider the case of a business that has had a very profitable year and has earned $1 million in profits. Can it distribute the $1 million to its owners (via dividends)? Maybe it can, and maybe it can't. It could if it had $1 million in cash at the end of the year. But it may have reinvested some of the cash in inventory or paid off some debts of the business, leaving its cash account balance near zero. In the second case, it cannot pay out $1 million to the owners.

Can the opposite be true? Can you *lose* money and still pay dividends? The answer is yes. A company could show a loss for the operating period, but have generated positive cash flow for the business, or it could have considerable cash from a previous period, enabling it to issue a dividend payment to its owners. For example, if the company had a large depreciation expense during the period—a noncash expense—the income statement could show a loss for the period. The cash account, however, may have grown enough during the same period so that there would be sufficient cash on hand for a dividend payment. It is important for you to understand this distinction between cash and profits.

We first introduced the difference between cash flow and profits in Chapter 2, where we examined the firm's income statement. Let's look again at an income statement and then modify this statement to illustrate the cash flow from operations. See Figures 10.1 and 10.2. It is important to understand that the $3,313 in Figure 10.1 is net income (profits) for Cogswell Cola, *not* the operating cash flow. Figure 10.2 shows the operating cash flow.

Let's again look at the difference between these two approaches. In accounting, we stop at net income or profits as in Figure 10.1. We also include interest expense as part of the statement. In finance, we remove interest expense as in Figure 10.2

FIGURE 10.1

Cogswell Cola Company Income Statement Year Ending December 31, 2011 ($ in thousands)	
Revenue	$25,112
Cost of goods sold	$11,497
Selling, general, and administrative expenses	$ 7,457
Depreciation	$ 1,112
EBIT	$ 5,046
Interest expense	$ 178
Taxable income	$ 4,868
Taxes	$ 1,555
Net income	**$ 3,313**

because we classify it as part of the firm's financing, not operating, decision. Then, to find cash flow from operations, we add back the noncash expenses—in this example, depreciation. What we end up with is the **operating cash flow (OCF)**, or the estimated cash flow that the business' basic operations generate. In Figure 10.2, we have the business' operating cash flow of $4,603 for the year, which is a sizable difference when we compare it with the net income of $3,313 for the year in Figure 10.1. So, when we estimate a project's cash flow, we will use the modified income statement approach so that we find the money flowing in and out from the project's operations.

A shortcut to finding the operating cash flow is the equation

$$\text{OCF} = \text{EBIT} + \text{depreciation} - \text{taxes}$$

Again, we typically use this OCF format for predicting the project's cash inflow. If you are unfamiliar with the four basic financial statements (income statement, balance sheet, statement of retained earnings, and the statement of cash flows), review Chapter 2.

Cogswell Cola Operating Cash Flow Year Ending December 31, 2011 ($ in thousands)	
Revenue	$25,112
Cost of goods sold	$11,497
Selling, general, and administrative expenses	$ 7,457
Depreciation	$ 1,112
EBIT	$ 5,046
Taxes	$ 1,555
Modified net income	$ 3,491
Add back depreciation	$ 1,112
Operating cash flow	**$ 4,603**

FIGURE 10.2

10.2 Estimating Cash Flow for Projects: Incremental Cash Flow

Our objective now is to estimate the timing and amount of cash flow of a proposed project so that we can apply one of the capital budgeting decision models from Chapter 9. These projected revenues and costs that form the basis of the potential for the project's acceptance or rejection are estimates of future activity. Often, these estimates will start with sales forecasts and the production costs associated with the sales forecast to arrive at the project's anticipated operating cash flow. We usually look at the project's initial outlay as its capital expenditure and determine depreciation from this capital expenditure.

At first glance, it would seem that we just want to estimate the annual cash flows from operations and capital spending and use those as the timing and amount of cash flow for the project. We want to be careful, however, to use only the additional or incremental cash flow that the firm would generate if it selected the project. **Incremental cash flow** is the increase in cash that a new project generates above the current cash flow with the addition of that specific new project. So, in some cases, projected sales revenue is not the proper revenue to use in the project's estimated income statement. To get to this point, we need to examine seven issues that affect the project's incremental cash flow:

1. Sunk costs
2. Opportunity costs
3. Erosion costs
4. Synergy gains
5. Working capital
6. Capital expenditures
7. Depreciation and cost recovery of divested assets

We will look at a potential Cogswell Cola project and illustrate these various cash flow issues. You will see that all but the first one (sunk costs) should be included in the incremental cash flow estimation.

Cogswell Cola is thinking about adding a new flavored cola to its product mix. We will need to find the timing and amount of incremental cash flow in order to decide whether this project is good for the company. We now turn to a consideration of the seven issues surrounding incremental cash flow. We look at the first five in the remainder of this section and the last two in the next section.

Sunk Costs

A project's **sunk costs** are those costs that the company has already incurred. They cannot be reversed or avoided. They can be costs that the company has contracted, but not yet paid. Because the company will incur these costs whether the project is accepted or rejected, they are not part of the decision to accept or reject the project. In our flavored-cola example, let's assume that Cogswell Cola commissions a marketing company to examine the potential market of a new flavored cola and agrees to pay $25,000 for the research results. The marketing company will estimate the potential market for Cogswell's new "Pulsar Cola," a cherry-flavored cola. The information that the marketing company produces will be critical input to the decision, but the expense—the marketing firm's $25,000 fee—is not relevant because it is a sunk cost. The eventual choice of accepting or rejecting the flavored-cola project will not change the fact that Cogswell Cola is obligated to pay the marketing firm $25,000 for its research. We do not consider this fee in estimating the project's incremental cash flow. It is irrelevant. The $25,000 fee is part of the company's income statement. It is just not part of the capital budgeting decision.

Opportunity Costs

When we focus on incremental cash flow, we usually think about all the future cash inflows and outflows. There may, however, be a cash flow that never occurs for a new project but that the company needs to add as a cost or outflow. This so-called **opportunity cost** is a benefit forgone due to the company's selection of a particular project.

For the new project, Cogswell Cola plans to use a bottling machine that the company purchased five years ago but has been sitting idle for the past two years. The bottling machine's original cost was $450,000. Should we include this cost as part of the Pulsar Cola project's cost? Clearly, the company has already spent this money, and whether we accept or reject the new project will not alter this fact. If, however, Cogswell Cola does not choose the Pulsar Cola project, the company can sell the idle bottling machine. This opportunity—to sell the idle machine—disappears if Pulsar Cola uses it. Should Cogswell add an additional $450,000 to the project's cash outflow as an opportunity cost? The answer is no. Cogswell should not add the original cost of $450,000, but it should determine what the machine could sell for today and then include that lost sale opportunity as part of the Pulsar Cola project's cash outflows. The sales price will be the going rate for a used bottling machine. This sales price is lost if the new project uses the equipment, so we want to be sure the new project will generate sufficient cash inflow to cover this lost opportunity. For example, let's assume Cogswell could sell the old bottling machine for $200,000. Let's also assume that the new cola will provide a net present value of $150,000 (if we exclude the cash flow from the sale of the old bottling machine). Now which project would you select? Cogswell Cola is better off selling the bottling machine rather than introducing the new cola product. Therefore, the new cola product must have a net present value of over $200,000 excluding the opportunity cost or a positive net present value if the company includes the $200,000 opportunity cost in the project's incremental cash flow.

When a new product's cash flows come at the expense of a company's already existing products, erosion costs occur.

Erosion Costs

If Cogswell Cola does market a new flavored cola, it may lose revenue from its other products, Cosmic Cola and Luna Lemon-Lime. Cogswell wants to capture part of the flavored-cola market, but some of its current customers may find that they prefer the new flavored cola to Cosmic Cola or Luna Lemon-Lime and may switch their cola choice within the Cogswell Cola family of soft drinks. Whenever a new product competes against a company's already existing products and reduces the sales of those products, **erosion costs** occur. You should include only the net *additional* revenue and costs—the *increase* in overall sales and costs to the company—in the incremental cash flow. Looking only at revenue figures in Table 10.1 for a moment, let's see the appropriate revenue increase with the new flavored-cola project.

We can see from the table's bottom line that the Pulsar Cola project will add only an additional $5 million of revenue because Pulsar Cola projects $7 million in sales at the expense of the other two products. Therefore, a large percent of the $12 million sales will come from existing customers, who will switch from one Cogswell product to another Cogswell product. It seems clear that existing product sales will erode with the introduction of Pulsar Cola. We sometimes refer to this phenomenon as "cannibalizing" existing sales.

One must be careful with erosion, however. If a competitor introduces a flavored cola that would take away existing customers from Cogswell's cola and lemon-lime products (see Table 10.2), the introduction of Pulsar Cola protects against the lost revenue from customers switching to the competitor's brand. In this scenario—that of a competitor as well as Cogswell Cola launching a flavored cola—the entire $12 million would be additional sales which the company should include in the incremental cash flow. A $7 million loss would take place whether or not Cogswell Cola introduced its new product. If current Cogswell Cola customers switch from Cosmic Cola and Luna Lemon-Lime to a competitor's cherry-flavored cola, the company would have sales of only $52 million. Therefore, the

TABLE 10.1 Annual Incremental Cash Revenues

	Revenue Before	Revenue After	Increase/Decrease
Cosmic Cola	$45 million	$40 million	−$5 million
Luna Lemon-Lime	$14 million	$12 million	−$2 million
Pulsar Cola	–	$12 million	+$12 million
Total	$59 million	$64 million	$5 million

TABLE 10.2 Annual Cash Revenues after Competitor Introduces Flavored Cola

	Revenue Before Competitor's Flavored Cola	Projected Revenue After Competitor's Flavored Cola	Change in Revenue
Cosmic Cola	$45 million	$40 million	−$5 million
Luna Lemon-Lime	$14 million	$12 million	−$2 million
Total	$59 million	$52 million	−$7 million

introduction of Pulsar Cola would prevent this $7 million sales loss, and the entire $12 million sales are incremental cash flow to Cogswell Cola. It would retain potential switching customers ($7 million in sales) as well as gain new ones ($5 million in sales).

Erosion can also provide cost savings. In the original scenario in which Cogswell introduces a flavored cola without a competitor doing so, the company might lose $7 million in revenue, but also avoids the cost of producing the regular colas and lemon-lime drinks that it associated with these lost sales. The $5 million in lost sales for Cosmic Cola and the lost sales of $2 million for Luna Lemon-Lime are also accompanied by a reduction in the costs to produce those products: a reduction in a cash outflow, which is an incremental cash inflow. If the production costs fall by $2.5 million for the lost $7 million in revenue for the current products, these cost savings are also part of the flavored-cola project's incremental cash flow.

EXAMPLE 10.1 Erosion costs

Problem Heavenly Foods makes pudding products. Its current sales are 2,000,000 units per year, with revenue of $1.29 per unit and cost of $0.63 per unit. Heavenly is thinking about introducing pudding pops. Estimated sales for pudding pops are 500,000 units at $1.45 per unit and cost of production of $0.88 per unit. By introducing pudding pops, however, the company estimates that regular pudding sales will drop by 300,000 units per year. What is the erosion cost per year of introducing pudding pops?

Solution Set up the revenue and production costs of the pudding sales before introduction of the new product and the total revenue and production costs of the two products after the introduction. The change is the incremental cash flow, and the reduction in pudding's contribution (margin before and after) is the erosion cost. The difference between revenue and production costs is the product's gross margin, which the following table notes as the margin.

Annual Erosion Costs of Pudding Pops for Heavenly Foods

	Pudding Before	Pudding After	Pudding Pops	Total After	Change After
Revenue	$2,580,000	$2,193,000	$725,000	$2,918,000	$338,000
– Cost	$1,260,000	$1,071,000	$440,000	$1,511,000	$251,000
= Margin	$1,320,000	$1,122,000	$285,000	$1,407,000	$ 87,000

The erosion costs are \$198,000 (\$1,320,000 margin of pudding before minus \$1,122,000 margin of pudding after), and the company needs to make up these lost dollars with pudding pops. Pudding pops contribute \$285,000 in margin, so the net contribution of adding pudding pops is only \$87,000 (\$285,000 − \$198,000).

Synergy Gains

In contrast to erosion costs, a new product that complements another current product and increases sales of the current product should include these additional sales as part of the project's sales. This addition is a **synergy gain**. Synergy is the "merger math" that says 2 + 2 = 5, that is, the combined parts are greater than the individual pieces. Therefore, you often see a company produce a series of products that are interrelated rather than a single product.

To see how synergy gains work, say that Gold Medal Sports currently has a line of baseball and softball gloves. It is now considering introducing baseballs and softballs to its product set. By adding baseballs and softballs, it may increase glove sales. When players go to a Gold Medal retail outlet store to purchase new baseballs and softballs, they will see the gloves and may buy them (impulse purchases). The additional glove sales (and additional net cash flow) are part of the baseball and softball project's incremental cash flow. Without the introduction of baseballs and softballs, the additional glove sales above the current level would not materialize. Therefore, the incremental cash flow includes the additional glove sales (and costs to produce the gloves). As nice as that may be, synergy gains may be one of the most difficult incremental cash flows to predict. It may be difficult to predict impulse purchases or sales increases for other existing products related to the introduction of a new product.

Working Capital

An often-neglected aspect of a project is the increase in working capital accounts necessary to support the project. These changes add upfront costs, but they also provide for cost reductions at the end of the project. In our first example, Cogswell Cola will need to purchase bottles for the production of Pulsar Cola. In a typical manufacturing process, the company will have to have a sufficient bottle supply for the production line. Once filled with soda, a bottle leaves the production line, and another empty bottle enters. Let's assume that the sales price per bottle is \$1, so the annual sales will require 12 million bottles. Let's also assume that each empty bottle costs 5 cents and the production line needs 20,000 empty bottles at all times. Therefore, during the first year, Cogswell Cola will purchase 12,020,000 bottles. Of these, they will eventually fill and sell twelve million bottles (thus recording these twelve million as cost of goods sold), but the inventory account will have 20,000 bottles or a \$1,000 increase (20,000 × \$0.05) as part of the company's current assets.

During the second year, the company will again buy 12 million bottles, using the 20,000 in the production line from the prior year and 11,980,000 of the current year purchases, and keep the last 20,000 purchased for the year in the production line. In other words, Cogswell will keep a steady state of 20,000 units in the production line or inventory account in the second year. Therefore, only the first year shows an increase in inventory for this project. Finally, if Cogswell decides to stop selling Pulsar Cola, it will draw the inventory account back to zero in the final year because the company will not want to hold on to 20,000 empty bottles. So, in year one, there is an increase in working capital that the company eventually recovers in the project's final operating year.

In Example 10.2, we assume a steady operating level of sales for a new project. In the real world, however, sales often increase from year to year, and working capital may correspondingly increase each year as inventories grow with sales. So, you may have additional investment in working capital each year of a project. We start with the simplest example to illustrate the recovery of the working capital at the end of a project with no increases or decreases in inventory over the life of the project.

EXAMPLE 10.2 Working capital cash flow

Problem College Doughnuts is a company that Julie, a college freshman, started to help pay her way through college. The company sells doughnuts every morning Monday through Friday from 7:30 to 9:30 to students on their way to morning classes. Julie anticipates keeping the business only for four years while an undergraduate. Julie projects annual sales at 12,000 doughnuts at $0.50 each. The production cost is $0.20 each. In addition, she needs to wrap each doughnut in waxed paper and place it in a bag for students to carry. The cost is $0.005 per doughnut for the waxed paper and $0.01 per bag. If this young entrepreneur wants to keep a minimum inventory of 300 bags and 300 sheets of waxed paper at all times, what is the working capital cash flow of her business?

Solution One way to understand the change in inventory of waxed paper wrappers and bags is to look at the sales flow and the cost of goods from each period or year and the inventory purchases that support the sales.

Inventory Flow and Cost of Wrappers and Bags

	Year 1	Year 2	Year 3	Year 4
Sales units	12,000	12,000	12,000	12,000
Purchased bags	12,300	12,000	12,000	11,700
Wrappers	12,300	12,000	12,000	11,700
Cost of goods sold	$180.00	$180.00	$180.00	$180.00
Inventory count	300	300	300	0
Inventory value change	$ 4.50	$ 0	$ 0	−$ 4.50
Cash flow out	$184.50	$180.00	$180.00	$175.50

By examining the table, we can see that in year one, Julie will purchase 12,300 bags and wrappers for $184.50 (12,300 × 0.015), allocating $180.00 (12,000 × $0.015) to the 12,000 sold doughnuts (cost of goods sold) and $4.50 (300 × $0.015) to inventory for an inventory increase of $4.50. Then, for the next two years, Julie will purchase only 12,000 bags and wrappers, using the 300 from the previous year's inventory plus purchases, and will still have 300 units left in inventory at the end of the year for a cash flow of $180.00 and no change in inventory. Julie will record this cash flow in the cost of goods that she sells as part of her company's operating cash flow. During the final year, the 12,000 wrappers and bags needed to come out of the 300 in inventory and the purchased 11,700, all of which end up as a cost of goods sold for $180.00. Because the inventory total is at zero at the end of the project, we must have a reduction in inventory the final year. Therefore, in the last year, there is an inventory or working capital account reduction of $4.50. Again, Julie has accounted for all cash flow: she has the cost of goods sold cash flow in the operating cash flow and the inventory piece in working capital. The net of these two accounts is $175.50, the actual cost of the inventory that she purchased in the fourth year. Working capital increases in the beginning and decreases in the last year.

FINANCE FOLLIES

Boston's "Big Dig" Gets Dug Under

In Chapter 9, you learned how to use quantitative models to evaluate capital projects. These models are mathematically precise and well grounded in finance principles. As you read this chapter, though, you will see that the results are only as reliable as the cash flow estimates that we used to compute them, which can be flawed.

Boston's Central Artery/Tunnel Project—or the Big Dig, as it is popularly known—was a three-decades-long project to put the city's major interstate highway underground and carve out a new underwater tunnel to the airport. Although the initial estimated cost of the project was $2.6 billion in 1982, by late 2006 the City of Boston and the Commonwealth of Massachusetts had spent a staggering $14.8 billion on the Big Dig, a whopping 469% over budget. The Big Dig was the costliest highway project in U.S. history. How could the initial estimate be so far off? As one observer noted, "Be careful with that first number, because it can become a permanent benchmark against which to measure success or failure."[1]

Rosy projections for the Big Dig at best assumed that nothing would go wrong and at worst ignored clear, early warnings of significant problems. Bechtel, the major contractor for Boston's Big Dig, knew early on that the project directors based engineering plans on outdated maps that omitted large new buildings standing in the project's path. Although Massachusetts initially secured federal funding, planners assumed that the cash spigots would permanently flow funding to a project of ever-increasing scope. When Uncle Sam instead put a cap on the cash flow, Massachusetts taxpayers were left with huge bills to foot. The saddest "cost" of all occurred when a shoddily constructed roof plate in the newly opened tunnel collapsed and killed a car passenger.

Is it possible that engineers at Bechtel actually believed or at least hoped that they could complete the Big Dig project within budget and on time? In a phenomenon known as *loss aversion*, people have difficulty cutting their losses. Terminating or curtailing a project, like selling a stock that has dropped in price, means realizing a sure loss. We may know intellectually that our losses are more likely to mount than to diminish, but we hang on to the hope that somehow our luck will change or that we will be able to find a solution. Managers and public officials may view terminating or curtailing a project as a failure that will negatively affect their careers. As things start to go wrong, people commit more time, energy, and resources to avoid failure. We call this tendency *incremental commitment*.

How can we avoid dysfunctional behaviors in capital budgeting decisions? One thing we can do is to ask what could go wrong with a project and then compute the net present value of the worst-case scenario as well as the best and most likely cases. Some firms use simulation software that considers many combinations of all the variables that they use in estimating project cash flows. It is good financial practice to agree on penalties for delays or cost overruns. In considering a project's risk, we must look not only at uncertainty, but at consequences. Negative outcomes for some projects might result in no more than a temporary blip in earnings, whereas others might have the potential to cause bankruptcy.

Finally, firms can control loss aversion and incremental commitment by establishing in advance concrete benchmarks that help curtail or terminate a project if things start to go wrong. Once a firm approves a project, it cannot allow it to take on a life of its own. It is important to have standard procedures in place that measure actual results against initial expectations.

[1]Quoted in Nicole Gelinas, "Lessons of Boston's Big Dig," *City Journal* (Autumn 2007); available online at www.city-journal.org.

We have illustrated the change in working capital with inventory accounts here, but it applies to all the net working capital accounts. Increases in accounts receivable constitute a use of cash flow because you are helping your customers finance their purchases. Increases in accounts payable constitute a source of cash flow because you are using your suppliers to help finance your business operations. Therefore, we look at the increase or decrease in net working capital as an important part of the timing and amount of a project's cash flow. If you offset the increase at the project's beginning by the reduction at the project's end, why do we consider working capital in the incremental cash flow? The answer is that these two cash flows occur at different points in time, and with the time value of money we must account for both: the value of the reduction in the future is not the same as the value of the initial cash outflow at the project's start.

The next two issues that affect the project's incremental cash flow—capital expenditures and depreciation—are more complex and deserve their own section for explanation. You may also be interested in reading the "Finance Follies" feature on page 305, which recounts how dysfunctional behavior can affect cash flow estimates.

10.3 Capital Spending and Depreciation

Continuing with our project of a flavored cola for Cogswell Cola, we need to examine the required cash flow to purchase new production equipment. For this project, the company will purchase a cola-syrup mixing system that will cost $2,000,000 and a water filtering machine that will cost $1,500,000. The company will need to purchase and install both machines prior to production; therefore, the cash outflow will occur at the start of the project. Let's assume that the installation cost of each machine is 10% of the value of the machines that Cogswell Cola purchased. Therefore, the company spends a total of $3,850,000 ($2,000,000 + $200,000 + $1,500,000 + $150,000) before it fills the first bottle with Pulsar Cola. The company will expense this cash outflow over a series of years through **depreciation**, which is the process of expiring the cost of a long-term tangible asset over its useful life. Essentially, we allocate a portion of the cost over each year to the product's production costs. The two reasons why we need to deal with depreciation are: (1) the tax flow implications from the operating cash flow and (2) the gain or loss at disposal of a capital asset.

There are two common ways to allocate the $3,850,000 through the years:

1. In **straight-line depreciation**, we depreciate capital assets by the same amount each year. We determine it by dividing the total initial cost by the number of years of useful life of tangible assets.
2. The **modified accelerated cost recovery system (MACRS)**, is a government-mandated accelerated depreciation system that depreciates the capital asset at the maximum accelerated amount allowed each year. MACRS classifies the useful "life" of every tangible asset in determining its depreciation cost for each year.

Let's look at the two methods in more detail.

Straight-Line Depreciation

Let's assume that the cola-syrup mixing machine has an expected useful life of five years and then the company will need to replace it. It will have no residual or salvage value at the end of five years. We'll also assume that the filtering machine has a useful life of twenty years and a residual or salvage value of $250,000. As we have seen, the cola-syrup mixing machine costs \$2,000,000 and the water filtering machine costs \$1,500,000, with an additional 10% of the purchase price as installation fees for each. How would the company allocate the depreciation costs each year for these two machines?

The annual depreciation expense is the total value (cost plus installation) minus any anticipated salvage value divided by the number of years of the machine's service (life). So, the annual depreciation of the cola-syrup mixing machine is

$$\frac{\$2{,}000{,}000 + \$200{,}000}{5} = \$440{,}000$$

and the annual depreciation of the water filtering machine is

$$\frac{\$1{,}500{,}000 + \$150{,}000 - \$250{,}000}{20} = \$70{,}000$$

Therefore, in straight-line depreciation, each year receives the same depreciation expense. If you were to graph the annual depreciation expense over time, it would appear on the graph as a horizontal line; hence the name straight-line depreciation. These "expired" costs each year, however, do not reflect cash flow because the machines' actual purchase and installation (outflow of dollars) have already taken place. The dollars are still important for determining the amount of taxable income, and therefore do have an effect on cash flow in subsequent years as a tax-reducing expense. We see this effect in the project's operating cash flow.

Modified Accelerated Cost Recovery System

In 1981, the federal government, as part of its tax changes, introduced a new system for depreciation, the accelerated cost recovery system (ACRS). Under this system, the government classifies all tangible assets into assigned groups with specific "lives" for the purpose of depreciation. Rather than refer to them as the useful "life" of the capital asset, it is probably more accurate to state that the assigned life class is the shortest allowable recovery period for allocating the capital expenditure costs and reducing taxes. The government modified the 1981 tax act in 1986 with longer asset life classifications. Table 10.3 displays the current asset life classifications under MACRS.

Once a firm establishes the assigned class life, it can expense a fixed percentage of the cost each year as depreciation. Table 10.4 lists the fixed percentages for three- to twenty-year lives.

Two special features of the fixed depreciation percentages are important to understand. First, the government allows a full depreciation of the capital expenditure (each column adds to 100%). Therefore, it is not necessary to estimate residual or salvage value. So, in the case of the water filtering machine, the \$250,000 salvage value at the end of year twenty is irrelevant when we use MACRS to estimate the annual depreciation expense. Second, for each recovery period, there appears to be an extra year of depreciation. For example, we depreciate the three-year class assets over four years, not three. What is actually happening is that the government is allowing a half-year of depreciation in the first year that the company places the equipment in production service and a half-year of depreciation in the last year of the recovery period. So, what we are really seeing is

$$\text{3-year class} = \tfrac{1}{2}\text{ year} + 1\text{ full year} + 1\text{ full year} + \tfrac{1}{2}\text{ year}$$

We can also use this same half-year convention with straight-line depreciation so that you see one-half a year's depreciation in the first year and one-half a year's depreciation in the final year.

TABLE 10.3 Property Classes under MACRS

Property Class (Recovery Period)	Types of Capital Assets
3 years	Research equipment and specialty tools
5 years	Computers, typewriters, copiers, duplicating machines, cars, light-duty trucks, qualified technological equipment, and other similar assets
7 years	Office furniture, fixtures, most manufacturing equipment, railroad track, and single-purpose agricultural and horticultural structures
10 years	Equipment used in petroleum refining or in the manufacturing of tobacco products and certain food products
15 years	Public utility properties, type 1
20 years	Public utility properties, type 2
27.5 years	Residential real property
39 years	Office buildings, shopping centers, warehouses, and manufacturing facilities
50 years	Railroad gradings and tunnel bores

TABLE 10.4 MACRS Fixed Annual Expense Percentages by Recovery Class

Year	3-Year	5-Year	7-Year	10-Year	15-Year	20-Year
1	33.33%	20.00%	14.29%	10.00%	5.00%	3.750%
2	44.45%	32.00%	24.49%	18.00%	9.50%	7.219%
3	14.81%	19.20%	17.49%	14.40%	8.55%	6.677%
4	7.41%	11.52%	12.49%	11.52%	7.70%	6.177%
5		11.52%	8.93%	9.22%	6.93%	5.713%
6		5.76%	8.93%	7.37%	6.23%	5.285%
7			8.93%	6.55%	5.90%	4.888%
8			4.45%	6.55%	5.90%	4.522%
9				6.56%	5.91%	4.462%
10				6.55%	5.90%	4.461%
11				3.28%	5.91%	4.462%
12					5.90%	4.461%
13					5.91%	4.462%
14					5.90%	4.461%
15					5.91%	4.462%
16					2.95%	4.461%
17						4.462%
18						4.461%
19						4.462%
20						4.461%
21						2.231%

TABLE 10.5 Annual Depreciation Expense of Equipment for Cogswell Cola

Year	Cola-Syrup Mixing Machine	Water Filtering Machine
1	\$2,200,000 × 0.1429 = \$314,380	\$1,650,000 × 0.1429 = \$235,785
2	\$2,200,000 × 0.2449 = \$538,780	\$1,650,000 × 0.2449 = \$404,085
3	\$2,200,000 × 0.1749 = \$384,780	\$1,650,000 × 0.1749 = \$288,585
4	\$2,200,000 × 0.1249 = \$274,780	\$1,650,000 × 0.1249 = \$206,085
5	\$2,200,000 × 0.0893 = \$196,460	\$1,650,000 × 0.0893 = \$147,345
6	\$2,200,000 × 0.0893 = \$196,460	\$1,650,000 × 0.0893 = \$147,345
7	\$2,200,000 × 0.0893 = \$196,460	\$1,650,000 × 0.0893 = \$147,345
8	\$2,200,000 × 0.0445 = \$ 97,900	\$1,650,000 × 0.0445 = \$ 73,425

Returning to our flavored-cola project for Cogswell Cola and the project's allowable depreciation expense each year, we see that both machines would fall into the seven-year class for manufacturing equipment. Therefore, both would use the seven-year recovery period expense percentages. In addition, as noted, the salvage value of \$250,000 for the water filtering machine is not part of the MACRS and we can ignore it for depreciation expense.

Table 10.5 shows the eight-year depreciation schedule for both machines. Notice that we have used the percentages that Table 10.4 outlines. We fully depreciate both machines at the end of the eighth year, even though we originally assumed that the cola-syrup mixing machine would last only five years and the water filtering machine would be around for twenty years and have a salvage value of \$250,000.

The advantage of MACRS over straight-line depreciation is that you can write off more of your capital costs in the earlier years. This accelerated write-off provides a taxable expense that reduces your taxes at a faster rate than you would get with straight-line depreciation. So, with the time value of money concepts that we have already placed in our financial tool kit, we can surmise that bigger tax cuts in the earlier years and lower tax cuts in the later years are better than a steady tax cut each year.

Depreciation, however, raises two important questions concerning cash flow:

1. What happens when we sell an asset before it is fully depreciated?
2. What happens when we sell an asset after it has been fully depreciated?

We will answer these two questions in the next section.

10.4 Cash Flow and the Disposal of Capital Equipment

When we sell a depreciable asset, we calculate a *tax gain* or *tax loss*, which we base on the asset's *book value* at the time of disposal. If there is a gain, we must pay taxes, and we have a cash outflow. If there is a loss, we record a tax credit or tax reduction, and we have a cash inflow. We want to identify those assets that the company sells from a specific project so that we can properly include the cash flow in the decision to accept or reject that project.

The asset's current book value serves as the basis for determining the gain or loss at disposal. **Book value** is the asset's original cost minus the accumulated depreciation. We recognize a gain on disposal when the asset's selling price is greater than the book value. We recognize a loss on disposal when the asset's selling price is less than the book value.

1. If the selling price is greater than the book value, there is a tax on the gain at the disposal of the asset. The after-tax cash flow is the selling price minus the taxes on the gain.
2. If the selling price is less than the book value, there is a tax credit as a result of the incurred loss at the disposal of the asset. The tax credit reduces the overall tax to the company and is therefore a cash inflow at disposal.

Let's look at an example.

EXAMPLE 10.3 Cash flow at disposal

Problem College Doughnuts purchases a deep-fat fryer for making doughnuts for $16,000. This machine qualifies as a seven-year recovery asset under MACRS. College Doughnuts has a tax rate of 30%. If the company sells the deep-fat fryer at the end of four years for $7,500, what is the cash flow from disposal? If the deep-fat fryer sells for $500 at the end of four years, what is the cash flow from disposal?

Solution For the four-year sale at $7,500, we must first establish the asset's book value to determine whether it has incurred a gain or loss at disposal. The depreciation schedule for the $16,000 deep-fat fryer is:

Year one: $16,000 × 0.1429 = $2,286.40

Year two: $16,000 × 0.2449 = $3,918.40

Year three: $16,000 × 0.1749 = $2,789.40

Year four: $16,000 × 0.1249 = $1,998.40

Accumulated depreciation = $2,286.40 + $3,918.40 + $2,789.40 + $1,998.40

Accumulated depreciation = $10,992.60

Book value of deep-fat fryer = $16,000.00 − $10,992.60 = $5,007.40

Gain on disposal = $7,500.00 − $5,007.40 = $2,492.60

Tax on gain = $2,492.40 × 0.30 = $747.78 (gain on disposal times tax rate)

After-tax cash flow at disposal = $7,500.00 − $747.78 = **$6,752.22**

For the four-year sale at $500, the book value is the same $5,007.40, but now the disposal price is less than the book value:

Loss on sale = $500.00 − $5,007.40 = −$4,507.40

If we assume that College Doughnuts, overall, makes money during the year, this $4,507.40 loss would reduce the company's taxable income and produce a tax credit or positive after-tax cash flow.

Tax credit = $4,507.40 × 0.30 = $1,352.22 (loss on disposal times tax rate)

After-tax cash flow at disposal = $500.00 + $1,352.22 = **$1,852.22**

Fully depreciated assets have a book value of zero, so any proceeds from sale at disposal are taxable gains. Anytime the proceeds equal the asset's book value, there is neither a taxable gain nor tax credit loss and the proceeds represent the after-tax cash flow at disposal.

In general, we can sum up after-tax cash flow at disposal as:

1. If the selling price is greater than the book value, the net after-tax cash flow is the *selling price minus the tax on gain.*
2. If the selling price is less than the book value, the net after-tax cash flow is the *selling price plus the tax credit on loss.*
3. If the selling price equals the book value, the net after-tax cash flow is the *selling price.*

Although we have taken a rather simple approach to the cash flow associated with disposal of assets, the tax rules for depreciation recapture are much more complicated. If you are selling off assets, be sure to work with a tax expert to establish any gain or loss at disposal.

10.5 Projected Cash Flow for a New Product

It is now time to put together all this cash flow knowledge and estimate the appropriate anticipated cash flow for our project both in terms of amount and timing of the incremental cash flow. We must use these elements when making a decision with the capital budgeting models: payback period, discounted payback period, net present value, internal rate of return, modified internal rate of return, and profitability index. Let's return to Cogswell Cola's flavored-cola project and estimate its incremental cash flow.

1. **Determine the initial capital investment for the project.** To start the process of identifying cash flow, begin with the required capital expenditure to start the project. In the case of Pulsar Cola, we know that we need to purchase two machines: a cola-syrup mixing machine and water filtering machine. Earlier, we estimated the total costs of these two machines (purchase and installation costs) at $2,200,000 and $1,650,000, respectively. In addition, we will need items for inventory that production will use. The required increase in net working capital to start the project will be $150,000. This $150,000 includes the increase in inventory for items such as bottles and labels. Note that we have not spelled out all the changes in working capital, but rather have quoted a number of $150,000 to complete the exercise. Therefore, the necessary total cash outflow to start this project is $4,000,000.

2. **Estimate the project's operating cash flows for each period.** To do so, typically, we would work through our modified income statement for each period with estimated revenues and costs. We would also consider the issues discussed earlier in the chapter such as sunk costs, erosion costs, and depreciation costs. For this example, we will simplify some of the issues and assume no erosion costs for the flavored-cola project. We assume that a competitor is also introducing a flavored-cola beverage. We will also pick a five-year horizon for the project so that we can illustrate what happens when a project terminates, and we will estimate operating cash flows first for year one. This estimate will be the map for the project's operating cash flows for the next four years. If we are estimating a project's cash flow, we would estimate every year's operating cash flow.

Recall that the estimated annual sales for Pulsar Cola are $12,000,000. We will assign a cost of goods sold of $0.25 per bottle. At a price of $1 per bottle, we estimate annual sales quantity at 12,000,000 bottles, so the total cost of sold goods

Operating Cash Flow for Pulsar Cola, Year One (Part 1: Calculating EBIT)	
Revenue	$12,000,000
Cost of goods sold	$ 3,000,000
Fixed costs	$ 1,500,000
Selling, general, and administrative expenses	$ 3,000,000
Depreciation expense	$ 550,165
EBIT	$ 3,949,835

FIGURE 10.3

is $3,000,000 (12,000,000 × $0.25). We also will incur annual fixed costs of $1,500,000 to run the operations. These fixed costs include, for instance, the lighting and heating of the building where we produce the new drink, salaries for workers, and transportation costs for distribution of the product. In addition, we will incur selling, advertising, and administrative expenses directly and indirectly related with this new product. How would we estimate all these costs in the real world? As we saw in Chapter 1, these projections would stem from a joint effort of managers from several different functional areas. At this point, the financial manager's functions and those of the marketing manager, production manager, human resources manager, and others come together to produce the best estimates of the future production costs and sales revenue of Pulsar Cola. For our example, Cogswell will have a large national marketing campaign, so the company will spend $3,000,000 annually on this new product, which would come from consulting with the marketing group on marketing plan costs.

Next, we would look at the depreciation costs for the first year for the two machines. Earlier, we used MACRS and estimated the first year's depreciation expenses at $314,380 and $235,785, for a total of $550,165. We can now estimate the EBIT of Pulsar Cola for the first year. See Figure 10.3.

If the tax rate for Cogswell Cola is 40%, we can produce the company's estimated operating cash flow for year one by estimating the taxes for this project and the modified net income and by adding back depreciation. See Figure 10.4. Once we have estimated the operating cash flow for year one, we would move to year two, then year three, and so on until we have estimated all the operating cash flow over the project's life. If we assume constant sales and costs over the next four years (admittedly, a big assumption for the purpose of the exercise), we would have the operating cash flow for years two through five as Figure 10.5 shows. With constant sales and costs, we can see the effect of the MACRS depreciation on the annual operating cash flow of the project.

3. **Determine the recaptured working capital and the cash flow from the disposal of assets at the end of the project.** Normally, we would continue to estimate operating cash flow for as long as Cogswell Cola produces Pulsar Cola. However, for the sake of this learning exercise, we assume that the project stops after five years. At that time, Cogswell Cola will recover the initial increases in working capital from the beginning of the project, $150,000. Also, Cogswell will dispose of the two production machines. In the case of the cola-syrup mixing machine, we assumed a practical life of five years, so we can only scrap the machine for serviceable parts for $25,000. However, the company can sell the water filtering machine for $500,000 to another firm. What is the cash flow from the disposal of these two assets?

Operating Cash Flow for Pulsar Cola, Year One (Part 2)	
EBIT	$3,949,835
Taxes (at 40%)	$1,579,934
Net income (modified)	$2,369,901
Add back depreciation	$ 550,165
Operating cash flow	$2,920,066

FIGURE 10.4

To answer this question, we first determine each asset's remaining book value. The cola-syrup mixing machine originally cost $2,200,000, and the water filtering machine cost $1,650,000. The remaining book value is the original cost minus accumulated depreciation over the first five years, or the asset's remaining depreciation at time of disposal. So,

FIGURE 10.5

Operating Cash Flow for Bottled Pulsar Cola				
	Year 2	Year 3	Year 4	Year 5
Revenue	$12,000,000	$12,000,000	$12,000,000	$12,000,000
Cost of goods sold	$ 3,000,000	$ 3,000,000	$ 3,000,000	$ 3,000,000
Fixed costs	$ 1,500,000	$ 1,500,000	$ 1,500,000	$ 1,500,000
Selling, general, and administrative expenses	$ 3,000,000	$ 3,000,000	$ 3,000,000	$ 3,000,000
Depreciation	$ 942,865	$ 673,365	$ 480,865	$ 343,805
EBIT	$ 3,557,135	$ 3,826,635	$ 4,019,135	$ 4,156,195
Taxes	$ 1,422,854	$ 1,530,654	$ 1,607,654	$ 1,662,478
Net income	**$ 2,134,281**	**$ 2,295,981**	**$ 2,411,481**	**$ 2,493,717**
Add back depreciation	$ 942,865	$ 673,365	$ 480,865	$ 343,805
Operating cash flow	$ 3,077,146	$ 2,969,346	$ 2,892,346	$ 2,837,522

$$\text{cola-syrup mixing machine book value} = \$2{,}200{,}000 - \$1{,}709{,}180 = \$490{,}820$$
$$\text{water filtering machine book value} = \$1{,}650{,}000 - \$1{,}281{,}885 = \$368{,}115$$

See Table 10.6 for the accumulated depreciation costs.

If an asset's disposal value is less than its current book value, a loss on disposal occurs. If an asset's disposal value is greater than its current book value, a gain on disposal occurs. Here we have both.

- We calculate the cash flow at disposal for the cola-syrup mixing machine as the $25,000 disposal plus the tax credit on the loss:

$$\text{tax loss} = \text{book value} - \text{disposal revenue}$$
$$\text{loss on disposal for cola-syrup mixing machine} = \$490{,}820 - \$25{,}000$$
$$= \$465{,}820$$
$$\text{tax credit} = \$465{,}820 \times 0.4 = \$186{,}328$$
$$\text{total cash flow at disposal} = \$25{,}000 + \$186{,}328 = \$211{,}328$$

  The tax credit is a reduction in taxes that Cogswell Cola pays.

- We calculate the cash flow at disposal for the water filtering machine as the $500,000 selling value minus the tax on the gain at disposal:

TABLE 10.6 Depreciation of Equipment for Cogswell Cola

Year	Cola-Syrup Mixing Machine	Water Filtering Machine
1	$2,200,000 × 0.1429 = $314,380	$1,650,000 × 0.1429 = $235,785
2	$2,200,000 × 0.2449 = $538,780	$1,650,000 × 0.2449 = $404,085
3	$2,200,000 × 0.1749 = $384,780	$1,650,000 × 0.1749 = $288,585
4	$2,200,000 × 0.1249 = $274,780	$1,650,000 × 0.1249 = $206,085
5	$2,200,000 × 0.0893 = $196,460	$1,650,000 × 0.0893 = $147,345
Total to date	$1,709,180	$1,281,885

$$\text{tax gain} = \text{selling price} - \text{book value}$$

$$\text{gain on disposal for water filtering machine} = \$500{,}000 - \$368{,}115 = \$131{,}885$$

$$\text{tax} = \$131{,}885 \times 0.4 = \$52{,}754$$

$$\text{total cash flow at disposal} = \$500{,}000 - \$52{,}754 = \$447{,}246$$

We can now put together all the incremental cash flows of the flavored-cola project for Cogswell Cola.

4. **Evaluate the proposed project using the NPV model.** The bottom line of Table 10.7 shows the appropriate after-tax incremental cash flow that we will use in making the decision as to whether to launch Pulsar Cola. We know from Chapter 9 that the NPV model is the preferred decision model. We will assume a 15% discount rate for this capital project and calculate the NPV of Pulsar Cola as follows:

$$NPV = -\$4{,}000{,}000 + \frac{\$2{,}920{,}066}{1.15} + \frac{\$3{,}077{,}146}{1.15^2} + \frac{\$2{,}969{,}346}{1.15^3} + \frac{\$2{,}892{,}346}{1.15^4} + \frac{\$3{,}646{,}101}{1.15^5} = \$6{,}284{,}810$$

Therefore, we recommend a "go" for the flavored-cola project using these incremental cash flows and the net present value decision model ($NPV > 0$).

The advantage of placing a project's incremental cash flow into a table is that we can easily pull the numbers into a spreadsheet and have the spreadsheet calculate the project's NPV, IRR, or MIRR. Entering the data in the spreadsheet is a simple task. We have noted the years in row one (T_0 through T_5) just for illustration. Figure 10.6 shows the spreadsheet application for Pulsar Cola.

First, we calculate the NPV by using the NPV function. Recall that you calculate the present value of cash flows from T_1 to T_5 with the discount rate in B9 and then subtract the initial capital investment at T_0. We find the value for the IRR by using the IRR function and the incremental cash flows for T_0 to T_5 [IRR (B7:G7)]. We can find the MIRR with the same cash flows and the reinvestment and discount rate of 15% from B9 [MIRR (B7:G7, B9, B9)].

The six financial decision models that you studied in Chapter 9 are valid only if one has the proper incremental cash flow for the project under consideration. The building of a project's incremental cash flow is the cornerstone of these models. The output of the capital budgeting decision models is only as good as the inputs that go into them.

You have now arrived at a point where you can synthesize the principles from previous chapters to make sound financial decisions, but there is one more tool that you will need. All along, we have provided you with the discount rate for the investments

TABLE 10.7 Incremental Cash Flow of Pulsar Cola

	T_0	T_1	T_2	T_3	T_4	T_5
Capital spending	−3,850,000					
Change in net working capital	−150,000					150,000
Operating cash flow		2,920,066	3,077,146	2,969,346	2,892,346	2,837,527
Salvage value						211,328
Filtering salvage value						447,246
Bottling incremental cash flow	−4,000,000	2,920,066	3,077,146	2,969,346	2,892,346	3,646,101

B10	*fx* =NPV(B9,C7:G7) + B7					
Using the incremental cash flow in the table of values and the NPV, IRR, and MIRR functions.						

	A	B	C	D	E	F	G
1		T_0	T_1	T_2	T_3	T_4	T_5
2	Capital Investment	($3,850,000.00)					
3	Change in Net Working Capital	($ 150,000.00)					$ 150,000.00
4	Operating Cash Flow		$2,920,066.00	$3,077,146.00	$2,969,346.00	$2,892,346.00	$2,837,527.00
5	Salvage of Syrup Machine						$ 211,328.00
6	Salvage of Filter Machine						$ 447,246.00
7	Incremental Cash Flow	($4,000,000.00)	$2,920,066.00	$3,077,146.00	$2,969,346.00	$2,892,346.00	$3,646,101.00
8							
9	Rate	0.15					
10	NPV	$ 6,284,810.29					
11	IRR	69.79%					
12	MIRR	38.91%					

FIGURE 10.6 Spreadsheet application for Pulsar Cola: Calculating NPV, IRR, and MIRR.

you have studied. For example, we gave you the discount rate of 15% earlier to calculate Pulsar Cola project's NPV. However, discount rates do not just fall out of the blue. How do we determine them? We answer that question in the next chapter.

To review this chapter, see the Summary Card at the end of the text.

Key Terms

book value, p. 310
cash flow, p. 298
depreciation, p. 306
erosion costs, p. 301
incremental cash flow, p. 299
modified accelerated cost recovery system (MACRS), p. 306
operating cash flow (OCF), p. 299
opportunity costs, p. 300
profits, p. 298
straight-line depreciation, p. 306
sunk costs, p. 300
synergy gains, p. 303

Questions

1. How is cash flow different from profit or net income?
2. Why is depreciation expense added back to the net income of a company to find the operating cash flow?
3. Why are owners of a business interested only in incremental cash flow for a project and not the total cash flow of a project?

4. Why are sunk costs excluded from the incremental cash flow of a project? Does that mean they were wasted expenses? Why or why not?
5. Give an example of an erosion cost. Explain why this cost is part of the incremental cash flow of a project. Is there a case in which a new product should get credit for additional revenue of another already existing product?
6. Give an example of an opportunity cost and explain how you would estimate the cost as it applies to a particular project.
7. Why must a company typically invest in working capital when starting a new project? Why is this investment in working capital recovered at the completion of the project?
8. How does depreciation spread the capital expenditure of a project over the life of the capital asset? Why is using MACRS usually beneficial to a company versus using straight-line depreciation?
9. Why is there typically a tax gain or tax loss at the disposal of capital assets?
10. All six decision models from Chapter 9 rely on the appropriate timing and amount of cash flow. What potential errors can a manager make if this information is not accurate?

Prepping for Exams

1. A major metric of a company's health and its prospects for a long life is how much ______________ it can generate.
   a. cash flow
   b. depreciation
   c. tax deferral
   d. net income

2. The revenue is $24,000, the cost of goods sold is $12,000, other expenses (from selling and administration) are $6,000, and depreciation is $2,000. What is the EBIT?
   a. $12,000
   b. $6,000
   c. $4,000
   d. $2,000

3. ______________ involve(s) a cash flow that never occurs, but we need to add it as a cost or outflow of a new project.
   a. Cost recovery of divested assets
   b. Capital expenditures
   c. Sunk costs
   d. Opportunity costs

4. Which of the statements below is *true*?
   a. The increase in working capital accounts necessary to support a project also provides for cost increases at the end of the project.
   b. An increase in working capital can be brought about by an increase in inventory or accounts receivable.
   c. Decreases in accounts receivable constitute a use of cash flow because you are helping your customers finance their purchases.
   d. Decreases in accounts payable constitute a source of cash flow because you are using your suppliers to help finance your business operations.

5. A firm is considering purchasing two assets. Asset A will have a useful life of fifteen years and cost $3 million. It will have installation costs of $400,000, but no salvage or residual value. Asset B will have a useful life of six years and cost $1.3 million. It will have installation costs of $180,000 and a salvage or residual value of $300,000. Which asset will have a greater annual straight-line depreciation?
   - **a.** Asset A has $30,000 more in depreciation per year.
   - **b.** Asset A has $40,000 more in depreciation per year.
   - **c.** Asset B has $30,000 more in depreciation per year.
   - **d.** Asset B has $40,000 more in depreciation per year.

6. The advantage of MACRS over straight-line depreciation is that you can write off more of your capital costs in the ____________ year(s).
   - **a.** first
   - **b.** last
   - **c.** later
   - **d.** earlier

7. Anthony, Ltd. purchases a duplicating machine for $15,000. This machine qualifies as a five-year recovery asset under MACRS. The company has a tax rate of 33%. If the company sells the machine at the end of four years for $4,000, what is the cash flow from disposal?
   - **a.** $3,535.36
   - **b.** $3,408.22
   - **c.** $2,592.00
   - **d.** $1,408.00

8. Which is *not* a step in the estimation of after-tax cash flow at disposal?
   - **a.** If selling price is greater than book value: selling price − tax on gain.
   - **b.** If selling price is less than book value: selling price + tax credit on loss.
   - **c.** If book value is less than selling price: selling price + tax credit on loss.
   - **d.** If selling price equals book value: selling price.

9. If we know the ____________ and the EBIT, we can estimate the taxes for a project for the year.
   - **a.** MACRS percentage
   - **b.** sunk costs
   - **c.** tax rate
   - **d.** salvage value

10. The building of the project's ________ cash flow is the cornerstone of the financial decision models.
    - **a.** depreciation
    - **b.** incremental
    - **c.** accounting
    - **d.** tax

Problems

These problems are available in MyFinanceLab.

1. ***Erosion costs.*** Fat Tire Bicycle Company currently sells 40,000 bicycles per year. The current bike is a standard balloon tire bike selling for $90, with a production and shipping cost of $35. The company is thinking of introduc-

ing an off-road bike with a projected selling price of $410 and a production and shipping cost of $360. The projected annual sales for the off-road bike are 12,000. The company will lose sales in fat-tire bikes of 8,000 units per year if it introduces the new bike, however. What is the erosion cost from the new bike? Should Fat Tire start producing the off-road bike?

2. ***Erosion costs.*** Heavenly Cookie Company reports the following annual sales and costs for its current product line:

	Chocolate Chip	Snicker-doodle	Peanut Butter	Lemon Drop	Cream-Filled
Volume	240,000	180,000	130,000	78,000	92,000
Price	$0.49	$0.49	$0.49	$0.49	$0.59
Cost	$0.19	$0.17	$0.15	$0.22	$0.31

Heavenly is thinking of adding Mississippi Mud brownies to the product line. The ultra-rich brownies would sell for $0.99 a piece and cost $0.81 to produce. The forecasted brownie volume is 250,000 per year. Introduction of brownies, however, will reduce cookie sales by 250,000 with the following drop in sales per cookie: 130,000 in chocolate chip, 60,000 in snickerdoodle, 40,000 in peanut butter, 10,000 in lemon drop, and 10,000 in cream-filled. What is the erosion cost of introducing the brownies? What is the net change in annual margin if Mississippi Mud brownies are added to the product line?

3. ***Opportunity cost.*** Revolution Records will build a new recording studio on a vacant lot next to the operations center. The land was purchased five years ago for $450,000. Today, the value of the land has appreciated to $780,000. Revolutionary Records did not consider the value of the land in its NPV calculations for the studio project (it had already spent the money to acquire the land long before this project was considered). The NPV of the recording studio is $600,000. Should Revolution Records have considered the land as part of the cash flow of the recording studio? If yes, what value should be used, $450,000 or $780,000? How will the value affect the project?

4. ***Opportunity cost.*** Richards Tree Farm Inc. has branched into gardening over the years and is now considering adding patio furniture to its product lineup. Currently, the area where the patio furniture is to be displayed is a vacant slab of concrete attached to the indoor shop. The company originally paid $8,500 to put in the slab of concrete three years ago. It would now cost $12,000 to put in the same slab of concrete. Should Richards consider the concrete slab when expanding its outdoor garden shop to include patio furniture? If yes, which value should it use?

5. ***Working capital cash flow.*** Cool Water Inc. sells bottled water. The firm keeps in inventory plastic bottles at 10% of the monthly projected sales. These plastic bottles cost $0.005 each. The monthly sales for the coming year are as follows:

January: 2,000,000
February: 2,200,000
March: 2,700,000
April: 3,000,000
May: 3,600,000
June: 5,500,000
July: 7,000,000
August: 9,000,000
September: 6,000,000
October: 4,000,000
November: 2,500,000
December: 1,300,000
January one year out: 2,200,000.

Show the anticipated cost of plastic bottles each month for these projected sales, the beginning inventory volume and ending inventory volume each month, and the monthly increase or decrease in cash flow for inventory given that an increase is a use of cash and a decrease is a source of cash.

6. ***Working capital cash flow.*** Tires for Less is a franchise of tire stores throughout the greater Northwest. It has projected the following unit sales per tire and costs of tires for the coming year:

	Snow Tires	Rain Tires	All-Terrain Tires	All-Purpose Tires
Cost per tire	$ 42	$ 31	$ 48	$ 37
Sales: Jan.	$44,000	$20,000	$ 4,000	$60,000
Sales: Feb.	$38,000	$36,000	$ 5,000	$54,000
Sales: Mar.	$14,000	$46,000	$ 7,000	$50,000
Sales: Apr.	$ 2,000	$22,000	$ 8,000	$60,000
Sales: May	$ 0	$40,000	$12,000	$65,000
Sales: Jun.	$ 0	$20,000	$30,000	$68,000
Sales: Jul.	$ 0	$ 2,000	$39,000	$75,000
Sales: Aug.	$ 0	$ 2,000	$22,000	$80,000
Sales: Sep.	$ 0	$ 2,000	$ 8,000	$70,000
Sales: Oct.	$ 0	$14,000	$ 2,000	$70,000
Sales: Nov.	$16,000	$18,000	$ 1,000	$65,000
Sales: Dec.	$82,000	$20,000	$ 3,000	$60,000
Sales: Jan.	$48,000	$22,000	$ 5,000	$60,000

The company policy is to have the next month's anticipated sales for each tire type in the warehouse. Shipments are made to the various stores throughout the Northwest from the central warehouse. Show the anticipated cost of tires each month for these projected sales by tire type, the beginning inventory volume and ending inventory volume each month for each tire, and the monthly increase or decrease in cash flow for inventory given that an increase is a use of cash and a decrease is a source of cash. Find the total cost of goods sold and the change in monthly working capital cash flow for all tires. What do you notice about the working capital change when you combine the cash flow of all four tires?

7. ***Depreciation expense.*** Brock Florist Company buys a new delivery truck for $29,000. It is classified as a light-duty truck.
   a. Calculate the depreciation schedule using a five-year life, straight-line depreciation, and the half-year convention for the first and last years.
   b. Calculate the depreciation schedule using a five-year life and MACRS depreciation.
   c. Compare the depreciation schedules from parts (a) and (b) before and after taxes using a 30% tax rate. What do you notice about the difference between these two methods?

8. ***Depreciation expense.*** Richards Tree Farm Inc. has just purchased a new aerial tree trimmer for $91,000. Calculate the depreciation schedule using the property class category of a single-purpose agricultural and horticultural structure (from Table 10.3) for both straight-line depreciation and MACRS.

Use the half-year convention for both methods. Compare the depreciation schedules before and after taxes using a 40% tax rate. What do you notice about the difference between these two methods?

9. ***Cost recovery.*** Brock Florist Company sold its delivery truck (see Problem 7) after three years of service. If MACRS was used for the depreciation schedule, what is the after-tax cash flow from the sale of the truck (continue to use a 30% tax rate) if

a. the sales price was $15,000?

b. the sales price was $10,000?

c. the sales price was $5,000?

10. ***Cost recovery.*** Jake Richards sold the tree trimmer (see Problem 8) after four years of service. If MACRS was used for the depreciation schedule, what is the after-tax cash flow from the sale of the trimmer (continue to use a 40% tax rate) if

a. the sales price was $35,000?

b. the sales price was $28,428.40?

c. the sales price was $21,000?

11. ***Operating cash flow.*** Grady Precision Measurement Tools has forecasted the following sales and costs for a new GPS system: annual sales of 48,000 units at $18 a unit, production costs at 37% of sales price, annual fixed costs for production at $180,000, and straight-line depreciation expense of $240,000 per year. The company tax rate is 35%. What is the annual operating cash flow of the new GPS system?

12. ***Operating cash flow.*** Huffman Systems has forecasted sales for its new home alarm systems to be 63,000 units per year at $38.50 per unit. The cost to produce each unit is expected to be about 42% of the sales price. The new product will have an additional $494,000 fixed costs each year, and the manufacturing equipment will have an initial cost of $2,400,000 and will be depreciated over eight years (straight line). The company tax rate is 40%. What is the annual operating cash flow for the alarm systems if the projected sales and price per unit are constant over the next eight years?

13. ***NPV.*** Using the operating cash flow information from Problem 11, determine whether Grady Precision Measurement Tools should add the GPS system to its set of products. The initial investment is $1,440,000 and is depreciated over six years (straight line) and will be sold at the end of five years for $380,000. The cost of capital is 10%, and the tax rate is still 35%.

14. ***NPV.*** Using the operating cash flow information from Problem 12, determine whether Huffman Systems should add the new home alarm system to its set of products. The manufacturing equipment will be sold off at the end of eight years for $210,000, and the cost of capital for this project is 14%.

15. ***Operating cash flow (growing each year; MACRS).*** Mathews Mining Company is looking at a project that has the following forecasted sales: first-year sales are 6,800 units and will grow at 15% over the next four years (a five-year project). The price of the product will start at $124 per unit and increase each year at 5%. The production costs are expected to be 62% of the current year's sales price. The manufacturing equipment to aid this project will have a total cost (including installation) of $1,400,000. It will be depreciated using MACRS and has a seven-year MACRS life classification. Fixed costs will be $50,000 per year. Mathews Mining has a tax rate of 30%. What is the operating cash flow for this project over these five years? *Hint:* Use a spreadsheet.

16. ***Operating cash flow (growing each year; MACRS).*** Miglietti Restaurants is looking at a project with the following forecasted sales: first-year sales quantity of 31,000 with an annual growth rate of 3.5% over the next ten years. The sales price per unit is $42.00 and will grow at 2.25% per year. The production costs are expected to be 55% of the current year's sales price. The manufacturing equipment to aid this project will have a total cost (including installation) of $2,400,000. It will be depreciated using MACRS and has a seven-year MACRS life classification. Fixed costs are $335,000 per year. Miglietti Restaurants has a tax rate of 30%. What is the operating cash flow for this project over these ten years? *Hint:* Use a spreadsheet.
17. ***NPV.*** Using the operating cash flow information from Problem 15, find the NPV of the project for Mathews Mining if the manufacturing equipment can be sold for $80,000 at the end of the five-year project and the cost of capital for this project is 12%. *Hint:* Use a spreadsheet.
18. ***NPV.*** Using the operating cash flow information from Problem 16, find the NPV of the project for Miglietti Restaurants if the manufacturing equipment can be sold for $140,000 at the end of the ten-year project and the cost of capital for this project is 8%. *Hint:* Use a spreadsheet.
19. ***Project cash flow and NPV.*** The managers of Classic Autos Incorporated plan to manufacture classic Thunderbirds (1957 replicas). The necessary foundry equipment will cost a total of $4,000,000 and will be depreciated using a five-year MACRS life. Projected sales in annual units for the next five years are 300 per year. If sales price is $27,000 per car, variable costs are $18,000 per car, and fixed costs are $1,200,000 annually, what is the annual operating cash flow if the tax rate is 30%? The equipment is sold for salvage for $500,000 at the end of year five. What is the after-tax cash flow of the salvage? Net working capital increases by $600,000 at the beginning of the project (year 0) and is reduced back to its original level in the final year. What is the incremental cash flow of the project? Using a discount rate of 12% for the project, determine whether the project should be accepted or rejected according to the NPV decision model.
20. ***Project cash flow and NPV.*** The sales manager has a new estimate for the sale of the classic Thunderbirds in Problem 19. The annual sales volume will be as follows:

    Year one: 240 Year four: 360
    Year two: 280 Year five: 280
    Year three: 340

    Rework the cash flow for operating cash flow with these new sales estimates and find the internal rate of return for the project using the incremental cash flow.

Advanced Problems for Spreadsheet Application

These problems are available in MyFinanceLab.

1. ***Erosion costs.*** Ice Cream City plans to introduce a new flavor, wild berry, to its current set of five flavors, which include vanilla, French vanilla, strawberry, chocolate, and mint chocolate. The new sales of wild berry are projected as follows:

Year	1	2	3	4	5	6	7	8	9
Units	$130,000	$145,000	$167,000	$192,000	$210,000	$230,000	$235,000	$230,000	$230,000

The expected sales will come from both new customers and current customers switching flavors. The current projected sales for the existing flavors (assuming no introduction of the new flavor) are:

Projected Sales

Year	1	2	3	4	5	6	7	8	9
Vanilla	$300,000	$300,000	$300,000	$320,000	$320,000	$320,000	$350,000	$350,000	$350,000
F-Van	$105,000	$110,000	$115,000	$115,000	$115,000	$120,000	$120,000	$120,000	$120,000
Straw	$230,000	$235,000	$245,000	$250,000	$260,000	$270,000	$280,000	$290,000	$300,000
Choc	$320,000	$330,000	$340,000	$350,000	$360,000	$360,000	$360,000	$360,000	$360,000
M-Choc	$160,000	$165,000	$170,000	$170,000	$175,000	$175,000	$180,000	$180,000	$185,000

However, if the company introduces wild berry, it will cut into the sales units of the original flavors based on the following estimates:

Percentage of Sales Erosion

Year	1	2	3	4	5	6	7	8	9
Vanilla	0.05	0.05	0.04	0.04	0.03	0.03	0.02	0.02	0.01
F-Van	0.025	0.025	0.02	0.01	0.00	0.00	0.00	0.00	0.00
Straw	0.45	0.40	0.35	0.30	0.25	0.25	0.25	0.25	0.25
Choc	0.15	0.10	0.05	0.00	0.00	0.00	0.00	0.00	0.00
M-Choc	0.025	0.02	0.01	0.00	0.00	0.00	0.00	0.00	0.00

Here are the revenue and cost per unit of ice cream for Ice Cream City:

Vanilla: current revenue $3.05 per unit and cost of $1.22 per unit

French vanilla: current revenue $3.15 per unit and cost of $1.38 per unit

Strawberry: current revenue $3.25 per unit and cost of $1.41 per unit

Chocolate: current revenue $3.25 per unit and cost of $1.57 per unit

Mint chocolate: current revenue $3.25 per unit and cost of $1.63 per unit

Wild berry: projected revenue $3.25 per unit and cost of $1.44 per unit

Find the annual erosion of revenue, the cost savings, and the net cash flow with the new ice cream.

2. ***Working capital impact on project.*** iCovers Incorporated wants to make covers for all the products that Apple manufactures. The company is looking at new covers for the iPhone, iPad, iPalm, iThumb, and the iEye. The initial investment in capital equipment will cost $10,000,000. The projected revenues and costs are:

	1	2	3	4	5	6
Revenue	$10,000,000	$13,000,000	$17,000,000	$23,000,000	$18,000,000	$12,000,000
Variable	$ 4,000,000	$ 5,200,000	$ 6,800,000	$ 9,200,000	$ 7,200,000	$ 4,800,000
Fixed	$ 1,500,000	$ 1,500,000	$ 1,500,000	$ 1,500,000	$ 1,500,000	$ 1,500,000
S,G & A	$ 1,250,000	$ 1,400,000	$ 1,750,000	$ 2,000,000	$ 2,000,000	$ 1,500,000

An initial investment in working capital is $2,000,000. However, working capital will increase or decrease each year so that it is always 20% of the anticipated revenue for the coming year. The equipment will depreciate as a five-year asset class asset using MACRS and there is no salvage value for the equipment at the end of the six-year project. The tax rate for iCovers is 37%.

Using a spreadsheet, set up the project's incremental cash flows showing the initial outlay (both capital and working capital), the operating cash flow each year, and the change in working capital each year. Note that the company will terminate the project in year six. Then, calculate the project's IRR and the NPV if the project's discount rate is 14%.

Mini-Case

BioCom, Inc.: Part 2, Evaluating a New Product Line

This mini-case is available in MyFinanceLab.

BioCom, Inc. is weighing a proposal to manufacture and market a fiber-optic device that will continuously monitor blood pressure during cardiovascular surgery and other medical procedures in which precise, real-time measurements are critical. The device will continuously transmit information to a computer via a thin fiber-optic cable and display measurements on several large monitors in view of operating room personnel. It will also store the data and display it graphically for review during or after procedures. BioCom would market various versions of the device, but manufacture all of them in the same facility using the same equipment. They would have similar markups and cost structures. If management decides to bring this device to market, BioCom will stop selling an earlier, less sophisticated version of the monitor. The product that BioCom will discontinue now contributes about $1,650,000 per year to operating cash flow, and projected sales are flat. BioCom focuses exclusively on cutting-edge applications, so it expects to discontinue the new monitor after five years. At that time, it will sell the technology and used manufacturing equipment to a foreign company for an estimated $2,400,000.

Cost analysts have collected the following figures and submitted them to the treasurer's office for additional study and a final decision on whether to proceed. You, as assistant to the treasurer, must compute and evaluate the basic capital budgeting criteria. The project will initially increase working capital by $480,000, which the company will recover at the end of the project when it sells remaining inventory and collects accounts receivable. The analysts are not quite sure if they should include $450,000 that the company already spent on research and development for the new product. They also disagree about whether the effect of the discontinued monitor on the company's overall operating cash flows is relevant to the decision on the new product line, so you must decide how to deal with these two items.

Cost of new plant and equipment	$24,000,000
Designs and prototypes	$ 450,000
Estimated salvage value of technology and equipment, end of year 5	$ 2,400,000
First-year sales forecast	$16,500,000
Projected annual rate of sales increases	6%
Cost of goods sold	40% of sales
Selling, general, and administrative expenses	5% of sales
Annual fixed cost	$600,000
Operating cash flow from current desk sales	$1,650,000
Economic life of the project	5 years
Initial change in net working capital	$480,000
Depreciation	5-year MACRS
Tax rate	34%
Discount rate = cost of capital	9%

Questions

1. What is the total relevant initial investment for BioCom's new product line? Would you include the designs and prototypes? Would you include the change in net working capital?
2. What is the cash flow resulting from disposal of the equipment at the end of the project?
3. Compute a schedule of depreciation for the plant and equipment.
4. Compute a schedule of operating cash flows for BioCom's new product.
5. Compute a schedule of incremental cash flows for BioCom's new product.
6. Compute the project's net present value.
7. Does your answer to Question 6 indicate that management should accept or reject the product?
8. **Challenge question**. Use a spreadsheet for this question.
   - **a.** Recompute your answers to Questions 4 through 7 assuming that sales grow at 12% per year.
   - **b.** Recompute your answers to Questions 4 through 7 assuming that sales grow at 0% per year.
   - **c.** Comment on the sensitivity of the NPV to the growth rate of sales.

Learning Objectives

LO1 Understand the different kinds of financing available to a company: debt financing, equity financing, and hybrid equity financing.

LO2 Understand the debt and equity components of the weighted average cost of capital (WACC) and explain the tax implications on debt financing and the adjustment to the WACC.

LO3 Calculate the weights of the components using book values or market values.

LO4 Explain how the capital budgeting models use WACC.

LO5 Determine a project's beta and its implications in capital budgeting problems.

LO6 Select optimal project combinations from a company's portfolio of acceptable projects.

Chapter 11
The Cost of Capital

When a company raises capital for its projects, it has a number of choices for the funding sources. Most companies will choose some combination of debt and equity. Each different financing source will present a different cost of capital, or required return. In this chapter, we examine how to calculate these various costs or rates and how to use the proportional percent financed from each source to come up with an overall cost of capital for the company, a rate that we call the weighted average cost of capital (WACC). We will continue to refine our financial tool kit by using tools from previous chapters to calculate components of the WACC. We will see that the discount rate in the NPV decision model, as well as the hurdle rate in the IRR model, is the weighted average cost of capital.

It may be useful to step back and look again at the big picture. In Chapter 9, you learned how to evaluate a capital budgeting project using a model such as net present value (NPV). We gave you both the project's future cash flows and the discount rate. In Chapter 10, you estimated the future cash flows, but we still gave you the discount rate. In this chapter, we will put the final tool in place by learning how to estimate the appropriate discount rate for the capital budgeting decision.

11.1 The Cost of Capital: A Starting Point

What is the cost of capital? The **cost of capital** is the cost of each financing component that the firm uses to fund its projects multiplied by that component's percent of the total funding amount. So, the very first question we want to ask is: From what sources can a company raise money?

Sources of funds include the following:

1. Commercial banks
2. Nonbank lenders
3. Owners of the company (common stockholders)
4. Preferred stockholders
5. Suppliers
6. The company itself, that is, the cash flow from operations

By looking closely at the list, we can see that these sources are the same individuals and institutions that have claims against the company: the firm's liability and equity accounts from the right side of the balance sheet. We will group together the liability accounts and simply call these sources *debt financing*. We will group together the owners' equity accounts, preferred shareholders, common shareholders, and retained earnings and call these sources *equity financing*. The choice of the various financing components of debt and equity makes up the firm's **capital structure**. In other words, capital structure refers to the way in which a company finances itself through some combination of loans, bond sales, preferred stock sales, common stock sales, and retention of earnings. Let's break down this concept into a bit more detail.

1. *Debt financing*. When a company borrows from a bank or sells bonds, we call it **debt financing**. We label this cost component R_d. A company will borrow money from banks in the form of loans or from individuals or other institutions by selling corporate bonds to them. The banks and the bond holders then become creditors of the company. Although it is a great simplification of the cost of debt, we typically look only at the company's long-term debt. We should include all the company's liabilities as part of the debt component. Besides these usual examples of bond sales and bank loans, money that the company owes suppliers also comes under the umbrella of debt financing. When a company orders supplies from a supplier but will pay for them at a later date, the company is, in effect, borrowing from the supplier. The company will eventually pay, but in the short term, the company books the transaction as an account payable, a debt of the company. When we calculate the cost of capital, we should include accounts payable. For simplicity, though, we usually focus on just the long-term debt, which is typically the overwhelming portion of debt financing.

2. *Equity financing*. When a company acquires capital by selling common stock or using internal funds, we call it **equity financing**. Common stockholders invest in the company with the anticipation that the company will provide a return over the initial contribution, either through dividend payments or through increasing stock prices. We label this cost component R_e, and it comprises two types: the cost of paid-in equity from the common shareholders and the cost of equity from using the company's retained and reinvested cash derived from earnings.

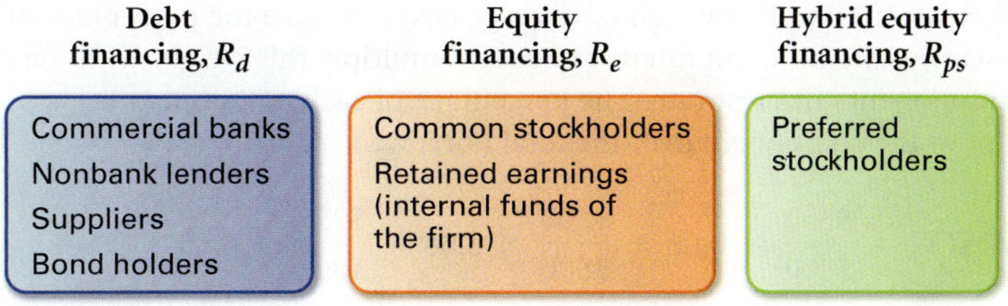

FIGURE 11.1 Component sources of capital.

3. *Hybrid equity financing.* When a company sells preferred stock, it is a hybrid form of equity financing. We label this cost component R_{ps}. It is a hybrid form of equity financing because we treat it like debt in terms of payment, with the annual dividend at a set rate like coupon payments on a bond. However, we also treat it like equity in that the company typically does not repay the principal. In addition, it does not have voting rights like common stock, although some preferred stock may eventually convert to common stock at a later date and therefore convert to a voting share. So, we consider it somewhere between debt financing and equity financing and call it **hybrid equity financing** to illustrate these features.

Figure 11.1 displays these three component sources of capital. We will associate a different cost of capital with each of these three financing components—debt, equity, and hybrid equity. The **weighted average cost of capital (WACC)** is the average of the costs of these financing sources weighted by the portion of the funds and is the cost of capital for the firm as a whole. Before we detail the WACC components and present the WACC formula, let's examine an intuitive example of the WACC, in which we use different sources of debt for a project.

EXAMPLE 11.1 The weighted average cost of capital

Problem Stan wants to buy a new lawn mower and start a grass cutting service in his neighborhood. Unfortunately, he does not have the required $800 for the new lawn mower, so he begins to ask his family and friends to invest in his new business. If they lend him money today, he will repay it, with interest, at the end of the year. Stan's mom says she will give him $350, but she wants repayment at 6% interest. Kyle, a friend, will loan Stan $200 but wants repayment at 8% interest. Chef, a business mentor, will loan Stan the remaining $250 but wants repayment at 12% interest. What is the cost of the $800 capital that Stan raised? What is the weighted average cost of this capital?

Solution The three different lenders require a different payment for their funds, and each lender provides a different amount. The total interest cost at the end of one year is

Mom's interest payment: $\$350 \times 0.06 = \$21.00$
Kyle's interest payment: $\$200 \times 0.08 = \$16.00$
Chef's interest payment: $\$250 \times 0.12 = \$30.00$
Total interest payments: $\$21.00 + \$16.00 + \$30.00 = \$67.00$

$$\text{Weighted average cost: } \frac{\$67.00}{\$800.00} = \mathbf{8.38\%}$$

Another way to find this weighted average cost is to take the percentage of each borrowing at the different interest rates and multiply this weight with the cost of that component's interest rate. The percentage of each component is just the loan amount of the component over the total borrowed:

$$\textbf{WACC} = \frac{\$350}{\$800} \times 0.06 + \frac{\$200}{\$800} \times 0.08 + \frac{\$250}{\$800} \times 0.12$$

$$= 0.4375 \times 0.06 + 0.25 \times 0.08 + 0.3125 \times 0.12$$

$$= 0.0263 + 0.0200 + 0.0375 = \mathbf{0.0838} \quad \text{or} \quad \mathbf{8.38\%}$$

Notice that the weights always add up to 1, or 100%, of the borrowed funds.

Finding the cost of capital helps Stan evaluate whether buying a new lawn mower and starting a neighborhood lawn-mowing service is a good business decision. If Stan anticipates the cash inflow over the year for the service to be $1,000 after all the operating costs, should he borrow the money, buy the lawn mower, and start the business?

The NPV approach tells Stan the answer. We can see that at the 8.38% cost of capital, it is yes:

$$NPV = -\$800.00 + \frac{\$1{,}000.00}{1.0838} = -\$800.00 + \$922.68 = \$122.68$$

The NPV is positive, so accept.

Using our IRR approach, the answer is again yes:

$$IRR\text{: } 0 = -\$800 + \frac{\$1{,}000.00}{1 + r}$$

Solve for r:

$$IRR = 25\%$$

$$= 25\% > \text{cost of capital} = 8.38\%$$

The IRR is greater than the cost of capital, so accept.

In this deliberately simple example, we calculated the average cost of debt for Stan. If we wanted to have an equity component for this example, it would have been necessary for Stan to put up some of his own money for the lawn mower. In this instance, stock ownership would reside in one person, Stan. We would also need to determine the cost of the equity financing, that is, what return Stan would require for his personal contribution to the purchase of the lawn mower. As we progress through this chapter, we will add the equity component to the WACC and examine ways to calculate the cost of equity.

Let's now look more formally at the cost of three financing components: debt, preferred stock, and equity. We will look back at the bond's yield to maturity to determine the *cost of debt*. We will look back at the constant dividend model to determine the *cost of preferred stock*. We will look back at the security market line and the dividend growth model to determine the *cost of equity*. These familiar models will provide the individual component costs for debt, preferred stock, and equity borrowing.

11.2 Components of the Weighted Average Cost of Capital

Recall the capital budgeting decision models (specifically, the NPV and the IRR) from Chapter 9. Although we did not explicitly state it, we needed the WACC as an integral input into whether we accept or reject capital projects. For the NPV, the WACC is the appropriate **discount rate** in the model, the rate that we use to determine the present value of the future cash flows:

$$\text{NPV} = -\text{investment} + \sum_{t=1}^{n} \frac{\text{cash flow}_t}{(1 + \text{WACC})^t} \qquad \textbf{11.1}$$

For the IRR, it is the hurdle rate:

Accept project if IRR $>$ WACC.
Reject project if IRR $<$ WACC.

Now that we have established the importance of the cost of capital as determined through the WACC, let's look at the WACC's various components—debt, preferred stock, and equity—in more detail.

Debt Component

The **cost of debt** is the return the bank or bond holder demands on new borrowing. Put another way, it is the rate a company pays on its current debt, or the cost of debt money. If a company borrows money from a bank, venture capitalist, or other lending source via a loan, the quote for the interest rate on the loan is R_d. Similarly, if a company borrows money by selling bonds, the yield to maturity (YTM) on the bonds is the cost of the bond, also R_d.

You have already studied the bond's yield to maturity. For a bond with annual coupon payments,

$$\text{price} = \text{par value} \times \frac{1}{(1 + YTM)^n} + \text{coupon} \times \frac{1 - [1/(1 + YTM)^n]}{YTM} \qquad \textbf{11.2}$$

The YTM is the cost of debt financing, R_d. It is best to solve for the YTM with a financial calculator or spreadsheet.

EXAMPLE 11.2 The cost of debt

Problem Stan has come a long way since his grass-cutting business. He now owns Stan's Plant and Tree Nursery and needs to raise $4 million for a major company expansion. Stan decides to sell a semiannual coupon bond with a coupon rate of 8%, a par value of $1,000, and a maturity of ten years. He receives $920 per bond. What is the yield of this bond? What is the cost of debt for Stan?

Solution The yield to maturity of this bond is the cost of debt.

We solve for the YTM via the Texas Instrument BA II Plus, using the TVM keys and the known variables of price, maturity date, coupon rate, and par value:

Mode: P/Y = 2 and C/Y = 2

Input	20	?	−920	40	1,000
Key	N	I/Y	PV	PMT	FV
CPT		**9.2430**			

The cost of debt for Stan's Plant and Tree Nursery is **9.243%**.

The solution to finding a bond's YTM is the cost of debt for borrowers selling bonds, but there is an important consideration: the bond's price in the marketplace and the sale's proceeds to the issuer are usually not the same. As we have seen, when a company issues a bond, it typically uses an investment banker to help with the sale. An investment banker facilitates the bond issuing and sale and receives a fee for the service. This fee is a reduction in the proceeds from the bond sale and the actual funds that the company selling the bond receives. Because the investment banker receives payment for his or her services, the *net proceeds* from the bond sale are the appropriate cash flow for determining the cost of debt. We call the costs to sell a security *flotation costs*, which apply to both debt and equity issues.

EXAMPLE 11.3 Net proceeds and the cost of debt capital

Problem Cartman Enterprises has hired Garrison Investment Bankers to help sell a new bond. The bond is a semiannual bond with a 6% coupon rate, $1,000 par value, and twenty years to maturity. Garrison Investment Bankers receives $25 compensation per bond sold. The bond sells in the market for $893. What is the cost of debt capital for Cartman Enterprises?

Solution The net proceeds from each bond is the market price minus the payment to the investment banker, $893 − $25 = $868. Using the net proceeds as the bond price, we solve for the YTM with the PV variable as the net proceeds to Cartman Enterprises, the market price minus commission to Garrison Bankers ($868), the coupon rate, the maturity date, and the par value using the TVM keys.

Mode: P/Y = 2 and C/Y = 2

Input	40	?	−868	30	1,000
Key	N	I/Y	PV	PMT	FV
CPT		**7.2614**			

The cost of debt for Cartman Enterprises is **7.2614%**.

The net proceeds determines the cost of the debt, not the bond's market price.

Preferred Stock Component

A second source of capital is from selling preferred stock. A quick review of the characteristics of preferred stock will reveal that the constant dividend model (Eq. 7.2) is a nice fit for the cash flow that a buyer of preferred stock can anticipate receiving. Preferred stock provides a constant cash dividend based on the preferred stock's original par value and the stated dividend rate. Because there is no maturity date on this kind of stock, the issuer does not anticipate repaying the stock's par value. Thus, preferred stock owners receive a perpetual constant dividend stream for their investment. Therefore, by rearranging the perpetuity model, we see that the **cost of preferred stock** is equal to the dividend divided by the price. Again, the price is the net price to the company for selling the preferred stock, not the market price. So,

$$\text{net price} = \frac{\text{dividend}}{R_{ps}} \qquad \textbf{11.3}$$

becomes

$$R_{ps} = \frac{\text{dividend}}{\text{net price}} \qquad \textbf{11.4}$$

EXAMPLE 11.4 Cost of preferred stock

Problem Cartman Enterprises will raise $2 million by selling preferred stock. The par value of the preferred stock is $100, and the annual dividend rate is 4%. A single share of Cartman Enterprises' preferred stock is currently selling for $38, with a flotation cost of $3 per share. What is the cost of capital?

Solution The annual dividend rate is 4%, so preferred shareholders will be receiving $4.00 ($100 × 0.04) annually as cash dividends. If a preferred shareholder paid $38 for this set of dividends and the company received $35 after paying the flotation cost of $3, the cost of this borrowing is

$$R_{ps} = \frac{\text{dividend}}{\text{net price}}$$

$$= \frac{\$4.00}{\$35.00} = \mathbf{0.1143} \quad \text{or} \quad \mathbf{11.43\%}$$

Again, as with bonds, the $35 for the preferred stock is the net proceeds to Cartman Enterprises, not the market price.

Equity Component

The third source of capital to consider is that of selling common stock. Investors buy shares at an *initial public offering* (IPO) of stock, a process that we will discuss in Chapter 15 on raising capital. Shareholders expect a positive return on their contribution of capital to the company, but in an uncertain stock market, just what is the expected return? There are two ways to determine the **cost of equity**, the rate of return that company shareholders require: the security market line

(SML), which we studied in Chapter 8; and the dividend growth model, which we studied in Chapter 7. We start with the SML, and use the expected return as the cost of equity, R_e.

The security market line approach to R_e Why is the expected return from the SML an appropriate cost of equity? The most direct answer is that potential shareholders have a large set of companies from which they can choose to invest. They will buy shares only in companies that provide an acceptable return for the perceived level of risk. Therefore, any company not "paying the going rate" will not attract potential investors. We determine the "going rate" by the riskiness of the future cash flow as measured by beta, the market risk premium, and the risk-free rate. The SML provides the required return for the level of risk, using beta as the measure of risk where *i* represents the individual stock's return and individual company's beta:

$$R_e = E(r_i) = r_f + [E(r_m) - r_f]\beta_i \qquad \textbf{11.5}$$

EXAMPLE 11.5 Cost of equity capital

Problem Kyle has a new business opportunity, but his company needs to raise an additional \$5,000,000 for the new project. Kyle wants to know the cost of this capital if he chooses to raise funds by selling common stock. He knows that the expected return on the market is 12% and the current risk-free rate is 3%. He also knows that his company and this project have a 0.8 beta.

Solution The market risk premium is the difference between the expected return on the market of 12% and the risk-free rate of 3%. Therefore, the cost of equity capital for any project with a beta of 0.8 is

$$R_e = E(r_i) = 0.03 + (0.12 - 0.03)0.8 = \mathbf{0.102} \quad \text{or} \quad \mathbf{10.2\%}$$

So, investors in Kyle's company will want an expected return of 10.2% on the stock that they buy.

The dividend growth model approach to R_e A second way to estimate the required return on equity is through the dividend growth model. Here we can rearrange the model and estimate R_e if we know the company's dividend pattern:

$$R_e = \frac{\text{Div}_0(1 + g)}{P_0} + g \qquad \textbf{11.6}$$

Here, Div_0 is the most recent dividend payment [recall that $\text{Div}_0 \times (1 + g) = \text{Div}_1$], g is the dividend stream's anticipated growth rate, and P_0 is the current stock price. A nice application of this model is that it is easy to include the flotation costs of a new equity issue. The formula adjusts to

$$R_e = \frac{\text{Div}_0(1 + g)}{P_0(1 - F)} + g \qquad \textbf{11.7}$$

where F is the flotation costs of the new issue as a percent of the stock's price.

Before we solve for the cost of equity with flotation costs, a quick word on the concept of flotation costs is warranted. **Flotation costs** are expenses that a company incurs when issuing stocks or bonds. Nearly all companies use an investment banker to help sell these issues, and, of course, the company must pay the investment banker for the services. Typically, the investment banker takes a cut from the sales price. So, the net cash flow to the company selling the stock or bond is the market price minus the flotation cost, or $P(1 - F)$, where the flotation cost is a percent of the sales price.

EXAMPLE 11.6 Cost of equity using the dividend growth model

Problem Kyle is still trying to raise $5,000,000 for his new project, and he has decided that he will issue additional common stock for the necessary funds. The current price of common stock is $15 per share, and the company has just paid a dividend of $0.70 per share with an anticipated growth rate of 3%. The company will issue new shares with a flotation cost of 6%. What is the cost of this new equity issue?

Solution First, we need to find D_1, the next dividend. It will be $0.70 × 1.03, or $0.721 per share. So, the cost of this equity is

$$R_f = \frac{\$0.721}{\$15 \times (1 - 0.06)} + 0.03 = \mathbf{0.0811} \text{ or } \mathbf{8.11\%}$$

In Example 11.5, using the SML, we saw that the cost of equity was 10.2%, but here in Example 11.6, using the dividend growth model, it is 8.11%. In fact, it is usual for the two different approaches to produce different R_e estimates. If data are available for both approaches, one technique is to average the two estimates. In this case, Kyle might use 9.155% for the cost of equity [(10.2% + 8.11%)/2]. Sometimes, based on your assessment of the data and reasonableness of the results, you will choose one method over the other. You may, however, base the approach of your choice on the availability of information and not necessarily on the best theoretical approach. For example, when a firm plans to issue capital for the very first time, it will not have a dividend history to use for the dividend model, so the only applicable approach is the SML approach.

Retained Earnings

Another potentially major equity source is the cash that the ongoing business generates itself and reinvests in the company. Because these retained earnings reflect the company's profit after it has satisfied all current liabilities, they technically belong to the public company's common stockholders. What cost should shareholders charge the company for using retained earnings to reinvest in the company on their behalf? Logically, it is the opportunity cost of capital for the shareholders if they were choosing to invest this capital into this or any other firm.

It may be best to illustrate the cost of retained earnings by examining its source and the distribution choice. When a company produces earnings, it has two choices: pay out the earnings to the owners in dividends or retain the earnings in the firm for reinvesting. Therefore, the **cost of retained earnings** is the loss of the dividend option for the owners. Now assume a company needs \$1 million for a new project. The company has just generated \$1 million in cash flow in the last business cycle. It can either "keep" the earnings to use in a new project or pay \$1 million out to the owners and then sell additional common stock to raise the needed \$1 million for the project. Therefore, the cost of keeping the retained earnings is the cost of issuing new stock. Retaining earnings, however, avoids the flotation costs of a new issue, so we will estimate the cost of using retained earnings as the cost of issuing new shares without flotation costs. We can estimate the cost of retained earnings with either the SML or the dividend growth model without an adjustment for flotation costs.

These three sources of capital—debt, preferred stock, and equity—are not the only sources of capital for a company. Again, firms indirectly "borrow" money from suppliers when they choose to pay for supplies at a later date; that is, they buy on credit. Because most of these other sources are relatively small amounts, standard practice is to look only at long-term debt, preferred stock, and common stock (which includes cash from operations that the firm retains) as the WACC components.

The debt component and taxes When we introduced estimating incremental cash flow in Chapter 10, we noted that we needed to work with after-tax cash flows. In addition, we modified the income statement and removed the interest expense. So far, we have not accounted for the tax implications of debt from this interest expense. When a company pays interest expense on borrowed funds, the expense is a deduction from taxable income, and there is a cost savings to the firm. For example, in the year 2007, PepsiCo paid out \$224 million in interest expense. PepsiCo also had a corporate tax rate of around 30%, and this \$224 million in interest expense therefore lowered its overall tax obligation by \$67 million. Because interest expense is a deductible business expense, the true cost of PepsiCo's debt borrowing was \$157 million in 2007: the cost of the \$224 million interest expense minus the \$67 million tax reduction. The net cash outflow of \$157 million is the after-tax cost of debt. So, if we need to incorporate the tax effect, how do we adjust the WACC cost of debt component?

We adjust the cost of debt by multiplying R_d by 1 minus the corporate tax rate. This adjustment, $1 - T_c$, shows that the tax savings on interest expense reduces the company's cost of debt. For PepsiCo, we can see that \$224 million multiplied by 1 minus the corporate tax rate gives the after-tax cash flow for the interest on debt: \$224 million times $(1 - 0.30)$ equals \$157 million. Once we build in the weights to the WACC, what we call adjusted WACC, we will use the after-tax cost of debt in the final form to reflect the corporation's tax rate deduction in interest costs:

$$\text{after-tax cost of debt} = R_d \times (1 - T_c) \qquad \mathbf{11.8}$$

11.3 Weighting the Components: Book Value or Market Value?

We have the component costs of capital, but as in our earlier example with Stan's lawn-mowing business, we typically use different amounts of funding from different sources. So, once we know the cost of each component, we must next determine the relative proportions of each component in the company's capital structure. Here we have two options: the book value of the funds or the market

FIGURE 11.2

Cartman Enterprises Balance Sheet Year Ending December 31, 2011 ($ in thousands)			
ASSETS		**LIABILITIES**	
Current assets		**Current liabilities**	
Cash	$ 300	Accounts payable	$ 0
Marketable securities	$ 200	**Total current liabilities**	**$ 0**
Accounts receivable	$ 500	Long-term liabilities	
Inventories	$ 900	Outstanding bonds	$12,000
Total current assets	**$ 1,900**	**Total liabilities**	**$12,000**
Long-term assets		**OWNERS' EQUITY**	
Net plant, property, and equipment	$22,040	Preferred stock	$ 1,300
		Common stock	$ 8,600
Intangible assets	$ 3,500	Retained earnings	$ 5,540
Total long-term assets	**$25,540**	**Total owners' equity**	**$15,440**
TOTAL ASSETS	**$27,440**	**TOTAL LIABILITIES AND OWNERS' EQUITY**	**$27,440**

value of the funds. We will examine book value first as a way to find the percentage of each component.

Book Value

The **book value** of a liability is its cost carried on the balance sheet. We could simply determine the weights or percentages of the various components by looking at their book values. Therefore, the balance sheet summarizes the current forms of financing for the firm and reflects the sources of the capital. We will look at the liabilities and the owners' equity section for Cartman Enterprises' funding sources.

Figure 11.2 presents Cartman Enterprises' balance sheet. Notice that the accounts payable line is at zero to illustrate the weights of the different capital components without consideration of the cost to use suppliers' funds or other current liability accounts. This keeps the balance sheet in balance for this exercise.

We can use the book values of each component to determine the company's financing mix. If we let D stand for debt, PS stand for preferred stock, and E stand for equity, we can see that total funding equals the firm's total assets or the firm's total value, V. We can imply that $E + PS + D = V$, which is the essence of the balance sheet, where the liabilities or debt ($12,000) plus the preferred stock or hybrid equity ($1,300) plus the equity or common stock and retained earnings ($8,600 + $5,540) equal the firm's assets ($27,440). The weights or percentages are:

$$\text{equity weight, } \frac{E}{V} = \frac{\text{common stock} + \text{retained earnings}}{\text{total assets}}$$

$$= \frac{\$8{,}600 + \$5{,}540}{\$27{,}440} = 51.53\%$$

$$\text{preferred stock weight, } \frac{PS}{V} = \frac{\text{preferred stock}}{\text{total assets}}$$

$$= \frac{\$1{,}300}{\$27{,}440} = 4.74\%$$

$$\text{debt weight, } \frac{D}{V} = \frac{\text{long-term debt}}{\text{total assets}}$$

$$= \frac{\$12{,}000}{\$27{,}440} = 43.73\%$$

Notice that the percentages add to 100%:

$$51.53\% + 4.74\% + 43.73\% = 100.00\%$$

Adjusted Weighted Average Cost of Capital

Let's assume that we have already calculated the cost of debt, preferred stock, and equity components for Cartman Enterprises at 10.30% for debt, 11.43% for preferred stock, and 13.56% for equity. In addition, we will need Cartman's corporate tax rate so that we can properly adjust the cost of debt. We will assume that the tax rate is 30%. Using the weights of each component, the costs of each component, and the adjustment for taxes on the interest payments for debt financing, we have the **adjusted weighted average cost of capital**:

$$WACC_{\text{adj}} = \frac{E}{V} \times R_e + \frac{PS}{V} \times R_{ps} + \frac{D}{V} \times R_d \times (1 - T_c) \qquad \textbf{11.9}$$

Plugging in the specific value components for Cartman Enterprises, we have

$$WACC = (0.5153 \times 0.1356) + (0.0474 \times 0.1143) + (0.4373 \times 0.103 \times (1 - 0.30)) = 10.68\%$$

So, we have now arrived at the cost of capital for Cartman Enterprises, the weighted average cost of capital. The WACC is a critical value in finance. We use it as the appropriate discount rate for a project in the NPV capital budget decision model and as the hurdle rate in the IRR capital budget decision model. In addition, because we use the after-tax cash flow in these models, we also use the adjusted WACC because we need to account for the interest expense from the debt funding. By adjusting the R_d cost by the corporate tax rate, we have successfully moved the funding decision to the WACC and out of the operating decision. So, we are consistent with the financial management view of separating the operating decisions from the funding decisions.

Market Value

Using book value is only one way to weight the funding components. A second way is by the current market value of the capital. **Market value** uses the current price of the debt or equity in the capital markets, the price at which investors currently buy or sell stocks and bonds. So, instead of book value for debt, we find the bond's current market price and multiply it by the number of outstanding bonds. Similarly, we find the preferred and common stocks' current prices and multiply them by the number of outstanding shares of the respective stocks. The variable V will now stand for the total market values of debt, preferred stock, and common stock.

EXAMPLE 11.7 Market value weights of capital components

Problem Stan's Plant and Tree Nursery has the following capital components and costs for each component.

Capital Components of Stan's Plant and Tree Nursery

	Debt	Preferred Stock	Common Stock
Market price	\$940	\$68	\$32
Outstanding	400 bonds	1,200 shares	8,000 shares
Market value	\$376,000	\$81,600	\$256,000
Cost of capital	9.0%	11.0%	14.0%

What is the WACC of Stan's Plant and Tree Nursery if its corporate tax rate is 35%?

Solution We use the market value of each component to determine the weight of the component. The total borrowing V is the sum of the debt market value D, the preferred stock market value PS, and the common stock market value E:

$$D = \$940 \times 400 = \$376{,}000$$

$$PS = \$68 \times 1{,}200 = \$81{,}600$$

$$E = \$32 \times 8{,}000 = \$256{,}000$$

$$V = D + PS + E$$

$$= \$376{,}000 + \$81{,}600 + \$256{,}000 = \$713{,}600$$

Therefore,

$$WACC = \frac{E}{V} \times R_e + \frac{PS}{V} \times R_{ps} + \frac{D}{V} \times R_d \times (1 - T_c)$$

$$= \frac{\$256{,}000}{\$713{,}600} \times 0.14 + \frac{\$81{,}600}{\$713{,}600} \times 0.11 + \frac{\$376{,}000}{\$713{,}600} \times 0.09 \times (1 - 0.35)$$

$$= (0.3587 \times 0.14) + (0.1143 \times 0.11) + (0.5269 \times 0.09 \times 0.65)$$

$$= 0.0502 + 0.0126 + 0.0308 = \mathbf{0.0936} \text{ or } \mathbf{9.36\%}$$

Which is the preferred way to estimate weights of the components, book value or market value? The preferred choice is market value, but with privately held companies it is not always possible to estimate market values. Therefore, if market values are not available, your only alternative is to use book values for estimating the weights of the components in the WACC.

In Chapter 16, we will introduce a third concept as we search for the firm's optimal capital structure. We will look at the best available funding combination and use that for the weights in the adjusted WACC. We leave this third concept for later because its fundamental underpinnings are complex. For now, then, let's move from the tool-building phase of the cost of capital to the application of the WACC.

11.4 Using the Weighted Average Cost of Capital in a Budgeting Decision

How does the adjusted WACC actually work in deciding which projects to accept and which to reject? Once we determine the adjusted WACC for a company, we select a decision model and use the adjusted WACC with a project's estimated future cash flows to determine if we should accept or reject the project.

To arrive at this accept-or-reject decision, let's return to Kyle's project, which will require an initial investment of $5 million. Kyle has estimated the incremental cash flow for the new project. Table 11.1 displays the data. If Kyle's company has an adjusted WACC of 12%, should Kyle accept or reject this project?

You know from Chapter 9 that we could choose among six capital budgeting decision models—payback period, discounted payback period, net present value, internal rate of return, modified internal rate of return, and profitability index—when deciding to accept or reject the project. Payback period does not require discounting the future cash flow, so using this capital budgeting decision model, we accept or reject regardless of the project or company's adjusted WACC. However, as we have seen, this model is not a firm's best choice for making large capital investments, and we again see that it does not account for risk because it does not use the WACC. Let's look at the two most popular decision models—the NPV and the IRR—instead.

When making a decision to accept or reject using the NPV model, we need an appropriate discount rate for the project's future cash flows. Using the 12% adjusted WACC as the appropriate discount rate, we have

$$NPV = -CF_0 + \frac{CF_1}{(1 + WACC)^1} + \frac{CF_2}{(1 + WACC)^2} + \frac{CF_3}{(1 + WACC)^3}$$

$$= -\$5{,}000{,}000 + \frac{\$2{,}000{,}000}{(1 + 0.12)^1} + \frac{\$2{,}000{,}000}{(1 + 0.12)^2} + \frac{\$2{,}640{,}000}{(1 + 0.12)^3}$$

$$= -\$5{,}000{,}000 + \$1{,}785{,}714 + \$1{,}594{,}388 + \$1{,}879{,}100 = \$259{,}202$$

Therefore, because the NPV is positive, Kyle should accept this project if his cost of capital is 12%.

Using the IRR as the capital budgeting decision model, we must first find the internal rate of return for the project cash flow:

$$\$0 = -CF_0 + \frac{CF_1}{(1 + r)^1} + \frac{CF_2}{(1 + r)^2} + \frac{CF_3}{(1 + r)^3}$$

$$= -\$5{,}000{,}000 + \frac{\$2{,}000{,}000}{(1 + r)^1} + \frac{\$2{,}000{,}000}{(1 + r)^2} + \frac{\$2{,}640{,}000}{(1 + r)^3}$$

TABLE 11.1 Incremental Cash Flow of a $5 Million Project

Category	T_0	T_1	T_2	T_3
Investment	−$4,400,000			
Net working capital	−$ 600,000			$ 600,000
Operating cash flow		$2,000,000	$2,000,000	$2,000,000
Salvage				$ 40,000
Total incremental cash flow	−$5,000,000	$2,000,000	$2,000,000	$2,640,000

Solving for r, the IRR, we have

$$IRR = 14.85\%$$

Again, because the IRR of 14.85% is greater than the adjusted WACC of 12%, Kyle should accept the project.

Individual Weighted Average Cost of Capital for Individual Projects

In previous sections, we hinted at the idea that not all company projects should have the same discount rate. If a company assigns all projects the same discount rate, some poor or incorrect management decisions about which projects to accept or reject could result. To illustrate the possible error types that can arise from assigning the same hurdle rate or cost of capital to every project, let's take a look at four projects facing Kenny, the CEO of West Park Industries:

1. Project 1: Waste management system for the manufacturing facilities of West Park Industries with a low level of risk and an 8% IRR.
2. Project 2: New manufacturing plant for manufacturing low-energy-impact lighting systems with a moderate level of risk and a 9% IRR.
3. Project 3: New manufacturing plant for manufacturing mountain bikes with a high level of risk and a 10% IRR.
4. Project 4: New manufacturing plant for manufacturing golf clubs with a very high level of risk and an 11% IRR.

If the weighted average cost of capital is 9.5% for West Park Industries and Kenny applies this rate to all projects regardless of the level of risk, we would have the acceptance and rejection recommendations for these projects as Figure 11.3 depicts. In the figure, notice that Projects 3 and 4, with their high IRRs, are a "go," whereas Projects 1 and 2 with their low IRRs are each a "no-go." It is not enough, however, to always accept high IRR projects and reject low IRR projects. Kenny, or any prudent business person, must assign the appropriate hurdle rate or cost of capital to each project that reflects the individual project's riskiness.

In principle, every project should have its own hurdle rate or opportunity cost of capital. Unfortunately, it is not always possible to estimate the appropriate adjusted WACC for each project. One way to assign a specific WACC is to use a subjective adjustment to the company's overall WACC. For low-risk projects, you would assign a lower WACC, and for high-risk projects, a higher WACC.

Another way to adjust for a project's riskiness is to use the SML and find an appropriate beta for a project. Recall that beta is the measure of an asset's risk in a well-diversified portfolio. So, we can make the connection that these projects are assets within the portfolio of projects, services, and activities for West Park

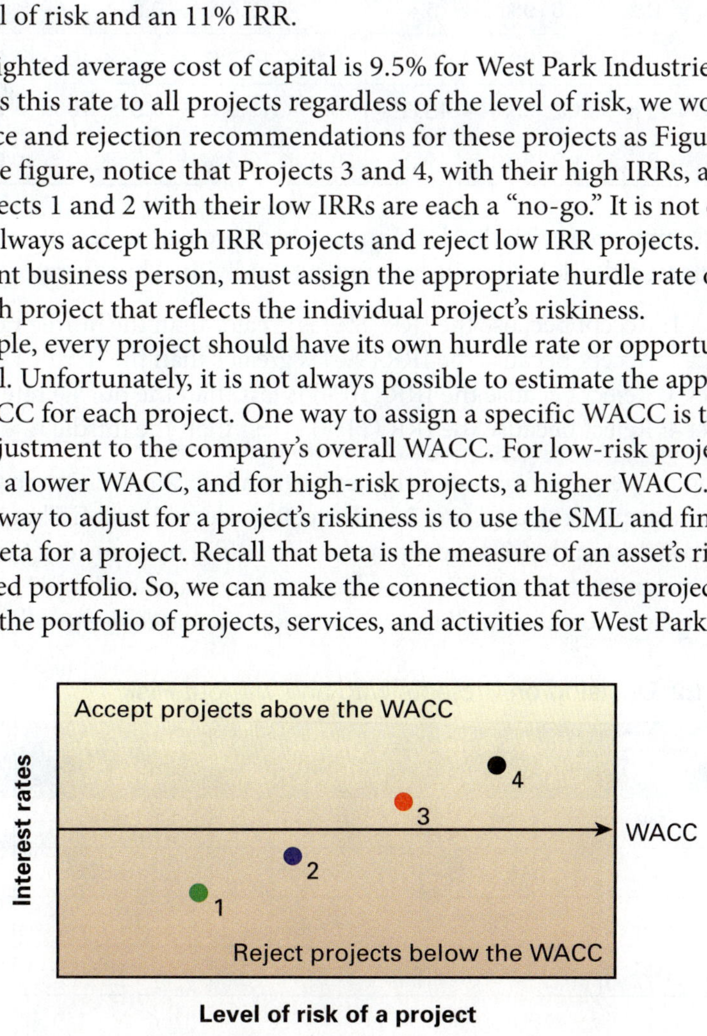

FIGURE 11.3 Capital project decision model without considering risk.

Industries. Their individual betas reflect their own unique level of riskiness. If we assign each project a beta and then work back through the adjusted WACC equation, we can come up with a project-specific hurdle rate and an appropriate decision about which projects to accept or reject while measuring both their return and risk.

For West Park Industries, we have the following information:

Sources of funding: equity 50%, debt 50%
Cost of debt financing: 10% before tax
Tax rate: 30%
Average risk of West Park Industries: 1.0 (beta)
Expected return on the market: 12%
Risk-free rate: 3%

The company hurdle rate is 9.5%:

$$WACC_{\text{adj}} = 0.5(12\%) + 0.5(10\%)(1 - 0.30) = 9.5\%$$

Using 9.5% for every project's hurdle rate, however, neglects to consider the risk level for the individual projects. If we assign each project a beta and then calculate the project's WACC based on that beta, we can apply a different hurdle rate for each project that reflects that project's risk level. The following table shows the betas, costs of equity, and respective risk-appropriate WACC for the four projects:

Project	Beta	Cost of Equity	Hurdle Rate or Adjusted WACC
1	0.6	$R_e = 3\% + 0.6\,(9\%) = 8.4\%$	$0.5 \times 8.4\% + 0.5 \times 10\% \times 0.7 = 7.7\%$
2	0.8	$R_e = 3\% + 0.8\,(9\%) = 10.2\%$	$0.5 \times 10.2\% + 0.5 \times 10\% \times 0.7 = 8.6\%$
3	1.2	$R_e = 3\% + 1.2\,(9\%) = 13.8\%$	$0.5 \times 13.8\% + 0.5 \times 10\% \times 0.7 = 10.4\%$
4	1.8	$R_e = 3\% + 1.8\,(9\%) = 19.2\%$	$0.5 \times 19.2\% + 0.5 \times 10\% \times 0.7 = 13.1\%$

Now, Kenny can revisit the decision on which projects to accept or reject using both the measured risk level with each project's individual hurdle rate and IRR:

Project 1: Accept because the IRR (8%) is greater than the hurdle rate (7.7%).
Project 2: Accept because the IRR (9%) is greater than the hurdle rate (8.6%).
Project 3: Reject because the IRR (10%) is less than the hurdle rate (10.4%).
Project 4: Reject because the IRR (11%) is less than the hurdle rate (13.1%).

Having properly incorporated risk and return into the decision making process, Kenny now accepts Projects 1 and 2 and rejects Projects 3 and 4. That is the opposite of the conclusion that Kenny reached when he did not consider the riskiness of the individual project. To see how this decision plays out, see Table 11.2 and Figure 11.4, which show how the hurdle rate of a project increases as the risk increases.

TABLE 11.2 Decision on Projects with and without Risk

Project	IRR	Hurdle Rate without Risk	Decision without Risk	Hurdle Rate with Risk	Decision with Risk
1	8%	9.5%	Reject	7.7%	Accept
2	9%	9.5%	Reject	8.6%	Accept
3	10%	9.5%	Accept	10.4%	Reject
4	11%	9.5%	Accept	13.1%	Reject

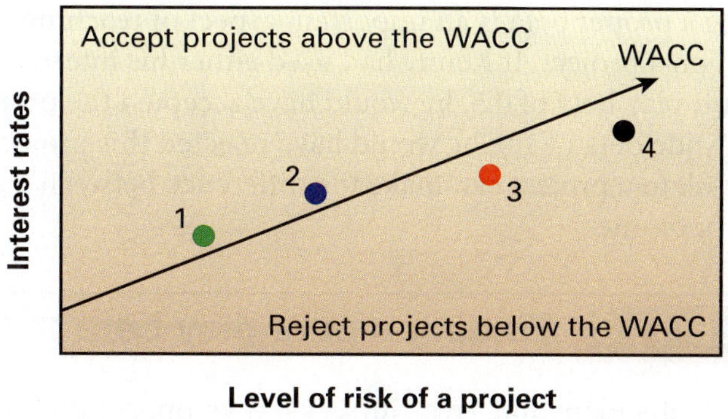

FIGURE 11.4 Capital project decision model with risk.

Figure 11.4 looks just like our discussion of the security market line, and, indeed, it is: we buy securities plotting above the SML and accept projects plotting above the WACC line. We sell securities plotting below the SML and reject projects plotting below the WACC line. Projects above the WACC line have positive NPVs, and projects below the WACC line have negative NPVs.

11.5 Selecting Appropriate Betas for Projects

If we return to our philosophy regarding capital budgeting decisions in which we accept all positive NPV projects and reject all negative NPV projects, we can view a company itself as a portfolio, a collection of projects. If we assume that we can obtain sufficient financing for all positive NPV projects, selecting the portfolio of projects for the company is straightforward: accept all positive NPV projects. One problem in assessing the project's risk level remains: how do we assign the appropriate beta? In the previous section, Kenny subjectively determined betas for each individual project and then found the appropriate hurdle rate or WACC for each. We now need to learn more formally how to assign betas to each project.

Assigning a beta is more of an art than a science. We call the simplest application **pure play**, which refers to matching the project to a company with a single business focus. As a manager, you would look for a firm whose sole business is similar to the business of your project, find the firm's beta, and assign it to your project. For example, if Kenny is looking at his waste management project and is trying to find the appropriate beta, he should first look for a firm or set of firms whose sole business activity is waste management. Kenny would then simply assign the beta of a waste management firm or the average beta of a set of waste management firms as the beta of his project. Pure play is particularly useful when a company wants to expand its current business operations into a brand new area and therefore has no internal projects it can use for estimating the new project's beta.

Say that Kenny looks for a single-focused waste management company and finds Waste Management Inc. The beta of Waste Management is 0.5. If Kenny assigns this beta to his waste management project, would he accept or reject the project? (Recall that the expected return on the market is 12%, the risk-free rate is 3%, and the source of the funding is 50% equity and 50% debt. The cost of debt is 10%, and the current tax rate is 30%.)

Project 1 equity cost with beta of 0.5: $R_e = 3\% + (12\% - 3\%)0.50 = 7.5\%$
Project 1 hurdle rate: $0.50 \times 7.5\% + [0.5 \times 10\% \times (1 - 0.3)] = 7.25\%$
Project 1: Accept because the IRR (8%) is greater than the hurdle rate (7.25%).

Assigning a proper beta is an important aspect of reaching the correct business decision on a project. If Kenny had used either his internally assigned beta of 0.6 or the pure-play beta of 0.5, he would have accepted the project. Had he used the companywide beta of 1.0, he would have rejected this project. Assigning the appropriate risk to a project can make the difference between a good business decision and a poor one.

EXAMPLE 11.8 Finding a pure play beta

Problem Stan's Plant and Tree Nursery has an opportunity to start a carbonated beverage business. This business component is unlike any other project or operations of the current business. What beta should Stan use for assessing the WACC of a carbonated beverage business?

Solution The company's current beta is not appropriate for a carbonated beverage business, so Stan needs to look at companies whose sole business or major portion of business is carbonated beverages. Stan uses PepsiCo and Coca-Cola as two businesses with a majority of their business in carbonated beverages. The beta of PepsiCo is 0.87, and the beta of Coca-Cola is 0.79. Stan decides to assign a beta of 0.83 to the carbonated beverage project, thereby reflecting the average beta of PepsiCo and Coca-Cola.

If pure play is not a viable choice, another method is to use a subjective modification of the company beta for individual projects. For example, a company may have an overall beta of 1.2 for its current portfolio of projects, but the company operates in a variety of business areas. The company partitions its potential projects into one of four categories: low risk, moderate risk, average risk, and high risk. The company assigns each category a beta based on the company's current overall beta. For example,

Low-risk projects: current company beta minus 0.4 unit of risk, $1.2 - 0.4 = 0.8$
Moderate-risk projects: current company beta minus 0.2 unit of risk, $1.2 - 0.2 = 1.0$
Average risk project: current company beta, 1.2
High-risk project: current company beta plus 0.4 unit of risk, $1.2 + 0.4 = 1.6$

Of course, this subjective assessment of projects and betas leaves much to be desired, but it may be a good first step in reviewing potential riskiness of projects and is better than just assigning the overall company beta to every project.

In other, more sophisticated models, companies use statistical analysis to assign betas to projects and integrate their actual capital structure weights into the analysis. We will not go into these more sophisticated models, but will remind you that projects, in general, will have varying levels of risk, and the project's cash flow risk is an integral part of the decision process. In addition, remember that you acquire the art of assigning a risk level to a project through time and practice.

11.6 Constraints on Borrowing and Selecting Projects for the Portfolio

Although it would be nice to have access to unlimited amounts of funds so that a company could fund all positive NPV projects, the practical side of capital budgeting is that there are limited funds, and a company can thus accept only a limited number of projects. A company must ration its capital over the available positive NPV projects. Capital rationing is the term we use to pick projects when a company has constraints on the amount of available capital. How do we select which projects to accept among all the projects with positive NPVs when capital is constrained? The choice is quite simple: take the set of projects that has the highest combined NPV without exhausting the available funds.

EXAMPLE 11.9 Selecting projects with a fixed amount of available funding

Problem You have a capital budget for the coming year of $5,000,000. You also have a list of all potential capital projects for the coming year:

Project A: Initial cost of $1,500,000 and NPV of $250,000
Project B: Initial cost of $2,000,000 and NPV of $200,000
Project C: Initial cost of $1,750,000 and NPV of $180,000
Project D: Initial cost of $750,000 and NPV of $60,000
Project E: Initial cost of $500,000 and NPV of $50,000
Project F: Initial cost of $900,000 and NPV of $25,000
Project G: Initial cost of $1,250,000 and NPV of $15,000

Which combination of projects is the best given the constraint that you can spend only up to $5,000,000?

Solution You must select the set of projects that has the highest total NPV without going over the $5,000,000 initial capital investment constraint. You have already completed the first step of finding the individual NPVs, so you now postulate all different project combinations that do not exceed the capital budget and add up their NPVs. Once you have listed all possible combinations that do not exceed your capital constraint you order these combinations by total NPV. You then pick Projects A, B, D, and E. The total initial cost is $4,750,000, and the total NPV is $560,000. All other viable combinations fall short of the $560,000 total NPV.

Table of Viable Combinations

Projects	Total Investment	Total NPV
A, B, D, and E	$4,750,000	**$560,000**
A, B, E, and F	$4,900,000	$525,000
A, B, and G	$4,750,000	$465,000
A, C, D, and E	$4,500,000	$540,000
A, C, D, and F	$4,900,000	$515,000
A, C, E, and G	$5,000,000	$495,000
A, D, E, F, and G	$4,900,000	$400,000
B, C, D, and E	$5,000,000	$490,000
B, C, and F	$4,650,000	$405,000
B, C, and G	$5,000,000	$395,000
C, D, E, and F	$3,900,000	$315,000
C, D, F, and G	$4,650,000	$280,000
C, E, F, and G	$4,400,000	$270,000

A frequent question when allocating capital funds to capital budgets is what to do with the unused dollars. In the previous example, you have chosen Projects A, B, D, and E, but this combination requires an investment of $4,750,000. What about the remaining $250,000? Because you do not have any other projects with a cost of $250,000 or less and a positive NPV, you can assume that the company either will invest the remaining dollars at the "going rate" (the company's WACC) or will return them to the debt and equity sources. All projects that meet the going rate have NPVs of zero; therefore, all remaining dollars provide no additional increase in firm value for the owners. If you are borrowing funds, the alternative is to forgo borrowing the entire $5,000,000 and to instead borrow only the necessary $4,750,000. If these funds are internally generated, you can pay the owners an additional $250,000 in dividends.

Looking back at another option, why not select Projects A, C, D, and E—an option that invests only $4,500,000, but has a combined NPV of $540,000, which is only $20,000 less than that of Projects A, B, D, and E? Selecting the optimal set of A, B, D, and E over A, C, D, and E nets $20,000 more for the company *above* the cost of capital. The investment of an additional $250,000 makes the company better off by $20,000 after paying for the additional funds.

So, we have come full circle here in the capital budgeting discussion. We know that there are six different capital budgeting models. We have seen that the NPV and the IRR models are the most popular and have concluded that the NPV is the most fundamentally sound model. We have examined the need for estimating a project's appropriate cash flows and determining the incremental cash flow for these models. In addition, we have examined how to find the appropriate discount rate or hurdle rate with the adjusted WACC. When selecting capital projects for a company, we can use these tools to make sound financial decisions.

To review this chapter, see the Summary Card at the end of the text.

Key Terms

adjusted weighted average cost of capital, p. 336
book value, p. 335
capital structure, p. 326
cost of capital, p. 326
cost of debt, p. 329
cost of equity, p. 331
cost of preferred stock, p. 331
cost of retained earnings, p. 333
debt financing, p. 326
discount rate, p. 329
equity financing, p. 326
flotation costs, p. 333
hybrid equity financing, p. 327
market value, p. 336
pure play, p. 341
weighted average cost of capital (WACC), p. 327

Questions

1. From what sources can a company raise capital? Do these different sources of capital all charge the same rate? Why or why not?
2. Why is the yield to maturity on a bond the appropriate cost of debt financing?
3. What are the two different ways to estimate the cost of equity for a firm?
4. Should retained earnings reinvested in the company have a zero cost of capital because it generates the funds internally and the company does not need to pay itself for borrowing money? If not, why?

5. When calculating the cost of capital, why is it that the company only adjusts the cost of debt for taxes?
6. What are two ways to estimate the percentage (weights) of funds that a company has received from lenders and owners? Which is more appropriate?
7. Why not use a single WACC for all company projects?
8. What are the types of errors that a manager can make if he or she does not assign individual WACCs to each potential project?
9. Why is selecting a beta for a project more of an art than a science?
10. If the capital budget is constrained by the amount of funds available for potential projects, what mistake might a manager make if he or she just lists the potential projects by highest to lowest NPV and picks the projects by moving down the list until the funds are exhausted?

Prepping for Exams

1. Which of the following would you classify as debt lenders for a firm?
   a. preferred shareholders, banks, and nonbank lenders
   b. nonbank lenders, common shareholders, and commercial banks
   c. preferred shareholders, common shareholders, and suppliers
   d. suppliers, nonbank lenders, and commercial banks

2. ______________ refers to the way a company finances itself through some combination of loans, bonds, preferred stock sales, common stock sales, and retention of earnings.
   a. Capital structure
   b. Cost of capital
   c. Working capital management
   d. NPV

3. The cost of debt could be which of the following?
   a. the required return on money borrowed as a long-term loan from a bank
   b. the required return on money borrowed from a venture capitalist
   c. the yield to maturity on money raised by selling bonds
   d. all the choices above

4. Your firm has preferred stock outstanding that pays a current dividend of $3.00 per year and has a current price of $39.50. You anticipate the economy to grow steadily at a rate of 3.00% per year for the foreseeable future. What is the market required rate of return on your firm's preferred stock?
   a. 10.82%
   b. 10.59%
   c. 7.59%
   d. There is not enough information to answer this question.

5. Use the dividend growth model to determine the required rate of return for equity. Your firm intends to issue new common stock. Your investment bankers have determined that you should offer the stock at a price of $45.00 per share and you should anticipate paying a dividend of $1.50 in one year. If you anticipate a constant growth in dividends of 3.50% per year and the

investment banking firm will take 7.00% per share as flotation costs, what is the required rate of return for this issue of new common stock?

a. 7.19%
b. 6.83%
c. 7.08%
d. There is not enough information to answer this question.

6. Elway Electronics has debt with a market value of $350,000, preferred stock with a market value of $150,000, and common stock with a market value of $450,000. If debt has a cost of 8%, preferred stock a cost of 10%, common stock a cost of 12%, and the firm has a tax rate of 30%, what is the WACC?

a. 8.64%
b. 9.12%
c. 9.33%
d. 10.04%

7. Your firm has an average-risk project under consideration. You choose to fund the project in the same manner as the firm's existing capital structure. If cost of debt is 9.50%, the cost of preferred stock is 10.00%, the cost of common stock is 12.00%, and the WACC adjusted for taxes is 11.50%, what is the project's NPV given the expected cash flows listed here?

Category	T_0	T_1	T_2	T_3
Investment	−$800,000			
Net working capital	−$ 50,000			$ 50,000
Operating cash flow		$350,000	$350,000	$350,000
Salvage				$ 20,000
Total incremental cash flow	−$850,000	$350,000	$350,000	$420,000

a. $1,150,904
b. $898,415
c. $300,904
d. $48,415

8. Takelmer Industries has a different WACC for each of three types of projects. Low-risk projects have an 8% WACC, average-risk projects a 10% WACC, and high-risk projects a 12% WACC. Which of the following projects do you recommend that the firm accept?

Project	Level of Risk	IRR
A	Low	9.50%
B	Average	8.50%
C	Average	7.50%
D	Low	9.50%
E	High	14.50%
F	High	17.50%
G	Average	11.50%

a. A, B, C, D, and G
b. B, C, E, F, and G
c. A, D, E, F, and G
d. A, B, C, D, E, F, and G

9. International Geographica is adding a new magazine project to the company portfolio and has the following information: the expected market return is 12%, the risk-free rate is 4%, and the expected return on the new project is 20%. What is the project's beta?

a. 1.00
b. 1.50
c. 1.75
d. 2.00

10. Your firm has $2,000,000 available for investment in capital projects. Which combination of projects is the best, given this budget constraint?

Project	Initial Investment	NPV
A	$ 750,000	$100,000
B	$1,500,000	$125,000
C	$ 500,000	$ 75,000
D	$ 500,000	$ 35,000

a. B and C
b. A, B, and C
c. A, B, C, and D
d. A, C, and D

Problems

These problems are available in MyFinanceLab.

1. *WACC.* Eric has another get-rich-quick idea, but needs funding to support it. He chooses an all-debt funding scenario. He will borrow $2,000 from Wendy, who will charge him 6% on the loan. He will also borrow $1,500 from Bebe, who will charge 8% on the loan, and $800 from Shelly, who will charge 14% on the loan. What is the weighted average cost of capital for Eric?

2. *WACC.* Grey's Pharmaceuticals has a new project that will require funding of $4 million. The company has decided to pursue an all-debt scenario. Grey's has made an agreement with four lenders for the needed financing. These lenders will advance the following amounts and interest rates:

Lender	Amount	Interest Rate
Stevens	$ 1,500,00	11%
Yang	$1,200,000	9%
Shepherd	$1,000,000	7%
Bailey	$ 300,000	8%

What is the weighted average cost of capital for the $4,000,000?

3. ***Cost of debt***. Kenny Enterprises has just issued a bond with a par value of $1,000, twenty years to maturity, and an 8% coupon rate with semiannual payments. What is the cost of debt for Kenny Enterprises if the bond sells at the following prices? What do you notice about the price and the cost of debt?

   a. $920
   b. $1,000
   c. $1,080
   d. $1,173

4. ***Cost of debt***. Dunder-Mifflin Inc. (DMI) is selling 600,000 bonds to raise money for the publication of new magazines in the coming year. The bonds will pay a coupon rate of 12% on semiannual payments. The bond's par value is $100, and the bond will mature in thirty years. What is the cost of debt to DMI if the bonds raise

   a. $45,000,000?
   b. $54,000,000?
   c. $66,000,000?
   d. $75,000,000?

5. ***Cost of debt with fees***. Kenny Enterprises will issue the same debt as in Problem 3, but will now use an investment bank that charges $25 per bond for its services. What is the new cost of debt for Kenny Enterprises at a market price of

   a. $920?
   b. $1,000?
   c. $1,080?
   d. $1,173?

6. ***Cost of debt with fees***. In Problem 4, Dunder-Mifflin Inc. hires an investment banker for the sale of the 600,000 bonds. The investment banker charges a 2% fee on each bond sold. What is the cost of debt to DMI if the proceeds below are before the banker's fees are deducted?

   a. $45,000,000
   b. $54,000,000
   c. $66,000,000
   d. $75,000,000

7. ***Cost of preferred stock***. Kyle is raising funds for his company by selling preferred stock. The preferred stock has a par value of $100 and a dividend rate of 6%. The stock is selling for $80 in the market. What is the cost of preferred stock for Kyle?

8. ***Cost of preferred stock***. Kyle hires Wilson Investment Bankers to sell the preferred stock from Problem 7. Wilson charges a 3% fee on the sale of preferred stock. What is the cost of preferred stock for Kyle using the investment banker?

9. ***Cost of equity: SML***. Stan is expanding his business and will sell common stock for the needed funds. If the current risk-free rate is 4% and the expected market return is 12%, what is the cost of equity for Stan if the beta of the stock is

   a. 0.75?
   b. 0.90?
   c. 1.05?
   d. 1.20?

10. ***Cost of equity: SML.*** Stan had to delay the sale of the common stock as outlined in Problem 9 for six months. When he finally did sell the stock, the risk-free rate had fallen to 3%, but the expected return on the market had risen to 13%. What was the effect on the cost of equity by waiting six months, using the four different betas from Problem 9? What do you notice about the increases in the cost of equity as beta increases?

11. ***Book value versus market value components.*** Compare Trout Inc. with Salmon Enterprises, using the following balance sheet of Trout and the market data of Salmon for the weights in the weighted average cost of capital.

Trout Inc.

Current assets:	$2,000,000	Current liabilities:	$1,000,000
Long-term assets:	$7,000,000	Long-term liabilities:	$5,000,000
Total assets:	$9,000,000	Owners' equity:	$3,000,000

Salmon Enterprises

Bonds outstanding: 3,000 selling at $980
Common stock outstanding: 260,000 selling at $23.40

If the after-tax cost of debt is 8% for both companies and the cost of equity is 12%, which company has the highest WACC?

12. ***Book value versus market value components.*** The CFO of DMI is trying to determine the company's WACC. Brad, a promising MBA, says that the company should use book value to assign the WACC's components percentage. Angela, a long-time employee and experienced financial analyst, says that the company should use market value to assign the components. The after-tax cost of debt is at 7%, the cost of preferred stock is at 11%, and the cost of equity is at 14%. Calculate the WACC using both the book value and market value approaches with the following information. Which do you think is better? Why?

DMI Balance Sheet ($ in thousands)

Current assets	$32,000	Current liabilities	$ 0
Long-term assets	$66,000	Long-term liabilities	
		Bonds payable	$54,000
		Owners' equity	
		Preferred stock	$12,000
		Common stock	$32,000
Total assets	**$98,000**	**Total liabilities and owners' equity**	**$98,000**

Market Information

	Debt	Preferred Stock	Common Stock
Outstanding	54,000	120,000	1,280,000
Market Price	$1,085	$95.40	$32.16

13. ***Adjusted WACC***. Lewis runs an outdoor adventure company and wants to know what effect a tax change will have on his company's WACC. Currently, Lewis has the following financing pattern:

Equity: 35% and cost of 14%
Preferred stock: 15% and cost of 11%
Debt: 50% and cost of 10% before taxes

What is the adjusted WACC for Lewis if the tax rate is

a. 40%?
b. 30%?
c. 20%?
d. 10%?
e. 0%?

14. ***Adjusted WACC***. Clark Explorers Inc., an engineering firm, has the following capital structure:

	Equity	Preferred Stock	Debt
Market price	$30.00	$110.00	$955.00
Outstanding units	120,000	10,000	6,000
Book value	$3,000,000	$1,000,000	$6,000,000
Cost of capital	15%	12%	9%

Using market value and book value (separately, of course), find the adjusted WACC for Clark Explorers at the following tax rates:

a. 35%
b. 25%
c. 15%
d. 5%

15. ***Apply WACC in NPV***. Brawn Blenders has the following incremental cash flow for its new project:

Category	T_0	T_1	T_2	T_3
Investment	−$4,000,000			
Net working capital change	−$ 300,000			$ 300,000
Operating cash flow		$1,500,000	$1,500,000	$1,500,000
Salvage				$ 250,000

Should Brawn accept or reject this project at an adjusted WACC of 6%, 8%, or 10%?

16. ***Apply WACC in IRR***. Leeward Sailboats is reviewing the following new boat line:

Category	T_0	T_1	T_2	T_3
Investment	−$9,000,000			
Net working capital change	−$ 600,000			$ 600,000
Operating cash flow		$3,200,000	$3,800,000	$4,500,000
Salvage				$ 400,000

At what adjusted WACCs will the company accept this project? *Hint:* Find the IRR of the project and use it as the maximum adjusted WACC for accepting the project.

17. ***Adjusted WACC.*** Ashman Motors is currently an all-equity firm. It has two million shares outstanding, selling for $43 per share. The company has a beta of 1.1, with the current risk-free rate at 3% and the market premium at 8%. The tax rate is 35% for the company. Ashman has decided to sell $43 million in bonds and retire half its stock. The bonds will have a yield to maturity of 9%. The company's beta will rise to 1.3 with the new debt. What was the adjusted WACC of Ashman Motors before selling bonds? What is Ashman Motor's new WACC after selling the bonds and retiring the stock with the proceeds from the bond sale? *Hint:* The weight of equity before selling the bonds is 100%.

18. ***Adjusted WACC.*** Thorpe and Company is currently an all-equity firm. It has three million shares selling for $28 per share. Its beta is 0.85, and the current risk-free rate is 2.5%. The expected return on the market for the coming year is 13%. Thorpe will sell corporate bonds for $28,000,000 and retire common stock with the proceeds. The bonds are twenty-year semiannual bonds with a 10% coupon rate and $1,000 par value. The bonds are currently selling for $1,143.08 per bond. When the bonds sell, the company's beta will increase to 0.95. What was Thorpe and Company's WACC before the bond sale? What is Thorpe and Company's adjusted WACC after the bond sale if the corporate tax rate is 40%? *Hint:* The weight of equity before selling the bonds is 100%.

19. ***Adjusted WACC.*** Hollydale's is a clothing store in East Park. It paid an annual dividend of $2.50 last year to its shareholders and plans to increase the dividend annually at 2%. It has 500,000 shares outstanding. The shares currently sell for $21.25 per share. Hollydale's has 10,000 semiannual bonds outstanding with a coupon rate of 7.5%, a maturity of sixteen years, and a par value of $1,000. The bonds are currently selling for $874.08 per bond. What is the adjusted WACC for Hollydale's if the corporate tax rate is 35%?

20. ***Adjusted WACC.*** Hollydale's will issue an additional 5,000 bonds with the help of an investment banker. The bonds will be semiannual bonds with thirty years to maturity. The coupon rate will be 8%, and the par value $1,000. The bonds will sell at $851.86 in the market, but the investment banker will receive a 4% commission on the sold bonds. The original bonds have sixteen years to maturity and are semiannual, with a coupon rate of 7.5% and a price of $874.08. There are 10,000 bonds outstanding with this senior issue. What is the new cost of capital for Hollydale's if the company still has 500,000 shares outstanding selling at $21.25 with an annual dividend growth rate of 2% and the last annual dividend of $2.50? The tax rate remains at 35%.

21. ***Beta of a project.*** Magellan is adding a project to the company portfolio and has the following information: the expected market return is 14%, the risk-free rate is 3%, and the expected return on the new project is 18%. What is the project's beta?

22. ***Beta of a project.*** Vespucci is adding a project to the company portfolio and has the following information: the expected market return is 12%, the risk-free rate is 5%, and the expected return on the new project is 10%. What is the project's beta?

23. ***Constraints on borrowing*****.** Country Farmlands Inc. is considering the following potential projects for this coming year, but has only $200,000 for these projects:

Project A: Cost $60,000, NPV $4,000, and IRR 11%

Project B: Cost $78,000, NPV $6,000, and IRR 12%

Project C: Cost $38,000, NPV $3,000, and IRR 10%

Project D: Cost $41,000, NPV $4,000, and IRR 9%

Project E: Cost $56,000, NPV $6,000, and IRR 13%

Project F: Cost $29,000, NPV $2,000, and IRR 7%

What projects should Farmlands pick?

24. ***Constraints on borrowing*****.** Runway Fashions Inc. is considering the following potential projects for the company but has only $1,000,000 in the capital budget. Which projects should it choose?

Project	Cost	NPV	IRR
Winter coats	$750,000	$95,000	13%
Spring dresses	$500,000	$45,000	9%
Fall suits	$500,000	$55,000	11%
Summer sandals	$400,000	$60,000	14%

These problems are available in MyFinanceLab.

Advanced Problems for Spreadsheet Application

1. ***Changing WACC and optimal choice*****.** Austin Enterprises is currently an all-equity firm. The firm is considering selling debt (bonds) and retiring some of the equity. However, at each level of debt, debt becomes more expensive (cost of debt is rising), and the riskiness of the equity also rises with more and more debt. Using a spreadsheet, determine the best combination of debt and equity for Austin Enterprises if:

Current beta of Austin Enterprises is 0.85

Current market return is 12%

Current risk-free rate is 3%

Total equity is 20,000,000 shares at $25 per share

Debt is sold in units of $2,000,000

First unit of debt has a cost of 7.5%

Tax rate of Austin Enterprises is 40%

For each additional unit of debt (each additional $2,000,000), the cost of debt rises by 0.85% and the beta of Austin Enterprises rises by 0.025.

Where is the WACC the lowest? Graph the results of the changing WACC.

2. ***Risk and cost of equity*****.** At the top of the next page is a list of projects in an all-equity firm. If the company has an average beta of 1.05, the expected return on the market is 11%, and the risk-free rate is 2.75%, which projects are accepted and which rejected? If the company chooses a hurdle rate for each project based on the project's listed beta, which projects does it now accept that it previously rejected and which projects does it now reject that it originally accepted? What is the final set of projects that the firm accepts, given the individual hurdle rates?

Project	IRR	Beta	Project	IRR	Beta
1	6.25%	0.35	7	12.84%	1.15
2	6.89%	0.65	8	13.01%	1.25
3	7.54%	0.55	9	13.66%	1.40
4	8.25%	0.70	10	14.21%	1.50
5	9.83%	0.85	11	17.85%	1.45
6	10.12%	0.95	12	18.93%	1.55

MINI-CASE

BioCom, Inc.: Part 3, A Fresh Look at the WACC

This mini-case is available in MyFinanceLab.

In the course of discussing the fiber-optic blood pressure monitor project that we introduced in Chapter 10, a recently hired financial analyst who is working on her MBA asks how the company arrived at 9% as the discount rate to use when evaluating capital budgeting projects. Her question is followed by an embarrassing silence that seems to last forever. Eventually, the comptroller, who has been with the company for many years, offers an explanation. When the company first began to use discounted cash flow methods for capital budgeting decisions in the 1980s, it hired a consultant to explain internal rate of return and net present value. The consultant used 10% in all his examples, so BioCom did the same. By the late 1990s, interest rates had fallen considerably and the company was rejecting some seemingly profitable projects because the hurdle rate was too high, so it lowered it to 9%. As far as he knew, that was the end of the story.

Interestingly, many participants in the discussion—even those who are not from accounting and finance—are aware of the weighted average cost of capital and have a good idea how to compute it, but no one had ever attempted to do so for BioCom. After a brief discussion, they ask the person who raised the question in the first place to analyze the company's debt and equity and report back in a week with her estimate of the company's weighted average cost of capital.

She begins by gathering the following information:

BioCom has two outstanding bond issues. Bond 1 matures in six years, has a par value of $1,000, has a coupon rate of 7% paid semiannually, and now sells for $1,031. Bond 2 matures in sixteen years, has a par value of $1,000, has a coupon rate of 8% paid semiannually, and now sells for $1,035. The preferred stock has a par value of $50, pays a dividend of $1.50, and has a current market value of $19. The common stock sells for $35 per share and recently paid a dividend of $2.50. The company expects dividends to grow at an average annual rate of 6% for the foreseeable future. The risk-free rate is 3%, the expected rate of return on the market portfolio is 12%, BioCom's beta is 1.2, and its marginal tax rate is 34%.

Assist the financial analyst by answering the questions on the next page.

BioCom's Capital by Percentages

Type of Capital	Percent of Book Value	Percent of Market Value
Bond 1	18%	15%
Bond 2	20%	20%
Preferred stock	20%	10%
Common stock	5%	Not available
Retained earnings	37%	Not available
Total common equity		55%

Continued

Continued

Questions

1. Compute the yield to maturity and the after-tax cost of debt for the two bond issues.
2. Compute BioCom's cost of preferred stock.
3. Compute BioCom's cost of common equity. Use the average of results from the dividend growth model and the security market line.
4. Compute BioCom's weighted average cost of capital. Should you use book values or market values for this computation?
5. BioCom could sell new bonds with maturities of fifteen to twenty years at approximately the same yield as Bond 2. It would, however, incur flotation costs of $20.00 per $1,000 of par value. Estimate the effective interest rate BioCom would have to pay on a new issue of long-term debt.
6. Some of BioCom's projects are low risk, some average risk, and some high risk. Should BioCom use the same cost of capital to evaluate all its projects, or should it adjust the discount rate to reflect different levels of risk?

Part 4

Financial Planning and Evaluating Performance

Learning Objectives

LO1 Understand the sources and uses of cash in building a cash budget.

LO2 Explain how companies use sales forecasts to predict cash inflow.

LO3 Understand how production costs vary in terms of cash flow timing.

LO4 Explain possible ways to cover cash deficits and invest cash surplus.

LO5 Prepare a pro forma income statement and a pro forma balance sheet.

Chapter 12

Forecasting and Short-Term Financial Planning

Is the future uncertain? Yes. Can we plan for it? Indeed! One task of a finance manager is to forecast for the coming period. Forecasting is the process of analyzing a company's current and historical data to estimate future events for the coming week, month, quarter, or year. The forecast is the foundation of a company's short-term financial action plan.

Companies use two tools to forecast and set in action a plan: (1) cash forecasts (often labeled cash budgets) and (2) pro forma financial statements (cash budget projections). As with considerable planning, these two financial forecasts begin with sales estimates and production schedules. Financial forecasts are seldom accurate, but they do provide a rational road map for the future and a yardstick by which a company can measure its adherence to or deviation from its short-term plan.

You may have experienced a deviation from a personal short-term financial plan yourself. It's likely that you've been in a situation in which you've come up a little short on cash. To handle the problem, you may have postponed buying something or perhaps asked a friend to cover you. Cash shortfalls can cause problems for a business as well. What do finance managers do in this situation? What do they do if their company faces the more pleasant scenario of an excess in cash? How do they forecast the timing of cash flow into and out of the company in the first place? We shall answer these questions in this chapter.

Before we begin our discussion of short-term financial planning, let's return for a moment to Chapter 9 and to our discussion of long-term and short-term financial planning. Here is a recap of the most important points.

In general, we can separate short-term and long-term financial decisions into three dimensions:

1. Length of effect
2. Cost
3. Degree of information gathering prior to the decision

The longer the effect and the higher the cost that we associate with a decision, the greater the time and degree we allot to gather information on choices and the more sophisticated or complex the decision model. With long-term financial decisions, we most likely devote more time to gathering information than with short-term financial decisions, and the amount of information that we gather is likely larger.

Businesses use this set of dimensions when making choices about how to allocate money to products, services, and company activities. We call capital budgeting decisions *long-term decisions* and typically view them as decisions that have long-term effects that we cannot easily reverse or change. An example of a long-term decision is determining the number of manufacturing facilities that the firm should operate.

Conversely, we view *short-term decisions* as decisions that have short-term effects and that we can change or modify at relatively low costs. An example of a short-term decision is determining the appropriate level of inventories that the firm should maintain. The firm can change the inventory amount with the next order if a product's sales are faster or slower than originally anticipated. As you can appreciate, it is much easier to adjust or change inventory levels than it is to open or close a manufacturing facility.

We are now ready to turn our focus from long-term capital budgeting decisions to short-term financial planning decisions.

12.1 Sources and Uses of Cash

The ultimate goal of cash management is to have sufficient cash—but not too much—on hand to meet business obligations in a timely and appropriate manner. This goal is similar to the personal finance goal that we face with our own daily inflow and outflow of cash. We do not want to be caught short when we need cash, nor do we want to carry too much cash, thereby losing earning power on our money.

The **cash budget** is the analytical tool that estimates the future timing of cash inflow and cash outflow and projects' potential shortfalls and surpluses. Although the cash management process will usually start with sales forecasting, we will first look at the "final product" to get an idea of where we are ultimately heading and why we look at sales forecasts and production schedules. To that end, Table 12.1 presents an abbreviated monthly cash budget for Bridge Water Pumps and Filters, a small manufacturing firm in Boise, Idaho. Bridge makes pumps and filters intended for rural homes that use well water for their domestic water supply.

As Table 12.1 shows, the cash budget's bottom line indicates by month when Bridge expects to have excess cash on hand and when it expects to have cash

TABLE 12.1 Bridge Water Pumps and Filters, Cash Budget for First Six Months of 2012 ($ in thousands)

Cash Flow	Jan.	Feb.	Mar.	Apr.	May	June
Cash receipts	$360	$330	$340	$365	$395	$374
Cash disbursements	$359	$325	$394	$379	$373	$359
Net cash flow	$ 1	$ 5	−$ 54	−$ 14	$ 22	$ 15
Beginning cash	$ 40	$ 41	$ 46	−$ 8	−$ 22	$ 0
Ending cash	$ 41	$ 46	−$ 8	−$ 22	$ 0	$ 15
Reserve for cash	$ 15	$ 15	$ 15	$ 15	$ 15	$ 15
Excess (shortfall)	$ 26	$ 31	($ 23)	($ 37)	($ 15)	$ 0

shortfalls (months for which the bottom row numbers are in parentheses, indicating a negative number). Bridge's cash budget for the first six months of 2012 indicates that the company will be fine in January and February in terms of cash, but it will need to borrow $23,000 in March and another $14,000 in April (the $37,000 shortfall by the end of April) to meet its cash needs and still have the appropriate reserves on hand. The $15,000 reserve is a "safety net" of cash for unanticipated emergencies, much like the extra cash that you might carry for your unexpected emergencies. May and June, however, produce sufficient cash inflow to pay back the shortfall and return the company to its $15,000 desired reserve level.

Although the budget for Bridge Water Pumps and Filters is only for illustration purposes and we have yet to explore the origin of the numbers, it gives you a necessary overview as we proceed through the different forecasting exercises that determine these numbers. We need to estimate anticipated cash receipts (inflows) each month as well as anticipated cash expenditures (outflows) to see if the receipts will be sufficient to handle the disbursements. An anticipated cash shortfall is easier to manage than one that is a surprise.

We will revisit cash forecasts later in the chapter. First, though, let's refresh your knowledge of the difference between the recording of revenue and the receipt of cash and the recording of expenses and the disbursement of cash.

What are the sources and uses of cash? We first looked at this issue in Chapter 10 when we studied incremental cash flow. Here we want to look *forward* to estimate future cash flow, anticipating excess and shortfall so that we can manage the company's cash flow in the best way possible. We do not want to get caught short at a time when we need cash or get caught holding excess cash that we could put to work for the company. Figure 12.1 illustrates a company's main cash inflows and outflows.

The listings of cash inflows and cash outflows in Figure 12.1 are not exhaustive, but they give a general overview of the kinds of items that go into each category. Our starting point for building the cash budget is the left side of the figure. We will begin with the cash receipts and specifically with sales forecasting. As we move through this process, we will address the difference between sales revenue and the receipt of cash from sales. We will then move to production and again focus on the difference between cost of goods sold and the timing of the cash outflow for the production of goods.

FIGURE 12.1 Cash inflows and cash outflows for a company.

Sources of cash

Cash sales from products and services
Accounts receivable (mainly credit sales)
Cash sales of equipment or other assets
Funding sources (bank loans, bond sales, stock sales)

Uses of cash

Cash purchases (supplies, inventories, raw materials, and so forth)
Accounts payable (to suppliers)
Wages and salaries
Rent, lease, or mortgage payments
Utility payments (sometimes called *overhead*)
Shipping costs
Interest payments
Dividend payments
Paying off debt (loans and bonds)
Repurchases of stock

12.2 Cash Budgeting and the Sales Forecast

We start the process of building a cash forecast with a prediction of the cash inflow from future sales, or the **sales forecast**. Remember that the *timing of the sale* and the *cash inflow from the sale* often happen at different times. So, we have two timing issues in sales forecasting:

1. When will the sales occur?
2. When will the firm receive the money for the sales?

The sales or marketing department usually provides the sales amount and timing. Then, based on the sales forecast, the finance manager estimates the receipt of cash based on cash and credit sales.

Before we look at our example company for this chapter, let's look first at McDonald's Corp. and its annual sales to understand why we need to start with a good sales forecast. Looking back at the recent history of McDonald's, we see the following revenues (in thousands) and percentage of growth in sales:

TABLE 12.2 McDonald's Sales Revenues 2008 to 2011

Year	Sales Revenues	Percentage Growth in Sales
2008	$23,522,400	—
2009	$22,744,700	−3.3%
2010	$24,074,600	5.8 %
2011	?	?

How should McDonald's estimate sales revenues for 2011? It could take one of three simple approaches:

1. Average the two previous growth rates (1.25% growth for $24,375,500).
2. Take only the prior year's growth rate (5.8% growth for $25,470,900).
3. Use the compounded average growth rate (1.167% growth rate for $24,328,200).

In sales forecasting, the time when a company records a sale is often different from the time that it actually receives cash because of credit arrangements. The collection or accounts receivable cycle deals with the timing of credit sales.

Using historical data is quick, but it does not necessarily give an accurate prediction. When we look at the actual revenue for McDonald's in 2011, will it show an increase as the world economy recovers from the 2008 recession? Will it show a growth as McDonald's expands into foreign markets? It is clear that McDonald's must use a more sophisticated model than just historical data to project its sales if it wants a reliable number.

Let's take a look at Bridge Water Pumps and Filters, our example company, to see how it determines its January sales forecast. Bridge has three sales representatives covering parts of eastern Washington, eastern Oregon, and most of southern Idaho. The sales representatives deal directly with home builders and homeowners. About 40% of Bridge's sales are to new construction homes, and about 60% are to homeowners who are replacing their current water pump and filter systems. Figure 12.2 provides some marketing background and assumptions.

Bridge will use two types of data sources, internal data and external data. **Internal data** are points of information that are unique or proprietary to the firm.

- New housing permits
  - Counts the new housing permits filed in each county
  - Classifies the permits based on the type of water system the home will use
  - Historical success rate on new houses is 30%
- Aging pump systems in market area
  - Tracks last installation of pumps and filters in rural homes
  - Target replacement period is every fifteen years
  - Replacement of prior Bridge systems at 85% rate
  - Replacement of other companies' systems at 10% rate
- Current estimates for January sales
  - Estimated Bridge systems ready for replacement in January: 105
  - Estimated other companies' systems ready for replacement in January: 260
  - Estimated new-home installations: 250

FIGURE 12.2 Marketing data for Bridge Water Pumps and Filters.

Here the data are the results of the firm's internal tracking of well-water systems and the replacement period of fifteen years. **External data** are points of information from outside the firm, often available to the public. Here the data are the housing permits that are filed with the county by home builders. Based on its external and internal data, the marketing department has projected the following January sales:

1. Newly filed permits in November 2011 with construction requiring well-water system installations in January 2012: 250 permits. Anticipated rate of sales is 30%: $250 \times 0.30 = 75$.
2. Estimated number of homes with current Bridge systems replacing their pumps in January 2012: 105 homes. Anticipated rate of sales is 85%: $105 \times 0.85 = 89$.
3. Estimated number of homes without Bridge systems replacing their pumps in January 2012: 260 homes. Anticipated rate of sales is 10%: $260 \times 0.10 = 26$.

Therefore, the total number of estimated systems to sell in January 2012 is $75 + 89 + 26 = 190$ units.

Cash Inflow from Sales

Once the finance manager obtains the sales estimate, he or she must estimate the cash flow from these sales in terms of timing. The two issues that we observed at the beginning of this section are at play here: When will the sales occur and when will the firm receive the money for the sales? Accrual-based accounting concepts will help us address the timing issues. We know that the company will record all cash and credit sales completed in January as sales revenue in January, but the actual cash flow will take place over a longer time period because of credit sales. To illustrate, let's look again at the January sales for Bridge and see how the finance manager estimates the cash flow timing from just these sales.

The marketing manager has estimated that the company will sell 190 units at \$2,000 per unit for a total sales revenue of \$380,000 for January 2012. Let's assume that Bridge's financial policy stipulates that replacements to existing homes are only on a cash basis. (We use the term *cash* loosely here. Most homeowners pay via credit cards.) Therefore, the 115 sales for replacement—89 to current Bridge customers and 26 to new Bridge customers—will generate cash flow in January 2012 of \$230,000 ($115 \times \$2{,}000$).

We know that the marketing manager has estimated 75 new-home sales for the month of January. However, the company typically does not receive proceeds for two months. Contractors who buy the systems pay upon house completion. Approximately two-thirds of the homes complete in the following month, and one-third complete two months later. Therefore, the January new-home sales will generate roughly \$100,000 ($\frac{2}{3} \times 75 \times \$2{,}000$) in February and \$50,000 ($\frac{1}{3} \times 75 \times \$2{,}000$) in March. The company will collect total January revenue of \$380,000 over a three-month period: \$230,000 in January, \$100,000 in February, and \$50,000 in March.

However, this estimate isn't the whole story. The finance manager wants to predict the cash receipts for January 2012 and therefore looks back to November and December credit sales from the previous year (Table 12.3) to estimate the percentage of these sales that will end up in January 2012 receipts. If we assume, as we did earlier, that the same percentages apply to cash and credit sales (60% and 40%) and the same timing of credit sales holds (two-thirds first month and one-third second month), we have the following January receipts:

TABLE 12.3 **Bridge Water Pumps and Filters Cash Flow from Sales: January, February, and March 2012 Cash Flow Estimates**

Sales	Nov. 2011	Dec. 2011	Jan. 2012	Feb. 2012	Mar. 2012
Forecasted sales	210 units	140 units	190 units	160 units	170 units
Replacement (60%)	$252,000	$168,000	**$230,000**	$192,000	$204,000
New home (40%)	—	—			
Prior month ($\frac{2}{3}$)	—	$112,000	**$ 74,000**	**$100,000**	$ 86,000
Two months prior ($\frac{1}{3}$)	—	—	**$ 56,000**	$ 38,000	**$ 50,000**
Total cash flow	—	—	$360,000	$330,000	$340,000

November sales of 210 units at 40% credit and one-third of credit sales collected two months later (in January): $210 \times 0.40 \times \frac{1}{3} \times \$2{,}000 = \$56{,}000$
December sales of 140 units at 40% credit and two-thirds of credit collected one month later (in January): $140 \times 0.40 \times \frac{2}{3} \times \$2{,}000 = \$74{,}667$

(For the December sales, we use only whole units, so we truncate this result to $74,000, which represents 37 units, not 37.33 units from the formula.)

With three months of forecasted sales, the finance manager can now estimate the January receipts at $360,000 ($230,000 + $56,000 + $74,000). Table 12.3 shows these numbers as well as the January sales broken out over January and the next two months and the following two months' receipts. We have not filled in the entire table (we do not show the cash inflow for November and December because it would require going back to September and October to get the credit sales for those two months). We do show the first quarter's cash flow by estimating February and March as well as January.

One other item may affect cash flow from sales: bad debts. The finance manager needs to know if the company will not collect credit sales from customers. This situation will entail a reduction in the cash flow estimate. In Chapter 13, we will look more closely at accounts receivable and issues surrounding the management of this account.

Other Cash Receipts

Although sales from a company's products and services are usually the main source of cash inflow, other activities can generate cash receipts. For instance, companies sell off equipment or other assets. We looked at this scenario in Chapter 10 with the selling off of equipment at the project's end. In that instance, calculating the actual cash flow for disposal required the finance manager to determine the asset's book value and compare it with the sale price to determine whether there was a gain or loss on disposal. The tax consequences of the gain or loss had an effect on the net cash flow from disposal. Just as with cash and credit sales for estimating the cash budget timing, however, the sale of the equipment might occur in one month and the tax consequence in another. The finance manager's job is to estimate the timing of each cash flow component in the appropriate month.

Companies also raise funds from various funding sources. We will look more closely at many aspects of raising capital in Chapter 15, but here you just need to understand that cash from these activities is also part of the cash budget.

We have now looked at the left side of Figure 12.1 and the sources of cash, or cash inflows and receipts. We now turn to the right side and the uses of cash, or cash outflows and expenditures.

12.3 Cash Outflow from Production

Because companies typically use sales forecasts for scheduling production, cash expenditures—or disbursements—are also closely tied to these forecasts. Product and service availability is necessary to meet customer needs. Therefore, companies usually base the production schedule on the timing of future sales.

Production costs include, among other items, expenditures such as workers' wages, the raw materials for manufacturing products, the overheads (such as electricity, water, and plant space), and shipping costs. For example, Bridge Water Pumps and Filters associates the following production costs with each $2,000 unit: $300 in labor, $500 in materials, $200 in overheads, and $100 in shipping costs, for a total of $1,100. Again, although we can estimate these production and shipping costs, it is up to the finance manager to estimate the *timing* of the cash outflows (expenditures) for these products. Remember that in accounting, the recording of the cost of goods sold occurs at the time of the sale, but the cash flow may take place over an extended time period.

EXAMPLE 12.1 Estimating cash outflow from a production schedule

Problem Bridge Water Pumps and Filters uses the sales forecast to plan production. The company produces the pumps one month in advance of the forecasted sale. Therefore, the company will schedule the January sales forecast of 190 units for December production. However, the company is well aware that sales forecasts and actual sales can differ, so it has a policy of retaining 10% in inventory to accommodate sales above forecast. Bridge acquires raw materials for pumps the month ahead (in this case, November), it pays wages in the current month of production (December), it pays utilities a month after production (January), and it pays shipping a month after the sale (two months after production, in February). Finally, an inventory count reveals that there are currently 15 units on hand above the projected sales for November (at the start of November when Bridge places the raw material order). When does the cash outflow take place for the January sales that Bridge will produce in December?

Solution If the January sales forecast is for 190 units and management has a 10% safety level of stock, it wants 190 + 19 or 209 units in inventory at the start of January. If Bridge anticipates the beginning inventory at 15 units above the November sales at the start of November when it orders raw materials, the December production schedule is for 194 units (209 − 15). Now, we can estimate the months of cash outflow for December production:

Raw materials: 194 × $500 = $97,000 paid in November
Wages: 194 × $300 = $58,200 paid in December
Utilities: 194 × $200 = $38,800 paid in January
Shipping: 190 × $100 = $19,000 paid in February

These estimates indicate when the December production for the anticipated January sales will manifest as cash outflow.

Once a company determines all the expenditures and receipts, a finance manager can estimate the probability of cash excess or cash shortfall in upcoming periods. We turn to those subjects next.

12.4 The Cash Forecast: Short-Term Deficits and Short-Term Surpluses

Having examined some of the cash inflow and cash outflow issues, we can now turn to the daily planning for cash, or the cash budget. We want to home in on the management of cash as it applies to a company's short-term borrowing or investing. The goal, of course, is to have sufficient cash on hand to pay bills without carrying excess cash. Excess cash is an asset that has an opportunity cost: lost earning power for the company.

We can condense the items that require cash outflow from Figure 12.1 into four categories:

1. Accounts payable for materials and supplies
2. Salaries, labor wages, taxes, and other operating expenses of the business
3. Capital expenditures
4. Long-term financing expenses (interest payments, dividend payments, issuing costs of debt and equity)

Although all four categories are important with respect to cash flow, we will concentrate on the first two because they apply to the firm's daily operating decisions. We now direct our attention to cash management as it pertains to the firm's operations, much as you do with your daily cash needs. Again, our objective is to determine the cash surplus (money the company can invest) or the cash deficit (money the company needs to borrow). Let's return to Bridge Water Pumps and Filters to understand this application of short-term cash management.

Bridge is a steady business, but it has monthly fluctuations in sales and collections. Table 12.4 shows the company's estimated monthly cash flow from operations. The company currently projects a balance of $40,000 in the company checking account at the start of January. This simple monthly cash flow estimate allows the managers of Bridge Water Pumps and Filters to anticipate periods when the company may need to borrow and periods when the company will have excess cash for investing. The table shows that, at the end of six months, Bridge has a positive cash balance of $15,000, which is equal to its desired reserve. What could go wrong?

The problem is that in the first three months of the year when sales are low, the company draws down the cash account to the point where it has a negative balance in March and April. That is, the company may have to delay payments to suppliers or employees. The second quarter shows stronger sales, which are eventually sufficient to replenish the cash account. Whenever a company foresees a potential cash deficit, it will need to determine how to finance this short-term cash need. Therefore, a company may need to borrow for the short-term to make ends meet. Companies that operate with seasonal fluctuations often face this problem of insufficient cash in one period and excess cash in another. A prominent example of a company with seasonal fluctuations is Mattel Inc. If you look at its quarterly sales revenues alone, you would see relatively low sales in its first two quarters (first quarter 2010: $952 million; second quarter 2010: $1,019 million), but a significant jump in the third and fourth quarters (third quarter: $1,833 million; fourth quarter: $2,125 million). An increase of 100% in sales in the last two

TABLE 12.4 Monthly Cash Budget for Bridge Water Pumps and Filters

Cash Flow	Jan.	Feb.	Mar.	Apr.	May	June
Beginning cash	$ 40,000	$ 41,000	$ 46,000	−$ 8,000	−$ 22,000	$ 0
Incoming						
Cash sales	$230,000	$192,000	$204,000	$220,000	$240,000	$230,000
Accounts receivable payments	$130,000	$138,000	$136,000	$145,000	$155,000	$144,000
Total in	$360,000	$330,000	$340,000	$365,000	$395,000	$374,000
Outgoing						
Accounts payable	$ 137,900	$ 110,000	$155,000	$152,000	$150,000	$138,000
Labor	$ 47,100	$ 41,000	$ 60,000	$ 48,000	$ 44,000	$ 42,000
Salaries	$170,000	$170,000	$175,000	$175,000	$175,000	$175,000
Interest	$ 4,000	$ 4,000	$ 4,000	$ 4,000	$ 4,000	$ 4,000
Total out	$359,000	$325,000	$394,000	$379,000	$373,000	$359,000
Net cash flow	$ 1,000	$ 5,000	−$ 54,000	−$ 14,000	$ 22,000	$ 15,000
Ending balance	$ 41,000	$ 46,000	−$ 8,000	−$ 22,000	$ 0	$ 15,000

quarters may have a significant effect on cash flow and make the cash budgeting process a major event for Mattel's finance manager.

Funding Cash Deficits

A company can handle cash shortfalls in four ways:

1. Cash from savings
2. Unsecured loans (letters of credit)
3. Secured loans (using accounts receivable or inventories)
4. Other sources (commercial paper, trade credit, or banker's acceptance)

By far, the simplest way to cover a cash deficit is to take money out of one's savings account—provided, of course, that one has sufficient savings to cover the shortfall. The most common way for a business to finance short-term cash deficits, however, is to obtain a bank loan. Often a company arranges these loans ahead of time as a **line of credit**, which is an unsecured bank loan whereby the bank agrees to lend a company up to a specific amount of cash, at the discretion of the company. "Unsecured" means that there is no pledge of specific assets backing the loan in case of default. So, a line of credit is simply a prearranged loan. Often, the bank will require the company to pay off the line of credit (return the balance to zero) and keep it there for a specific period of time each year. We call this the **clean-up period**. For example, a bank requirement might be that the line of credit remains at a zero balance for at least one sixty-day period each year. Banks require a clean-up period so that this temporary loan does not turn into a permanent loan. The parallel in your personal finances is a credit card. The credit card gives you a prearranged borrowing amount up to a maximum. You also agree to pay a fee for the use of the money. With lines of credit, this fee (interest rate) typically floats, based on the prevailing market interest rates, whereas your credit card rate is generally fixed.

Companies can also apply for **secured loans**, in which they pledge assets against borrowed funds as collateral for the loan. In personal finance, car loans and home mortgages are secured loans because the borrower pledges the car and home as collateral for the loan. Should you fail to make a loan payment, the lender can seize your car or home to recover the cost of the loan. Likewise, in business, companies can pledge receivables or inventories against their loans.

For inventories to qualify as a pledge on a loan, businesses need to easily transfer them to the lender and the lender needs to have the ability to easily convert the inventory into cash. Bridge may be able to easily transfer the water pump and filter systems to the bank, but the bank might not be able to easily convert them into cash to cover the loan. The more generic the inventory, the better it serves as a pledge against a loan.

As businesses grow and become more established, other short-term financing options emerge. For example, companies with strong histories and good reputations can borrow short-term funds directly from the investing public or investment companies. **Commercial paper** is a financial asset that a company sells directly to investors, like bonds and common stock, but with very short maturity dates. Typically, commercial paper has a maturity date of less than 90 days. The maximum maturity date is 270 days; otherwise, companies must register any commercial paper that exceeds 270 days with the Securities and Exchange Commission.

Another way to finance operations is through a **banker's acceptance**, which is much like a postdated check that the bank guarantees. Banker's acceptances are for self-liquidating inventories. For example, a car dealer may finance the purchase of imported cars with a banker's acceptance. As the dealer sells the imported cars and generates cash flow, the car dealer pays off the banker's acceptance. The imported cars are self-liquidating in that the dealer sells them as part of the normal business operation. On the other hand, a business that uses delivery trucks to perform a vital business function cannot use a banker's acceptance to acquire the delivery trucks because the trucks will not be sold as part of the normal business operations to generate cash to pay off the banker.

Finally, just knowing how to speed up receivables and slow down payables (legally, of course!) may be sufficient to survive cash deficit times. For example, Bridge's finance manager may delay payments to suppliers for a week or two until sufficient cash is available. Of course, this tactic puts a burden on one's suppliers and may sour them in terms of doing future business with the company. It is a choice of the manager to either borrow from the bank or delay payments.

Investing Cash Surpluses

When a company has excess funds, it has four options:

1. Put the surplus in a savings account or invest it in marketable securities.
2. Repay lenders and owners (retire debt early or pay extra dividends).
3. Replace aging assets (reinvest the money in company assets).
4. Invest in new company projects (accept positive net present value projects).

The simplest thing to do with a surplus is to hold it in anticipation of cash deficits. Companies can either keep the money as cash or invest it in financial assets. We call such assets **marketable securities** because the company plans to turn these security holdings back into cash in a short period of time.

If the company does not need the excess cash to cover future cash deficits, it can use it to pay down, or "retire," current debt. Another option is to give the cash back to the owners via extra dividend payments. The auto industry used to pay special one-time dividends to owners when companies had a strong cash performance. We used to see this practice of special dividends by Ford Motor Company prior to its suspension of its cash dividend as it would pay large one-time special dividends when earnings were high.

Companies also use excess cash to replace aging assets. Here again, managing the timing of replacement comes into play. When cash flow is tight, a company often extends maintenance and replacement. On the other hand, when cash flow is abundant, a company can complete replacement and maintenance programs at a faster pace. Ultimately, the speed of replacement and the maintenance of assets are both functions of cash available and the company's operating needs.

Finally, a company can use surpluses to invest in its growth through internal funding of positive net present value projects. As you have seen in previous chapters, growing a firm through its profits from such projects can be very beneficial to owners because their wealth increases without additional contributions to the company.

12.5 Planning with Pro Forma Financial Statements

Another important aspect of short-term financial planning is forecasting operating cash flow and, ultimately, the company's profitability in the coming period. This type of financial planning typically uses forecasted income statements, balance sheets, and statements of cash flow. We call these forecasted accounting statements pro forma financial statements, or pro formas for short. A **pro forma financial statement**—whether a balance sheet, statement of cash flow, income statement, or retained earnings statement—sets out the company's financial predictions on an "as if" basis; that is, it projects future financial performance based on a set of operating and sales assumptions. There are many ways to produce pro formas, but the statements usually rely on two primary inputs:

1. The prior year's financial statements and the relationship of the account balances to each other
2. The projected sales for the coming year

We use the prior year's financial statements to find the relationship or relative percentage of each line (accounting category) to either the sales revenue or the firm's total assets. We use the projected sales for the coming year as the starting point for all the income statement lines. To illustrate, let's stay with Bridge Water Pumps and Filters. First, we look at last year's income statement and the relative percentage of each line to sales.

Pro Forma Income Statement

Figure 12.3 provides the prior year's income statement with each line's actual dollar amount and percentage of total sales. What does it tell us? Among other things, it indicates the following:

- For every sales dollar, it took a little more than \$0.50 to produce the product (cost of goods sold at 50.42%).
- For every sales dollar, approximately \$0.125 ended up as net income (12.42%).
- For every sales dollar, shareholders received about \$0.05 in dividends (4.96%).

The next objective is to estimate the firm's potential performance for the coming year. Typically, we start with the sales forecast from the marketing

FIGURE 12.3

Bridge Water Pumps and Filters Income Statement Year Ending December 31, 2011 ($ in thousands)		
	Amount	Percentage of total
Sales		
Cash sales	$2,880	60.00%
Credit sales	$1,920	40.00%
Total sales	**$4,800**	**100.00%**
Returns	$ 24	0.50%
Net sales revenue	$4,776	99.50%
Cost of goods sold		
Materials	$1,200	25.00%
Labor (wages)	$ 732	15.25%
Overhead (electric and water)	$ 488	10.17%
Total cost of goods sold	$2,420	50.42%
Depreciation	$ 218	4.54%
Selling, general, and administrative	$ 931	19.40%
Operating profits (EBIT)	$1,207	25.15%
Interest expense	$ 291	6.07%
Taxable income	$ 916	19.08%
Taxes (federal and state)	$ 320	6.67%
Net income	**$ 596**	**12.42%**
Common stock distributions (dividends)	$ 238	4.96%
Retained earnings	$ 358	7.46%

department and prepare a pro forma income statement using the percentages of the prior year for each category. Thus, if we have a forecasted growth in sales of 6% from the marketing department, total sales will be $5,088,000 for the coming year (1.06 × $4,800,000). Using the exact same percentages from the 2011 income statement, we can project a pro forma for Bridge Water Pumps and Filters for 2012 as depicted in Figure 12.4.

Although this method suggests that the company will generate $632,000 in profit (net income) this coming year if it hits its sales forecast of $5,088,000, it may be a little too simplistic. Let's look more closely at a few specific line items in Figure 12.4. On the depreciation line item, the company uses 4.54% of sales revenue for the coming year. Depreciation tends to go down each year with the modified asset cost recovery system (see Chapter 10), not up with sales. Unless there is a change to investments in plant, property, and equipment that will increase the depreciation line item, using the same percentage as that of the previous year may prove erroneous. So, the finance manager should modify the pro forma income statement to accommodate the actual estimate of depreciation for the coming year based on the company's capital budget.

The cost of goods sold line suggests that production costs will stay in line with revenue. With competition from other firms and new technologies, however, the production costs can rise faster than revenue, so the company may need to

FIGURE 12.4

Bridge Water Pumps and Filters Pro Forma Income Statement Year Ending December 31, 2012 ($ in thousands)	Amount	Percentage
Forecasted sales revenue		
Cash sales	$3,053	60.00%
Credit sales	$2,035	40.00%
Total sales	**$5,088**	**100.00%**
Returns	$ 25	0.50%
Net sales revenue	$5,063	99.50%
Cost of goods sold		
Materials	$1,272	25.00%
Labor (wages)	$ 776	15.25%
Overhead (electric and water)	$ 517	10.17%
Total cost of goods sold	$2,565	50.42%
Depreciation	$ 231	4.54%
Selling, general, and administrative	$ 987	19.40%
Operating profits (EBIT)	$1,280	25.15%
Interest expense	$ 309	6.07%
Taxable income	$ 971	19.08%
Taxes (federal and state)	$ 339	6.67%
Net income	**$ 632**	**12.42%**
Common stock distributions (dividends)	$ 252	4.96%
Retained earnings	$ 380	7.46%

adjust costs upward. Another issue is fixed versus variable costs. As sales increase, if the company has some fixed costs (and these costs are truly fixed and do not vary with production or sales), a higher percentage of sales dollars flows to the bottom line. Another adjustment may be necessary for selling, general, and administrative expenses in line with known changes in these expenses that may not correspond directly to sales or production. The finance manager will work with the basic pro forma income statement and known adjustments to fine-tune the company's expected performance outcome for the coming year.

Pro Forma Balance Sheet

We can take a similar approach for projecting the coming year's balance sheet. The company looks at the prior year's balance sheet and finds each line's percentage of total assets. It then forecasts the coming year's total assets based on known changes such as the completion of capital projects, desired levels of certain accounts such as cash and inventories, and additional borrowing for capital projects. Again, the finance manager uses these changes as the starting point and then adjusts the individual lines for known changes or relative amounts. For example, if the company will complete a large capital project in the coming year and the plant, property, and equipment line will grow significantly, its percentage of total assets should increase. Therefore, other asset lines such as cash, accounts receivable, and possibly inventories should fall as a percentage of total assets in the coming year. This type of adjustment holds true for the liabilities and owners' equity account lines as well. Financing a capital project may require additional debt financing. Therefore, the percentage of long-term debt will rise above its prior year's percentage of total assets.

EXAMPLE 12.2 A pro forma balance sheet for Bridge Water Pumps and Filters

Problem Bridge Water Pumps and Filters requires $500,000 for a plant expansion. Some of this funding will come from operations (the equity owners' contribution through retained earnings), some from changes in the company's current assets and current liabilities, and the remainder through debt via a bank loan. The lending bank wants the current balance sheet and a pro forma balance sheet for the coming year as part of the documents for the loan application. Prepare the pro forma balance sheet with the following assumptions and targets and determine the needed increase in long-term debt for the coming year:

Net fixed assets will increase by $500,000 (capital expenditure).
Cash balance account will be at $150,000.
Accounts receivable will be 6% of forecasted sales, or $305,000.
Total inventories will be 15% of prior year's sales, $4,800,000, with one-third in raw materials and two-thirds in finished goods.
All new financing will be long-term debt.
Increase in retained earnings will be $380,000 (from the pro forma income statement).

Figure 12.5 depicts the current balance sheet.

Bridge Water Pumps and Filters Balance Sheet for the Period Ending 12/31/2011 ($ in thousands)					
ASSETS	Amount	Percentage	**LIABILITIES**	Amount	Percentage
Current assets			**Current liabilities**		
Cash	$ 130	2.15%	Accounts payable	$ 358	5.92%
Accounts receivable	$ 245	4.05%	Taxes payable	$ 242	4.00%
Inventories			**Total current liabilities**	**$ 600**	**9.91%**
			Long-term debt	$2,702	44.65%
Raw materials	$ 324	5.35%	**Total liabilities**	**$3,302**	**54.56%**
Finished goods	$ 400	6.61%	**OWNERS' EQUITY**		
Total inventory	$ 724	11.96%	Common stock	$ 62	1.02%
Total current assets	**$1,099**	**18.16%**	Retained earnings	$2,688	44.42%
Net fixed assets	$4,953	81.84%	**Total owners' equity**	**$2,750**	**45.44%**
TOTAL ASSETS	**$6,052**	**100.00%**	**TOTAL LIABILITIES AND OWNERS' EQUITY**	**$6,052**	**100.00%**

FIGURE 12.5

Solution Figure 12.6 shows the solution. To get to the solution, first fill in the asset side of the balance sheet with amounts that you calculate from the assumptions:

> Cash is \$150,000.
> Accounts receivable is \$305,280 (\$5,088,000 × 0.06 = \$305,280), rounded to \$305,000.
> Total inventory is \$720,000 (\$4,800,000 × 0.15 = \$720,000).
> Raw materials are one-third of total inventory (\$720,000 × $\frac{1}{3}$ = \$240,000).
> Finished goods are two-thirds of total inventory (\$720,000 × $\frac{2}{3}$ = \$480,000).
> Net fixed assets are \$4,953,000 + \$500,000 = \$5,453,000.
> The total assets are now \$6,628,000.

Fill in the liabilities based on the same percentages as those of last year except for the common stock, which will not change (all new financing is debt); a targeted reduction in accounts payable to 5% of assets; and an increase in retained earnings (\$380,000) projected by the pro forma income statement:

> Accounts payable reduces to 5.0% of \$6,628,000, or \$331,400 (round to \$331,000).
> Taxes payable will be 4.00% of \$6,628,000, or \$265,120 (round to \$265,000).
> Retained earnings are \$380,000 + \$2,688,000 = \$3,068,000.
> Common stock will remain at \$62,000.

So, for the balance sheet to balance, long-term debt must be \$2,902,000 (\$6,628 − \$331 − \$265 − \$62 − \$3,068 = \$2,902.) Therefore, the long-term

Bridge Water Pumps and Filters
Pro Forma Balance Sheet for the Period Ending December 31, 2012
(\$ in thousands)

ASSETS	Amount	Percentage	LIABILITIES	Amount	Percentage
Current assets			**Current liabilities**		
Cash	\$ 150	2.26%	Accounts payable	\$ 331	5.00%
Accounts receivable	\$ 305	4.60%	Taxes payable	\$ 265	4.00%
Inventories			**Total current liabilities**	**\$ 596**	**9.00%**
Raw materials	\$ 240	3.62%	Long-term debt	\$2,902	43.78%
			Total liabilities	**\$3,498**	**52.78%**
Finished goods	\$ 480	7.24%	**OWNERS' EQUITY**		
Total inventory	\$ 720	10.86%	Common stock	\$ 62	0.94%
Total current assets	**\$1,175**	**17.72%**	Retained earnings	\$3,068	46.29%
Net fixed assets	\$5,453	82.27%	**Total owners' equity**	**\$3,130**	**47.23%**
TOTAL ASSETS	**\$6,628**	**100.00%**	**TOTAL LIABILITIES AND OWNERS' EQUITY**	**\$6,628**	**100.00%**

FIGURE 12.6

debt account needs to increase by $200,000 ($2,902,000 − $2,702,000). To complete the $500,000 funding for the project, the company will need outside funding of $200,000. The other funding will come from internal funding sources.

Example 12.2 reflects the finance manager's best estimates, given inputs from marketing and the company's history. The funding of the $500,000 capital project will come from a variety of sources (mainly new debt and cash retained through operations), and the pro forma balance sheet reflects the needed amount from outside funding if the company does not plan to increase equity funding through sale of common stock. To see all the sources and uses anticipated for the coming year, the company prepares a pro forma statement of cash flow. Although we will not build the pro forma statement of cash flow step by step, Figure 12.7 shows the one for Bridge Water Pumps and Filters for the coming year. Note that the bottom line of $20 (thousand) is the change in the cash account from 2011 to 2012 (from $130,000 to $150,000).

A company uses pro forma financial statements as tools to forecast its profitability and potential financial performance for the coming year. The statements help highlight areas that the company should monitor as part of its short-term financial planning. The key to remember is that the foundation of these statements comes from the sales forecast.

The quality of financial forecasts depends heavily on the reliability of the inputs. To see how technology figures in the art and science of forecasting and financial planning, see the nearby "Putting Finance to Work" feature.

In the next chapter, we explore more details of cash management as we examine ways to manage accounts receivable, accounts payable, and inventories. We can then maximize the efficiency of the company's short-term financial planning.

Bridge Water Pumps and Filters Pro Forma Statement of Cash Flow for 2012 ($ in thousands)		
Sources and (uses): Operating activities		
Operating cash flow	$1,172	
Increase in current assets excluding cash	$ 56	
Decrease in current liabilities	$ 4	
Total: Sources and (uses) from operating activities		$1,112
Sources and (uses): Investing activities		
Increase in capital spending	$ 731	
Total: Sources and (uses) from investing activities		$ 731
Sources and (uses): Financing activities		
Interest expense	$ 309	
Dividends	$ 252	
Increase in long-term liabilities	$ 200	
Increase in common stock	$ 0	
Total: Sources and (uses) from financing activities		$ 361
Net sources and (uses) or change in cash account		**$ 20**

FIGURE 12.7

Putting Finance to Work

Information Technology

The quality of short-term financial plans and forecasts depends completely on the quality of information that goes into them. The cash flow forecast requires us to know what inventory we have on hand, where it is, how long we expect to hold it before we sell it, and how long it takes us to replace it. It requires us to know how much money our customers owe us and when we expect them to pay. The sales forecast requires data on what we sold recently, what we sold in the same period last year, and what trends are developing. For a company like McDonald's that handles thousands of transactions a minute in every corner of the globe, an apparently simple question such as "How much cash do we have on hand?" is not that simple.

These data requirements present a challenge even for relatively uncomplicated businesses that manufacture just a few products like furniture or that retail a single product like automobiles. For a company such as Proctor and Gamble that manufactures an array of consumer products from many different raw materials in many locations, or for retailers such as CVS or Walgreen's that seem to sell everything from alarm clocks to zinc tablets, the problem stretches the imagination. Without such information, our plans and forecasts are little more than a shot in the dark.

Fortunately, financial executives can usually retrieve accurate and timely data with a few keystrokes or clicks of the mouse. Business software can produce many types of reports, including financial statements. Financial planners can enter various assumptions to turn reports into forecasts, budgets, and pro forma financial statements. They can modify critical assumptions to analyze hypothetical scenarios.

It's clear that a company's information is one of its most important assets. The vital tasks of storing, protecting, transmitting, and retrieving such information lie in the realm of information technology, or IT. Those who work in the management of information go by many names, including systems analysts, business analysts, information technology specialists, information managers, and database managers. Whatever we call them, their role is critical to an organization's financial management. They design, develop, implement, and support the systems that make this information usable, retrievable, and secure. Depending on their area of specialization, they may design or adapt software to specific requirements, and they can play a key role in choosing and supporting hardware to run the systems. Because they work closely with managers and staff in the major business functions such as marketing, operations, accounting, and finance, IT specialists must have a good understanding of those functions and their needs. Often, different functions such as finance and marketing will need the same information, but in different formats.

College students who major in computer science, computer engineering, or management information systems prepare for careers in information technology. Some schools offer information technology as a concentration within the business major. These programs, and others with similar names, overlap considerably, but computer science and computer engineering usually require more mathematics and science, whereas programs in the management of information systems require more business courses, especially in accounting, economics, and finance.

IT specialists typically enjoy excellent salaries and job mobility as well as nonmonetary rewards. Those who quickly resolve hardware and software problems for stressed-out coworkers earn their undying gratitude.

To review this chapter, see the Summary Card at the end of the text.

Key Terms

banker's acceptance, p. 367
cash budget, p. 358
clean-up period, p. 366
commercial paper, p. 367
external data, p. 361
internal data, p. 361
line of credit, p. 366
marketable securities, p. 367
pro forma financial statements, p. 368
sales forecast, p. 360
secured loans, p. 367

Questions

1. What are a company's main sources of cash? What are a company's main uses of cash?
2. What are two key timing issues with respect to predicting cash inflow for a sales forecast?
3. What are some of the production costs that are tied to the sales forecast?
4. What is a line of credit? Why would a bank require a company with a line of credit to have a zero balance in its line of credit for at least sixty days a year?
5. What is the difference between a secured loan and an unsecured loan?
6. Why can excess cash be an opportunity cost for a company?
7. If a pro forma income statement has 5% for the net income line, what does that mean in terms of a company's total sales and per dollar sales?
8. In a pro forma income statement, why would a finance manager make changes in the prior year's percentages for different line items? Give an example of a line item that you would expect to vary in percentage every year as sales forecasts grow.
9. In a pro forma balance sheet, what line item would you expect to be constant from year to year in dollar terms and decreasing in terms of percentage of total assets? When would this line item have a significant change in percentage?
10. Why are cash management and cash budgeting important to a company's survival?

Prepping for Exams

1. One function of a finance manager is ______________.
   a. to forecast for the coming period
   b. to forecast for the present period
   c. to forecast for the past period
   d. to forecast for the present and past periods

2. For March, Heavenly Hotel will have cash receipts of $365,000 and cash disbursements of $370,000. If its beginning cash is $4,000 and its reserves are $3,000, what will be its shortfall in cash for the month?
   a. There is no shortfall in cash, but an excess of cash.
   b. −$3,000
   c. −$4,000
   d. −$5,000

3. ______________ consist of items such as number of sales personnel in the field and average sales per representative, competitors and alternative products, and production capabilities and schedules, as well as other factors that the company mainly knows.
   a. External data
   b. Product data
   c. Employee data
   d. Internal data

4. The sales for October, November, and December are \$10,000, \$12,000 and \$18,000, respectively. For any particular sales month, the company receives the following percentages over time in cash: 20% in cash from that same sales month, 50% in cash from the previous month's sales, and 30% in cash from the sales from two months ago. What amount of cash will the company receive during December?
   a. \$12,600
   b. \$12,000
   c. \$9,600
   d. \$9,000

5. Which one of the following costs is *not* a production cost?
   a. wages paid to workers
   b. raw materials for manufacturing products
   c. dividends paid to shareholders
   d. shipping costs that get the product to the customer

6. A company estimates the following expenditures: preferred dividends payout of \$22,200, wages to workers of \$49,600, overhead costs of \$24,300, raw material costs of \$45,000, and shipping costs of \$12,100. What are the total production costs?
   a. \$131,000
   b. \$134,500
   c. \$142,100
   d. \$153,200

7. Depreciation tends to ______________ each year with the modified asset cost recovery system when sales increase.
   a. increase
   b. remain the same
   c. increase exponentially
   d. decrease

8. Which is *not* true of depreciation per the pro forma statement?
   a. Depreciation tends to decrease each year with the modified asset cost recovery system, not increase with sales.
   b. Unless there is a change to investments in plant, property, and equipment, increasing the depreciation line item, using the same percentage as the previous year may prove erroneous.
   c. The finance manager should keep the pro forma income statement constant to accommodate the actual estimate of depreciation for the coming year based on the company's capital budget.
   d. Statements a through c are *not* true.

9. We can condense the items that require cash outflow into basic categories. Which of the following is a basic category?

a. wages (but not commissions)
b. accounts receivable
c. long-term financing expenses (interest payments, dividend payments, issuing costs of debt and equity)
d. choices a through c

10. The following information is for Auxiliary Inc. for the month of May: cash sales of $200,000, accounts receivable payments of $200,000, accounts payable of $200,000, wages and salaries of $100,000, and interest payments of $50,000. There are no other cash inflows or outflows for the month of May, and its beginning monthly cash balance is $50,000. What is Auxiliary's ending cash balance for May?

a. –$50,000
b. $50,000
c. $100,000
d. $150,000

Problems

These problems are available in MyFinanceLab.

1. ***Sales forecasts.*** For the prior three years, sales for National Beverage Company have been $21,962,000 (2007), $23,104,000 (2008), and $24,088,000 (2009). The company uses the prior two years' average growth rate to predict the coming year's sales. What were the sales growth rates for 2008 and 2009? What is the expected sales growth rate using a two-year average for 2010? What is the sales forecast for 2010?
2. ***Sales forecasts.*** For the prior three years, sales for California Cement Company have been $20,011,000 (2009), $21,167,000 (2010), and $22,923,000 (2011). The company uses the prior two years' average growth rate to predict the coming year's sales. What were the sales growth rates for 2010 and 2011? What is the expected sales growth rate using a two-year average for 2012? What is the sales forecast for 2012?
3. ***Sales forecast based on external data.*** Raspberry Phones uses external data to forecast the coming year's sales. The company has 8% of all new-phone sales in the United States and 6% of all replacement phones. Industry forecasts predict an additional eighteen million new-phone buyers and replacement sales of thirty-one million phones in 2012. If the average Raspberry phone costs $85, what sales revenue is the company forecasting for 2012?
4. ***Sales forecast based on external data.*** Nelson Heating and Ventilating Company estimates the coming year's sales revenue based on external data. The company's main business is new shopping mall construction, and it uses the square footage of each mall as a "yardstick" for many financial statements and projections. The company does business in four Midwest states. Last year, it completed heating and ventilating systems on four shopping malls with an average size of 3,000,000 square feet for sales revenues of $9,600,000. Nelson is the primary contractor for one-third of the new malls in the four-state area. This coming year, nine new malls are under construction with an average size of 4,500,000 square feet. What is Nelson's anticipated sales revenue for the coming year?
5. ***Sales receipts.*** National Beverage Company anticipates the following first-quarter sales for 2010: $1,800,000 (January), $1,600,000 (February), and $2,100,000 (March). It posted the following sales figures for the last quarter of 2009: $1,900,000 (October), $2,050,000 (November), and $2,200,000 (December). The company sells 40% of its products on credit, and 60% are cash sales. The company collects credit sales as follows: 30% in the following

month, 50% two months later, 18% three months later, and 2% defaults. What are the anticipated cash inflows for the first quarter of 2010?

6. ***Sales receipts.*** California Cement Company anticipates the following fourth-quarter sales for 2009: $1,800,000 (October), $1,600,000 (November), and $2,100,000 (December). It posted the following sales figures for the third quarter of 2009: $1,900,000 (July), $2,050,000 (August), and $2,200,000 (September).The company sells 90% of its products on credit, and 10% are cash sales. The company collects credit sales as follows: 60% in the following month, 20% two months later, 19% three months later, and 1% defaults. What are the anticipated cash inflows for the last quarter of 2009?
7. ***Production cash outflow.*** National Beverage Company produces its products two months in advance of anticipated sales and ships to warehouse centers the month before sale. The inventory safety stock is 10% of the anticipated month's sale. Beginning inventory in October 2009 was 267,143 units. Each unit costs $0.25 to make. The average selling price is $0.70 per unit. The cost is made up of 40% labor, 50% materials, and 10% shipping (to warehouse). The company pays labor the month of production, shipping the month after production, and raw materials the month prior to production. What is the production cash outflow for the month of October 2009 production, and in what months does it occur? *Note:* October production is based on December anticipated sales. Use the fourth-quarter sales forecasts from Problem 5.
8. ***Production cash outflow.*** California Cement Company produces its products two months in advance of anticipated sales and ships to warehouse centers the month before sale. The inventory safety stock is 20% of the anticipated month's sale. Beginning inventory in September 2009 was 33,913 units. Each unit costs $2.80. The average sales price per unit is $5.75. The cost is made up of 30% labor, 65% materials, and 5% shipping (to warehouse). The company pays labor the month of production, shipping the month after production, and raw materials the month prior to production. What is the production cash outflow for the month of September 2009 production, and in what months does it occur? *Note:* September production is based on November anticipated sales. Use the fourth-quarter sales forecasts from Problem 6.
9. ***Pro forma income statement.*** Given the following income statement for National Beverage Company for 2009 and the sales forecast from Problem 1, prepare a pro forma income statement for 2010.

National Beverage Company Income Statement for 2009	
Sales revenue	$24,088,000
Costs of goods sold	$ 8,164,000
Selling, general, and administrative expenses	$ 7,616,000
Depreciation expenses	$ 2,388,000
EBIT	$ 5,920,000
Interest expense	$ 220,000
Taxable income	$ 5,700,000
Taxes	$ 2,498,000
Net income	**$ 3,202,000**

10. *Pro forma income statement.* Given the following income statement for California Cement Company for 2009 and the sales forecast from Problem 2, prepare a pro forma income statement for 2010.

California Cement Company Income Statement for 2009	
Sales revenue	$22,923,000
Cost of goods sold	$11,713,000
Selling, general, and administrative expenses	$ 4,043,000
Depreciation expenses	$ 1,420,000
EBIT	$ 5,747,000
Interest expense	$ 173,000
Taxable income	$ 5,574,000
Taxes	$ 1,723,000
Net income	**$ 3,851,000**

11. *Pro forma balance sheet.*

National Beverage Company Balance Sheet for the Year Ending December 31, 2009			
ASSETS		LIABILITIES	
Current assets		**Current liabilities**	
Cash	$ 2,440,000	Accounts payable	$ 5,622,000
Marketable securities	$ 1,656,000	Other current liabilities	$ 3,268,000
Accounts receivable	$ 2,704,000	**Total current liabilities**	**$ 8,890,000**
Inventories	$ 1,641,000	Long-term liabilities	
Total current assets	**$ 8,441,000**	Long-term debt	$ 1,314,000
Long-term assets		Other long-term liabilities	$ 2,839,000
		Total long-term liabilities	**$ 4,153,000**
Plant, property, and equipment	$13,686,000	**Total liabilities**	**$13,043,000**
		OWNERS' EQUITY	
Goodwill	$ 1,403,000	Common stock	$ 6,861,000
Intangible assets	$ 6,433,000	Retained earnings	$10,059,000
Total long-term assets	**$21,522,000**	**Total owners' equity**	**$16,920,000**
TOTAL ASSETS	**$29,963,000**	**TOTAL LIABILITIES AND OWNERS' EQUITY**	**$29,963,000**

Next year, National Beverage Company will increase its plant, property, and equipment by $4,000,000 with a plant expansion. The inventories will grow by 30%, accounts receivable will grow by 20%, and marketable securities will reduce by 50% to help finance the expansion. Assuming that all other asset accounts remain the same and the company will use long-term debt to finance the remaining expansion costs (no change in common stock or retained earnings), prepare a pro forma balance sheet for 2010. How much additional debt will the company need using this pro forma balance sheet?

12. ***Pro forma balance sheet.***

California Cement Company Balance Sheet for the Year Ending December 31, 2010			
ASSETS		**LIABILITIES**	
Current assets		**Current liabilities**	
Cash	$ 1,447,000	Accounts payable	$ 6,125,000
Marketable securities	$ 1,129,000	Other current liabilities	$ 1,198,000
Accounts receivable	$ 3,769,000	**Total current liabilities**	**$ 7,323,000**
Inventories	$ 2,601,000	Long-term liabilities	
		Long-term debt	$ 2,488,000
Total current assets	**$ 8,946,000**	Other long-term liabilities	$ 1,524,000
Long-term assets		**Total long-term liabilities**	**$ 4,012,000**
Plant, property, and equipment	$ 6,760,000	**Total liabilities**	**$11,335,000**
		OWNERS' EQUITY	
Goodwill	$ 4,082,000	Common stock	$ 2,493,000
Intangible assets	$ 1,506,000	Retained earnings	$ 7,466,000
Total long-term assets	**$12,348,000**	**Total owners' equity**	**$ 9,959,000**
TOTAL ASSETS	**$21,294,000**	**TOTAL LIABILITIES AND OWNERS' EQUITY**	**$21,294,000**

Next year, California Cement Company will increase its plant, property, and equipment by $6,000,000 with a plant expansion. The inventories will grow by 80%, accounts receivable will grow by 70%, and the company will reduce marketable securities by 60% to help finance the expansion. Assuming all other asset accounts remain the same and the company will use long-term debt to finance the remaining expansion costs (no change in common stock or retained earnings), prepare a pro forma balance sheet for 2011. How much additional debt will the company need using this pro forma balance sheet?

These problems are available in MyFinanceLab.

Advanced Problems for Spreadsheet Application

1. ***Cash flow forecasting.*** Regional Homes Construction Company has a very seasonal business that puts a high demand on cash flow management. Prepare a cash flow for the coming year by month for Regional Construction on a spreadsheet based on the following information:

Projected Housing Starts for the Coming Year 2012

Jan.	Feb.	Mar.	Apr.	May	Jun.	Jul.	Aug.	Sep.	Oct.	Nov.	Dec.
12	12	16	20	32	32	30	24	22	18	12	4

It takes four months to complete a house. All houses are custom built, and the company receives payment the month following completion. The average sales price per home is $450,000. The average cost to build a home is:

Raw materials: 52% of the sales price and paid equally over the first three months of construction
Labor: 28% of the sales price and paid equally over the four months of construction
Fees and permits: 4% of the sales price and paid the month before construction begins
Legal fees and title transfer: 3% of the sales price and paid at completion of the house
Housing starts from the previous year (2011): Sep. 18, Oct. 16, Nov. 11, and Dec. 7
Projected housing starts for Jan. 2013 the following year: 14

What is the total cash flow in and out for 2012 and in which months does Regional Construction Company have negative cash flow?

2. ***Pro forma income statements.*** Green Planet, a restaurant supply company, has the following income statement accounts for 2011:

Revenue	$12,345,000	Sales Returns $185,175	COGS $5,555,250
Fixed Costs	$1,975,200	SG & A Costs $1,481,400	Depreciation $988,320
Interest Expense $ 802,425			

Construct the income statement for 2011 with a tax rate of 38%. Then construct a pro forma statement for the years 2012, 2013, and 2014 if the company expects projected sales to rise annually at 4.5% and all the accounts have the same percent of sales as 2011. Redo the pro forma statements for 2012, 2013, and 2014 if fixed costs are truly fixed and remain at $1,975,200 but all other accounts listed will be at the same percent of sales for the next three years. Find the growth in net income each year.

MINI-CASE

Midwest Properties: Quarterly Forecasting

This mini-case is available in MyFinanceLab.

Dennis Clarkson manages several buildings for Midwest Properties, which owns and manages apartment buildings in university cities such as Madison, Wisconsin, and Champaign-Urbana, Illinois. Midwest's tenants are overwhelmingly students, and the buildings are private, for-profit university residence halls. As a result of this specialized clientele, Midwest's revenues and expenses follow a predictable seasonal pattern. From September through May, vacancy rates are negligible, but they rise rapidly in June, July, and August.

The summer months require careful cash flow planning. The company schedules cleaning, painting, repairs, and renovations when vacancies are highest, so expenses for supplies, materials, temporary student labor, and outside contractors peak when revenues are at their low point for the year.

Dennis is preparing his budget for July, August, and September to submit to headquarters in Chicago. His budgeting forms include adjusted figures for the preceding quarter.

Cash Inflows

Dennis is responsible for 200 rental units: 75% are direct rentals at $600 per month, and 25% are contracted to Mendota University at $500 each per month. Direct rentals pay on the first of the month, and the university makes quarterly payments at the end of each quarter regardless of whether the apartments are occupied. Rents are scheduled to increase by 5% in September; the increase will affect both direct rentals and the university's payment at the end of the month. By law, rental companies must segregate security and

Continued

Continued

damage deposits from operating funds and return them to tenants with interest when they vacate apartments, so these funds are not included in the budget, but Dennis nonetheless assumes an average damage assessment of $100 per vacating tenant. These funds become available in the following month and should contribute $7,500 to cash flows in June and $2,500 in July, August, and September.

Cash Outflows

Salaries are $8,000 per month. Labor and outside contractors average $2,000 per month for most of the year, but $10,000 per month in June, July, and August. Supplies and materials purchases are normally $5,000 per month, but that number triples in June, July, and August. The company pays for supplies and materials one month after they purchase them. Utilities average $80 per occupied apartment. Only half of the 50 contracted apartments are actually occupied June through August. The company pays utilities in the following month. Payments of $210,000 on debt, $31,500 for property taxes, and $15,500 for insurance are due in the last month of each quarter.

Questions

1. Complete the following table of cash collections for the months of July, August, and September. Use Table 12.1 as a model.

	Apr.	May	June	July	Aug.	Sept.
Occupied direct rental units	150	150	100	75	50	150
Collections from direct rentals	$90,000	$90,000	$ 60,000			
Contract rental payments			$ 75,000			
Damage assessments	0	0	$ 7,500			
Total cash flow	$90,000	$90,000	$142,500			

2. Complete the following table of cash outflows for the months of July, August, and September.

	Apr.	May	June	July	Aug.	Sept.
Total occupied units	200	200	125	100	75	200
Payments for supplies and materials purchases	$ 5,000	$ 5,000	$ 5,000			
Salaries	$ 8,000	$ 8,000	$ 8,000			
Labor	$ 2,000	$ 2,000	$ 10,000			
Payments for utilities	$16,000	$16,000	$ 16,000			
Payment on debt			$150,000			
Property taxes			$ 31,500			
Insurance			$ 15,500			
Total cash outflow	$31,000	$31,000	$228,000			

3. Complete the following monthly cash flow estimate for the months of July, August, and September. Use Table 12.4 as a model.

Cash Flow	Apr.	May	June	July	Aug.	Sept.
Beginning cash	$25,000	$ 84,000	$143,000			
Incoming collections from direct rentals	$90,000	$ 90,000	$ 60,000			
Contract rental payments			$ 75,000			
Damage assessments	0	0	$ 7,500			
Total in	$90,000	$ 90,000	$142,500			
Outgoing payments for supplies and materials purchases	$ 5,000	$ 5,000	$ 5,000			
Salaries	$ 8,000	$ 8,000	$ 8,000			
Labor	$ 2,000	$ 2,000	$ 10,000			
Payments for utilities	$16,000	$ 16,000	$ 16,000			
Payment on debt			$150,000			
Property taxes			$ 31,500			
Insurance			$ 15,500			
Total out	$31,000	$ 31,000	$236,000			
Net cash flow	$59,000	$ 59,000	($ 93,500)			
Ending balance	$84,000	$143,000	$ 49,500			

4. Your monthly cash flow estimate should show a small cash shortage at the end of September. Is this shortage a cause for concern? Based on Midwest's collection and payment patterns, would you expect a cash deficit or surplus by the end of October? No calculations are required, but briefly explain your prediction.

5. Construct a pro forma income statement for the properties managed by Dennis for the third quarter (July, August, and September). Use Figure 12.4 as a model. Show dollar amounts and percent of revenues. September's expenses include $5,000 for supplies and materials and $16,000 for utilities. The payment on debt includes $105,000 in interest and $45,000 toward retirement of the principal. Midwest's tax rate is 34%. Remember that the income statement is based on accrual rather than cash flow principles.

6. Does the period July through September fairly represent Midwest's profitability?

Learning Objectives

LO1 Model the cash conversion cycle and explain its components.

LO2 Understand why the timing of accounts receivable is important and explain the components of credit policy.

LO3 Understand the float concept and its effect on cash flow and explain how to speed up receivables and slow down disbursements.

LO4 Explain inventory management techniques and calculate the economic order quantity (EOQ).

LO5 Account for working capital changes in capital budgeting decisions.

Chapter 13

Working Capital Management

In Chapter 12, we focused on cash inflow and outflow: the natural flow of funds into and out of a company through the sale of products or services; the collection of revenue from customers; and the payment of labor, utilities, and supplies. We looked at cash flow from a forecasting perspective. In this chapter, we examine models and tools that will help us *manage* this flow of funds.

We examine techniques such as credit policies, payment styles, and inventory management that speed up cash inflow and slow down cash outflow. As background, we first examine the cash conversion cycle, and in so doing we take a closer look at the "march to cash." For a typical manufacturing company, this march to cash travels up the company's current assets on the balance sheet. A company must first produce a product (create finished goods), then sell the product (turn inventory into accounts receivable), and finally collect on those sales (turn accounts receivable into cash).

13.1 The Cash Conversion Cycle

You learned in Chapter 2 that working capital consists of a company's current assets and liabilities. Managing these assets and liabilities in such a way as to improve the company's flow of funds is what **working capital management** is all about. This strategy focuses on maintaining efficient levels of both current assets and current liabilities so that a company has greater cash inflow than cash outflow. It is not only the *amount of cash flow* that is important, but also the *timing of the cash flow*.

Managing working capital is the operational side of budgeting. When we put a budget together, we anticipate future cash flow and the timing of that cash flow. When we manage working capital, we are trying to ensure that we produce the required level of cash inflow at the appropriate time to handle the cash outflow. To achieve this, a company must decide when and what to order, when to extend credit, when to write off bad debts, and when to make payments on accounts. In this chapter, we turn to the models that help us make informed short-term financial decisions.

In general, we know that a company must build the product before it can sell the product, so we need to understand how long a company must finance its operation before a customer pays. The *cash conversion cycle* helps determine that length of time by measuring the amount of time money is tied up in the production and collection processes before the company can convert it into cash. Three different cycles constitute the company's overall cash conversion cycle:

1. The **production cycle**: the time it takes to build and sell the product
2. The **collection cycle**: the time it takes to collect from customers (collecting accounts receivable)
3. The **payment cycle**: the time it takes to pay for supplies and labor (paying accounts payable)

These three cycles combine to form the **cash conversion cycle (CCC)**, or the time between the initial cash outflow and the final cash inflow of a product. This is the time a company must cover in order to finance its operations. In other words, the CCC begins when a company first pays out cash to its suppliers and ends when it receives cash in from its customers. Essentially, it measures how quickly a company can convert its products or services into cash. We can show the relationship as

$$\text{cash conversion cycle} = \text{production cycle} + \text{collection cycle} - \text{payment cycle} \qquad \textbf{13.1}$$

We should make one further distinction within the CCC: the *business operating cycle*. This cycle starts at the time production begins and ends with the collection of cash from the sale of the product. It is the core of the business: making and selling the product and collecting the revenue from the customers. In other words, the business operating cycle has two components: the production cycle and the collection cycle. If you recall the "march to cash" in the opening of this chapter, the operating cycle describes this movement up the balance sheet from inventory to accounts receivable to cash. We "pull out" the CCC's operating cycle to focus only on what it takes to move from cash outlay (the payment cycle) to cash recovery. Figure 13.1 shows various graphical relationships of the CCC.

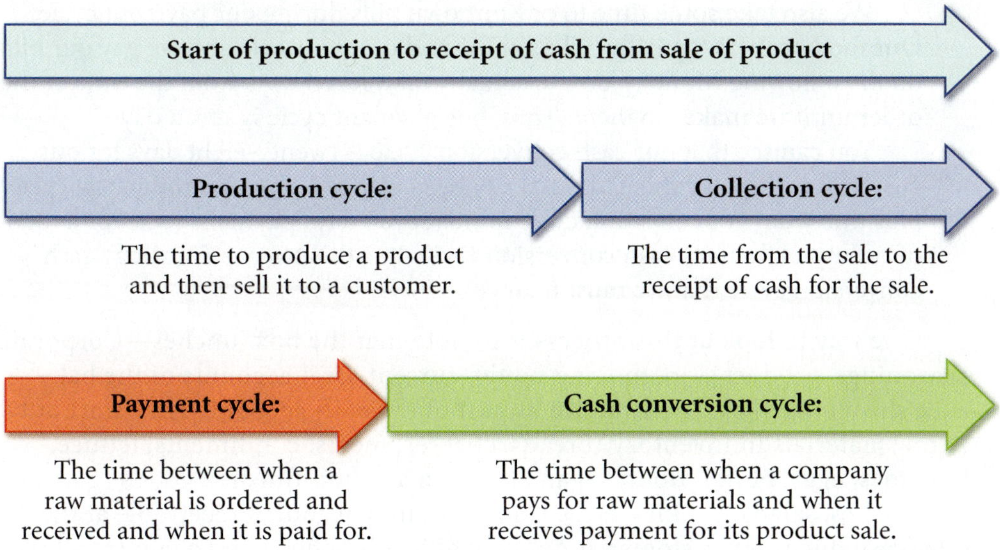

FIGURE 13.1 The cash conversion cycle.

Let's look at the different cycles in Figure 13.1 and the overall CCC through the experiences of a small company, Corporate Seasonings, a catering company. Corporate Seasonings caters mainly to the business community by providing box lunches and breakfast food trays. The company typically receives food orders three days to a week in advance of an event. Customers pay after delivery, but the company receives some payments immediately and some over the next few months. Because Corporate Seasonings receives payment after production, it must figure out how to finance its daily operations. Let's have the owner explain her business in her own words.

> When a customer calls and places an order, our business operating cycle begins. For example, on Monday morning, a customer calls and places an order for a dozen box lunches to be delivered on Friday at 11:30 a.m. for a business luncheon. The order includes the standard items of a gourmet sandwich, a small salad, a dessert, and a soft drink or bottled water. Once we receive the order, our production cycle begins. Our production cycle is five days.
>
> During the production cycle, we must order the appropriate breads and ingredients to fill the order. We have working relationships with various food brokers for the main ingredients, and we have our own kitchen staff for food preparation. The ingredients are typically delivered a day or two before the order will be delivered to our customer.
>
> On delivery day, the lunches arrive at our customer's business, and the order is signed for by a company representative. The delivery driver returns the signed order to our office. At this point, the production process (production cycle) is complete. Now our *collection cycle* begins.
>
> Some companies pay via credit cards, so our collection is immediate, but we still have some customers who must cut us a check for the lunches, and the check processing at our customer's company could take up to thirty days. If all our customers paid by check thirty days later, our total business cycle would be thirty-five days: five days for production and thirty days for collection.

We also take some time to pay our own bills during our payment cycle. Our food brokers typically bill us at the end of each week, and we pay our bills on the following Monday. So, we actually take seven days from the time of the order until we make payment. Thus, our payment cycle is seven days.

You can see that our cash conversion cycle is twenty-eight days for our customers who take thirty days to pay by check: five days of production cycle plus thirty days of collection cycle minus seven days payment cycle for a total of twenty-eight days cash conversion cycle. It is this twenty-eight-day cash conversion cycle that we must finance.

One way to look at this process is to note that the box lunches—Corporate Seasonings' product—are moving up the current asset accounts of the balance sheet until they finally arrive as part of the cash account. They start out as raw materials in inventory (breads, cheeses, meats, condiments, lettuce, tomatoes, eggs, butter, flour, sugar, etc.), convert into finished goods (gourmet sandwiches, salads, cookies, etc.), transform into accounts receivable at the sale (cash due from customer at delivery of box lunches), and again transform into cash when the accounts receivable payment arrives (the customer's check arrives and the company deposits it into its bank account). This process is a business cycle, producing product that eventually winds up as cash for the company.

Because the company receives some customer orders with shorter or longer lead times and some customers pay for their orders at different times, it is necessary to get general estimates for the average time. Let's now turn to an estimation of the averages, first for the average production cycle, second for the average collection cycle, and third for the average payment cycle. We will then have the firm's average cash conversion cycle. To find these averages, we look at the company's income statement and balance sheet accounts at different points in time. Figure 13.2 shows the abbreviated income statement and balance sheet for Corporate Seasonings for 2011.

Average Production Cycle

The first component of the company's average cash conversion cycle is the average production cycle. There are three steps in calculating the average production cycle, each building on the previous one:

1. We first calculate the average inventory for the year. One simple way is to assume inventories do not vary much during the year, so a quick estimate is

$$\text{average inventory} = \frac{\text{beginning inventory} + \text{ending inventory}}{2} \qquad \textbf{13.2}$$

   For Corporate Seasonings, then,

$$\text{average inventory} = \frac{\$8{,}000 + \$5{,}000}{2} = \$6{,}500$$

2. Determine how quickly the company turns over the inventory. To do so, we take the cost of goods sold (COGS) for the year and divide by the average inventory and get the number of times inventory turns over:

$$\text{inventory turnover} = \frac{\text{cost of goods sold}}{\text{average inventory}} \qquad \textbf{13.3}$$

FIGURE 13.2

Selected Income Statement Items, 2011	
Cash sales	$115,000
Credit sales	$450,000
Total sales	$565,000
Cost of goods sold	$312,000

Selected Balance Sheet Accounts	12/31/11	12/31/10	Change
Accounts receivable	$18,000	$16,000	$2,000
Inventory	$ 8,000	$ 5,000	$3,000
Accounts payable	$ 7,000	$ 5,000	$2,000

So, for Corporate Seasonings,

$$\text{inventory turnover} = \frac{\$312{,}000}{\$6{,}500} = 48 \text{ times}$$

3. Estimate the average production period in days by taking the number of days in the year and dividing by the inventory turnover rate:

$$\text{production cycle} = \frac{365}{\text{inventory turnover}} \qquad \textbf{13.4}$$

So, for Corporate Seasonings,

$$\text{production cycle} = \frac{365}{48} = 7.6 \text{ days}$$

Therefore, Corporate Seasonings receives the average order about seven and one-half days prior to required delivery time. For this firm, the proper interpretation is that it takes, on average, 7.6 days to produce and sell the company product.

Average Collection Cycle

The second component of a company's average cash conversion cycle is the average collection cycle, or average **accounts receivable cycle**. To estimate it, we ask how long, on average, it takes to collect from our customers. Only customers who pay *after* the company delivers the box lunches—the credit sales customers—are part of the collection cycle. Customers who pay cash on delivery are not part of the collection cycle. Therefore, it is necessary to track both cash sales and credit sales. In 2011, total sales for Corporate Seasonings amounted to $565,000, of which $450,000 was credit sales. Again, we have three steps to calculate the average collection cycle, and again, each step builds on the previous one:

1. Determine the average accounts receivable for the year:

$$\text{average accounts receivable} = \frac{\text{beginning accounts receivable} + \text{ending accounts receivable}}{2} \qquad \textbf{13.5}$$

For Corporate Seasonings,

$$\text{average accounts receivable} = \frac{\$18{,}000 + \$16{,}000}{2} = \$17{,}000$$

2. Determine the accounts receivable turnover rate and get the number of times accounts receivable turns over:

$$\text{accounts receivable turnover} = \frac{\text{credit sales}}{\text{average accounts receivable}} \tag{13.6}$$

For Corporate Seasonings,

$$\text{accounts receivable turnover} = \frac{\$450{,}000}{\$17{,}000} = 26.5 \text{ times}$$

3. Estimate the average collection cycle in days by dividing the number of days in a year by the accounts receivable turnover rate:

$$\text{collection cycle} = \frac{365}{\text{accounts receivable turnover rate}} \tag{13.7}$$

For Corporate Seasonings,

$$\text{collection cycle} = \frac{365}{26.5} = 13.8 \text{ days}$$

On average, the credit customers take nearly two weeks to pay their Corporate Seasonings bills.

Average Payment Cycle

The third and final component of a company's average cash conversion cycle is the average payment cycle. Corporate Seasonings pays its suppliers after delivery, so cash does not flow out of the company at the same time that it places orders with suppliers. We call this delayed outflow the **accounts payable cycle**. There are three steps to estimating the average payment cycle, and as with the other two cycles, each step builds on the previous one:

1. Determine the average accounts payable for the year:

$$\text{average accounts payable} = \frac{\text{beginning of year accounts payable} + \text{end of year accounts payable}}{2} \tag{13.8}$$

For Corporate Seasonings,

$$\text{average accounts payable} = \frac{\$7{,}000 + \$5{,}000}{2} = \$6{,}000$$

2. Determine the accounts payable turnover rate. To do so, we use the cost of goods sold as the cost of production and get the number of times the accounts payable turns over:

$$\text{accounts payable turnover} = \frac{\text{cost of goods sold}}{\text{average accounts payable}} \tag{13.9}$$

For Corporate Seasonings,

$$\text{accounts payable turnover} = \frac{\$312{,}000}{\$6{,}000} = 52 \text{ times}$$

3. Determine the number of days it takes the company to pay its suppliers:

$$\text{accounts payable cycle} = \frac{365}{\text{accounts payable turnover}} \qquad \textbf{13.10}$$

So, for Corporate Seasonings,

$$\text{accounts payable cycle} = \frac{365}{52} = 7.0 \text{ days}$$

Therefore, Corporate Seasonings takes an average of one week to pay its suppliers.

Putting It All Together: The Cash Conversion Cycle

By putting together a company's average production cycle, the average collection cycle, and the average payment cycle, we can answer the question "How long does it *typically* take between the outflow of needed cash to start production and the receipt of payment for the credit sales?" In other words, what is the average cash conversion cycle in days for a company's credit sales?

$$\text{average cash conversion cycle} = \text{production cycle} + \text{collection cycle} - \text{payment cycle} \qquad \textbf{13.11}$$

For Corporate Seasonings,

$$\text{average cash conversion cycle} = 7.6 + 13.8 - 7.0 = 14.4 \text{ days}$$

The 14.4 days for Corporate Seasonings' CCC means that, on average, the company must finance its credit sales for two weeks. Recall that the company's owner stated that the cash conversion cycle was twenty-eight days for the customers who took up to thirty days to pay their bills. So, we need to understand that estimating the average CCC is just that, an average. Some customers will still take longer to pay and may require additional incentives to pay their bills sooner. We now move to the topic of managing a company's credit sales or, as we more commonly call it, managing accounts receivable.

13.2 Managing Accounts Receivable and Setting Credit Policy

When we first start to interpret the business effects of the cash conversion cycle, we note that accounts receivable and accounts payable play major roles in determining the number of days in the cycle. In Section 13.1, we took a simple approach—smooth or steady cash flow—to find the average collection cycle and the average payment cycle. Cash flow, however, is usually not smooth or steady, but rather is often influenced by seasonal and weekly fluctuations. We will see these fluctuations as we turn to accounts receivable and ways to speed up the receipt of future cash payments.

Collecting Accounts Receivable

A company's future cash inflow from the sale of its products or services—accounts receivable—and the anticipated timing of this inflow are part of its short-term cash flow planning and management. As you saw in Chapter 12, correct estimates for the timing of cash inflow from sales are important. Let's look at our example company, Corporate Seasonings, to see the cash inflow from sales and the actual time of collection of credit sales.

EXAMPLE 13.1 Collection of accounts receivable

Problem When Corporate Seasonings delivers an order, it attaches an invoice for payment. Some customers pay at delivery with a credit card or cash; some with a check at the invoice due date (thirty days after delivery); and some pay late, taking more than thirty days. Any payment that a customer makes at delivery is a cash sale. Any payment that a customer makes after delivery is a credit sale. Estimate the monthly cash inflow for Corporate Seasonings for the first quarter of the year, given the following monthly sales and payment percentages:

Sales by Month for Corporate Seasonings

	Nov.	Dec.	Jan.	Feb.	Mar.
Sales	$48,000	$57,000	$39,000	$49,000	$51,000
Cash	21%	17%	23%	20%	20%
When due	66%	64%	71%	65%	66%
Late	13%	19%	6%	15%	14%

Solution To see the cash flow each month, we need to see the timing of collection of each month's sales. For example, the company will collect the November sales of $48,000 over three months: in November (cash sales), in December (due credit sales), and in January (late credit sales). So, looking at the first quarter, we have the following cash collections:

Monthly Cash Collections for Corporate Seasonings

Cash Inflow	Jan.	Feb.	Mar.
November late	$48,000 × 0.13 = $6,240.00		
December on time	$57,000 × 0.64 = $36,480.00		
December late		$57,000 × 0.19 = $10,830.00	
January cash	$39,000 × 0.23 = $8,970.00		
January on time		$39,000 × 0.71 = $27,690.00	
January late			$39,000 × 0.06 = $2,340.00
February cash		$49,000 × 0.20 = $9,800.00	
February on time			$49,000 × 0.65 = $31,850.00
March cash			$51,000 × 0.20 = $10,200
Total	$51,690.00	$48,320.00	$44,390.00

The interesting part of the cash inflow from first-quarter sales is that January has the lowest sales but the highest cash inflow, and March has the highest sales but the lowest cash inflow, illustrating why estimating the timing and amount of the cash inflow from sales is so important. Doing so helps a company anticipate any shortfalls in cash so that it can use the most effective means of covering such shortfalls. Corporate Seasonings may "save" some of the extra January cash inflow to cover the additional outflow in February and March with higher sales and presumably higher production costs to support these higher sales.

Corporate Seasonings' first-quarter cash inflow is the anticipated inflow based on anticipated sales. The company will monitor actual cash inflow so that deviations from the estimates can help the company anticipate potential cash shortfalls and avoid costly surprises.

Credit: A Two-Sided Coin

In Section 13.1, we looked at Corporate Seasonings' accounts receivable and its cash conversion cycle. Let's briefly recap its 14.4-day average CCC. The 14.4 days includes the time it takes to produce the goods for sale (production cycle) plus the time it takes to collect on the sale (collection cycle divided by accounts receivable) minus the time it takes to pay for the raw materials (payment cycle divided by accounts payable). When a company deals only in cash transactions (from one's customers and to one's suppliers), the CCC comprises only the production cycle. It is credit—either for one's customers or from one's suppliers—that has an effect on the CCC. Let's now turn to an examination of credit issues.

We can see from our Corporate Seasonings example that if the collection cycle lengthens, the company will need to finance operations over a longer period of time. On the other hand, if Corporate Seasonings can extend the time to pay its suppliers, it can shorten the financing period. Therefore, in managing the credit portion of the CCC, we have two options:

1. Speed up receivables
2. Slow down payments

Note an interesting aspect of credit: one company's accounts receivable is another's accounts payable. So, when we speed up our receivables, we are inherently speeding up someone else's payments, and when we slow down our payments, we are slowing down someone else's receivables. As we look at credit, remember that it is a two-sided coin. What's good for our own company is not always good for our suppliers or customers and vice versa.

When a company sells a product or service to a customer, it has the option to require payment upon delivery or to allow the customer to pay for services or products at a later date—in other words, to grant credit. Extending credit to a customer has three major components:

1. The company must have a policy on how customers will *qualify* for credit.
2. Once a company extends credit, it must have a policy on the *payment* plan for the creditors.
3. When customers do not pay on time, the company must have procedures and policies for attempting to *collect* overdue bills.

Although we examine these three items separately, they actually all fall under one umbrella: credit policy. We must integrate the three components to make the credit policy effective.

Qualifying for Credit

In setting credit policy, the first question a company must answer is which customers should receive credit, that is, which ones it will allow to pay later for product delivered today. Obviously, a company loses money if a customer takes delivery but never pays for the product. In accounting terms, those are a company's bad debts. The amount of potential business from a customer and the background of the customer are essential components that a company uses to determine whether it should extend credit. In addition, the common practices of competing firms will also influence the extension of credit. If a competitor is granting more generous credit terms on purchases, a company may need to modify its own credit policy to compete. Still, some customers are good credit risks and some are not, and companies may choose to use credit screening before offering credit. There are different levels of credit screening, and the costs vary across different levels. The rationale for increasing the cost to review a potential customer's creditworthiness is to eliminate bad debts, but the benefits from denying credit may come at too high a cost: lost sales. The company may be worse off if it tightens credit too much and loses good customers. The challenge is to determine the appropriate level of credit-screening costs so that good customers are not turned away when potential bad customers do not receive credit.

We call the process of distinguishing good customers from bad customers **credit screening**. A credit screen can be as simple as filling out a credit application to provide the company with information on which to base a decision to extend or not extend credit. It may be a very long and detailed process. For example, a bank reviewing a loan application for a mortgage will require the applicant to provide personal financial statements, proof of employment, credit history, appraisal of the property, and property inspection before granting a loan. This is a very expensive credit screen process. In Example 13.2, we look at what is a reasonable cost for a credit screen.

EXAMPLE 13.2 Credit screening costs and business profits

Problem Winkler Water Works makes small recreational boats. The recreational boats are inflatable with the option of attaching sails, a small outboard motor, or rowing equipment. The boats typically sell for $1,500. Many of Winkler's customers cannot pay cash for their boats, but are willing to make monthly payments over a two-year period. The company's financing department has estimated the following profile for its small recreational boats and customer base:

Annual sales:	16,000 inflatable boats
Annual production costs:	$1,100 per boat
Profit margin per boat:	$400
Lost sales if credit is not provided for all customers:	7,000 boats
If credit is provided for all customers:	0.5% of customers default (80)

If credit screening can eliminate bad-credit customers, what is the maximum credit-screening cost per customer that Winkler should pay? Let's assume that

Winkler has 9,000 customers who are ready to pay cash and 7,000 customers who will need credit. Let's further assume all 16,000 buyers will opt for credit if Winkler allows credit.

Solution First, let's compare the "profit margin" of no-credit sales with that of all-credit sales and no screening activities by Winkler Water Works. With cash only or no-credit sales, we have

$$\text{profit margin cash-only customers} = 9{,}000 \times \$400 = \$3{,}600{,}000$$

With credit sales (and assuming all customers buy on credit and 0.5% then fail to pay), we have

$$\text{profit margin all credit} = (15{,}920 \times \$400) - (80 \times \$1{,}100) = \$6{,}280{,}000$$

The previous equation shows that 15,920 customers buy a boat and then pay for it later, providing Winkler with a \$400 profit margin on these sales. In addition, it shows that 80, or 0.5%, of the customers ($16{,}000 \times 0.005 = 80$) buy a boat that cost \$1,100 to produce, but do not pay. The difference between the two policies is

$$\text{policy difference} = \$6{,}280{,}000 - \$3{,}600{,}000 = \$2{,}680{,}000$$

So, the extra profit with credit sales is \$2,680,000, which is a substantial sum. The company is losing $80 \times \$1{,}100 = \$88{,}000$ in bad credit. If Winkler implements a credit-screening process that would identify these 80 bad-debt customers prior to extending them a credit sale, what is the maximum charge per customer that Winkler should pay to eliminate the bad debts?

Benefits of credit screening: save \$88,000

Cost to screen per customer: $\frac{\$88{,}000}{16{,}000} = \$5.50$ per customer

Winkler Water Works could spend up to \$5.50 per customer for credit screening and would be better off allowing credit with a screen than allowing credit without one. Of course, we assume that the credit screening is 100% accurate, denying only the bad-debt customers and giving credit to all the good-debt customers. For example, if credit screening cost \$5.00 per customer and is 100% accurate, the profit margin on the boats is

$$\text{profit margin} = (15{,}920 \times \$400) - (16{,}000 \times \$5) = \$6{,}288{,}000$$

Therefore, credit screening at this rate adds only \$8,000 to the profit margin.

It seems highly unlikely that Winkler Water Works could screen for as little as \$5.50 per applicant as in Example 13.2 and have a 100% accurate screen. If the cost of credit screening exceeds \$5.50, Winkler would add credit sales, but not credit screening for customers. The addition of 7,000 more customers with only 80 defaults drives the profits well above the cash-only 9,000 customers. If, however, Winkler had a higher rate of default—say 4%—the cost of screening could go as high as \$44 per customer before it would be cost-ineffective.

$$\begin{aligned}\text{Bad credit customers at 4\% default rate} &= 16{,}000 \times 0.04 = 640\\ \text{Loss due to bad credit customers} &= \$1{,}100 \times 640 = \$704{,}000\\ \text{Maximum credit screen cost per customer} &= \$704{,}000/16{,}000 = \$44.00\end{aligned}$$

Setting Payment Policy

The second phase of granting credit is to set the credit terms, which specify when a company requires payment and what reductions to the bill are available in return for early payment. When one business buys on credit from another business, often the seller will offer an extended payment period for the product or service and an incentive to pay the bill early. In formulating their discounts for early payment, companies often take into account what their competitors are offering.

Figure 13.3 shows an invoice that Space Lumber Company sent to Peak Construction for purchased materials "on account" for a major deck remodeling project. According to the terms in the lower-right corner of the invoice, Peak Construction has sixty days to make payment, but if it chooses, it can pay the bill in the first ten days and deduct 1% of the invoice total for paying early. The term "1/10 net 60" is actually an option to take a 1% deduction and pay 99% of the invoice within the first ten days or pay the entire amount within sixty days.

If you are the owner or manager of Peak Construction, when should you pay this bill? The choice is to pay either the entire bill of \$7,572.00 on August 30 (sixty days later) or the discounted amount of \$7,496.28 on July 11 (ten days later), thereby saving \$75.72. You would pay only on one of these two dates—July 11 or August 30—because taking the discount prior to July 11 or paying the net prior to August 30 has an implied opportunity cost for your funds. So, which choice is better, July 11 or August 30? See Figure 13.4.

If we return to the time value of money principles, the real question here is, "What is the implied interest rate on the loan from Space Lumber Company?" You could also approach this question from another perspective: What interest would you have to earn on the \$7,496.28 over the fifty days between your two payment

Peak Construction Invoice #07010922

Space Lumber Company
945 North 9th Avenue; Portland, OR 97330
555-767-5555

Customer	Vendor Number	Materials and Costs
Peak Construction 24444 Old Peak Road Salem, OR 97370	9293280	Treks Decking Material:

1 × 2 300 @ \$2.10 each =	\$630.00
2 × 6 600 @ \$9.45 each =	\$5,670.00
4 × 4 120 @ \$8.10 each =	\$972.00
Brackets 50 boxes @ \$6.00 each =	\$300.00
TOTAL DUE	**\$7,572.00**

Invoice number **07010922**
Date: July 1, 2009 **TERMS: 1/10 net 60**

FIGURE 13.3

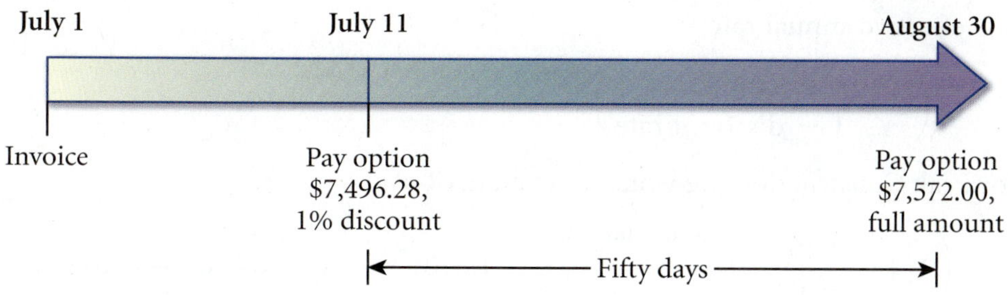

FIGURE 13.4 Invoice payment options, amounts, and dates for Peak Construction's bill from Space Lumber Company.

dates to make you indifferent about the payment dates? You already have the answer: the difference between the two payment amounts. Therefore, the interest required over fifty days is

$$\$7{,}572.00 - \$7{,}496.28 = \$75.72$$

So, you could either write a check to Space Lumber on July 11 for $7,496.28 or you could invest the $7,496.28 in an interest-earning account for fifty days. At the end of the fifty days, you would take the money out of the interest-bearing account and pay the net amount of $7,572.00. You would be better off paying on August 30 only if you were able to earn more than $75.72 interest over the fifty days between the two payment dates. What interest rate would you need to earn to break even? The holding period of fifty days would return

$$\frac{\$75.72}{\$7{,}496.28} = 0.010101 \quad \text{or} \quad 1.01\%$$

Now, what is 1.01% interest over fifty days stated on an annual basis? Recall from Chapter 5 that there are two ways to annualize a holding period return: the annual percentage rate (APR), which is a simple interest rate without compounding, and the effective annual rate (EAR), which is a compounded interest rate. For Peak Construction, the APR is

$$0.0101 \times \frac{365}{50} = 0.0737 \quad \text{or} \quad 7.37\%$$

So, Peak Construction should pay this bill on July 11 if it cannot earn at least 7.37% (APR) on the account over the next fifty days. If it can earn more than 7.37%, it should keep the money in the account for another fifty days and pay the invoice on August 30.

There are a number of different types of discounts, and we can find the implied interest rate for each type by using the following definition:

$$\text{annual percentage rate} = \frac{\text{discount rate}}{1 - \text{discount rate}} \times \frac{365}{\text{days between payment dates}} \qquad \textbf{13.12}$$

For Peak Construction, the APR is

$$\frac{0.01}{1 - 0.01} \times \frac{365}{60 - 10} = 0.07373 = 7.37\%$$

If we use the effective annual rate, which implies compounding, as the appropriate interest rate, we get effective annual rate =

$$\left(1 + \frac{\text{discount rate}}{1 - \text{discount rate}}\right)^{365/\text{days between payment dates}} - 1 \qquad \textbf{13.13}$$

For Peak Construction, we would have an EAR of

$$\left(1 + \frac{0.01}{1 - 0.01}\right)^{365/(60-10)} - 1 = 1.0101^{7.3} - 1 = 0.0761 = 7.61\%$$

As noted, there are two sides to the credit coin, and now you have seen that there are two sides to every invoice. The company receiving the invoice can choose to take the discount and pay early or to pay the full amount on time. Paying on time is a choice to slow down outflow (accounts payable) if the discount terms are not sufficiently high. On the other hand, the company issuing the discount option is trying to speed up inflow (payment on accounts receivable); because the discount is the cost of speeding up receivables, it should not be too high. Therefore, the company bases the early payment terms on the competition's credit terms as well as on the degree of the need to speed up receivables.

Using a discount option can have nontrivial ramifications. Consider a personal finance example, a property tax bill. Often, homeowners receive a discount offer from their county assessor if they pay their property tax early. A modestly populated county on the West Coast, for example, offers a 3% discount for early payment. The total property tax assessment for the county is $150 million. If all homeowners take the 3% discount and pay early, the county loses $4.5 million of tax income, but it has the use of revenues six months early. Is the early receipt of the property tax worth the cost? There is no definitive answer, but in effect, the early cash receipts constitute short-term funding to cover any cash shortfalls the county might experience.

Collecting Overdue Debt

The final issue with granting credit involves formulating a collection policy for a company's bad-debt accounts. If a customer fails to pay on time, the account becomes delinquent and the company must either take action or write off the debt as uncollectible.

What actions can a company take? The first is likely a letter to the customer stating that the account is past due and that it has assessed a financing charge or fee. For example, a customer may receive a letter stating

1. The balance of the account that is past due
2. The additional finance charge assessment
3. A new payment date for the past due amount and finance charge
4. Additional assessment charges if the company does not receive payment by the new due date.

The success of this letter may vary. If it fails to get the proper response—payment of the past-due bill—the company may need to escalate its collection activities. If the customer in question is one who does repeat business, the next response may be to suspend that customer's credit activity until the customer pays the account. This loss of credit could encourage payment but may also lose business from repeat customers, who may be temporarily under cash management problems of their own. If the delinquency letter or loss of credit does not get a response, the company may have to escalate its collection activities and resort to other methods such as

A collection agency
Court action
Writing off the bill as bad debt

When a company turns over an account to a collection agency, the agency usually takes a percentage of the account as its fee. A typical fee is one-third of the collected amount. Thus, the company will get only two-thirds of the account. This route is fairly expensive, but it is better to get two-thirds of the cash than nothing.

An even more expensive route is to take the customer to court. Because the court costs may significantly reduce the account's final collection, the net cash flow involved may not be worth legal action in the first place.

The final choice may simply be to write off the account as a bad debt. A bad debt means that the company has given up pursuing the collection of the account, but it is also a business expense that reduces taxes. The tax benefit is a small portion of the lost collection, but is some consolation for losing the cash.

Each escalation of the collection policy is more expensive than the previous one and correspondingly reduces the revenues from the credit sales more and more. Therefore, a company should select credit-screening choices, credit terms, and collection action plans to create a credit policy that maximizes benefits over costs.

13.3 The Float

When individuals or companies use a checking account to make payments or receive payments from customers, there is a time delay between when they write the check and when funds are available to the payee. We call the lag time involved in the process of clearing a check the **float**. The float also represents the difference between the cash balance on the company's books and the cash balance in its bank account. It is the same difference that you see between your bank account balance and your checkbook balance: there is often a difference between what the bank says you have and what your checkbook says you have. Although a law called Check Clearing for the 21st Century Act, or Check 21 (passed in October 2003; effective October 2004), has eliminated some of the float, several features remain. To set the stage for how check processing enables a firm (or you) to slow down payments, let's return to the period before Check 21 to see the historical float and then the eliminated portion.

Figure 13.5 illustrates the time delay between when you first write a check and when the money is made available to the payee. As the figure shows, the float, from your perspective as the buyer of a product and check writer, is a five-day *disbursement float*. On day 1, you pay a $100 invoice from a store where you have made a purchase by writing a check. Although you may feel as if you have paid for the goods by writing the check, the money does not leave your checking account until day 5, meaning that the $100 may still be working for you in an interest-bearing account until the financial institution actually transfers funds to the store's account at the store's bank. This delay (in our example, five days) between writing a check and transferring funds from your account is the **disbursement float**. From the store's perspective as the agent receiving the check, it is a three-day **collection float**. The store receives the check on day 3 but does not collect the actual funds from your bank until day 5.

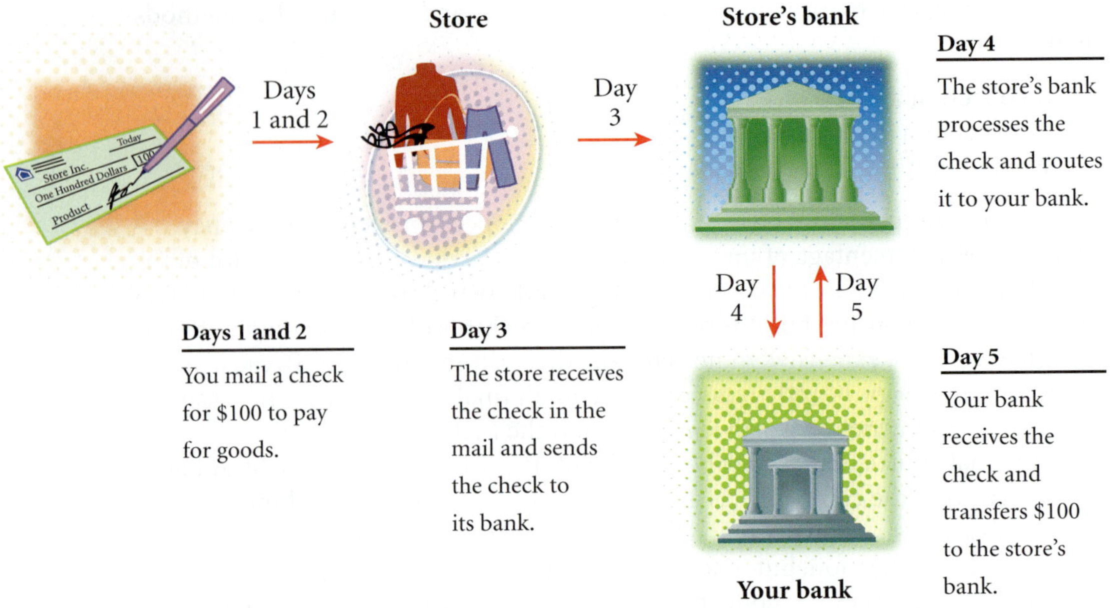

FIGURE 13.5 Disbursement and collection float.

Some businesses and individuals engage in playing the float when they have cash flow problems. For example, they may write a check to pay a bill with funds that they do not currently have and then deposit cash later to cover the check. If the timing is off, the financial institution of the check writer will return the check to the payee's bank (the company that sold the product) marked "NSF," meaning there are "not sufficient funds" to cover the check. The payee, in turn, will probably charge a fee to their customer for the returned check and require payment for the goods with cash.

From your cash management viewpoint, the longer the disbursement float, the more time money is in your account working for you. From the seller's cash management viewpoint, the shorter the collection float, the sooner the money is in its account working for it. Therefore, an important cash management objective is to lengthen the disbursement float and reduce the collection float or, put another way, pay as late as possible and collect as soon as possible. There are numerous techniques to accomplish this objective. We will look at a few of the common and legal ways to speed up the collection or extend the disbursement float shortly.

With the high use of debit cards and online checking, has the float evaporated? The answer is no. Even in the age of debit accounts and e-checks (online checks from your checking account), the float is still present. Banks, however, are playing the float to their advantage now. When a customer goes online and "writes" an e-check to pay a bill, the financial institution removes funds from the customer's account, but it may not deliver the funds for up to a week. Where are the funds while this e-check is in route? They are still at the customer's bank, but they are not collecting interest for the customer. The bank has reduced its interest expense with the e-check option. Check processing, however, is still big business when we look at companies and their cash management activities.

Speeding Up the Collection (Shortening the Lag Time)

To speed up the collection float means having cash available sooner. In Section 13.2, we looked at credit policies to encourage customers to pay early. With the collection float, we are concerned about processing customers' payments faster.

One way to do so is to reduce the handling and mail time of checks. Many companies use lockboxes to speed up the delivery of checks into their bank accounts. A **lockbox** is a post office box at a central post office near a company's bank. Rather than a customer's payment check being received at the company itself, it goes to the post office, where collections from the lockbox by the company's bank take place early in the business day. The bank forwards a copy of the check to the company's accounts receivable department to credit the appropriate customer account at the store. Because the actual check goes directly to the bank and into the company's bank account, the company streamlines receipts by reducing the collection float processing time. It can capture more payments more quickly. In today's e-commerce world, lockboxes are increasingly image based; that is, the bank scans payments in your lockbox so that you can view them online on the same day that they arrive.

Electronic funds transfer has substantially limited the collection float for businesses and the disbursement float for customers. Online banking has all but eliminated lag time because of the instantaneous transfer of funds from one bank account to another.

Today, companies process a large portion of collections via electronic transfers. **Electronic funds transfer (EFT)** is a system of transferring funds from one bank account directly to another. No paper checks change hands. Customers authorize their banks to transfer funds from their accounts to the business's bank account. This "e-approach" substantially eliminates the collection float for the business and the disbursement float for the customer. For example, many utility companies set up direct payment with banks for all the bank's customers who elect to pay their bills online. Funds transfer directly from a customer's checking account to the utility company's bank, eliminating the paper check that a customer would traditionally send for bill payment. Many companies that routinely bill their customers will set up direct payment to avoid the delay of receiving the paper check that a bank sends when a customer pays via the online check option.

Slowing Down Payment (Lengthening the Lag Time)

For many businesses, the advent of Check 21 legislation, EFT direct payments, and the use of debit cards—in which a customer's checking account reduces immediately and the funds electronically transfer to the retail merchant—have virtually eliminated the disbursement float. The main technique left to slow down payment, or lengthen the lag time, is through the use of credit. For a customer, a credit card purchase is an extended disbursement float. A retail purchase via a credit card can delay cash outflow for more than a month. Many businesses use credit cards to pay for many of their retail purchases, effectively delaying their cash outflow.

A number of other practices speed up or slow down payments. Such trade-offs are part of the business-customer relationship. Such methods may be effective and legal, but they may also hurt the relationship between the business and the customer. Losing a good customer or a trusted supplier over a credit policy may not be a good business practice. It is important to look at the overall credit policy, not just the individual pieces. Optimizing the pieces does not necessarily optimize the whole.

13.4 Inventory Management: Carrying Costs and Ordering Costs

Inventory is one of the most important business assets because it generates revenue. It includes the raw materials that go into the making of the company's products, work-in-progress products, and finished goods. Holding too much inventory for too long is usually not a good thing, however, because of the storage costs, potential spoilage, and obsolescence. So, firms must choose the appropriate level of inventories to support their operations. How do they do it? What determines the right inventory size for a business? When is "too many toys" a bad thing for Toys"R"Us, and when is "too few toys" a bad thing?

We can view the appropriate inventory level as a trade-off between the additional costs of carrying too many items in inventory and the lost sales resulting from inventories running out or stoppage costs resulting from raw materials running out. Consider the case of a production line that requires bottles for packaging beverages. If the bottles are out of stock, the production process comes to a halt. Stopping and then restarting the production process is costly, and running out of bottles therefore increases the cost of producing beverages. It is necessary to manage the timing and number of bottles that the company receives from the supplier to avoid production stoppage.

For a retailer, out-of-stock inventory results in lost sales. A customer that finds the store out of the product they want will seek the product in another store. If this happens too often for the customer's convenience, the customer may stop going to the store. On the other hand, too much inventory may also be costly. For example, if the supermarket's dairy section manager orders too many gallons of milk, the product could spoil before it sells, resulting in a loss. Or consider the seemingly optimal scenario of when demand for a product is high. Perhaps the company has to build additional storage facilities to house the increased quantity. Will the increased sales be sufficient to offset the new storage facilities' increased cost, or is the firm better off running out of stock occasionally?

Let's now look at four aspects of inventory management designed to minimize the costs that we associate with inventory or production:

1. The ABC inventory management model
2. Redundant inventory
3. The economic order quantity (EOQ) method
4. The just-in-time (JIT) method

ABC Inventory Management

One simple inventory management technique is the ABC inventory management system, which divides inventory into three categories:

- A type: large-dollar items, or critical inventory items
- B type: moderate-dollar items, or essential inventory items
- C type: small-dollar items, or nonessential inventory items

The different groupings of inventory items require different levels of monitoring as well as different amounts of items in inventory. We can count inventory items in Type A daily or on a perpetual inventory monitoring system. We can count inventory items in Type B on a periodic basis. We can monitor inventory items in Type C infrequently and order them only when the inventory level hits zero.

TABLE 13.1 Inventory Categories for Corporate Seasonings

Category A	Category B	Category C
Meats	Spreads: mayonnaise, mustard, ketchup	Cleaning supplies
Cheeses	Containers	Menus
Drinks	Plasticware	Invoices
Breads	Cooking utensils	Office supplies

Let's return to Corporate Seasonings and see how this catering business might classify its inventories into three groups and what monitoring process it will use for each inventory item. Table 13.1 shows how the company groups the items.

The owner of Corporate Seasonings explains her inventory system:

> The items in Category A are critical to the daily production of box lunches and have high spoilage. It is important for the business to check these food supplies daily so that the following day's production can be completed and any spoiled items removed quickly from the refrigerator. Category B items are essential to the business, but spoilage is not an issue; therefore, the cost to store these items is relatively cheap compared with those in Category A, which need to be refrigerated. Sometimes an item will shift from one category to another. Once we open a bottle of ketchup, mayonnaise, or mustard, it must be refrigerated and moves from Category B to Category A. Category C items are ordered as supplies hit zero or near the last item. The soap for washing the cooking utensils is ordered by the case (twelve bottles to a case), and we order a new case whenever we start using the last bottle. Other items like menus and invoices in Category C are printed when we run out. The printing is done next door, and our orders are filled immediately.

Redundant Inventory Items

Another inventory management issue to consider is redundant inventory items. A redundant inventory item is an item that a company does not use in current operations but serves a backup role just in case the current item fails during operations. Engineers often require redundant items in cases in which, if a critical item fails, it is costly or prohibitive to replace that item in a timely fashion. An extreme example is that of NASA engineers designing a redundant energy system for the Mars Rover. In January 2004, the Mars Rover landed and rolled out onto the surface of Mars. The Rover's mission was to send data back to Earth so that scientists could evaluate and learn more about our neighboring planet. After eighteen days of transmitting, the Rover suddenly stopped sending data. If the sudden stoppage were due to a dead battery, a $400 million mission would have been doomed. If engineers had built a redundant backup system into the Rover, NASA could simply switch to the other energy source and continue transmitting data. The cost of the second battery was cheap compared to the loss of the Rover's ability to transmit data. It's not easy or cheap to send someone to Mars to put in a new battery! The Rover's story does have a happy ending. The engineers were able to correct the problem, and Rover gathered additional data, which it sent back for evaluation.

Although the Mars Rover is an extreme example of "planning for failure," companies may need to keep critical inventory items as redundant items to avoid expensive delays or stoppages in production. In other words, a second battery is a very cheap insurance policy, and the optimal level of inventory may include redundant parts.

Economic Order Quantity

To determine the appropriate level of inventory, we must weigh the trade-off between the *carrying costs* and the *ordering costs* of the inventory. A common method that we use to determine the appropriate inventory levels is the **economic order quantity (EOQ)** model. The EOQ is the result of trading off carrying costs and ordering costs. In the EOQ model, we ignore the *actual cost* of the item because we are trying to determine only the proper level of inventories. Instead, we consider the costs associated with *holding inventory*. We divide inventory costs into two categories:

1. The cost of ordering and delivery the inventory
2. The cost of storage or carrying the inventory item until sold or used in production

One EOQ model assumption concerns the rate of production or sale of an inventory item. This model assumes that usage or the inventory item's sales rate is constant. This assumption works well with a production cycle that turns out the same number of products each period, but not as well with sales rates that vary daily, monthly, or seasonally for a particular inventory item.

The Trade-off between Ordering Costs and Carrying Costs What, exactly, is the trade-off? When companies order inventories in large batches instead of small batches, the number of required deliveries each period is lower and the delivery order costs are typically lower per item. When companies order in smaller batches, they receive more deliveries and the cost of ordering typically goes up per item. Think of ordering DVDs from Amazon.com. For each order that you place, Amazon.com charges you handling and shipping fees. If you order one DVD at a time, Amazon.com charges you a handling and shipping fee for each DVD. If you order a large batch of DVDs, you receive only one handling and shipping charge. So, it is better to order in larger batches and spread the fixed handling and shipping charges over the number of DVDs in the same package.

On the other hand, with large inventories, the cost to store or carry the inventory increases as you require more space and facilities. With small orders, you require less space and fewer facilities, so the cost to carry the inventory decreases. The EOQ model lets us estimate the happy medium between the small orders and large orders. Let's see how it all works.

Measuring Ordering Costs The cost of ordering is the number of orders placed per period multiplied by the cost of ordering and delivery, or

$$\text{total annual ordering cost} = OC \times \frac{S}{Q} \qquad \textbf{13.14}$$

where OC is the cost of each individual order, S is the annual sales, and Q is the quantity of each order, or order size.

EXAMPLE 13.3 Total annual ordering costs

Problem Marge is in charge of ordering the cartridges for all printers at Clinko's Fast Printers. Whenever Marge orders cartridges, Clinko's supplier charges $10.95 for shipping and handling, regardless of how many cartridges that she orders. Currently, Clinko's uses 12,000 cartridges a year. What is the total annual ordering cost if Marge orders in quantities of 400, 300, 200, or 100?

Solution The costs per order using Equation 13.14 are

$$\text{400 cartridges at a time} = \$10.95 \times \frac{12{,}000}{400} = \mathbf{\$328.50}$$

$$\text{300 cartridges at a time} = \$10.95 \times \frac{12{,}000}{300} = \mathbf{\$438.00}$$

$$\text{200 cartridges at a time} = \$10.95 \times \frac{12{,}000}{200} = \mathbf{\$657.00}$$

$$\text{100 cartridges at a time} = \$10.95 \times \frac{12{,}000}{100} = \mathbf{\$1{,}314.00}$$

Marge should order in large quantities (400) to save the company ordering costs.

The cost of ordering is only one factor to consider. We also need to look at the cost of storing those orders.

Measuring Carrying Costs How much does it cost to store inventory for the year? The cost of carrying or holding the inventory is the order quantity Q divided by two and then multiplied by the average carrying cost per item per year, or CC:

$$\text{total annual carrying cost} = CC \times \frac{Q}{2} \tag{13.15}$$

Why do we divide the order quantity Q by two in Equation 13.15? One assumption of the EOQ model is that we use inventory at a constant rate. So, we want to know how much inventory we have *on average*. If we order 100 units, we assume that we use up these units at a constant rate, and we order another 100 units when we hit zero. On average, we have 50 units in inventory as we constantly go from 100 to 0 and then reorder. Figure 13.6 illustrates this

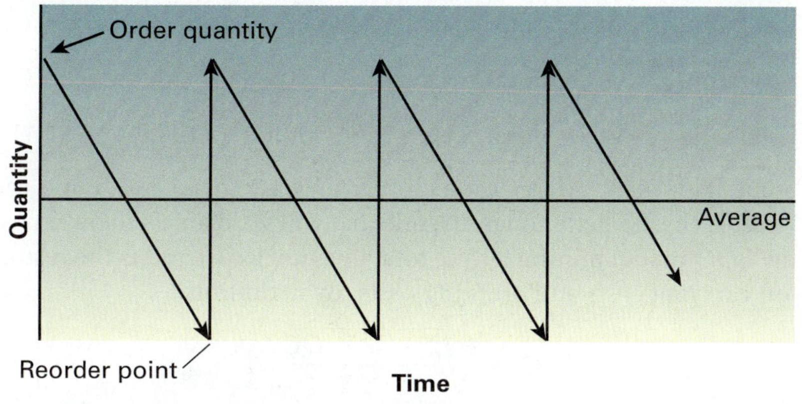

FIGURE 13.6 Inventory flow.

constant use of inventory over time and the jump in inventory with each new order when we hit zero. Therefore, the average inventory is $Q/2$, or one-half the order quantity.

EXAMPLE 13.4 Total annual carrying costs

Problem Marge has determined that it costs the company $2.00 per year to hold one cartridge in inventory. If she orders 400, 300, 200, or 100 cartridges at a time, what are the total annual carrying costs for cartridges?

Solution Using Equation 13.15, we can find the annual carrying costs as follows:

$$\text{400 units per order} = \$2.00 \times \frac{400}{2} = \$400.00$$

$$\text{300 units per order} = \$2.00 \times \frac{300}{2} = \$300.00$$

$$\text{200 units per order} = \$2.00 \times \frac{200}{2} = \$200.00$$

$$\text{100 units per order} = \$2.00 \times \frac{100}{2} = \$100.00$$

It looks now like Marge should order in small quantities (100) to save the company money, whereas in Example 13.3 it looked like she should order in large quantities (400). Large quantities carry higher storage costs and lower ordering costs, and small quantities carry lower storage costs and higher ordering costs. What should Marge really do?

Examples 13.3 and 13.4 have shown the ordering costs and carrying costs for cartridges at Clinko's Fast Printers for various order sizes. What is the best ordering quantity for Clinko's to use? To find out, we need to add ordering and carrying costs to find the total inventory costs for each order size. We can define the total ordering cost as

$$\text{total cost} = \text{ordering costs} + \text{carrying costs} \qquad \textbf{13.16}$$

Applying Equation 13.16 to Marge's dilemma, we have

$$\text{400 units per order, total costs} = \$328.50 + \$400.00 = \$728.50$$

$$\text{300 units per order, total costs} = \$438.00 + \$300.00 = \$738.00$$

$$\text{200 units per order, total costs} = \$657.00 + \$200.00 = \$857.00$$

$$\text{100 units per order, total costs} = \$1{,}314.00 + \$100.00 = \$1{,}414.00$$

At this point, it looks like Marge should order in larger lots of 400, but is that the optimal size? Is there a better quantity, one that will yield an even lower cost total? Again, the EOQ model minimizes the total inventory cost and is the result of trading off carrying costs and ordering costs. By definition,

$$EOQ = \sqrt{\frac{2 \times S \times OC}{CC}} \qquad \textbf{13.17}$$

where S is the annual sales, OC is the cost of each individual order, and CC is the carrying cost of each inventory item. If Marge applied this model for ordering to find her optimal order size, how many cartridges would she order at a time? Let's use Equation 13.17:

$$\text{EOQ of cartridges} = \sqrt{\frac{2 \times 12{,}000 \times \$10.95}{\$2.00}} = 362.4914 \text{ cartridges}$$

Is this result better than 400 per year? Let's check the total cost at 362.4914 versus 400:

Total cost of 362.4914 units per order:

$$\frac{\$10.95 \times 12{,}000}{362.4914} + \frac{\$2.00 \times 362.4914}{2} = \$362.50 + \$362.50 = \$725.00$$

Total cost of 400 units per order: $328.50 + $400.00 = $728.50

So, it does pay off to decrease the order size to 362.4914 units per order. Of course, we can't order 0.4914 unit of a cartridge and may want to round to 360 or so, but the EOQ model does tell us the optimal order size. An interesting feature of the EOQ model is that it finds the quantity for which the total annual carrying costs and the total annual ordering costs are the same, and we can diagram this result.

Figure 13.7 illustrates the growing carrying costs and the decreasing ordering costs as the order quantity increases. The total inventory costs are the sum of these two costs. The lowest point of the total inventory costs is the point where the ordering costs and carrying costs are the same. It is also where we find the optimal order quantity, the quantity that produces the lowest total inventory cost.

Reorder Point and Safety Stock Although we expect orders to arrive on time, delays can occur. Therefore, a company faces two issues when ordering inventories: the natural lead time for an order and unexpected order delays. Open six days a week, Marge knows that Clinko's Fast Printers uses 24,000 boxes of paper per year, or 2,000 boxes per month, or about 80 boxes per day. If it takes five business days to receive a paper order, at what inventory level should Marge reorder?

We use the term **reorder point** to represent the level of inventories at which a company should place an order. If we keep a constant count of the paper in inventory, we reorder a new supply when the inventory falls to the reorder point, which we can define as

$$\text{reorder point} = \text{days of lead time} \times \text{daily usage rate}$$

For Clinko's, we have

$$\text{paper reorder point} = 5 \text{ days} \times 80 \text{ boxes per day} = 400$$

So, Marge should place her monthly order of 2,000 boxes of paper when the inventory level hits 400 and should allow five days for the new shipment to arrive. Over these five days, the company uses the last 400 units in inventory while the new shipment is in route.

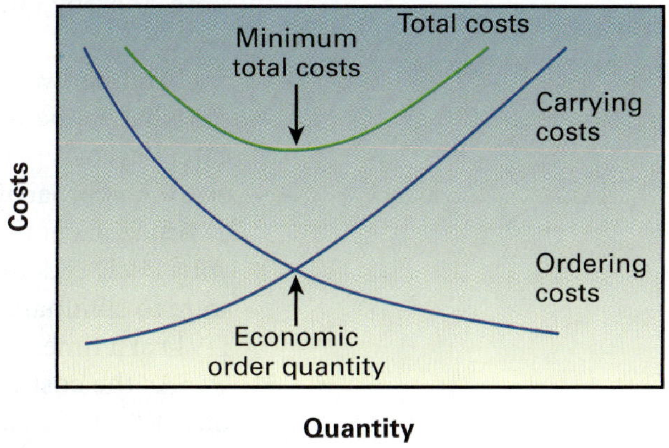

FIGURE 13.7 Inventory costs.

Marge is also aware that although orders take five days on average for delivery, it is not uncommon for deliveries to take up to seven days. If Clinko's runs out of paper, printing stops, which is costly for the company because customers expect their printing jobs on time, every time. Late print jobs usually mean lost customers. Marge must take into account the high cost of stock outages, so she adds two extra days of safety stock. **Safety stock** is the additional inventory on hand so that if an inventory order is delayed in arrival, the current inventory is sufficient to cover the delay. If Marge thinks shipments that normally take five days could be delayed as much as two additional days, she will need to keep an extra two days' production usage in inventory. The reorder point is now 560 boxes of paper: 400 for the normal five days for delivery and 160 safety stock for potential shipment delays. Keeping these extra 160 units on the shelf year round increases the average inventory level from 1,000 boxes to 1,160 boxes. We can define the average inventory as follows:

$$\text{average inventory} = \frac{\text{EOQ}}{2} + \text{safety stock} \qquad \textbf{13.18}$$

So, for Clinko's, applying Equation 13.18 gives us the necessary number of units for average inventory if Marge orders 2,000 boxes at a time (monthly order):

$$\frac{2{,}000}{2} + (2 \text{ day's safety stock} \times 80 \text{ per day}) = 1{,}160 \text{ units}$$

Just in Time Because both excess inventories and stock outages are costly to a company, management needs to address lead time and safety stock issues in order to reduce any excess inventories. A fourth inventory management system is **just-in-time (JIT)** inventory management. JIT attempts to minimize inventory carrying costs by having companies work with both their suppliers and their customers to reduce the time that items are in inventory as finished goods and the overall amount of inventory that a company carries.

Working with suppliers, a company using the JIT system tries to ensure that all deliveries are on time, every time, and that the quality of the materials meets production standards. On the other end, the company needs to work with customers to ensure that once a product is finished, it can ship it to the customer without delay. Eliminating the uncertainty about the timing of deliveries from suppliers and to customers to ensure that it ships finished goods immediately reduces the inventory carrying costs. So, we can consider JIT to be the inventory management system that attempts to produce only the necessary items with only the necessary raw materials at the necessary time, thereby eliminating waste and improving productivity. It is "lean manufacturing."

Another way to view JIT is to look back at the EOQ model (Eq. 13.17) and see what happens when the ordering costs per order increasingly decrease or the carrying costs per inventory item increasingly increase. As the cost per order decreases, approaching zero, the optimal order quantity approaches 1. For example, as Amazon.com reduces its handling and shipping costs, you reduce the size of your DVD order because you prefer to order one DVD at a time. If Amazon.com were to eliminate the handling and shipping cost entirely, you would order one DVD at a time.

As the cost to carry an item in inventory increases, the optimal order quantity decreases. If it becomes increasingly expensive to store inventory, you will want to reduce the amount that you hold. For example, consider cash as an inventory item. We know that if we are holding cash, it is not working for us by earning interest. The higher the current interest rate, the greater the opportunity or carrying cost of cash. Thus, with higher interest rates (higher carrying costs), you will want to reduce your cash holdings. So, JIT is just an application of EOQ by looking at the ordering costs and the carrying costs for inventory.

To see how the real world uses inventory management techniques, see the "Putting Finance to Work" feature on the next page.

13.5 The Effect of Working Capital on Capital Budgeting

When we introduced working capital management, we said that it is the operational side of the budgeting process. We also need to understand how this operational part of working capital affects the capital budgeting decision process. When a new project or business begins, it is necessary to consider the funding of the working capital that is part of the project. In Chapter 12, we noted how the increase of working capital at the beginning of a project was offset by a reduction of the same amount at the end of a project. To see further how working capital has an effect on the capital budgeting decisions of a company, let's look at Corporate Seasonings again.

When Corporate Seasonings was just in the planning stages, the owner needed to borrow money to start up the company. The capital assets that the company needed were a functional industrial kitchen and an office. The capital equipment included the following:

Range and stove
Walk-in refrigerator
Storage racks for food and cooking utensils
Tables
Cleaning equipment
Sinks
Office equipment

In addition, the company could not start shipping box lunches to customers without other items, including:

Boxes
Plastic utensils
Napkins

This latter set of items is not part of the capital assets of the firm; rather, they are *current assets* because the company will use up these items during the year. On the other hand, *capital assets*, such as the walk-in refrigerator, have useful lives much greater than one year. Start-up costs for Corporate Seasonings were $75,000, with $70,000 allocated to capital assets and $5,000 to working capital. Working capital does not "depreciate" like capital assets, however, and the company constantly reorders supplies. How does one account for this fact when looking at the company's cash flow?

Putting Finance to Work

Operations Management

Business people sometimes describe finance and operations managers as "night birds." No one sees them when everything is going well, but they come out when companies get into trouble. Managers and investors first notice declining profits. A closer look reveals higher production costs, declining margins, slower asset turnover, bulging inventories, and a decline in operating cash flow.

Ford Motors is a good case in point. In 2006, a good year for the U.S. economy, Ford lost more than $12.6 billion from continuing operations and its lots were bulging with unsold vehicles. A new CEO, Alan Mulally, had to close plants and lay off employees to raise cash. His philosophy was to direct this realized cash from downsizing into improving operations. Ford studied the manufacturing and design methods of its successful competitors Toyota and Mazda. The company implemented lean manufacturing, lean design, and Six Sigma quality control measures. It also worked diligently with its suppliers to improve communication within its supply chain. Within a year, Ford shortened the time from design to production by 50% and improved quality by 35%. Asset turnover ratios and other measures of operating efficiency quickly improved, and shortly thereafter, so did measures of profitability. By fiscal 2009, a terrible year for the U.S. economy, Ford rebounded financially and for fiscal 2010, earned profits from continuing operations of $6.6 billion. Ford was, of course, the only U.S. auto manufacturer not to need or accept government bailout money in 2009.

Operations management combines knowledge from engineering, management, economics, and, of course, finance. Typical responsibilities include the management of purchasing, inventory control, quality control, and logistics. Modern operations managers are concerned with implementing lean manufacturing, a central feature of which is just-in-time inventory management, or lean design, which greatly reduces the required time to bring products to market, managing supply chains for efficiency and adaptability, and statistical quality control strategies such as Six Sigma, which, taken literally, would result in a percentage of defects almost too small to measure.

These days, operations management is not just for manufacturing companies, companies in trouble, or even fast-growing companies. The ultimate objective of operations management is to do more with less. Lessons learned from lean manufacturing and design have led to lean processes in general and are equally valuable to service-oriented companies and nonprofit organizations. Businesses such as Amazon and Wal-Mart owe much of their competitive advantage and financial success to their eagerness to adopt operational innovations. A focus on efficient operations makes the balance sheets of most major companies look very different than they did a decade ago, with much less capital tied up in current assets, resulting in higher rates of return on investment.

Students interested in operations management should consult the website of the Association for Operations Management (www.apics.org). The Web site has a wealth of information on educational requirements, certifications such as the Certification in Integrated Resource Management (CIRM) and Certification in Production and Inventory Management (CPIM), as well as information on career opportunities and salaries.

Source: Jeffrey Liker and James Morgan, "Lean Product Development as a System: A Case Study of Body and Stamping Development at Ford," *Engineering Management Journal*, March 2011, vol. 23, pp. 16–28.

Inventories and Daily Operations

To understand how working capital eventually affects a company's cash flow, we must look back at general accounting practices and understand how expenses eventually reach the income statement and affect operating cash flow, or OCF. When Corporate Seasonings orders supplies and pays out cash to suppliers, the cost goes into an asset account (inventories, supplies). When Corporate Seasonings eventually sells its goods, the transaction moves the goods from the inventory account to the cost of goods sold (COGS) and records the expense.

When the inventory account is decreased, the company expenses this amount for the period on the income statement. However, Corporate Seasonings must maintain its inventory level, so it "replaces" the inventory as it sells. So, costs are constantly being added to inventory and subtracted from inventory, keeping the account constant. What we then have in the project's start-up period is an initial increase in inventory to support the project. Although OCF captures the sales side, the company needs to capture the increase in working capital as cash outflow as well.

As long as we remain in operations and stay at the same level, the usage of supplies each period will show up in COGS for our operating cash flow and the inventory level will remain constant as we consistently replace the inventory that production and sales use. Imagine a continuous process in which we sell a supply item as part of the product sale on the back end and purchase a supply item on the front end to replace the used inventory. Inventory remains constant and we see that it has no impact on cash flow.

Not until we close the business will we recapture the original working capital outlay. In the final operating period, we will not order supplies on the front end to replenish the inventory, but instead will draw the inventory down to zero and show the usage of inventories in COGS. For a project or business, this final period shows a "recapture" of working capital or a cash inflow in the working capital accounts. Actually, this inflow is a reduction in the cash outflow that we associate with COGS because the company purchased the supplies in the prior period. We actually have no cash flow in the period, but we overstated cash outflow in the COGS on the income statement as an expense. Therefore, the reduction in inventory is treated as a cash inflow to offset this overstated cash outflow.

To see how working capital affects a capital budgeting decision, let's look at a new business project for Corporate Seasonings and evaluate whether the company should accept or reject this project. We will use the net present value (NPV) model for the decision. This final example in this chapter combines material from previous chapters with the estimation of incremental cash flows for a project, including the operating cash flow, working capital cash flow, capital expenditures, and salvage cash flow. Once we know the incremental cash flows, we apply the NPV capital budget decision model. Of course, we use a positive NPV as the rationale for accepting the project.

EXAMPLE 13.5 Net present value decision with working capital

Problem Corporate Seasonings is investigating the possibility of adding pick-up evening meals to its current product portfolio. The idea is to have customers order a home-cooked meal such as a casserole that they can pick up at the close of the day, take home, heat in a microwave, and serve within ten minutes. The customer benefit is the elimination of cooking at the end of a long day but still getting a balanced, home-cooked meal. A typical meal for a family of four would cost $20.00, excluding drinks, and would include an entrée, a salad, a vegetable, and a dessert. Corporate Seasonings anticipates offering this product for three years. Here are the estimated costs:

Annual revenue: 1,200 meals at $20.00 per meal = $24,000

Annual COGS: 1,200 meals at $12.00 per meal = $14,400

Capital expansion costs for kitchen:	$16,000 (add second walk-in refrigerator, with a MACRS life of five years); refrigerator will be sold for $6,000 at the end of the third year
Working capital costs:	$2,000 for packing supplies
Cost of capital for Corporate Seasonings:	8%
Corporate tax rate:	40%

Solution First, determine the project's incremental cash flow. The capital outlay is $16,000, and depreciation schedule from MACRS is

$$\text{Year 1: } \$16{,}000 \times 0.20 = \$3{,}200$$
$$\text{Year 2: } \$16{,}000 \times 0.32 = \$5{,}120$$
$$\text{Year 3: } \$16{,}000 \times 0.192 = \$3{,}072$$

With the depreciation expenses for each year, we can determine the annual operating cash flow.

Annual Operating Cash Flows

	Year 1	Year 2	Year 3
Revenue	$24,000	$24,000	$24,000
– Cost of goods sold	$14,400	$14,400	$14,400
– Depreciation	$ 3,200	$ 5,120	$ 3,072
= EBIT	$ 6,400	$ 4,480	$ 6,528
–Taxes	$ 2,560	$ 1,792	$ 2,611
= Net income	$ 3,840	$ 2,688	$ 3,917
+Depreciation	$ 3,200	$ 5,120	$ 3,072
Operating cash flow	$ 7,040	$ 7,808	$ 6,989

Then, determine the cash flow of recapture of depreciation for the refrigerator:

$$\text{Book value} = \$16{,}000 - \$3{,}200 - \$5{,}120 - \$3{,}072 = \$4{,}608$$
$$\text{Sale price} - \text{book value} = \text{gain on sale} = \$6{,}000 - \$4{,}608 = \$1{,}392$$
$$\text{Tax on gain} = \$1{,}392 \times 0.40 = \$557$$
$$\text{Cash flow at disposal} = \$6{,}000 - \$557 = \$5{,}443$$

Once we have the salvage cash flow, we can determine the project's incremental cash flow.

Incremental Cash Flows for the Project

	Year 0	Year 1	Year 2	Year 3
Capital investment	–$16,000			
Working capital	–$ 2,000			$ 2,000
Operating cash flow		$7,040	$7,808	$ 6,989
Salvage				$ 5,443
Total cash flow	–$18,000	$7,040	$7,808	$14,432

We can now determine the net present value:

$$NPV = -\$18{,}000 + \frac{\$7{,}040}{1.08} + \frac{\$7{,}808}{1.08^2} + \frac{\$14{,}432}{1.08^3}$$

$$= -\$18{,}000 + \$6{,}519 + \$6{,}694 + \$11{,}457 = \mathbf{\$6{,}669}$$

Therefore, Corporate Seasonings should offer take-home meals.

How would the decision change had we neglected to consider the working capital changes?

NPV without considering working capital is:

$$NPV = -\$16{,}000 + \frac{\$7{,}040}{1.08} + \frac{\$7{,}808}{1.08^2} + \frac{\$12{,}432}{1.08^3} = \mathbf{\$6{,}923}$$

In this second case, the project's net present value was overstated by $254. So the mistake of failing to consider the working capital cash flow would not have produced the wrong decision. However, that may not always be the case. Remember that changes in working capital often have a significant effect on capital projects.

To review this chapter, see the Summary Card at the end of the text.

Key Terms

Questions

1. Explain the three components of the cash conversion cycle.
2. Why should a company attempt to speed up its receivables and slow down its payables?
3. How can a company "encourage" its slow-paying customers to pay their outstanding bills?
4. What is credit screening? When would it be appropriate for a company to use credit screening? When would it be appropriate to not use credit screening?
5. Why is it often a good practice to simply write off a bad debt rather than pursue payment from a credit customer?
6. Should a company take all discounts offered by its suppliers? What criteria should a company use when accepting or rejecting a discount on an invoice?
7. What is the float? Why does it take time between when you write a check and when the funds come out of the account?

8. When might it be detrimental to a company to have too many items in inventory? When might it be detrimental to have too few?
9. What is an economic order quantity? What cost does it attempt to minimize?
10. Why might a company have extra inventory on hand above the amount suggested by the economic order quantity? Make a case for a redundant inventory item in a business setting.
11. Why is it necessary to consider changes to working capital accounts as part of the capital budgeting decision?
12. What are some potential pitfalls of poor short-term financial planning?

Prepping for Exams

1. The production cycle ______________.
   - **a.** is the net period from the start of cash outflow for producing a product or service until the associated cash inflow materializes from the sale of that product or service
   - **b.** begins at the time that a firm first starts to make a product and lasts until the time that the customer buys the product
   - **c.** starts when production begins and ends with the collection of cash from the sale of the product
   - **d.** starts when the customer takes delivery of the product and ends when the firm receives payment for the product

2. Using the following information, the inventory turnover for the company is ______________.
   - **a.** 23.53 times
   - **b.** 53.33 times
   - **c.** 48.00 times
   - **d.** 60.00 times

   2009 Selected Income Statement Items for Perfect Purchase Electronics

Cash sales	$1,500,000
Credit sales	$7,500,000
Total sales	$9,000,000
Cost of goods sold	$6,000,000

2009 Selected Balance Sheet Accounts of Perfect Purchase Electronics

	12/31/2009	12/31/2008	Change
Accounts receivable	$270,000	$240,000	$30,000
Inventory	$125,000	$100,000	$25,000
Accounts payable	$110,000	$ 90,000	$20,000

3. BarnBurner Music, a music publishing firm located in Tennessee, bills its clients on the first of the month. For example, any sale that it makes in the month of July it bills on August 1 with payment due on September 1. Clients traditionally pay as follows: 50% at the end of the first month, 40% at the end of the second month, and 8% at the end of the third month; 2%

default on their bills. The dollar value of collected January billings in April is ______________.

a. $7,040
b. $29,600
c. $5,920
d. $0.00

First-Quarter Actual Billings			Second-Quarter Anticipated Billings		
Jan.	Feb.	Mar.	Apr.	May	June
$88,000	$74,000	$96,000	$99,000	$82,000	$63,000

4. Extending credit to a customer has three major components: ______________.
a. a policy on how customers will qualify for credit, a policy on the payment plan allowed creditors, and a policy for collecting overdue bills
b. a policy on how customers will qualify for credit, a policy on paying commissions on sales, and a policy for collecting overdue bills
c. a policy on how customers will qualify for credit, a policy on the payment plan allowed creditors, and a policy on accounting for depreciation
d. a policy on how customers will qualify for credit, a policy on accounting for depreciation, and a policy on paying commissions on sales

5. Travel and Tow Trailers Inc. makes small trailers for light-duty towing behind SUVs and small pickup trucks. Its trailers typically sell for $2,500. Many of its customers have asked for credit terms to aid in purchasing the trailers. The firm's finance department has estimated the following profile for its light-duty trailers and customer base:

Annual sales:	10,000 trailers
Annual production costs per trailer:	$1,500
Lost sales if credit is not provided for customers:	2,000 trailers
Default rate if all customers purchase on credit:	3.00%

What is the profit margin if the firm has a cash-only policy?
a. $9,250,000
b. $25,000,000
c. $8,000,000
d. $15,000,000

6. Which of the following does *not* reduce the length of time of collection float for a firm?
a. electronic fund transfers (EFT)
b. lockboxes
c. direct payment via online checking
d. Choices (a) through (c) all reduce the length of time of collection float for a firm.

7. When using the ABC inventory management system, type A items are ______________.
a. small-dollar items
b. nonessential inventory items
c. large-dollar or critical inventory items
d. moderate dollar items

8. The optimal order quantity as determined by the EOQ occurs when _______________.

a. ordering costs equal carrying costs
b. ordering costs are exactly one-half carrying costs
c. ordering costs are exactly twice as much as carrying costs
d. None of answers (a) through (c) is accurate.

9. The Hannibal Homers minor league baseball club is considering an expansion of its stadium to increase capacity by 2,000 seats. Management estimates increased revenue from ticket and concession sales at $600,000 per year for the next five years. The cost of expansion is $750,000, with an additional $50,000 in working capital. The working capital increase is permanent (will not be recovered after five years). The club expects annual costs to increase by $200,000 per year, the club's cost of capital is 14%, and its tax rate is 30%. If the club depreciates the stadium addition in a straight line to a value of $0.00 over five years, what is the net present value of this project rounded to the nearest dollar? Ignore any revenues or costs associated with the project's terminal value after five years.

a. $165,751
b. $365,751
c. $315,751
d. $1,115,751

10. Of the following items, which is working capital as opposed to a capital asset?

a. disposable parts that aid in installation and ship with each sale
b. a CAD/CAM machine used in the manufacturing process
c. an addition to the existing building designed to facilitate a new product line
d. None of answers (a) through (c) is a working capital asset.

These problems are available in MyFinanceLab.

Problems

1. ***Business operating cycle.*** Kolman Kampers has a production cycle of thirty-five days, a collection cycle of twenty-one days, and a payment cycle of fourteen days. What are Kolman's business operating cycle and cash conversion cycle? If Kolman reduces the production cycle by one week, what is the effect on the cash conversion cycle? If Kolman decreases the collection cycle by one week, what is the effect on the cash conversion cycle? If Kolman increases the payment cycle by one week, what is the effect on the cash conversion cycle?

2. ***Business operating cycle.*** Stewart and Company currently has a production cycle of forty days, a collection cycle of twenty days, and a payment cycle of fifteen days. What are Stewart's current business operating cycle and cash conversion cycle? If Stewart and Company wants to reduce its cash conversion cycle to thirty-five days, what action can it take?

Use the following account information for Problems 3 through 8.

2007 and 2008 Selected Balance Sheet Accounts of Rian Company

	12/31/08	12/31/07	Change
Accounts receivable	$38,000	$46,000	$8,000
Inventory	$55,000	$59,000	$4,000
Accounts payable	$27,000	$25,000	$2,000

2008 Selected Income Statement Items for Rian Company

Cash sales	$298,000
Credit sales	$672,000
Total sales	$970,000
Cost of goods sold	$570,000

3. ***Average production cycle.*** Find the average production cycle for Rian Company.
4. ***Average production cycle.*** For the coming year, Rian Company wants to reduce its average production cycle to thirty days. If the target-ending inventory for 2009 is $61,000, what cost of goods sold will the company need to reach its goal?
5. ***Average collection cycle.*** What is the average collection cycle for Rian Company?
6. ***Average collection cycle.*** Rian Company had a target of twenty days for the collection cycle for the year 2008. If total sales had remained at $970,000, how much of the sales revenue would have needed to be cash sales for the company to meet the collection goal?
7. ***Average accounts payable cycle.*** Calculate Rian Company's average accounts payable cycle.
8. ***Average accounts payable cycle.*** Rian Company had a target of fifteen days for its payment (accounts payable) cycle. What would the ending balance in the accounts payable account need to be to reach this target (holding all other accounts the same)?
9. ***Cash flow of accounts receivable.*** Myers and Associates, a famous law office in California, bills it clients on the first of each month. Clients pay in the following fashion: 40% pay at the end of the first month, 30% pay at the end of the second month, 20% pay at the end of the third month, 5% pay at the end of the fourth month, and 5% default on their bills. Myers wants to know the anticipated cash flow for the first quarter of 2009 if the past billings and anticipated billings follow this same pattern. The actual and anticipated billings are as follows:

Fourth Quarter Actual Billings			First Quarter Anticipated Billings		
Oct.	Nov.	Dec.	Jan.	Feb.	Mar.
$392,000	$323,000	$296,000	$340,000	$360,000	$408,000

10. ***Cash flow of accounts receivable.*** Myers and Associates (from Problem 9) has hired a new accountant, who promises to increase the speed of payment by clients. The new collection times will be 60% at the end of the first month, 25% at the end of the second month, and 10% at the end of the third month. The uncollectible accounts will remain at 5%. What cash flow improvement will this change generate for the first quarter if the new system takes effect in January? Assume payments from the fourth quarter will stay on the old payment schedule.
11. ***Credit screening.*** Tennindo Inc. is starting up its new, cost-efficient gaming system console, the yuu. Tennindo currently has 4,000 cash-paying customers and makes a profit of $60 per unit. Tennindo wants to expand its customer base by allowing customers to buy on credit. It estimates that credit sales will bring in an additional 1,200 customers per year, but that there will also be a

default rate on credit sales of 5%. It costs $260 to make a yuu, which retails for $320. If all customers (old and new) buy on credit, what is the cost of bad debt without credit screening? What is the most Tennindo would pay for credit screening that accurately identifies bad-debt customers prior to the sale? What are the increased profits by adding credit sales for customers with and without credit screening? Should Tennindo offer credit sales if credit screening costs $10 per customer?

12. ***Credit screening.*** Screendoor Inc. is a credit-screening consulting firm. Screendoor advises Tennindo Inc. (from Problem 11) that it can offer a credit-screening device that is 90% accurate and costs $5.00 per customer to apply. Using the data in Problem 11, determine whether Tennindo should use Screendoor's credit-screening system.

13. ***Credit terms.*** As manager of Fly-by-Night Airlines, you decide to allow customers 90 days to pay their bills. To encourage early payment, though, you allow them to reduce their bills by 1.5% if they pay within the first 30 days. At what implied effective annual interest rate are you loaning money to your customers? What if you extend the discount to 60 days and allow full payment up to 180 days?

14. ***Credit terms.*** Find the effective annual rate of the following credit terms:

    a. 2% discount if paid within ten days or net within thirty days
    b. 1% discount if paid within thirty days or net within sixty days
    c. 0.5% discount if paid within fifteen days or net within forty-five days
    d. 1.0% discount if paid within twenty days or net within thirty days

15. ***Economic order quantity (EOQ).*** Tennindo Inc. believes that it will sell 4 million zen-zens, an electronic game, this coming year. Note that this figure is for annual sales. The inventory manager plans to order zen-zens forty times over the next year. The carrying cost is $0.03 per zen-zen per year. The order cost is $600 per order. What are the annual carrying cost, the annual ordering cost, and the optimal order quantity for the zen-zens? Verify your answer by calculating the new total inventory cost.

16. ***Economic order quantity (EOQ).*** It turns out that the marketing manager in Problem 15 has underestimated the zen-zen market. The zen-zens are a smash, and current estimates are that the company will sell 8 million of them per year. Should the inventory manager simply double the order quantity from Problem 15? Find the new EOQ and verify that it is the correct order quantity by finding the new carrying cost and new ordering cost.

17. ***Working capital and capital budgeting.*** Farbuck's Tea Shops is thinking about opening another tea shop. The incremental cash flow for the first five years is as follows:

    Initial capital cost = $3,500,000
    Operating cash flow for each year = $1,000,000
    Recovery of capital assets after five years = $250,000

    The hurdle rate for this project is 12%. If the initial cost of working capital is $500,000 for items such as teapots, teacups, saucers, and napkins, should Farbuck's open this new shop if it will be in business for only five years? What is the most it can invest in working capital and still have a positive net present value?

18. ***Working capital and capital budgeting.*** Working capital investment is 25% of the anticipated first year sales for Wally's Waffle House. The first-year sales are

currently projected at $4,300,000. The incremental cash flow (not including working capital investment) is

Initial cash flow = $13,700,000 outflow

Cash flow years 1 through 10 = $2,850,000

What is the internal rate of return of the ten-year project with working capital factored into the cash flow? What is the net present value at 15% weighted average cost of capital? What is the maximum investment in working capital for an acceptable project with a 15% weighted average cost of capital?

Advanced Problems for Spreadsheet Application

These problems are available in MyFinanceLab.

1. ***Cash flow timing for accounts receivable.*** Zenotech Incorporated sells business software to a variety of companies. The payment for products and services varies across the Zenotech customers. In addition, as Zenotech increases its sales, it has more default customers due to the lack of screening for credit. Zenotech also uses discounts to incentivize customers to pay early on their accounts. Currently it is offering 1.5%/30 or net 60 days on all accounts. Following are the projected sales per month for the coming year in thousands of dollars:

Jan.	Feb.	Mar.	Apr.	May	Jun.	Jul.	Aug.	Sep.	Oct.	Nov.	Dec.
1,010	1,608	1,974	2,005	2,608	3,501	4,070	5,280	3,547	2,411	1,604	1,233

For monthly sales of less than $2,000,000, the following payments take place:

default 1.25%, take discount 48%, pay at 60 days 39%, pay 30 days late 7.5%, pay 60 days late 4.25%

For monthly sales of $2,000,000 to $4,999,999.99, the following payments take place:

default 2.5%, take discount 41%, pay at 60 days 42%, pay 30 days late 9%, pay 60 days late 5.5%

For monthly sales of $5,000,000 or more, the following payments take place:

default 4.0%, take discount 37%, pay at 60 days 41.5%, pay 30 days late 11%, pay 60 days late 6.5%

Assume that Zenotech records all sales on the last day of the month for this problem rather than equally throughout the month. If sales for the last half of the previous year are:

Jul.	Aug.	Sep.	Oct.	Nov.	Dec.
3,866	4,209	3,113	1,979	1,543	1,137

what are the monthly anticipated cash inflows from accounts receivable/sales for the coming year?

2. ***Economic order quantity.*** Exact Copies Incorporated currently orders paper every month for its operations and stores them at a central warehouse. Annually the company uses 12,000,000 reams of paper. Each order cost $450 for delivery to the warehouse. Exact also estimates that the average cost per year to store a ream of paper is $0.05. Using a spreadsheet, determine the

total annual inventory cost of ordering every week, every other week, monthly, every other month, and quarterly. Find the economic order quantity (EOQ) for Exact Copies. How often should it order? Finally, visually prove the EOQ by calculating the total order cost for order sizes at 25,000 increments (up and down) over a range of 500,000 (EOQ − 250,000 to EOQ + 250,0000) with the EOQ as the midpoint by graphing total inventory costs, total annual ordering costs, and total annual carrying costs.

MINI-CASE

Cranston Dispensers, Inc.: Part 1

This mini-case is available in MyFinanceLab.

In the early 1990s, Cranston Dispensers, Inc. was quick to realize that concern for the environment would cause many consumer product manufacturers to move away from aerosol dispensers to mechanical alternatives that pose no threat to the ozone layer. In the following decades, most countries banned the most popular aerosol propellants, first chlorofluorocarbons and then hydrochlorofluorocarbons. As the leading manufacturer of specialized pump and spray containers for a variety of products in the cosmetics, household cleaning supplies, and pharmaceutical industries, Cranston experienced a rapid increase in sales and profitability after it made this strategic move. At that time, the firm focused much of its attention on capturing market share and keeping up with demand.

For most of 2009 and 2010, however, Cranston's share price was falling while shares of other companies in the industry were rising. At the end of fiscal 2010, the company hired Susan McNulty as the new treasurer, with the expectation that she would diagnose Cranston's problems and improve the company's financial performance relative to that of its competitors. She decided to begin the task with a thorough review of the company's working capital management practices.

While examining the company's financial statements, she noted that Cranston had a higher percentage of current assets on its balance sheet than other companies in the packaging industry. The high level of current assets caused the company to carry more short-term debt and to have higher interest expense than its competitors. It was also causing the company to lag behind its competitors on some key financial measures, such as return on assets (net income divided by total assets) and return on equity (net income divided by total equity), which we discuss in Chapter 14.

In an effort to improve Cranston's overall performance, Susan has decided to conduct a comprehensive review of working capital management policies, including those related to the cash conversion cycle, credit policy, and inventory management. Cranston's financial statements for the three most recent years follow.

Income Statements			
	2010	2009	2008
Sales	$3,784.00	$3,202.00	$2,760.00
Cost of goods sold	$2,568.00	$2,172.00	$1,856.00
Gross profit	$1,216.00	$1,030.00	$ 904.00
Selling, general, and administrative expenses	$ 550.00	$ 478.00	$ 406.00
Depreciation	$ 247.00	$ 230.00	$ 200.00
EBIT	$ 419.00	$ 322.00	$ 298.00
Interest expense	$ 20.50	$ 24.70	$ 14.30
Earnings before taxes	$ 398.50	$ 297.30	$ 283.70
Taxes	$ 119.55	$ 89.19	$ 85.11
Net income	**$ 278.95**	**$ 208.11**	**$ 198.59**

Questions

1. Determine Cranston's average production cycles for 2009 and for 2010.
2. Determine Cranston's average collection cycles for 2009 and for 2010. Assume that all sales are credit sales.
3. Determine Cranston's average payment cycles for 2009 and for 2010.
4. Using your answers to Questions 1 through 3, determine Cranston's cash conversion cycles for 2009 and for 2010.
5. Cranston now bills its customers with terms of net 45, meaning that payment is due on the forty-fifth day after the company ships the goods. Although most customers pay on time, some routinely stretch the payment period to sixty or even ninety days. What steps can Cranston take to encourage clients to pay on time? What is the potential risk of implementing penalties for late payment?
6. Suppose Cranston institutes a policy of granting a 1% discount for payment within fifteen days with the full amount due in forty-five days (1/15, net 45). Half the customers take the discount; the other half take an average of sixty days to pay.
   a. What is the length of Cranston's collection cycle under this new policy?
   b. In dollars, how much would the policy have cost Cranston in 2010?
   c. If this policy had been in effect during 2010, by how many days would Cranston have shortened the cash conversion cycle?
7. An image-based lockbox system could accelerate Cranston's cash collections by three days. Cranston can earn an annual rate of 6% on the cash freed by accelerated collections. Using sales for 2010, determine the most that Cranston should pay per year for the lockbox system.
8. One of Cranston's principal raw materials is plastic pellets, which it purchases in lots of 100 pounds at $0.35 per pound. Annual consumption is 8,000,000 pounds. Within a broad range of order sizes, ordering and shipping costs are $120 per order. Carrying costs are $1.50 per year per 100 pounds. Compute the EOQ for plastic pellets. Cranston can order the pellets only in whole lots of 100 pounds, so use 8,000,000/100 as *S* in Equation 13.17. If Cranston used the EOQ model, how often would it order pellets?

Balance Sheets

ASSETS	2010	2009	2008	LIABILITIES	2010	2009	2008
				Current liabilities			
Cash	$ 341.00	$ 276.00	$ 236.00	Accounts payable	$ 332.00	$ 288.00	$ 204.00
				Accrued expenses	343.00	335.00	192.00
Accounts Receivable	722.00	642.00	320.00	Short-term debt	503.00	491.00	243.00
Inventory	595.00	512.00	388.00	**Total current liabilities**	**$1,178.00**	**$1,114.00**	**$ 639.00**
				Long-term debt	398.00	324.00	289.00
				Other liabilities	239.00	154.00	147.00
Total current assets	**$1,658.00**	**$1,430.00**	**$ 944.00**	**Total liabilities**	**$1,815.00**	**$1,592.00**	**$1,075.00**
				OWNERS' EQUITY			
Net fixed assets	1,822.00	1,691.00	1,572.00	Common equity	1,665.00	1,529.00	1,441.00
TOTAL ASSETS	**$3,480.00**	**$3,121.00**	**$2,516.00**	**TOTAL LIABILITIES AND OWNERS' EQUITY**	**$3,480.00**	**$3,121.00**	**$2,516.00**

Learning Objectives

LO1 Create, understand, and interpret common-size financial statements.

LO2 Calculate and interpret financial ratios.

LO3 Compare different company performances using financial ratios, historic financial ratio trends, and industry ratios.

Chapter 14
Financial Ratios and Firm Performance

In the opening of the 1984 movie *Ghostbusters,* Dan Aykroyd tries to explain to Bill Murray the difference between the academic world and the real world with this insightful analysis:

> *Personally, I liked the university. They gave us money and facilities. We didn't have to produce anything. You've never been out of college. You don't know what it's like out there. I've worked in the private sector. They expect results!*

The real world does, indeed, expect results. In the business world, managers need to be able to measure past performance and predict future performance if they want to deliver positive results.

A company's financial statements are the primary sources of information that communicate its financial results, both internally and externally. Every company's financial statements tell a story about the value of the business. No one financial statement tells the complete story, but together they can help us analyze a company's performance over time and help predict future performance. It is critical to know how to use these financial statements properly. Although they contain much useful information, we need to know the limitations of that information so that we do not fall into the trap of relying on numbers without informed analysis.

In this chapter, we return to the financial statements that we first introduced in Chapter 2 and used in forecasting in Chapter 12. Here we will learn how to conduct ratio analysis, a series of financial measurements that help us piece together the story behind the numbers and point us in the right direction to discover more information about specific areas of a company's performance. In the process, we may discover some warning flags or unearth some gold nuggets. The financial tools from the first few chapters and the decision models of the last few chapters have given you the necessary background for using financial statements. Here we put them to work in multiple ways to help analyze and interpret the performance of companies.

14.1 Financial Statements

We first studied two primary financial statements in Chapter 2. We now return to these statements and their relationship to the performance of the firm. The two financial statements are:

1. Statement of financial position (balance sheet)
2. Income statement

In this chapter, we look again at Cogswell Cola Company from Chapter 10 and first scrutinize the company's two financial statements, starting with the balance sheet (Figure 14.1). Here, and throughout the chapter, when we use numbers from the balance sheet, we color-key the numbers in blue.

The balance sheet is the listing of all assets and all claims against the assets of a company. We use the term *balance sheet* because the following *accounting identity* (Eq. 2.1) must always hold:

$$\text{assets} \equiv \text{liabilities} + \text{owners' equity}$$

The *income statement* is the recording of the business activities over the past business cycle. Usually, this business cycle is one year, but companies often prepare income statements monthly for internal use and quarterly for external reporting. Here, and throughout the chapter, when we use numbers from the income statement, we color-key the numbers in red. Figure 14.2 shows Cogswell Cola's income statement in abbreviated form. The last line, the company's earnings per share (EPS), is the net income divided by the number of outstanding shares. The term *diluted* refers to the number of shares, including all currently outstanding shares and any items that we can convert into shares such as convertible bonds, convertible preferred shares,

Cogswell Cola Company Balance Sheet
Year Ending December 31, 2011
($ in thousands)

ASSETS	2011	2010	Change	LIABILITIES AND OWNERS' EQUITY	2011	2010	Change
Current assets				**Liabilities**			
Cash and equivalents	$ 1,638	$ 683	$ 955	Accounts payable	$ 6,052	$ 4,998	$1,054
Short-term investments	$ 207	$ 966	−$ 759				
Accounts receivable	$ 2,531	$ 2,142	$ 389	Long-term liabilities	$ 8,131	$ 8,023	$ 108
Inventories	$ 1,342	$ 1,310	$ 32	**Total liabilities**	**$14,183**	**$13,021**	**$1,162**
Prepaid expenses	$ 695	$ 752	−$ 57	**OWNERS' EQUITY**			
Total current assets	**$ 6,413**	**$ 5,853**	**$ 560**	Common stock	$ 1,517	$ 1,309	$ 208
Net plant, property, and equipment	$16,390	$14,879	$1,511	Retained earnings	$ 7,774	$ 7,368	$ 406
Other long-term assets	$ 671	$ 966	−$ 295	**Total owners' equity**	**$ 9,291**	**$ 8,677**	**$ 614**
TOTAL ASSETS	**$23,474**	**$21,698**	**$1,776**	**TOTAL LIABILITIES AND OWNERS' EQUITY**	**$23,474**	**$21,698**	**$1,776**

FIGURE 14.1

warrants, and stock options. The diluted EPS is therefore the net income divided by all potential outstanding shares.

Cogswell Cola Company Income Statement Year Ending December 31, 2011 ($ in thousands)	
Revenue	$25,112
Cost of goods sold	$11,497
Selling, general, and administrative expenses	$ 7,457
Depreciation	$ 1,112
EBIT	$ 5,046
Interest expense	$ 178
Taxable income	$ 4,868
Taxes	$ 1,555
Net income	**$ 3,313**
Earnings per share (diluted)	$ 1.85

FIGURE 14.2

Benchmarking

We will use the balance sheet and the income statement to analyze the performance of Cogswell Cola. Before we launch into this analysis, however, you should understand the concept of benchmarking. **Benchmarking** compares a company's current performance against its own previous performance or that of its competitors. It provides a standard of comparison for measurement. Let's look at benchmarking for Cogswell Cola in terms of its past performance first.

One of the most important aspects of analyzing performance is to look at trends over time. If we want to see if Cogswell Cola is improving its market share over time, we might look at its sales trends. If sales are increasing year after year, we would tend to view this increase as a positive performance. If we want to know how well managers are performing, we may want to look at net income over time. If net income is falling year after year, we would view this decrease as a negative sign. To look at trends over time requires that we examine a series of financial statements over a specific time period. We often look at the past five years of financial statements to establish trends and then predict future performance based on those trends. What, for example, is your prediction of the upcoming net income of Cogswell Cola given the historical financial statements (in abbreviated form) listed in Table 14.1?

TABLE 14.1 Cogswell Cola's Abbreviated Income Statements ($ in thousands)

Account	2007	2008	2009	2010	2011	Annual % Δ
Sales	$18,460	$19,934	$21,529	$23,252	$25,112	+8.0%
Cost of goods sold	$ 7,853	$ 8,638	$ 9,502	$10,452	$11,497	+10.0%
Selling, general, and administrative	$ 4,739	$ 5,307	$ 5,945	$ 6,658	$ 7,457	+12.0%
Depreciation	$ 1,300	$ 1,250	$ 1,202	$ 1,156	$ 1,112	−3.8%
EBIT	$ 4,568	$ 4,739	$ 4,880	$ 4,986	$ 5,046	+2.5%
Interest	$ 178	$ 178	$ 178	$ 178	$ 178	0.0%
Taxes	$ 1,402	$ 1,456	$ 1,502	$ 1,536	$ 1,555	–
Net income	$ 2,988	$ 3,105	$ 3,200	$ 3,272	$ 3,313	+2.6%

Based on the previous five years of income statements, you can see in Table 14.1 that earnings have been increasing annually at an overall rate of 2.6% $[(\$3,133/\$2,988)^{1/4} - 1]$. So, if we wanted to predict next year's earnings, we could use this five-year trend:

$$\text{predicted net income 2012} = \$3,313 \times (1 + 0.026) = \$3,400$$

We could also construct an income statement for 2012 using the trends of sales (8.0% annual growth); COGS (10.0% annual growth); selling, general, and administrative, or SG&A (12.0% annual growth); depreciation (−3.8% annual reduction); interest (constant); and taxes at 31.92% of taxable income. It would produce the following predictions for 2012:

Sales revenue	$27,121
Cost of goods sold	$12,647
Selling, general, and administrative	$ 8,352
Depreciation	$ 1,069
EBIT	$ 5,053
Interest	$ 178
Taxable income	$ 4,875
Taxes	$ 1,557
Net income	**$ 3,318**

Which is the better prediction, the one based solely on net income or the one based on all the individual accounts? If we use more information than just the trend in net income, we will probably have a better comfort level with the predicted number. Using the trends of the individual accounts, we can see that profit is eroding by rising production costs (COGS) and support costs (SG&A) that are growing at a rate faster than the sales growth rate. This observation is one of the warning flags that can arise from doing a trend analysis. If we believe these trends are going to continue, we will probably trust the $3,318 predicted net income for 2012 more than the $3,400 of the annual 2.6% net income gain and begin to investigate why the cost of production is growing faster than the sales rate.

A second way to measure a company's financial performance is to benchmark against the financial performance of its competition. A problem arises when we use financial statements of different firms, however. Because firms are often different sizes, comparisons may be troubling. To aid in comparing against other companies, we restate financial statements into **common-size financial statements**, in which we express all line items as percentages of a common base figure. For income statements, it is usually sales. In essence, we compare percentages, not actual numbers.

Figure 14.3 presents both the actual income statements (dollars) and the common-size statements (percentage of revenue or sales) for Cogswell Cola and its competitor, Spacely Spritzers. Let's do a quick analysis of what these numbers are telling us. There are some important indicators in Figure 14.3 that tell the story of a bigger firm versus a smaller firm and that illustrate the effects of economies of scale. First, note that COGS is higher as a percentage of sales for Spacely Spritzers, the smaller firm, than for Cogswell (48.85% for Spacely versus 45.78% for Cogswell), which means that it costs Spacely more to produce its product in terms of revenue dollars. Larger companies like Cogswell Cola can often realize economies of scale in their COGS numbers. Larger production runs result in lower costs per individual product produced.

Cogswell Cola spends a higher percentage than Spacely in SG&A per sales dollar (29.69% for Cogswell versus 26.25% for Spacely), which may be a function

FIGURE 14.3

Income Statements and Common-Size Income Statements Year Ending December 31, 2011 ($ in thousands)				
	Cogswell	Percent	Spacely	Percent
Revenue	$25,112	100.00%	$ 8,403	100.00%
Cost of goods sold	$11,497	45.78%	$ 4,105	48.85%
Selling, general, and administrative expenses	$ 7,457	29.69%	$ 2,206	26.25%
Depreciation	$ 1,112	4.43%	$ 618	7.35%
EBIT	$ 5,046	20.09%	$ 1,474	17.54%
Interest expense	$ 178	0.71%	$ 214	2.55%
Taxable income	$ 4,868	19.39%	$ 1,260	14.99%
Taxes	$ 1,555	6.18%	$ 403	4.80%
Net income	**$ 3,313**	**13.19%**	**$ 857**	**10.20%**
Earnings per share (diluted)	$ 1.85		$ 1.46	

of a more expansive marketing program or a larger administrative staff. Cogswell may want to revisit its marketing plan or its administrative organization. Cogswell also has a lower depreciation percentage (4.43% for Cogswell versus 7.35% for Spacely), which could represent a lower amount of fixed assets per sales dollar or older equipment. If it is true that Cogswell Cola's equipment is older and will need replacing in the near future, management may want to start formulating plans for timely replacement of key equipment.

The combination of all these factors gives a higher EBIT for the larger Cogswell Cola (20.09% for Cogswell versus 17.54% for Spacely). One way to interpret this EBIT percentage is that for every dollar of sales, Cogswell Cola generates 20 cents to cover interest and taxes, whereas Spacely Spritzers generates only 17.5 cents to cover the same.

Spacely is more heavily debt-financed (see the interest expense line) and therefore has a higher interest expense percentage. Finally, the net income percent of Cogswell Cola states that for every dollar in sales, it generates a little more than 13 cents for net income. Spacely Spritzers is generating only 10 cents per sales dollar at net income. In general, the larger Cogswell Cola seems to be outperforming the smaller Spacely Spritzers. This analysis, though, is just a quick comparison of the two cola companies' income statements. Now, let's look at the balance sheet comparisons.

To convert a balance sheet into a common-size balance sheet statement, we restate all the numbers as percentages of total assets. Figure 14.4 shows common-size statements for Cogswell Cola and Spacely Spritzers. Note that Spacely Spritzers is about one-third the size of Cogswell Cola in terms of assets. Note also the new line for *prepaid expenses*. These expenses are items, such as rent or insurance, that the company pays at the start of the coverage period and therefore reflect an asset (use of a facility or insurance coverage). The company expenses these items over the business cycle and they end up in the income statement in lines such as SG&A expenses.

From the percentage comparisons in Figure 14.4, we see that these two different-size companies have quite comparable balance sheets, with Spacely using a little more debt financing for its operations than Cogswell (long-term liabilities

Common-Size Balance Sheet Year Ending December 31, 2011 ($ in thousands)									
ASSETS	Cogswell	Percent	Spacely	Percent	**LIABILITIES AND OWNERS' EQUITY**	Cogswell	Percent	Spacely	Percent
Current assets					**Liabilities**				
Cash and equivalents	$ 1,638	6.98%	$ 383	5.15%	Accounts payable	$ 6,052	25.78%	$ 1,784	24.00%
Short-term investments	$ 207	0.88%	$ 330	4.44%	Long-term liabilities	$ 8,131	34.64%	$ 2,972	39.98%
Accounts receivable	$ 2,531	10.78%	$ 457	6.15%					
Inventories	$ 1,342	5.72%	$ 860	11.57%	**Total liabilities**	**$14,183**	**60.42%**	**$ 4,756**	**63.98%**
Prepaid expenses	$ 695	2.96%	$ 188	2.53%	**OWNERS' EQUITY**				
Total current assets	**$ 6,413**	**27.32%**	**$1,835**	**24.69%**	Common stock	$ 1,517	6.46%	$ 1,309	17.61%
Net plant, property, and equipment	$16,390	69.82%	$5,162	69.45%	Retained earnings	$ 7,774	33.12%	$ 1,368	18.40%
Other long-term assets	$ 671	2.86%	$ 436	5.87%	**Total owners' equity**	**$ 9,291**	**39.58%**	**$ 2,677**	**36.02%**
TOTAL ASSETS	**$23,474**	**100%**	**$7,433**	**100%**	**TOTAL LIABILITIES AND OWNERS' EQUITY**	**$23,474**	**100%**	**$ 7,433**	**100%**

FIGURE 14.4

39.98% for Spacely versus 34.64% for Cogswell). We can also see that Spacely has more current assets in inventories (11.57% for Spacely versus 5.72% for Cogswell) versus the higher accounts receivables for Cogswell Cola (10.78% for Cogswell versus 6.15% for Spacely). Reflecting on Chapter 13 and working capital management issues, we might conclude that the cash position of Cogswell Cola is stronger than that of Spacely Spritzers because, ordinarily, accounts receivables will generate cash flow much more quickly than inventories.

Is there any other percentage difference that might suggest a different operating style or a better-managed company? For one thing, Cogswell may have too high a balance in cash and cash equivalents (6.98%), suggesting that the company needs to review its cash management, but this quick overview would need much more analysis before jumping to action. Again, we would use the tools from Chapter 13 to evaluate the proper or optimal quantity of cash for Cogswell Cola.

This exercise is just a quick review of the potential of common-size statements for benchmarking firms against their competitors. In reality, to discover superior management skills, advantages due to economies of scale, or areas of concern for a management team, you would do a much more thorough analysis. Often, benchmarking is a starting point for analysis and directs the management team or potential investors to areas of the company that may be performing well or poorly.

14.2 Financial Ratios

Our first set of financial analysis tools looked directly at individual accounts on the financial statements. We now add another set of financial tools—ratios—that we can employ to analyze a company's performance or to compare it with the performance of competitors. **Financial ratios** are relationships between different accounts from financial statements—usually the income statement and the balance sheet—that serve as performance indicators. We can look at a company's specific performance areas by selecting key pieces of information from the financial statements and by analyzing this information at a point in time or over a specific time horizon. We again either look at trends over time of an individual company or compare ratios of different companies at a specific point in time. We will now build some of the key financial ratios from our financial statements for Cogswell Cola and Spacely Spritzers and relate them back to the key performance areas. We look specifically at the following five types of ratios and the questions these ratios try to answer:

1. *Liquidity ratios:* Can the company meet its obligations over the short term?
2. *Solvency ratios (also known as financial leverage ratios):* Can the company meet its obligations over the long term?
3. *Asset management ratios*: How efficiently is the company managing its assets to generate sales?
4. *Profitability ratios*: How well has the company performed overall?
5. *Market value ratios*: How does the market (investors) view the company's financial prospects?

We will then look at a special case of one ratio developed by DuPont. It breaks down the return on equity into three components. As we work with these ratios, be sure to note the unit of measurement (dollar or number), because it will be a major help in trying to interpret the information in the ratio.

Short-Term Solvency: Liquidity Ratios

In Chapters 10 and 13, you learned that positive cash flow is critical to a company's success; one of the key areas for financial ratio analysis will be the firm's liquidity. **Liquidity ratios** measure a company's ability to meet its short-term debt obligations in a timely fashion. Liquidity ratios deal with the short term, so firms use current assets and current liabilities accounts. These accounts track the assets that we expect to turn into cash in the near future and the liabilities that we expect will come due in the near future. If a company is unable to meet its short-term cash obligations, it may find itself in bankruptcy.

To gauge the liquidity of the firm, we have a few key ratios to help us understand the potential near-term cash flow:

$$\text{current ratio} = \frac{\text{current assets}}{\text{current liabilities}} \qquad \textbf{14.1}$$

$$\text{quick ratio (or acid ratio test)} = \frac{(\text{current assets} - \text{inventories})}{\text{current liabilities}} \qquad \textbf{14.2}$$

$$\text{cash ratio} = \frac{\text{cash}}{\text{current liabilities}} \qquad \textbf{14.3}$$

Using the data from Cogswell Cola and Spacely Spritzers in Figures 14.3 and 14.4, we can compute each of these three ratios:

1. For Cogswell Cola, we have the following liquidity ratios for 2011:

$$\text{current ratio} = \frac{\$6{,}413}{\$6{,}052} = 1.0596 \text{ times}$$

TABLE 14.2 Liquidity Ratios 2011 for Cogswell Cola and Spacely Spritzers

2011 Liquidity Ratio	Cogswell Cola	Spacely Spritzers
Current ratio	1.0596	1.0286
Quick ratio or acid ratio test	0.8379	0.5465
Cash ratio	0.2707	0.2147

$$\text{quick ratio} = \frac{\$6{,}413 - \$1{,}342}{\$6{,}052} = 0.8379 \text{ time}$$

$$\text{cash ratio} = \frac{\$1{,}638}{\$6{,}052} = 0.2707 \text{ time}$$

2. For Spacely Spritzers, we have the following liquidity ratios for 2011:

$$\text{current ratio} = \frac{\$1{,}835}{\$1{,}784} = 1.0286 \text{ times}$$

$$\text{quick ratio} = \frac{\$1{,}835 - \$860}{\$1{,}784} = 0.5465 \text{ time}$$

$$\text{cash ratio} = \frac{\$383}{\$1{,}784} = 0.2147 \text{ time}$$

Table 14.2 displays the ratios for ease of comparison across the two companies. How would you rate the liquidity of these two companies?

Computing the liquidity ratios is straightforward. Interpreting them is more complex. Let's analyze each one:

The *current ratio* tells us that Cogswell has its current liabilities covered 1.05 times over by its current assets and Spacely has its current liabilities covered 1.02 times over.

The *quick ratio* or *acid ratio test* uses the same accounts of current assets and current liabilities, but subtracts inventories.

The *cash ratio* indicates the percent of current liabilities covered by the current cash on hand.

We usually look at all ratios within a range to understand performance. For instance, a current ratio greater than 1 tells us that the current assets should generate enough cash to cover the current liabilities coming due and keep the company out of short-term cash problems. If this number is much greater than 1, however, we may have too much capital tied up in current assets. We had mentioned earlier that Cogswell Cola may be carrying too high a balance in cash, and its liquidity ratios are stronger than those of Spacely Spritzers. The question is, "Are they *too* strong?" Cash is an unemployed asset of a company, and Cogswell Cola may be incurring an opportunity cost here by not investing more of it. Although not a ratio, the net working capital of the company is, in fact, another way to look at the current ratio. Recall that net working capital is current assets minus the current liabilities. Therefore, when the current ratio is greater than 1, we are also saying that net working capital is positive because current assets are greater than current liabilities. That is usually a good thing. If the current ratio is less than 1, current liabilities are greater than current assets and net working capital is negative. That can be a bad thing.

We will return to the issue of acceptable ratio ranges when we look at external uses of financial statements later in this chapter. For now, we certainly can see a difference between the cash management activities of Cogswell Cola and Spacely Spritzers. Cogswell may be holding too much cash, or Spacely Spritzers may not be holding enough cash. A more in-depth look at the cash forecast (our analytical tool from Chapter 12) could provide the needed clues as to which company is in better liquidity shape.

Long-Term Solvency: Solvency or Financial Leverage Ratios

Financial leverage ratios measure a company's ability to meet its long-term debt obligations. With financial leverage ratios, we want to know whether a company can handle interest expenses from debt with normal operations or will need to seek additional capital just to meet them. Failing to meet this obligation may mean bankruptcy—or at least a major change in operations. To gauge the long-term solvency of a business, we can use the following ratios:

$$\text{debt ratio} = \frac{\text{total assets} - \text{total equity}}{\text{total assets}} \text{ or } \frac{\text{total liabilities}}{\text{total assets}} \quad \textbf{14.4}$$

$$\text{times interest earned} = \frac{\text{EBIT}}{\text{interest expense}} \quad \textbf{14.5}$$

$$\text{cash coverage ratio} = \frac{(\text{EBIT} + \text{depreciation})}{\text{interest expense}} \quad \textbf{14.6}$$

Let's look at the ratios in this area for both Cogswell Cola and Spacely Spritzers:

1. For Cogswell Cola, we have the following financial leverage ratios for 2011:

$$\text{Cogswell Cola's debt ratio} = \frac{\$14{,}183}{\$23{,}474} = 0.6042$$

$$\text{Cogswell Cola's times interest earned} = \frac{\$5{,}046}{\$178} = 28.3483$$

$$\text{Cogswell Cola's cash coverage} = \frac{\$5{,}046 + \$1{,}112}{\$178} = 34.5955$$

2. For Spacely Spritzers, we have the following financial leverage ratios for 2011:

$$\text{Spacely Spritzers' debt ratio} = \frac{\$4{,}756}{\$7{,}433} = 0.6398$$

$$\text{Spacely Spritzers' times interest earned} = \frac{\$1{,}474}{\$214} = 6.8879$$

$$\text{Spacely Spritzers'cash coverage} = \frac{\$1{,}474 + \$618}{\$214} = 9.7757$$

Table 14.3 puts these financial leverage ratios together for easy reference.

TABLE 14.3 Financial Leverage Ratios 2011 for Cogswell Cola and Spacely Spritzers

2011 Financial Leverage Ratios	Cogswell Cola	Spacely Spritzers
Debt ratio	0.6042	0.6398
Times interest earned	28.3483	6.8879
Cash coverage	34.5955	9.7757

How do we interpret financial leverage ratios? Let's look at each one:

1. *Debt ratio:* One way to look at the debt ratio is to see it as the amount in debt for every dollar of assets. In this case, it is 60 cents of every dollar for Cogswell and 64 cents for Spacely.
2. *Times interest earned ratio:* We can interpret the times interest earned ratio as the number of times over a company has its interest obligation covered by its earnings before it pays its interest expense and taxes. For Cogswell, it is 28 times, and for Spacely, about 7 times.
3. *Cash coverage ratio:* The cash coverage ratio indicates a company's ability to generate cash from operations to meet its financial obligations. We add depreciation expense back to EBIT because depreciation is a noncash expense, and we want to determine the cash from operations available to cover the interest expense. Cogswell has these obligations covered about thirty-five times, and Spacely about ten times.

We see a major difference in the times interest earned and cash coverage ratios of the two firms. Cogswell Cola appears to have the capacity to use more debt financing in its operations because it can cover its interest expense many times over. The question here becomes one of management choice. Management may have chosen to minimize its debt financing and rely on cash from operations for funding all growth. At one time, that was the choice of Coors, expanding only as fast as its cash would allow. Later this philosophy changed, and Coors was able to expand at a much faster rate, keeping up with its competitors by leveraging its growth.

What is the "best" financing mix for a company? Should it use debt, use equity, or rely exclusively on its cash from operations? Chapter 16, in which we look at optimal capital structure, explores this topic. Here, you can use your intuition and ask, "Is debt good?" Consumers constantly borrow money for college, cars, homes, and other items. Debt is good in these cases because it allows people to enjoy the benefits of college education, a car, or a home long before they have the cash to pay for the asset. When we use too much debt, however, we can get into real financial stress. The solvency ratios help us analyze whether a company is moving toward financial stress or is using debt to benefit the company and ultimately the owners of the company. Here, Spacely Spritzers may be doing a better job of using debt, whereas Cogswell Cola has the capacity to use more debt.

Asset Management Ratios

Asset management ratios measure how efficiently a company uses its assets to generate revenue or how much cash is tied up in other assets like inventory or receivables. Let's look to the balance sheets and income statements for Cogswell Cola and Spacely Spritzers for our inputs:

$$\text{inventory turnover} = \frac{\text{cost of goods sold}}{\text{inventory}} \quad \textbf{14.7}$$

$$\text{days' sales in inventory} = \frac{365}{\text{inventory turnover}} \quad \textbf{14.8}$$

$$\text{receivables turnover} = \frac{\text{sales}}{\text{accounts receivable}} \quad \textbf{14.9}$$

$$\text{days' sales in receivables} = \frac{365}{\text{receivables turnover}} \quad \textbf{14.10}$$

$$\text{total asset turnover} = \frac{\text{sales}}{\text{total assets}} \tag{14.11}$$

1. For Cogswell Cola, we have the following asset management ratios for 2011:

$$\text{Cogswell Cola's inventory turnover} = \frac{\$11{,}497}{\$1{,}342} = 8.5671$$

$$\text{days' sales in inventory} = \frac{365 \text{ days}}{8.5671} = 42.6050 \text{ days}$$

$$\text{Cogswell Cola's receivables turnover} = \frac{\$25{,}112}{\$2{,}531} = 9.9218$$

$$\text{days' sales in receivables} = \frac{365 \text{ days}}{9.9218} = 36.7878 \text{ days}$$

$$\text{Cogswell Cola's total asset turnover} = \frac{\$25{,}112}{\$23{,}474} = 1.0698$$

2. For Spacely Spritzers, we have the following asset management ratios for 2011:

$$\text{Spacely Spritzers' inventory turnover} = \frac{\$4{,}105}{\$860} = 4.7733$$

$$\text{days' sales in inventory} = \frac{365 \text{ days}}{4.7733} = 76.4677 \text{ days}$$

$$\text{Spacely Spritzers' receivables turnover} = \frac{\$8{,}403}{\$457} = 18.3873$$

$$\text{days' sales in receivables} = \frac{365 \text{ days}}{18.3873} = 19.8506 \text{ days}$$

$$\text{Spacely Spritzers' total asset turnover} = \frac{\$8{,}403}{\$7{,}433} = 1.1305$$

Table 14.4 summarizes these asset management ratios. Notice that they are all turnover ratios, which we use to measure efficiency of asset management (total assets, inventory, or receivables). Let's look at each ratio.

1. *Inventory turnover:* Cogswell sold and restocked the entire inventory about eight times during the year. Spacely sold and restocked about five times.
2. *Days' sales in inventory:* Inventory was "on the shelf" forty-three days at Cogswell and an average of seventy-six days at Spacely before it sold.

TABLE 14.4 Asset Management Ratios 2011 for Cogswell Cola and Spacely Spritzers

Asset Management Ratio	Cogswell Cola	Spacely Spritzers
Inventory turnover	8.5671	4.7733
Days' sales in inventory	42.6050	76.4677
Receivables turnover	9.9218	18.3873
Days' sales in receivables	36.7878	19.8506
Total asset turnover	1.0698	1.1305

3. *Receivables turnover:* The receivables turnover ratio is similar in orientation to inventory turnover. It measures the number of times per year the companies collected payment on credit accounts. For Cogswell, it was about ten times, and for Spacely, about eighteen times.
4. *Days' sales in receivables:* Customers took an average of thirty-seven days at Cogswell and an average of twenty days at Spacely to pay for their credit purchases.
5. *Total asset turnover:* The total asset turnover ratio relates sales to assets. We call this the management efficiency ratio because it indicates how well a company uses assets to generate revenue.

We looked at some of these ratios in Chapter 13—specifically, accounts payable turnover—as we examined the firm's cash cycle. Comparing these two firms, we see from the inventory turnover ratios that Cogswell Cola moves its inventories much faster than Spacely Spritzers. Cogswell Cola turns its inventory over eight times a year, whereas Spacely Spritzers manages to turn its inventory over just short of four times a year, which is potentially a long shelf time for its products. Using receivables turnover, we see that Spacely Spritzers' customers pay much faster than Cogswell Cola's customers. Maybe the two management teams could learn something from each other: Cogswell could learn how to speed up payments, and Spacely could learn how to reduce shelf time for its inventories. Both companies seemingly could improve their cash flow management by exercising some of the working capital management strategies that we explored in Chapter 13.

Profitability Ratios

Profitability ratios measure how effectively the company is turning sales or assets into income. Ultimately, what we want to know is how well the company has performed overall, that is, how the company has generated profits. The following ratios help us analyze that overall performance:

$$\text{profit margin} = \frac{\text{net income}}{\text{sales}} \tag{14.12}$$

$$\text{return on assets} = \frac{\text{net income}}{\text{total assets}} \tag{14.13}$$

$$\text{return on equity} = \frac{\text{net income}}{\text{total owners' equity}} \tag{14.14}$$

1. For Cogswell Cola, we have the following profitability ratios for 2011:

$$\text{Cogswell Cola's profit margin} = \frac{\$3{,}313}{\$25{,}112} = 0.1319$$

$$\text{Cogswell Cola's return on assets} = \frac{\$3{,}313}{\$23{,}474} = 0.1411$$

$$\text{Cogswell Cola's return on equity} = \frac{\$3{,}313}{\$9{,}291} = 0.3563$$

2. For Spacely Spritzers, we have the following profitability ratios for 2011:

$$\text{Spacely Spritzers' profit margin} = \frac{\$857}{\$8{,}403} = 0.1020$$

TABLE 14.5 Profitability Ratios 2011 for Cogswell Cola and Spacely Spritzers

Profitability Ratio	Cogswell Cola	Spacely Spritzers
Profit margin	0.1319	0.1020
Return on assets	0.1411	0.1153
Return on equity	0.3566	0.3201

$$\text{Spacely Spritzers' return on assets} = \frac{\$857}{\$7{,}433} = 0.1153$$

$$\text{Spacely Spritzers' return on equity} = \frac{\$857}{\$2{,}677} = 0.3201$$

Table 14.5 summarizes these ratios.

We can make some general observations about these profitability ratios. Notice that they all have net income in the numerator and that each denominator changes the focus to the profit per dollar of sales, profit per dollars invested in assets, or profit for the equity owners. Let's look at each ratio:

1. *Profit margin:* Cogswell Cola is generating 13 cents of profit from every sales dollar, and Spacely Spritzers is generating 10 cents.
2. *Return on assets (ROA):* The ROA indicates how well the assets (investment in plant, property, equipment, and so forth) are generating income. The assets of Cogswell Cola are generating 14 cents per investment dollar in profit, whereas the assets of Spacely Spritzers are generating 11.5 cents per investment dollar.
3. *Return on equity (ROE):* The ROE is a key ratio for the company's owners. It indicates how much profit the company generates for the owners based on their ownership claim. Both firms are returning more than 30% to the owners.

You saw the profit margin when we first looked at common-size income statements at the beginning of the chapter. Recall that the percentage on the net income line of the income statement is the profit margin. It is the percentage of sales dollars that reaches net income on the common-size statements. The other two performance measures provide information on how well the company employs assets to generate income. Cogswell seems to be able to generate a higher percentage of income with its assets than Spacely Spritzers, but we must be careful not to read too much into this difference. Cogswell may have older equipment in place and, as such, is carrying a relatively low value on the financial statements. Cogswell may need to replace these assets soon with higher valued assets that will lower the company's ROA. Again, we use these ratios to direct our attention to potentially good and potentially poor performance areas. We often interpret the ROE as the return to shareholders. In our two-company example, both are producing returns of greater than 30%.

Market Value Ratios

One other area that potential investors often review is the market value of the firm; that is, does the share price of the firm appear reasonable based on its performance? **Market value ratios** measure the firm's performance against the firm's perceived value from the trading value of the shares or number of shares. The financial statements do not contain all the necessary information we need to calculate some of the market value ratios. We will also need to look at the price at which common stock is trading to produce the price to earnings (P/E) ratio and the **price/earnings to growth (PEG) ratio**. The common stock's current market price is not typically available from an income statement, so for the following calculations, we provide the prices for these ratio calculations. (Prices are readily available from exchanges such as the NYSE for publicly traded firms.) The earnings per share (EPS) is on most income statements, such as the EPS of $1.85 for Cogswell Cola and $1.46 for Spacely Spritzers from Figures 14.2 and 14.3. Given the earnings per share and the net income, we can determine the outstanding shares by simply rearranging the EPS ratio:

$$\text{earnings per share} = \frac{\text{net income}}{\text{number of outstanding shares}} \tag{14.15}$$

$$\text{price to earnings ratio} = \frac{\text{price per share}}{\text{earnings per share}} \tag{14.16}$$

$$\text{price/earnings to growth ratio} = \frac{\text{price/earnings per share}}{\text{earnings growth rate} \times 100} \tag{14.17}$$

$$\text{market to book value} = \frac{\text{market value per share}}{\text{book value per share}} \tag{14.18}$$

For Cogswell Cola, we know that the current EPS is $1.85 per share, so given a net income of $3,313,000, we must have 1,790,811 shares outstanding ($3,313,000/$1.85). For Spacely Spritzers, we have 586,986 shares outstanding ($857,000/$1.46). Let's assume that Cogswell Cola shares are trading at $28.50 per share and Spacely Spritzers shares are trading at $19.00 per share. Therefore,

$$\text{Cogswell Cola's P/E ratio} = \frac{\$28.50}{\$1.85} = 15.4054$$

$$\text{Spacely Spritzers' P/E ratio} = \frac{\$19.00}{\$1.46} = 13.0137$$

One way to interpret P/E ratios is that they tell you how long it will be before you double your money if you buy the stock at the current price and you receive the earnings each year at the current earnings per share. Here it means that it will take fifteen years for Cogswell Cola and thirteen years for Spacely Spritzers to double your money. If we take the reciprocal, $^1/_{(P/E)}$, we get the return on buying the stock: Cogswell Cola is 6.49% and Spacely Spritzers is 7.68%. Both of these returns look low when we look back at the returns from Chapter 8 for equity investments. So, what is the P/E ratio really telling a potential investor?

Financial analysts have many ways to interpret the P/E ratio. One standard interpretation is that firms with high P/E ratios should be growth companies and those with low P/E ratios should be mature, stable companies. Firms with really high P/E ratios—above 50—may have great growth and earnings potential not yet demonstrated in current earnings. Again, though, use caution here because the stock price could simply be out of line with the firm's earnings potential.

Equation 14.17 gives the PEG ratio, an adjustment to the recently developed P/E ratio to account for growth. For Cogswell Cola and Spacely Spritzers, we would need to estimate the growth rate of earnings from the historical data. Typically, we would want a few years of earnings to avoid an unusual swing in the past year. For illustration, we will set the recent growth rate for Cogswell Cola at 12% and for Spacely Spritzers at 15%. Therefore,

$$\text{Cogswell Cola's PEG} = \frac{\$28.50/\$1.85}{0.12 \times 100} = 1.2838$$

$$\text{Spacely Spritzers' PEG} = \frac{\$19.00/\$1.46}{0.15 \times 100} = 0.8676$$

One interpretation of the PEG ratio is that firms with a PEG ratio of less than 1 are undervalued, firms with a PEG ratio near 1 are properly valued, and firms with PEG ratios above 1 are overvalued. Here it would seem that Spacely Spritzers is undervalued (a good buy) and Cogswell Cola overvalued (a good sell).

What we do know is that firms with high P/E ratios need to have high growth rates in earnings to justify the current price. By estimating an appropriate growth rate for companies (whether we use historical growth or some anticipated growth rate), we can modify the high P/E ratio firms to see which firms have reasonable prices. If the growth rate is insufficient to bring the PEG ratio near 1, it may signal a need to take a much closer look at the company's earnings potential.

Equation 14.18 gives the market-to-book ratio, yet another ratio in the profit category. The market value per share is, of course, the current stock price. The book value per share is the total owners' equity divided by the number of outstanding shares. So, for our example,

$$\text{Cogswell Cola's book value per share} = \frac{\$9{,}291{,}000}{1{,}790{,}811} = \$5.19$$

$$\text{Spacely Spritzers' book value per share} = \frac{\$2{,}667{,}000}{586{,}986} = \$4.56$$

The market-to-book values are therefore

$$\text{Cogswell Cola's market-to-book value} = \frac{\$28.50}{\$5.19} = 5.4913$$

$$\text{Spacely Spritzers' market-to-book value} = \frac{\$19.00}{\$4.56} = 4.1667$$

A value of less than 1 would be troubling because it would signal that the firm has not been able to generate earnings for the owners. A low market-to-book ratio may indicate that the market for shares of the company stock is depressed. "Depressed" in this sense means that prices are low and the market's expectations of turning larger profits in the future are also low. Both Cogswell Cola and Spacely Spritzers, however, are turning the investment of the owners into earnings because they have high market-to-book ratios, which is a good thing.

DuPont Analysis

Let's return to one of the profitability ratios, return on equity, and apply some more analysis with this widely used ratio. We will use a technique that E. I. du Pont de Nemours and Company developed. DuPont has gone one step further in analyzing financial performance by breaking down ROE into three components of the firm: (1) **operating efficiency**, as measured by the profit margin (net income/sales); (2) **asset management efficiency**, as measured by asset turnover (sales/total assets); and (3) **financial leverage**, as measured by the equity multiplier (total assets/total equity). If we multiply the three ratios, we have return on equity:

$$\text{return on equity} = \frac{\text{net income}}{\text{sales}} \times \frac{\text{sales}}{\text{total assets}} \times \frac{\text{total assets}}{\text{total equity}}$$

$$= \frac{\text{net income}}{\text{total equity}} \qquad \textbf{14.19}$$

One benefit of the DuPont identity is that it can focus management on an area that might be less efficient in terms of producing a higher ROE. For example, if asset management is underperforming because of high levels of inventory and cash, the company may want to review its inventory and cash management operations to lower the amount of capital committed to current assets. The reduction in inventories could provide an option to use cash for investing in other areas that could lead to an increase in sales.

Let's break down Cogswell Cola's and Spacely Spritzers' ROE for an inside look at the firms' operating efficiency, asset management efficiency, and financial leverage:

$$\text{Cogswell Cola's ROE} = \frac{\$3{,}313}{\$25{,}112} \times \frac{\$25{,}112}{\$23{,}474} \times \frac{\$23{,}474}{\$9{,}291} = \frac{\$3{,}313}{\$9{,}291}$$

$$= 0.1319 \times 1.0698 \times 2.5246$$

$$= 0.3566 \quad \text{or} \quad 35.66\%$$

$$\text{Spacely Spritzers' ROE} = \frac{\$857}{\$8{,}403} \times \frac{\$8{,}403}{\$7{,}433} \times \frac{\$7{,}433}{\$2{,}677} = \frac{\$857}{\$2{,}677}$$

$$= 0.1020 \times 1.1305 \times 2.7766$$

$$= 0.3201 \quad \text{or} \quad 32.01\%$$

The DuPont identity suggests that Cogswell Cola is more operationally efficient, but Spacely Spritzers is more asset efficient and uses more financial leverage. Cogswell Cola is more efficient at moving sales dollars to net income (it gets 13.19 cents of every sales dollar to the bottom line, which is nearly 3 cents per dollar better than Spacely Spritzers at 10.20 cents of every sales dollar). Spacely Spritzers, however, is able to get more of its earnings to the shareholders because it uses its assets better and has used more debt to finance the company's operations. So once again, we see that using debt can be good for company owners. Recall that Cogswell has considerable debt capacity. This analysis may spur the management team at Cogswell to use debt to finance more of its activities.

These financial ratios are not the only ones that are useful in analyzing a company's performance, but they are among the most common. The real key is that whatever financial ratios you select, you should use them in a systematic and focused approach. The ratios may not provide all the answers that you are seeking, but they can point you in the right direction for further investigation.

14.3 External Uses of Financial Statements and Industry Averages

Once financial statements are made public, financial analysts begin their external analysis of the company. Why do they have such a keen interest in the performance of a company? Why should a finance manager be concerned with how external analysts view the company? Remember the opening comment in Chapter 1 about financial management and the field of finance. Finance is about making decisions, what to buy and what to sell, and when to buy and when to sell. Financial analysts provide recommendations to their clients about what company to buy (invest) and what company to sell (divest). Such recommendations have a direct effect on the finance manager because they ultimately affect the company's ability to raise funds to support its operations. A firm that is considered a bad investment will have trouble raising capital from banks and bond holders as well as raising new equity capital.

With the wide variety of business activities of different companies, how do these analysts determine the good buys from the bad buys or the good sells from the bad sells? Let's take some of the financial ratios of two beverage giants—PepsiCo and Coca-Cola—and see if we can use them to help us analyze and compare their individual performances.

Cola Wars

Which is the better investment, PepsiCo or Coca-Cola? To analyze these companies as buying prospects, we will compare a set of financial ratios (Table 14.6) to see if we can determine which company is in a better position to deliver future performance.

The ratios and accounts for these two companies are fairly similar, except that Coke seems to have a better ROE and stronger profit performance with a much higher net income and earnings per share. We can see that Coca-Cola is placing more burdens on its equity borrowing in its lower debt-to-equity ratio. Gross margin is sales minus cost of goods sold. If we were to end the analysis here, it would indicate that Coke is a better buy. PepsiCo's price is also higher; with lower performance indicators it seems that Coke is winning the Cola Wars in terms of financial performance.

TABLE 14.6 Key Financial Ratios and Accounts for PepsiCo and Coca-Cola (as of December 31, 2010)

Ratio or Account	PepsiCo	Coca-Cola
Return on equity	29.51%	38.09%
Return on assets	9.30%	16.19%
Current ratio	1.10	1.17
PEG ratio	1.79	1.93
Market-to-book value	5.85	6.62
Inventory turnover	7.88	4.79
Debt-to-equity ratio	2.17	1.35
Net income (in millions)	$6,338	$11,809
Gross margin	54.05%	63.86%
Earnings before taxes margin	14.23%	40.55%
Earnings per share	$ 3.91	$ 5.12
P/E ratio	16.20	12.10
Current price	$63.36	$ 61.95

TABLE 14.7 Some Key Ratios for PepsiCo and Coca-Cola (Five-Year Period)

Ratio	Company	2006	2007	2008	2009	2010
Gross margin	PepsiCo Coca-Cola	55.2% 66.1%	54.3% 63.9%	52.9% 64.4%	53.5% 64.2%	54.1% 63.9%
Inventory turnover	PepsiCo Coca-Cola	8.18 4.98	7.88 3.83	8.07 5.20	7.68 4.71	7.88 4.79
Current ratio	PepsiCo Coca-Cola	1.33 0.94	1.31 0.92	1.23 0.94	1.44 1.28	1.11 1.17
Return on assets	PepsiCo Coca-Cola	18.85% 16.95%	16.34% 13.82%	14.29% 14.33%	15.00% 14.02%	9.30% 16.19%
Return on equity	PepsiCo Coca-Cola	36.53% 30.02%	32.66% 27.51%	42.14% 28.37%	34.28% 27.52%	29.51% 38.09%
Debt-to-equity ratio	PepsiCo Coca-Cola	0.94 0.77	1.00 0.99	1.95 0.98	1.28 0.96	2.17 1.35
Earnings per share	PepsiCo Coca-Cola	$3.34 $2.16	$3.41 $2.59	$3.21 $2.51	$3.77 $2.95	$3.91 $5.12

If we look at only one year of data, though, we may be getting the wrong picture. What we need to know is not only what the ratios are, but also what the *trend* is over time and how these two companies have compared in performance over the past five years. Table 14.7 shows some key ratios from 2006 to 2010 for these same two companies. Here the picture changes, as we see that Pepsi has historically outperformed Coke in earnings per share, ROE, and inventory management.

One of the first things we notice in looking over the five years of data is how similar many of the ratios are from year to year, showing remarkable consistency for these two companies. We also can see that the gross margin for Coca-Cola is consistently higher that that of PepsiCo. The debt-to-equity ratio of both firms jumped substantially in 2010 from historic norms. One question we must now address is how the two companies used the newly acquired debt in 2010. PepsiCo used the funds to acquire Pepsi Bottling Company and PepsiAmericas in 2010. Coca-Cola used its new debt to acquire Coca-Cola Enterprises North America businesses and pay off its commercial paper. We also can see that ROE has been very good for both companies, although historically better for PepsiCo. Finally, PepsiCo has very strong and growing earnings per share over this period, outperforming Coca-Cola's EPS every year except 2010. Part of this higher EPS is due to PepsiCo using more debt to finance the company and thus providing leverage for the equity holders.

So, which is the better investment? This quick analysis using financial ratios and trend analysis does not give a clear picture. These ratios and their trends over long periods of time give the potential buyer some indication of the best buy, but not a complete picture. Part of the explanation is that most of the information is historical, and your investment performance is tied to future performance of the company. In other words, it's not what you have done that counts, but what you are going to do. So will PepsiCo use its new acquisitions, Pepsi Bottling Company and PepsiAmericas, to return a stronger position in terms of EPS and ROE in the coming years? Past performance would support a strong future with its newly acquired companies. Picking a winner is tough, and it is a much easier task to taste-test the two colas and see which one you prefer to drink. As for financial ratio analysis, it is more of an art than a science.

Industry Ratios

Although used often by financial analysts, financial ratios can vary across industries. Therefore, it is important to benchmark these ratios by industry. Let's look at a few industries and some key financial ratios in Table 14.8 to get a sense of the benchmarking process for firms in particular industries.

Table 14.8 shows just a few ratios and a few industries, but it is enough to demonstrate that there are some major differences across industries. For example, both the airline and the retail industries use debt financing more than other industries (debt-to-equity ratios greater than 1 for airlines and 0.81 for retail). Why would these industries tend to borrow so much more money compared with other industries? First, these are very capital-intensive industries, with large fixed asset requirements (airplanes and stores). Second, these assets can be used as collateral for the loans.

We see the lowest gross margins in the airline and auto industries, two industries that have struggled significantly over the past few years. Retail is also low in gross margin, but this is due to the business model of this industry, which has a very high volume and significant inventory turnover. At the other end of the gross margin is the pharmaceutical industry, in which COGS represents less than one-third the sales price of a drug. Profit margins are lowest for the airline industry, where for every $1 of sale, less than 1 cent makes it to net income. The profit margin ratio line shows that the computer hardware industry converts the greatest amount of sales dollars into profits, with more than 17 cents of every $1 making it to the bottom line. Both the computer hardware and oil and gas industries have returns on equity above 20%, making them desired investment targets for equity investors.

The issue at hand is not a judgment of industry performance but an understanding that industries operate differently in terms of borrowing, cash management, capital intensity (required fixed-asset investments), labor intensity, competition, and regulation. When one begins to compare companies from different industries and does not consider their different norms, the evaluation may lead to a poor buying or selling decision. For example, if one were to compare Pfizer (a leading pharmaceutical firm) and ExxonMobil (a large oil and gas company), the low gross margin of ExxonMobil compared with that of Pfizer might lead one to assume that Pfizer has a much higher profit potential and is thus a better buy than ExxonMobil. Looking at the ROE, however, we get a different story about the oil and gas industry, which—with its higher leverage—is able to produce a higher ROE. So, once again, we must understand that these ratios are just starting points for analysis. The real work begins once we compute these ratios to find the areas we need to explore for an evaluation of the company.

TABLE 14.8 Financial Ratios: Industry Averages

Ratio or Account	Airlines	Auto	Pharmaceuticals	Oil and Gas	Retail	Computer Hardware
P/E	22.44	7.38	87.80	5.39	34.29	20.97
Gross margin	19.28%	21.77%	59.54%	47.47%	24.51%	43.54%
Profit margin	0.75%	3.79%	14.85%	12.14%	2.94%	17.08%
Current ratio	0.92	0.32	2.77	1.11	1.23	2.86
Debt-to-equity ratio	1.69	0.34	0.11	0.19	0.81	0.19
Return on assets	0.70%	3.57%	9.40%	12.11%	6.31%	18.22%
Return on equity	0.77%	10.17%	14.71%	20.10%	16.82%	26.24%

Source: Data from Reuters (www.investors.reuters.com).

Finance Follies

Cooking the Books at Enron and WorldCom

Before the spectacular bankruptcies of investment banks like Lehman Brothers and other financial institutions in 2008, there were other company implosions that had their roots in questionable accounting practices. Two of these companies, Enron and WorldCom, had remarkably similar histories. Both were founded in the 1990s; both were for a time the darlings of celebrity media analysts; and both were audited by the same Big Five accounting firm, Arthur Andersen, which built its reputation on honesty and strict adherence to accounting principles.

Enron was a leading energy company; WorldCom was a telecommunications giant. Throughout the 1990s, the stocks of both companies rose to dizzying heights, making fortunes for their executives, employees, and lucky investors. They were included in the major stock indexes and were widely held by mutual funds, pension funds, and other institutional investors. In 2001, however, the party was over when it was revealed that both companies, in collusion with their auditors, had engaged in "creative" financial reporting and questionable accounting practices, some outright fraud and some so outlandish that no one had ever thought to prohibit them. In general, the companies' financial statements were manipulated to create the illusion of growth and profitability when in fact they were bleeding cash.

"Cooking the books" occurs when a company knowingly and deliberately includes incorrect information on its financial statements, manipulating various items to improve the appearance of earnings per share. Such statements may keep existing stockholders happy and attract new ones, especially because Wall Street analysts use company financial statements to determine whether they can recommend the stock. Glamour firms in the media spotlight are particularly under pressure to meet analysts' expectations based on their past performance, but the reality is that businesses cannot grow faster than the overall economy for extended periods. Sales and profits that grow at two or three times the rate of the gross domestic product, or GDP, quarter after quarter, year after year, might indicate an exceptional company, but should also be examined with a degree of skepticism.

In Enron's case, many of its recorded assets and profits were inflated, fraudulent, or nonexistent. One ploy was to make some liabilities "off-sheet" or "off-shore"—that is, not part of the financial statements—to understate debts and losses. An assortment of complex partnerships set up by Enron officers enabled massive amounts of debt to be concealed by transferring it on paper to these partners and simultaneously recognizing the partners' revenues on the Enron financial statements. This fraudulent accounting technique was later dubbed *enronomics.* It made Enron look far more profitable than it actually was. Its stock spiraled up to artificially high prices, and many investors bought in. At the high point, some Enron executives who knew about the hidden losses began to unload their stock while cashing in was optimal. Inevitably, the price plummeted. The SEC launched an investigation into Enron's accounting procedures and partnerships, and the house of cards came tumbling down. Enron—the "crooked E"—filed for bankruptcy in 2001, employees lost jobs, retirement nest eggs cracked, and *Enron* became a byword for willful corporate fraud.

WorldCom, too, engaged in irregularities on its financial statements. While its rival AT&T was losing money, WorldCom was supposedly making enormous profit. When the SEC stepped in to investigate, it was discovered that in an effort to increase its revenue and meet analysts' expectations, the company had—among other things—shifted billions of dollars of operating expenses to long-term capital investments to meet its earnings targets. WorldCom, too, eventually toppled and became one of the largest bankruptcies yet.

Business cycles, competition, and even the weather cause fluctuations in the sales and profits of normal companies. Most firms "manage" earnings to some extent by shifting revenues and expenses from one period or category to another to smooth growth, but some of these practices amount to outright deception and violate sound accounting practices.

How can the wary investor or creditor detect these empty transactions? The great thing about double-entry accounting is that errors or deceptions in one account usually show up in another. For example, the WorldCom transaction just described caused net income to improve, but the capital expenditures ratio (cash from operations/capital expenditures) moved in the opposite direction. Another cash measure that signals impending problems is the cash coverage ratio (EBIT + depreciation)/interest expense. At Enron, this ratio plummeted in the months preceding the firm's collapse. Other clues to watch for are high earnings combined with low dividends or no dividends and low tax payments in relationship to net income.

Financial statements do tell stories, and with some diligent digging and analysis, sometimes we discover that the stories just don't add up.

Sources: Alex Berenson, *The Number* (New York: Random House, 2004); Frank Partnoy, *Infectious Greed* (New York: Holt, 2003).

It turns out that the real world does indeed expect results. Measuring past performance and predicting future performance are major activities for financial analysts, potential lenders, and you (as you manage your own investment portfolio). For an account of financial statements that told stories that couldn't be trusted, see the "Finance Follies" feature.

To review this chapter, see the Summary Card at the end of the text.

Key Terms

asset management efficiency, p. 437
asset management ratios, p. 432
benchmarking, p. 425
common-size financial statements, p. 426
financial leverage, p. 437
financial leverage ratios, p. 431
financial ratios, p. 429
liquidity ratios, p. 429
market value ratios, p. 435
operating efficiency, p. 437
price/earnings to growth (PEG) ratio, p. 436
profitability ratios, p. 434
solvency ratios, p. 431

Questions

1. What is the accounting identity?
2. What does analyzing companies over time tell a finance manager?
3. What does restating financial statements into common-size financial statements allow a finance manager or financial analyst to do?
4. What are liquidity ratios? Give an example of a liquidity ratio and how it helps evaluate a company's performance or future performance from an outsider's view.
5. What are solvency ratios? Which ratio would be of most interest to a banker considering a debt loan to a company? Why?
6. What are asset management ratios? For retail firms, what is one of the key management ratios? Why?
7. What does the P/E ratio tell an outsider about a company? Why might this ratio not provide very compelling evidence on the firm's performance?
8. What are the three components of the DuPont identity? What do they analyze?
9. What does analyzing companies against their industry tell a finance manager or financial analyst?
10. What does analyzing a company against firms in other industries tell a finance manager or financial analyst?

Prepping for Exams

1. Which of the following statements is *false*?
   a. Financial statements are a collection of a company's historical and current activities.
   b. The collection of value over time in financial statements requires us to pay attention to how we construct financial ratios so as to glean information for analysis.

c. Businesses construct all financial statements with the same accounting principles, so you can always compare different firms based solely on these statements.
d. We want to analyze financial statements so as to compare different companies and their performance relative to our company.

2. Businesses often prepare income statements _______________.
   a. monthly for external use and quarterly for internal reporting
   b. annually for internal use and quarterly for external reporting
   c. monthly for internal use and quarterly for external reporting
   d. monthly for internal use and annually for external reporting

3. Comparing two companies using _______________ may point out differences in management styles.
   a. common-size financial statements
   b. sales growth
   c. historical share prices
   d. earnings per share

4. *True* or *false*: The higher the current ratio, the better.

5. Debt is good when _______________.
   a. we pay for everything later, allowing more positive cash flow today
   b. we enjoy the benefits of acquiring an asset early, but can still pay for it over time
   c. we borrow at low rates
   d. we use it very sparingly

6. _______________ break(s) the ROE into three components.
   a. The DuPont identity
   b. Market value ratios
   c. Profitability ratios
   d. Asset management ratios

7. Which of the following statements is *true*?
   a. The current ratio is current assets divided by current liabilities.
   b. Total asset turnover is net income divided by total assets.
   c. The cash coverage ratio equals cash divided by current liabilities.
   d. The quick ratio equals current assets minus current liabilities divided by current liabilities.

8. The debt-to-equity ratios for Firm 1, Firm 2, Firm 3, and Firm 4 are 0.2, 0.3, 0.35, and 0.4, respectively. The earnings per share for Firm 1, Firm 2, Firm 3, and Firm 4 are $4, $3, $2.5, and $2, respectively. Everything else being equal, which firm is placing the most burdens on its borrowing?
   a. Firm 1
   b. Firm 2
   c. Firm 3
   d. Firm 4

9. Because financial ratios can vary across industries, it is _______________ these ratios by industry.
   a. not necessary to study
   b. unimportant to benchmark

c. important to benchmark
d. futile to examine

10. Which industry has the highest average debt-to-equity ratio?
a. airlines
b. oil and gas
c. auto
d. pharmaceuticals

Problems

These problems are available in MyFinanceLab.

1. ***Income statement.*** Fill in the missing numbers on the following annual income statements for Barron Pizza Inc.

Barron Pizza Inc.
Abbreviated Income Statements for the Years Ending 2009–2011
($ in thousands, except earnings per share)

Account	Year Ending 2011	Year Ending 2010	Year Ending 2009
Revenue	$917,378	$946,219	
Cost of goods sold		$669,382	$656,215
Gross profit	$169,441		$315,017
Selling, general, and administrative expenses	$ 70,505		$193,000
Research and development	$ 5,469	$ 7,129	$ 3,521
Depreciation		$ 34,579	$ 35,713
Operating income	$ 60,540	$ 81,427	
Other income	$ 672		$ 1,958
EBIT		$ 82,553	$ 84,741
Interest expense	$ 6,851		$ 8,857
Income before tax		$ 74,876	$ 75,884
Taxes	$ 20,385	$ 28,079	
Net income		**$ 46,797**	**$ 47,245**
Shares outstanding	16,740,000		16,740,000
Earnings per share	$ 2.03	$ 2.78	

2. ***Income statement.*** Construct the Barron Pizza Inc. income statement for the year ending 2011 with the following information:

Shares outstanding: 16,740,000

Tax rate: 37.5%

Interest expense: $6,114

Revenue: $889,416

Depreciation: $31,354

Selling, general, and administrative expense: $77,572

Other income: $1,253

Research and development: $4,196

Cost of goods sold: $750,711

3. ***Balance sheet.*** Fill in the missing information on the annual balance sheet statements for Barron Pizza Inc.

Baron Pizza Inc.
Balance Sheet as of December 31, 2009, 2010, and 2011
($ in thousands)

ASSETS	2011	2010	2009	LIABILITIES	2011	2010	2009
Current Assets				**Current liabilities**			
Cash	$ 7,071	$ 9,499	$ 17,609	Accounts payable		$ 74,467	$ 66,209
Accounts receivable	$ 26,767		$ 25,877	Short-term debt	$ 250		$ 225
Inventory		$ 16,341	$ 12,659	**Total current liabilities**	**$ 80,917**	**$ 74,702**	
Other current	$ 11,590	$ 10,955		Long-term debt	$ 61,000		$185,085
Total current assets	**$ 62,458**	**$ 57,433**	**$ 65,131**	Other liabilities		$ 28,970	$ 20,288
Long-term investments	$ 19,102		$ 20,998	**Total liabilities**	**$187,942**	**$243,522**	
				OWNERS' EQUITY			
Net plant, property, and equipment	$203,818	$223,599		Common stock		$102,421	$102,107
Goodwill		$ 48,756	$ 48,274	Retained earnings	$ 39,371		$ 13,525
Other assets	$ 13,259	$ 13,817	$ 14,091	**Total owners' equity**			
TOTAL ASSETS	**$347,214**	**$365,469**	**$387,439**	**TOTAL LIABILITIES AND OWNERS' EQUITY**	**$347,214**	**$365,469**	

4. ***Balance sheet.*** Construct the Barron Pizza Inc. balance sheet statement for December 31, 2011, with the following information:

   Retained earnings: $43,743
   Accounts payable: $74,633
   Accounts receivable: $34,836
   Common stock: $119,901
   Cash: $8,344
   Short-term debt: $210
   Inventory: $23,455
   Goodwill: $48,347
   Long-term debt: $80,207
   Other noncurrent liabilities: $42,580
   Plant, property, and equipment: $192,465
   Other noncurrent assets: $16,838
   Long-term investments: $22,331
   Other current assets: $14,658

5. ***Predicting net income.*** Abbreviated income statements for Wal-Mart appear on the next page. Predict the net income for the period ending January 31, 2010, by determining the growth rates of sales, COGS, SG&A, and interest expense. Use a tax rate of 37%.

Wal-Mart Inc. Abbreviated Income Statements for the Years Ending 2007–2010 ($ in Millions)				
Account	1/31/2007	1/31/2008	1/31/2009	1/31/2010
Sales	$348,650	$378,799	$405,607	
Cost of goods sold	$264,152	$286,515	$306,158	
Selling, general, and administrative expenses	$ 63,721	$ 69,983	$ 76,367	
EBIT	$ 20,777	$ 22,301	$ 23,082	
Interest expense	$ 1,809	$ 2,103	$ 2,184	
Taxes	$ 7,684	$ 7,468	$ 7,498	
Net income	**$ 11,284**	**$ 12,731**	**$ 13,400**	

6. ***Predicting net income.*** Below are abbreviated income statements for Starbucks. Predict the net income for the period ending September 30, 2009, by determining the growth rates of sales, COGS, interest expense, and SG&A. Use a tax rate of 37%. Then look up the numbers for Starbucks for 2009 and see how you did.

Starbucks Abbreviated Income Statements for the Years Ending 2006–2009 ($ in Millions)				
Account	9/30/2006	9/30/2007	9/30/2008	9/30/2009
Sales	$7,786	$9,411	$10,383	
Cost of goods sold	$3,179	$3,999	$ 4,654	
Selling, general, and administrative expenses	$3,701	$4,356	$ 5,216	
EBIT	$ 906	$1,056	$ 513	
Interest expense	$ 0	$ 0	$ 53	
Taxes	$ 342	$ 384	$ 145	
Net income	**$ 564**	**$ 672**	**$ 315**	

7. ***Common-size financial statements.*** Prepare common-size income statements for Wal-Mart and Starbucks using the January 2009 and September 2008 information provided in Problems 5 and 6. Which company is doing a better job of getting sales dollars to net income? Where is the one company having an advantage over the other company in turning revenue into net income?

8. ***Common-size financial statements.*** The next page shows the balance sheet information for two companies. Prepare a common-size balance sheet for each company. Review each company's percentage of total assets. Are these companies operating with similar philosophies or in similar industries? What appears to be the major difference in financing for these two companies?

ASSETS	Balance Co. 1	Percent of Total Assets	Balance Co. 2	Percent of Total Assets
Current assets				
Cash	$ 5,377		$ 299	
Investments	$ 4,146		$ 354	
Accounts receivable	$ 8,100		$ 221	
Inventory	$ 5,372		$ 494	
Total current assets	**$22,995**		**$1,368**	
Long-term investments	$ 84		$ 307	
Net plant, property, and equipment	$ 9,846		$1,471	
Goodwill	$ 5,390		$ 69	
Intangible	$ 6,149		$ 27	
Other	$ 3,799		$ 86	
TOTAL ASSETS	**$48,263**	**100.00%**	**$3,328**	**100.00%**

LIABILITIES	Balance Co. 1	Percent of Total Assets	Balance Co. 2	Percent of Total Assets
Current liabilities				
Accounts payable	$12,309		$ 661	
Short-term debt	$ 1,139		$ 0	
Other short-term liabilities	$ 0		$ 122	
Total current liabilities	**$13,448**		**$ 783**	
Long-term debt	$ 2,955		$ 4	
Other liabilities	$ 4,991		$ 54	
Total liabilities	**$21,394**		**$ 841**	
OWNERS' EQUITY				
Common stock	$ 3,120		$1,026	
Treasury stock	($ 6,754)		$ 0	
Retained earnings	$30,503		$1,461	
Total owners' equity	**$26,869**		**$2,487**	
TOTAL LIABILITIES AND OWNERS' EQUITY	**$48,263**	**100.00%**	**$3,328**	**100.00%**

For Problems 9 through 12, use the following data:

Tyler Toys Inc.
Income Statement for Years Ending December 31, 2010 and 2011

	2011	2010
Revenue	$14,146,700	$13,566,400
Cost of goods sold	$ 8,449,100	$ 8,131,300
Selling, general, and administrative expenses	$ 999,320	$ 982,160
Depreciation	$ 1,498,980	$ 1,473,240
EBIT	$ 3,199,300	$ 2,979,700
Interest expense	$ 375,000	$ 356,100
Taxes	$ 1,093,300	$ 1,041,500
Net income	**$ 1,731,000**	**$ 1,582,100**

Tyler Toys Inc.
Balance Sheet as of December 31, 2010 and 2011

ASSETS	2011	2010	LIABILITIES	2011	2010
Current assets			**Current liabilities**		
Cash	$ 191,000	$ 188,900	Accounts payable	$ 1,545,700	$ 1,455,100
Investments	$ 182,300	$ 121,800	Short-term debt	$ 311,500	$ 332,600
Accounts receivable	$ 669,400	$ 630,400	**Total current liabilities**	**$ 1,857,200**	**$ 1,787,700**
Inventory	$ 587,500	$ 563,600	Long-term liabilities		
Total current assets	**$ 1,630,200**	**$ 1,504,700**	Debt	$ 8,658,400	$ 7,934,400
Long-term assets			Other liabilities	$ 1,462,100	$ 1,345,100
Investments	$ 3,052,000	$ 2,827,900	**Total liabilities**	**$11,977,700**	**$11,067,200**
			OWNERS' EQUITY		
Plant, property, and equipment	$ 8,498,900	$ 8,481,500	Common stock	$ 1,457,900	$ 1,453,400
Goodwill	$349,000	$ 348,700	Retained earnings	$ 1,253,800	$ 1,598,900
Intangible assets	$ 1,159,300	$ 956,700	**Total owners' equity**	**$ 2,711,700**	**$ 3,052,300**
TOTAL ASSETS	**$14,689,400**	**$14,119,500**	**TOTAL LIABILITIES AND OWNERS' EQUITY**	**$14,689,400**	**$14,119,500**

9. ***Financial ratios: Liquidity.*** Calculate the current ratio, quick ratio, and cash ratio for Tyler Toys for 2010 and 2011. Should any of these ratios or the change in a ratio warrant concern for the managers of Tyler Toys or the shareholders?

10. ***Financial ratios: Financial leverage.*** Calculate the debt ratio, times interest earned ratio, and cash coverage ratio for 2010 and 2011 for Tyler Toys. Should any of these ratios or the change in a ratio warrant concern for the managers of Tyler Toys or the shareholders?

11. ***Financial ratios: Asset management.*** Calculate the inventory turnover, days' sales in inventory, receivables turnover, days' sales in receivables, and total asset turnover ratios for 2010 and 2011 for Tyler Toys. Should any of these ratios or the change in a ratio warrant concern for the managers of Tyler Toys or the shareholders?

12. ***Financial ratios: Profitability***. Calculate the profit margin, return on assets, and return on equity for 2010 and 2011 for Tyler Toys. Should any of these ratios or the change in a ratio warrant concern for the managers of Tyler Toys or the shareholders?

13. ***DuPont identity***. For the following firms, find the return on equity using the three components of the DuPont identity: operating efficiency, as measured by the profit margin (net income/sales); asset management efficiency, as measured by asset turnover (sales/total assets); and financial leverage, as measured by the equity multiplier (total assets/total equity).

Financial Information ($ in millions, 2009)

Company	Sales	Net Income	Total Assets	Liabilities
PepsiCo	$43,251	$5,142	$35,994	$23,888
Coca-Cola	$31,994	$5,807	$40,519	$20,047
Starbucks	$10,383	$ 315	$ 5,673	$ 3,182

14. ***DuPont identity***. Go to a Web site such as Yahoo.com and find the sales, net income, total assets, and total equity of the following five actively traded companies: Microsoft (MSFT), Boeing (BA), Wal-Mart (WMT), Procter and Gamble (PG), and Waste Management (WMI). Use the three components of the DuPont identity—operating efficiency, as measured by the profit margin (net income/sales); asset management efficiency, as measured by asset turnover (sales/total assets); and financial leverage, as measured by the equity multiplier (total assets/total equity)—to find the return on equity for these five companies. Based on these components and the ROE, which company do you think is doing the best job for its shareholders?

15. ***Company analysis***. Go to a Web site such as Yahoo.com and find the financial statements of Disney (DIS) and McDonald's (MCD). Compare these two companies using the following financial ratios: times interest earned, current ratio, asset turnover, financial leverage, profit margin, PEG ratio, and return on equity. Which company would you invest in, either as a bond holder or a stockholder?

16. ***Company analysis***. Go to a Web site such as Yahoo.com and find the financial statements of General Motors (GM) and Ford Motor Company (F). Compare these two companies using the following financial ratios: times interest earned, current ratio, asset turnover, financial leverage, profit margin, PEG ratio, and return on equity. Which company would you invest in, either as a bond holder or a stockholder?

Advanced Problems for Spreadsheet Application

These problems are available in MyFinanceLab.

1. ***DuPont analysis***. Go to a Web site such as Yahoo.com and find the financial statements for Exxon-Mobil (XOM), Chevron (CVX), Conoco-Phillips (COP), Marathon Oil (MRO), and Occidental Petroleum (OXY). From the income statements for the three previous years, retrieve the sales revenue and the net income. From the balance sheets for the three previous years, retrieve the total assets and total equities. Calculate the operating efficiency, the asset management efficiency, financial leverage, and the return on equity for the last three years for each company. Verify the DuPont ROE by multiplying each of the three component ratios and comparing that ROE to the ROE found by dividing net income by total equity. Calculate these same financial ratios as if these five companies represent the industry average. Use an equal weighting of each company for the industry average. Use a bar graph to display the change in the ROE over the years for each of the firms. The bar graph should show each company grouped together each year and each year displayed as one unit.
2. ***Common-size statements: Proctor & Gamble and Johnson & Johnson and their ratios***. In a spreadsheet, enter the income statement data and the balance sheet data for Proctor & Gamble and Johnson & Johnson for the past three years. Ignore minority interest for this exercise. Compare the two companies using common-size statements for each of the three years (see Figures 14.3 and 14.4). Then calculate the financial ratios for Proctor & Gamble and Johnson & Johnson and complete the key ratios in Table 14.7 for the most recent three years. Be sure to look up the outstanding shares for each company. Which ratios have changed the most over the years? For the income statement and balance sheet, use the information from Yahoo and use only the revenues and expenses from Yahoo and calculate the EBIT and net income from the provided numbers. You will have a difference with the reported net income in Yahoo. For inventory turnover, use the operating expenses as the cost of goods sold.

Mini-Case

Cranston Dispensers, Inc.: Part 2

These problems are available in MyFinanceLab.

In the Chapter 13 mini-case, you learned that Cranston Dispensers, Inc. manufactures specialized pump and spray containers for a variety of products in the cosmetics, household cleaning supplies, and pharmaceutical industries.

For most of 2009 and 2010, the price of Cranston's shares was falling while shares of other companies in the industry were rising. The CFO has charged Susan McNulty, the recently appointed treasurer, with diagnosing Cranston's problems and improving the company's financial performance relative to its competitors. She has already reviewed Cranston's working capital management policies and will continue her analysis with a thorough review of the financial statements.

She has gathered financial statements for the three most recent years. Her assistant also found a ratio analysis for fiscal 2008 and 2009 and updated industry benchmarks from published sources.

Continued

Continued

Income Statements

Account	2010	2009	2008
Sales	$3,784.00	$3,202.00	$2,760.00
Cost of goods sold	$2,568.00	$2,172.00	$1,856.00
Gross profit (margin)	$1,216.00	$1,030.00	$ 904.00
Selling, general, and administrative expenses	$ 550.00	$ 478.00	$ 406.00
Depreciation	$ 247.00	$ 230.00	$ 200.00
EBIT	$ 419.00	$ 322.00	$ 298.00
Interest expense	$ 20.50	$ 24.70	$ 14.30
Earnings before taxes	$ 398.50	$ 297.30	$ 283.70
Taxes	$ 119.55	$ 89.19	$ 85.11
Net income	**$ 278.95**	**$ 208.11**	**$ 198.59**

Balance Sheets

ASSETS	2010	2009	2008	LIABILITIES	2010	2009	2008
Current assets				**Current liabilities**			
				Accounts payable	$ 332.00	$ 288.00	$ 204.00
Cash	$ 341.00	$ 276.00	$ 236.00	Accrued expenses	$ 343.00	$ 335.00	$ 192.00
				Short-term debt	$ 503.00	$ 491.00	$ 243.00
Accounts receivable	$ 722.00	$ 642.00	$ 320.00	**Total current liabilities**	**$1,178.00**	**$1,114.00**	**$ 639.00**
Inventory	$ 595.00	$ 512.00	$ 388.00	Long-term debt	$ 398.00	$ 324.00	$ 289.00
				Other liabilities	$ 239.00	$ 154.00	$ 147.00
Total current assets	**$1,658.00**	**$1,430.00**	**$ 944.00**	**Total liabilities**	**$1,815.00**	**$1,592.00**	**$1,075.00**
				OWNERS' EQUITY			
Net fixed assets	$1,822.00	$1,691.00	$1,572.00	Common equity	$1,665.00	$1,529.00	$1,441.00
TOTAL ASSETS	**$3,480.00**	**$3,121.00**	**$2,516.00**	**TOTAL LIABILITIES AND OWNERS' EQUITY**	**$3,480.00**	**$3,121.00**	**$2,516.00**

Additional Information

	2010	2009	2008
Stock price per share	$33.00	$38.00	$32.00
Dividend per share	$ 1.00	$ 0.84	$ 0.70
Shares outstanding (millions)	143	143	143

Questions

1. Following are Cranston's common-size income statements and balance sheets for 2009 and 2008. Prepare common-size statements for 2010.
2. Complete the 2010 table of financial ratios for Cranston.

Income Statements

	2010	2009	2008
Sales		100.00%	100.00%
Cost of goods sold		67.83%	67.25%
Gross profit		32.17%	32.75%
Selling, general, and administrative expenses		14.93%	14.71%
Depreciation		7.18%	7.25%
EBIT		10.06%	10.80%
Interest expense (net of interest income)		0.77%	0.52%
Earnings before taxes		9.28%	10.28%
Taxes		2.79%	3.08%
Net income		**6.50%**	**7.20%**

Balance Sheets

ASSETS	2010	2009	2008	LIABILITIES	2010	2009	2008
Current assets				**Current liabilities**			
				Accounts payable		9.23%	8.11%
Cash and cash items		8.84%	9.38%	Accrued payables		10.73%	7.63%
				Short term debt		15.73%	9.66%
Accounts receivable		20.57%	12.72%	**Total current liabilities**		**35.69%**	**25.40%**
				Long-term debt		10.38%	11.49%
Inventory		16.40%	15.42%	Other liabilities (e.g., deferred taxes)		4.93%	5.84%
Total current assets		**45.82%**	**37.52%**	**Total liabilities**		**51.01%**	**42.73%**
				OWNERS' EQUITY			
Net fixed assets		54.18%	62.48%	Common equity		20.15%	21.50%
				Total owners' equity		**48.99%**	**57.27%**
TOTAL ASSETS		**100.00%**	**100.00%**	**TOTAL LIABILITIES AND OWNERS' EQUITY**		**100.00%**	**100.00%**

Continued

Ratio Analysis *Continued*

	Cranston			Industry Averages 2010
	2010	2009	2008	
Liquidity				
Current ratio		1.28	1.48	2.10
Quick ratio or acid ratio test		0.82	0.87	1.10
Cash ratio		0.25	0.37	0.39
Financial leverage ratios				
Debt ratio		0.51	0.43	0.25
Times interest earned		13.04	20.84	19.00
Cash coverage		22.35	34.83	35.00
Asset management				
Inventory turnover		4.24	4.78	5.20
Days' sales in inventory		86.04	76.30	70.19
Receivables turnover		4.99	8.63	6.81
Days' sales in receivables		73.18	42.32	53.60
Total asset turnover		1.03	1.10	1.80
Profitability ratios				
Profit margin		6.50%	7.20%	8.60%
Return on total assets		6.67%	7.89%	15.48%
Return on equity		13.61%	13.78%	20.59%
Market				
Earnings per share (EPS)		$ 1.46	$ 1.39	Not meaningful
Price/earnings (P/E)		26.11	23.04	21.00
Earnings growth rate		4.79%	17.45%	18.00%
PEG		5.45	1.32	1.17
Book value		$10.69	$10.08	Not meaningful
Market/book		3.55	3.18	4.26

3. Use the common-size statements and the ratio analysis that you have prepared to comment on Cranston's:
   a. liquidity
   b. solvency
   c. asset management
   d. profitability
   e. market performance

   Indicate whether the ratios are improving or deteriorating over the three-year period and whether they are better or worse than the 2010 industry averages.
4. Express Cranston's ROE in terms of the DuPont identity. Which ratios are contributing to Cranston's below-average ROE?
5. Based on your analyses in Questions 1 through 4, why do you think Cranston's recent stock performance has been disappointing?

Part 5

Other Selected Finance Topics

Learning Objectives

LO1 Describe the life cycle of a business.

LO2 Understand the different sources of capital available to a start-up business and to a growing business.

LO3 Explain the funding available to a stable or mature business.

LO4 Explain how companies sell bonds in a capital market.

LO5 Explain how companies sell stocks in a capital market.

LO6 Examine some special forms of financing: commercial paper and banker's acceptance.

LO7 Describe the options and regulations for closing a business.

Chapter 15
Raising Capital

It takes money to make money. Every business needs capital: to start up, to grow, to thrive, to expand, to compete, to survive. Where do firms obtain the cash they need to fund their projects and services? You already know that businesses generate cash through their operations and raise money by borrowing it from a lending institution like a bank (debt financing), selling off part of the ownership (equity financing), or combining both sources. Raising capital is a structured process. To understand this process, it helps to look at the various ways to raise capital across a firm's life cycle as it moves through different stages of growth.

15.1 The Business Life Cycle

Every firm has a **business life cycle**. There are a number of classifications of the business life cycle. Here we use the five active phases of start-up, growth, maturity, decline, and closing, as Figure 15.1 shows. Each phase brings with it unique problems and opportunities related to managing the business and financing it. In this chapter, we look particularly at funding sources that businesses typically use at the first three stages.

The birth of a firm comes about when a business idea reaches the implementation stage. The idea could come from a single individual or a group, but either way, the business starts when actions begin the process of producing a product or service to sell to customers. Once the business is "born," it will move through one or more of the four remaining stages.

Some businesses will move to the final stage—closing the business—very rapidly, even skipping the middle ones. According to the U.S. Census Bureau's Business Information Tracking System, three out of every five employer businesses (businesses that employ others besides the owners) close within their first six years. Others move through the first two stages, start-up and growth, and settle into the mature stage for many years. Some of the best-known companies fit this description. Each stage presents different management issues as well as different financing sources for a business. These different financing sources at various stages of a firm's life cycle are the subject of this chapter. We devote much of the chapter to the mature business, but we begin with start-up and growing firms.

The classification of business life-cycle stages and various types of financing is not rigid. There can be and often is overlap. The life-cycle approach is a convenient way of examining different sources of capital in the stage of business development where the borrowing source is most *typical*.

15.2 Borrowing for a Start-up and Growing Business

A business can use five sources of capital to start a business and fuel its initial growth:

1. Personal funds
2. Borrowed funds from family and friends
3. Commercial bank loans
4. Borrowed funds through business start-up programs like the U.S. Small Business Administration (SBA)
5. Angel investor or venture capitalist funds

Personal Funds and Family Loans

Personal funds and family loans are by far the most common types of start-up financing, even though such loans limit the initial size of the business to the

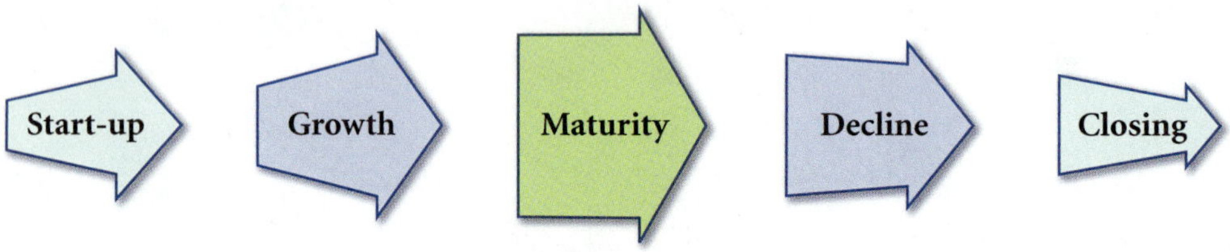

FIGURE 15.1 The business life cycle.

funding capabilities of the owner and the owner's family. Recall from Chapter 1 that among the different types of business organizations, self-funded businesses are usually proprietorships, which mix the assets of a company with the personal assets of the owner. One advantage of this form of business is that the owner or manager can make all the business decisions and enjoy all the profits. One disadvantage is that the limitation of capital may add significant constraints to growth and to the potential success of the business.

Loans from family and friends may be informal agreements or formal contracts with specific repayment schedules. Although many entrepreneurs want to avoid borrowing from family and friends, the next source for borrowing—banks and other lending institutions—may look favorably on family funding as a positive sign for the business. After all, if you can't convince your family and friends that you have a good business idea, how can you convince a stranger?

Commercial Bank Loans

Probably the first place one would think to look for outside funding for a start-up business is the local commercial bank. Many banks have lending officers who approve funds for businesses in their area, but the vast majority of these funds are for businesses with a solid history. Start-up ventures do not fit the typical lending model of commercial banks. Often, a loan for a start-up venture takes place only when the borrower has sufficient income or sufficient assets outside the new business that the borrower can pledge as collateral for the loan. Loans to start-ups without sufficient outside resources for collateral are the exception for commercial banks. This type of lending is usually left to the SBA.

Commercial Bank Loans through the Small Business Administration

The **U.S. Small Business Administration (SBA)** is a government agency with three different loan programs designed to cover a wide array of businesses and their particular needs. These loans are delivered by SBA's partners, not directly by the SBA. The partners are commercial banks that receive some guarantee from the SBA. The program we discuss here is the most common of these programs, the basic 7(a) Loan Guaranty Program.

The 7(a) Loan Guaranty Program administers business loans to individuals or businesses that might not be eligible for a loan through the normal lending agencies. The borrower can use loan proceeds for working capital and fixed assets, with repayment schedules extending up to twenty-five years. Commercial lenders deliver these loans and the SBA guarantees them.

Although the requirements may vary, a typical scenario is that an applicant applies for a loan at a commercial lending institution and demonstrates or provides the following:

- Evidence of good character
- Evidence of management capability
- Collateral and owner's contribution
- A viable business plan
- A personal financial statement
- Business financial statements, including projected cash flows

The commercial lenders decide whether their bank will make the loan or whether there is a weakness in the application that will require an SBA guaranty. If the SBA makes a guaranty on the loan, the guaranty is only to the lending institution. If the original borrower defaults, the government will repay the obligation up to the percentage of the SBA guaranty. The original borrower remains obligated for the remaining outstanding balance of the loan.

One of the key elements of the loan is collateral. An individual who owns more than 20% of the business must personally guarantee the loan. In other words, it may be necessary to use one's personal assets as a pledge against the loan.

What are the rates for an SBA guaranty loan? The commercial banks loaning the funds provide them at the current market rates for business loans. There is really no advantage to the borrower in terms of rates or repayment schedules by going through the SBA. The real benefit is to the lending bank that has a portion of the loan backed by the SBA. As part of the monitoring function of the SBA, however, it does review the rates and does set a maximum rate for guaranteed loans.

So what exactly does the SBA do for the small business owner? As mentioned, the SBA's objective is to help small business owners qualify for loans when they may not be able to qualify through the normal lending policies of a commercial lender. The lender receives a guaranty from the SBA, thereby lowering the default risk on the loan. The SBA aids borrowers only when lending institutions will not approve their applications through normal channels.

Angel Financing and Venture Capital

Sometimes, some of the best business ideas come from individuals who have little experience and even less money. Such business ideas often do not fit the commercial lending process or the SBA loan program. Upstart entrepreneurs seeking money to start an operation may end up proposing their business ideas to an angel investor. **Angel investors** are lenders who provide funding for new, high-risk ideas. The term does not refer to a well-defined set of lenders, but is a generic term applied to individuals or groups that seek to support new start-up business ventures. As such, an angel financier is usually a wealthy individual or collection of individuals with pooled funds. Angel financing is usually limited to early development of the business, and often an angel will commit up to $2 million, depending on his or her personal wealth or the pooled funds of the group. It is not an exact dollar limit—some angels provide more and some less—but it is a common upper limit.

Angel investors typically invest their own funds in start-up, high-risk ideas and therefore require higher rates of return.

Angel financiers are rare for most business ideas. It is usually difficult to catch the eye of an angel. If one does, the cash infusion is generally for the medium term, not the long term, and often includes some part of equity ownership in the company for the angel. The angel plans on a **liquidity event** occurring in a relatively short amount of time, that is, an event that allows the angel to cash out all or some of his or her ownership

TABLE 15.1 **Differences between Angel Investors and Venture Capitalists**

Angel Investors	Venture Capitalists
Individual or group of individuals	Corporate entities
Invest own money	Invest pooled money from range of investors
Focus on early stages of business	All stages of development
Investment may be tied to individual or group expertise	Investment may be tied to high-growth opportunities, with focus on technology and innovation

Source: Adapted from LBO Advisers, "Essential Differences between Angel Investors and Venture Capital," www.lbo-advisers.com.

shares to realize a profit in short fashion. Such an event could be an initial public offering (see Section 15.5) or a direct acquisition by another company. Financing that will require more than ten years for repayment is not attractive to most angels. The longer the funds are tied up in the business idea, the higher the probability that the borrower may not pay back funds in full and the longer the angel must wait to look for other business ideas that could use financial support.

As a business starts growing and has initial success, it may require additional funding beyond the capacity of the angel investor, typically in excess of $5 million. The new business may seek out **venture capitalist firms** or **funds**. Like angel investors, venture capitalists are not a well-defined group of lenders. Rather, venture capitalism is a general term that we apply to groups or institutions that provide funding at a level higher (larger loans) than most angel investors. Funds that borrowers obtain from a venture capitalist may come in segments over time, with the new business needing to meet certain specific targets before the investor makes the next set of funds available. To help distinguish between angels and venture capitalists, Table 15.1 presents some general characteristics of the two lenders.

Let's say you have come up with an entrepreneurial idea for a new home video gaming system, which you have dubbed the "yuu." At this stage, all you have is an idea, a product profile, a set of drawings, and a big dream. You do not have the personal wealth or collateral to appeal to a bank, so you must seek out an angel or venture capitalist or both to finance your idea. In this case, your idea is too expensive for angels to fund the whole process, but they are the appropriate source to provide the initial investment. Once you move successfully through the first two stages of development, you will have a strong case for appealing to venture capitalists, who may then fund the second two stages. Both the angel financier and the venture capitalist will present you with a set of short-term targets as well as a funding schedule whose target dates you must meet before they invest additional cash. Table 15.2 provides the set of goals.

Table 15.2 shows that the entire project has a funding plan of $8.5 million spread over four years. One major issue with an angel (or venture capital firm) is the rate at which an idea will use up funds. This use rate is called the **burn rate** or **bleed rate** and lets the financier know the timing of necessary future funding to support the idea, as well as funds that the investor can retain for other promising ventures. Ventures with high burn rates may require more monitoring, more performance benchmarks, and more time from the financier, and thus will affect the actual decision to fund a venture.

TABLE 15.2 Yuu Home Video Gaming System Targets and Funding Amounts

Stages	Funding Description	Funding Type	Length of Time for Stage
Stage 1	Design prototype	Seed money: $800,000	Six months
Stage 2	Small-scale production	Production I phase money: $1,600,000	Twelve months
Stage 3	Marketing and distribution in selected markets	Marketing and distribution money: $1,600,000	Six months
Stage 4	Full-scale operations	Production II phase money: $4,500,000	Twenty-four months

Table 15.2 also indicates that the angel seeds the first stage with only $800,000 to enable you to complete and test a successful prototype of the system. The angel puts up this relatively small amount to lower the risk if you cannot develop the prototype and sets a short time frame (six months) to encourage you to devote your full time and energy to the project. If your project doesn't take off within the first six months, the angel will stop supporting the project and will lose the initial $800,000 investment. The angel will now look elsewhere with his or her remaining funds, leaving you without capital for the next stage. From the angel's point of view, the name of the game is to minimize exposure and timing of funds to projects that do not work and move on to projects that have a higher probability of success.

Let's say that you clear the first hurdle. The angel will then release the next set of funds so that you can set up a small-scale production facility to manufacture the video gaming system. Again, if successful, you move forward with more funding and more goals. As long as you continue to meet your goals at the different stages, the investor will make funds available until the business is ready to move to full-scale operations. Full-scale production support may be beyond the capability of the angel investor, however, and you may need to find a venture capitalist to provide larger funding.

If your entrepreneurial idea is appealing to a wide number of potential angels or venture capitalists, you may be lucky enough to select from a set of different interested parties. In such a case, you will need to look at three important areas:

1. Financial strength of the angel or venture capitalist
2. Contacts of the angel or venture capitalist
3. Exit strategy of the angel or venture capitalist

Financial Strength Not all angels or venture capitalists are alike in terms of the depths of their funding capabilities. Some may have very deep pockets, so with sequential funding programs there is a high probability that future funds will be available at the appropriate time. Others may have limited funds, and if other projects the angel or venture capitalist is supporting do not produce substantial incomes, future funding for your project may be in jeopardy, even if your project appears to be moving forward. Therefore, given a choice, you will, of course, want to pick an angel or venture capitalist with plenty of funding ability.

Contacts Angels and venture capitalists often supply more than money to a business idea. Many times, they have contacts that will help the entrepreneur reach his or her goals. It may even be the case that the funds are contingent on the entrepreneur using these contacts. For example, when you hit stage three, marketing and distribution, you may be required as part of the funding agreement to work with a specific marketing firm. At the full production phase, the venture capitalist may have access to other sources that will aid you in moving from a small, regional market to a national or international one. Access to these special contacts increases the probability of success for your project, thereby making you and your funding sources better off in the long run.

Exit Strategy As we have already noted, angels and venture capitalists are medium-term lenders, and they need a liquidity event to get their money out of the new business and convert the investment into cash so they can move on to the next business idea. Because many new ventures fail, they need to get a high return on successful ventures. Therefore, the exit strategy is critical to both the lender and the borrower. In your case, the venture capitalist may end up lending $4.5 million over the two-year production II phase and may then look for a liquidity event to take as much as $10 million to $20 million out of the new business. This substantial payback may critically affect the company's long-run survival. Thus, the venture capitalist may take a large equity position during the funding stage instead of receiving cash directly from the business. If you want to maintain ownership of the new company, you may need to raise substantial capital to buy back the equity position from the venture capitalist. If you can't, the venture capitalist may sell his or her equity position to someone else to recover the investment.

Although there is a long list of venture capitalists (to see a list, go to www.vfinance.com) with access to a substantial amount of funding, the probability of actually getting funding for one's business idea is relatively small. Angels and venture capitalists may see hundreds of solicitations, many of which are directed straight to the wastebasket.

Because the probability of failure is so high, what kind of return does an angel or venture capitalist need to generate from a successful venture? Let's look at what it would take for a venture capitalist to stay in the business of supporting start-up companies.

EXAMPLE 15.1 Required rate of return for a venture capitalist

Problem Columbia Venture Capitalists (CVC) has a success rate of one out of every six ventures funded. The average funding for a new business venture is $5 million, and the average length of time for recovery of funds is three years. What return rate must CVC get on a successful new venture if the company wants to earn 15% on its invested capital?

Solution If we assume that CVC disburses all the funds up front (that is, we are not sequencing the funding), we have an initial outlay of $30 million for the six projects. At the end of three years, we will need a payoff that earns 15% annually on the $30 million investment. So, in this case, we determine the future value as we did in Chapter 3 (Eq. 3.2):

$$FV = \$30{,}000{,}000 \times 1.15^3 = \$45{,}626{,}250$$

Statistically speaking, only one venture will be successful, so this one venture must be able to return $45,626,250 in three years from its funds of $5 million to the venture capitalist. Thus, the new venture must "borrow" the $5 million at the following cost:

$$\text{cost of capital} = \left(\frac{\$45{,}626{,}250}{\$5{,}000{,}000}\right)^{1/3} - 1 = \mathbf{108.97\%}$$

This cost of capital is very expensive, but it may be the only capital an entrepreneur can get for starting up the business.

Although at first glance a 109% annual interest rate looks extremely high, it is important to realize that the venture capitalist is really a partner (not a loan officer) who is taking an equity stake in the venture. The payoff for the financier comes from selling off his or her ownership position when the company makes good. One angel in the Pacific Northwest has a target return of ten times the initial value in the first three to five years. That is, if this financier lends $1 million to a firm, he expects to sell his ownership position for $10 million in three to five years from his liquidity event, which is an annual rate of 60% to 100% return on his investment. Of course, some ventures pay off the full amount, some pay off a portion, and some ventures never materialize and are a complete loss. On average, though, an annual return of 60% to 100% on their successful investments is quite typical for angels or venture capitalists.

Because starting a business may require money the owner does not have, the borrowing options may play a major role in the success or failure of the business in its infant stage. Even with the backing of a venture capitalist, the business still has a long way to go from start-up to growth to reach the next stage of the business life cycle, the stable and mature stage.

15.3 Borrowing for a Stable and Mature Business: Bank Loans

The second phase of borrowing is usually connected directly with commercial banks through lines of credit, bank loans, and syndicated loans. Many times, these borrowing arrangements are intended for the operations of the firm (short-term financing) and not necessarily for the firm's long-term growth or expansion. As we saw in Chapter 12, some types of loans, such as lines of credit, are intended to enable a company to work through the short-term fluctuations of cash on a daily basis rather than provide funding for expansion. Larger loans from banks or syndicate loans (explained later) are intended for business expansion. The loans that we look at in this section are mostly for the short term.

Straight Loans

Let's start with the simplest of the borrowing avenues, a bank loan. To secure a bank loan for a mature business, a company owner or manager goes through an application process. The commercial loan officer reviews the business operations and evaluates the potential of the business to generate sufficient cash to maintain operations and pay back the loan. If the officer approves the loan, the firm can then borrow the funds. There are a few ways to set up the loan:

- Straight loan with preset payment schedule
- Discount loan
- Letter of credit or line of credit
- Compensating balance loan

Each of these loans acts a little differently, and the quoted interest rates for each are not the actual rates. Let's review a straight loan first.

EXAMPLE 15.2 Straight bank loan

Problem McCarty Manufacturing, a manufacturer of baseball equipment, is a stable business. The company has just signed a deal with Keen Sports to make baseball bats with the Keen insignia. To make the required number of bats, McCarty will need to expand its production facilities. The cost of such an expansion is $2,500,000. The company applies for a loan from its local banker. The commercial loan officer approves the loan, quoting an APR of 7% and required monthly repayments over the next five years. What are the monthly payment (principal and interest) and effective interest rate (EAR) on this bank loan?

Solution For a calculator solution of the monthly payment,

Mode: P/Y = 12 and C/Y = 12

Input	60	7.0	−2,500,000	?	0
Key	N	I/Y	PV	PMT	FV
CPT				**49,503**	

The effective annual rate of this 7% APR is therefore

$$EAR = \left(1 + \frac{0.07}{12}\right)^{12} - 1 = 0.0723 \text{ or } \mathbf{7.23\%}$$

Discount Loans

Now, let's examine a discount loan. With a discount loan, the bank "discounts" or subtracts the interest charges from the loan up front and allows the company to borrow the face amount of the loan minus the interest on it. It is a loan without a series of repayments to the bank. Instead, it has a lump sum up front (principal borrowed) and a lump-sum payment at maturity (principal and interest). It gets somewhat confusing because we categorize the bank loan by the size of the repayment, not the principal. The bank quotes the loan rate as the discount rate, but that is an understatement of the loan's actual cost. Just like a Treasury bill, a discount loan pays the face value at maturity, but the face value reflects both the initial price (principal) and the interest. The price of the Treasury bill is the discounted face value. Here the loan amount is the discounted face value of the loan, the stated final repayment amount.

EXAMPLE 15.3 Discount loan

Problem Sunvold Systems makes shot clocks for basketball games. The state of Missouri has decided to use shot clocks for all high school games and has awarded the contract to Sunvold Systems. Sunvold Systems needs a loan of \$495,000 to buy all the additional materials to make the shot clocks. The company applies for a loan from Doone County Bank, and the bank says that Sunvold can borrow under a "discount loan" with a 10% discount rate payable at the end of the year. What is the size of the loan Sunvold Systems needs from the bank? What is the effective interest rate of the loan?

Solution Doone County is going to discount the available funds by 10%, so the bank divides the needed funds of \$495,000 by 1 minus the loan rate of 10%:

$$\text{loan size} = \frac{\$495{,}000}{1 - 0.10} = \mathbf{\$550{,}000}$$

Sunvold Systems will receive the needed \$495,000 today, but will repay \$550,000 at the end of the year. The interest is therefore \$55,000 (\$550,000 − \$495,000), and the interest rate is

$$\text{interest rate} = \frac{\$55{,}000}{\$495{,}000} = \mathbf{11.11\%}$$

Discount loans are usually very short-term loans.

Letter of Credit or Line of Credit

We already met the next type of loan, a letter of credit or line of credit, in Chapter 12. A **letter of credit** or **line of credit** is a preapproved borrowing amount that works much like a credit card. The company can borrow money at a preset rate from the bank at any time without seeking additional approval of the loan each time it needs funds. The bank, however, receives compensation on the outstanding balance of the loan. The compensation can be a fixed interest rate, but often is a floating interest rate tied to a benchmark interest rate. This borrowing style has changing balances and changing interest rates, so it is difficult to state the effective rate on the loan.

Compensating Balance

The fourth way to borrow from a bank is with a **compensating balance**. This type of loan works much like a line of credit, but only a portion of the loan is available for the company and it pays interest on the face value of the loan. For example, a company may borrow 85% of its credit line, leaving 15% with the bank as its compensating balance. The effective rate increases as the size of the compensating balance increases. To illustrate, say a company has a credit line of \$800,000 in a 15% compensating balance arrangement and the bank charges a 6% interest rate on the credit line. In other words, the company must leave \$120,000 of the credit line in the bank at all times. Although the company borrows only \$680,000, the bank applies the 6% interest rate to the face amount of the loan (\$800,000 × 0.06 = \$48,000). The true rate of this loan is higher than 6%. It is

\$48,000/\$680,000, or 7.06%. We can also calculate the true rate by dividing the quoted rate by 1 minus the compensating balance percent:

$$\text{actual interest rate} = \frac{0.06}{1 - 0.15} = 0.070588 \quad \text{or} \quad \approx 7.06\%$$

What happens when a company needs more funding than a single bank is willing or able to loan? The company can try to find a bank that has more lending capacity, or the bank can try to enlist other banks to support the loan. A **syndicated loan** is a loan from a set of multiple banks that join together and make the loan to a single company, sharing both the income from the loan and the risk of default. Syndicated loans are usually reserved for large and mature businesses, and are for the long term rather than the short term.

Now that we have explored the different types of loans, you may wonder if some situations call for particular types of loans or if borrowers prefer certain loan types in certain situations. There is no exact formula for the right kind of loan in every situation; rather, the loan is usually tailored to the needs of the business and the uncertainty of the future needs for funding. For example, if a firm is buying a piece of equipment as part of an expansion and the total outlay is certain, a straight loan is usually the best match. On the other hand, if a firm is expanding its business gradually over an extended period of time and knows the amount that it needs, but cannot predict when it needs the funds, a line-of-credit loan is a good match. Lending institutions will customize loans to the firm's needs, the capacity of the bank, and the prevailing interest rates.

15.4 Borrowing for a Stable and Mature Business: Selling Bonds

Once a business grows to a certain size and has established itself in an industry, the capital markets become an available financing source. The two main ways to raise funds in the capital markets are through bond sales and through equity sales. We have already looked at the pricing of bonds and stocks in Chapters 6 and 7. We will now examine the issuing process for these two kinds of securities. Let's start with bonds. In contrast to the loans that you studied in the previous section, which were mostly for the short term, bonds generally have maturities of twenty or thirty years; we view them as long-term financing.

A financial institution may issue bonds either in a public auction or through a private placement. With a public auction, the SEC regulates the process. The U.S. government created the SEC with the passage of the 1934 Securities Exchange Act, which carried the authority to enforce and regulate both the 1933 Securities Act and the 1934 Securities Exchange Act. These acts set the standards for issuing securities (both bonds and stocks) and subsequent selling of securities in secondary markets.

How does a bond auction work? There are five steps:

1. The company selects an investment bank to help design and market the bond. An **investment bank** is an agent that works with the firm to meet all the listing requirements of the bond issue, the design of the bond terms, the marketing of the bond, and the auction of the bond.
2. The company and investment bank register the bond with the SEC, providing a prospectus and referencing the indenture for the bond (discussed shortly). (We touched on the indenture in Chapter 6.)

3. An agency such as Standard & Poor's or Moody's rates the bond to help potential buyers determine an appropriate price. (We also discussed these ratings in Chapter 6.)
4. The investment bank markets the bond to prospective buyers prior to the auction, using the prospectus as the key information on the bond.
5. The investment bank conducts an auction to sell the bond.

Two documents are required for a bond sale, a prospectus and an indenture. The **prospectus** contains much of the information filed in the registration, and the bank uses it to inform potential buyers about the bond. The **indenture** is the formal contract for the bond between the issuing company and the eventual buyer. It includes vital information about the bond, such as the coupon rate, payment schedule, maturity date, and par value as well as other provisions, including those that restrict the activities of the issuing firm to increase the bond's safety in the eyes of potential buyers.

The company will base the total funds that it raises on the authorized number of bonds that it can sell through the registration process and the price buyers are willing to pay.

EXAMPLE 15.4 Bond proceeds

Problem Alsip Glass and Mirror is about to issue a bond with the help of Becker Investment Bank. The bond will be a twenty-year, semiannual bond with a 7% coupon rate and a $5,000 par value. A rating agency has given the bond an AA1 rating. Bonds with a twenty-year maturity and this rating are currently selling to yield 8.5%. Alsip Glass and Mirror has requested authorization from the SEC to sell 2,000 of these bonds. If Becker Investment Bank is receiving a 2.5% commission on the sale of these bonds, what will the total proceeds be for Alsip? What is the cost of these bonds to Alsip in terms of cost of capital?

Solution First, the 8.5% yield for these bonds will produce the following retail or market price per bond. For a calculator solution,

Mode: P/Y = 2 and C/Y = 2

Coupon payment = 0.07 × $5,000/2 = $175

Input	40	8.5	?	175	5,000
Key	N	I/Y	PV	PMT	FV
CPT			4,284.60		

$$\text{gross revenue} = 2{,}000 \times 4{,}284.60 = \$8{,}569{,}200$$

The commission for Becker Investment Bank is 2.5% of the proceeds, so

$$\text{commission} = \$8{,}569{,}200 \times 0.025 = \$214{,}230$$

The net proceeds of the sale per bond to Alsip Glass and Mirror is

$$\text{net proceeds per bond} = \frac{\$8{,}569{,}200 - \$214{,}230}{2{,}000} = \mathbf{\$4{,}177.485}$$

Using the net proceeds, we next find the cost of the bonds to Alsip Glass and Mirror.

Solving for the yield to maturity, (I/Y = YTM), with the TVM keys, we have

Mode: P/Y = 2 and C/Y = 2

Input	40	?	4,177.485	−175	−5,000
Key	N	I/Y	PV	PMT	FV
CPT		8.757%			

Once Alsip Glass and Mirror sell the bonds, what is its future cash flow obligation? The 2,000 bonds have a semiannual interest payment of

$$\frac{2{,}000 \times \$5{,}000 \times 0.07}{2} = \$350{,}000$$

and a final cash payment for the principal of

$$2{,}000 \times \$5{,}000 = \$10{,}000{,}000$$

at maturity.

The company can easily cover the semiannual interest payment total of $350,000, but the repayment of $10,000,000 at maturity may be difficult. Alsip Glass and Mirror has two options to handle this future outflow: borrow again at maturity and swap out old debt for new debt, or put away some money each year to handle this future large outflow.

A company can put away money each year into a special fund for retirement of debt, called a **sinking fund**. The sinking fund allows the company to reduce the effect of the large cash outflow at the bond's maturity. Some companies opt to use their annual contribution to the sinking fund to buy back the bonds prior to maturity.

15.5 Borrowing for a Stable and Mature Business: Selling Stock

In Chapter 7, you saw that when a company sells common stock to the public, it is raising funds by selling part of the firm's ownership rights. The common stockholders become owners, have voting rights, and receive a distribution of the company's earnings when it declares and pays dividends. The process of selling stock for the first time is called the initial public offering (IPO), which the SEC and the 1933 Securities Act govern.

Stock ownership has its advantages and disadvantages. Owners enjoy the firm's success through a rise in the stock share price and received dividends, but they also bear the risk of poor company performance. We do not base performance solely on company managers' decisions, but also on the economy itself. Events such as the advent of World Wars I and II; the September 11, 2001, terrorist attacks; and, most recently, the subprime mortgage fiasco have all led to downturns in the stock market, some quite steep. So, equity holders do in fact bear risk.

Initial Public Offerings and Underwriting

The process underlying the selling of common stock to the public is usually unfamiliar to companies, so they seek out and hire an *investment bank*. The investment bank partners with the company and guides it through the selling process. Investment banks are required to perform **due diligence** in ensuring that all information that they release during the process is accurate. Failing to perform this due diligence task puts the investment bank and the company at risk for litigation after the sale of the stock.

There are two ways to hire an investment bank: through a competitive bid process or through a direct selection process, which usually involves negotiation of terms. The terms include how the client will compensate the investment bank for its services. An investment bank determines compensation by either a preset funding arrangement or the number of shares sold, the share price, and the spread on the securities. The **spread** is the difference between the stock sale price to the public and the sale proceeds that the investment bank pays to the company.

There are two types of compensation for the investment bank. We base the first type of compensation on the number of shares sold and the spread, which we call a best efforts basis. In a **best efforts arrangement**, the investment bank pledges to use its best efforts to sell all the authorized shares and takes a cut on each individual share that it sells, but provides no guarantee as to how many shares it will sell. The more shares it sells, the higher the payoff to the investment bank.

The second type of compensation does not rely on the actual number of shares that sell at the auction. Instead, the investment bank guarantees a certain dollar amount to the company regardless of how many shares it actually sells. The bank keeps the difference between the actual proceeds from the sale and the guaranteed amount. We call this arrangement a firm commitment. In a **firm commitment arrangement**, the investment bank guarantees a preset amount of money to the company. A firm commitment takes away the uncertainty of the financial outcome for the issuing company because the investment bank must make up any shortfalls in the proceeds from the auction. We use **underwriter** or *underwriting* to describe the function of an investment bank. By making a firm commitment, the investment bank is buying the entire issue (underwriting it) and then selling it to the public. The initial act of buying the whole issue means that the investment bank is paying the firm a fixed amount up front (although actual payment comes after the public sale). The investment bank retains all the shares that it does not sell at auction.

When we compare these two compensation methods, it is clear that the company would prefer the firm commitment method and the investment bank the best efforts method. To compensate for the risk, we usually see that with a firm commitment arrangement, the investment bank gets a larger spread than with the best efforts method.

EXAMPLE 15.5 Firm commitment versus best efforts arrangements

Problem The "yuu" home video gaming system is a big success. You have started Video Action Company, and you now want to sell common stock in the company to raise capital for expansion of the business and paying off the venture capital firm. Future View Investment Bank is proposing two types of compensation arrangements. The first is a firm commitment of $15,000,000. The second is a best efforts arrangement in which Future View will receive $2.00 for every share of stock it sells up to $1,750,000 for the 875,000 shares that it will offer to the public. The offer price to the public is $20.00 per share. If Future View sells 100% of the shares, what are your proceeds? What is the payment to Future View under each method of issuing securities? What if it sells 80% of the shares? At what percentage of sold shares are the proceeds to you the same under the two compensation arrangements? At what percentage is the payment to Future View the same?

Solution

1. For a 100% sale of the 875,000 shares at $20.00 per share to the public, the proceeds are $17,500,000

   Firm commitment funds to you: $15,000,000
   Firm commitment compensation to Future View:
   $\$20 \times 875{,}000 - \$15{,}000{,}000 = \$2{,}500{,}000$
   Best efforts to you: $(\$20 - \$2) \times 875{,}000 = \mathbf{\$15{,}750{,}000}$
   Best efforts to Future View: $\$2 \times 875{,}000 = \mathbf{\$1{,}750{,}000}$

Therefore, if the security is 100% sold, you are better off with a best effort and Future View is better off with a firm commitment.

2. For an 80% sale of the 875,000 shares, the proceeds are $14,000,000

   Firm commitment funds to you: $15,000,000
   Firm commitment compensation to Future View: $\$20 \times 875{,}000(0.8) - \$15{,}000{,}000 = -\$1{,}000{,}000$ (and Future View now holds 20% of the shares, but must pay Video Action Company $1,000,000 above the funds collected from the sale).
   Best efforts to you: $(\$20 - \$2) \times 875{,}000 \times (0.8) = \mathbf{\$12{,}600{,}000}$
   Best efforts to Future View: $\$2 \times 875{,}000 \times (0.8) = \mathbf{\$1{,}400{,}000}$

Therefore, if the security is 80% sold, you are better off with a firm commitment and Future View is better off with a best effort in terms of immediate cash flow.

3. What is the break-even point in sales percent between firm commitment and best efforts for you?

$$\text{Firm commitment } \$ = \text{best effort } \$ \text{ per share sold}$$
$$\$15{,}000{,}000 = \$18 \times 875{,}000 \times X\%$$
$$X\% = \frac{\$15{,}000{,}000}{\$18 \times 875{,}000}$$
$$= \frac{\$15{,}000{,}000}{\$15{,}750{,}000} = \mathbf{95.2381\%}$$

So, you will be better off selecting best efforts only if more than 95.2381% of the stock sells at the auction.

We can also see that we have the same break-even point in sales for Future View with the $15,000,000 firm commitment:

$$\$20 \times 875{,}000 \times (X\%) - \$15{,}000{,}000 = \$2.00 \times 875{,}000 \times X\%$$
$$\$15{,}000{,}000 = (\$20 - \$2) \times 875{,}000 \times X\%$$
$$X\% = \frac{\$15{,}000{,}000}{\$15{,}750{,}000} = \mathbf{95.2381\%}$$

So, for Future View Investment Bank, best efforts is a better way unless it believes it can sell more than 95.2381% of all authorized shares.

Registration, Prospectus, and Tombstone

Long before the price is set and the auction process takes place, the investment bank and firm must register the sale with the SEC, provide a prospectus for the sale to potential buyers, and advertise the equity sale. The process on average takes from four to six months to complete. The preliminary registration that it files with the SEC contains, among other items,

- Financial expectations of the company
- Description of the issue to be sold
- Listing of all individuals and firms involved in the sale
- All material information regarding the company

There is some colorful terminology that we associate with the IPO process, which we will touch on as we continue our discussion of the IPO process. One such term is **red herring**, the first filing of the prospectus. Its name derives from the red ink in which the word "preliminary" appears across the face of the prospectus.

At this point, the investment bank may begin the marketing process of the issue, but it cannot actively solicit buying commitments. The SEC, meanwhile, reviews the filed documents. If all materials are on file and in order, the SEC approves the issue for sale after a waiting period that generally lasts from twenty to forty days. This waiting period is the **quiet period** or **cooling-off period** and may be longer than forty days because the SEC does not explicitly set a standard quiet period for all issues. During the cooling-off period, the investment bank typically does not advertise the price and promotional activity is banned. Analysts cannot make recommendations about the stock to potential investors during the waiting period.

If there is missing information, the SEC issues a **letter of comment** to the company and the investment bank. The company and investment bank then make the necessary corrections to the registration and refile the new registration. At this time, the waiting period for approval starts again. At the end of this waiting period, if the SEC requires no further action, the bank moves forward with the issue for sale to the general public. The SEC approval simply means that the necessary information is on file, not that this issue is a good investment prospect for a buyer. The assessment of whether it is a good or bad investment opportunity remains the obligation of each potential buyer.

The advertisement of the issue after the waiting period is the tombstone, so called because firms used to print it in heavy black type within thick black borders. The **tombstone** contains the name of the issuing firm, some details about the issue, and the list of involved investment banks. The ad lists banks by level of participation in the issue in brackets. It lists the lead banks in largest print, and thereafter the brackets reduce in print size, suggesting less involvement in the issue. The ad lists banks with only a marketing function in the last bracket. Figure 15.2 gives some idea of how a tombstone looks for Video Action Company, the company manufacturing the yuu.

There are two major exceptions to the requirement to file with the SEC. The first is if the issue will mature in less than nine months (270 days). The second is if the issue is for less than $5 million. This second exemption, **Regulation A**, is also known as the small business exception and requires only a brief offering statement.

The Marketing Process: Road Show

The marketing of the issue is a short-lived but intense process in which the investment bank attempts to attract buyers of the issue and get a read on the potential issue price. The investment bank may enlist other investment banks in the marketing effort to form a syndicate for the issue. The marketing process may occur through exclusive solicitation of current clients, but to expand the potential sales pool, the investment bank may seek additional buyers via a road show.

A **road show** is an effort to gain sales momentum for the issue by holding information sessions on the upcoming new equity issue in several major cities. The presentation will touch on many aspects of the company and the forthcoming issue, such as the history of the company, the vision for the product, industry trends, and how it will use the funds to grow or sustain the company. Following the

FIGURE 15.2 Tombstone for Video Action Company.

session, the presenters solicit audience members for their reactions and potential buying interest. At the end of the day, the managers, accountants, and bankers pack up their presentations and head to another city for another day of presentations.

The road show may last two weeks, with stops in a dozen cities to solicit potential buying interest. At the completion of the road show, the investment bankers, in consultation with the company managers and owners, try to establish the potential for the issue. If the issue has received insufficient interest to go forward with the actual auction, it is stopped at this time. If, however, the road show has generated sufficient interest, the investment bank sets a price for the auction and the issue proceeds forward.

The Auction

The auction itself is held on a single day, during which buyers submit bids for a specific quantity of shares. All shares sell at the preset auction price. If the bid is undersubscribed (bid quantity is less than the offered shares), all bidders get their requested shares. If the bid is oversubscribed, each bidder is supposed to receive a **pro-rata share** of his or her bid. For example, in the case of Video Action Company's 875,000 shares offered for sale to the general public, if the bids total 1,093,750 shares, each bidder should receive 80% of his or her bid ($875{,}000/1{,}093{,}750 = 0.80$). Once the auction is completed, the investment bank notifies bidders of their share allocation and it issues shares upon receipt of the funds.

The Aftermarket: Dealer in the Shares

Once the auction is completed, the company's new outstanding equity shares are traded on the secondary market. One of the remaining functions of the lead investment bank is to become a dealer in the stock. The investment bank typically deals in the stock for a minimum of eighteen months and will continue to function as a dealer after the initial required period as long as it remains a profitable business for the bank. These stocks typically trade on regional exchanges such as the Chicago, Pacific, or Boston Stock Exchanges or the online trading system which the National Association of Securities Dealers, the NASDAQ, maintains.

To maintain the investment bank's ability to function as a dealer in the stock, there is usually a green-shoe provision as part of its contract to take the company public. The **green-shoe provision** typically allows the investment bank to purchase up to 15% of additional shares over a thirty-day period beyond those offered to the public during the auction. The ability to purchase additional shares is especially important when an issue is oversubscribed. If demand for the stock is higher than expected, the investment bank can acquire an inventory of shares for selling in the secondary market to customers who did not get their desired quantity of shares. The industry uses the somewhat odd name of "green shoe" because the first company to issue this kind of provision was, in fact, the Green Shoe Company.

Another standard agreement is a **lock-up agreement**, which requires the original owners of the firm to maintain their shares of stock for 180 days. The original owners may hold a substantial number of shares—more than issued in the public sale—if they want to maintain a majority interest in the company. This arrangement prevents the original managers from dumping shares on the market immediately after the sale and driving down the price of the new shares. In addition, the firm may issue venture capitalists equity shares as payment for their funding in an earlier business stage, and they, too, must wait the 180 days before starting to sell stock to recover their investment. If you look back at the Tombstone for Video Action, the company stock offer in Figure 15.2, you will see that there are 3,000,000 authorized shares, but only 875,000 offered to the public.

The firm will distribute the other 2,125,000 shares to the current owners, use the green-shoe provision, or hold for future sales. It is not uncommon for the original owner to try to maintain control of the company by keeping more than 50% of the stock in his or her own name.

EXAMPLE 15.6 Issuing securities

Problem You have hired Future View Investment Bank to take your company public. Future View has formed a syndicate with Astro Investments and Cartman Bank and has also hired other investment banks to participate in the marketing phase. Future View will remain lead banker and will do a best effort for the shares, with a $2.00 commission on each share sold. The SEC has authorized you to issue 3,000,000 shares of stock. You plan to keep 1,500,000 shares of stock, selling 875,000 to the public, paying off your venture capitalist (Angel Venture Capitalists) with 500,000 shares, and holding back 125,000 shares for Future View's green-shoe provision. The price set for the auction is $20.00 per share. The lock-up agreement prevents Angel Venture or you from selling your shares for six months. At the auction, the bank receives the following bids, and due to the over-subscribed quantity, each bidder receives a pro-rata share or 80% of his or her bid (875,000/1,093,750):

Bidder	Quantity	Pro-rata Share	Shares Received
ABC Pension	300,000	80%	240,000
Farm Insurance	250,000	80%	200,000
D. Trump	53,000	80%	42,400
RET of Oregon	490,000	80%	392,000
Gaius Baltar	750	80%	600
Total	**1,093,750**		**875,000**

Future View decides to exercise its green-shoe provision and buy an additional 125,000 shares at $18.00 apiece. What are the total proceeds for your company? What is the value of the stock held by Angel Venture Capitalists following the auction?

Solution Your company receives $18 per share from the public sale portion and the additional shares of the green-shoe provision:

$$\text{company proceeds} = \$18 \times (875{,}000 + 125{,}000) = \mathbf{\$18{,}000{,}000}$$

Future View Investment Bank nets the following:

$$\text{cash proceeds} = \$2 \times 875{,}000 - \$18 \times 125{,}000 = -\$500{,}000$$

but they own stock worth

$$\text{equity position} = \$20 \times 125{,}000 = \$2{,}500{,}000$$

Angel Venture Capitalists owns stock worth

$$\text{equity position} = \$20 \times 500{,}000 = \mathbf{\$10{,}000{,}000}$$

The key is whether the stock will continue to trade at $20 in the future so that both Future View Investment Bank and Angel Venture Capitalists can get their money back out of future stock sales in the secondary market. If prices should rise, they are better off. If prices should fall, they are, of course, worse off.

As you have seen, the process of raising capital for both start-up and mature companies can require special expertise. One such specialized kind of knowledge required is legal. See the "Putting Finance to Work" feature for a brief overview of the area of corporate law.

Putting Finance to Work

Corporate Law

Raising capital is a highly regulated process in which all participants have complex legal interests to protect. Lawyers with an in-depth knowledge of business and finance are involved at every stage. Although some lawyers spend much of their time in contentious adversarial relationships, corporate lawyers who specialize in financial issues are more likely to be involved in *cooperative* efforts. A business needs capital, and an investor wants to invest. The corporate lawyer's function is to guide them through a complex maze of regulations, documentation, and due diligence so that they can complete the deal.

Although some investors in start-ups may be "angels," their business hardly consists of performing random acts of kindness. The loans that they provide to jump-start businesses have complex structures designed to ensure a high rate of return if the business makes it to the next level and to minimize losses to the extent possible in an inherently high-risk venture. Corporate lawyers for these lenders draft contracts that include myriad details such as benchmarks for progress, conditions under which the companies can terminate the agreement, collateral provisions, and guarantees for loans. As you have seen in this chapter, most venture capital loans include mechanisms for the lender to obtain an equity position in the business and to participate in the initial public offering. The lawyers for venture capitalists conduct due diligence to ensure that the firm has provided complete and accurate financial information, and they also review documents that the borrower's legal representative prepared.

Companies that survive the venture capital stage will at some point issue stock to the public. More established firms regularly borrow money through new bond issues. In both cases, the firms will seek the services of an investment banking firm. As you have seen, the SEC tightly regulates the initial public offering process. Because of the complexities involved, investment banks must employ lawyers who specialize in securities law. Again, they must perform due diligence because any misrepresentation of financial facts can have serious legal consequences.

Lawyers who work with venture capitalists and investment banks usually have degrees from top law schools and work in a few large cities. Opportunities for lawyers with business expertise, however, exist everywhere. Either in a specialized practice or as part of a general practice, lawyers draw up partnership agreements; form corporations; arrange financing between individuals and groups; and advise clients on real estate transactions, taxes, bankruptcies, and a host of other matters requiring business and financial expertise. Almost all medium-sized and large businesses have a legal department. Lawyers with a good background in finance also work for government regulatory and law enforcement agencies. Business, accounting, and finance have become popular majors for students planning to attend law school, and many law schools offer interdisciplinary programs culminating in both doctor of jurisprudence and master of business administration degrees.

15.6 Other Borrowing Options for a Mature Business

So far, we have looked at the mainstream financing of a business as it progresses through the business life cycle. Once a firm reaches a mature business stage, there are many other borrowing opportunities. We will take a look at two of those options: commercial paper and banker's acceptance. We mentioned these concepts briefly in Chapter 12 and will look at them in depth here.

One exception to the requirement of registering with the SEC is if the maturity of the issue is less than nine months, or 270 days. Many large companies are able to use their strong reputations to borrow directly from the public without going through the SEC approval process. One such way that companies can accomplish short-term borrowing directly from the markets is by issuing commercial paper. As its name implies, companies issue **commercial paper** for commercial purposes. It is a discounted note that a company sells directly to an investor with both principal and interest repaid within 270 days. Because the standard face value of commercial paper is typically $100,000, it is out of the reach of most small investors. We generally assume that institutions and sophisticated investors purchase commercial paper. The reason firms issue commercial paper over other forms of borrowing is that they can get lower rates than through commercial banks.

EXAMPLE 15.7 Commercial paper

Problem General Robotics Inc., a large and well-known company, is about to issue $5,000,000 worth of commercial paper. The paper has a maturity of six months (182 days), and the market is willing to pay 97% of par value for it. It will sell the paper with a face or par value of $100,000. How many commercial papers will it sell? What is the cost of this borrowing to General Robotics?

Solution The $5,000,000 quote is usually the face or par value of the entire commercial paper issue, and if it is selling at 97% of par, the proceeds from the sale will be

$$\text{proceeds} = \$5{,}000{,}000 \times 0.97 = \$4{,}850{,}000$$

The cost of this borrowing is

$$\text{six-month interest rate} = \frac{\$5{,}000{,}000 - \$4{,}850{,}000}{\$4{,}850{,}000} = 0.0309$$

Stated annually, we have

$$\text{annual percentage rate} = 0.0309 \times 2 = 0.0618 \quad \text{or} \quad \mathbf{6.18\%}$$

$$\text{effective annual rate} = (1 + 0.0309)^2 - 1 = 0.0628 \quad \text{or} \quad \mathbf{6.28\%}.$$

The total number of sold "papers" will be

$$\text{number issued} = \frac{\$5{,}000{,}000}{\$100{,}000} = \mathbf{50}$$

Another financing technique is the use of a banker's acceptance. A **banker's acceptance** is a short-term credit arrangement created by a firm and guaranteed by a bank, and firms ordinarily use it to finance inventories or other assets that will self-liquidate over a relatively short period of time. Its specific purpose is to promote trade. The best way to describe a banker's acceptance is through an example.

Say a local car dealer wants to expand its car listings to include BMWs, but the local dealer is not large enough or financially strong enough to self-finance the acquisition. The car dealer does have a good banking relationship with the local banker, and the banker is willing to underwrite the purchase of the BMWs from the manufacturer. The manufacturer is in Germany, however, and does not deal with the local car dealer's bank, preferring to work with its own bankers. The dilemma is how to get the local bank's backing to the foreign bank so that BMW is willing to ship the cars to the U.S. car dealer.

The first step is for the U.S. car dealer to negotiate directly with BMW for the price and quantity of cars it wants to buy. For our example, let's assume that the car dealer wants twelve BMWs at an average cost of €50,000 each. BMW will ship the cars as soon as it has a guarantee that the dealer or dealer's agent will pay for the cars.

Next, the car dealer goes to the local bank and shows the banker the order for the cars and the prices. The banker agrees to "loan" the funds to purchase the cars, and the car dealer pledges the cars as collateral for the loan. This agreement is stated in an official letter, which sets forth all the loan details, including that the bank will pay for the cars if the dealer defaults. A bank's acceptance is typically a discount loan, so the letter will state the loan amount and the repayment amount, which includes both principal and interest. For this example, we will say that the repayment is €650,000 at the end of the period.

The car dealer then sends the letter to BMW requesting release of the cars. BMW, in turn, takes the letter of agreement to its bank and asks the bank to "pay for the cars," keeping the loan agreement as its collateral on the purchase of the cars. The foreign bank will issue payment to BMW of €50,000 per car, or €600,000 total (at shipment), and will then deal directly with the U.S. car dealer's bank for reimbursement. The foreign bank "accepts" the transaction by stamping "accepted" on the letter, so that the loan agreement now becomes a tradable asset, *a banker's acceptance*. The foreign bank can hold it for payment or can sell it to another investor. The foreign bank takes titles to all the cars that BMW is going to ship because these cars are the stated collateral on the loan.

The foreign bank notifies BMW that it can ship the cars to the U.S. dealer and that it will pay BMW €600,000. BMW ships the cars and presents the shipping documents (bill of lading) and titles to the foreign bank and in return receives €600,000. The foreign bank is now in possession of the titles and the bill of lading, which represents the collateral for the banker's acceptance.

After the cars ship, the foreign bank will typically sell the banker's acceptance back to the car dealer's bank, say, in this case, for €615,000 (the value of the cars plus a portion of the discounted loan, for a €15,000 profit on the transaction). If the U.S. bank "buys back" the banker's acceptance, the foreign bank is now paid off and ships the loan agreement, bill of lading, and titles to the U.S. bank.

When the cars arrive in the United States, the car dealer goes to the local bank and gets the bill of lading so that importation services can release the cars and move them to the dealer's car lot. The bank retains the titles of the cars. As the dealer sells the cars, it pays back the bank against the loan agreement (banker's acceptance) and gets title to the cars for title transfer to the new owner. When the dealer sells the last of the twelve cars, the local bank has turned over all titles and has received payment of €650,000 or, more likely, the U.S. dollar equivalent of the euros. If the local bank had purchased the banker's acceptance at €615,000, then it will have a profit of €35,000 once all the cars sell. The U.S. car dealer is selling the cars for more than €650,000, and the dealer's profit is the difference between the total sales revenue and the €650,000 payment to the local bank.

Without the banker's acceptance, the U.S. car dealer could not "buy" the BMWs for resale in the United States. In addition, the banker's acceptance is financing a self-liquidating inventory and promoting trade between the United States and Germany.

Commercial paper and banker's acceptances are two of the most common and interesting ways for financing the operations of a mature business.

15.7 The Final Phase: Closing the Business

Both successful and unsuccessful businesses eventually cease operations. When a successful business decides to stop operations, it will sell off its remaining assets, pay off its liabilities, and distribute any remaining funds to the owners. An unsuccessful business may elect to cease operations or may be forced to cease operations. Usually it declares **bankruptcy**, a state of financial distress in which the company cannot pay its debts. There are two paths through bankruptcy for companies, Chapter 7 and Chapter 11, and both are overseen by a court.

Chapters 7 and 11 (Chapter 13 is for personal bankruptcy) of the Federal Bankruptcy Reform Act of 1978 (latest information at www.bankruptcydata.com) are the two chapters for commercial businesses to handle financial difficulties. **Chapter 7** of the Federal Bankruptcy Reform Act of 1978 deals with **straight liquidation**, the selling of the firm's assets. In Chapter 7 filings, the company is ceasing all business operations, and the final act of selling all remaining assets and distributing these proceeds to the legal claimants is governed by a bankruptcy court. A **Chapter 11** filing entails reorganization of a company's business affairs and restructuring of its debt. The company, in effect, asks the court to step between it and its legal claimants to provide the company with an opportunity to work out its financial difficulties without the claimants taking action. Chapter 11 is for a specific time period only and is not a permanent solution to a company's financial difficulties. During this time period, however, the owners cannot try to get their money out of the company, and legal claimants (such as bond holders, suppliers, and employees) are held at bay. The Bankruptcy Abuse and Prevention and Consumer Protection Act of 2005 deals mainly with personal bankruptcy, but does restrict transfers to insiders of any funds or assets of a corporation in distress.

Straight Liquidation: Chapter 7

When a firm can no longer pay its creditors on time, the company or the creditors may file for Chapter 7. If Chapter 7 is granted, an orderly process to close down the business begins. The bankruptcy court judge usually appoints a trustee to oversee the disposition of the assets and payment of the claimants. The order of payment is as follows:

1. Proceeds from the sale of the collateralized assets or transfer of actual assets to secured creditors to settle their claims
2. The trustee's expenses in administering the sale of assets and payment of claims
3. Payment to claimants whose claims result from activities after Chapter 7 filing
4. Company wage earners for unpaid wages (there are limits for this class of claims)

5. Claims for unpaid portions of benefit plans for employees (again, there are limits for this class of claims)
6. Unsecured claims from customer deposits (up to a certain amount)
7. Federal, state, and local unpaid taxes
8. Unfunded pension plans
9. General unsecured creditors (unsecured bank loans, bond holders, and so forth)
10. Preferred stockholders up to the par value of their stock
11. Common stockholders (all remaining funds)

Usually, by the time the trustee reaches the common stockholders, few—if any—funds remain for this last or residual class of claimants.

Reorganization: Chapter 11

Firms do not always opt for Chapter 7, especially if there appears to be a case for reorganization such that the claimants would be better off in the long run compared with estimated payments under Chapter 7 liquidation. A typical Chapter 11 reorganization might proceed as follows. First, either a company voluntarily files a petition for Chapter 11 or a legal claimant (such as a creditor) files the petition involuntarily for the company. A bankruptcy court judge either accepts or denies the petition. Once the judge accepts the petition, he or she then sets a date for all claimants to show proof of their claims. It is necessary to establish all claimants because as the process moves forward, the claimants will have a voice and vote in determining the company's reorganization plan.

The company presents a reorganization plan to the court. The majority of the claimant class members (all bond holders are lumped into one class, all employees are lumped into one class, all shareholders are lumped into one class, and so forth) must approve the plan. If the claimants cannot agree on the reorganization plan, the judge may issue a ruling on all or parts of a plan and thus "decree" the reorganization plan. If a minority of classes does not agree to the plan, the judge may listen to their objections and alter the reorganization plan.

Often, the current managers continue to run the business while it operates under the reorganization plan, but the court may also appoint a trustee to oversee the operations and protect the rights of the claimants during this period of time. The reorganization plan may allow the issuance of new securities and thus add another set of claimants to the firm. Old debt may be restructured in terms of both maturity and rates. The plan itself holds off claimants while the company tries to reorganize and come out of bankruptcy as a new operating firm. If a firm fails to make the reorganization plan work, it will probably fall into Chapter 7 bankruptcy.

We have taken a journey through the life cycle of the firm from the perspective of the most typical financing sources that companies use at each stage. Our view, though, has by no means been an exhaustive one. An important point to take away from the chapter is that at the earlier stages of the business life cycle, there may be limited access to various financing sources. As a firm grows and matures, however, more areas of financing such as bank loans, the bond market, and the stock market become available. The key to successful financing is the ability of a business to generate sufficient cash to pay back its borrowings in a timely fashion.

To review this chapter, see the Summary Card at the end of the text.

Key Terms

angel investor, p. 460
banker's acceptance, p. 478
bankruptcy, p. 479
best efforts arrangement, p. 470
bleed rate, p. 461
burn rate, p. 461
business life cycle, p. 458
Chapter 7, p. 479
Chapter 11, p. 479
commercial paper, p. 477
compensating balance, p. 466
cooling-off period, p. 472
due diligence, p. 470
firm commitment arrangement, p. 470
green-shoe provision, p. 473
indenture, p. 468
investment bank, p. 467
letter of comment, p. 472
letter of credit, p. 466
line of credit, p. 466
liquidity event, p. 460
lock-up agreement, p. 473
pro-rata share, p. 473
prospectus, p. 468
quiet period, p. 472
red herring, p. 472
Regulation A, p. 472
road show, p. 473
sinking fund, p. 469
spread, p. 470
straight liquidation, p. 479
syndicated loans, p. 467
tombstone, p. 472
underwriter, p. 470
U.S. Small Business Administration (SBA), p. 459
venture capitalist firms or funds, p. 461

Questions

1. What are the five stages of a business life cycle? Do all companies go through all five stages?
2. According to the U.S. Census Bureau's Business Information Tracking System, what is the failure rate of companies over the first six years?
3. What is the function of the Small Business Administration in regard to business loans? Who receives the guaranty on the loans?
4. What is the difference between an angel investor and a venture capitalist? What event do these investors want to see happen? Why?
5. What is a letter of credit or line of credit? How does it work?
6. What is the role of an investment bank in selling bonds?
7. What is the role of an investment bank in selling stock?
8. What is commercial paper? Why does it not need SEC approval?
9. Banker's acceptance supports lending for what type of activities? Explain how collateral works in a banker's acceptance arrangement.
10. What is the difference between Chapter 7 and Chapter 11 bankruptcies? Why might Chapter 11 be better for claimants than Chapter 7?

Prepping for Exams

1. In the life cycle of a business, we most closely identify a stable business with ____________.
   - **a.** old age
   - **b.** youth
   - **c.** maturity
   - **d.** infancy

2. Banks and other lending institutions ____________.
   a. frown on family funding for start-up businesses
   b. have lending models better fitted for start-up businesses compared with established businesses
   c. are in competition with the Small Business Administration for start-up loans
   d. are often next sources of financing for businesses after personal and family contributions

3. If the SBA makes a loan guaranty, the guaranty is only ____________. If the original borrower defaults, the government will repay the obligation up ____________.
   a. to the borrower; to the loan balance
   b. to the public at large; to the percentage of the SBA guarantee
   c. to the lending institution; to the percentage of the SBA guarantee
   d. to the lending institution; to the loan balance

4. You have agreed to a $50,000 fixed-rate loan from First National Bank today and promise to repay the loan with thirty-six equal monthly payments at an APR of 6.50%. How large are your monthly payments?
   a. $1,388.89
   b. $1,479.17
   c. $1,532.45
   d. $1,677.71

5. A *letter of credit* or *line of credit* is a preapproved borrowing amount that works much like a ____________.
   a. premium loan
   b. discount loan
   c. syndicated loan
   d. credit card

6. The ____________ is the formal contract for the bond between the issuing company and the buyer.
   a. debenture
   b. sinking fund
   c. indenture
   d. prospectus

7. The process for selling stock for the very first time is ____________.
   a. an initial public offering
   b. a primary market
   c. a first refusal rights
   d. a rookie offering

8. The Bull Bows (BB) investment banking firm has proposed two types of payment plans for the IPO that Johnson JerryRig, a manufacturer of oil drilling equipment, is considering. The first is a firm commitment of $10,000,000. The second is a best effort in which BB will receive $3.00 for every sold share up to a maximum of $1,200,000 for the 400,000 shares offered. How much

money will BB earn under the best efforts method if it is able to sell only 90% of the offering at a price of $30.00 per share?

a. $800,000
b. $1,080,000
c. $1,200,000
d. $2,000,000

9. Asian Motors Inc. plans to issue $3 million of commercial paper with a six-month maturity at 98% of par value. What is the six-month interest rate?

a. 2.00%
b. 4.00%
c. 2.04%
d. 4.08%

10. ____________ bankruptcy allows a company to attempt reorganization under court supervision without claimants taking action.

a. Chapter 7
b. Chapter 11
c. Liquidation
d. None of choices (a) through (c)

Problems

These problems are available in MyFinanceLab.

1. ***Venture capital required rate of return.*** Blue Angel Investors has a success ratio of 10% with its venture funding. Blue Angel requires a rate of return of 20% for its portfolio of lending, and the average length on its loan is five years. If you were to apply to Blue Angel for a $100,000 loan, what is the annual percentage rate you would have to pay for this loan?

2. ***Venture capital required rate of return.*** Red Devil Investors has a success rate of one project for every four funded. Red Devil has an average loan period of two years and requires a portfolio return of 25%. If you borrow from Red Devil, what is your annual cost of capital?

3. ***Straight bank loan.*** Left Bank has a standing rate of 8% (APR) for all bank loans and requires monthly payments. What is the monthly payment if a loan is for (a) $100,000 for five years, (b) $250,000 for ten years, or (c) $1,000,000 for twenty-five years? What is the effective annual rate of each of these loans?

4. ***Straight bank loan.*** Right Bank offers EAR loans of 9.38% and requires a monthly payment on all loans. What is the APR for these monthly loans? What is the monthly payment for (a) a loan of $200,000 for six years, (b) a loan of $450,000 for twelve years, or (c) a loan of $1,250,000 for thirty years?

5. ***Discount loan.*** Up-Front Bank uses discount loans for all its customers who want one-year loans. Currently, the bank is providing one-year discount loans at 8%. What is the effective annual rate on these loans? If you were required to repay $250,000 at the end of the loan for one year, how much would the bank give you on your loan at the start of the loan?

6. ***Discount loan.*** Up-Front Bank is now offering a two-year discount loan for 10%. Working backward, what are the available funds at the start of the loan and the implied balance at the end of the first year if the total lump-sum repayment at the end of the second year is $400,000? What is the EAR of this loan?

7. ***Letter of credit or line of credit.*** As We Go Bank offers its customers a line of credit loan in which each month's outstanding balance requires a 12% APR. What are the required monthly interest payments on the following loans and total interest paid for the year on these loans with a $100,000 credit line?

Month	Outstanding Balance Loan A	Outstanding Balance Loan B	Outstanding Balance Loan C	Outstanding Balance Loan D
January	$22,500	$68,000	$ 0	$53,500
February	$31,000	$82,500	$ 0	$ 0
March	$16,000	$96,000	$ 0	$40,300
April	$24,300	$45,000	$98,000	$ 0
May	$31,500	$13,200	$92,000	$80,100
June	$48,600	$ 0	$95,000	$ 0
July	$37,000	$ 0	$60,000	$65,900
August	$28,900	$ 0	$54,000	$ 0
September	$23,300	$22,000	$36,000	$48,000
October	$24,700	$36,700	$22,000	$ 0
November	$27,600	$48,200	$ 0	$46,100
December	$18,500	$55,900	$ 0	$ 0

8. ***Letter of credit or line of credit.*** In Problem 7, Loan A and Loan D borrow the same amount each year. Loan A, however, borrows every month, and Loan D borrows every other month (note that the borrowing for Loan D for January equals the borrowing for Loan A for January and February). If As We Go Bank charges its customers for the unused balance, which loan strategy is better if the unused balance is charged 3% APR per month by the bank? Which loan borrowing strategy is better for the customer?

9. ***Selling bonds.*** Astro Investment Bank has the following bond deals under way:

Company	Bond Yield	Commission	Coupon Rate	Maturity
Gravity belts	8.0%	2% of sale price	8.0%	10 years
Invisible rays	9.0%	3% of sale price	12.0%	10 years
Solar glasses	7.0%	2% of sale price	5.0%	20 years
Spaceships	12.0%	4% of sale price	0.0%	20 years
Lunar vacations	10.0%	3% of sale price	10.0%	50 years

Determine the net proceeds of each bond and the cost of the bonds for each company in terms of yield. The bond yield in the table is the market yield before the bank charges commission. Assume that all bonds are semiannual and issued at a par value of $1,000.

10. ***Selling bonds.*** Lunar Vacations needs to raise $6 million for its new project (a golf course on the moon). Astro Investment Bank will sell the bond for a commission of 2.5%. The market is currently yielding 7.5% on twenty-year semiannual bonds. If Lunar wants to issue a 6% semiannual coupon bond, how many bonds will it need to sell to raise the $6 million?

11. ***Selling bonds.*** Berkman Investment Bank has the following bond deals under way:

Company	Bond Yield	Commission	Coupon Rate	Maturity
Rawlings	7.0%	2% of sale price	0.0%	20 years
Wilson	7.5%	3% of sale price	8.5%	20 years
Louis Sluggers	7.5%	2% of sale price	9.0%	10 years
Spalding	8.0%	4% of sale price	7.0%	20 years
Champions	8.5%	3% of sale price	6.5%	30 years

Determine the net proceeds of each bond and the cost of the bonds for each company in terms of yield. The bond yield in the table is the market yield before the bank charges commission. Assume that all bonds are semiannual and issued at a par value of $1,000.

12. ***Selling bonds.*** Rawlings needs to raise $40 million for its new manufacturing plant in Jamaica. Berkman Investment Bank will sell the bond for a commission of 2.5%. The market is currently yielding 7.5% on twenty-year zero-coupon bonds. If Rawlings wants to issue a zero-coupon bond, how many bonds will it need to sell to raise the $40 million?

13. ***Firm commitment versus best efforts.*** Astro Investment Bank offers Lunar Vacations the following options on its initial public sale of equity: (a) a best efforts arrangement whereby Astro will keep 2.5% of the retail sales or (b) a firm commitment arrangement of $10,000,000. Lunar plans on offering 1,000,000 shares at $12 per share to the public. If it sells 100% of the shares, which is the better choice for Lunar Vacations? Which is the better choice for Astro Investment Bank?

14. ***Firm commitment versus best efforts.*** Using the information in Problem 13, what is the break-even sales percentage for Lunar Vacations? What are the proceeds to Lunar Vacations and Astro Investment Bank at the break-even sales percentage?

15. ***Issuing securities.*** Bruce Wayne is going public with his new business. Berkman Investment Bank will be his banker and is doing a best efforts sale with a 4% commission fee. The bank has authorized Wayne 5,000,000 shares for this issue. He plans to keep 1,000,000 shares for himself, holding back an additional 200,000 shares for a green-shoe provision for Berkman Bank, paying off Venture Capitalists with 500,000 shares, and selling the remaining shares at $16 a share. Given the bids at the auction (shown on the next page), distribute

the shares to all bidders using a pro-rata share procedure and assume that Berkman Bank takes its green-shoe provision. What is the total cash flow to Wayne after the sale? To Berkman Bank?

Bidder	Quantity Bid
Gotham Pension Fund	2,000,000
Clark Kent Investors	1,100,000
Central City Insurance	600,000
Arthur Curry	400,000
Barry Allen	300,000

16. ***Issuing securities.*** Use the same information from Problem 15. What if the auction bids total only 2,640,000 shares as follows:

Bidder	Quantity Bid
Gotham Pension Fund	1,200,000
Clark Kent Investors	500,000
Central City Insurance	400,000
Arthur Curry	300,000
Barry Allen	240,000

What is the distribution of the shares and cash flow to Bruce Wayne if Berkman Investment Bank declines its green-shoe provision?

17. ***Commercial paper.*** Criss-Cross Manufacturers will issue commercial paper for a short-term cash inflow. The paper is for ninety-one days and has a face value of $50,000, and the company anticipates it to sell at 96% of par value. Criss-Cross wants to raise $3,000,000. What is the cost of this borrowing (annual terms)? How many "papers" will it sell?

18. ***Commercial paper.*** Criss-Cross has decided it will need to raise more than $3,000,000 in commercial paper (see Problem 17). Criss-Cross must now raise $5,000,000, and the paper will have a maturity of 182 days. If this paper has a maturity value of $50,000 and is selling at an annual interest rate of 9%, what are the proceeds from each paper; that is, what is the discount rate on the commercial paper?

19. ***Bankruptcy, Chapter 7.*** Gigantic Furniture is having its annual "Going Out of Business Sale." If Gigantic Furniture is filing under Chapter 7, will it be back next year for another going out of business sale?

20. ***Bankruptcy, Chapter 7.*** A customer and an employee are waiting for payment from Gigantic Furniture after the company has filed for bankruptcy under Chapter 7. The employee's claim against Gigantic Furniture is for $500 for health care benefits that it did not pay to the health care carrier during the last month of company operations, plus $300 for the pension plan. The customer's claim is for $400 for a deposit on a specialty sofa that never shipped. In what order will the bankruptcy courts pay these claims?

Advanced Problems for Spreadsheet Application

These problems are available in MyFinanceLab.

1. ***Issuing stock with an undersubscribed or oversubscribed issue.*** McEwing Investment Bank has worked with Yuu Gaming Company for its initial public auction. The auction is still two weeks away, but McEwing is looking at different scenarios for the upcoming auction. After completing the road show, it has estimated six different scenarios with potential bids for each of its interested clients. It believes that there is a small chance for an undersubscribed sale and it will buy all the remaining shares so that Yuu Gaming Company gets the firm commitment of $35,000,000. The auction is for 2,000,000 shares at $19.00 per share. Here are the anticipated bids from the customers:

Client	Scenario 1	Scenario 2	Scenario 3	Scenario 4	Scenario 5	Scenario 6
A	400,000	400,000	500,000	500,000	600,000	650,000
B	120,000	160,000	200,000	200,000	260,000	350,000
C	630,000	630,000	630,000	630,000	630,000	630,000
D	180,000	220,000	220,000	280,000	280,000	370,000
E	130,000	160,000	200,000	240,000	280,000	400,000
F	140,000	230,000	250,000	350,000	350,000	400,000
TOTAL	1,600,000	1,800,000	2,000,000	2,200,000	2,400,000	2,800,000

For each scenario, determine the allocation of shares and the cost to clients A through F and the number of shares and cost to McEwing. Determine the proceeds for Yuu Gaming in each scenario.

2. ***Firm commitment versus best efforts.*** McEwing Investment Bank have been approached by a new client for issuing stock. McEwing is considering how to structure its compensation for the initial public offering for the client. If McEwing makes a firm commitment, the company would receive $20,000,000 from the stock sale. If McEwing offers to do the sale on a best efforts compensation basis, McEwing will receive a 3.5% commission on all sold stock. The anticipated sale is for 4,000,000 shares at $5.50 per share. Calculate the proceeds to the client and the compensation to McEwing under both methods at 100,000 share increments from 3,000,000 shares (75% of the available shares) to 4,000,000 shares. Find the break-even point in terms of best efforts and firm commitment for McEwing Investment Bank. Graph the two choices (best efforts vs. firm commitment) over the range of potential sales volume using the compensation to McEwing.

MINI-CASE

AK Web Developers.com

This mini-case is available in MyFinanceLab.

From aluminum Christmas trees to ZZ Top's greatest hits: if you can think of it, you can buy it on the Internet. The visible faces of e-commerce are the millions of Web sites that serve as online stores for merchants who may be multibillion-dollar businesses like Amazon.com or individual entrepreneurs working out of a spare bedroom in their home. As computer science majors in 1992, Anastasia Kropotkin and Kristina Petrovich were quick to realize that the supply of aspiring online entrepreneurs greatly exceeded the supply of skilled Web site developers.

Continued

Continued

Anastasia and Kristina became close friends in college. Both had come from Russia to the United States as teenagers, bringing with them strong foundations in math and science. In college, Kristina picked up spending money helping students and faculty members develop individual Web pages. Anastasia worked briefly as the "world's most inept telemarketer," as she styled it, but managed to get transferred to accounting, where she acquired an in-depth knowledge of telephone credit card transactions.

During their senior year, the friends answered an ad pinned to the department bulletin board by the forward-looking owner of several automobile dealerships. He wanted to be the first automotive dealer in the city to have a Web site. His simple requirements at that time were to post phone numbers and locations of his dealerships, store hours, and announcements of special sales and promotional events along with photos of himself, the sales staff, and the latest new car offerings. The dealer was so impressed with Anastasia's and Kristina's work that he referred them to several business associates and provided "angel" financing to start their new business, incorporated as AK Web Developers. He became something of a mentor, offering useful advice on marketing, financial controls, and other management issues.

Fifteen years later, AK Web Developers offers comprehensive e-commerce services, including shopping carts, search engine optimization, graphic design, consulting services for setting up merchant accounts and credit card processing with affiliated banks, and Web site hosting. The business employs nearly 100 programmers, graphic designers, business consultants, and support staff. It has clients throughout North America and a growing business in Eastern Europe.

Five years ago, AK repaid the original $2,000,000 loan given to it by its angel investor. Instead of interest, AK's angel accepted 500,000 shares in the fledgling company. AK then obtained a $6,000,000 loan from MR Venture Capital. The loan required annual interest payments at 5% above the one-year Treasury bill rate. After five years, the venture capitalists had the option of converting the loan principal into 6,000,000 common shares with a par value of $1.00 each. Anastasia, Kristina, the angel, and the venture capitalist group all anticipated that AK would have a liquidity event or initial public offering at that point.

Questions

1. The one-year Treasury bill rates for 2002 through 2006 are as follows:

Year	Rate
2002	2.00%
2003	1.24%
2004	1.89%
2005	3.62%
2006	4.94%

   How much interest did MR Venture Capital receive each year? What was the average interest rate that AK Web Developers paid over the five-year period?

2. O'Brien Brothers Investment Bankers has offered AK Web Developers two options for its initial public offering. In addition to the 500,000 shares held by the original angel and the 6,000,000 shares held by the venture capitalists, AK will offer 5,000,000 shares to the public at $20 per share. O'Brien Brothers is willing to either make a best efforts offering and keep 4% of the retail sales or make a firm commitment offer of $95,000,000. If AK Web Developers expects to sell at least 95% of the shares, which offer should it accept?
3. Describe the steps the investment bankers and the firm must take before and after the initial public offering.
4. The provider of the original angel financing loaned AK Web Developers $2,000,000 at the end of 1994. At the end of 2001, AK repaid the $2,000,000 principal on the loan and gave him 500,000 shares in lieu of interest. At the end of 2007, he sold the 500,000 shares at an average price of $22. What was his rate of return on the original loan? *Hint:* Construct a time line of the cash flows and find the internal rate of return.
5. If MR Venture Capital sold its shares at the end of 2007 for the same $22 price, what was the rate of return on its investment? Include the interest payments calculated in Question 1.
6. Assume AK Web Developers is a typical investment for MR Venture Capital, but only one investment in six is actually successful. What is MR's average overall rate of return? For the sake of simplicity,

assume the five (out of six) investments that fail never make any payments to MR.

7. AK Web Developers also needs to raise $2,000,000 in short-term loans for working capital needs. Which of the following loan offers should it accept?
   a. Interbank offers an annual percentage rate of 6%, but AK must repay the loan in twelve equal monthly installments. This arrangement is acceptable to AK because the need for working capital will decline during the year. Compute the monthly payment and the EAR for this loan.
   b. Bancnet offers a one-year loan discounted at 6%. How much would AK need to borrow to meet its initial need for $2,000,000? What is the EAR for this loan?
   c. Webster Bank offers a one-year loan at 6% add-on interest with a compensating balance of 10%. How much would AK need to borrow to meet its initial need for $2,000,000? What is the EAR for this loan?

Learning Objectives

LO1 Explain why borrowing rates are different based on ability to repay loans.

LO2 Demonstrate the benefits of borrowing.

LO3 Calculate the break-even EBIT for different capital structures.

LO4 Explain the appropriate borrowing strategy under the pecking order hypothesis.

LO5 Develop the arguments for the optimal capital structure in a world of no taxes and no bankruptcy and in a world of corporate taxes with no bankruptcy costs.

LO6 Understand the static theory of capital structure and the trade-off between the benefits of the tax shield and the cost of bankruptcy.

Chapter 16
Capital Structure

You've now seen how a firm raises capital during different stages of its development. How, though, does a firm decide whether to use debt, equity, or a combination of both? In this chapter, we look at how a company finances its operations and growth through various debt combinations (short term and long term), equity, and other securities, a composition that we call its *capital structure*.

In a so-called perfect financial world—one without taxes, bankruptcy, and other imperfections—a company's value is independent of its capital structure; that is, it doesn't matter how the firm is financed. To understand this ideal theoretical construct, think of the firm's value as a giant pie cut into various pieces. The size of the pie doesn't change if you slice it into eighths, sixths, or quarters. It doesn't matter how you slice it. The pie is the same. The same holds true (theoretically) for the firm's value. It doesn't matter how you dice up debt and equity. The firm's value is the same. We'll go into this scenario in more detail later in the chapter when we study two famous financial propositions advanced by two Nobel laureates. Of course, we all know that in the real world there are, indeed, taxes, bankruptcy, and all sorts of financial imperfections, but by looking at capital structure in a perfect world where these imperfections don't exist, we can gain insight on which to build.

After understanding the theory, we'll look at the real, imperfect world and see that capital structure can indeed make a significant difference, especially in regard to taxes. We will explore whether there is a best combination of debt and equity that maximizes the firm's value, creating what we call an *optimal capital structure*.

Before we examine these important financial theories, let's review capital markets and the benefits of borrowing.

16.1 Capital Markets: A Quick Review

In Chapter 8, we looked at the different rates of return over time for some different investment choices. The lowest returns were for short-term government securities, and the highest returns were for small company stocks. In general, the debt market (bonds) had lower returns and lower variances (they were less risky) than the equity markets (stocks). Now we want to flip the coin from the buyer or investor side to the seller or borrower side.

Because a public company is a separate entity, it can acquire funds from all types of investors: banks, bond holders, preferred stockholders, and company owners (the shareholders). These sources of capital, regardless of their classification, all consider their purchases as investments, for which they hope to make a positive return.

First, note that the *return to the investor is the cost to the seller of the financial asset*. So, restating the capital market returns from the seller's perspective, the lowest cost to pay back to the investor is typically in the debt markets, and the highest cost to pay back to the investor is typically in the equity markets. In other words, the highest return to the investor is the highest cost for the seller and vice versa.

Second, not all markets are open to all sellers (companies). The government bond market is open only to the federal government as issuer. The municipal bond market is open only to state and local government agencies as issuers. Obviously, a firm cannot issue debt such as Treasury bills in the government debt market, yet as we saw in Chapter 15, firms can borrow from financial institutions such as banks, sell bonds, or sell stock to raise the necessary capital to fund a project. In that chapter, we took an in-depth look at the different markets available to firms at different stages in their life cycle. Here we want to revisit the cost of capital from the firm's perspective when it raises capital.

When issuing debt, banks quote different borrowing rates to firms, depending on the riskiness of the project.

Two different individuals or companies could go to the very same bank and request exactly the same amount of funding for their projects yet end up paying different costs for their funds. Why? The reason is that one borrower may not have the same resources as the other borrower to pay back the funds. The "riskier" borrower will most likely have to pay a higher cost for funds. In the bond market, we see these different rates as the different yields on bonds for different companies. In the equity market, we see these different rates as the different required returns for companies due to their different betas. In general, the cost of funds for an individual or company will be directly related to the lender's view of the risk of fund repayment. Let's look at two angel investors in Example 16.1 and see why they charge different amounts for their funding to different borrowers.

EXAMPLE 16.1 Different borrowing rates

Problem Angel investors Larry and Sherry see a steady stream of customers wanting funds. On average, they lend $100,000 to each new idea that they think will fly. Larry historically selects low-risk projects or ideas that hit 40% of the time. Sherry historically takes on high-risk projects that hit 10% of the time. What is the minimum rate that Larry and Sherry will offer to their customers on these $100,000 loans?

Solution With Larry's success rate, we know that four out of ten projects are successful and that Larry recoups the loan four out of ten times. Therefore, he must get enough cash from the four successful projects to cover the funding, plus funding for the six failed projects. If he makes ten loans of $100,000 each, he needs to recover $1,000,000 from the four successful projects just to break even. Thus, each successful project must repay $250,000:

$$\frac{\$1{,}000{,}000}{4} = \$250{,}000$$

Therefore, the loan "return" rate must be, at a minimum,

$$\frac{\$250{,}000 - \$100{,}000}{\$100{,}000} = 150\%$$

With Sherry's success rate of 10%, with one successful project out of every ten, we have

$$\frac{\$1{,}000{,}000}{1} = \$1{,}000{,}000$$

So, the loan return rate must be, at a minimum,

$$\frac{\$1{,}000{,}000 - \$100{,}000}{\$100{,}000} = 900\%$$

For Sherry, the one successful project's revenues must cover the funding for all ten projects. Therefore, the rates that Larry and Sherry charge their two customers vary because of the probability of repayment. Larry's rate is 150%, or 6/4 (ratio of failed projects to successful projects), and Sherry's rate is 900%, or 9/1 (ratio of failed projects to successful projects).

Of course, these interest rates allow Larry and Sherry only to break even. If they want to earn a profit on their loan portfolio (investments), they will need to increase their rates. Larry's rate will exceed 150%, and Sherry's will exceed 900%. Larry's rate may seem reasonable compared with those of other angel investors, but Sherry's rate looks extremely high. Why would someone want to borrow from Sherry at a rate above 900%? We will see why in the next section. In short, a borrower who has few borrowing choices may have to go to a source that charges a higher rate.

16.2 Benefits of Debt

Why would anyone ask to borrow money from Sherry at the whopping 900% rate or higher? Let's see how it might play out. Say you have a project that has a 25% chance of paying off $5,000,000 and a 75% chance of paying off $0, but you need

$100,000 for funding no matter what. On average, are you better off borrowing at 900% from Sherry or forgoing this project?

Let's dissect this scenario. The expected payoff from the new project is

$$\text{expected payoff (project)} = 0.25 \times \$5{,}000{,}000 + 0.75 \times \$0 = \$1{,}250{,}000$$

and the expected profit if you borrow from Sherry and will repay $1,000,000 for the loan is

$$\text{expected profit (project)} = \$1{,}250{,}000 - \$1{,}000{,}000 = \$250{,}000$$

So, if you need $100,000 for the project and have no other source of capital but Sherry, and she offers the money at the extraordinary rate of 900%, you are, on average, better off taking the loan. The expected payoff is positive, but your actual payoff is one of two outcomes. Your outcome will either be $4,000,000 profit ($5,000,000 minus the loan repayment of $1,000,000) or a default of $100,000. Sherry will either receive $1,000,000 in repayment and make $900,000 or she will lose the $100,000.

What we see here is the advantage of **financial leverage**, the degree to which a firm or individual uses borrowed money to make money. You are able to make $4,000,000 if the project is successful, but Sherry, the lender, has a maximum profit of $900,000 ($1,000,000 repayment minus the original loan of $100,000). If successful, you are able to borrow the $100,000 at the 900% rate and invest it into a project that earns a 4,900% return ($[\$5{,}000{,}000 - \$100{,}000]/\$100{,}000$). In the investment world, we commonly refer to borrowing funds at one rate and investing at a higher rate to benefit the owner of a new idea as "using other people's money." The more debt a company uses, the greater the leverage it employs on behalf of its owners. We call firms with substantial debt *highly levered*, and we call firms with no debt *unlevered*.

Earnings per Share as a Measure of the Benefits of Borrowing

How do we measure the advantage of financial leverage to the company's owners? One way to see the effect is to examine the company's earnings per share (EPS) before and after borrowing from debt lenders.

Let's examine three companies, identical in every way except in terms of their choice of financing (see Table 16.1). Company 1 is an all-equity-financed firm. Company 2 is funded by 50% debt and 50% equity. Company 3 is 100% debt-financed. Each company produces the same EBIT (earnings before interest and taxes).

TABLE 16.1 Capital Structure of Three Identical Firms

	Company 1	Company 2	Company 3
Assets	$10,000	$10,000	$10,000
Debt	$ 0	$ 5,000	$ 9,975
Equity	$10,000	$ 5,000	$ 25
Share price	$ 25	$ 25	$ 25
Shares	400	200	1

TABLE 16.2 Earnings per Share of Firms with Different Funding Structures

	Company 1	Company 2	Company 3
EBIT	$2,000.00	$2,000.00	$2,000.00
Interest	$ 0.00	$ 500.00	$ 997.50
Net income	$2,000.00	$1,500.00	$1,002.50
Shares	400	200	1
Earnings per share	$ 5.00	$ 7.50	$1,002.50

Now, let's see what the capital structure of each company looks like if each sells its shares at $25 per share and the total required funding for each company is $10,000. The all-equity firm, Company 1, sells 400 shares of stock. Company 2 sells 200 shares and uses $5,000 of debt financing. Company 3 does not issue common stock. Technically, Company 3 cannot exist without an owner, so we will say that the owner here owns a single share of stock worth $25 so that all the income after it pays the interest goes to that single shareholder. We then have Company 3 with one share of common stock and $9,975 of debt financing, making it essentially an all-debt company.

Let's examine the EPS of each firm if EBIT is $2,000 in a world with no taxes. We base the interest payment on the total debt issued. We will assume a cost of debt at 10%.

Table 16.2 shows that when earnings (EBIT) are at $2,000, the more debt the company has sold, the better off the shareholders. Such is the case when the earnings reflect a return greater than the 10% cost of debt.

It can also be the case that selling debt can hurt the shareholders. Let's look at the case when earnings (EBIT) are only $800 for the year as in Table 16.3. Now the advantage swings to the owners of Company 1, the all-equity firm. The earnings are less than the cost of debt, so the more debt, the lower the percentage of earnings available for distribution to the owners.

What have we demonstrated here? We can see that sometimes more debt is good and sometimes more debt is bad. Leverage magnifies both gains and losses. If a firm uses debt to finance an investment and it fails, the loss is greater for the firm and the shareholders than it otherwise might be because of the interest expense. So, leverage depends on how well the company is performing. When a company performs well, it can handle more debt and benefit the owners. Borrowing from debt lenders at one rate and investing the money in the business and making a higher rate are good for the owners. Again, the firm makes money by using other people's money. When a company does not perform well, however, debt amplifies the losses.

TABLE 16.3 Earnings per Share of Firms with Different Funding Structures

	Company 1	Company 2	Company 3
EBIT	$800.00	$800.00	$800.00
Interest	$ 0.00	$500.00	$ 997.50
Net income	$800.00	$300.00	−$ 197.50
Shares	400	200	1
Earnings per share	$ 2.00	$ 1.50	−$ 197.50

16.3 Break-Even Earnings for Different Capital Structures

From the previous section, we see that the three capital structures have different earnings per share as we vary EBIT. We can also solve for the EBIT that produces the same EPS for any two comparable firms. Finding this break-even EBIT will then determine at what level the company should consider using debt. Below the break-even amount, there is no benefit in debt financing. Above the break-even amount, the owners benefit from financial leverage. We will start with the all-equity firm, Company 1 (with no debt financing), and Company 2, with the 50/50 capital structure. We begin by calculating the EPS for each firm:

$$\text{Company 1's EPS} = \frac{\text{EBIT}}{400}$$

$$\text{Company 2's EPS} = \frac{\text{EBIT} - \$500}{200}$$

We then set the two right-hand sides equal to each other and solve for the EBIT that produces the same EPS:

$$\frac{\text{EBIT}}{400} = \frac{\text{EBIT} - \$500}{200}$$

Solving for EBIT, we have

$$200\ \text{EBIT} = 400\ (\text{EBIT} - \$500)$$

$$200\ \text{EBIT} = 400\ \text{EBIT} - \$200{,}000$$

$$\text{EBIT} = \frac{\$200{,}000}{200} = \$1{,}000$$

So, when the EBIT is $1,000, the capital structure is irrelevant to the owners of an all-equity firm or a firm with 50% debt financing and 50% equity financing. Below $1,000 EBIT, the all-equity firm has a higher EPS for the owners, and above $1,000 EBIT, the leveraged firm has a higher EPS for the owners.

We can follow this same procedure with the two other pairings (Company 1 and Company 3 or Company 2 and Company 3), and for this example will find that the $1,000 EBIT has the same EPS across these companies; that is, $EPS_1 = EPS_2 = EPS_3$. So, no matter what the capital structure of the firm, at EBIT of $1,000 owners have the same EPS, as we can see in Table 16.4. The firms' capital structures recall our opening pie example. No matter how you slice the $1,000, the firm's value is the same.

TABLE 16.4 Earnings per Share of Firms with Different Capital Structures

	Company 1	Company 2	Company 3
EBIT	$1,000.00	$1,000.00	$1,000.00
Interest	$ 0.00	$ 500.00	$ 997.50
Net income	$1,000.00	$ 500.00	$ 2.50
Shares	400	200	1
Earnings per share	$ 2.50	$ 2.50	$ 2.50

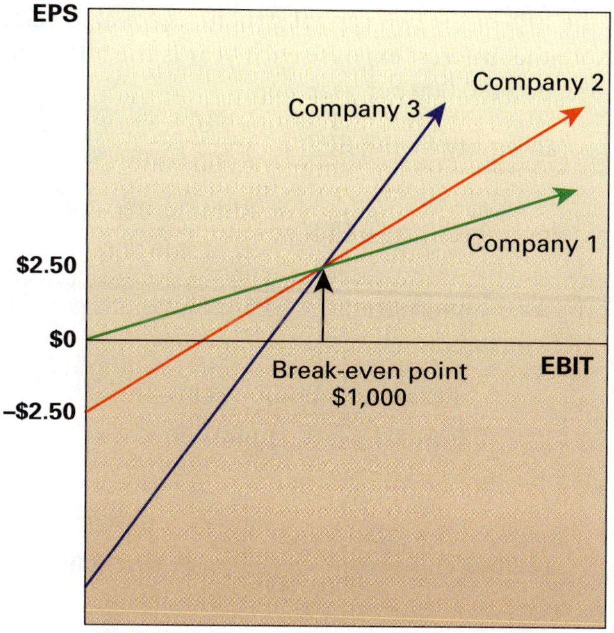

FIGURE 16.1 Earnings per share and earnings for three different capital structures.

The decision on capital structure is related to the company's expected earnings: *the more the earnings, the more debt we should use to finance the company*. The graph of the EPS compared with EBIT in Figure 16.1 illustrates this statement.

All firms on this graph intersect at the $1,000 EBIT and EPS of $2.50. Above $1,000 EBIT, the company with the greatest financial leverage (Company 3) will have the highest EPS. Below $1,000, the company with the least amount of financial leverage (Company 1) will have the greatest EPS.

EXAMPLE 16.2 Capital structure choice without corporate taxes

Problem (A) Jordan Enterprises is looking at two possible capital structures in a world without taxes. Currently, the firm is an all-equity firm, with $12 million in assets and 2 million shares outstanding. The market value of each stock is $6.00. The CEO of Jordan Enterprises is thinking of leveraging the firm by selling $6 million of debt financing and retiring stock in a debt for equity swap. The cost of debt is 8% annually. What is the break-even EBIT for Jordan Enterprises with these two possible capital structures?

Capital Structure Options

	Current	Proposed
Assets	$12,000,000	$12,000,000
Liabilities (debt)	$ 0	$ 6,000,000
Equity	$12,000,000	$ 6,000,000
Outstanding shares	2,000,000	1,000,000
Interest expense	$ 0	$ 480,000
Earnings per share	?	?

Solution Set the EPS of the two capital structures equal to each other and solve for EBIT. Note that interest expense each year is the total outstanding debt of \$6,000,000 at 8%, or \$480,000 per year. So,

$$\text{all-equity firm's EPS} = \frac{\text{EBIT}}{2{,}000{,}000}$$

$$\text{leveraged firm's EPS} = \frac{\text{EBIT} - 480{,}000}{1{,}000{,}000}$$

Setting the two proposed capital structure EPS calculations equal to each other and solving for EBIT, we have

$$\frac{\text{EBIT}}{2{,}000{,}000} = \frac{\text{EBIT} - 480{,}000}{1{,}000{,}000}$$

Solving, we have

$$\text{EBIT} = \frac{\$9{,}600{,}000{,}000{,}000}{1{,}000{,}000} = \mathbf{\$960{,}000}$$

The two EPS calculations are

$$\text{all-equity firm's EPS} = \frac{\$960{,}000}{2{,}000{,}000} = \$0.48$$

$$\text{leveraged firm's EPS} = \frac{\$960{,}000 - 480{,}000}{1{,}000{,}000} = \$0.48$$

Problem (B) Which capital structure should Jordan Enterprises choose if the anticipated EBIT for the coming years is \$1,000,000?

Solution If Jordan Enterprises' philosophy is to take care of the shareholders, select the capital structure with the highest EPS:

$$\text{all-equity firm's EPS} = \frac{\$1{,}000{,}000}{2{,}000{,}000} = \mathbf{\$0.50}$$

$$\text{leveraged firm's EPS} = \frac{\$1{,}000{,}000 - 480{,}000}{1{,}000{,}000} = \mathbf{\$0.52}$$

The leveraged capital structure is better, as we should have known from the calculation of the break-even EBIT. Above \$960,000, the firm is better off using more debt financing.

Financial leverage can make shareholders better off in terms of EPS when earnings are sufficiently high to offset the interest expense of debt. In simple terms, the owners are better off if the company makes more money from the funds it borrowed than the cost of the money it borrowed. In finance terms, the essence of a business is to earn a return on capital that exceeds the cost of capital.

We now turn to the bigger issues of *how much* debt a company should carry and *from whom* the company should obtain funds given a set of potential sources of capital. The company must decide from among all available sources of funds which combination provides the greatest benefit to the firm's owners.

16.4 Pecking Order

Does it matter from what source the company obtains funding? Is there a preferred financing order?

Simple logic tells us we should use the cheapest source first, and then move to the next cheapest source. One theory, in fact, holds that companies do tend to prioritize their sources of financing. According to the theory, they proceed from internal funding to debt and finally to equity as a last resort. This movement from one source of funding to another in a preferred order we call the **pecking order hypothesis**. At its base, the pecking order hypothesis builds from the concept of **asymmetric information**. Information is asymmetric when one party in a transaction has a different set of information from the other party in the transaction. In our context here, asymmetric information means that managers or company owners know more about the company's future performance than do potential outside lenders, which is a realistic assumption.

Thus, with the background ideas of using the cheapest source first and the effect of asymmetric information, we will examine two main predictions of the pecking order hypothesis:

1. Firms prefer internal financing (retained earnings) first.
2. If a firm requires external financing, it will choose to issue the safest or cheapest security first, starting with debt financing and using equity as a last resort.

Let's now take a look at the logic behind these two predictions of the pecking order hypothesis.

Firms Prefer Internal Financing First

Firms tend to use internal funds, or retained earnings, first. To see why, consider your personal finances. What is your cheapest source of money? For many younger students, it is their parents. If parents are typically the cheapest borrowing source, why not exhaust this external source of funds before using up your own internal cash? The reason you would not is that the implicit cost of borrowing from parents may be too high. You are likely to have to field questions about why you need the money, what you did with the money that you received last week, and how much money you have in your account. It may be more efficient to spend your own money first if you have sufficient funds, thereby avoiding the need to answer these questions. In essence, you may prefer not to reveal certain types of information to your sources of capital.

Companies face similar concerns when seeking funding from outside sources. External sources of capital generally require the company to provide private information about the company's plans, current operations, and past performance. If this information is proprietary or if the company does not want to deal with an outside source that requires information about its activities, the company may choose to use only internal funds (assuming they are sufficient for funding a new project).

Firms Choose to Issue Cheapest Security First and Use Equity as a Last Resort

Of course, some projects are too expensive for one's current income, and external funding is eventually necessary. To use a personal finance example once again, the cost of college is one of these expensive "projects" for many and is beyond their current financial capabilities. So, what is the first source of funding to seek? Following is the preferred order—or, more appropriately, the "pecking order"—of college funding:

1. *Scholarships*: These provide money to a student with no requirement to repay the principal and no interest charge.
2. *Parents*: Parents provide money to a student. They may not require repayment, but it may have implicit charges.
3. *Work-study*: This program provides money to a student who repays through labor capital.
4. *Student federal loans*: These loans provide money to a student who begins repayment after completing college with an interest rate generally lower than that of private lenders.
5. *Private loans*: This is a last resort for most students who may begin repayment immediately after receiving the funds and with an interest rate higher than that of student federal loans.

Given a choice, most of us would exhaust the cheapest source of external funding first before moving to the next cheapest source. There are, however, limited dollars available from these sources, and we must compete for them. Students with the best qualifications receive the scholarship funds.

It is the same for companies seeking external funding: they go to the cheapest source first. From our review of capital markets, we have seen that debt is cheaper than equity. Therefore, it follows that firms should first seek debt financing. These lenders (banks or bond holders), however, will have many firms competing for limited dollars, so a firm will need to demonstrate why it is more qualified to receive the lender's money than another potential borrower.

Even if equity is cheaper than debt, could a company still benefit by selling debt when it has debt capacity? To answer this question, let's consider two seemingly identical companies seeking external funding in Example 16.3. These companies appear identical to the outside world, that is, to the potential external debt and equity funding sources. Both companies have **debt capacity**, the ability to add debt financing to the firm's current borrowing and still be able to make interest and principal repayments on time. The managers of the two companies know more about their companies than does the outside world, however, which is the asymmetric information foundation for the pecking order hypothesis.

EXAMPLE 16.3 Debt or equity funding in an asymmetric world

Problem Rogen Industries and Rudd Corporation have new growth opportunities, but both companies are risky. Outside equity investors believe the stocks of the two companies could go as high as $50 over the coming year or fall as low as $35 a share. The consensus, however, is that the shares are probably worth $42. Both companies need to raise $50 million and can seek either debt or equity funding.

The CEO of Rogen Industries knows that the company has a major breakthrough on a new product and the stock will surely rise to at least $50. Much of the information, however, must remain private until the company launches its new product so that the company will not lose market share to competitors. The

CEO knows that if the company is first to market, it will enjoy a long lead time as the only supplier of the product and does not want to divulge any more information than necessary to get the $50 million funding.

Rudd Corporation also has a new product to launch with the $50 million, but it will not cause a major rise in stock price. The CEO knows that any initial surge in market share for a new product is temporary because competitors will quickly be able to imitate it. The company's current value, however, is such that $42 is a fair price for the shares.

How should Rogen Industries and Rudd Corporation raise the $50 million, with debt or equity?

Solution If investors could read the minds of the two managers, they would correctly set the price of Rogen Industries at $50 a share and Rudd Corporation at $42 per share, but the cost to fully inform the investing public may be too much (giving away technology secrets, product designs, marketing plans, and so forth). The CEO of Rogen Industries realizes that the true value of his company stock is $50, but new equity investors are only willing to pay $42, and the CEO chooses to issue debt instead of equity. The CEO refuses to sell stock that is undervalued.

Rudd's CEO, at first, decides to sell stock for the $50 million and wants to issue 1,200,000 shares at $42 a share, but investors realize that a manager will sell stock only if the manager believes it is overpriced when the company still has debt capacity. Therefore, investors assume that this stock is probably worth $35 and will only pay $42 million for the 1,200,000 shares, leaving Rudd Corporation short of its funding needs. So, the CEO must also seek debt financing to get the necessary $50 million.

The end result is that both companies will seek debt financing in a world of asymmetric information when companies have debt capacity.

In summary, there are three implications of the pecking order hypothesis:

1. Profitable companies will borrow less (because they have more internal funds available) and may have lower **debt-to-equity ratios**—ratios showing the proportional mix of debt and equity funding—because they have more debt capacity.
2. Less profitable companies will need more external funding and will first seek debt financing in an asymmetric world, avoiding the equity market.
3. As a last resort, firms will sell equity to fund investment opportunities.

16.5 Modigliani and Miller on Optimal Capital Structure

We now turn to a theoretical model of capital structure that begins with a simple assumption: a firm's investing decision and financing decision are separable. Firms first select what products or services that they will produce (the investing decision) and then select how best to finance these products or services (the financing decision). Although the initial decision of what products and services it should produce has a much larger effect on the firm's profitability, the financing decision is still an important consideration.

Capital Structure in a World of No Taxes and No Bankruptcy

In 1956, two finance professors examined optimal capital structure and concluded that the financing decision was irrelevant in valuing the firm. The professors, Franco Modigliani and Merton Miller, later won a Nobel Prize in Economics for their work. Their first venture into the optimal capital structure question began with a simple model and a hypothetical world of *no taxes* and *no bankruptcy*. As you shall see, they would later modify this initial model and *reverse* their original conclusion. We will now work through their models and examine how the optimal capital structure issue plays out.

M&M Proposition I In their initial work, Modigliani and Miller (M&M) concluded that it is irrelevant how the firm finances its operations in determining its value. They labeled this conclusion **M&M Proposition I**. This first proposition, illustrated in Figure 16.2, assumes a world of no taxes and no bankruptcy. We also represent this proposition in an equation in which the value of an all-equity firm (V_E) is equal to the value of a levered firm (V_L):

$$V_E = V_L \qquad \textbf{16.1}$$

Assume that we have two firms that have selected identical investing choices (in Fig. 16.2, they have the same set of products and services, so the circles of value are of identical size). The only difference lies in their financing choices. Firm E chooses an all-equity financing structure. Firm L chooses to finance with 50% debt and 50% equity. The size of the pie (circle) represents the value of each firm and is determined solely by the cash flow that the selection of products and services generates, not by the capital structure. The value of the unlevered firm is the same as the value of the levered firm.

M&M Proposition I simply states that *the value of a firm does not depend on its capital structure*. In other words, it doesn't matter how you slice it, the value is the same. We can capture the essence of M&M Proposition I with a convenient "Yogi-ism," an expression made famous by or attributed to former New York Yankees catcher Yogi Berra, who fractured the English language in amusing and interesting ways: "Yogi ordered a pizza and when the pizza was ready to be served, the server asked Yogi if he should cut the pizza into four or eight slices. Yogi replied, 'Four, I don't think I can eat eight.'"[1] The size of the pie is the same, no matter how it is sliced. In fact, Miller explained Proposition I to a group of television reporters with just that, a pie metaphor.

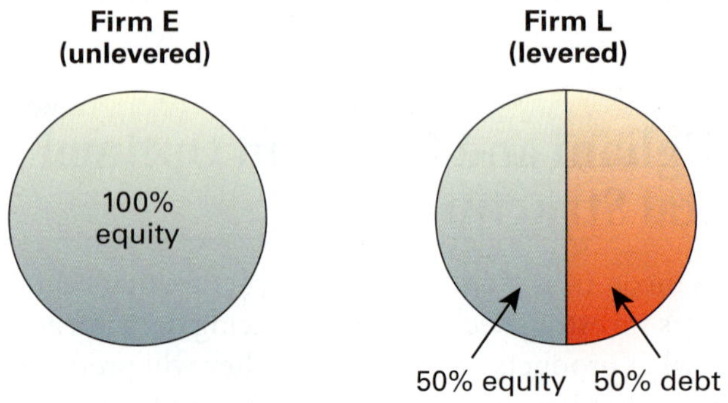

FIGURE 16.2 Value of firms according to Modigliani and Miller's Proposition I in a world of no taxes.

[1]Yogi Berra, *The Yogi Book: I Really Didn't Say Everything I Said* (New York: Workman, 1988), p. 80.

M&M Proposition II If the firm's value doesn't depend on how it structures its financing, then on what *does* it depend? **M&M Proposition II** states that it depends on three things:

1. The required rate of return on the firm's assets (which is the same for firms with identical assets or investment choices)
2. The cost of debt to the firm
3. The firm's debt-to-equity ratio

Recall the weighted average cost of capital (WACC) from Chapter 11. There we noted that WACC is the appropriate discount rate for projects and that it varies as we vary debt and equity weights. Taking the WACC formula and rearranging it twice will get us to the essence of Proposition II.

To illustrate, let's return to our two firms, E and L. We will first determine the value of these two companies from a standard cash flow analysis. We will assume that the companies are in business forever (a perpetual cash flow) and each firm generates \$100,000 in annual cash flow. The cash flow is a simple perpetuity:

$$\text{value} = \frac{\$100{,}000}{r}$$

where r is the desired return of the company owners. If we set r at 8%, we then have

$$\text{value} = \frac{\$100{,}000}{0.08} = \$1{,}250{,}000$$

Now r is both the expected return (from the investor's perspective) and the cost of capital (from the firm's perspective). So, r is the firm's cost of capital, or its WACC. Looking back at the WACC and remaining in a world of no taxes and no bankruptcy, we have

$$WACC = \left(\frac{E}{V} \times R_e\right) + \left(\frac{D}{V} \times R_d \times (1 - T_c)\right) \qquad \textbf{16.2}$$

where E is the equity value, V is the firm's value, D is the debt value, and the corporate tax rate, T_c, is zero. The WACC is also the required return on the firm's assets (the investor's expected return), which we can express as R_a. So, taking out the tax factor (because we are still in a model world of no taxes and no bankruptcy), we can rewrite Equation 16.2 as

$$WACC = R_a = \left(\frac{E}{V} \times R_e\right) + \left(\frac{D}{V} \times R_d\right) \qquad \textbf{16.3}$$

Notice that Equation 16.3 is our first rearrangement of the WACC formula to which we alluded previously: it is the WACC without the tax factor. As we have already stated, M&M Proposition II says that the cost of equity is a function of three things: (1) the required return on the assets (which is the same for firms with identical assets or investment choices), (2) the cost of debt, and (3) the firm's debt-to-equity ratio. We can see this proposition when we rearrange Equation 16.2 a second time by moving the cost of equity to the left-hand side of Equation 16.3 (knowing that $V = E + D$):

$$R_e = R_a + (R_a - R_d) \times \frac{D}{E} \qquad \textbf{16.4}$$

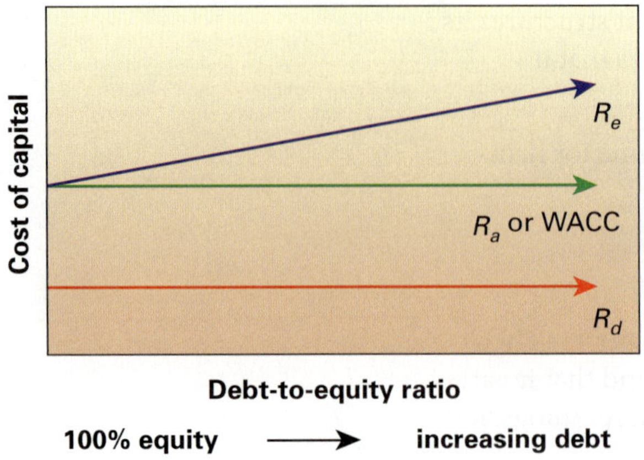

FIGURE 16.3 M&M Proposition II.

The contribution of Modigliani and Miller comes from the constant trade-off ratio between debt and equity. When a firm adds more low-cost debt, it automatically increases the cost of equity so that the overall cost of capital remains constant (the WACC does not change as the funding choice changes). Figure 16.3 illustrates this trade-off and Equation 16.4. Think of the constant trade-off as the slope of the line in Equation 16.4, D/E.

Figure 16.3 plots the debt-to-equity ratio on the x-axis and the cost of equity capital (R_e) on the y-axis. We can see that no matter what the debt-to-equity ratio is, the firm's R_a (or WACC) does not change. *Thus, the firm's value is insensitive to the funding choice between debt and equity.* As a company borrows more and increases its debt-to-equity ratio, the owners raise their required rate of return. Shareholders demand a higher rate of return on equity, shown as the upward-sloping line R_e. To clarify these relationships, let's look at firms E and L in a simple example in which we add more and more cheaper debt and see the rise in the cost of equity that keeps the firm's value constant.

EXAMPLE 16.4 Cost of capital in a world of no taxes

Problem Firm E is an all-equity firm with a required return on its assets of 8%. Firm L is a levered firm and can borrow in the debt market at 6%. Both companies operate in a world of no taxes and no bankruptcy (no risk). If M&M Proposition II holds, what is the cost of equity as Firm L borrows more and more in the debt markets? Solve for each of the following three capital structures: **(A)** 100% equity, **(B)** 50% equity and 50% debt, and **(C)** 10% equity and 90% debt. The firms earn $100,000 every year forever.

Solution Given these three different capital structures, it is necessary to find the required cost of equity, R_e, and then the WACC for each capital structure. The capital structure with the lowest WACC is the best choice. We start with Firm E and use the all-equity firm as the benchmark.

Step 1: Use Equation 16.4 to find the required cost of equity for each capital structure.

(A) All-equity firm E: $R_e = 8\% + (8\% - 6\%) \times \frac{0}{1} = 8\%$

(B) 50/50 firm L: $R_e = 8\% + (8\% - 6\%) \times \frac{0.5}{0.5} = 10\%$

(C) 90/10 firm L: $R_e = 8\% + (8\% - 6\%) \times \frac{0.9}{0.1} = 26\%$

Step 2: Use Equation 16.3 to find the weighted average cost of capital for each capital structure.

(A) All-equity firm E: $WACC = \left(\frac{1}{1} \times 8\%\right) + \left(\frac{0}{1} \times 6\%\right) = 8\%$

(B) 50/50 firm L: $\text{WACC} = \left(\frac{1}{2} \times 10\%\right) + \left(\frac{1}{2} \times 6\%\right) = 8\%$

$$\textbf{(C)}\ \ 90/10 \text{ firm L: WACC} = \left(\frac{1}{10} \times 26\%\right) + \left(\frac{9}{10} \times 6\%\right) = 8\%$$

Step 3: Find the firm's value (using WACC as the appropriate discount rate).

$$\textbf{(A)}\ \ \text{All-equity Firm E: } \frac{\$100{,}000}{0.08} = \$1{,}250{,}000$$

$$\textbf{(B)}\ \ 50/50 \text{ Firm L: } \frac{\$100{,}000}{0.08} = \$1{,}250{,}000$$

$$\textbf{(C)}\ \ 90/10 \text{ Firm L: } \frac{\$100{,}000}{0.08} = \$1{,}250{,}000$$

So, the choice of borrowing does *not* affect the firm's value because the rising required return on equity offsets the lower cost of debt as the firm uses more and more debt in its capital structure. Therefore, capital structure is irrelevant with no taxes and no bankruptcy, and M&M Proposition II holds.

Capital Structure in a World of Corporate Taxes and No Bankruptcy

Modigliani and Miller followed up their initial work with a new model that incorporated a world *with* corporate taxes. The inclusion of taxes turned their original results upside down! So why did we look at a world of no taxes first when we know that taxes are a fact of life? The reason is that to understand how taxes affect the financing choice, we need to have a benchmark against which to measure. Unsurprisingly, it turns out that taxes do indeed turn the original M&M utopian world upside down. So we now progress to a world of taxes and see why leverage is good. You will end up learning that because it takes a smaller piece of the pie every time we add more debt for the government's share (tax collector), the government provides the advantage to leverage.

The two famous M&M propositions with the added tax element are as follows:

Proposition I, with taxes: All debt financing is optimal.
Proposition II, with taxes: The firm's WACC falls as it adds more debt.

Again, we can illustrate the two famous conclusions with simple diagrams. Figure 16.4 shows pie diagrams of two firms—Firm E (unlevered) and Firm L (levered)—each with a 25% corporate tax rate.

Figure 16.4 shows that with the all-equity or unlevered firm (firm E), the company must "distribute" 25% (the quarter wedge) of the firm's value to the government in taxes. When we add debt to the firm as in Firm L, it reduces the government share from its original 25% of the firm's value because the interest the firm pays to the debt holders is tax-deductible. So, in a firm with 50% debt, we have created a tax shield for some of the firm's value. The **tax shield** is a tax-deductible expense that lowers taxes and, all other things held constant, increases the firm's value. It is this tax shield that the firm distributes to its equity holders. Therefore, reducing the government's share of the firm increases the firm's value to the equity holders. The more debt it sells, the greater the tax shield and the smaller the government's share of the firm.

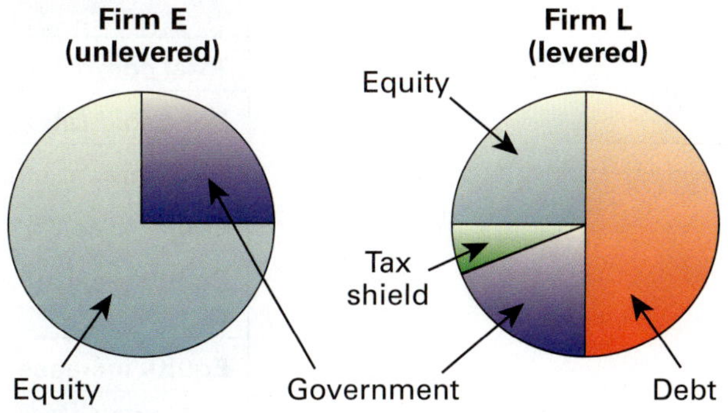

FIGURE 16.4 Value of firms in a world of corporate taxes.

TABLE 16.5 EBIT Distribution to Claimants under Different Funding Structures

	Firm E All-Equity	Firm L 50/50	Firm L 90/10
EBIT	$100,000	$100,000	$100,000
Interest	$ 0	$ 50,000	$ 90,000
Taxable income	$100,000	$ 50,000	$ 10,000
Taxes	$ 25,000	$ 12,500	$ 2,500
Net income	$ 75,000	$ 37,500	$ 7,500
Equity share	$ 75,000	$ 37,500	$ 7,500
Debt share	$ 0	$ 50,000	$ 90,000
Government share	$ 25,000	$ 12,500	$ 2,500
Total value	$100,000	$100,000	$100,000

Debt and the Tax Shield

Let's again return to EBIT to see exactly how the tax shield works. Table 16.5 shows the wealth distributions for three firms with $100,000 EBIT each, but with different debt structures in a world of corporate taxes.

Notice that the three types of firms in Table 16.5 each have the same size of pie—the $100,000 EBIT—to split between the owners, the debt holders, and the government. Think once again of the firm cut into slices: the equity slice, the debt slice, the government slice, and, with taxes, a fourth slice, the tax-shield slice. The equity share gets a smaller and smaller slice of the annual cash flow (the EBIT) as the debt holders receive their interest payments. The government's slice also gets smaller because the cash flow after the interest payment is smaller and it applies taxes after the interest payment. The debt holders, however, must buy their slice of the pie from the equity holders.

Table 16.6 shows the same firms as in Table 16.5 from the equity holders' perspective. Here, we account for the price that the debt holders must pay for their slice of the firm. In the all-equity firm with a 25% tax rate, the government gets one-fourth of the value of the firm. If the firm is making $100,000 per year and the cost of capital is at 8%, the firm's value for both the equity holders and the government is $1,250,000 ($100,000/0.08). The equity holders get three-fourths—$937,500—after taxes, and the government gets $312,500 (the present

TABLE 16.6 Total Equity Wealth

	Firm E All Equity	Firm L 50/50	Firm L 90/10
Total company	$1,250,000	$1,250,000	$1,250,000
Debt sold (*a*)	$ 0	$ 625,000	$1,125,000
Government slice	$ 312,500	$ 156,250	$ 31,250
Equity slice (*b*)	$ 937,500	$ 468,750	$ 93.750
Equity wealth (*a* + *b*)	$ 937,500	$1,093,750	$1,218,750
Equity increase	N/A	$ 156,250	$ 281,250
Tax shield	$ 0	$ 156,250	$ 281,250

value of the future tax stream, \$25,000/0.08). If the equity holders decided to "sell" half the cash flows to bond holders and the bond holders pay \$625,000 for this half of the company, the government's share is now reduced to 25% of the remaining equity holders' portion. So, the government's share shrinks to 25% × \$625,000, or \$156,250 (the perpetuity of the tax flows: \$12,500/0.08 = \$156,250). The government gives up half its share. The equity holders capture this reduction in the government's slice of the pie. So, coupled with the funds it receives from the bond holders, the equity holders' new wealth is \$468,750 (0.75 × \$625,000) plus \$625,000 (from the bond holders) for a total of \$1,093,750. This gain of \$156,250 in value represents the reduced share to the government. If the firm adds more debt, the equity holders will continue to capture the government's lost portion.

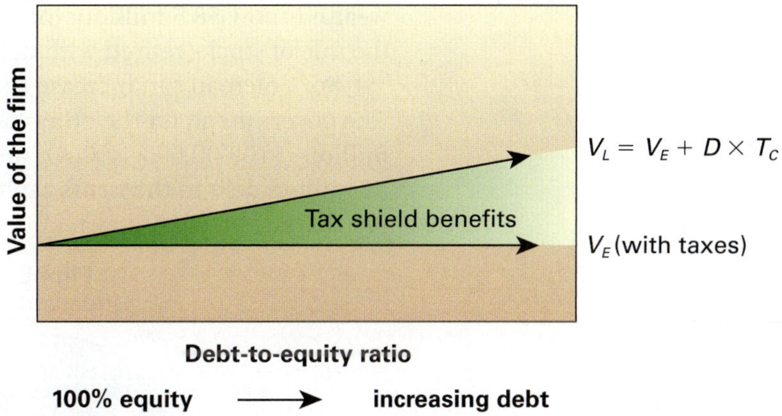

FIGURE 16.5 M&M Proposition II with taxes, where V_E represents the value of an unlevered or 100% equity-financed firm and V_L represents the value of the levered firm.

We can now summarize M&M Proposition I with taxes from the equity holders' perspective as

$$V_L = V_E + (D \times T_c) \qquad \textbf{16.5}$$

where the value of the levered firm V_L is equal to the value of the all-equity firm V_E plus the tax shield, $D \times T_c$. Simply stated, Equation 16.5 says that the value to the owner of a levered firm is equal to the value of that same firm unlevered plus the tax shield from selling debt. When we look at M&M Proposition II with taxes via the WACC (Eq. 16.2), we have (with $T_c > 0$)

$$WACC = \left(\frac{E}{V} \times R_e\right) + \left(\frac{D}{V} \times R_d \times (1 - T_c)\right)$$

Again, we see that as the firm adds more debt, the tax break lowers the overall cost of capital, thereby increasing the firm's value to the equity holder. Figure 16.5 graphically illustrates this point.

EXAMPLE 16.5 Equity value in a leveraged company

Problem Coleman Enterprises resides in a country with a 30% corporate tax rate. Coleman Enterprises currently uses no debt to finance its operations and has a value of \$10 million before taxes. The company's WACC is 20%. Can Coleman increase the firm's value for the equity holders by selling debt? What if the company chooses to have \$5 million in debt? How would that affect the firm's value if it used the proceeds to buy up stock?

Solution The firm's current value is \$10 million. The equity value is currently \$7 million, and the government's value is currently \$3 million at the given tax rate of 30%. So, if Coleman chooses to sell debt of \$5 million, it will have a pretax value of \$5 million for the equity holders and the government. The government's slice is 30% of the \$5 million, or \$1.5 million. The firm's pie is now split \$3.5 million equity, \$5 million debt, and \$1.5 million government. The equity holders' wealth is now \$8.5 million: the \$2 million equity value, the \$5 million cash from the sale of stock (retired with debt proceeds), and the \$1.5 million tax shield.

So, Coleman can increase the firm's value to the equity holders by selling debt. The government, on the other hand, is squeezed out of its original share of \$3 million (\$10,000,000 × 0.30) and gets only \$1.5 million when Coleman adds the \$5 million debt to the firm's capital structure. We can illustrate this result with our pie charts:

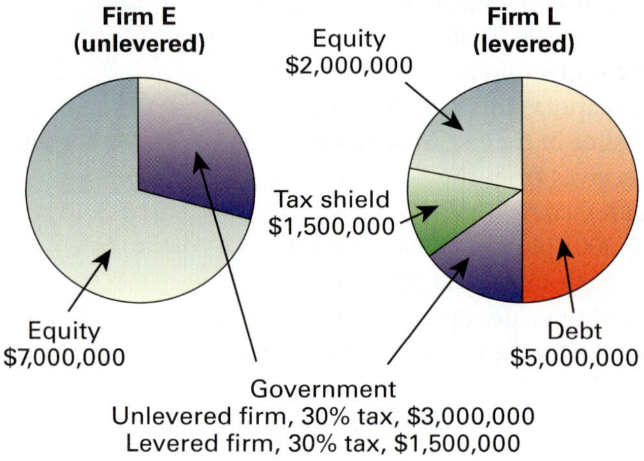

The pie diagrams of Example 16.5 show that as a company adds debt in a world of taxes, the value of the levered firm, from the owners' perspective, increases by the size of the tax shield ($D \times T_c$). The logical conclusion is to add as much debt as possible to increase the firm's value to the equity holders by squeezing the government, but does that make financial sense? This outcome works only in a world of no bankruptcy or, more pointedly, no risk. So, we must add bankruptcy to the model to account for the increasing risk to the equity holders: the rising R_E as we add more debt. Whereas before we saw the tax shield in isolation, we now begin to see the trade-off between its benefits and the potential risk of bankruptcy as the company increases debt. Risk completes the picture, and it is to risk that we now turn.

16.6 The Static Theory of Capital Structure

Although the work of Modigliani and Miller in a world of taxes produced a desired near-100% debt mix for firms, the actual borrowing mix by firms falls well short of approaching 100% debt. In fact, across many different companies, the debt-to-equity ratio hovers closer to 50/50. Why would companies not want to exploit leverage all the way to 100% debt financing? The answer, in a word, is *bankruptcy*. When we introduce risk into the model, we find that the equity holder cannot fully exploit the benefits of the tax shield.

Bankruptcy

As a company adds debt to its financing mix, equity holders reap the benefit of the interest tax shield, but they also bear the risk of potential loss of the company itself. **Bankruptcy** is the point at which the equity value of the firm is zero.

That is, at that point, the value of the assets is equal to or less than the value of the firm's liabilities. We discussed the mechanics of bankruptcy in some detail in Chapter 15. Here we are interested more in the theoretical viewpoint that accounts for the risk that the shareholders bear in a levered company.

With bankruptcy, the equity holders have lost all their value and the debt holders now "own" the company. In practice, bankruptcy takes place when a firm can no longer make its scheduled payments to debt holders. One problem with having considerable debt and thus debt payments (interest expense on bonds, for example) is that when the firm's cash flow is not constant from year to year, the company may be short in meeting its obligations in a down year. Our example of $100,000 EBIT forever assumed that we would generate enough earnings every year to pay the interest on the firm's debt, but what would happen if the firm had a bad year and could not make those payments? If that happens, the firm is in default. Once a firm goes into default, legal proceedings that officially remove the equity holders as owners of the firm may start. A financial institution usually oversees the firm's liquidation and uses the proceeds from selling the assets to pay off the liability claims. In essence, the equity holders lose the firm to the debt holders. Therefore, with uncertainty about future earnings, the possibility of bankruptcy may limit the amount of debt funding a firm chooses to use.

Bankruptcy entails both direct and indirect costs. When a firm cannot meet its debt payments on time and moves through the legal process to turn over its assets to the debt holders, legal and administrative fees arise, called the **direct costs of bankruptcy**. Such costs also reduce funds available to pay the debt holders because administrative fees are first in line for payment in bankruptcy.

Prior to bankruptcy proceedings, the shareholders still remain in control of the firm and the firm's assets. Knowing that in bankruptcy the shareholders may lose all their wealth in the firm, managers acting in the interest of shareholders try to avoid it. As managers' attention turns from running the business to saving the business, additional costs—the **indirect costs of bankruptcy**, which we call **financial distress costs**—arise. During times of financial distress, a firm may lose sales, valuable employees may leave, customers may lose confidence in the firm's products and services, and projects with good long-term future payouts are forgone to preserve cash. The greater the amount of debt that a firm carries, the greater the chance of bankruptcy and therefore the higher the potential financial distress costs.

To see how high levels of leverage can lead to financial distress and bankruptcy, see the nearby "Finance Follies" feature about high leverage investments.

Static Theory of Capital Structure

The optimal capital structure comes at the point where the additional tax-shield benefit of adding one more dollar of debt financing is equal to the direct and indirect costs of bankruptcy from that extra dollar of debt. Past this point, adding one more dollar of debt financing makes the equity holder worse off. We find this balance of benefits and costs of debt financing at the **optimal debt-to-equity ratio** the **static theory of capital structure**. So, once the firm fixes (static) the assets and operations, we can consider the optimal way to finance the firm. Figure 16.6 demonstrates that, theoretically, there is an optimal debt-to-equity ratio at the point where the marginal benefits of the tax shield equal the marginal costs of bankruptcy. Thus, the optimal capital structure of a firm falls somewhere short of 100% debt financing.

FIGURE 16.6 The static theory of finance.

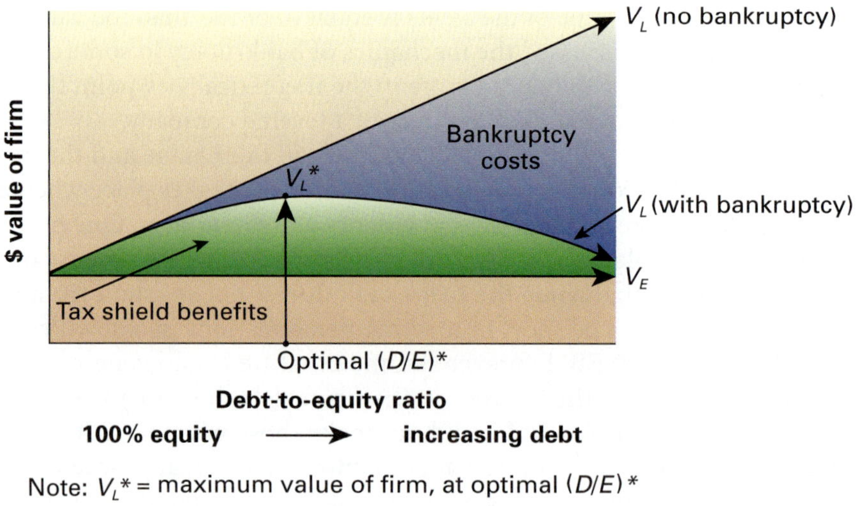

FINANCE FOLLIES

Hedge Funds: Some Really Smart Guys Get into Big Trouble

The verb *hedge* means to protect by leaving an escape route or taking an offsetting position. The early hedge funds employed conservative and relatively simple strategies such as simultaneously buying and selling the same security to make a small gain if the bet was successful, but limiting losses if it was not. Another typical transaction involved nearly identical bonds selling at slightly different prices. By buying the under-priced bonds and selling the overpriced bonds, a fund could make a small profit when the prices eventually converged. It was like betting that the odds-on favorite in a horse race would finish in third place or better. You might have a good chance of winning such a bet, but your payoff would never be very large.

Unlike mutual funds, hedge funds are private investment pools, open only to "qualified investors," defined by law as individuals with a net worth of $1 million or more or institutions with more than $5 million. Under the dubious assumption that wealthy clients must be sophisticated investors, the Securities and Exchange Commission does not regulate the investment activities of hedge funds or require them to disclose their portfolios or to exercise prudence in managing their risks.

The ability to operate secretly in an unregulated environment attracts brilliant eccentrics with an appetite for risk. One of the most famous is Ed Thorp, University of California math professor and author of a famous book on blackjack strategy that got him banned from Las Vegas casinos. He was a founding partner of Princeton/Newport Partners, which used arcane mathematical strategies to achieve 15% returns for several years. The fund dissolved in 1988 after then U.S. Attorney General Rudolph Giuliani charged several partners, but not Thorp, in a junk bond insider trading scandal. Another is Ken Griffin, a computer programming prodigy who began trading stocks as a Harvard undergraduate and was still in his twenties when he founded Citadel, a hedge fund that initially produced market-beating returns by using computing power and mathematical techniques to find mispriced convertible bonds. Griffin built Citadel into a huge, diversified investment firm, but it came close to bankruptcy in 2008. To save the firm, Griffin refused to allow investors to withdraw funds.

Perhaps no hedge fund ever employed more brain power than Long-Term Capital Management (LTCM). The name certainly suggests a cautious, patient approach to wealth creation. John Meriwether, one of Wall Street's most successful and experienced executives, founded the firm, which at one time boasted a staff of more than twenty Ph.D.s, including Myron Scholes and Robert Merton, who shared the Nobel Prize in Economics in 1997. Only four years after its founding in 1994, however, LTCM began to lose such spectacular amounts of money for its elite institutional clientele that the Federal Reserve Bank was obliged to intervene to prevent an international financial disaster. Six years after its founding, the fund had failed and was gone.

Through skill or luck, LTCM did very well in its first three years, averaging annual returns of close to 40%. It used these returns and the reputation of its principals to justify fees that were twice those charged by other hedge funds. In 1997, however, LTCM returned only 17%. In that same year, a relatively conservative investment in the Standard & Poor's 500 stock index would have earned more than 30%. By 1998, hedge fund competition was intense, low-risk trades were hard to find, and LTCM's luck was running out. To match its earlier performance, it was not enough for LTCM to make riskier trades; it had to use increasing amounts of leverage. Of course, every student who has made it this far in the study of finance knows that leverage works both ways, multiplying profits and losses equally. By August 1998, LTCM's debt-to-equity ratio was 50; in other words, it had a bit more than 98 cents of debt for every $1.00 of assets. A mere 2% operating loss would completely wipe out its equity.

That same month, the market turned completely against LTCM's positions, and the fund lost $600 million in two days. That was enough for anxious investors, who insisted on withdrawing their funds. Of course, LTCM did not have the cash to meet their demands. With $300 billion under LTCM's management, Alan Greenspan, then chairman of the Federal Reserve Bank, feared the hedge fund's failure could trigger an international financial panic. With a persuasive combination of bribes and threats, he convinced a group of the largest financial institutions to orchestrate a painful but orderly plan to sell LTCM's remaining assets and dissolve the fund. Meriwether, Scholes, and Merton, who had recently been multimillionaires on paper, lost their entire personal stakes in LTCM.

Rather than learn from LTCM's failure, over the next decade, hedge funds engineered ever more novel ways to increase their leverage. The internal hedge funds at once staid investment banks like Bear Sterns, Lehman Brothers, and Merrill Lynch used short-term debt to buy derivative investments such as credit default swaps that are intrinsically highly leveraged, meaning that a small change in the value of the underlying assets (mortgage pools) could cause huge changes in the value of the derivative. In other words, they leveraged their balance sheets to buy leveraged investments. When real-estate prices started to decline, the outcome was inevitable. Early in 2008, J. P. Morgan bought Bear Stearns, which traded at $170 per share a year earlier, for $10 per share, technically saving it from bankruptcy. Merrill Lynch met a similar fate in a forced sale to Bank of America. Later in the year, the Federal Reserve allowed Lehman Brothers to fail. The shareholders and bond holders lost everything.

For the time being, risky investments are out of fashion; conservative balance sheets are in. But the surviving hedge funds remain unregulated, still operate in the dark, and still recruit the best mathematical and programming talent from elite universities around the world. These highly paid financial engineers are not cooking up novel ways to earn average returns with a minimum of risk to their firms and financial markets.

Sources: Scott Patterson, *The Quants* (New York: Crown Business, 2010); Sebastian Mallaby, *More Money than God* (New York: Penguin, 2010).

Figure 16.6 shows that the firm achieves its highest value at the optimal debt-to-equity ratio (D/E^*). At this point, the cost of capital (WACC) is the lowest for the firm, implying the maximum benefit to the firm from financial leverage. Past this point, the WACC begins to rise when the firm adds more debt to its financing structure. This is due to the costs associated with the increasing possibility of bankruptcy. A rising WACC reduces the value of the firm's future cash flows and thus its present value.

There is one final question: Do all companies have the same optimal debt-to-equity structure? The answer is no. Think about different industries and their ability to carry debt based on the volatility of their cash flows and recall our Chapter 14 comparison of different financial ratios across different industries. Table 16.7 shows financial ratios across some different industries, with the debt-to-equity ratio highlighted in red.

Table 16.7 shows that the airline industry, in general, uses the most debt and the pharmaceutical industry uses the least amount of debt. One can understand why airlines use so much debt with the requirement to lease a large fleet of airplanes to provide their service and the airplanes serving as collateral for the debt. The pharmaceutical industry, with so much of its activities in research, has a lower asset base for collateral on its debt.

TABLE 16.7 Financial Ratios: Industry Averages

	Airlines	Auto	Pharmaceutical	Oil and Gas	Retail	Computer Hardware
Price-to-earnings ratio	22.44	7.38	87.80	5.39	34.29	20.97
Gross margin*	19.8%	21.77%	59.54%	47.47%	24.51%	43.54%
Profit margin*	0.75%	3.79%	14.85%	12.14%	2.94%	17.08%
Current ratio	0.92	0.32	2.77	1.11	1.23	2.86
Debt-to-equity ratio	1.69	0.34	0.11	0.19	0.81	0.19
Return on assets*	0.70%	3.57%	9.40%	12.11%	6.31%	18.22%
Return on equity*	0.77%	10.17%	14.71%	20.10%	16.82%	26.24%

*Five-year average
Source: Reuters, www.investors.reuters.com.

We can now review the three scenarios of optimal capital structure with the M&M propositions and bankruptcy.

1. *No taxes, no bankruptcy*. In a world of no taxes and no bankruptcy, the firm's value is indifferent to its capital structure because the cost of capital is constant across all potential debt-to-equity ratios.
2. *Taxes, no bankruptcy*. In this world of taxes and no bankruptcy, the firm's value is greatest with 100% debt financing. The optimal capital structure and lowest cost of capital occur when the firm uses only debt financing.
3. *Taxes, bankruptcy.* In a world of taxes and bankruptcy, the firm's maximum value is the point where the marginal benefit of financial leverage (the tax shield) is equal to the marginal cost of bankruptcy (financial distress costs). It is where the cost of capital is lowest.

In conclusion, the optimal capital structure falls short of the choice of 100% debt financing. The company's **optimal capital structure** is the combination of debt and equity from various funding sources that provides the lowest overall cost of capital, or the lowest WACC. It is a function of the cost of capital of the different funding components, the tax structure, and the potential for bankruptcy.

To review this chapter, see the Summary Card at the end of the text.

Key Terms

Questions

1. What is the difference between the return to an investor or lender and the cost to the borrower?
2. Why would one lender charge more for a loan to different borrowers? Why would two different lenders charge different rates to the same borrower?
3. What is the advantage of financial leverage, the degree to which a firm or individual uses borrowed money to make money?
4. How do we measure the advantage of financial leverage to the company's owners?
5. In what way is the decision on capital structure related to the company's expected earnings?
6. What is asymmetric information? How does it affect the prioritization of financing sources under the pecking order hypothesis?
7. What does it mean when one states that the operating and financing decisions are separate from each other? How do we view the financing decision in terms of the magnitude of effect?
8. Explain why M&M Proposition I in a world of no taxes and no bankruptcy states that the firm's value does not depend on its capital structure.
9. Who loses out on a company's cash flow when it adds more and more debt to the financing structure? Who gains as a company adds more and more debt?
10. In a world of taxes and no bankruptcy, why is a company's optimal capital structure all debt? What happens when a company adds bankruptcy to the world of taxes with regard to the optimal capital structure?
11. In the static theory of capital structure, what is static?
12. In the static theory of capital structure, how do you find a firm's optimal capital structure? In other words, what benefit are you receiving as you add debt, and what cost are you incurring when you add debt?

Prepping for Exams

1. The return to the investor is the ______________.
   - **a.** reward to the borrower
   - **b.** cost to the borrower
   - **c.** cost to the manager
   - **d.** internal rate of return

2. Investors Al and Bea lend $100,000 to each new idea. Al historically selects low-risk projects or ideas that hit 80% of the time. Bea historically takes on high-risk projects that hit 40% of the time. What rate of return must each successful project pay Al and Bea for them to break even?
   - **a.** Al's rate is 150%, and Bea's rate is 25%.
   - **b.** Al's rate is 40%, and Bea's rate is 40%.
   - **c.** Al's rate is 25%, and Bea's rate is 150%.
   - **d.** Al's rate is 30%, and Bea's rate is 150%.

3. Buck Stops Here Inc. has a project that costs $900,000. It has a 50% chance of paying off $2,000,000 and a 50% chance of paying off $0. What is its expected payoff and its expected profit or loss from the new project?

a. The expected payoff is $1,000,000, and the expected loss is $10,000.
b. The expected payoff is $100,000, and the expected profit is $10,000.
c. The expected payoff is $100,000, and the expected loss is $100,000.
d. The expected payoff is $1,000,000, and the expected profit is $100,000.

4. Donat Corp. is a small company looking at two possible capital structures. Currently, the firm is an all-equity firm with $600,000 in assets and 100,000 shares outstanding. The market value of each share is $6.00. The CEO of Donat is thinking of leveraging the firm by selling $300,000 of debt financing and retiring 50,000 shares, leaving 50,000 shares outstanding. The cost of debt is 5% annually, and the current corporate tax rate for Donat is 30%. The CEO believes that Donat will earn $50,000 per year before interest and taxes. Which of the statements below is true?

a. The all-equity EPS is $0.35.
b. 50/50 debt to equity EPS is $0.49.
c. Shareholders will be better off with a price of $0.14 per share under a firm with $300,000 in debt financing versus a firm that is all equity.
d. Statements (a) through (c) are all true.

5. Moving from one source of funding to another in a particular order is the ______________.

a. pecking order hypothesis
b. barnyard order hypothesis
c. funding order hypothesis
d. capital market hypothesis

6. M&M Proposition I states that, in a world of no taxes and no bankruptcy, ______________.

a. the cost of debt increases with leverage
b. the choice of financing is relevant to determining the firm's value in the short run
c. how the company finances its operations affects the firm's value
d. how the company finances its operations does not affect the firm's value

7. M&M Proposition II suggests that in a world of no taxes and no bankruptcy, ______________.

a. no matter what the debt-to-equity ratio is, the firm's R_a or the WACC increases with debt
b. the firm's value is sensitive to the funding choice between debt and equity
c. in simple terms, as the firm adds more debt to the financing mix, the shareholders require a higher and higher return on equity such that it exactly offsets the use of the cheaper debt.
d. Statements (a) through (c) are all incorrect.

8. Consider Modigliani and Miller's world of corporate taxes. An unleveraged (all-equity) firm's value is $100 million. By adding debt, the annual interest expense is $10 million, the corporate tax rate is 40%, and the discount rate on the tax shield is 10%. What is the gain from leverage or the value added from issuing debt?

a. $100 million
b. $120 million

c. $140 million
d. $160 million

9. The indirect costs of bankruptcy can include which of the following?
   a. setting aside projects with good NPVs
   b. lost sales
   c. loss of confidence in the firm's products and services
   d. all of the above

10. When a firm adds bankruptcy to Modigliani and Miller's world of capital structure, which of the following statements is *true* as the firm adds more debt to its financing mix?
    a. Equity holders increase their rate of return.
    b. The advantage of the tax shield starts to be offset by financial distress costs.
    c. The company's WACC starts to increase past a certain level of debt.
    d. Statements (a) through (c) are all correct.

Problems

These problems are available in MyFinanceLab.

1. ***Different loan rates.*** Winthrop Enterprises is a holding company (a firm that owns all or most of some other companies' outstanding stock). Winthrop has four subsidiaries. Each subsidiary borrows capital from the parent company for projects. Ervin Company is successful with its projects 85% of the time, Morten Company 92% of the time, Richmond Company 78% of the time, and Garfield Company 83% of the time. What loan rates should Winthrop Enterprises charge each subsidiary for loans?
2. ***Different loan rates.*** Keith Peterson is the CFO of Springfield Soups and Sauces. The company's typical success rate for new products is 88%. Keith wants to improve this success rate to 94%. What loan improvement (in terms of rates) would do that for Springfield Soups and Sauces?
3. ***Benefits of borrowing.*** Wilson Motors is looking to expand its operations by adding a second manufacturing location. If successful, the company will make $450,000. If it fails, the company will lose $250,000. Wilson Motors is trying to decide whether it should borrow the $250,000 given the current bank loan rate of 15%. Should Wilson Motors borrow the money if
   a. the probability of success is 90%?
   b. the probability of success is 80%?
   c. the probability of success is 70%?
4. ***Benefits of borrowing.*** What is the break-even probability of success at the 15% borrowing rate in Problem 3? What is the break-even probability of success if the loan rate is 20%?
5. ***Break-even EBIT (with and without taxes).*** Alpha Company is looking at two different capital structures, one an all-equity firm and the other a leveraged firm with $2 million of debt financing at 8% interest. The all-equity firm will have a value of $4 million and 400,000 shares outstanding. The leveraged firm will have 200,000 shares outstanding.
   a. Find the break-even EBIT for Alpha Company using EPS if there are no corporate taxes.

b. Find the break-even EBIT for Alpha Company using EPS if the corporate tax rate is 30%.
c. What do you notice about these two break-even EBITs for Alpha Company?

6. ***Break-even EBIT (with taxes).*** Beta, Gamma, and Delta companies are similar in every way except for their capital structures. Beta is an all-equity firm with $3,600,000 of value and 100,000 shares outstanding. Gamma is a levered firm with the same value as Beta, but $1,080,000 in debt at 9% and 70,000 shares outstanding. Delta is a levered firm with $2,160,000 in debt at 12% and 40,000 shares outstanding. What are the break-even EBITs for Beta and Gamma, Beta and Delta, and Gamma and Delta companies if the corporate tax rate is 40% for all three companies?

7. ***Pecking order hypothesis.*** Rachel can raise capital from the following sources:

Source of Funds	Interest Rate	Borrowing Limit
Parents	0%	$10,000
Friends	5%	$ 2,000
Bank loan	9%	$15,000
Credit card	14.5%	$ 5,000

What is Rachel's weighted average cost of capital if she needs to raise
a. $10,000?
b. $20,000?
c. $30,000?

8. ***Pecking order hypothesis.*** Ross Enterprises can raise capital from the following sources:

Source of Funds	Interest Rate	Borrowing Limit
Small business bureau	6%	$50,000
Bank loan	8%	$40,000
Bond market	11%	$60,000
Owners' equity (stock)	16%	$80,000

Ross has a new project that has an estimated IRR of 12%, but will require an investment of $200,000. Should Ross borrow the money and invest in the new project?

9. ***Finding the WACC.*** Monica is the CFO of Cooking for Friends (CFF) and uses the pecking order hypothesis philosophy when she raises capital for company projects. Currently, she can borrow up to $600,000 from her bank at a rate of 8.5%, float a bond for $1,100,000 at a rate of 9.25%, or issue additional stock for $1,300,000 at a cost of 17%. What is the WACC for CFF if Monica chooses to invest:
a. $1,000,000 in new projects?
b. $2,000,000 in new projects?
c. $3,000,000 in new projects?

10. ***Finding the WACC.*** Chandler has been hired by Cooking for Friends to raise capital for the company. Chandler increases the funding available from the bank to $900,000, but with a new rate of 8.75%. Using the data in Problem 9, determine what the new WACC is for borrowing $1,000,000, $2,000,000, and $3,000,000.

11. ***Modigliani and Miller's world of no taxes.*** Air Seattle is looking to change its capital structure from an all-equity firm to a leveraged firm with 50% debt and 50% equity. Air Seattle is a not-for-profit company and therefore pays no taxes. If the required rate on the assets (R_a) of Air Seattle is 20%, what is the current required cost of equity? What are the new required costs of equity if the cost of debt is 10%?

12. ***Modigliani and Miller's world of no taxes.*** Roxy Broadcasting Inc. is currently a low-leveraged firm with a debt-to-equity ratio of 1/3. The company wants to increase its leverage to 3/1 for debt to equity. If the current return on assets is 14% and the cost of debt is 11%, what is the current and new cost of equity if Roxy operates in a world of no taxes?

13. ***Modigliani and Miller's world of taxes.*** Air Seattle from Problem 11 has lost its not-for-profit status, and the corporate tax rate is now 35%. If Air Seattle's value was $5,000,000 as an all-equity firm, what is its value under a 50/50 debt-to-equity ratio? Assume the $5,000,000 is the after-tax value of the unlevered firm.

14. ***Modigliani and Miller's world of taxes.*** Roxy Broadcasting in Problem 12 was originally an all-equity firm with a value of $25,000,000. Roxy now pays taxes at a 40% rate. What is the value of Roxy under the 1/3 debt to equity capital structure? Under the 3/1 capital structure?

15. ***Size of tax shield.*** Using the information from Problems 11 and 13 on Air Seattle, determine the size of the tax shield with a corporate tax rate of 15%, 25%, 35%, and 45% if Air Seattle's capital structure is 50/50 debt to equity.

16. ***Size of tax shield.*** Using the information from Problems 12 and 14 on Roxy Broadcasting, determine the size of the tax shield with a corporate tax rate of 15%, 25%, 35%, and 45% if Roxy's capital structure is 1/3 debt to equity. Determine the same if the capital structure is 3/1.

17. ***Equity value in a levered firm.*** Air Seattle has an annual EBIT of $1,000,000, and the WACC in the unlevered firm is 20%. The current tax rate is 35%. Air Seattle will have the same EBIT forever. If the company sells debt for $2,500,000 with a cost of debt of 20%, what is the value of equity in the unlevered firm and in the levered firm? What is the value of debt in the levered firm? What is the government's value in the unlevered firm and in the levered firm?

18. ***Equity value in a levered firm.*** Roxy Broadcasting has an annual EBIT of $3,500,000 and a WACC of 14%. The current tax rate is 40%. Roxy will have the same EBIT forever. The company currently has debt of $6,250,000 with a cost of debt of 14%. Roxy will sell $12,500,000 more of debt and retire stock with the proceeds. What is the value of equity in the higher-levered firm? What is the government's value in the higher-levered firm?

Advanced Problems for Spreadsheet Application

These problems are available in MyFinanceLab.

1. ***Break-even EBIT for different capital structures in a world of no taxes.*** Jordan Enterprises is looking at five different capital structures. Each structure uses an increasing amount of debt financing. The first structure is an all-equity structure whereby Jordan Enterprises will raise $40,000,000 by selling 10,000,000 shares of stock for $4 each. The next structure uses $5,000,000 of debt at a cost of 7.5% annually and reduces the number of shares outstanding

to 8,750,000 shares. Each successive capital structure will add $5 million in debt and reduce the number of shares outstanding by 1,250,000 shares. In the final capital structure model, there is 50% debt ($20,000,000) and 50% equity (5,000,000 shares outstanding). For potential values of EBIT between $25 million and $35 million at $500,000 increments, find the earnings per share (EPS) at each increment. At what EBIT do all five capital structures give the same EPS? Graph the EPS for each capital structure across the EBIT range of $0 to $5,000,000. Based on the graph and EPS at each EBIT, what capital structure should Jordan Enterprise choose?

2. ***Break-even EBIT for different capital structures in a world of taxes.*** Jordan Enterprises is looking at five different capital structures. Each structure uses an increasing amount of debt financing. The first structure is an all-equity structure whereby Jordan Enterprises will raise $40,000,000 by selling 10,000,000 shares of stock for $4 each. The next structure uses $5,000,000 of debt at a cost of 7.5% annually and reduces the number of shares outstanding to 8,750,000 shares. Each successive capital structure will add $5 million in debt and reduce the number of shares outstanding by 1,250,000 shares. In the final capital structure model, there is 50% debt ($20,000,000) and 50% equity (5,000,000 shares outstanding). The tax rate for Jordan Enterprises is 35%. For potential values of EBIT between $25 million and $35 million at $500,000 increments, find the EPS at each increment. At what EBIT do all five capital structures give the same EPS? Graph the EPS for each capital structure across the EBIT range of $0 to $5,000,000. Based on the graph and EPS at each EBIT, what capital structure should Jordan Enterprise choose?

Mini-Case

General Energy Storage Systems: How Much Debt and How Much Equity?

This mini-case is available in MyFinanceLab.

General Energy Storage Systems (GESS) was founded in 2002 by Ian Redoks, a Ph.D. candidate in physics who was interested in "outside-the-box" solutions to the problem of storing electrical energy. Redoks had obtained several patents with potential applications for plug-in hybrid cars, off-grid home electrical systems, and large-scale storage of commercial electricity, produced by conventional means from excess capacity at off-peak hours or from non-fossil-fuel sources such as solar power and wind power.

The timeliness of Redoks's research has quickly attracted investors. For example, GESS has won contracts from an automobile company to manufacture batteries for a limited-production plug-in hybrid. It is also ready to begin commercial production of storage components for off-grid home electrical systems. More product means more storage space, however. To acquire the necessary manufacturing facilities, GESS needs to obtain additional financing.

Up to this point, GESS's primary source of funds has been from the sale of stock. The company is entirely equity-financed except for current liabilities incurred in the course of day-to-day operations. There are 200,000 shares outstanding, which are mostly owned by large, diverse technology companies that may wish to partner with or even acquire GESS at some point in the future. The shares trade occasionally in the NASDAQ over-the-counter market at an average price of $20.00.

The investment bankers who placed the stock have suggested that an all-debt plan would minimize taxes, but it would be risky and leave little room for future borrowing. Instead, they recommend staying close to the industry averages for debt-to-assets and debt-to-equity ratios. They have proposed two alternative plans:

a. plan A calls for $2,000,000 of new equity (100,000 new shares at the firm's current stock price of approximately $20.00) and $4,000,000 of privately placed debt at 9%

b. plan B calls for $4,000,000 of new equity (200,000 new shares at the current stock price of $20.00) and $2,000,000 of privately placed debt at 8%

Under either plan, GESS's combined state and federal marginal tax rate will be 40%.

Questions

1. Why should GESS expect to pay a higher rate of interest if it borrows $4,000,000 rather than $2,000,000?
2. Estimate earnings per share for plan A and plan B at EBIT levels of $800,000, $1,000,000, and $1,200,000.
3. How do taxes affect your findings in Question 2? By how much would the value of GESS increase or decrease as a result of choosing plan A or plan B?
4. At what level of EBIT would EPS be the same under either plan?
5. Suppose GESS's management is fairly confident the EBIT will be at least $1,000,000. Which plan would the firm be most likely to choose?
6. Assume GESS has no internal sources of financing and does not pay dividends. Under these conditions, would the pecking order hypothesis influence the decision to use plan A or plan B?
7. We assumed the decision to use more or less debt did not change the price of the stock. Under real-life conditions, how would the decision be likely to affect the stock price at first, and later, if management's optimism turned out to be justified?
8. **Challenge question.** What if 40% of GESS's stock was owned by a large pharmaceutical company and this company also purchased 40% of the privately placed debt? Would this situation influence the decision to use plan A or plan B?

Learning Objectives

LO1 Understand the formal process for paying dividends and differentiate between the most common types.

LO2 Explain individual preferences and issues surrounding different dividend policies.

LO3 Explain how a company selects its dividend policy.

LO4 Understand stock splits and reverse splits and why companies use them.

LO5 Understand stock repurchases and dividend reinvestment programs.

Chapter 17

Dividends, Dividend Policy, and Stock Splits

Dividends—payment of cash or stock to company owners—are not as straightforward as they may seem. For instance, you might think that the more dividends, the merrier, and that all investors want the maximum amount of dividends possible. Such is not the case. This chapter will show you that there are different "dividend clienteles" for different firms. Some investors prefer large and frequent dividends, some are happy with small but steady dividends, and some want no dividends at all.

Why do companies pay cash dividends to shareholders in the first place? Is it better not to pay dividends at all and instead invest the money in positive net present value projects and increase the overall value of the company? A policy of retaining all funds avoids taxes for the shareholders until they sell their shares and lets the company pursue more growth through adding positive net present value projects. Or, is it better to distribute cash to shareholders each year, even though they must pay taxes immediately on this distribution?

In this chapter, we answer these and other questions. We examine both the mechanics of dividends and the rationale for choosing different dividend policies for a company. The mechanics of dividends are straightforward, but a company's choice of dividend policy is not. It is more subjective than objective and—surprise—may not be important at all. That is, any dividend policy may be as good as any other dividend policy. As you read this chapter, keep in mind that what is important to individuals—especially company owners—is the after-tax cash flow they receive, in terms of both the timing and amount of cash that they receive.

17.1 Cash Dividends

Cash dividends are payments of cash to the owners of a company. As such, they are taxable as income. At one time, nearly 85% of all firms listed on the NYSE paid cash dividends on a regular basis. With the downturn in the economy in the early 2000s, that number fell to around 65%, and it has continued to fall since the financial meltdown of 2008. Yet a majority of the largest U.S. firms still pay regular quarterly cash dividends. There is a formal process for the paying and timing of dividends in a typical firm, and we now turn to those mechanics.

Buying and Selling Stock

Before turning to an examination of dividends per se, we need to look at the process of buying stocks to understand when ownership—and therefore entitlement to dividends, if any—takes place. If you want to buy shares in a company today, you need to find a current owner who is willing to sell. You can put in an order through your broker to trade for shares at an organized exchange like the NYSE, or you can go through a dealer and buy through NASDAQ. Let's review a typical trade and follow the mechanics that accompany such a transaction.

Say you are seeking 100 shares of PepsiCo and decide to place an order to buy these shares through your stockbroker. PepsiCo is listed on the NYSE, so your stockbroker then submits the order to the NYSE via the SuperDOT system. SuperDOT matches you with a seller, and the trade goes through at a price to which both you and the seller agree. Now all that is necessary is to exchange the 100 shares for the money. This transaction will take place two days after the agreed-upon trade on the **settlement date**, when your brokerage firm will transfer the funds to the seller (or the seller's brokerage firm) out of your brokerage account, and the seller's brokerage firm will send the 100 shares of stock to your broker. After the settlement date, you are the new stock owner and are entitled to all the rights and privileges as the owner, including dividend payments.

A common practice today is to hold the shares in **street name**, the name of the broker listed as the owner, rather than you. Keeping the shares in the broker's name makes transferring the shares easier and helps facilitate meeting the settlement date in the future when you decide to sell the shares. The brokerage firm records these shares in your individual brokerage account, and you become the **beneficiary owner**, or ultimate owner, of the stock. The brokerage company is the **owner of record** of the stock and receives all distributions and communications from PepsiCo. The brokerage firm immediately transfers distributions and communications to the beneficiary owner when it receives them.

Declaring and Paying a Cash Dividend: A Chronology

We now turn to dividends themselves and the mechanics that we associate with their declaration and payment. It is important to understand the various dates with these processes. We will look at these dates in the context of an example, PepsiCo's declaration of a dividend in February 2009. There are four key dates to consider, all of which are noted in Figure 17.1: the declaration date, the ex-date, the record date, and the payment date.

1. *Declaration date:* The decision to pay a cash dividend is within the jurisdiction of the firm's board of directors—in this case, PepsiCo. The board authorizes a specific dividend payment to current shareholders. The day on which

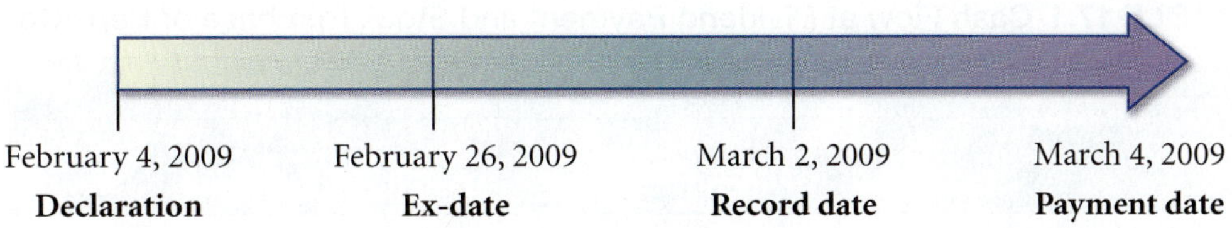

FIGURE 17.1 PepsiCo dividend dates.

they do so is the **declaration date**. The board will indicate the amount per share and other specifics. In PepsiCo's case, the declaration date was February 4, 2009. The press release on February 5, 2009, might read as follows: PepsiCo will pay a $0.425 dividend per share to all shareholders on record as of March 2, 2009, and payment will be mailed on Wednesday, March 4, 2009.

2. *Ex-dividend date:* The important ex-dividend date—informally called the **ex-date**—is the date that establishes the recipient of the dividend. It is two days before the date of record (which we discuss next). If you buy before the ex-date, you get any declared dividend. The seller does not. If you buy on or after the ex-date, the seller gets any declared dividend. You do not. This date is also an important one for price because the price on the morning of the ex-date will reflect the stock trading ex-dividend, without the dividend. Prior to the ex-date, the price reflects the stock trading *with* a declared dividend. Theoretically, the stock price will fall by the size of the declared dividend on the morning of the ex-date. Of course, other factors affect price as well, so we don't always see a price reduction equal to the dividend on the morning of the ex-date. In Figure 17.1, Thursday, February 26, 2009, is listed as the ex-date for PepsiCo.
3. *The record date:* The **record date** determines the shareholders entitled to receive a dividend. The issuer of the security establishes a list of the owners of record as of this date. With PepsiCo, it was Monday, March 2, 2009. This date is essentially a marker that ensures that the company sends dividend checks to the correct owners of record.
4. *Payment date:* The **payment date** is the actual day on which the company pays the declared cash dividend. For PepsiCo, it was March 4, 2009.

Why is this time frame on the buying, selling, and recording of the stock ownership important to understand? The answer has to do with ownership rules and the payment of cash dividends. It is important that a company pays the "true" stock owner and specifies the record date for dividend payments. If you buy a stock today, the brokerage executes the order today, but you do not become the official shareholder for another two business days, which is when the actual trade completes, the issuing company receives notification, and the ownership (title of the stock) changes hands. Thus, if a company pays a dividend to the shareholders of record and your personal settlement date is after the record date, it goes to the previous share owner, not to you. Recognizing this fact will alter the price that you are willing to pay for the acquisition of 100 shares of PepsiCo if the board of directors has already declared a dividend payment. If you settle after the record date, the dividend goes to the seller, but you pay a lower price for the stock. If you settle before the record date, the dividend comes to you, but you pay a higher price for the stock.

Let's return to the ex-date and examine its effect on the "true price" to the buyer and seller of a stock with a declared dividend (see Table 17.1). If you purchased the stock at the close on Wednesday, February 25, while the stock was trading with dividend, you would have paid $49.43 per share. You would have been

TABLE 17.1 Cash Flow at Dividend Payment and Stock Purchase of PepsiCo

	Before Ex-Date			After Ex-Date		
	Cash flow	Dividend	Net cash flow	Cash flow	Dividend	Net cash flow
New owner	−$49.43	+$0.43	−$49.00	−$49.00		−$49.00
Old owner	$49.43		$49.43	$49.00	+$0.43	$49.43

entitled to the $0.43 dividend, so the effective cost to you would have been $49.43 − $0.43, or $49.00. Your settlement date would be on Friday, February 27, so you would have made the list of current owners in time to receive the dividend. The seller's proceeds would have been $49.43, the price he or she received from you.

What would happen had you waited until the morning of Thursday, February 26, to buy the stock, the day of the ex-date? The price of the stock would have fallen (the price at the opening of the market on February 26 was $49.00). Now, though, your personal settlement date will be after the close of business on Monday, March 2, 2009—after the date of record—and you would not be on the list of owners for the dividend. So, the seller would have received $49.00 from you and stayed on the ownership list long enough to receive the $0.43 dividend, thereby increasing his or her net proceeds to $49.43. Our example has simplified the actual prices on these dates, and if there had been no other issues overnight, the first price of the morning on the ex-date would be lower by just the size of the dividend. So, if you purchased the stock after the dividend declaration date, you would have paid $49.00 net either before or after the ex-date. The seller would have received a net of $49.43 whether the sale took place before or after the ex-date. From Table 17.1, we can see that the seller always gets $49.43 and the buyer always pays $49.00. We used prices that reflect only the dividend. So, the dividend of $0.43 always goes to the owner at the declaration date.

The stock traded with the dividend prior to the ex-date, so a new buyer was paying for both the stock and the cash dividend and implicitly paying the seller for both of them. Beginning on the morning of the stock's ex-date, however, the stock traded without the dividend. So, the new buyer was simply paying for the stock, and the issuer would eventually send the declared cash dividend to the original owner. It did not matter to the original owner whether he or she collected the dividend directly from PepsiCo or indirectly from the new owner. Cash is cash.

Different Types of Dividends

Dividends come in different forms and with different names, but there are four common types:

1. Regular cash dividends
2. Special or extra cash dividends
3. Stock dividends
4. Liquidating dividends

Regular cash dividends A **regular cash dividend** is a dividend that a company pays out routinely to shareholders, often quarterly and often the same from quarter to quarter. When we first looked at dividends in Chapter 7, we examined the

TABLE 17.2 PepsiCo Quarterly Cash Dividend History

Date of Dividend	Amount of Dividend per Share
June 2007	$0.375
September 2007	$0.375
December 2007	$0.375
March 2008	$0.375
June 2008	$0.425
September 2008	$0.425
December 2008	$0.425
March 2009	$0.425
June 2009	$0.45
September 2009	$0.45
December 2009	$0.45
March 2010	$0.45
June 2010	$0.48
September 2010	$0.48
December 2010	$0.48
March 2011	$0.48

annual cash dividend, which was simply the sum of the four quarterly cash dividends for many of the companies.

Table 17.2 shows quarterly cash dividends for PepsiCo from June 2008 to March 2011. Notice the consistent amount for four consecutive quarters. This dividend pattern is typical, with the same quarterly dividend for four consecutive quarters and then a slight increase in the cash dividend each June. Based on this pattern, could you predict the cash dividends from PepsiCo for June 2011? If you guessed an increase to $0.515, you are correct.

Some companies choose to raise dividends every fourth quarter by the same percentage amount, some by the same dollar (cent) amount, and others by at least the prior increase and occasionally more. Most companies try not to reduce the annual increase or forgo an increase once they establish a pattern. When companies reduce their dividends, we often interpret it as a signal of bad times ahead. Investors are inclined to interpret the lowered dividends as a sign that the company does not believe it can maintain the current payout level into the future.

Special or extra cash dividend Some companies follow this basic dividend pattern, but then add a special or extra dividend during periods of good company performance. This **special or extra dividend** is a dividend that the company does not guarantee in the following period; in fact, by using the term *special* or *extra dividend*, the board of directors is implying that the dividend is a one-time, nonrecurring payment. We usually associate these dividends with periods of unusually strong company performance.

Stock dividends A **stock dividend** is exactly what the term states: a dividend in the form of shares of stock instead of cash. In the case of stock dividends, the board authorizes distribution of a specified number of new shares to shareholders based on their current holdings. For example, a 10% stock dividend means that you will receive one new share of common stock for every ten shares that you currently hold. In terms of the record date for ownership, the stock dividend process is the same as that for sending out of a cash dividend, but no actual dollars are involved.

Liquidating dividends Shareholders receive a **liquidating dividend** when the company is discontinuing operations or when a company has sold off a major portion of the business. Once the firm ceasing operations has paid all debts, the remaining funds belong to the shareholders. The final distribution of cash to shareholders as the business closes is the liquidating dividend. For an individual owner, though, the liquidating dividend can also be the selling price because that is the day the owner liquidates his or her holdings of that company.

17.2 Dividend Policy

The declaration and payment of dividends are important events for a company, but is the size of the dividend important? That's the question we really want to answer. A company can pay a large dividend, or it can pay a small one, or none at all, and invest more in the business. Dividend policy deals with whether the firm should pay out a large amount now or invest more in the company. It is actually just a matter of timing of the dividends.

The declaration of an actual cash dividend is the culmination of a company's dividend policy. So, why *do* some firms pay large cash dividends and others pay small cash dividends or none at all? Is there an optimal dividend policy? Does it matter what dividend policy a company chooses? We turn first to a consideration of why firms have different payout patterns.

Dividend Clienteles

One simple answer to why some firms choose their specific cash dividend pattern is individual preferences. Different investors have different needs. Some may want high dividend payouts; others low or none at all. Some owners like high-dividend payouts because they are using the dividend stream as income. That may be the case, for example, for those living on fixed incomes, such as retirees.

On the other hand, some investors have an incentive to want small dividends or even no dividends at all because the government taxes dividends as income when distributed to owners. They want to avoid paying taxes on these distributions in the present and thus seek a firm with a low-dividend-payout policy. These individuals, some of whom are wealthy, want to postpone taxes. In addition, these shareholders believe pouring more money back into the company will raise the stock price. When they sell their stock, they will realize a sizable taxable gain, but the government often taxes this gain at a lower rate than that of dividends. Therefore, they not only postpone taxes, but they may also actually *reduce* their taxes.

We call these different groups of shareholders with different desires on dividend policies **dividend clienteles**. Companies may select their dividend policy based on what type of clienteles currently own the company shares or on what type of owner clientele they want. Typically, a company may have a variety of clienteles and not be able to satisfy all owners. The important point is that different investors have different preferences when it comes to the timing of the dividend stream.

Dividend Policy Irrelevance

We turn now to an issue raised in the opening to the chapter: whether one dividend policy may be just as good as any other. To examine this question, we will adopt the perspective of the shareholder and start in a very simple world (as we did in Chapter 16 on optimal capital structure): a world of no taxes and no transaction costs.

Dividend policy in a world of no taxes and no transaction costs Say you currently have no income except the dividend stream that you receive from owning 10,000 shares of Stark Industries. The board of directors for Stark is considering two dividend policies. Policy 1 is a high-dividend-payout policy in which the company will declare a $2 annual cash dividend, and Policy 2 is a no-dividend-payout policy in which the company will reinvest all earned money rather than pay it out to the shareholders. Stark asks you your dividend policy preference. To the board's surprise, you state that the dividend policy is irrelevant to you and that you can create any dividend policy you want on your own. How can that be? Let's examine your acute financial logic.

EXAMPLE 17.1 Illustration of dividend-policy irrelevance (Part 1)

Problem Assume that you have a target income of $20,000 per year. How can you attain this income (in a world of no taxes) if your only wealth is the 10,000 shares of Stark Industries?

Policy 1: $2 annual dividend; current price per share is $10 before cash dividend, with the price after the cash dividend falling to $8.
Policy 2: No cash dividend; current price is and will remain at $10 per share.
Dividend objective: You want to receive $20,000 income from your current 10,000 shares of Stark. Your current paper wealth is $10 × 10,000 shares, or $100,000.

Solution

Action under Policy 1: You will receive $20,000 cash dividend ($2 × 10,000) from your shares and will maintain your 10,000 shares at $8 a share for a total wealth of $20,000 cash + $80,000 paper, or $100,000.
Action under Policy 2: You need to sell 2,000 shares of Stark to get your $20,000. You are left with 8,000 shares of stock at a value of $10 per share. You now have wealth of $20,000 cash + $80,000 paper, or $100,000.

So, under either policy, you end up with $20,000 cash and $80,000 in stock. You achieve your dividend objective under either scenario and in the process have rendered the dividend policy irrelevant.

What if you want only $10,000 income for the year, not $20,000? How could you *undo* the two dividend policies in Example 17.1 and meet your desired income?

EXAMPLE 17.2 Illustration of dividend-policy irrelevance (Part 2)

Problem Assume that you have a target income of $10,000 per year. How can you attain this income (in a world of no taxes) if your only wealth is the 10,000 shares of Stark Industries?

Policy 1: $2 annual dividend; current price per share is $10 before cash dividend, with the price after the cash dividend falling to $8.
Policy 2: No cash dividend; current price is and will remain at $10 per share.
Dividend objective: You want to receive $10,000 income from your current 10,000 shares of Stark. Your current paper wealth is $10 × 10,000 shares, or $100,000.

Solution

Action under Policy 1: You initially receive the dividend stream of $20,000, but keep only $10,000 in cash. With the other $10,000, you "buy back" $10,000 of stock in Stark after the cash dividend distribution (at the $8 per share price, which reflects the drop in price due to the $2 cash dividend). You can purchase 1,250 shares of Stark ($10,000/$8 = 1,250). Your wealth is now $10,000 cash + $ 90,000 (11,250 shares × $8) paper, or $100,000.
Action under Policy 2: You need to sell only 1,000 shares of Stark to get your $10,000. You are left with 9,000 shares of stock at a value of $10 per share. You now have $10,000 cash + $90,000 (9,000 shares × $10) paper, or $100,000.

You can therefore undo any dividend policy of Stark Industries to get the dividend policy that meets your personal cash flow needs. Each scenario will render identical cash balances and paper wealth balances, regardless of the overall dividend policy.

Thus, it is irrelevant to you what dividend policy the company in our examples chooses. The *dividend irrelevancy theory*, proposed by Merton Miller and Franco Modigliani in 1961[1] and more properly called the **dividend policy irrelevance theory**, says that a company's dividend policy is irrelevant to investors because they can buy back shares with the cash dividend or sell a portion of their shares to attain their desired current cash flow.

Dividends in a world of taxes Our previous scenario took place in a hypothetical "perfect" world of no taxes and no transaction costs. We are quite familiar with taxes. **Transaction costs** are the costs that investors pay to complete a transaction that reduces the net cash flow to a buyer or seller. We know that we live in a "messy" world where taxes apply and where there are costs to complete a transaction. How does your perspective specifically change if we add taxes to the mix? We could add transaction costs as well, but we want to emphasize the tax effect first. We will also add one more assumption: the original stock purchase price is the current stock price before the dividend payment. We later relax this assumption.

It turns out that your perspective will change when taxes enter the picture, if we assume the same tax rate for dividends and stock price appreciation and if the original stock purchase price equals the current price. If we add a tax rate

[1]M. Miller and F. Modigliani, "Dividend Policy, Growth, and the Valuation of Shares," *Journal of Business* (October 1961): 411–433.

of 25% for both ordinary income (the dividend distribution) and for capital gains (profit from sale of the stock), the dividend policy becomes relevant to you as long as we assume that the stock price still falls by the size of the dividend and not by the size of the after-tax cash dividend. Let's look at these assumptions in more detail.

EXAMPLE 17.3 Dividends in a world of taxes and no capital gains

Problem You have a target income of $10,000 for the year, and Stark Industries still has the same two policies under consideration: $2 dividend per share or no dividends for the year. You originally purchased the stock for $10, and the before-dividend-payout price is $10.

Solution

After-tax cash flow under Policy 1: Dividend income is $20,000, and tax on this income is $5,000 ($20,000 × 0.25), so net cash flow from the dividends is $15,000. If the after-tax cash flow target remains at $10,000, you will reinvest $5,000. If the stock price falls only by the cash dividend of $2.00 per share, you can buy 625 shares at the $8.00 share price, and your wealth is now $10,000 cash + $85,000 paper (10,625 shares × $8.00). Note the government has collected $5,000 from you, so your total wealth is now $95,000.

After-tax cash flow under Policy 2: Again, you must sell 1,000 shares to get $10,000, but by selling shares of stock, you now face potential taxes on the capital gain from the sale. Here is where the assumption that the current stock price is the same as your original purchase price comes in. If you originally purchased the stock at $10 per share, you have no capital gain on the stock sale and therefore no taxes. Thus, you keep the entire $10,000 proceeds from the sale. Your net cash flow after the sale is $10,000. You also have 9,000 shares left at $10 per share, and your wealth remains the same, as you have avoided paying any taxes: $10,000 cash + $90,000 (9,000 × $10) paper, or $100,000.

In a world of taxes (on ordinary income) and no capital gains, you would prefer the no-dividend policy.

Let's now change the assumption about the original stock purchase price. What happens if you must pay a gain on the sale? What happens if you bought the stock years ago at $5.00 per share?

In a world of taxes, things do get messy and complicated quite quickly. The dividend policy irrelevance proposition may not hold as we incorporate the timing and amount of taxes under each policy. Let's look at the case where you have a gain on sale of $5.00 per share.

EXAMPLE 17.4 Dividends in a world of taxes and capital gains at sale of stock

Problem As before, you have a target of $10,000 after-tax income, and Stark Industries has the same two potential dividend policies: Policy 1 with $2 per share dividend, and Policy 2 with no dividend payment.

Solution Policy 1 remains the same with cash and paper wealth because you do not sell any of the stock to get your \$10,000 cash flow, so your wealth remains \$10,000 after-tax cash and \$85,000 paper wealth. In Policy 2, however, you will need to sell enough shares to get your \$10,000 and pay the capital gains tax. For every share that you sell, you pay the following tax:

$$\text{tax per share} = (\$10.00 - \$5.00) \times 0.25 = \$1.25$$

You can now determine your wealth under Policy 2.

Net cash flow per share: $\$10.00 - \$1.25 = \$8.75$

Shares to sell: $= \dfrac{\$10{,}000}{\$8.75} = 1{,}142.8571$

Shares after sale: $= 10{,}000 - 1{,}142.8571 = 8{,}857.1429$

Wealth: \$10,000 cash + \$88,571.43 (8,857.1429 shares × \$10) paper = \$98,571.43

Total taxes paid on your capital gain is $1{,}142.8571 \times \$1.25 = \$1{,}428.57$, which is your loss in wealth from the original \$100,000.

You would want Policy 2, the no-dividend policy, which would lead to a drop in your wealth of \$1,428.57 for the capital gains taxes versus a \$5,000 loss of wealth with the tax on the dividend distribution. So, it seems that in a world with taxes, the preferred policy will be the no-dividend policy.

Let's not go so fast, though. Having studied finance, you realize that stock prices change and prices can go down as well as up in the future and that future dividends are not guaranteed. A cash dividend now may be worth more than the potential cash dividend in the future. So, current cash distribution matters.

With taxes, potential capital gains, and company reinvestment opportunities, the dividend policy *does* become relevant to you and to all other shareholders. The answer to the preferred policy must now incorporate not only your desired income level but also your personal marginal tax rates, original stock basis, and expectations about the future stock price. Thus, the optimal dividend policy will take into account these differentials and will vary for different shareholders. We can now see that our original observation on dividend clienteles—that different shareholders have different preferences about the firm's dividend policy—makes sense.

Reasons Favoring a Low- or No-Dividend-Payout Policy

There are three commonly cited reasons for a low- or no-dividend-payout policy:

1. The avoidance or postponement of taxes on distributions for shareholders
2. Higher potential future returns for shareholders
3. Less need for additional costly outside funding

Let's discuss each in turn.

Advantages A common reason for low-dividend-payout policies is the tax advantage to shareholders. Taxes historically have been higher on ordinary income than on capital gains, and because investors do not pay taxes on capital gains until they realize them, they can postpone taxes until they sell the shares. So, if we think that the dividend policy is just timing of the cash flows, we would prefer more of the distribution to come through stock appreciation (the lower capital gains rate) and to postpone the taxes into the future.

Higher potential returns from positive net present value projects Let's change the perspective for a moment and look at the dividend policy from the point of view of the company's cash needs. Return to Stark Industries' two potential dividend policies: assume that the firm has 100,000 shares outstanding and the value is $10 before the dividend distribution. The firm will pay out $200,000 in total dividends if it declares a $2-per-share dividend. These dollars are no longer available for investing in the firm's positive net present value projects. Under the no-dividend policy, however, the firm retains these funds for reinvesting, thereby creating more potential that the firm's value will increase and, with it, the stock value. Shareholders will not realize this price gain until they sell their shares, so they can postpone taxes into the future.

Less need for outside funding A corollary to the previous point is that if a good project comes along, a low- or no-dividend-payout policy will allow the company to invest without seeking new outside funding, which is an expensive proposition. On the other hand, a high-dividend-payout policy may require outside funding. In Chapter 16, you saw that outside funding can be more expensive (higher cost of capital), and as you know from our study of capital budgeting and the NPV model, a higher cost of capital lowers the project's overall contribution to the company.

Reasons Favoring a High-Dividend-Payout Policy

There are two commonly cited reasons for a high-dividend-payout policy:

1. Avoidance of transaction costs for selling shares
2. Cash payments today versus uncertain cash payments tomorrow

Freedom from transaction costs One advantage to a shareholder in a firm with a high-dividend-payout policy is a steady income stream free of the aforementioned transaction costs, those costs that occur with various financial procedures, such as brokerage commissions. Dividend payout does not require selling shares through a broker to get a cash stream. In our initial example, you received your desired $20,000 income without any transaction fees. In fact, today firms pay dividends directly into shareholders' checking or savings accounts, thereby minimizing any hassle or time delays in receiving a dividend distribution.

Certainty versus uncertainty Another reason that a shareholder may prefer a high-dividend-payout policy lies in the certainty of a payment today versus the uncertainty of a future payment. With high-dividend yields, a shareholder receives payment today versus waiting for an uncertain higher future payout. If the company performs well, it may be worth the wait, but if the company does not perform well, it may be better to get some cash distribution now while the firm can still afford to pay out cash. Payment today removes uncertainty about future firm performance and future payments.

Optimal Dividend Policy

Is there an optimal dividend policy, and is dividend policy relevant to an investor? The answer currently remains buried in the beliefs and desires of individual investors and their tax status. It is clear that the optimal dividend policy for one shareholder may be quite different from that of another shareholder. Shareholders will differ based on their personal income tax status, the current capital gains rate versus ordinary tax rate, stock basis (original purchase price), and their beliefs about the firm's future performance. A company can have only one dividend policy, however, and it must choose one that fits a large percentage of its shareholders. So, we now look at what other issues affect the choice of the dividend policy from the firm's perspective.

17.3 Selecting a Dividend Policy

Prior to selecting a dividend policy, a firm should review its cash flow requirements and future funding requirements. The goal is to produce sufficient cash flow to pay off debts in a timely fashion, maintain operations, and provide cash for reinvesting. Once the firm covers these three areas, it can distribute the remaining cash flow from operations to owners through dividends. When the firm pays out the funds left to shareholders, we call this distribution a residual dividend policy.

In a **residual dividend policy**, the firm issues dividend payments from leftover equity (the "residual") only after it meets all other capital requirements. So, one viable dividend policy might simply be a fluctuating cash dividend each year based on the excess of cash inflow over cash outflow. We rarely see this type of policy, however. Why? The answer lies in another common policy choice that we call **sticky dividends**.

Looking back at the PepsiCo dividends from June 2007 to March 2011 (in Table 17.2), we see a pattern: the company raises its quarterly dividends once a year and then maintains this level for the next three quarterly dividends. In other words, it "sticks" to the new, raised level for three periods before raising the dividend again. Why does it follow this pattern?

One theory is that investors do not like dividend fluctuations, especially decreases. There are a number of reasons to explain this reaction, but we commonly cite two. First, individuals living off their dividend streams do not like reductions in their quarterly payments; on the contrary, they like to see an annual increase to offset inflation. Second, a cut in dividends may signal poor future performance or the company's inability to maintain a given level of dividends in the future. To avoid these two negative situations, a company will set its dividend policy low enough so that it can continually meet the cash dividend's distribution level despite variances in cash flow from operations, maintenance, and investing. The quarterly dividend is set well below the excess cash flow level so that cash can accumulate for down periods and not require a reduction in dividends.

Investors tend to view cuts in dividends as a negative signal of a company's future performance and ability to sustain the level of dividend payments. This is one reason why companies set their dividend policies low enough so they can continually meet the expectations of given dividend streams.

EXAMPLE 17.5 Selecting a dividend payout rate: Residual versus sticky

Problem Thumbnail Industries, makers of thumb drives for data storage, shows the following anticipated cash inflow and outflow over the next four years. The company has estimated best-case and worst-case scenarios in their cash flow projections in which operating inflow varies by 20%. In the best-case scenario, the company assumes inflow will be up 20%. In the worst-case scenario, it assumes inflow will be down 20%.

Cash Flow Expectations for Thumbnail Industries

	Year 1	Year 2	Year 3	Year 4
Normal				
Operations	$2,000,000	$2,200,000	$2,400,000	$2,700,000
Maintenance	−$ 350,000	−$ 450,000	−$ 500,000	−$ 650,000
Investing	−$ 500,000	−$ 500,000	−$ 600,000	−$ 900,000
Expected excess	$1,150,000	$1,250,000	$1,300,000	$1,150,000
Best case				
Operations	$2,400,000	$2,640,000	$2,880,000	$3,240,000
Maintenance	−$ 350,000	−$ 450,000	−$ 500,000	−$ 650,000
Investing	−$ 500,000	−$ 500,000	−$ 600,000	−$ 900,000
Expected excess	$1,550,000	$1,690,000	$1,780,000	$1,690,000
Worst case				
Operations	$1,600,000	$1,760,000	$1,920,000	$2,160,000
Maintenance	−$ 350,000	−$ 450,000	−$ 500,000	−$ 650,000
Investing	−$ 500,000	−$ 500,000	−$ 600,000	−$ 900,000
Expected excess	$ 750,000	$ 810,000	$ 820,000	$ 610,000

Currently, 2,000,000 shares are outstanding, and Thumbnail Industries pays annual cash dividends. What are the highest dividends Thumbnail can pay each year under the anticipated cash flow, the best-case scenario, and the worst-case scenario if it maintains a residual dividend policy? If Thumbnail wants to avoid cutting dividends and use a sticky dividend policy, what is the largest dividend it should declare considering the income in the worst-case scenario?

Solution Under the residual dividend policy, the company simply divides the expected excess under the different scenarios by the number of outstanding shares—in this case, 2,000,000—and pays it out in dividends. The dividends will vary from $0.305 per year to $0.89 per year, depending on the cash flow outcome, as the table on the next page illustrates.

Residual Dividends for Thumbnail Industries

	Year 1	Year 2	Year 3	Year 4
Normal				
Expected excess	$1,150,000	$1,250,000	$1,300,000	$1,150,000
Dividend	$ 0.5750	$ 0.6250	$ 0.6500	$ 0.5750
Best case				
Expected excess	$1,550,000	$1,690,000	$1,780,000	$1,690,000
Dividend	$ 0.7750	$ 0.8450	$ 0.8900	$ 0.8450
Worst case				
Expected excess	$ 750,000	$ 810,000	$ 820,000	$ 610,000
Dividend	$ 0.3750	$ 0.4050	$ 0.4100	$ 0.3050

Under the sticky dividend policy that incorporates no reductions in cash flow, however, the company will declare a $0.3050 dividend and not raise the dividend until it saves sufficient cash to cover the downside potential of the fourth year's worst-case scenario.

Some Further Considerations in the Selection of a Dividend Policy

From the firm's perspective, there are some other considerations in selecting a dividend policy.

Restrictions on legal capital In most states, there are legal constraints on the size of the dividend. Firms cannot pay out cash dividends from their legal capital. We can think of **legal capital** as the owner's original cash contributions. It consists of the par value and the paid in excess of par on the common shares. Paid-in-excess is the difference between the stock's original selling price at the initial public sale and the stock's par value. To protect creditors, states do not allow reduction of the legal capital. The concern is that exorbitant dividend payments will not leave enough to pay the company's bills, thereby placing the claims of suppliers, customers, and employees at risk. It is the equity holders who still assume the final risk on firm performance.

Restrictive bond covenants Bond holders may have covenants stating that a company cannot pay dividends unless sufficient cash is currently available to cover the next coupon payments. Other constraints may prohibit dividends above a certain percentage of current earnings. The covenants are another way to ensure that the owners have some capital at risk.

Cash availability Dividends may also be constrained by the amount of cash the company has accumulated. Remember that net income (earnings) and retained earnings do not reflect the amount of cash in the bank. Although firms may be able to borrow funds to pay dividends, most lenders prefer that companies use loans to grow or expand the firm, not to make payments that go to current shareholders and that add no value to the firm.

17.4 Stock Dividends, Stock Splits, and Reverse Splits

A stock dividend is a payment of shares to current shareholders in which the payment is less than 25% of the currently held shares. For example, a 10% stock dividend means that a shareholder with 100 shares of stock will receive an additional 10 shares. With stock dividends, however, there is no real change in wealth. Only a paper transaction has occurred.

In a **stock split**, a company divides its existing shares into multiple shares, with the total dollar value remaining the same. When a company declares a 2-for-1 stock split, it is like changing a $20 bill into two $10 bills. In a stock split, the number of outstanding shares increases by the declared split ratio. The most common split is 2-for-1, in which the number of outstanding shares doubles. With a 2-for-1 split, an individual who owned 100 shares before the split owns 200 shares after the split. The share's value after the split is half the share's value before the split. Stock splits come in a variety of ratios. Some other common splits are 3-for-1, 4-for-1, and 5-for-1.

Table 17.3 shows the company's total equity value and that of an individual owner after a 2-for-1 stock split. Before the split, the value of one share of stock is $50. The company has 2 million shares outstanding. The company's equity value is $100 million. After the split, the equity value remains at $100 million, even though there are now 4 million shares outstanding. The value of one share of stock is now $25 instead of $50. So, for individual shareholders, their shares increase, but their wealth and ownership percentage in the company remain the same.

The process of declaring a stock split is the same as that for a cash dividend declaration and follows the same chronology.

1. The company will announce its intentions to split the stock (declaration date). The company will announce the actual split factor, that is, 2-for-1, 3-for-1, 4-for-1, and so forth.
2. The market will assign an ex-date for the stock split. The ex-date tells potential new shareholders that if they buy shares before this date, they will receive the new shares as the holders of record for the split, but if they buy on or after this date, they will not receive the shares directly from the company. The brokerage will add a "due bill" to the sale, requiring the seller to forward

TABLE 17.3 Stock Split Value Changes on a 2-for-1 Split

	Before Split	After Split
Company		
Shares outstanding	2,000,000	4,000,000
Value per share	$ 50.00	$ 25.00
Total equity value	$100,000,000	$100,000,000
Individual owner		
Shares owned	20,000	40,000
Value per share	$ 50.00	$ 25.00
Total equity value	$ 1,000,000	$ 1,000,000
Percentage ownership	1%	1%

the new shares to the buyer of the stock. On the morning following the ex-date, the shares will trade at the after-split price.

3. The new shares will go to those who are current shareholders of record as of a specific date (record date).
4. The company mails the new shares on a subsequent date (payment date).

Reasons for Stock Splits

If stock splits are of no value to the shareholder, why go to all the trouble to engineer them in the first place? Three popular explanations as to why firms split stocks have emerged.

Preferred trading range One explanation is the **preferred trading range**, which is the span between the highest and lowest prices at which investors prefer to buy stock. To understand this concept, a bit of background is necessary. Historically, the average price on the NYSE has hovered in the $20 to $40 range. Thus, the average price to buy 100 shares (a **round lot**) is $2,000 to $4,000. Investors can buy in less than 100 share units (**odd lot**), but the commissions can be higher. Moreover, the quoted prices are good for a round lot, but not necessarily for an odd lot. When a stock price begins to rise and move above this range, the cost of a round lot moves out of the range of many small retail traders. Firms do not want to limit the set of potential investors, so they elect to reduce the share price back to this average or preferred price by splitting the stock.

Looking at more than 400 stock splits in the early 1990s, researchers found that companies that split their stock generally had an after-split price in the $20 to $40 range. Table 17.4 shows that prior to the stock split, more than 80% of the firms were trading above $40, but after the split, more than 60% of the firms were trading in the $20 to $40 range. Although there remains a debate about the economic effect of splitting shares, it is clear that when companies do so, shares tend to move back into this preferred trading range of $20 to $40.

On the other hand, a little intuition renders this argument weak. It's like saying people prefer to carry $10 bills over $20 bills. If that were the case, people would constantly be changing their $20 bills into $10 bills and the government would supply more $10 bills than $20 bills, and that is not the case. If we extend this reasoning to companies, we would see companies constantly splitting their shares to this preferred range, but again, that is not the case. Companies price stocks across a broad spectrum of prices, and even after a split, 28% of the firms in Table 17.4 are trading above $40 per share.

TABLE 17.4 Prices Before and After Stock Splits

Presplit Price	Frequency	Percentage	Postsplit Price	Frequency	Percentage
$ 0 to $15	0	0%	$ 0 to $15	22	5%
$15 to $20	3	1%	$15 to $20	24	6%
$20 to $25	5	1%	$20 to $25	73	18%
$25 to $30	19	5%	$25 to $30	71	17%
$30 to $35	22	5%	$30 to $35	62	15%
$35 to $40	32	8%	$35 to $40	41	10%
Above $40	327	80%	Above $40	113	28%

Signaling hypothesis A second explanation for why stock splits occur comes from the **signaling hypothesis**. According to this theory, current management can signal information to both current and potential shareholders that the strong past performance that caused the price to rise out of the preferred trading range will continue into the future. The stock price will therefore not fall back naturally into the preferred trading range, and it will thus be necessary to split the stock. This "good news signal" is generally accepted because we see stock prices, in general, continue to rise after splits. Thus, stock splits signal continued strong performance to the public.

Increased liquidity A third rationale offered to explain stock splits is the increased liquidity argument. The intuition is that when companies split stocks to trade in a preferred trading range, there will be more shares available and more buyers and sellers will be interested. Therefore, it will be easier to buy and sell the shares in a shorter time frame. The speed at which one can buy or sell an asset is one dimension of liquidity. Although the intuition seems sound, proof has been slow in coming for this argument.

Reverse Splits

If it makes no difference to trade a $20 bill for two $10 bills, what about trading two $10 bills for a $20 bill? The latter is an everyday example of a reverse split. A **reverse split** is the division of a company's stock into a lesser number of outstanding shares. Whereas companies often use a straight stock split to engineer the stock price *down* into the preferred trading range, they can also use the reverse split to engineer the stock price *up* into the preferred trading range to meet listing standards and avoid delisting. As a result of a reverse split, the stock price rises, but the company's value remains the same. It is a legal, although artificial, way of raising the stock price. There are two reasons for reverse splits.

The first reason concerns trading activity and stock attractiveness. If a company's stock trades below the preferred trading range, it may be a sign that the market believes the company is not competitive. As noted previously, the argument goes that if the company uses a reverse split, the price rises and investors will view the company more positively, but this explanation does not have much empirical evidence to back it up. One reason that we may not see evidence supporting this explanation is that if the liquidity argument is true for a regular split, a reverse split would lower liquidity because there are fewer shares to trade.

The second explanation is institutional and is much more direct. If a firm is trading below $1 for more than thirty days, NASDAQ has the option to delist the stock. Reverse splits increased in the early 2000s following the bursting of the technology bubble. Many of the Internet start-up companies that went public prior to the meltdown in March 2000 found their share prices falling toward the $1 level or lower. A reverse split was a quick and efficient way to jump the price up and avoid possible delisting.

Perhaps the most extreme proposed reverse stock split occurred in the financial press on May 5, 2009, when General Motors stated that it was contemplating a 1-for-100 reverse split. The price of a single share was at $1.85, and with a reverse split, the motor vehicle company would reissue every 100 shares with 1 share trading at $185. Shortly after floating this idea in public, GM filed for Chapter 11 bankruptcy, making the proposed reverse stock split moot.

17.5 Specialized Dividend Plans

We now consider two specialized dividend plans: stock repurchases and dividend reinvestment programs.

Stock Repurchase

Many companies forgo the formal cash dividend process and instead use the cash that they would normally use to pay dividends to buy back their own shares on the open market. This process constitutes a **stock repurchase plan**. The effect is to reduce the number of shares outstanding and increase earnings per share. Clearly, a company's EPS increases when you reduce the number of shares outstanding, but the firm's value does not change.

EXAMPLE 17.6 Share repurchase, EPS, and firm value

Problem Storm Guard Inc., an all-equity firm, shows the following abbreviated income and balance sheet:

Income Statement	
Revenue	$5,000,000
Cost of goods sold	$3,000,000
Taxes	$1,000,000
Net income	**$1,000,000**
Earnings per share	$ 5.00
Number of shares outstanding	200,000

Balance Sheet			
Cash	$ 250,000	Liabilities	$ 0
Other assets	$ 9,750,000	Owners' equity	$10,000,000
TOTAL ASSETS	**$10,000,000**	**TOTAL LIABILITIES AND OWNERS' EQUITY**	**$10,000,000**

The current price per share is $10,000,000/200,000, or $50.00.

Storm Guard can do either a stock repurchase for $250,000 and buy back 5,000 shares, or it can pay out a dividend of $1.25 resulting in a total distribution of $250,000 ($1.25 × 200,000 shares). What is the change in EPS, stock price, and the firm's value with the stock repurchase and cash dividend scenarios?

Solution

Scenario 1: Stock repurchase

With the stock repurchase, the EPS is now $1,000,000/195,000 = $5.13, and the current stock price remains at $50 per share. The balance sheet is as follows:

Balance Sheet			
Cash	$ 0	Liabilities	$ 0
Other assets	$9,750,000	Owners' equity	$9,750,000
TOTAL ASSETS	**$9,750,000**	**TOTAL LIABILITIES AND OWNERS' EQUITY**	**$9,750,000**

Scenario 2: Cash dividend payout

With a cash dividend, the EPS is still $5.00 per share ($1,000,000/200,000), but the stock price has fallen to $48.75 ($9,750,000/200,000). The balance sheet is as follows:

Balance Sheet			
Cash	$ 0	Liabilities	$ 0
Other assets	$9,750,000	Owners' equity	$9,750,000
TOTAL ASSETS	**$9,750,000**	**TOTAL LIABILITIES AND OWNERS' EQUITY**	**$9,750,000**

The EPS does go up with a share repurchase, but the firm's value is the same. Shareholders are no better off with a share repurchase versus a cash dividend. The wealth with share repurchase per share becomes

Sell share, $50 cash
Don't sell, share $50 paper

The wealth with cash dividend per share becomes

$$\$1.25 \text{ cash} + \$48.75 \text{ paper} = \$50$$

So, a share repurchase is the same as a cash dividend except that shareholders will choose how much cash that they want by the number of shares that they choose to sell.

Firms announce stock repurchase plans ahead of time so that the market is aware that the company has targeted a number of shares for purchase. The plan typically sets a specific time frame and dollar figure for repurchase. Figure 17.2 shows a press release from a hypothetical company, Freese Corporation, on its intentions to repurchase its own common stock.

Freese's announcement of a stock repurchase plan illustrates another way to pay cash dividends and let shareholders select their own dividend amount. At the time of this announcement, Freese shares were selling for $27.50 per share. If Freese bought back the full 5,000,000 shares, the committed funds would have been $27.50 × 5,000,000, or $137,500,000. The company could have used the same funds instead to pay out cash dividends to current shareholders. By electing the share repurchase plan, Freese in effect allowed its current shareholders to select their own dividend. Those who wanted a high-dividend payout would sell enough shares to generate their desired cash flow. Those who wanted a low- or no-dividend payout would sell very few or no shares to generate their desired cash flow.

If this type of dividend offers shareholders the ability to create their own dividend payments, why not always offer share repurchases instead of cash

FIGURE 17.2 Stock repurchase plan announcement by Freese.

Press Release **Source: Freese**

Freese Announces Stock Repurchase Plan

Freese announced today that its board of directors authorized the Company to purchase up to 5,000,000 shares of its common stock between now and November 2, 2012. The Company said that repurchases will be made from time to time in the open market, at the discretion of management. Shares purchased under this plan will be used for the Company's employee stock option and purchase plans.

About Freese

Freese is a global leader in cold package shipping and storage, primarily for food products. Freese also helps independent enterprises of all sizes and types to ensure the safety of their products. Freese serves more than 10,000 customers in more than 30 countries, including the world's 5 largest food service companies. Freese (NYSE: FRS) is a member of the S&P 500 and has annual revenues of $11 billion.

BUSINESS WIRE, ST. LOUIS, Mo.— Freese (NYSE: FRS–News)—Thursday November 2, 2011, 5:43 pm ET

dividends? For one thing, shareholders who want dividends must sell their shares. This process is costly, and shareholders may incur a sizable tax if the original cost of the share is low compared with the current price. Typically, long-time shareholders have a low basis (low original purchase price) in their stock and prefer cash dividends. For shareholders whose current share price is near the original purchase price and for whom the tax rates on capital gain are lower than those for ordinary income, however, the share repurchase allows for avoidance or reduction of taxes.

One of the rules surrounding share repurchases, though, is that their sole purpose cannot be to avoid taxes for shareholders. These plans must have a business reason. Looking back at Freese's announcement, we see that according to Freese, it will use the repurchased shares for management stock options and the share purchasing program for employees, a business purpose.

Not all stock repurchase plans are completed. A company has no legal obligation to act on the repurchase plan, once announced. In fact, of the announced programs like Freese's, 35% never start and 35% are only partially used. Companies typically complete only 30% of announced share repurchase plans.

Dividend Reinvestment Plans

A recent innovation in dividend policies is the **dividend reinvestment plan (DRIP)**—the automatic reinvestment of the shareholder's cash dividend in more shares of the company stock. The shareholder chooses to reinvest rather than receive a cash distribution, and the company distributes the equivalent number of shares directly to the shareholder. Many DRIPs provide shares commission-free, so they are an attractive way to increase holdings in a company over time without going to the secondary market to buy additional shares.

EXAMPLE 17.7 Dividend reinvestment plan (DRIP)

Problem John Watson currently owns 1,000 shares in Holmes, Ltd. Holmes has a dividend policy of \$0.25 per quarter per share or the option to reinvest the cash dividend into additional shares of company stock. The current stock price (ex-dividend) is \$25.00. If John elects the DRIP option, what can he expect in additional shares by reinvesting his dividend directly in the company?

Solution John will have his current cash dividend go directly to the purchase of additional shares:

$$\text{entitled dividend} = 1{,}000 \times \$0.25 = \$250$$

$$\text{share received via DRIP} = \frac{\$250}{\$25 \text{ per share}} = \textbf{10 shares}$$

What are the advantages to selecting a DRIP? In Example 17.7, John Watson was able to buy ten shares directly from the company and thus avoid transaction fees on the purchase of these shares. Most companies with dividend reinvestment plans charge little or no fee for purchasing stock through these programs. If he had taken the cash dividend and gone through a broker for more shares, he probably would have ended up with fewer than ten shares because a portion of the \$250 would have gone to commission and other transaction fees. Also, by electing a DRIP option, he automatically buys additional shares in Holmes, Ltd. on a regular basis, a procedure that may turn out to be a very prudent investment strategy.

Some companies offer **optional cash purchase plans** attached to DRIPs in which a shareholder can purchase additional shares through the DRIP for a small fee and small initial investment. Such a plan permits shareholders to buy additional shares in relatively small amounts—sometimes as little as \$10—which would not be available through normal brokerage trading channels. These small cash purchases are over and above the DRIP shares, thereby adding to the number of new shares available to a current shareholder.

We can find DRIPs in three types of investment programs:

1. *Company-run programs* are usually administered from the company's investor relations department, which deals directly with each shareholder. Again, the company charges little or no fees for purchasing company shares with the automatically reinvested cash dividends.
2. *Transfer-agent-run programs* are administered by financial institutions on behalf of a company. A financial institution can use its large resources over a large number of customers to provide a more efficient DRIP for the company than the company would be able to do on its own. Boston EquiServe, Chicago Trust, and Chase Mellon are three of the largest transfer agents that run DRIPs for companies.
3. *Brokerage-run programs* may offer broker clients the option to reinvest their dividends. Recall that stocks are usually stored in street name rather than the actual owner's name. Thus, when a company pays dividends, they are sent to the brokerage firm (the listed owner) rather than to the shareholder (beneficiary owner). The brokerage firm will credit the owner's account for the cash or will allow the shareholder to use the funds to purchase more of the company's stock, even if the company itself does not have a DRIP. The brokerage firm will take the cash dividend of its customer and immediately purchase additional shares in the market, adding them to the individual customer's brokerage account.

DRIPs allow shareholders a convenient way to reinvest their cash dividends in a company. The government still treats the cash dividend as ordinary income, however, so these convenient purchases do not avoid that tax liability. The exception is if the investor holds these shares in a tax-deferred account like an IRA or a 401(k) plan.

To review this chapter, see the Summary Card at the end of the text.

Key Terms

beneficiary owner, p. 522
cash dividends, p. 522
declaration date, p. 523
dividend clienteles, p. 526
dividend policy irrelevance theory, p. 528
dividend reinvestment plans (DRIPs), p. 540
dividends, p. 522
ex-date, p. 523
legal capital, p. 534
liquidating dividend, p. 526
odd lot, p. 536
optional cash purchase plans, p. 541
owner of record, p. 522
payment date, p. 523
preferred trading range, p. 536
record date, p. 523
regular cash dividend, p. 524
residual dividend policy, p. 532
reverse split, p. 537
round lot, p. 536
settlement date, p. 522
signaling hypothesis, p. 537
special or extra dividend, p. 525
sticky dividends, p. 532
stock dividend, p. 526
stock repurchase plans, p. 538
stock split, p. 535
street name, p. 522
transaction costs, p. 528

Questions

1. When you agree to buy a stock on the NYSE or NASDAQ, how much time after the agreed-upon sale do you have to provide the necessary funds for the purchase? What is the name given to the actual delivery of funds and stocks for exchange?
2. What does it mean to be a beneficiary owner of stock? Why would individuals find this ownership stake convenient?
3. Explain why we use the term *ex-date* when pricing a stock that has a declared dividend.
4. How does a stock dividend differ from a cash dividend? Is one better than the other from the shareholder's perspective?
5. In a world of no taxes and no transaction costs, is dividend policy relevant? Why or why not?
6. In a world of taxes when the capital gains tax and the ordinary income tax rates are the same, is dividend policy relevant? Why or why not?
7. Contrast a residual dividend program with a sticky dividend program.
8. Does a stock split provide an increase in wealth for a shareholder? If yes, how? If no, why not?
9. Under what condition would a shareholder prefer a share repurchase over a cash dividend? Under what condition would a shareholder prefer a cash dividend over a share repurchase?
10. Why is a dividend reinvestment program attractive to a shareholder who plans to increase his or her holdings in a company?

Prepping for Exams

1. Typically, shares of stock are stored in the vault of the brokerage firm, and you, as owner, will not take physical possession. Under these circumstances, the brokerage firm is the ____________ and you are the ____________.
   a. street owner; settlement owner
   b. settlement owner; street owner
   c. owner of record; beneficiary owner
   d. beneficiary owner; owner of record

2. Identify each of the following dates associated with the payment of a dividend by Jefferson State Timber Company: August 15, September 5, September 7, and September 22.
   a. declaration date, ex-dividend date, record date, payment date
   b. ex-dividend date, declaration date, record date, payment date
   c. record date, declaration date, ex-dividend date, payment date
   d. declaration date, record date, payment date, ex-dividend date

3. Investors who wish to avoid paying taxes in the present are typically ____________.
   a. low-dividend clientele
   b. high-dividend clientele
   c. drawn to firms that have erratic dividend policies
   d. None of choices (a) through (c)

4. Which of the following is a reason for a high-dividend-payout policy?
   a. Dividends are generally taxed at a lower rate than capital gains.
   b. All investors prefer high dividend payments over low dividend payments.
   c. Cash payments today are preferred over uncertain payments in the future.
   d. More cash is left in the company for investing in company projects.

5. Surf City Inc. has decided on a 3-for-1 stock split. If the firm currently has 900,000 shares outstanding, how many shares will be outstanding after the stock split?
   a. 3,600,000 shares
   b. 2,700,000 shares
   c. 1,200,000 shares
   d. 300,000 shares

6. Surf City Inc. has decided on a 20% stock dividend. If the firm currently has 900,000 shares outstanding, how many shares will be outstanding after the stock dividend?
   a. 4,500,000 shares
   b. 1,080,000 shares
   c. 720,000 shares
   d. 180,000 shares

7. Surf City Inc. has decided on a 5-for-1 reverse stock split. If the firm currently has 20,000,000 shares outstanding, how many shares will be outstanding after the stock split?
   a. 100,000,000 shares
   b. 20,000,000 shares

c. 5,000,000 shares
d. 4,000,000 shares

8. Historically, the average price on the ______________ has traded in the $20 to $40 per share range.
   a. Dow Jones Industrial Average
   b. New York Stock Exchange
   c. Standard & Poor's 500
   d. Wilshire 2000

9. Firms use reverse splits when they ______________.
   a. decide to divide the company's stock into a fewer number of outstanding shares
   b. want to change directions in product development
   c. are reversing complex derivative security contracts
   d. None of choices (a) through (c)

10. Maggie owns 100 shares of FloorMart Inc. The firm has a semiannual dividend policy of $0.75 per share or the option to reinvest the cash dividends into additional shares of company stock. If the stock is selling for $55.00 per share, how many shares of stock will Maggie receive each dividend period if she chooses the dividend reinvestment plan?
   a. 0.73 shares
   b. 1.36 shares
   c. 7.33 shares
   d. 13.64 shares

These problems are available in MyFinanceLab.

Problems

1. ***Time line of cash dividend.*** Atlantis Manufacturing Inc. issues the following press release: "Atlantis Manufacturing will pay a quarterly dividend of $0.50 per share to record holders as of the 10th of this month on the 20th of this month." The company made this announcement on July 3, 2009. Draw a time line of the dates around this dividend payment with a two-day settlement for stock transactions. Label the declaration date, the ex-date, the record date, and the payment date.
2. ***Time line of cash dividend.*** Camelot Manufacturing Inc. issues the following press release: "Camelot Manufacturing will pay a quarterly dividend of $1.00 per share on the 20th of the following month to record holders as of the 20th of this month." The company made this announcement on September 3, 2009. Draw a time line of the dates around this dividend payment. Draw a time line of the dates around this dividend payment with a two-day settlement for stock transactions. Label the declaration date, the ex-date, the record date, and the payment date.
3. ***Stock price around dividend.*** Using the information in Problem 1, determine what the stock price of Atlantis Manufacturing will be after the cash dividend announcement in a world of no taxes. Assume that the current price is $47.12 per share and the price does not change between July 3 and July 20 other than for the cash dividend. On what day does the price change? What is the cost to a buyer after the announcement? What is the sales revenue to a seller after the announcement?

4. ***Stock price around dividend.*** Jenny plans to sell 200 shares of ExxonMobil stock. ExxonMobil has just declared a $0.45 cash dividend per share payable in forty days to registered owners twenty days from now. If on the ex-date the price of ExxonMobil is $61.55 per share, show the total proceeds and the source of the proceeds to Jenny if she sells before the close on the ex-date or waits until the morning after the ex-date. Assume a world of no taxes.
5. ***Dividend pattern.*** Refer to Table 17.2 and predict the next dividend using a percent change pattern, a dollar change pattern, and your expectation given the actual pattern change.
6. ***Dividend pattern.*** Go to a Web site source such as Yahoo.com and find the recent dividend payment history of Coca-Cola. Predict Coca-Cola's next dividend change in size and timing.
7. ***Creating own dividend policy.*** Erik owns 2,000,000 shares of Wiseguy Entertainment. Wiseguy just declared a cash dividend of $0.05 per share. The stock is currently selling for $5.00. If Erik wants an annual "dividend income" of $50,000, $100,000, or $250,000 from his stock holdings, what must he do to get these levels of income? What is his wealth in paper and cash for each level of desired dividend income level? Assume a world of no taxes.
8. ***Creating own dividend policy.*** Carmen owns 300,000 shares of Wiseguy Entertainment. Wiseguy has just declared a $0.20 per share dividend on a stock selling at $25.20. What must Carmen do if she wants no cash dividends at this time, $40,000 worth of dividends, or $80,000 worth of dividends? Show her wealth in paper and cash under each scenario. Assume a world of no taxes.
9. ***Change to low-dividend-payout policy.*** Scott currently owns 500 shares of Twelve Colonies Inc. Twelve Colonies has a high-dividend-payout policy and this year will pay $2.00 cash dividend on its shares selling currently at $18.00. Scott wants a low-dividend-payout policy of 2% of the stock price. What will Scott need to do to convert this high-dividend-payout policy to a low-dividend-payout policy for himself? Assume a world of no taxes.
10. ***Change to high-dividend-payout policy.*** Kevin currently owns 800 shares of Cylon Inc. Cylon has a low-dividend-payout policy and this year will pay $0.35 cash dividend on its shares selling currently at $21.00. Kevin wants a high-dividend-payout policy of 6% of the stock price. What will Kevin need to do to convert this low-dividend-payout policy to a high-dividend-payout policy for himself? Assume a world of no taxes.
11. ***Change to low-dividend-payout policy in world of taxes.*** Refer to Problem 9. Assume that Scott pays 20% tax on dividend distribution and 20% on capital gains. Assume also that Scott originally paid $18 for these shares. If Scott only wants to receive $200 after tax, is his wealth affected by changing this dividend policy from a high-dividend-payout policy to a low-dividend-payout policy?
12. ***Change to high-dividend-payout policy in world of taxes.*** Refer to Problem 10. Now assume that Kevin bought the stock at $17.00 per share and his tax rates are 30% on dividends and 15% on capital gains. If Kevin changes the dividend policy from a low-dividend-payout policy to a high-dividend-payout policy, how does his wealth change?
13. ***Stock split.*** If a company declares a 3-for-1 stock split and the price before the split is $90 and the price after the split is $30, show that a current shareholder is no better off after the split.

14. ***Reverse stock split.*** If a company declares a 1-for-5 reverse stock split and the price before the split is $5 and the price after the split is $25, show that a current shareholder is no better off after the split.

15. ***Stock price around stock split.*** Southwest Tires declares a 4-for-1 stock split. The current price is $82.00 per share, and you own 300 shares. What is the expected after-share price? What is your wealth before the split? After?

16. ***Stock price around stock split.*** Northeast Tires announces a reverse split. The company will consolidate outstanding shares through a 1-for-5 split. That is, the company will consolidate every five shares that you currently own into one share. The current stock price is $2.50 per share. What is the after-share price? If you own 10,000 shares, how many will you have after the reverse split? What is your wealth in stock after the split?

17. ***Stock repurchase plan.*** Northern Railroad has announced that it will buy back 1 million of its 30 million shares over the next year. If the stock is selling for $23.40, what is the equivalent cash dividend that the company could pay? If you owned 300 shares of stock, how many would you need to sell to get this cash-equivalent dividend?

18. ***Stock repurchase plan.*** Southern Railroad has announced a $5,000,000 stock repurchase plan over the next month. The current price of Southern Railroad is $18.50 per share, and 15,000,000 shares are outstanding. How many shares is Southern expecting to buy? What is an equivalent cash dividend for this repurchase? If you were a shareholder with 600 shares, how many shares would you need to sell back to have the same cash dividend as the cash-equivalent dividend?

19. ***DRIPs.*** Eastern Railroad has a dividend reinvestment program for shareholders. From 2007 to 2011, the company had the following share prices and the following dividends:

Year	Share Price after Dividend	Dividend per Share
2007	$48.00	$2.50
2008	$50.75	$2.75
2009	$55.15	$3.00
2010	$60.50	$3.50
2011	$61.25	$4.00

If you started with 100 shares of stock at $46 per share and participated fully in the DRIPs program, how many shares of stock would you have at the end of 2011? What is the total value of your shares?

20. ***DRIPs.*** Western Railroad has a dividend reinvestment program for shareholders. From 2007 to 2011, the company had the following share prices and the following dividends:

Year	Share Price after Dividend	Dividend per Share
2007	$28.00	$2.50
2008	$30.75	$2.75
2009	$35.15	$3.00
2010	$40.50	$3.50
2011	$41.25	$4.00

If you started with 100 shares of stock at $20 per share and participated fully in the DRIPS program, how many shares of stock would you have at the end of 2011? What would be the total value of your shares?

Advanced Problems for Spreadsheet Application

These problems are available in MyFinanceLab.

1. ***Dividend irrelevancy problem (no taxes).*** Third Street Music Company has just announced a new dividend policy. It will pay shareholders $1.50 per share this year (it pays dividends annually). The previous policy was not to pay dividends (no-cash-dividend policy). Some members of the board of directors are concerned that some of the shareholders will be upset by the switch. Demonstrate to the board of directors that shareholders view the dividend policy as irrelevant by using the following five shareholders. Show the shareholders' wealth before and after a no-cash-dividend policy and the new $1.50 cash dividend policy. The price before the dividend distribution for the stock was $28.50 and the price after the dividend distribution will be $27.00. If the company had not declared a cash dividend, the price would have remained at $28.50.

   Shareholder No. 1: Owns 5,000 shares of stock and annually takes a home made dividend of $8,000.
   Shareholder No. 2: Owns 25,000 shares of stock and annually takes a homemade dividend of $45,000.
   Shareholder No. 3: Owns 5,000 shares of stock and annually does not take a dividend.
   Shareholder No. 4: Owns 25,000 shares of stock and annually does not take a dividend.
   Shareholder No. 5: Owns 90,000 shares of stock and annually takes a homemade dividend of $100,000.

   Are any shareholders better off under the new cash dividend policy?

2. ***Dividend irrelevancy problem (with personal taxes).*** One of the board members of Third Street Music (from Problem 1) stated that the analysis in a world of no taxes was correct, but our shareholders live in a world of taxes and therefore the change in dividend policy to a cash dividend of $1.50 has an impact on the shareholders' wealth. The board member asks that the company review the analysis of wealth before and after the switch from the no-cash-dividend policy to the cash-dividend policy in a world of personal taxes. Assume that all shareholders pay a 25% tax rate on distributed cash dividends (but no taxes on capital gains) and that the stock price falls by the after-tax cash dividend following the dividend payment (falls by $\$1.50 \times (1 - 0.25)$ or only $1.125 per share). Are any shareholders better off under the new cash dividend policy?

MINI-CASE

East Coast Warehouse Club

This mini-case is available in MyFinanceLab.

Frank O'Connor, CFO of East Coast Warehouse Club, was reviewing notes from the annual shareholders' meeting the week before. Most of the meeting was routine: greetings from the CEO and chairman of the board, review of last year's results, plans for the coming year, election of directors (no surprises), ratification of the auditors, and so on. The only unexpected incident occurred during a question-and-answer period with the CFO when a major institutional shareholder asked if and when the company expected to start paying dividends.

Continued

Continued

The question was met with loud applause and a few cheers of "Hear, hear!" Frank answered, not quite truthfully, that the matter was being discussed internally and was on the agenda for the next board of directors' meeting. In any case, it was on the agenda now.

When the directors met the following month, they looked over a report they had asked the CFO to compile on the pros and cons of instituting dividends. The report first provided a review of the company's financial situation. A recent economic downturn and high energy prices had been devastating for other retailers, but had actually been good for East Coast because hard-pressed consumers looked for the lowest prices on everything from groceries to computers to automobile tires and batteries. East Coast had recently added gas pumps to many locations and could sell gasoline for a few cents less per gallon than other retailers. The gas business was thriving, and company research showed that gas sales brought customers to the stores for other purchases. On the other hand, East Coast's growth policy had become cautious. Its extensive real estate holdings were losing value in a declining market, and the company was unwilling to build stores so close together that it would be competing with itself or so far from its regional base that distribution would become inefficient. Ten percent of total assets were now in cash and short-term investments. Long-term debt had fallen from 35% of assets a few years ago to less than 20%. Cash flow from operations was more than double the investment in new assets.

There was no question that East Coast *could* pay a dividend, but *should* it? Frank wondered what some of his bright young staffers—several of whom had used East Coast's generous educational benefits to obtain MBAs—would have to say about this question, so he put it on the agenda for the regular Wednesday afternoon staff meeting.

Questions

1. The following is a partial list of comments made by staffers at the meeting. To help Frank make a decision, identify the dividend policy or theory they reflect and comment on the usefulness of each.
   - **a.** "What difference does it make if we pay dividends or not? Shareholders can always sell a few shares and make their own dividends." Response: "That works for the big shareholders, but what about the little guys?"
   - **b.** "From a tax perspective, our shareholders would be better off paying the capital gains tax than paying the tax on dividends."
   - **c.** "Stock prices go up and down due to market factors we can't control. A dividend is something you can count on."
   - **d.** "Some of our shareholders want dividends. You heard that at the shareholders' meeting." Response: "That's right, but of course maybe some of them don't. They might prefer that we try to grow the business faster."
   - **e.** "Our business has been doing well, but we're in tough times. A lot of retailers are hurting, and the market is down. By paying a dividend, we send a message to our shareholders that we expect to stay strong for the foreseeable future."
   - **f.** "Before we think of paying dividends, we should be sure we have enough cash to cover our operating expenses and capital budget." Response: "That's right, and once we start paying dividends, we will never be able to cut them."
2. When Frank thought he had gathered enough ideas about dividend theory and policy, he asked the following question: "Let's say we decide that our shareholders want some kind of distribution. What's the best way to do it?" Evaluate the merits of the following suggestions.
   - **a.** "How about a 20% or 30% stock dividend? They will feel as if they're getting something, and it won't use any cash."
   - **b.** "Our stock has been trading between $65 and $80 for the last year. How about a 2-for-1 or 3-for-1 stock split?"
   - **c.** "What about a stock repurchase plan?"
   - **d.** Frank: "Nice thoughts, but the institutional investors seem to be the ones asking for dividends. They won't be easily fooled. Let's focus on cash dividends for now."
3. Assume an investor holds 1,000 shares of East Coast stock, which is trading at $72 per share immediately before the following actions. Calculate the probable value of the stock, the amount of cash received, and total investor wealth immediately after the following actions. Consider each action independently.
   - **a.** East Coast pays a 20% stock dividend.
   - **b.** East Coast splits its stock 3-for-1.
   - **c.** East Coast pays a $2.00 per share cash dividend. The tax rate on dividends is 15%.
   - **d.** East Coast pays a $2.00 per share cash dividend. The investor holds her shares in a tax-sheltered retirement account.
   - **e.** The investor sells 100 shares, which were purchased for $52 per share. The tax rate on capital gains is 15%.
4. The following table shows (in thousands of dollars) normal, best-case, and worst-case projections for East Coast's cash flow from operations,

maintenance costs, investments in new assets, and excess cash for the next four years.

a. If East Coast adopts a sticky dividend policy, what is the highest dividend it will pay in year 1?

b. If it grows dividends at a constant percentage rate, what is the highest sustainable rate it can adopt?

c. East Coast has 42.5 million shares outstanding. If it decides to increase dividends by a constant amount rather than a constant percentage, how much will it increase the dividend per share in year 2?

d. Suppose East Coast adopts a strict residual dividend policy. Year 1 ends up with the excess projected in the best-case scenario, but year 2 ends up with the worst-case scenario. What would be the dividend per share in each year? Why might such a policy not be desirable?

	Year 1	Year 2	Year 3	Year 4
Normal				
Operations	$175,000	$196,000	$ 217,560	$239,316
Maintenance	−$ 36,000	−$ 40,320	−$ 44,755	−$ 49,231
Investing	−$ 44,000	−$ 49,280	−$ 54,701	−$ 60,171
Expected excess	$ 95,000	$106,400	$ 118,104	$129,914
Best case				
Operations	$192,500	$215,600	$239,316	$263,248
Maintenance	−$ 39,600	−$ 44,352	−$ 49,231	−$ 54,154
Investing	−$ 48,400	−$ 54,208	−$ 60,171	−$ 66,188
Expected excess	$104,500	$ 117,040	$129,914	$142,906
Worst case				
Operations	$ 157,500	$166,950	$176,967	$ 187,585
Maintenance	−$ 32,400	−$ 34,344	−$ 36,405	−$ 38,589
Investing	−$ 39,600	−$ 41,976	−$ 44,495	−$ 47,164
Expected excess	$ 85,500	$ 90,630	$ 96,068	$101,832

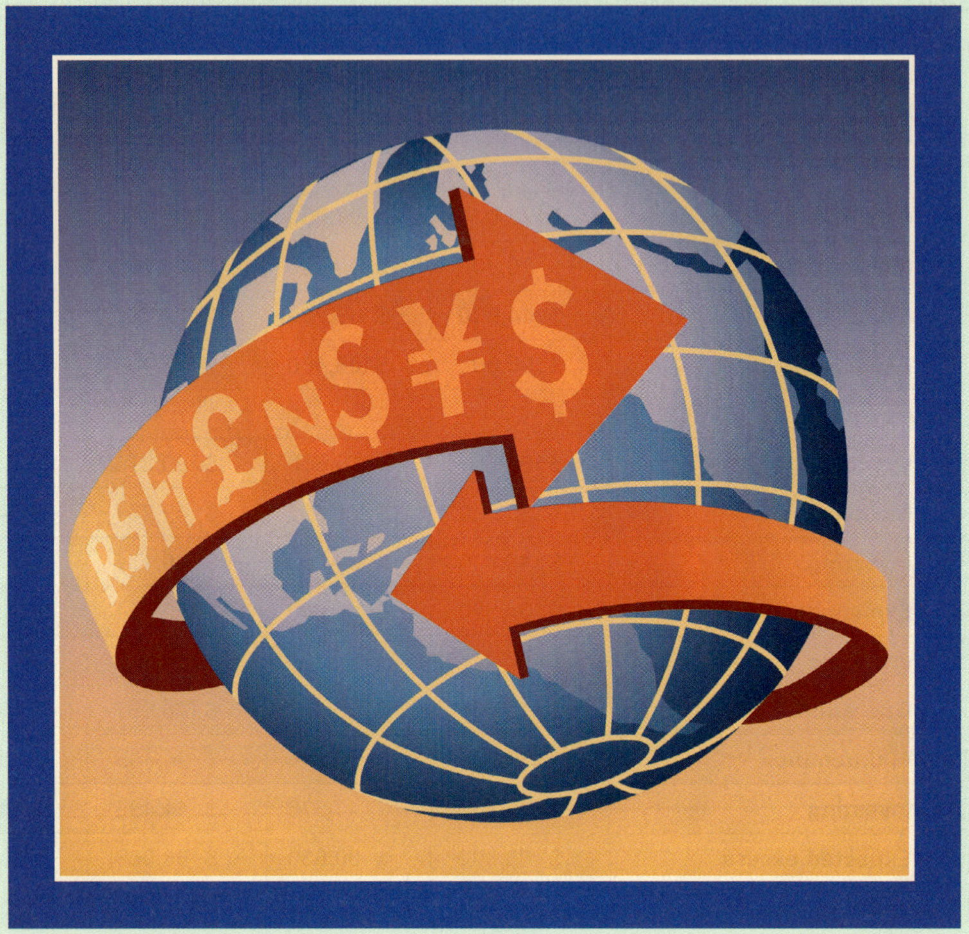

Learning Objectives

LO1 Understand cultural, business, and political differences in business practices.

LO2 Calculate exchange rates, cross rates, and forward rates.

LO3 Understand transaction exposure, operating exposure, and translation exposure.

LO4 Apply net present value to foreign projects.

Chapter 18
International Financial Management

The Big Mac has become an American food icon, right up there with apple pie and corn on the cob. Although it may seem quintessentially American, the Big Mac is, in fact, a world traveler, popular in approximately 120 different countries around the world. The golden arches, in effect, span the globe. In the globalization process, McDonald's has developed customized regional specialties for its otherwise standard American menus. For example, spicy shaka shaka chicken is among the choices in Singapore, and McAloo Tikki, a blend of potatoes and vegetables, is a specialty in India. McDonald's has also set up tailor-made programs and initiatives to benefit the local communities that host the restaurants. So pervasive is the Big Mac presence around the world that ever since 1986, the *Economist* has published a so-called Big Mac index that provides an informal way of making exchange rates "digestible." We'll look at this index later in this chapter.

Managing a business around the globe presents a host of opportunities and a myriad of problems for the management team, some familiar and some unique. The world is shrinking from a business point of view, with links forged every day with multiple business transactions, but within the global community, there are still different cultures, perspectives, and currencies. In this chapter, we look at some of the most basic cultural and financial aspects of managing multinational operations. The area of international finance is vast, so we can touch on only the most essential topics here.

18.1 Managing Multinational Operations

Imagine that you are managing two separate business facilities. You may feel like you have to be in two places at one time. Now imagine that those two facilities are in two different countries. You probably now feel like the complexities have increased tenfold. So it is with **multinational firms**, businesses that operate in more than one country.

The difficulties of managing international business operations stem from three special issues:

1. Cultural risk that can stem from cultural differences
2. Business risk that can arise from differences in business practices
3. Political risk

Aside from the problems facing a manager for a domestic firm on a day-to-day basis, these additional complexities can make the management of all aspects of the multinational firm challenging. In this section, we take a brief look at some of the cultural, business, and political differences to consider when operating a multinational enterprise. Naturally, they are huge and complex issues, so our discussion provides only a brief snapshot. Although they are not directly financial in nature, an appreciation of these issues provides a good backdrop against which to begin to understand international exchange rates and other aspects of international finance.

Cultural Risk

The first issue that can make the management of international business operations a complex enterprise is that of cultural risk. **Cultural risk** arises from differences in customs, social norms, attitudes, assumptions, and expectations of the local society in the host country. We could consider many different issues in a discussion of cultural risk, but here we shall explore five specific issues relating to cultural differences:[1]

1. Differences in ownership structure
2. Differences in human resource norms
3. Religious heritage of the host country
4. Nepotism and corrupt practices in the host country
5. Intellectual property rights

Differences in ownership structure The cultural norms of a country may demand local business ownership. Such norms may even work their way into laws and regulations so that the host country's interests take precedence over the foreign country's interest, the original home of the business. Many times, in order to start a business operation in a foreign country, it will be necessary to use a joint venture business form. Although this practice is now quite common in developing countries, some governments are starting to drop or lower these requirements. However, some industries remain heavily protected against foreign ownership. In the United States, for example, there are laws about foreign investment in areas that are important to national defense, financial markets, and agriculture. This

[1]This typology comes from David K. Eiteman, Arthur I. Stonehill, and Michael H. Moffett, *Multinational Business Finance*, 11th ed. (Boston: Pearson Education, 2007). Here we have added the issue of religious differences and omitted the issue of protectionism.

situation can restrict a company's ownership structure once the business ventures overseas and faces the additional constraint of meeting ownership requirements of more than one government.

Differences in human resource norms Differences in human resource norms can also present problems. In particular, two aspects loom large: hiring and firing practices and policies for management positions.

The hiring of local citizens instead of foreign expatriates is often a necessary part of conducting business abroad. Even if the skill sets of local workers are insufficient, the local cultures of some countries will not allow foreigners to fill certain local jobs. Even in countries where there aren't such restrictions, foreign expatriates may find it difficult living and working in communities where locals view them as taking away wages and livelihoods from local citizens. An additional consideration is that businesses must train unskilled local workers beyond the typical training in a domestic operation.

A second problem can arise from different cultural attitudes toward women or minorities in the workplace. For example, in some areas of the Middle East, women are not allowed to participate at management levels. Thus, local promotions and reward systems may not be consistent with those of the home office and the company must alter them to maintain positive relations with local employees, customers, and government officials.

Religious heritage of the host country Religious differences can also affect the ways in which companies manage employees. Issues surrounding religious observances and dress are part of the daily management issues facing a company conducting business in a foreign country. Businesses can avoid many of the potential conflicts with common sense and respect for the religious heritage of the workforce. Part of management's responsibility is to ensure that the workforce does not have to make a choice between religious beliefs and service to the company.

Nepotism and corrupt practices in the host country The Foreign Corrupt Practices Act, passed during President Jimmy Carter's administration, makes it illegal for U.S. citizens to pay bribes to foreign officials or leaders to facilitate business operations. In many countries, however, bribes are part of the natural flow of cash that makes transactions and business ventures "go." The real issue surrounding bribery arises when a company is competing with other companies not operating under the same set of domestic laws. What should the foreign manager do if bribes are a part of the host country's business practice, competitors are paying them, and domestic laws prohibit them? Unfortunately, that is not an easy question to answer. If the company does not have a competitive advantage so that it can operate successfully without paying a bribe, it may be best to look somewhere else to extend business operations. Another potential solution is to work with local officials or a local advisor to circumvent the traditional bribes. Although some companies will choose to pay the bribe to facilitate business relations, such a policy is illegal for U.S. companies.

Another issue close to that of bribery is the hiring of relatives, a practice known as **nepotism**. In this practice, companies are forced by a local government official to hire specific individuals and place them in positions of control. In so doing, the local official maintains a degree of control over the business, and the ability to reward constituents increases the local official's power. Nepotism was particularly rampant during the reign of the Suharto government in Indonesia. However, it is not restricted to foreign or corrupt officials. In the United States, it is not uncommon to place family members in positions of authority, regardless of their skills or talents. Many a business has tumbled into bankruptcy after ill-prepared family members were given lead management roles. The foreign practice of nepotism can, however, be more intrusive because it may be a requirement before a business can operate locally.

Intellectual property rights Probably the biggest issue in cultural risk is that of intellectual property rights. Property rights, in general, refer to the right of an individual to use his or her talents and properties (assets) for personal gain. The use of physical property, such as one's truck, is restricted to the truck's owner so that he or she can generate revenue from using it in a business. Others cannot legally use another's property (the truck) without the owner's permission. **Intellectual property rights** are similar, but they refer to the product or service that the talents of an individual create. For instance, a composer receives compensation when a performer uses his or her song. Typically, the composer receives a royalty when the sheet music sells. Individuals or entities in foreign countries often violate the rights to retain ownership of such copyrighted creative materials. They also often ignore the rights to patented technology.

The United States and China have been at odds over this issue for several years because the ability to copy and disseminate intellectual property has far outpaced the ability to control distribution. Intellectual property rights are established through patents and copyrights to protect the goods and services of the original developer and the revenues pertaining to them. Some societies view intellectual property rights as critical to the development of new and innovative practices, the creation of art and music, or other types of inspirational activities. Other societies believe that there should be little residual value accorded to the creator and that the idea, product, or service should be free to copy or replicate for the benefit of all.

This issue becomes especially pertinent as firms with specific technological advantages move their businesses into cultures where the exclusive use of the technology may be lost because local governments do not respect or honor copyright or patent laws. Therefore, firms must make a decision when moving overseas about whether to exploit or lose a comparative advantage when it becomes available to competitors through foreign channels.

Many developed nations, including China, signed a 2001 worldwide treaty protecting intellectual property rights. Whether this treaty will alter the landscape of cultural differences on intellectual property rights is still unknown.

Copyrights and patents designed to protect intellectual property may be at risk in some countries.

Business Risk

Another major aspect of operating a business in foreign countries is the assumption of business risk. **Business risk** arises from differences in economic factors and business practices of the host country. Such differences can have critical effects on the profits of a foreign operation.

When we look at a domestic-only company and analyze these areas, we tend to assign "forecasting errors" to the differences between actual performance and anticipated performance. When we look at foreign operations, we need to expand such analysis to include changes in foreign markets that can affect performance. For example, the inflation rate in a foreign economy may be twice that of the domestic economy and can drain company profits. We will look at this issue more closely when we talk about foreign currency transaction risk.

In Chapter 8, we looked at systematic risk and defined it as the risk of doing business, the risk that we cannot diversify away. We can eliminate some firm-specific risks by expanding the breadth of selection of investments in a portfolio (diversification). As a firm moves from domestic operations to international operations, it can, likewise, potentially receive a diversification benefit, but its *total* risk can also increase as it first starts to expand overseas and is not well diversified globally.

For example, a severe drought in a foreign country may have a major effect on a multinational company's ability to meet its sales projections if the company is not well diversified. A sudden rise in interest rates in the host country may affect the multinational's ability to finance operations. A shift in the country's currency exchange rates may have a negative effect on the profits of the multinational firm after it has converted the money back to the domestic currency. The level of international diversification of a multinational business can be a major factor in determining the degree to which specific economic conditions in foreign countries affect the firm. For an example, see the Finance Follies feature on the following pages.

Political Risk

Political risk involves the changes in a foreign government that can have far-reaching effects—both positive and negative—on a multinational company. At one end of the spectrum is a government policy that encourages foreign investment and gives breaks to companies willing to move operations locally. In this case, additional profits are possible as the local government tries to entice firms to move there and help grow the local economy.

At the other extreme is the case in which a local government "takes over" the assets of the company and **nationalizes** it. In this case, the original company often does not receive compensation for the loss of these assets to the ruling government. How does a company guard against the extreme case of nationalized assets? Three basic defensive mechanisms can protect against this type of loss:

1. Keeping critical operations private
2. Financing operations and assets with local money
3. Receiving primary inputs outside the local economy

One way to minimize the potential of nationalization is to *maintain key or critical elements of operations safely within the firm.* If, for example, only the company knows a key process and without this specific knowledge the assets cannot operate properly, the assets are then of no value to the foreign government without the company operating them. If the local government takes over the assets and the company takes its intellectual property home, the assets are no longer able to produce product and, therefore, are of no value to the local government.

Finance Follies

Rino International

What could be hotter than a Chinese company that manufactures pollution control equipment? Investors who bought shares of Rino International in 2007 and 2008 apparently found the combination of China and environment irresistibly seductive. But what did they really know about this company?

Like many foreign companies seeking a listing on the U.S. stock exchanges, Rino was not eager to submit to the intense scrutiny that accompanies a conventional IPO. Instead, it used an obscure procedure known as a reverse merger. To execute a reverse merger, a company arranges for a shell company to purchase it. The shell company has a ticker-tape symbol, but no other significant operations or assets. The company desiring acquisition arranges the financing for its own takeover. The new entity resulting from the merger can then begin to trade on NASDAQ under the old symbol. This maneuver is perfectly legal. Initially well-known companies such as Berkshire-Hathaway, Occidental Petroleum, and Turner Broadcasting used reverse mergers to circumvent the normal IPO process. More recently, foreign companies—especially Chinese and Brazilian firms—have made extensive use of reverse mergers to gain access to U.S. capital markets. In 2010, Chinese companies accounted for 83 reverse mergers, a third of the U.S. total.

In 2007, Rino merged with the shell company American Jade Mountain. On May 9, 2009, a press release announced that American Jade Mountain Corporation was changing its name to Rino Environmental Engineering Science Co. Shortly after, NASDAQ allowed Rino to change its ticker symbol to RINO, completing the transformation. The press release claimed that Rino maintained ISO 9001 Quality Management Certification and implied that the company had many contracts to provide wastewater treatment and other pollution abatement equipment to Chinese iron and steel manufacturers.

The following table shows Rino's NASDAQ stock price on selected dates.

Date	Price
Oct. 1, 2007	$ 2.40
Dec. 2, 2008	$12.25
Aug. 3, 2009	$15.73
Oct. 1, 2009	$21.16
Dec. 1, 2009	$35.00
Dec. 1, 2010	$ 6.07
Aug. 3, 2011	$ 0.38

In August 2010, Rino issued "guidance" forecasting revenues between $221 and $229 million for the year. A month later, the popular investing Web site Motley Fool (www.fool.com) called Rino "undervalued in light of expected earnings." But in November 2010, the Hong Kong–based investment research firm Muddy Waters issued a report declaring that Rino International was an outright fraud. Unlike many U.S.-based firms, Muddy Waters had the distinct advantage of employing analysts who could speak and read Mandarin and who knew how to access the official accounting data that Rino filed with Chinese authorities. Milbery LLP filed a class action suit in December 2010 alleging that Rino's reports to the SEC and the information it provided to analysts included fake contracts, fanciful growth projections, and revenues 90% higher than those it reported to Chinese authorities. The table shows that Rino's stock price began to collapse immediately after Muddy Waters blew the whistle. NASDAQ delisted the stock a short time later and it now trades over the counter at around $0.40 per share.

Without a doubt, foreign investments offer some extraordinary opportunities. Emerging economies like China and India are growing much faster than the mature economies of North America, Western Europe, or Japan. Investments in emerging countries often move independently of or even opposite investment returns in the United States, so they can diversify portfolios more efficiently than domestic investments. At the same time, the Rino example illustrates the many perils of international investing, especially in emerging economies. Official accounting data reported to Chinese authorities are not easily available in the United States. Even if analysts were able to access such data, it would be in Mandarin and employ Chinese accounting practices and conventions, which can be quite different from generally accepted Western accounting practices.

Rino, a tiny mom-and-pop business operating from an industrial park in Dalian, China, did not arrange a reverse merger all by itself. The company employed the services of a New York law firm and a boutique investment banking firm that specializes in advising foreign companies on how to gain access to U.S. capital markets. There are even U.S. investors who specialize in buying up defunct or nearly defunct U.S. companies so that they can sell their SEC registrations and NASDAQ listings to foreign companies looking for reverse mergers. Some of the many lawsuits spawned by the Rino incident claim that these intermediaries also misled investors because they failed to exercise competent due diligence. The intermediaries have countered that competent investors who buy the stocks of newly listed Chinese companies should expect a high level of risk and volatility. This is wise advice, even if it comes a little late for the investors who watched their high-flying investment in Rino crash in the blink of an eye.

Sources: David Barboza and Azam Ahmed, "China to Wall St.: The Side Door Shuffle," *New York Times*, July 24, 2011, Bu1; Karina Frayter, "Questionable China Deals Not Fatal to Reverse Mergers," CNBC.com, June 27, 2011; Jade Mountain Press Release, Reuters, May 9, 2008.

A second defense is to *finance the assets locally*. If the government chooses to take the assets, the company can simply default on its debt payment, thereby leaving the financial burden of the nationalization to the local banker. In this case, the banker will likely lobby the local government to leave the assets in place under the foreign firm's operation. The local banker may have a much stronger tie to the local government than to the foreign company and may be able to influence the local government not to nationalize the assets.

Finally, if possible, it may be that the foreign operation must *rely on inputs from outside the country* to make the assets valuable. For example, if the company can obtain integral parts of the production only from the parent company and without them it cannot produce the desired end products, the assets are no longer valuable under nationalization.

Political risk is not unique to multinational firms. It is also a risk that domestic companies face when domestic government regulations or laws change. Federal, state, and local governments constantly change rules and regulations on the conduct of business. Some of these changes encourage business development, others restrict types of operations, and still others swing the competitive advantages from one business to another. Thus, domestic firms also face political risk, but we tend to think that the stakes are much higher with foreign operations.

In today's international environment, companies must also be concerned with the stability or instability of local governments and the acts of terrorists. Firms may be operating in a country with a friendly and positive government one day only to witness a political coup that changes the relationship overnight. In addition, foreign assets in foreign countries may be easy targets for terrorists. So, the stability of the local government and its ability to provide a safe work environment are critical in expanding operations to foreign countries.

Following this brief snapshot of the risks involved in going global, we now move back to the financial aspects of international finance. We start with foreign currency issues and exchange rates.

18.2 Foreign Exchange

Each country around the world issues currency for use in economic transactions. In England, the currency is the pound sterling (symbol £); in Japan, the yen (¥); in Mexico, the peso; and so on. Nearly every country around the world has its own currency. The exception is the euro (€), a currency that presently seventeen members of the European Union (EU) use, as well as six nonparticipating members of the European Union. Three EU members (Romania, Sweden, and England) continue to use their own currencies. Introduced in 1999, the euro is now the second-most-traded currency in the world, behind the U.S. dollar. As any world traveler knows, when you go from one country to another, you need to exchange your current currency into the currency of the country that you are entering. The world traveler also knows that it's not a direct one-for-one exchange. So, why is one country's currency not equivalent to another country's currency?

To begin to answer this question, we need to understand the concept of an **exchange rate**, the price of one country's currency in units of another country's currency. For example, let's say that you can exchange one U.S. dollar for ninety Japanese yen. Why is an exchange rate of \$1 for ¥90 an acceptable rate? Underlying exchange rates is a basic economic principle called purchasing power parity, a concept that can help us answer this question.

Purchasing Power Parity

Purchasing power parity means that the price of similar goods is the same regardless of which currency one uses to buy the goods. Thus, purchasing power becomes a constant (achieves "parity") among currencies. Let's start with a simple example and see if we can justify the exchange rate of \$1 for ¥90.

Say that you can buy a pair of shoes for \$65.00 in the United States (using U.S. dollars). These shoes are identical in every way, shape, and form to a pair of shoes for sale in Japan. You can order these shoes with direct shipment to you from either the U.S. company or the Japanese company. We will assume that both pairs of shoes will arrive on the same day and transportation costs are included in the total price. You have \$65.00 in U.S. cash. The price of the shoes in Japan is ¥6,010. So, from whom should you order the shoes?

Recall that the philosophy in finance is to buy low and sell high. Thus, you want to buy these shoes at the lowest possible price. If you could exchange your dollars for yen at a rate of \$1 for ¥100, it would cost you only \$60.10 for the shoes if you bought them from the Japanese manufacturer:

$$\text{cost of Japanese shoes} = \frac{¥6{,}010}{¥100/\$1} = \$60.10$$

On the other hand, if you could only get ¥80 per dollar, you would order the shoes from the U.S. company because the Japanese shoes now cost the equivalent of \$75.125:

$$\text{cost of Japanese shoes} = \frac{¥6{,}010}{¥80/\$1} = \$75.125$$

If you could get ¥92.46 per dollar, you would be indifferent because the exchange rate would be set at the point where your purchasing power is the same in Japan as it is in the United States. Thus, the exchange rate is actually set by the ratio of the price of the shoes in Japanese yen to the price of the shoes in U.S. dollars:

$$\text{exchange rate} = \frac{¥6{,}010}{\$65} = \frac{¥92.46}{\$1} \text{ or } ¥92.46 \text{ to } \$1$$

It would be naive to think that all exchange rates around the world are based on the price of a pair of shoes, but the concept of purchasing power parity does help set these rates. An easy-to-understand, rather lighthearted index of purchasing power parity is the so-called Big Mac index published by the *Economist*. Although only an approximation, it provides an intuitive understanding of the concept that a commodity costs

The concept of purchasing power parity means that identical products or services in different countries should cost the same regardless of the currency.

TABLE 18.1 Big Mac Index

Country	Cost of Big Mac	In U.S. Dollars	Purchasing Power	Exchange Rate Foreign Currency per $1
United States	$4.07			
Argentina	Peso 20.0	$4.84	4.92	4.13
Australia	A$4.56	$4.56	1.12	0.92
Brazil	Real 9.50	$6.16	2.34	1.54
Britain	£2.39	$3.89	1.70	1.63
China	Yuan 14.7	$2.27	3.60	6.45
Euro[a]	€3.44	$4.93	1.18	1.43
Hong Kong	HK$15.1	$1.94	3.71	7.79
Japan	¥320	$4.08	78.7	78.4
Mexico	Peso 32.0	$2.74	7.87	11.7
Russia	Ruble 75.0	$2.70	18.5	27.8
Sweden	SKR 48.4	$7.64	11.5	6.34
Turkey	Lire 6.50	$3.77	1.60	1.72

[a]Euro is a weighted average price of a Big Mac across Europe.
Source: "Big Mac Index," August 4, 2011, www.economist.com.

the same no matter what currency one uses to buy it. The index takes the price of a Big Mac in several countries throughout the world and adjusts each price in terms of that country's exchange rate. Table 18.1 shows the Big Mac index for August 4, 2011. Notice that the price of a Big Mac in U.S. dollars was $4.07, whereas in Sweden, it cost the equivalent of $7.64 (or 48.4 Swedish krona), and in China it cost the equivalent of $2.27 (or 14.7 yuan).

The second column of Table 18.1 gives the price of the Big Mac in the local currency. The price in U.S. dollars is in the third column. The current foreign exchange rate is in the far right column. If the Big Mac were the sole good used in the exchange rate of countries, the exchange rates would be equal to the purchasing power column (price in the foreign currency divided by the price of the Big Mac in the United States: $4.07). By comparing the purchasing power column and the actual exchange rate column, you can see how well the Big Mac would fare as the basis for all exchange rates. You can also see how far off the Big Mac is as an exchange rate benchmark. Rather than a single good for the exchange rate, economists use the concept of a basket of goods as the price base for the exchange rate. In general, the rate at which we can exchange money between currencies should allow us to purchase the same basket of goods in any country with the same dollars.

Currency Exchange Rates

Table 18.2 shows selected exchange rates for August 9, 2011. The second column shows the **direct rate**, or **American rate**, which reflects the rate or amount of U.S. dollars required to purchase one unit of a foreign currency. For example, the index quotes the Mexican peso at 0.0810, which means it took a little more than eight U.S. cents to buy one Mexican peso. The far right column shows the **indirect rate**, or **European rate**,

TABLE 18.2 Exchange Rates on August 9, 2011

Country	Direct	Indirect
Argentina (peso)	0.2402	4.1630
Australia (dollar)	1.0167	0.9836
Brazil (real)	0.6126	1.6324
Britain (pound)	1.6228	0.6162
China (yuan)	0.1555	6.4311
Euro	1.4241	0.7022
Hong Kong (dollar)	0.1280	7.8095
Japan (yen)	0.0130	77.1550
Mexico (peso)	0.0810	12.3383
Russia (ruble)	0.0334	29.9220
Sweden (krona)	0.1527	6.5477
Turkey (lire)	0.5639	1.7735

which is the amount of foreign currency that you need to buy one U.S. dollar. For example, it took just over one and a half Brazilian reals to buy one U.S. dollar.

Let's look for a moment at the simple mathematics behind these rates. For direct exchange rates, we list in the numerator the number or amount of domestic currency (U.S. dollars) needed to purchase one unit of the foreign currency. We then list one unit of the foreign currency in the denominator. So, for a direct American rate, we state the amount of U.S. dollar units that we require to buy one foreign currency (FC):

$$\text{direct or American rate} = \frac{\text{U.S. \$}}{\text{1 FC}} \qquad \textbf{18.1}$$

An example is

$$\text{American rate on Mexican pesos} = \frac{\$0.0810}{\text{1 peso}}$$

You can think of the denominator as what we want to buy and the numerator as the price in U.S. dollars (hence, the American rate or American price). In conversation, we often restate this direct rate and say that one peso can buy approximately eight U.S. cents. When you think about converting a peso into dollars, this wording makes sense, just as it makes sense to say it takes only eight cents to buy a peso.

The relationship between the American or direct rate and the European or indirect rate is simply a reciprocal, with the base as one U.S. dollar in the denominator. Thus,

$$\frac{1}{\text{American rate}} = \text{European rate} = \frac{\text{FC}}{\$1} \qquad \textbf{18.2}$$

An example is

$$\text{European rate on Brazilian real} = \frac{\text{Real 1.6324}}{\$1}$$

Thus, it takes just over one and one-half Brazilian reals to buy one U.S. dollar. Again, we often hear that one dollar can buy about one and a half Brazilian reals.

Cross Rates

A cross rate is the exchange rate between two foreign currencies. You can determine it by using the direct and indirect rates of the home currency and the two foreign currencies.

So far, we've looked at the exchange rates between the U.S. home currency rate and the currency rate of another country. For those living in the United States, the use of the U.S. dollar as the base rate makes perfect sense, but what if we want to determine the exchange rate between the British pound sterling (£) and Japanese yen (¥)? We do not have a rate for this exchange in Table 18.2, but we know that British citizens travel to Japan and that Japanese citizens travel to England. Without an exchange rate listed for pounds to yen, how can you determine the exchange rate between these two currencies?

We turn to cross rates to determine the exchange rate between two non-U.S. currencies, using U.S. direct and indirect rates. A **cross rate** is an exchange rate for a non-U.S. currency expressed in terms of another non-U.S. currency. Let's see how it works.

We can use a three-step process to determine the rate:

1. We first convert pounds (£) into U.S. dollars. Using the direct rate from Table 18.2, we see that £1 buys \$1.6228.
2. We then convert our dollars into yen at the indirect rate of ¥77.155 per dollar. So, \$1.6228 times 77.155 buys ¥125.2071.
3. We now have an exchange rate for pounds to yen via the U.S. dollar. That is, if we start with £1, we will end up with ¥125.2071:

$$\text{cross rate (pounds to yen)} = \frac{\pounds 1}{¥125.2017}$$

If you lived in England, you would call this rate the British indirect rate, the amount of Japanese yen that you could purchase with one pound sterling. If we want to go from yen to pound (the British direct rate), we could follow the same three steps, starting with the yen and ending in pounds. Or, we could realize that the stated cross rate—the amount that one pound can buy in yen—is the reciprocal of the amount that one yen can buy in pounds:

$$\text{cross rate (yen to pounds)} = \frac{\pounds 1}{¥125.2017} = \frac{¥1}{\pounds 0.0079868}$$

$$\text{British direct rate for yen} = \frac{\pounds\ 0.0079868}{¥1}$$

We can compute all cross rates using this setup with American rates and European rates with the U.S. dollar as the home currency. To find a foreign currency's indirect rate of another foreign currency, take the direct or American rate of the first foreign currency and multiply it by the indirect or European rate of the second foreign currency:

$$\text{direct rate foreign currency 1} \times \text{indirect rate foreign currency 2}$$
$$= \text{cross rate of foreign currency 1 to foreign currency 2} \qquad \textbf{18.3}$$

$$\text{cross rate (pounds to yen)} = 1.6228 \times 77.155 = 125.2017$$

TABLE 18.3 International Cross Rates

Country	Australia	Britain	China	Euro	Japan	Sweden
Australia	—	0.6265	6.5385	0.7139	78.4435	6.6570
Britain	1.5962	—	10.4364	1.1395	125.2017	10.6256
China	0.1529	0.0958	—	0.1092	11.9976	1.0182
Euro	1.4007	0.8776	9.1582	—	109.8764	9.3246
Japan	0.0127	0.0080	0.0833	0.0091	—	0.0849
Sweden	0.1502	0.0941	0.9822	0.1072	11.7816	—

The reciprocal states

¥1 buys £0.0079868

Table 18.3 displays a set of cross rates from some of the countries listed in Table 18.2. You should be able to confirm these cross rates. If you go down a column, you will see a country's cross rate in the foreign country, that is, the currency of that home country necessary to buy one unit of currency in the foreign currency. If you go across a row, you will see the cross rate that is the amount of foreign currency that it takes to buy one unit of the home currency.

You should recognize that one black rate is the reciprocal of the corresponding red rate between two foreign currencies. For example, the Euro-to-Australia rate (0.7139) is the reciprocal of the Australia-to-Euro rate (1.4007).

Arbitrage Opportunities

What happens if this relationship does not hold, that is, if the cross rate between two foreign currencies does *not* equal the direct rate of currency 1 times the indirect rate of currency 2? When the cross rates are out of line, we have what is known as **arbitrage**, that is, an opportunity to make a profit without risk. In this case, we call it **triangular arbitrage** because it is an opportunity to make a profit without risk by exchanging three currencies. An example will clarify this concept.

EXAMPLE 18.1 Triangular arbitrage

Problem You are preparing to spend two months in Europe following your college graduation. You receive a graduation gift of $5,000. You plan to spend the first two weeks in London and then move on to Paris, Munich, and Vienna. You want to know what the exchange rate will be for your dollars as you convert to pounds and then what the pound-to-euro rate will be for your next exchange. Finally, you want to know what your euro-to-dollar rate will be at the end of your trip. (For convenience, we will use Tables 18.2 and 18.3 in our calculations.)

First, look up the indirect rate for dollars to pounds and see 0.6162 (using the indirect rate from Table 18.2). Then look for the cross rate for pounds to euros and see 1.1395 (using the rates from Table 18.3). Finally, look at the direct rate for dollars and euros and see 1.4241 (Table 18.2).

What if you see that the cross rate for pounds to euros in Table 18.3 is off, however? That is, say that the rate quote is 1.3674. What can you do to exploit this situation?

Solution The answer is that you can perform triangular arbitrage and increase your current $5,000 cash holding without risk. Notice that the quoted cross rate of 1.3674 is above the implied cross rate of 1.1395 from Table 18.3. So, you will want to convert dollars to pounds to euros and back to dollars to take advantage of this undervalued exchange.

You will proceed in three steps.

1. Convert your dollars to pounds:

$$\$5{,}000 \times 0.6162 = £3{,}081$$

2. Then convert your pounds to euros (at the undervalued quoted cross rate):

$$£3{,}081 \times 1.3674 = €4{,}213$$

3. Finally, convert your euros to dollars:

$$€4{,}213 \times 1.4241 = \$6{,}000$$

You are now better off by $1,000 without leaving home. If these rates continue to exist, you will keep on doing this arbitrage, making 20% each time you complete the three exchanges because the rate is overstated by (1.3674/1.1395 − 1), or 20%. Of course, you must be careful not to go in reverse order—dollars to euros, euros to pounds, and pounds to euros—because you would lose money with this exchange order. When cross rates are out of line, one path can lead you to riches and another to ruin!

Why is this particular arbitrage called triangular arbitrage? Figure 18.1 illustrates the process as well as the triangular nature of the path. Starting from the very top of the triangle with an initial $5,000 and moving clockwise, you can see on each side of the triangle the currency exchange rate and the resulting amount in the new currency. The current exchange rates are listed on the respective sides of the triangle for our example problem. If we were to replace the incorrect quoted cross rate of pounds to euros with the correct or implied cross rate of 1.1395, we would have the result depicted in Figure 18.2.

Forward Rates

Although we can go to the market today and exchange one currency for another, travelers or businesses may want to know what rate they can get in the future.

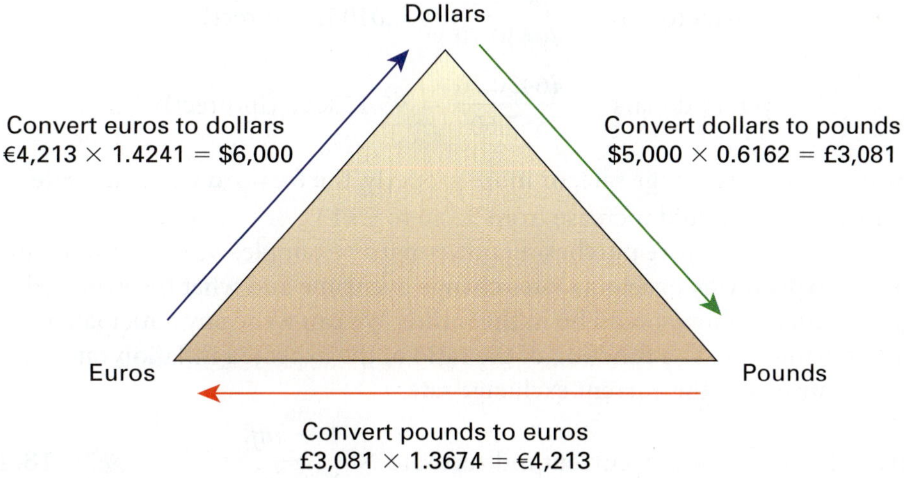

FIGURE 18.1 Triangular arbitrage with three currencies.

FIGURE 18.2 Appropriate cross-rates prevent triangular arbitrage.

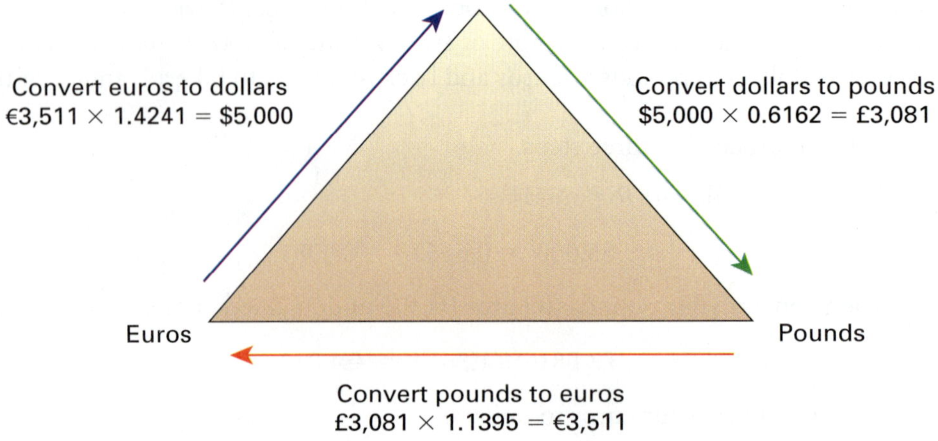

Do exchange rates vary over time, or are they fixed? In 1944, at the Bretton Woods International Monetary Conference, participants fixed the U.S. dollar against foreign currency so that the rate was always the same. When the United States abandoned the gold standard in the early 1970s, as economic conditions changed, new policies allowed the dollar to "float" against other currencies. Today, most currencies float and are thus in a constant state of change.

To address why exchange rates vary over time, let's return to our shoe example and apply the principles of purchasing power parity again. This time, though, let's look at the price of the shoes one year later in the United States and Japan. Recall that the beginning-of-the-year prices were \$65 and ¥6,010, respectively, which would have produced an exchange rate of ¥92.46 per \$1. We know prices in the United States and Japan will change over the coming year due to inflation. If we assume that inflation in the United States (our home country, inf_h) will be 4% and inflation in Japan (our foreign country, inf_f) will be 7%, what will the price of the shoes be at the end of the year? We can solve with equations:

$$\text{U.S. shoe price} = \$65 \times (1 + inf_h) = \$65 \times 1.04 = \$67.60$$

$$\text{Japanese shoe price} = ¥6{,}010 \times (1 + inf_f) = ¥6{,}010 \times 1.07 = ¥6{,}430.70$$

If we apply purchasing power parity at the end of the year, the exchange rate should be set for dollars and yen so that end-of-the-year shoe prices reflect this exchange rate:

$$\text{dollars to yen} = \frac{\$67.60}{¥6430.70} = 0.010512 \text{ (direct)}$$

$$\text{yen to dollars} = \frac{¥6430.70}{\$67.60} = 95.128698 \text{ (indirect)}$$

The future indirect exchange rate, or more properly, the **forward exchange rate** one year from now, should increase from 92.46 to 95.13.

From this simple future purchasing power parity example, we get a powerful tool to help explain why exchange rates change over time and what the expected change in exchange rates should be in the future. We can write any anticipated forward exchange rate as a function of the ratio of the expected inflation rates of the two countries and the current exchange rate:

$$\text{forward indirect rate} = \text{current indirect rate} \times \frac{1 + inf_f}{1 + inf_h} \qquad \textbf{18.4}$$

A word of caution: The inflation rates (inf_f for the foreign country and inf_h for the home country) are expected inflation rates. We do not know what they actually will be, so the forward rate is just a prediction of the forward exchange rate. Also, we could look at the forward rate one year from now, two years from now, or for shorter or longer periods of time.

Let's take our shoe example one more time. If we assume the same inflation rates, but now want to look farther down the road, what is the forward exchange rate two years from now or three years from now?

Again, we simply find the price of the shoes in both countries two and three years from now and imply the forward rate from the future prices:

Two years from now:

$$\text{U.S. shoe price} = \$65.00 \times (1.04)^2 = \$70.304$$

$$\text{Japanese shoe price} = 6{,}010 \times (1.07)^2 = 6880.849$$

$$\text{two-year forward rate} = \frac{¥6880.849}{\$70.304} = \frac{¥97.87}{\$1}$$

Three years from now:

$$\text{U.S. shoe price} = \$65.00 \times (1.04)^3 = \$73.11616$$

$$\text{Japanese shoe price} = ¥6{,}010 \times (1.07)^3 = ¥7{,}362.5084$$

$$\text{three-year forward rate} = \frac{¥7{,}362.5084}{\$73.11616} = \frac{¥100.69}{\$1}$$

So, we can find any forward rate by taking the current rate and the expected inflation rates of the two countries with respect to the number of years. We can alter Equation 18.4 to show any future rate by adding the time to the equation:

$$\text{forward indirect rate}_T = \text{current indirect rate} \times \left(\frac{1 + inf_f}{1 + inf_h}\right)^T \qquad \textbf{18.5}$$

where T is the number of years and the inflation rates are the expected annual inflation rates.

Let's look again at the United States and Japan with a current rate of ¥92.46 per \$1 and see some near- and far-term exchange rates implied by a 4% home country inflation rate and a 7% foreign country inflation rate:

$$\text{90-day forward rate} = 92.46 \times \left(\frac{1 + 0.07}{1 + 0.04}\right)^{90/365} = 92.46 \times 1.0070367 = 93.11$$

$$\text{180-day forward rate} = 92.46 \times \left(\frac{1 + 0.07}{1 + 0.04}\right)^{180/365} = 92.46 \times 1.014123 = 93.77$$

$$\text{2-year forward rate} = 92.46 \times \left(\frac{1 + 0.07}{1 + 0.04}\right)^{2} = 92.46 \times 1.0585244 = 97.87$$

$$\text{3-year forward rate} = 92.46 \times \left(\frac{1 + 0.07}{1 + 0.04}\right)^{3} = 92.46 \times 1.0890588 = 100.69$$

Using Forward Rates

Why do forward rates play an important part in currency exchange? The answer is that you can lock in future currency exchanges with these forward rates. When you convert your currency today, you are exchanging currency in the **spot market** at the current or **spot rate**. When you agree to the exchange at a future point in time at a preset exchange rate (the forward rate), however, you are in fact participating in a **forward contract**. From a business perspective, these forward contracts are "hedging" tools. Through hedging, companies can lock in an exchange rate and avoid the riskiness of market fluctuations and adverse exchange rate movements. We look at this issue later in the chapter when we look at operating exposure and transaction exposure.

Because inflation rates are different around the world, can you leverage them to your own benefit? Why not find a country with the highest inflation rate, convert all your excess cash to that currency, invest it to grow at this high rate, and then at the end of the year convert it back to your domestic currency and outperform domestic returns? You can indeed try to do so. The process is called **covered interest arbitrage**: investing in different currencies with different expected inflation rates to make a profit. The only problem with exploiting this arbitrage is the uncertainty of the end-of-year exchange rate. To remove this uncertainty, you must lock in your future exchange rate when you first start the process. Let's see how it works.

EXAMPLE 18.2 Exploiting higher international interest rates

Problem You have saved \$20,000 for investing purposes. You see that the CD rate in Japan is 9% for the coming year and only 6% in the United States. You also see that the current indirect exchange rate is ninety yen to one dollar (¥90 to \$1). You also note that the one-year forward indirect rate is 92.5472. Can you exploit this situation to your gain?

Solution You have two choices: invest in the United States and get a 6% increase on your \$20,000, or invest in Japan at 9% with the need to convert current cash at ninety yen per dollar and the ability to convert future cash at 92.5472 with a forward exchange rate contract. Here are the two scenarios.

1. Year-end results of U.S. investing:

$$\$20{,}000 \times 1.06 = \$21{,}200$$

2. Year-end results of Japanese investing:

$$\text{convert on day 1: } \$20{,}000 \times 90 = ¥1{,}800{,}000$$

$$\text{investment growth in Japan: } ¥1{,}800{,}000 \times 1.09 = ¥1{,}962{,}000$$

$$\text{convert back at end of year: } \frac{¥1{,}962{,}000}{92.5427} = \$21{,}200$$

Apparently, the rising exchange rate offsets any potential gain that you might realize from investing your money in the country with the higher inflation rate.

Again, we must be careful because there are various interest rates for various investments in both countries. Here we are using a nominal risk-free rate. If we return for a moment to the basics of interest rates and revisit the Fisher effect (see Chapter 5), we can rewrite this equation and derive the **International Fisher effect** on real interest rates. Recall that the approximate nominal risk-free rate is inflation plus the real rate. If we substitute back into Equations 18.4 and 18.5 and solve, we get the approximate real rates:

$$\text{nominal rate}_h - \text{inflation rate}_h = \text{nominal rate}_f - \text{inflation rate}_f$$

or

$$\text{real rate}_{\text{home country}} = \text{real rate}_{\text{foreign country}} \quad \textbf{18.6}$$

What the International Fisher effect tells us is that real interest rates the world over are the same and that one cannot exploit different inflation rates across different countries.

With this knowledge about exchange rates and forward rates, how do we use it to benefit the management of multinational business operations? We explore some of the business applications and issues in the next two sections.

18.3 Transaction, Operating, and Translation Exposures

If you manage a business, one of the first things that you will realize is that customers often pay for a product or service long after they receive it. A major current asset of many businesses is accounts receivable, the anticipated payment for products that they sell or services that they render. In a domestic-only company, you can manage this asset with some basic short-term cash management tools, but when a foreign operation is involved, you face the added problem of fluctuating exchange rates.

Two problems can arise. First, anticipated cash inflows may fall in value if unexpected movements in the exchange rate hurt your ability to convert the foreign currency into domestic currency. Second, the future anticipated cash flows of the foreign business now will be producing less domestic currency upon conversion. We call the first problem—reduction in the conversion of future currency—transaction exposure. We call the second problem—reduction in the value of future cash flow from operations—operating exposure.

Transaction Exposure

Let's look first at transaction exposure. **Transaction exposure** is the potential loss in home currency value of future foreign currency payments. Assume that you manage a firm that manufactures and sells bicycles around the world. You have just completed a sale of 5,000 bicycles to a chain of stores in Sweden at a cost of 1,880 krona per bicycle. You are now awaiting payment.

The exchange rate today is 6.5477 krona per dollar, so your anticipated sales receipt of 9,400,000 krona will convert into $1,435,619 at this rate. However, the company will not make the payment for another ninety days. Over the next ninety days, the indirect exchange rate unexpectedly moves from 6.5477 to 6.7500. Now the sale of the 5,000 bicycles will produce domestic revenue of only $1,392,593, or a difference of $43,026 between anticipated revenue and actual revenue. Of course, the exchange rate could unexpectedly move in your favor and produce more revenue than expected. Either way, the potential unexpected change in exchange rates affects the cash flow of the business. Therefore, you must try to manage this uncertainty.

One way to hedge the future conversion of known sales is to enter at the time of the sale into a *forward currency contract*, an agreement to exchange currencies at a preset exchange rate (the *forward rate*) at some future point in time. In this way, you lock in the anticipated conversion of the foreign currency to U.S. dollars. In this setting, at the time the company sells the bicycles to the Swedish client, the company enters into a forward contract with a set exchange rate in anticipation of the receipt of the 9,400,000 krona. The forward rate will be the current spot rate multiplied by the ratio of the anticipated inflation rates of Sweden and the United States. Such a contract removes the uncertainty around the cash flow in dollars when the company converts the bicycle revenue from krona ninety days after the initial sale.

Operating Exposure

A second problem in our example is that of operating exposure. **Operating exposure** is the risk of the effect of unfavorable exchange rate movements on the long-run viability of a foreign operation of a multinational business. To understand this potential problem, just expand the bicycle scenario to future production and sales. Let's assume that we have expanded operations overseas and the bicycles that the company manufactures in Sweden are assembled with local materials and labor at a cost of 1,200 krona per bicycle. The price per bicycle remains at 1,880 krona. If we assume a modest inflation rate of 5% per year for both production and sales in Sweden and the same inflation rate in the United States, things are fine. A smaller 3.25% inflation rate in the United States, however, will cause a rising indirect exchange rate. Watch what happens in Tables 18.4 (same inflation rates) and 18.5 (different inflation rates) to the future cash flow in terms of domestic profit over time. The revenue and cost for each successive year are the prior year's revenue or cost multiplied by 1 plus the inflation rate.

TABLE 18.4 Dollar Profit per Swedish Bicycle Sale: No Change in Exchange Rate (inflation the same in both countries)

	Year 1	Year 2	Year 3	Year 4
Revenue	$ 1,880	$ 1,974	$2,072.70	$2,176.33
Cost	$ 1,200	$ 1,260	$1,323.00	$1,389.15
Krona profit	$ 680	$ 714	$ 749.70	$ 787.33
Exchange rate	6.5477	6.5477	6.5477	6.5477
Dollar profit	$103.85	$109.05	$ 114.50	$ 120.25

TABLE 18.5 Dollar Profit per Swedish Bicycle Sale: Increase in Exchange Rate Due to Different Inflation Rates

	Year 1	Year 2	Year 3	Year 4
Revenue	$ 1,880	$ 1,974	$2,072.70	$2,176.33
Cost	$ 1,200	$ 1,260	$1,323.00	$1,389.15
Krona profit	$ 680	$ 714	$ 749.70	$ 787.33
Exchange rate	6.5477	6.6587	6.7715	6.8863
Dollar profit	$103.85	$107.23	$ 110.71	$ 114.33

Table 18.5 shows that the anticipated growth in profits is not keeping up with the Swedish inflation rate of 5% when the company converts profits to dollars with increasing indirect exchange rates (see the exchange rate line in both tables). These increasing exchange rates reduce the growth of the business. Again, the opposite can materialize with declining exchange rates that increase the growth of the foreign operations.

For management purposes, the value of the operations is at risk, and even though the company could use forward rates to hedge this lower profit margin, in terms of real domestic dollars, the company has one more added risk exposure when dealing with foreign operations. If you examine the two tables closely, you will see that the dollar profit growth is 3.25% for Table 18.5, or the same as the U.S. inflation rate, despite a 5% growth rate in Sweden.

What would happen if the inflation rates in both countries remained constant and we could anticipate fully the exchange rate increase? Would we then have no loss in value? Not all products and costs inflate at the same rate as the overall inflation rate of a country. We could still have a lower inflation rate for bicycle revenue and a higher rate for labor costs than the overall inflation rate of Sweden and could therefore still lose value in the foreign operation.

Translation Exposure

A third issue is **translation exposure** or **accounting exposure**, the risk of a negative effect on financial statements due to different countries' rules for translating foreign financial statements into consolidated reports of both foreign and domestic operations. At issue here is the translation of different accounts with different exchange rates. It would seem that the best way to translate foreign statements for consolidation with domestic statements is to use the current exchange rate on all accounts and then add them into the domestic account totals. Unfortunately, rules governing consolidation of foreign accounts are not that simple. Translation principles in many countries require the use of historical exchange rates for certain equity, fixed asset, and inventory accounts, but current exchange rates for current assets, current liabilities, and income accounts. Therefore, when the companies process everything, the result can be in an account imbalance. In other words, the companies can violate the accounting identity during translation and consolidation. This imbalance cannot exist when reporting the consolidated financial statements, so accounting practices take the difference to either current income or an equity reserve account. Either way, it can have a negative effect on the financial statements.

Do the challenges of transaction, operating, and translation exposures that we have just discussed change the way we make decisions on foreign projects, or do we remain faithful to the basic financial tools that we already possess and make decisions based on the project's net present value? That is the next issue that we address.

18.4 Foreign Investment Decisions

Multinational capital budgeting is a straightforward application of the NPV model with one twist: we can do the analysis in either domestic currency or foreign currency. The inputs are identical to any other project in that we need to know the timing and amount of all incremental cash flow and must select the appropriate discount rate for the project.

However, we should consider two important issues as we extend capital budgeting into a multinational setting. The first is the derivation of the appropriate discount rate, which must take into account different inflation rates in different countries. The second is the exchange rate, with which we are now familiar.

In terms of finding the appropriate discount rate, we must take inflation into account because inflation rates vary with the economies of various countries. To select the appropriate discount rate for a project, we would build the rate as follows:

$$\text{discount rate} = \text{real rate} + \text{inflation} + \text{risk premium of project} \qquad \textbf{18.7}$$

The only variable that would be different across the two currencies is the anticipated inflation rate for the two countries. Therefore, the discount will reflect the inflation rate for the currency that we pick for the project.

The second issue is the exchange rate, which we can handle rather easily. If we are using foreign currency for the NPV decision, we just restate all the foreign incremental cash flow in terms of present value and use the current exchange rate. We already discount all incremental cash flow to the present with the NPV model anyway, so we just add this small step in the process. If we choose to use the domestic currency, we will have to convert incremental cash flow at different points in time. If we know the two different inflation rates, however, we can calculate the forward rates for each of the future conversion years. Again, it is an added step, but one that we can easily accomplish.

For verification, we will examine a proposed foreign project and its net present value in Example 18.3, using both the foreign currency and the domestic currency approaches.

EXAMPLE 18.3 Domestic currency and foreign currency approaches for an NPV decision

Problem Surfboards U.S.A. wants to produce and sell surfboards in Mazatlan, Mexico. The company has calculated the following after-tax incremental cash flow in pesos using a five-year project window:

- Initial investment of 120,000,000 pesos
- Operating cash flow

  Year 1: 30,000,000 pesos
  Year 2: 45,000,000 pesos
  Year 3: 56,000,000 pesos
  Year 4: 48,000,000 pesos
  Year 5: 34,000,000 pesos

- Working capital increases or decreases

  Investment increase in working capital: 6,000,000 pesos
  Recovery (decrease) in working capital, Year 5: 6,000,000 pesos

The appropriate discount rate for this project would be 12% in the United States. The anticipated inflation rate in the United States is 4%, and the anticipated inflation rate in Mexico is 7%. Let's assume a current indirect exchange rate of 13.5 pesos per dollar.

Solution

Domestic Currency Approach

Step 1: Calculate the forward exchange rates.

$$\text{Year 1: } 13.25 \times \frac{1.07}{1.04} = 13.6322$$

$$\text{Year 2: } 13.25 \times \left(\frac{1.07}{1.04}\right)^2 = 14.0254$$

$$\text{Year 3: } 13.25 \times \left(\frac{1.07}{1.04}\right)^3 = 14.4300$$

$$\text{Year 4: } 13.25 \times \left(\frac{1.07}{1.04}\right)^4 = 14.8463$$

$$\text{Year 5: } 13.25 \times \left(\frac{1.07}{1.04}\right)^5 = 15.2745$$

Step 2: Convert all pesos into dollars using current and forward exchange rates.

$$\text{Year 0 cash outflow: } \frac{-120{,}000{,}000 - 6{,}000{,}000}{13.25} = -\$9{,}509{,}434$$

$$\text{Year 1 cash inflow: } \frac{30{,}000{,}000}{13.6322} = \$2{,}200{,}670$$

$$\text{Year 2 cash inflow: } \frac{45{,}000{,}000}{14.0254} = \$3{,}208{,}454$$

$$\text{Year 3 cash inflow: } \frac{56{,}000{,}000}{14.4300} = \$3{,}880{,}796$$

$$\text{Year 4 cash inflow: } \frac{48{,}000{,}000}{14.8463} = \$3{,}233{,}133$$

$$\text{Year 5 cash inflow: } \frac{34{,}000{,}000 + 6{,}000{,}000}{15.2745} = \$2{,}618{,}737$$

Step 3: Convert all future dollars into present value with the *domestic discount rate* of 12%.

Year 0: $-\$9{,}509{,}434$

$$\text{Year 1: } \frac{\$2{,}200{,}670}{1.12} = \$1{,}964{,}884$$

$$\text{Year 2: } \frac{\$3{,}208{,}454}{1.12^2} = \$2{,}557{,}760$$

$$\text{Year 3: } \frac{\$3{,}880{,}796}{1.12^3} = \$2{,}762{,}274$$

$$\text{Year 4: } \frac{\$3{,}233{,}133}{1.12^4} = \$2{,}054{,}715$$

$$\text{Year 5: } \frac{\$2{,}618{,}737}{1.12^5} = \$1{,}485{,}942$$

Step 4: Add the net present value of the outflow and inflow.

$$NPV = -\$9{,}509{,}434 + \$1{,}964{,}884 + \$2{,}557{,}760 + \$2{,}762{,}274$$

$$+ \$2{,}054{,}715 + \$1{,}485{,}942 = \mathbf{\$1{,}316{,}140}$$

Step 5: Accept the project because the net present value is positive.

Foreign Currency Approach

Step 1: Find the appropriate foreign discount rate.

$$\text{rate}_f = (1 + \text{U.S. discount rate}) \times \left(\frac{1 + \text{foreign inflation}}{1 + \text{U.S. inflation}}\right) - 1$$

$$\text{foreign discount rate} = 1.12 \times \frac{1.07}{1.04} - 1 = 15.2307692\%$$

Step 2: Find the present value of cash flow in pesos using the foreign discount rate.

Year 0: $(-120{,}000{,}000 - 6{,}000{,}000) = -126{,}000{,}000$ pesos

Year 1: $\dfrac{30{,}000{,}000}{1.1523} = 26{,}034{,}712.95$ pesos

Year 2: $\dfrac{45{,}000{,}000}{1.1523^2} = 33{,}890{,}313.92$ pesos

Year 3: $\dfrac{56{,}000{,}000}{1.1523^3} = 36{,}600{,}131.34$ pesos

Year 4: $\dfrac{48{,}000{,}000}{1.1523^4} = 27{,}224{,}968.95$ pesos

Year 5: $\dfrac{34{,}000{,}000 + 6{,}000{,}000}{1.1523^5} = 19{,}688{,}729.22$ pesos

Step 3: Find the net present value in pesos (add up the present value of the cash outflow and inflow).

$$NVP = -126{,}000{,}000 + 26{,}034{,}712.95 + 33{,}890{,}313.92 + 36{,}000{,}131.34$$

$$+ 27{,}224{,}968.95 + 19{,}688{,}729.22 = 17{,}438{,}856.38$$

Step 4: Convert pesos to dollars using the current exchange rate.

$$NPV = \frac{17{,}438{,}856.38}{13.25} = \mathbf{\$1{,}316{,}140}$$

Step 5: Accept the project because the NPV is positive.

Notice in Example 18.3 that it did not matter which approach we used as long as we made the proper adjustment for forward exchange rates and the appropriate discount rate for the domestic and foreign approaches. The answer is always the same. One must be careful, of course, to avoid differences with rounding of exchange rates, discount rates, and cash flow to produce the exact same value. We changed the cash flow and rates here to present value and converted from foreign to domestic with a spreadsheet, where rounding is not a problem.

One item that we rushed by in the previous calculations was the appropriate foreign discount rate. In Example 18.3, it was Step 1 where we found the appropriate discount rate when using pesos. With the foreign currency approach, if we know the appropriate discount rate in the home country and the expected inflation rates in the two countries, we can determine the appropriate foreign discount rate. We used the ratio of the inflation rates just as we did when we looked at the forward exchange rates and different interest rates between countries. This ratio does not reflect a higher risk premium or a higher real rate of interest, but only the difference in anticipated inflation of the two countries. The foreign discount rate adjusts to accommodate the project's operating exposure over its entire life.

Numerous other issues fall into the category of international financial management, but they will be left to other books and other classrooms because of their vast scope.

To review this chapter, see the Summary Card at the end of the text.

Key Terms

accounting exposure, p. 569
arbitrage, p. 562
business risk (foreign business risk), p. 554
covered interest arbitrage, p. 566
cross rate, p. 561
cultural risk, p. 552
direct (American) rate, p. 559
exchange rate, p. 558
forward contract, p. 566
forward exchange rate, p. 564
indirect (European) rate, p. 559
intellectual property rights, p. 554
International Fisher effect, p. 566
multinational firm, p. 552
nationalize, p. 555
nepotism, p. 553
operating exposure, p. 568
political risk, p. 555
purchasing power parity, p. 558
spot market, p. 565
spot rate, p. 566
transaction exposure, p. 567
translation exposure, p. 569
triangular arbitrage, p. 562

Questions

1. What effect can cultural differences have on the ownership structure of a foreign operation of a multinational business?
2. What are intellectual property rights? How have changes in technology affected the ability to protect intellectual property rights?
3. What does it mean to nationalize a business? How can a domestic company minimize the risk of nationalization of its foreign operations?
4. Explain how purchasing power parity determines the exchange rate between two currencies.
5. Why are currency exchange rates constantly changing over time?
6. What is a cross rate? How can you find the cross rate of two foreign currencies if you know only the direct and indirect rates of those two foreign currencies with respect to your home currency?
7. Why should a company be concerned about a change in future exchange rates if it has already delivered and sold product in a foreign country?
8. How can a changing exchange rate affect a company's profits on one of its foreign operations?
9. Explain how translating a foreign balance sheet for inclusion in a multinational's domestic balance sheet can violate the accounting identity.

10. Is it better to calculate the net present value of a foreign project in the foreign currency or in the domestic currency?

Prepping for Exams

1. Specific issues related to cultural differences can arise in the management of a multinational enterprise. All of the following are related to cultural differences except ________.

a. a requirement to have local management
b. issues with promotion of women into management positions
c. issues with observation of religious holidays
d. nationalization of the company's assets by the foreign government

2. As we go from home operations to international operations, we can potentially receive a ________, but we can also see our ________ increase.

a. diversification benefit; systematic risk
b. diversification disadvantage; total risk
c. diversification disadvantage; systematic risk
d. diversification benefit; total risk

3. ________ means that the price of similar goods is the same, regardless of which currency one uses to buy the goods.

a. Interest rate parity
b. Purchasing power parity
c. Currency parity
d. Expectation parity

4. Assume that you are the manager of an American company and that you face an exchange rate of ¥150 per $1. Whenever you receive an order, rather than ship from your production facilities, you call in the order to a Japanese company and have it ship the bill to you directly. If the bill the company ships to you is ¥7,500 and you can collect $55 per item that you sell to your customer, what is your profit if you pay the Japanese company ¥7,500?

a. $5.00 per time
b. $4.75 per time
c. $4.50 per time
d. $4.00 per time

5. If £1 buys ¥200, then the reciprocal states that ¥1 buys what?

a. £0.00491
b. £0.00494
c. £0.00500
d. £0.00512

6. We can write any ________ as a function of the difference between the expected inflation rates of two countries and the current or spot exchange rate.

a. anticipated forward exchange rate
b. known forward exchange rate
c. anticipated spot rate
d. unanticipated forward exchange rate

7. Anticipated cash inflows may fall in value if unexpected movements in the exchange rate hurt your ability to convert the foreign currency into domestic currency. We call this reduction in the conversion of future payments ________.

   a. translation exposure
   b. transaction exposure
   c. conversion exposure
   d. operating exposure

8. Assume that you manage a firm that faces transaction exposure. Your company manufactures and sells tricycles around the world. You have just completed a large tricycle sale to a chain of stores in Sweden and received a promised payment of 375 krona per tricycle. You have already sold 3,000 tricycles and are now awaiting payment. The exchange rate today is 7.5 krona per dollar. Over the next ninety days, the indirect exchange rate unexpectedly moves from 7.5 to 7.7. What is the fall in domestic revenue due to this unexpected move in the exchange rate?

   a. $389
   b. $1289
   c. $2896
   d. $3896

9. Which of the following statements is *true*?

   a. Multinational capital budgeting is a more complicated application of the NPV model because we can only do the analysis in foreign currency.
   b. The application of the NPV model to multinational firms is different from any other project in that we must always find the appropriate discount rate for the project in the foreign country rate.
   c. When performing multinational capital budgeting, the appropriate discount rate varies based on the currency that you choose to analyze the project.
   d. It is impossible to tell the actual NPV in the home currency because foreign cash flows are from different time periods.

10. Say that the current indirect exchange rate is 12 pesos per dollar. The cash inflow in pesos is 100,000 in two years, and the discount rate is 10%. During this time, the anticipated annual inflation rate is 6% in the United States and 14% in Mexico. What is the present value of the 100,000 pesos in U.S. dollars after conversion from pesos to dollars if you are using current and forward exchange rates?

   a. $5,984.35
   b. $5,954.36
   c. $5,924.46
   d. $5,936.54

Problems

These problems are available in MyFinanceLab.

1. ***Foreign exchange and commodity prices.*** While traveling in the following countries you see twenty-ounce plastic bottles of Coca-Cola. You know the price in the United States for a coke is $1.09, but the countries have the following prices:

   Canada: C$1.50
   Japan: ¥125
   England: £0.60
   European Union: €0.90

   What is the implied exchange rate for U.S. dollars and these four currencies?

2. ***Foreign exchange and commodity prices.*** While traveling in various countries, you occasionally resort to U.S. food. You pay the following prices for a Big Mac:

   India: 210 rupee
   Kuwait: 1.39 dinar
   Sweden: 34.90 krona
   Ukraine: 133 rubles

   If the price of a Big Mac is $4.59 in the United States, what are the implied exchange rates for these currencies?

3. ***Currency exchange rates.*** You are taking a trip to six European countries. It is a ten-day trip, and you are taking $3,500. The current direct conversion rate is 1.2150 for euros. While in Europe, you spend €2638.30. You convert your remaining euros back to U.S. dollars upon your return. If the exchange rates remained the same over your trip, how much do you have left in U.S. dollars?

4. ***Currency exchange rates.*** On the day you arrive in England, the exchange rate for U.S. dollars and British pounds is $1:£0.58. While you remain in England for the next two weeks, the exchange rate falls to $1:£0.54. When you entered England, you converted $4,200 to pounds. As you leave England, you have £135. How much did you spend in England in U.S. dollars? Did the movement in the exchange rate help or hurt you?

5. ***Cross rates.*** You plan to travel to Japan and China on a business trip. You will first stop in Japan, where the current direct exchange rate is 0.0092. You will next stop in China, where the current direct exchange rate is 0.1285. As you leave Japan, you have ¥980,000 and need to convert to yuan. What is the cross rate for yuan? How many yuan do you get for your yen? Verify by converting yen back to dollars and then dollars to yuan.

6. ***Cross rates.*** Fill in the missing cross rates and direct rates in the following table.

International Cross Rates

Country	$	Euro	Pound	Peso	Yen	C$
Canada	1.3689					—
Japan	109.48				—	
Mexico	11.3921			—		
United Kingdom	0.5460		—			
Euro	0.8222	—				
United States	—					

7. ***Triangular arbitrage.*** Great Exchanges Inc. is a currency exchange company located at most international airports. Today, a clerk has made a mistake on one of the currency exchanges and has posted the following rates:

$ for £	£ for €	€ for $	£ for $	€ for £	$ for €
0.5310	1.4435	1.3046	1.8832	0.9628	0.7665

   Which corresponding rates do not match? If you had $1,000, how much could you make on one pass through the currencies?

8. ***Triangular arbitrage.*** Using the data from Problem 7, determine what you would lose if you went the wrong way for the arbitrage. Explain this result.

9. ***Forward rates.*** Your company has posted you on an eighteen-month overseas assignment in Budapest, Hungary. You will be living on the Buda side of the river, but will be spending much of your time on the Pest side. The current indirect rate for the Hungarian forint is 187.90. If the anticipated inflation rate in the United States is 3% and the anticipated rate in Hungary is 8.5% (annually), what exchange rate do you anticipate at the end of your assignment?

10. ***Forward rates.*** The *Wall Street Journal* lists forward rates for Japanese yen. Say that the current listings are

    one-month forward rate (indirect) 103.17
    three-month forward rate (indirect) 102.68
    six-month forward rate (indirect) 101.88

    First, is the anticipated inflation rate higher or lower in Japan compared with that in the United States? Second, if the current indirect rate is 103.37, what do the six-month rate and the current rate imply about the relative difference in the anticipated annual inflation rates? Finally, using the current indirect rate and the six-month forward rate, determine the annual anticipated inflation rate for Japan if the anticipated U.S. inflation rate is 3.45%.

11. ***Real rates.*** Determine the real interest rates in the following countries given their nominal interest rates and inflation rates:

    Canada: Inflation is 4.5%, and the nominal risk-free interest rate is 6.0%.
    Switzerland: Inflation is 1.25%, and the nominal risk-free interest rate is 3.75%.
    United States: Inflation is 3%, and the nominal risk-free interest rate is 4.50%.

12. ***Real rates.*** Determine the nominal rates for the three countries listed if they have the following inflation rates and the real rate the world over is 1.25%:

    Canada: Inflation is 4.5%.
    Switzerland: Inflation is 1.25%.
    United States: Inflation is 3%.

13. ***Transaction exposure.*** International Products Inc. has ordered 10,000 leather coats from Argentina for delivery in six months. The contracted cost of a coat is 122 pesos. International Products will pay for the coats upon delivery. The current indirect exchange rate is $1 for 1.2902 pesos. The anticipated inflation rate is 3% in the United States and 7% in Argentina. In U.S. dollars, how much will the 10,000 leather coats cost International Products at delivery?

14. ***Transaction exposure.*** International Products has contracted for 5,000 winter hats from Russia. The contract price is 1,375 rubles per hat. The current direct exchange rate is 0.03562. The expected inflation rate for the next nine months is 5% in the United States and 2% in Russia. If International Products will pay for the hats at delivery and scheduled delivery is nine months away, what is the cost of the hats in U.S. dollars? Did waiting the nine months to pay increase or decrease the payment (in U.S. dollars)? If so, by how much?

15. ***Operating exposure.*** Copy-Cat Inc. has signed a deal to make vintage Nissan 240-Z sports cars for the next three years. The company will build the cars in Japan and

ship them to the United States for sale. The current indirect rate is 103.50 for dollars and yen. The anticipated inflation rate for parts and labor in Japan is 2.5% over the next three years, and the anticipated overall inflation rate for Japan is 3.5% over the next three years. The expected overall inflation rate in the United States is 4.0% over the next three years. (The stated rates are on an annual basis.) If Copy-Cat plans to sell 500 cars a year at an initial price of $45,000 and the cost of production is ¥4,036,500, what is the annual profit in real dollars for Copy-Cat? Assume that it takes one year for production and all sales revenues and production costs are at the end of the year. Is this profit rising or falling each year? Why?

16. ***Operating exposure.*** Just before Copy-Cat Inc. starts the project outlined in Problem 15, the government announces new anticipated inflation numbers. For Japan, the estimate is a higher inflation rate of 5%. For the United States, the estimate is a lower projection of 3.0%. If the production cost inflation rate remains at 2.5%, will these new anticipated inflation rates affect the production of vintage 240-Zs?

17. ***Domestic NPV approach.*** Surfboards U.S.A. wants to expand its operations to Australia. The current indirect exchange rate is 1.45 for U.S. and Australian dollars. The anticipated inflation rate is 3% in the United States, but only 1.5% in Australia. The discount rate in the United States for the expansion project is 14%. If the company has forecasted the following Australian dollars for the expansion project, should Surfboards U.S.A. expand to Australia? Use the domestic currency approach.

    Investment: A$40,000,000
    Year 1 cash flow: A$5,000,000
    Year 2 cash flow: A$9,000,000
    Year 3 cash flow: A$16,000,000
    Year 4 cash flow: A$20,000,000
    Year 5 cash flow: A$8,000,000
    Year 6 cash flow: A$3,000,000

18. ***Domestic NPV approach.*** Farbucks is thinking of expanding to South Korea. The current indirect rate for dollars and South Korean won is 1025. The expected inflation rate in South Korea should hover near 0.5% for the next five years. The expected U.S. inflation rate should stay around 3.0%. The discount rate for expanding is 15% for Farbucks. Given the following projected cash flows for the expansion project and using the domestic NPV approach, should Farbucks expand to South Korea?

    Year 0: initial investment costs of 82,000,000 won per coffee shop
    Year 1 cash flow: Won 25,000,000
    Year 2 cash flow: Won 30,000,000
    Year 3 cash flow: Won 70,000,000
    Year 4 cash flow: Won 90,000,000
    Year 5 cash flow: Won 45,000,000

19. ***Foreign currency NPV approach.*** Verify your answer to Problem 17 using the foreign currency approach.

20. ***Foreign currency NPV approach.*** Verify your answer to Problem 18 using the foreign currency approach.

Advanced Problems for Spreadsheet Application

These problems are available in MyFinanceLab.

1. ***Find the triangular arbitrage across six currencies (three way pairs).*** Can you find the triangular arbitrage? Below is a table of direct rates (U.S. dollars to foreign currency) in the first column, indirect rates (U.S. dollars to foreign currency) in the top row, and the corresponding cross rates for each set of foreign currencies. One of the cross rates is incorrect. Using a spreadsheet, verify each cross rate and find the incorrect cross rate. Then using $1,000 to start, show the order of currency conversion (assuming no transaction costs) and the profit from one round trip through the three currencies for the arbitrage. Note that the exchange rates are rounded to the nearest four decimal points, so format the cells to the nearest four decimal points for your verification.

	$	C $	Peso	Euro €	HK $	AUS $	JAP ¥	Pound £
$	—	1.3333	16.0000	0.7407	6.4725	1.4545	98.0392	0.6466
C $	0.7500	—	12.0000	0.5556	4.8544	1.0909	73.5294	0.4850
Peso	0.0625	0.0833	—	0.0463	0.4045	0.0909	6.1275	0.0404
Euro €	1.3500	1.8000	21.6000	—	8.7379	1.9636	132.3529	0.8729
HK $	0.1545	0.2060	2.4720	0.1144	—	0.2247	15.1471	0.0999
AUS $	0.6875	0.9167	14.0000	0.5093	4.4498	—	67.4020	0.4466
JAP ¥	0.0102	0.0136	0.1632	0.0076	0.0660	0.0148	—	0.0066
Pound £	1.5465	2.0620	24.7440	1.1456	10.0097	2.2495	151.6176	—

2. ***NPV in foreign and home currency.*** O'Brien Athletic Equipment has a potential project in Australia for manufacturing and selling specialty athletic equipment for outdoor recreational use. The project manager has determined that this project has a fifteen-year horizon and has estimated the following incremental cash flow for the project in Australian dollars (AUS$):

Year 0–Investment of AUS $325,000,000

Year	Cash Flow	Year	Cash Flow	Year	Cash Flow
1	12,000,000	6	86,000,000	11	102,000,000
2	36,000,000	7	92,000,000	12	104,000,000
3	58,000,000	8	95,000,000	13	105,000,000
4	74,000,000	9	97,000,000	14	94,000,000
5	81,000,000	10	99,000,000	15	63,000,000

The current direct exchange rate is $0.6875, with the anticipated inflation rate in Australia estimated at 3.75% for the next fifteen years and 3.25% in the United States for the next fifteen years. If the appropriate discount rate for this project in the United States is 16%, determine if the project should be accepted using both the foreign currency approach and the home currency approach.

Mini-Case

Scholastic Travel Services, Inc.

This mini-case is available in MyFinanceLab.

Twelve years ago, Réjean Rondeau and Carmella DiStefano founded Scholastic Travel Services. They began their careers teaching foreign languages in suburban New York high schools. They were both active in professional associations and worked on committees to stimulate interest in language studies. Their first endeavors involved week long trips to Mexico and Rondeau's native Québec during school breaks. These trips were extremely successful, and within a few years, they were organizing summer courses for Advanced Placement credit in the United Kingdom, France, Italy, and Spain. Eventually, they realized that what started as a volunteer activity had become a business, except that the compensation for their work and the unique expertise they had developed barely covered their expenses. They faced a choice between burning out and hoping someone else would pick up the challenge, or leaving their day jobs and turning the study trips into a full-time business.

They had gained enough confidence from their volunteer activities to believe they could turn the trips into a successful business. With financing from home equity loans, they incorporated as Scholastic Travel Services and began organizing study trips with enough surplus built into the fees to provide decent incomes and some profits to grow the business. In 2010, Scholastic offered its first program in Beijing, which sold out within a month.

A unique aspect of Scholastic Travel's programs was that it charged students a single fee, out of which the company paid for housing, tuition, an optional meals plan, side trips, and activities. Most students and their parents preferred student housing with a resident director who either lived in the country or was an experienced American academic to the typical, but risky, placement with compensated host families. Once they paid the fee, students would be responsible only for their personal spending money.

Students typically booked—meaning paid in full—Scholastic Travel's programs six to nine months in advance. Scholastic disbursed funds as necessary, before, during, and after the programs, so it often held funds for six months to a year before it made actual payments. This arrangement had obvious advantages because a prorated system of refunds protected it from untimely withdrawals. However, Scholastic had to convert dollars to foreign currencies before paying individual and institutional vendors. In the early years of the business, a strengthening dollar worked very much in its favor, sometimes bringing unexpected profits. However, in recent years, a weakening dollar has been troublesome. At first, it tried to cope by building a "margin for error" into its prices, but in 2009, the business lost money due to foreign exchange rate losses.

Questions

1. In the summer of 2011, a budget crisis in Greece sparked occasionally violent protest demonstrations in Athens. A few weeks later, a right-wing extremist in Norway bombed government buildings in Oslo and then went on a shooting spree, killing sixty-nine young campers. In early August, violent riots broke out in London after police shot and killed twenty-nine-year old Mark Duggan while attempting to arrest him. Shortly before the start of the fall term, anxious families withdrew more than a third of the students enrolled in the UK programs and requested full refunds, even though their contract with Scholastic Travel specified a 50% refund for withdrawals after June 30. Scholastic Travel also faced a higher than normal withdrawal rate from other programs in Western Europe.
   - **a.** What types of risk are illustrated by this incident?
   - **b.** How should Scholastic Travel respond to the requests for refunds?
2. Ashley and Michaela are participating in a Scholastic college program in Turin, Italy. On a weekend trip to Switzerland, they stop at an outdoor café for coffee and pastry and to observe the Geneva sidewalk scene. The two *cafés au lait* and two chocolate croissants came to 19.25 Swiss francs. Because they had not had a chance to exchange any currency, they ask if they can pay in dollars or euros. The server says that the price will be the same either way, \$14.56 or €10.26.
   - **a.** What exchange rates between dollars and Swiss francs and dollars and euros do these prices imply?
   - **b.** What is the implied cross rate between euros and Swiss francs?
   - **c.** The actual exchange rates at the time set \$1.00 equal to €0.705 or SF1.374. Why might these rates differ slightly from the rates calculated in Question 2a?
   - **d.** Should Ashley and Michaela pay in dollars or euros?
   - **e.** At a Starbucks in the Boston, Massachusetts, suburb of Newton, Ashley and Michaela's home town, a latte costs \$3.50 and a chocolate croissant costs \$2.50. If these orders are close substitutes for what they ordered at the Swiss café, does purchasing power parity prevail? Why or why not? Is arbitrage possible?

3. On February 1, 2011, Scholastic received $25,000 in fees from students for a summer program in Angers, France. Directly related to these fees, Scholastic will have to pay €3,525 for facilities rental on June 1 and €7,050 in staff salaries at the end of August. The current exchange rates are the same as in Question 2. The estimated future inflation rate in France is 0.124% per month; the estimated future U.S. inflation rate is 0.231% per month.

   a. What is the expected exchange rate on June 1 and on August 31 (use five months and seven months to compute the forward rates)?

   b. What is the cost of rents and salaries in dollars at the current exchange rate?

   c. What is the expected cost of rents and salaries in dollars if exchange rates equal actual exchange rates?

   d. What is the cost of salaries in dollars if the dollar unexpectedly strengthens to €0.80 or weakens to €0.60? What do your answers imply about transaction risk?

4. What measures can Scholastic Travel take to protect the business from exchange rate risk?

Appendix 1

Future Value Interest Factors

$$FVIF = (1 + r)^n$$

(where r is the periodic interest rate and n is the number of periods)

$n\backslash r$	0.005	0.01	0.015	0.02	0.03	0.04	0.05	0.06
1	1.0050	1.0100	1.0150	1.0200	1.0300	1.0400	1.0500	1.0600
2	1.0100	1.0201	1.0302	1.0404	1.0609	1.0816	1.1025	1.1236
3	1.0151	1.0303	1.0457	1.0612	1.0927	1.1249	1.1576	1.1910
4	1.0202	1.0406	1.0614	1.0824	1.1255	1.1699	1.2155	1.2625
5	1.0253	1.0510	1.0773	1.1041	1.1593	1.2167	1.2763	1.3382
6	1.0304	1.0615	1.0934	1.1262	1.1941	1.2653	1.3401	1.4185
7	1.0355	1.0721	1.1098	1.1487	1.2299	1.3159	1.4071	1.5036
8	1.0407	1.0829	1.1265	1.1717	1.2668	1.3686	1.4775	1.5938
9	1.0459	1.0937	1.1434	1.1951	1.3048	1.4233	1.5513	1.6895
10	1.0511	1.1046	1.1605	1.2190	1.3439	1.4802	1.6289	1.7908
11	1.0564	1.1157	1.1779	1.2434	1.3842	1.5395	1.7103	1.8983
12	1.0617	1.1268	1.1956	1.2682	1.4258	1.6010	1.7959	2.0122
13	1.0670	1.1381	1.2136	1.2936	1.4685	1.6651	1.8856	2.1329
14	1.0723	1.1495	1.2318	1.3195	1.5126	1.7317	1.9799	2.2609
15	1.0777	1.1610	1.2502	1.3459	1.5580	1.8009	2.0789	2.3966
16	1.0831	1.1726	1.2690	1.3728	1.6047	1.8730	2.1829	2.5404
17	1.0885	1.1843	1.2880	1.4002	1.6528	1.9479	2.2920	2.6928
18	1.0939	1.1961	1.3073	1.4282	1.7024	2.0258	2.4066	2.8543
19	1.0994	1.2081	1.3270	1.4568	1.7535	2.1068	2.5270	3.0256
20	1.1049	1.2202	1.3469	1.4859	1.8061	2.1911	2.6533	3.2071
24	1.1272	1.2697	1.4295	1.6084	2.0328	2.5633	3.2251	4.0489
30	1.1614	1.3478	1.5631	1.8114	2.4273	3.2434	4.3219	5.7435
36	1.1967	1.4308	1.7091	2.0399	2.8983	4.1039	5.7918	8.1473
48	1.2705	1.6122	2.0435	2.5871	4.1323	6.5705	10.401	16.394
60	1.3489	1.8167	2.4432	3.2810	5.8916	10.520	18.679	32.988
120	1.8194	3.3004	5.9693	10.765	34.711	110.66	348.91	1088.2

n\r	0.07	0.08	0.09	0.10	0.12	0.15	0.20
1	1.0700	1.0800	1.0900	1.1000	1.1200	1.1500	1.2000
2	1.1449	1.1664	1.1881	1.2100	1.2544	1.3225	1.4400
3	1.2250	1.2597	1.2950	1.3310	1.4049	1.5209	1.7280
4	1.3108	1.3605	1.4116	1.4641	1.5735	1.7490	2.0736
5	1.4026	1.4693	1.5386	1.6105	1.7623	2.0114	2.4883
6	1.5007	1.5869	1.6771	1.7716	1.9738	2.3131	2.9860
7	1.6058	1.7138	1.8280	1.9487	2.2107	2.6600	3.5832
8	1.7182	1.8509	1.9926	2.1436	2.4760	3.0590	4.2998
9	1.8385	1.9990	2.1719	2.3579	2.7731	3.5179	5.1598
10	1.9672	2.1589	2.3674	2.5937	3.1058	4.0456	6.1917
11	2.1049	2.3316	2.5804	2.8531	3.4785	4.6524	7.4301
12	2.2522	2.5182	2.8127	3.1384	3.8960	5.3503	8.9161
13	2.4098	2.7196	3.0658	3.4523	4.3635	6.1528	10.699
14	2.5785	2.9372	3.3417	3.7975	4.8871	7.0757	12.839
15	2.7590	3.1722	3.6425	4.1772	5.4736	8.1371	15.407
16	2.9522	3.4259	3.9703	4.5950	6.1304	9.3576	18.488
17	3.1588	3.7000	4.3276	5.0545	6.8660	10.761	22.186
18	3.3799	3.9960	4.7171	5.5599	7.6900	12.375	26.623
19	3.6165	4.3157	5.1417	6.1159	8.6128	14.232	31.948
20	3.8697	4.6610	5.6044	6.7275	9.6463	16.367	38.338
24	5.0724	6.3412	7.9111	9.8497	15.1786	28.625	79.497
30	7.6123	10.063	13.268	17.449	29.960	66.212	237.38
36	11.424	15.968	22.251	30.913	59.136	153.15	708.80
48	25.729	40.211	62.585	97.017	230.39	819.40	6319.7
60	57.946	101.26	176.03	304.48	897.60	4384.0	56348
120	3357.8	10253	30987	92709	805680	19219445	3175042374

Appendix 2

Present Value Interest Factors

$$PVIF = \frac{1}{(1 + r)^n}$$

(where r is the periodic interest rate and n is the number of periods)

$n \backslash r$	0.005	0.01	0.015	0.02	0.03	0.04	0.05	0.06
1	0.9950	0.9901	0.9852	0.9804	0.9709	0.9615	0.9524	0.9434
2	0.9901	0.9803	0.9707	0.9612	0.9426	0.9246	0.9070	0.8900
3	0.9851	0.9706	0.9563	0.9423	0.9151	0.8890	0.8638	0.8396
4	0.9802	0.9610	0.9422	0.9238	0.8885	0.8548	0.8227	0.7921
5	0.9754	0.9515	0.9283	0.9057	0.8626	0.8219	0.7835	0.7473
6	0.9705	0.9420	0.9145	0.8880	0.8375	0.7903	0.7462	0.7050
7	0.9657	0.9327	0.9010	0.8706	0.8131	0.7599	0.7107	0.6651
8	0.9609	0.9235	0.8877	0.8535	0.7894	0.7307	0.6768	0.6274
9	0.9561	0.9143	0.8746	0.8368	0.7664	0.7026	0.6446	0.5919
10	0.9513	0.9053	0.8617	0.8203	0.7441	0.6756	0.6139	0.5584
11	0.9466	0.8963	0.8489	0.8043	0.7224	0.6496	0.5847	0.5268
12	0.9419	0.8874	0.8364	0.7885	0.7014	0.6246	0.5568	0.4970
13	0.9372	0.8787	0.8240	0.7730	0.6810	0.6006	0.5303	0.4688
14	0.9326	0.8700	0.8118	0.7579	0.6611	0.5775	0.5051	0.4423
15	0.9279	0.8613	0.7999	0.7430	0.6419	0.5553	0.4810	0.4173
16	0.9233	0.8528	0.7880	0.7284	0.6232	0.5339	0.4581	0.3936
17	0.9187	0.8444	0.7764	0.7142	0.6050	0.5134	0.4363	0.3714
18	0.9141	0.8360	0.7649	0.7002	0.5874	0.4936	0.4155	0.3503
19	0.9096	0.8277	0.7536	0.6864	0.5703	0.4746	0.3957	0.3305
20	0.9051	0.8195	0.7425	0.6730	0.5537	0.4564	0.3769	0.3118
24	0.8872	0.7876	0.6995	0.6217	0.4919	0.3901	0.3101	0.2470
30	0.8610	0.7419	0.6398	0.5521	0.4120	0.3083	0.2314	0.1741
36	0.8356	0.6989	0.5851	0.4902	0.3450	0.2437	0.1727	0.1227
48	0.7871	0.6203	0.4894	0.3865	0.2420	0.1522	0.0961	0.0610
60	0.7414	0.5504	0.4093	0.3048	0.1697	0.0951	0.0535	0.0303
120	0.5496	0.3030	0.1675	0.0929	0.0288	0.0090	0.0029	0.0009

$n\backslash r$	0.07	0.08	0.09	0.10	0.12	0.15	0.20
1	0.9346	0.9259	0.9174	0.9091	0.8929	0.8696	0.8333
2	0.8734	0.8573	0.8417	0.8264	0.7972	0.7561	0.6944
3	0.8163	0.7938	0.7722	0.7513	0.7118	0.6575	0.5787
4	0.7629	0.7350	0.7084	0.6830	0.6355	0.5718	0.4823
5	0.7130	0.6806	0.6499	0.6209	0.5674	0.4972	0.4019
6	0.6663	0.6302	0.5963	0.5645	0.5066	0.4323	0.3349
7	0.6227	0.5835	0.5470	0.5132	0.4523	0.3759	0.2791
8	0.5820	0.5403	0.5019	0.4665	0.4039	0.3269	0.2326
9	0.5439	0.5002	0.4604	0.4241	0.3606	0.2843	0.1938
10	0.5083	0.4632	0.4224	0.3855	0.3220	0.2472	0.1615
11	0.4751	0.4289	0.3875	0.3505	0.2875	0.2149	0.1346
12	0.4440	0.3971	0.3555	0.3186	0.2567	0.1869	0.1122
13	0.4150	0.3677	0.3262	0.2897	0.2292	0.1625	0.0935
14	0.3878	0.3405	0.2992	0.2633	0.2046	0.1413	0.0779
15	0.3624	0.3152	0.2745	0.2394	0.1827	0.1229	0.0649
16	0.3387	0.2919	0.2519	0.2176	0.1631	0.1069	0.0541
17	0.3166	0.2703	0.2311	0.1978	0.1456	0.0929	0.0451
18	0.2959	0.2502	0.2120	0.1799	0.1300	0.0808	0.0376
19	0.2765	0.2317	0.1945	0.1635	0.1161	0.0703	0.0313
20	0.2584	0.2145	0.1784	0.1486	0.1037	0.0611	0.0261
24	0.1971	0.1577	0.1264	0.1015	0.0659	0.0349	0.0126
30	0.1314	0.0994	0.0754	0.0573	0.0334	0.0151	0.0042
36	0.0875	0.0626	0.0449	0.0323	0.0169	0.0065	0.0014
48	0.0389	0.0249	0.0160	0.0103	0.0043	0.0012	0.0002
60	0.0173	0.0099	0.0057	0.0033	0.0011	0.0002	0.0000
120	0.0003	0.0001	0.0000	0.0000	0.0000	0.0000	0.0000

Appendix 3

Future Value Interest Factors of an Annuity

$$FVIFA = \frac{(1 + r)^n - 1}{r}$$

(where r is the periodic interest rate and n is the number of periods)

$n \backslash r$	0.005	0.01	0.015	0.02	0.03	0.04	0.05	0.06
1	1.0000	1.0000	1.0000	1.0000	1.0000	1.0000	1.0000	1.0000
2	2.0050	2.0100	2.0150	2.0200	2.0300	2.0400	2.0500	2.0600
3	3.0150	3.0301	3.0452	3.0604	3.0909	3.1216	3.1525	3.1836
4	4.0301	4.0604	4.0909	4.1216	4.1836	4.2465	4.3101	4.3746
5	5.0503	5.1010	5.1523	5.2040	5.3091	5.4163	5.5256	5.6371
6	6.0755	6.1520	6.2296	6.3081	6.4684	6.6330	6.8019	6.9753
7	7.1059	7.2135	7.3230	7.4343	7.6625	7.8983	8.1420	8.3938
8	8.1414	8.2857	8.4328	8.5830	8.8923	9.2142	9.5491	9.8975
9	9.1821	9.3685	9.5593	9.7546	10.1591	10.5828	11.0266	11.4913
10	10.2280	10.4622	10.7027	10.9497	11.4639	12.0061	12.5779	13.1808
11	11.2792	11.5668	11.8633	12.1687	12.8078	13.4864	14.2068	14.9716
12	12.3356	12.6825	13.0412	13.4121	14.1920	15.0258	15.9171	16.8699
13	13.3972	13.8093	14.2368	14.6803	15.6178	16.6268	17.7130	18.8821
14	14.4642	14.9474	15.4504	15.9739	17.0863	18.2919	19.5986	21.0151
15	15.5365	16.0969	16.6821	17.2934	18.5989	20.0236	21.5786	23.2760
16	16.6142	17.2579	17.9324	18.6393	20.1569	21.8245	23.6575	25.6725
17	17.6973	18.4304	19.2014	20.0121	21.7616	23.6975	25.8404	28.2129
18	18.7858	19.6147	20.4894	21.4123	23.4144	25.6454	28.1324	30.9057
19	19.8797	20.8109	21.7967	22.8406	25.1169	27.6712	30.5390	33.7600
20	20.9791	22.0190	23.1237	24.2974	26.8704	29.7781	33.0660	36.7856
24	25.4320	26.9735	28.6335	30.4219	34.4265	39.0826	44.5020	50.8156
30	32.2800	34.7849	37.5387	40.5681	47.5754	56.0849	66.4388	79.0582
36	39.3361	43.0769	47.2760	51.9944	63.2759	77.5983	95.8363	119.121
48	54.0978	61.2226	69.5652	79.3535	104.408	139.263	188.025	256.565
60	69.7700	81.6697	96.2147	114.052	163.053	237.991	353.584	533.128
120	163.879	230.038	331.288	488.258	1123.70	2741.56	6958.24	18119.8

*n**r*	0.07	0.08	0.09	0.10	0.12	0.15	0.20
1	1.0000	1.0000	1.0000	1.0000	1.0000	1.0000	1.0000
2	2.0700	2.0800	2.0900	2.1000	2.1200	2.1500	2.2000
3	3.2149	3.2464	3.2781	3.3100	3.3744	3.4725	3.6400
4	4.4399	4.5061	4.5731	4.6410	4.7793	4.9934	5.3680
5	5.7507	5.8666	5.9847	6.1051	6.3528	6.7424	7.4416
6	7.1533	7.3359	7.5233	7.7156	8.1152	8.7537	9.9299
7	8.6540	8.9228	9.2004	9.4872	10.0890	11.0668	12.9159
8	10.2598	10.6366	11.0285	11.4359	12.2997	13.7268	16.4991
9	11.9780	12.4876	13.0210	13.5795	14.7757	16.7858	20.7989
10	13.8164	14.4866	15.1929	15.9374	17.5487	20.3037	25.9587
11	15.7836	16.6455	17.5603	18.5312	20.6546	24.3493	32.1504
12	17.8885	18.9771	20.1407	21.3843	24.1331	29.0017	39.5805
13	20.1406	21.4953	22.9534	24.5227	28.0291	34.3519	48.4966
14	22.5505	24.2149	26.0192	27.9750	32.3926	40.5047	59.1959
15	25.1290	27.1521	29.3609	31.7725	37.2797	47.5804	72.0351
16	27.8881	30.3243	33.0034	35.9497	42.7533	55.7175	87.4421
17	30.8402	33.7502	36.9737	40.5447	48.8837	65.0751	105.931
18	33.9990	37.4502	41.3013	45.5992	55.7497	75.8364	128.117
19	37.3790	41.4463	46.0185	51.1591	63.4397	88.2118	154.740
20	40.9955	45.7620	51.1601	57.2750	72.0524	102.444	186.688
24	58.1767	66.7648	76.7898	88.4973	118.155	184.168	392.484
30	94.4608	113.283	136.308	164.494	241.333	434.745	1181.88
36	148.913	187.102	236.125	299.127	484.463	1014.35	3539.01
48	353.270	490.132	684.280	960.172	1911.59	5456.00	31593.7
60	813.520	1253.21	1944.79	3034.82	7471.64	29219.99	281733
120	47954.1	128150	344289.1	927081	6713994	128129627	15875211864

Appendix 4

Present Value Interest Factors of an Annuity

$$PVIFA = \frac{1 - [1/(1 + r)^n]}{r}$$

(where r is the periodic interest rate and n is the number of periods)

$n \backslash r$	0.005	0.01	0.015	0.02	0.03	0.04	0.05	0.06
1	0.9950	0.9901	0.9852	0.9804	0.9709	0.9615	0.9524	0.9434
2	1.9851	1.9704	1.9559	1.9416	1.9135	1.8861	1.8594	1.8334
3	2.9702	2.9410	2.9122	2.8839	2.8286	2.7751	2.7232	2.6730
4	3.9505	3.9020	3.8544	3.8077	3.7171	3.6299	3.5460	3.4651
5	4.9259	4.8534	4.7826	4.7135	4.5797	4.4518	4.3295	4.2124
6	5.8964	5.7955	5.6972	5.6014	5.4172	5.2421	5.0757	4.9173
7	6.8621	6.7282	6.5982	6.4720	6.2303	6.0021	5.7864	5.5824
8	7.8230	7.6517	7.4859	7.3255	7.0197	6.7327	6.4632	6.2098
9	8.7791	8.5660	8.3605	8.1622	7.7861	7.4353	7.1078	6.8017
10	9.7304	9.4713	9.2222	8.9826	8.5302	8.1109	7.7217	7.3601
11	10.6770	10.3676	10.0711	9.7868	9.2526	8.7605	8.3064	7.8869
12	11.6189	11.2551	10.9075	10.5753	9.9540	9.3851	8.8633	8.3838
13	12.5562	12.1337	11.7315	11.3484	10.6350	9.9856	9.3936	8.8527
14	13.4887	13.0037	12.5434	12.1062	11.2961	10.5631	9.8986	9.2950
15	14.4166	13.8651	13.3432	12.8493	11.9379	11.1184	10.3797	9.7122
16	15.3399	14.7179	14.1313	13.5777	12.5611	11.6523	10.8378	10.1059
17	16.2586	15.5623	14.9076	14.2919	13.1661	12.1657	11.2741	10.4773
18	17.1728	16.3983	15.6726	14.9920	13.7535	12.6593	11.6896	10.8276
19	18.0824	17.2260	16.4262	15.6785	14.3238	13.1339	12.0853	11.1581
20	18.9874	18.0456	17.1686	16.3514	14.8775	13.5903	12.4622	11.4699
24	22.5629	21.2434	20.0304	18.9139	16.9355	15.2470	13.7986	12.5504
30	27.7941	25.8077	24.0158	22.3965	19.6004	17.2920	15.3725	13.7648
36	32.8710	30.1075	27.6607	25.4888	21.8323	18.9083	16.5469	14.6210
48	42.5803	37.9740	34.0426	30.6731	25.2667	21.1951	18.0772	15.6500
60	51.7256	44.9550	39.3803	34.7609	27.6756	22.6235	18.9293	16.1614
120	90.0735	69.7005	55.4985	45.3554	32.3730	24.7741	19.9427	16.6514

n\r	0.07	0.08	0.09	−0.10	0.12	0.15	0.20
1	0.9346	0.9259	0.9174	0.9091	0.8929	0.8696	0.8333
2	1.8080	1.7833	1.7591	1.7355	1.6901	1.6257	1.5278
3	2.6243	2.5771	2.5313	2.4869	2.4018	2.2832	2.1065
4	3.3872	3.3121	3.2397	3.1699	3.0373	2.8550	2.5887
5	4.1002	3.9927	3.8897	3.7908	3.6048	3.3522	2.9906
6	4.7665	4.6229	4.4859	4.3553	4.1114	3.7845	3.3255
7	5.3893	5.2064	5.0330	4.8684	4.5638	4.1604	3.6046
8	5.9713	5.7466	5.5348	5.3349	4.9676	4.4873	3.8372
9	6.5152	6.2469	5.9952	5.7590	5.3282	4.7716	4.0310
10	7.0236	6.7101	6.4177	6.1446	5.6502	5.0188	4.1925
11	7.4987	7.1390	6.8052	6.4951	5.9377	5.2337	4.3271
12	7.9427	7.5361	7.1607	6.8137	6.1944	5.4206	4.4392
13	8.3577	7.9038	7.4869	7.1034	6.4235	5.5831	4.5327
14	8.7455	8.2442	7.7862	7.3667	6.6282	5.7245	4.6106
15	9.1079	8.5595	8.0607	7.6061	6.8109	5.8474	4.6755
16	9.4466	8.8514	8.3126	7.8237	6.9740	5.9542	4.7296
17	9.7632	9.1216	8.5436	8.0216	7.1196	6.0472	4.7746
18	10.0591	9.3719	8.7556	8.2014	7.2497	6.1280	4.8122
19	10.3356	9.6036	8.9501	8.3649	7.3658	6.1982	4.8435
20	10.5940	9.8181	9.1285	8.5136	7.4694	6.2593	4.8696
24	11.4693	10.5288	9.7066	8.9847	7.7843	6.4338	4.9371
30	12.4090	11.2578	10.2737	9.4269	8.0552	6.5660	4.9789
36	13.0352	11.7172	10.6118	9.6765	8.1924	6.6231	4.9929
48	13.7305	12.1891	10.9336	9.8969	8.2972	6.6585	4.9992
60	14.0392	12.3766	11.0480	9.9672	8.3240	6.6651	4.9999
120	14.2815	12.4988	11.1108	9.9999	8.3333	6.6667	5.0000

Appendix 5

Answers to Prepping for Exam Questions

Chapter 1

1. c.
2. a.
3. a.
4. b.
5. c. The proper mix of stocks and bonds to hold for financing assets is a capital structure question.
6. b. The current price of a share of stock is the present value of expected future cash flows.
7. c.
8. b. Sole proprietorships have *unlimited* liability.
9. c.
10. d

Chapter 2

1. b.
2. c.
3. d.
4. d. The income statement begins with revenue and subtracts various operating expenses until arriving at earnings before interest and taxes (EBIT). Next, interest expense is subtracted to find the taxable income for the period. Then the appropriate taxes are calculated and subtracted. We finally arrive at the net income, the so-called bottom line of the income statement.
5. c. The finance manager uses the framework of the income statement to find the operating income of the company (an accounting measure) and then makes adjustments to find the true cash flow from operations. In accrual-based accounting, revenue is recorded at the time of sale, whether or not the revenue has been received in cash. Generally accepted accounting principles (GAAP) in the United States do allow the use of accrual accounting to record revenue.
6. a. Change in net working capital = ending net working capital − beginning net working capital; net capital spending = ending net fixed assets + beginning net fixed assets + depreciation; cash flow from assets = operating cash flow − net capital spending − change in net working capital.
7. c. Total current liabilities = accounts payable + short-term debt + other current liabilities = \$5,173 + \$288 + \$1,401 = \$6,862.
8. c.
9. c. In Yahoo! Finance's presentation of the balance sheet, you will find items that are new to this book's balance sheet discussion. Such items include goodwill, deferred long-term asset charges, and treasury stock.
10. a.

Chapter 3

1. d.

2. b. $FV = PV \times (1 + r)^n = \$7{,}500 \times (1.0525)^5 = \$9{,}687$

3. c. $PV = FV/(1 + r)^n = \$10{,}000/(1.03875)^{15} = \$5{,}654$

4. c.

5. a.

6. c. $r = (FV/PV)^{1/n} - 1 = (2418/3071)^{1/5} - 1 = -4.67\%$

7. d. $r = (FV/PV)^{1/n} - 1 = (\$28{,}960/\$1{,}970)^{1/60} - 1 = 4.58\%$

8. b. $n = \ln (FV/PV)/\ln (1 + r) = \ln (\$16{,}950/\$600)/\ln (1.0573)$
$= 59.96$ years

9. a. $72/6 = 12\%$ via the Rule of 72

10. b. Unit sales doubled from 125,000 to 250,000 and doubled again to 500,000 in eight years. Thus, at a doubling rate of every four years, the Rule of 72 suggests an annual rate of $72/4 = 18\%$. Via the formula, the actual growth rate is 18.92% per year.

Chapter 4

1. b. $FV = PV \times (1 + r)^n = \$50{,}000 \times (1.10)^2 + \$25{,}000 \times (1.10)^1 + \$10{,}000 \times (1.10)^0 = \$98{,}000$

2. b.

3. d. Choice 1: $FV = PMT \times [(1 + r)^n - 1]/r = \$3{,}000 \times [(1.10)^7 - 1]/0.10 \times (1.10)^{40} = \$1{,}288{,}146.89$;
choice 2: $\$3{,}000 \times [(1.10)^{39} - 1]/0.10 = \$1{,}204{,}343.33$

4. a. $PV = PMT \times \{[1 - 1/(1 + r)^n]/r\}/(1 + r)^n =$
$\$500 \times \{[1 - 1/(1.04)^{10}]/0.04\}/(1.04)^1 = \$3{,}899.47$

5. b. $PV = PMT \times \{[1 - 1/(1 + r)^n]/r\} \times (1 + r) =$
$\$50{,}000 \times \{[1 - 1/(1.032)^{15}]/0.032\} \times (1.032) = \$607{,}180.14$

6. a. Discount loans pay in full at maturity.

7. d.

8. c. via calculator, I/Y $= 6.0$, $PV = \$1{,}000{,}000$, $PMT = -\$87{,}500$ and compute n, $n = 19.86$ years

9. a. Solving for the rate is an iterative (trial-and-error) process. Solve using the RATE function in Excel or via calculator (via calculator, $n = 20$, $PV = \$67{,}000$, $PMT = -\$5{,}000$ and compute I/Y, I/Y $= 4.16\%$).

10. b. Solving for the rate is an iterative (trial-and-error) process. Solve using the RATE function in Excel or via calculator (via calculator, $n = 20$, $PV = \$5{,}734{,}961$, $PMT = -\$500{,}000$ and compute I/Y, I/Y $= 6.0\%$).

Chapter 5

1. a.

2. c. Explanation: a. When you buy a CD, the bank promises to repay both the principal and interest due. b. When you buy a CD, the bank is not lending money to you but borrowing money from you. d. When you buy a CD, the bank is renting or borrowing money from you and thus it *is* borrowing.

3. b.

4. c. Explanation: All other answers besides c have at least one word that disagrees with the correct words found in c.

5. d.

6. c. Explanation: We can see that an inflation rate of 4% is one-half of our 8% investment rate. Thus, one-half of the \$800, or \$400, is the real increase in your purchasing power.

7. c.

8. c.

9. c. Explanation: With a house, the potential loss due to default is less than a car because the growing value of the asset should be sufficient to cover the outstanding balance (principal) of the loan.

10. b. Explanation: From 1950 to 1999, inflation averaged 1.28%, the real rate has averaged 1.18%, the maturity premium has averaged 0.71% (for twenty-year maturity differences), and the default premium has averaged 0.49% (for equity over government bonds).

Chapter 6

1. b.

2. d.

3. a.

4. a.

5. c.

6. a.

7. a.

8. b. $100,000 × {1 − [(90/360) × 0.0425]} = $98,937.50

Chapter 7

1. b. Stocks and bonds are both major sources of funds. Bonds do not represent residual ownership. Bonds, unlike stocks, give owners legal claims to payments. Stocks, unlike bonds, represent voting ownership.

2. b.

3. d. Most companies do not have the resident expertise to complete an initial public offering or first public equity issue.

4. a. The fair price is the present value of the selling price plus the present value of the dividend stream. Thus, today's price (P) = (future price × *PVIF*) + (dividend stream × *PVIFA*) = ($30 × 0.620921) + ($6 × 3.790787) = $18.628 + $22.745 = $41.372, or about $41.37.

5. d. When computing a perpetuity, we have to make sure both the payment and the discount rate represent the same period. In this problem, let us use three months as our period. Thus, we restate the annual required rate of 9.25% as a quarterly (or three-month) rate of 9.25%/4 = 2.3125% (or 0.023125). Applying the constant dividend forever formula with the quarterly rate of return and a quarterly dividend of $1.77, we get: $1.77/0.023125 = $76.54. We can get the same answer using annual data. For example, the annual dividend is 4 × $1.77 = $7.08. Thus, price = $7.08/0.0925 = $76.54.

6. a. The constant growth dividend model states that $P_0 = \text{Div}_0 \times (1 + g)/(r - g) = \text{Div}_1/(r - g)$. Inserting our values gives: P_0 = $1.80 × 1.06/(0.12 − 0.06) = $1.908/0.06 = $31.80.

7. a. We use the formula $P_{15} = \text{Div}_{15} \times (1 + g)/(r - g)$. Inserting our given values, we get P_{15} = $2.00 × (1 + 0.07)/(0.12 − 0.07) = $2.14/0.05 = $42.80.

8. d. The preferred stock usually has a stated or par value, but, unlike bonds, this par value is not repaid at maturity because preferred stocks do not have a maturity date. The only time this par value would be paid to the shareholder is if the company ceases operations or retires the preferred stock. The cash dividend due each year is based on the stated dividend rate times the par value of the stock.

9. c. Dividend models do not focus on past and present cash flows but, rather, on future cash flows that are discounted by a required rate of return.

10. c. The dealers make money on the difference between what they buy the stock for and what they sell it for, much like a car dealer makes money by buying a used car at one price and then selling the car later at a higher or marked-up price. A bull market is a prolonged rising market, one in which stock prices in general are increasing. A bear market is a prolonged declining market, one in which stock prices in general are decreasing.

Chapter 8

1. a. Profit or loss = ending price − beginning price + cash flows

Profit = \$27.65 − \$31.50 + \$0.85 = −\$3.00

$$HPR = \frac{\text{ending price} - \text{beginning price} + \text{cash flows}}{\text{beginning price}}$$

$$= \frac{\$27.65 - \$31.50 + \$0.85}{\$31.50} = -9.52\%$$

2. b.

3. d.

4. c. Variance $= (0.30)(1.00 - 0.0667)^2 + (0.70)(-0.333 - 0.0667)^2$

$= 0.3733$, or 37.33%

5. b. $E(r) = \sum (P_s \times r_s)$

$= 0.25 \times -20\% + 0.60 \times 10\% + 0.15 \times 35\% = 6.25\%$

6. d.

7. d.

8. a.

9. c. $\beta_p = \sum (B_i \times w_i) = 0.95 \times 40\% + 1.20 \times 35\% + 1.35 \times 25\%$

$= 1.1375$

10. b. The slope is $(15\% - 12\%)/(1.7 - 1.1) = 5\%$.

The equation for the SML is

$E(r_i) = r_f + (E(r_m) - r_f)B_i$, $15\% = r_f + 5\% \times 1.7$, $r_f = 6.50\%$

Chapter 9

1. a.

2. c. After three years, we will have paid back \$900,000. Thus, we only need \$100,000 in after-tax cash flows in the fourth year. Because we get \$200,000 in the fourth year, the rule of thumb is to divide what is needed by what cash inflows we will get next period and add the result to the number of previous periods of cash inflows, for example, (\$100,000 divided by \$200,000) + 3, which gives 3.500. Thus, the payback period is 3.5 years.

3. b. The discounted payback period method is the time it takes to recover the initial investment in *current* dollars.

4. a. Projects are mutually exclusive if picking one project eliminates the ability to pick the other project even if both projects have positive net present values. This mutually exclusive situation can arise for one of two reasons: (1) there is need for only one project, and both projects can fulfill that current need; or (2) there is a scarce resource that both projects need, and by using it in one project, it is not available for the second project.

5. d. $$NPV = -CF_0 + \frac{CF_1}{(1+r)^1} + \frac{CF_2}{(1+r)^2} + \frac{CF_3}{(1+r)^3} + \frac{CF_4}{(1+r)^4}$$

$$= -\$80{,}000 + \frac{\$40{,}000}{(1.12)^1} + \frac{\$40{,}000}{(1.12)^2} + \frac{\$30{,}000}{(1.12)^3} + \frac{\$30{,}000}{(1.12)^4}$$

$= -\$80{,}000 + \$35{,}714.29 + \$31{,}887.76 + 21{,}353.41 + \$19{,}065.54$

$= -\$80{,}000 + \$108{,}020.99 = \$28{,}020.99$. Thus, Dweller accepts the project because it has a positive NPV.

6. d. Using a financial calculator or software program like Excel or trial and error, we get $IRR = 28.89\%$ if we round to two digits.

7. b.

8. c. **Step 1:** Find the future values of all the cash inflow by reinvesting the cash inflow at the appropriate cost of capital. We can use the future value annuity formula, given that the cash inflow streams are identical. Thus, $FV = \$1{,}900{,}000 \times [(1 + r)^n - 1]/r = \$1{,}900{,}000 \times [(1 + 0.095)^7 - 1]/0.095 = \$1{,}900{,}000 \times 9.342648$. Multiplying out, we get: $FV = \$17{,}751{,}032$.]

Step 2: Find the present value of the cash outflow by discounting at the appropriate cost of capital. It is the initial cash outflow of $10,200,000 because all investment is made at the start of the project. Expressing the cash outflow in absolute terms gives $PV = \$10{,}200{,}000$.

Step 3: Find the interest rate that equates the present value of the cash outflow with the future value of the cash inflow given as $MIRR = (FV/PV)^{\frac{1}{n}} - 1 = (\$17{,}751{,}032/\$10{,}200{,}000)^{\frac{1}{7}} - 1 = (1.740297)^{\frac{1}{7}} - 1 = 1.082368 - 1 = 0.082368$ or about 8.24%.

9. b.

10. a.

Chapter 10

1. a.

2. c. EBIT = revenue − cost of goods sold − other expenses − depreciation = $24,000 − $12,000 − $6,000 − $2,000 = $4,000. Interest is not considered when computing the EBIT.

3. d.

4. b. The increase in working capital accounts necessary to support a project also provides for cost reductions at the end of the project. An increase in working capital can be brought about by an increase in any short-term or current assets account, including inventory or accounts receivable (similarly, a decrease in working capital can be brought about by a decrease in any short-term or current liabilities account). Increases in accounts receivable constitute a use of cash flow because you are helping your customers finance their purchases. Increases in accounts payable constitute a source of cash flow because you are using your suppliers to help finance your business operations.

5. a. Annual depreciation for asset A = (asset cost + installation cost − salvage value)/useful life = ($3 million + $0.4 million − 0)/15 years = $226,666.67 or about $226,667 per year. Annual depreciation for asset B = (asset cost + installation cost − salvage value)/useful life = ($1.3 million + $0.18 million − $0.3 million)/6 years = $196,666.67 or about $196,667 per year. Thus, asset A has $226,667 − $196,667 = $30,000 more in depreciation per year.

6. d.

7. a. The four-year sale is at $4,000. To begin with, the book value of the machine must be established to determine if a gain or loss has been incurred at disposal. The depreciation schedule for the $15,000 machine is

Year 1: $15,000 × 0.2000 = $3,000

Year 2: $15,000 × 0.3200 = $4,800

Year 3: $15,000 × 0.1920 = $2,880

Year 4: $15,000 × 0.1152 = $1,728

Accumulated depreciation = $3,000 + $4,800 + $2,880 + $1,728 = $12,408

Book value of machine = $15,000 − $12,408 = $2,592

Gain on disposal = $4,000 − $2,592 = $1,408

Tax on gain = gain on disposal × tax rate = $1,408 × 0.33 = $464.64

After-tax cash flow at disposal = $4,000 − $464.64 = $3,535.36

8. c. In general, we have the following steps in the estimation of after-tax cash flow at disposal: (1) If selling price is greater than book value: selling price – tax on gain. (2) If selling price is less than book value: selling price + tax credit on loss. (3) If selling price equals book value: selling price. *Note:* If book value is less than selling price: selling price − tax on gain.

9. c.

10. b.

Chapter 11

1. d. Preferred stockholders are hybrid equity lenders, common shareholders are owners, and the rest of the choices may be considered a form of debt lender.

2. a.

3. d.

4. c. $R_p = \frac{D}{P} = \frac{\$3.00}{\$39.5} = 7.59\%$. *Note:* The growth rate in the economy is a red herring and has no bearing on the answer.

5. c. $R_e = \frac{D_1}{P_0 \times (1 - F)} + g,$

$$R_e = \frac{\$1.50}{(\$45.00)(1 - 0.07)} + 0.035 = 0.03584 + 0.035 \approx 7.08\%.$$

6. c. $WACC = \frac{D}{V} \times R_d \times (1 - T_c) + \frac{PS}{V} \times R_p + \frac{E}{V} \times R_e$

$$= \frac{\$350{,}000}{\$950{,}000} \times 8\% \times (1 - 0.30) + \frac{\$150{,}000}{\$950{,}000} \times 10\% + \frac{\$450{,}000}{\$950{,}000} \times 12\% = 9.33\%.$$

7. d. $NPV = PV$ of cash inflows − initial investment; $PMT = \$350{,}000$, $FV = \$420{,}000 - \$350{,}000$, $N = 3$, $I/Y = 11.50\%$, $NPV = \$898{,}415 - \$850{,}000 = \$48{,}415$.

8. c.

9. d. $R_e = r_f + [E(r_m) - r_f]\beta$; therefore, $\beta = \frac{R_e - r_f}{E(r_m) - r_f} = \frac{20\% - 4\%}{12\% - 4\%} = 2.00.$

10. d.

Chapter 12

1. a.

2. c. Its net cash flow for the month is cash receipts minus cash disbursements = \$365,000 − \$370,000 = −\$5,000. Its ending cash is net cash flow plus beginning cash = −\$5,000 + \$4,000 = −\$1,000. Its short-fall is ending cash minus reserves = −\$1,000 − \$3,000 = −\$4,000.

3. d. The amount of sales a company predicts is a function of external data, internal data, or a combination of both. External data consist of items such as the current interest rates, housing starts, gross national product, disposable income estimates, and other economic indicators. Internal data consist of items such as number of sales personnel in the field, average sales per representative, competitors and alternative products, and production capabilities and schedules as well as other factors known mainly to the company.

4. a. Cash received during or by the end of December is 0.2 × December sales + 0.5 × November sales + 0.3 × October sales = 0.2 × \$18,000 + 0.5 × \$12,000 + 0.3 × \$10,000 = \$3,600 + \$6,000 + \$3,000 = \$12,600.

5. c. Production costs include the wages paid to workers, the raw materials for manufacturing products, the overhead (such as electricity, water, and plant space), and the shipping costs to get the product to the customer.

6. a. Production costs include the wages paid to workers, the raw materials for manufacturing products, the overhead (such as electricity, water, and plant space), and the shipping costs to get the product to the customer. Thus, the total production costs are \$49,600 + \$24,300 + \$45,000 + \$12,100 = \$131,000. Preferred dividends are considered a financing cost that is often paid in quarterly payments.

7. d.

8. c. The finance manager *should modify* the pro forma income statement to accommodate for the actual estimate of depreciation for the coming year based on the capital budget of the company.

9. c. We can condense the items that require cash outflow into four categories: accounts payable for materials and supplies; wages, taxes, and other operating expenses of the business; capital expenditures; and long-term financing expenses (interest payments, dividend payments, issuing costs of debt and equity).

10. c. The total incoming cash flow for May = cash sales for May + accounts receivable payments for May = \$200,000 + \$200,000 = \$400,000. The total outgoing cash flow for May = accounts payable for May + wages and salaries for May + interest payment for May = \$200,000 + \$100,000 + \$50,000 = \$350,000. Thus, its net cash flow for May is total incoming cash flow for May − total outgoing cash flow for May = \$400,000 − \$350,000 = \$50,000. The ending cash balance for May = beginning cash for May + net cash flow for May = \$50,000 + \$50,000 = \$100,000.

Chapter 13

1. b.

2. b. Inventory turnover = COGS/average inventory
= \$6,000,000/[(\$125,000 + \$100,000)/2]
= 53.33 times.

3. a. 8% of January sales are collected in April = \$88,000 × 0.08 = \$7,040

4. a.

5. c. Trailers sold × (price − cost) = 8,000 × (\$2,500 − \$1,500)
= \$8,000,000.

6. d. All speed up the collection float.

7. c.

8. a.

9. c.

Year	0	1	2	3	4	5
Initial						
Investment	−\$750,000					
Change in NWC	−\$ 50,000					
Revenues		\$600,000	\$600,000	\$600,000	\$600,000	\$600,000
Costs		\$200,000	\$200,000	\$200,000	\$200,000	\$200,000
Depreciation		\$150,000	\$150,000	\$150,000	\$150,000	\$150,000
Net cash flow	−\$800,000	\$325,000	\$325,000	\$325,000	\$325,000	\$325,000
PV CF		\$285,088	\$250,077	\$219,366	\$192,426	\$168,795
NPV	\$315,751					

10. a.

Chapter 14

1. c. It would be nice if all companies and all industries could be compared by looking at financial statements, but differences in size and industry practices mean interpreting the financial statements will vary across firms and industries.
2. c.
3. a.
4. False; if current ratio is too high it can indicate poor cash management.
5. b. It is the best answer because even borrowing at low rates when you have excess debt is bad, and when you borrow very sparingly, you miss opportunities that are very beneficial.
6. a.
7. a.
8. d.
9. c.
10. a.

Chapter 15

1. c.
2. d. Banks tend to look favorably upon family funding for start-up businesses, have lending models better fitted for established businesses, and work with the Small Business Administration for start-up loans.
3. c.
4. c. Via financial calculator: $PV = -\$50{,}000$, $I/Y = 6.50$, $N = 36$, $FV = 0$. Solve for PMT $= \$1{,}532.45$. Note: $P/Y = 12$.
5. d.
6. c.
7. a.
8. b. Best efforts cash flow = # of shares offered × percent sold × commission per share sold = 400,000 × 0.90 × \$3.00 = \$1,080,000.
9. c. Rate = Interest due ÷ Discounted amount = (\$3,000,000 × (1 − 0.98))/(\$3,000,000 × 0.98) = 2.04%.
10. b.

Chapter 16

1. b.
2. c. With Al's rate of success, we know that eight out of ten projects are successful and that Al has repaid the loan eight out of ten times. Therefore, we must get enough funding from the eight successful projects to cover all ten projects. If we make ten loans of \$100,000 each, we need to recover \$1,000,000 from the eight successful projects. Thus, each successful project must repay = \$1,000,000/8 = \$125,000. Therefore, the loan "return" rate on each successful project must be
$$\frac{\$125{,}000 - \$100{,}000}{\$100{,}000} = 25\%.$$
With Bea's rate of success of 40%, we have four successful projects out of every ten, so \$1,000,000/4 = \$250,000 needs to be recovered, giving a loan return rate of: $\frac{\$250{,}000 - \$100{,}000}{\$100{,}000} = 150\%$ from the four successful projects.
3. d. Expected payoff = (0.5) × \$2,000,000 + (0.5) × \$0 = \$1,000,000. Expected profit = \$1,000,000 − \$900,000 = \$100,000.

4. d. Find the EPS under the two financing structures with an EBIT of $50,000:

$$\text{With all equity: EPS} = \frac{\$50{,}000\ (1 - 0.30)}{\$100{,}000} = \$0.35.$$

$$\text{With 50/50 debt to equity: EPS} = \frac{(\$50{,}000 - \$15{,}000)\ (1 - 0.30)}{\$50{,}000} = \$0.49.$$

So, the shareholders will be better off with a price of $0.14 per share under a firm with $300,000 in debt financing versus a firm that is all equity. The CEO of Donat should add debt to the firm because it would benefit the owners of the company.

5. a.
6. d.
7. c.
8. c. We first compute the tax shield: interest expense × tax rate/discount rate = $10,000,000 × 0.4/0.1 = $40,000,000. We can now compute firm value: $V_L = V_E$ + tax shield = $100 million + $40 million = $140 million.
9. d.
10. d.

Chapter 17

1. c.
2. a.
3. a.
4. c.
5. b.
6. b. Additional shares 0.20 × 900,000 = 180,000 and new total outstanding is 900,000 + 180,000 = 1,080,000.
7. d.
8. b.
9. a.
10. b. Cash value of the dividends = the per share dividend × the number of shares owned = $0.75 × 100 shares = $75.00. At $55 per share, Maggie can purchase $75/$55 = 1.36 shares.

Chapter 18

1. d. It is a political risk, not a cultural risk.
2. d.
3. b.
4. a. By paying the Japanese company, you are converting yen into dollars and getting ¥7,500/(¥150/$1) = $50 per item. Because you collect $55 per item sold to your customer, your profit per item is $55 − $50 = $5 per item.
5. c. £1/¥200 = £0.00500 per yen
6. a.
7. b.
8. d. 3,000 tricycles at 375 kronas per tricycle = 1,125,000 kronas is your sales receipt. At today's exchange rate, these kronas will convert to 1,125,000/7.5 = $150,000. At the indirect exchange rate, these kronas will convert to 1,125,000/7.7 = $146,104. That is a difference of $150,000 − $146,104 = $3,896.
9. c.
10. b. Comment: First, we compute the forward exchange rate: $12 \times (1.14/1.06)^2 =$ 13.879672. Second, we convert all pesos into dollars using forward exchange rates: 100,000/13.879672 = $7,204.78. Third, we discount the dollar cash flow at the home discount rate: $(7{,}204.78/1.10)^2$ = $5,954.36.

Glossary

1933 Securities Act The original federal legislation that regulated the trading of primary securities.

1934 Securities Exchange Act An act that created the U.S. Securities and Exchange Commission and regulated the trading of securities in secondary markets.

accounting exposure See *translation exposure.*

accounting identity The basic accounting definition wherein assets always equal liabilities plus owners' equity.

accounts payable cycle The average time it takes to pay suppliers after delivery.

accounts receivable cycle The average time it takes to collect from credit customers.

accrual-based accounting A process in which revenues or costs are recognized and recorded at the time of sale regardless of whether revenues have been received in cash or costs have been paid out in cash.

adjusted weighted average cost of capital ($WACC_{adjusted}$) The weighted average cost of capital adjusted for the tax deduction on interest paid on debt by the firm.

agency cost A term used in agency theory for an extra cost paid to an agent on behalf of a principal.

agency theory The study of principal-agent problems and how to align the actions of agents with the interests of principals.

agent Individual acting in the interest of another person, the principal.

American rate See *direct rate.*

American Stock Exchange (AMEX) One of the three well-known secondary stock markets (see also *New York Stock Exchange* and *National Association of Securities Dealers Automated Quotation system*).

amortization schedule The listing of the periodic interest expense, the reduction in principal each period, and the ending balance for each period.

amortized loan A loan in which the principal and interest are paid each period.

angel investor A lender who provides funding for a new, high-risk idea.

annual percentage rate (APR) The yearly uncompounded rate of interest.

annual percentage yield (APY) See *effective annual rate.*

annuity A series of equal cash flows at regular intervals across time.

annuity due A series of equal and regular payments in which the payments occur at the beginning of each period.

arbitrage An opportunity to make a profit without risk.

ask price The price at which an authorized stock dealer is willing to sell shares.

asset management efficiency One of the three DuPont equation components, measured by the asset turnover, that measures how efficiently a company uses its assets to generate revenue.

asset management ratios Financial ratios that measure how efficiently a company uses its assets to generate revenue.

assets Items of economic value the company owns.

asymmetric information The state in which different parties have different information about an event or value of an asset.

auction market A market in which assets are sold to the highest bidder.

authorized shares The maximum number of shares that a firm is allowed to issue.

balance sheet The set of assets owned by a company and all claims against those assets.

banker's acceptance A self-liquidating financing arrangement guaranteed by a bank.

bankruptcy A state of financial distress in which the equity value of the firm is zero and the company cannot pay its debts.

basis point One-hundredth of a percentage point.

bear market A prolonged market period in which stock prices in general are decreasing.

bearer bond A bond for which proof of ownership is simply possession.

benchmarking Comparing a company's current performance against its own previous performance or against that of its competitors.

beneficiary owner The ultimate owner of the stock, even though the stock is kept in the street name of the brokerage firm.

best efforts A compensation package wherein the investment banker pledges his or her best efforts in trying to sell the shares of an initial public offering, taking a small percentage of the sale of stock.

beta A statistical measure of the volatility of an individual security in comparison to the market as a whole; the measure of the risk of an asset in a well-diversified portfolio.

bid-ask spread See *spread.*

bid price A price at which an authorized stock dealer is willing to buy shares.

bleed rate See *burn rate.*

bond A long-term debt instrument in which a borrower promises to pay back the principal with interest on specific dates in the future.

bond equivalent yield (BEY) The annual percentage rate converted from the bank discount rate on a Treasury bill.

book value The original cost of the asset minus the accumulated depreciation; the accounting or balance sheet value, as opposed to market value.

bull market A prolonged period in which stock prices in general are rising.

burn rate (bleed rate) The rate at which a new idea will use up funds provided by an angel or venture capitalist investor.

business life cycle The five phases of a business in which it starts up, grows, matures, declines, and closes.

business risk (foreign business risk) The risk of changes in foreign markets that affect performance.

callable bond A bond that the issuer has the right to buy back prior to maturity at a predetermined price.

capital asset pricing model (CAPM) The relationship between the systematic risk of the market and the expected return on an individual asset based on its perceived risk.

capital budgeting The process of planning, evaluating, comparing, and selecting the long-term operating projects of the company.

capital markets Markets for financial assets with maturities longer than one year.

capital structure The relative weights of debt and equity that a firm uses to finance its operations and growth.

cash account The currency, checking accounts, and savings accounts of a company that are available for paying liabilities, dividends, or new acquisitions.

cash budget A firm's estimate of the future timing of its cash inflows and outflows.

cash conversion cycle (CCC) The time between the initial cash outflow and the final cash inflow of a product that determines how long a company must finance its operations.

cash dividends Payments of cash to the owners of the company.

cash flow An actual inflow or outflow of money; the increase or decrease in cash for the period.

cash flow identity A definition in which the cash flow from assets is always equal to the cash flow to creditors and owners.

Chapter 7 A state of financial distress in which the company ceases all business operations and goes through bankruptcy court proceedings.

Chapter 11 A reorganization plan in which the bankrupt company continues to operate while trying to resolve its financial difficulties with creditors.

chief financial officer (CFO) The top financial officer of a company, who oversees all the company's financial activities.

clean-up period (resting the line) A requirement that a line of credit remain at a zero balance for a number of days each year.

collateral Assets that support a loan should the borrower fail to make the obligated payments on time and that can be transferred to the lender to satisfy loan repayment.

collection cycle The time it takes a firm to collect payment from its customers.

collection float The time delay between when a check is first written and when the money is made available to the seller.

commercial paper A short-term financial asset sold by a company directly to investors with a maturity of less than 270 days.

common-size financial statements Financial statements in which all line items are expressed as a percentage of a common base figure. For income statements, the base figure is usually sales.

common stock A financial asset signifying ownership in a company.

compensating balance A specific amount of a loan not available to the borrower.

compounding The earning of interest on interest into the future.

compounding period The period in which interest is applied.

compounding periods per year (*C/Y* or *m*) The frequency of times interest is added to an account each year.

compound interest The interest earned in subsequent periods on the interest earned in prior periods.

consols Stocks that pay interest forever, have no date of maturity, and make no promise to repay the principal. They are priced as perpetual bonds.

constant annual dividend A dividend payment that is the same year after year.

constant growth A growth pattern in which the percentage increase in the stock dividend is the same each year.

convertible bond A bond that gives the bond holder the right to swap the bond for another asset, usually common stock in the company, at a preset conversion ratio under certain conditions.

cooling-off period See *quiet period.*

corporate finance The set of financial activities that support the operations of a corporation or business.

corporate governance The way in which a company conducts its business and implements controls to ensure proper procedures and ethical behavior.

corporation A business form in which the company is a legal entity that is separate from the owners.

corpus A bond with the coupons clipped off, representing only the principal.

correlation A measure of how stocks perform relative to one another in different states of the economy.

correlation coefficient A measure of the co-movement between two variables that ranges from -1 to $+1$.

cost of capital The cost of each financing component used by the firm to fund its projects multiplied (weighted) by that component's percent of the total funding amount.

cost of debt The rate of return that the bank or bond holder demands on funds.

cost of equity The rate of return required by shareholders of the company.

cost of preferred stock The rate of return that preferred stockholders require on preferred shares.

cost of retained earnings The rate of return required from shareholders for internal funds.

coupon The regular interest payment of a bond.

coupon rate The interest rate for the bond coupons, expressed in annual percentage terms.

covered interest arbitrage Investing in different currencies with different expected inflation rates to make a profit.

credit screening A process that attempts to verify the creditworthiness of a customer prior to granting credit.

crossover rate The discount rate at which two different projects have the same NPV.

cross rate An exchange rate for a non-U.S. currency expressed in terms of another non-U.S. currency.

cultural risk The risk that arises from differences in business policies due to customs, social norms, attitudes, assumptions, and expectations of the local society.

cumulative (dividends) A preferred stock provision in which missed dividends must be made up.

current yield The annual bond coupon payment divided by the current price.

cycle of money The movement of money from lender to borrower and back again.

dealer market The market in which individuals or firms buy and sell securities out of their own inventory.

debentures Unsecured bonds.

debt capacity The ability to add debt financing to the current borrowing of the firm and still be able to make interest and principal repayments on time.

debt-equity ratios The mix of debt and equity funding in firms.

debt financing A company's borrowing from a bank or selling bonds to raise capital.

declaration date The date on which a company's board of directors announces the next quarterly cash dividend to the public.

deed of trust See *indenture.*

default premium The portion of a borrowing rate that compensates the lender for the higher risk of default.

depreciation The process of amortizing the cost of a long-term tangible asset over its useful life; a current expense of a cash outflow from a previous period.

direct costs of bankruptcy The legal and administrative fees that are first in line in bankruptcy proceedings.

direct rate (American rate) The amount of U.S. dollars required to purchase one unit of a foreign currency.

disbursement float The time delay between when a check is first written and when the money is made available to the payee.

discount bond A bond for which the price is below par.

discounted payback period A capital budgeting model that calculates the amount of time it takes to recover an initial investment in current dollars.

discounting The compounded reduction in value from future values to present values.

discount loan A loan wherein all interest and principal are repaid at maturity.

discount rate The rate used to determine the present value of future cash flows.

diversifiable risk Risk that can be eliminated by forming a diversified portfolio.

diversification The spreading of wealth over a variety of investment opportunities in order to eliminate some risk.

dividend clienteles Different groups of shareholders with different desires on dividend policies.

dividend policy irrelevance theory The theory that company dividend policy is irrelevant to the dividend holder.

dividend reinvestment plans (DRIPs) The automatic reinvestment of the shareholders' cash dividends into more shares of the company stock.

dividends Payments of cash or stock to the owners of the company.

double-entry accounting The accounting process that matches an equal debit and credit for every transaction.

double-entry bookkeeping See *double-entry accounting.*

due diligence A duty of the investment banker to ensure all relevant information is disclosed prior to the sale of stock.

earnings before interest and taxes (EBIT) Revenue minus operating expenses.

economic order quantity (EOQ) The quantity of inventory ordered each period that minimizes the sum of inventory ordering and holding costs.

effective annual rate (EAR) The compounded rate of interest per year.

efficient markets Stock markets in which costs are minimal and prices are current and fair to all traders.

electronic funds transfer (EFT) An electronic system of transferring funds from one bank account to another; substantially eliminates collection float for businesses and disbursement float for customers.

equity What the company owners receive after the liabilities have been satisfied.

equity claim An ownership claim to all the assets and cash flows of a company once debt claimants have been paid.

equity financing Acquiring capital by selling common stock or using internal funds.

equity value The value of the company to the owners.

equivalent annual annuity (EAA) An annuity version of a project that has the same net present value as the project's original uneven cash flows.

erosion costs The loss of sales of existing products due to the introduction of a new competing product by the same company.

European rate See *indirect rate.*

ex-ante Before the fact.

exchange rate The price of one country's currency in units of another country's currency.

ex-date The first day to buy stock and not have one's name on record for receiving the declared dividend; the date that establishes the recipient of the dividend.

exotic bond A bond with special features distinct to that particular bond.

ex-post After the fact.

external data Information gathered outside the firm and often available to the public.

fallen angel A bond originally issued as investment grade that has been downgraded to a speculative bond.

finance The art and science of managing wealth.

financial assets Intangible assets such as stocks and bonds.

financial distress costs See *indirect costs of bankruptcy.*

financial institutions and markets The organized financial intermediaries and the forums that promote the cycle of money.

financial intermediary An institution that acts as a middleman between borrowers and lenders.

financial leverage The degree to which a firm or individual utilizes borrowed money to make money. Also, one of the three DuPont equation components, measured by the equity multiplier (total assets/total equity).

financial leverage ratios Ratios that measure a company's ability to meet its long-term debt obligations.

financial management Those activities that create or preserve the economic value of the assets of an individual, small business, or corporation.

financial portfolio An investor's total investment set.

financial ratios Relationships between different accounts on financial statements that serve as performance indicators.

firm commitment A guarantee by an investment banker to sell the entire stock issue of an initial public offering (IPO) at a preset amount of money for the company.

Fisher effect The relationship in which the nominal interest rate is a function of the real rate, inflation, and the product of the real rate and inflation.

float The lag time involved in the process of clearing a check.

floating rate bond A bond with a changing coupon rate.

flotation cost An expense incurred by a company in issuing stock or bonds.

foreign bond A bond issued by a foreign corporation or foreign government.

forward contract An agreement to exchange an asset or currency at a preset value or rate at some specific future point in time.

forward exchange rate The predicted future exchange rate at some point in time.

free cash flow The remaining funds after paying for the operations and capital spending of a firm that are free to distribute to security holders such as bond holders, preferred stock owners, and shareholders.

future value (FV) The cash value of an asset in the future that is equivalent in value to a specific (lower) amount today.

future value interest factor (FVIF) The growth rate raised to the power of a number of periods $(1 + r)^n$, where r is the interest rate and n is the number of periods.

future value interest factor of an annuity (FVIFA) The mathematical factor, $[(1 + r)^n - 1]/r$, used to multiply the annuity to calculate the future value of the annuity stream.

general partners Those individuals in a partnership who operate the daily business.

generally accepted accounting principles (GAAP) The set of accounting standards, procedures, and principles companies follow when assembling their financial statements.

Gordon model A stock valuation model that determines the value of a stock based on a future stream of dividends growing at a constant rate forever.

green-shoe provision A provision that allows the investment bankers to purchase up to 15% of additional shares of those being issued.

growth rate The annual percentage increase (of dividends, investment values, and so forth).

holding period return The return from the initial purchase to the final sale of an investment regardless of the investment period.

hurdle rate The interest rate that represents the lowest required return that must be exceeded when using the internal rate of return (IRR) model for accepting or rejecting a project.

hybrid equity financing Financing with securities that have characteristics of both debt and equity.

income bond A bond that pays coupons based on the income of a company.

income statement An accounting document that measures a company's financial performance over a specific period of time.

incremental cash flow The increase in cash generated by a new project above the company's current cash flow.

indenture The formal contract for a bond between the issuing company and the buyer. It includes vital information about the bond and its provisions.

indirect costs of bankruptcy The costs of lost sales, employees leaving, loss of customer confidence, and forgone good projects while the company is in financial distress.

indirect rate (European rate) The amount of foreign currency needed to buy one U.S. dollar.

informational efficiency A measure of how quickly information is reflected in the available prices for trading.

initial public offering (IPO) The process of selling stock for the first time.

intellectual property rights The exclusive rights of an individual to use his or her products created by his or her own intellectual talents for personal gain.

interest The amount the lender charges for borrowing money.

interest-only loan A loan in which the interest is paid regularly and the principal and final interest payment are repaid at the end of the loan.

internal data Information unique or proprietary to the firm.

internal rate of return (IRR) The discount rate that produces a zero net present value for a given set of cash flows.

international finance The study of when and what to buy and sell, taking into account country differences in currencies, institutions, and laws.

International Fisher effect The proposition that, in equilibrium, real interest rates are the same in all countries.

investment bank An agent that works with the firm to design, market, list, and sell its securities.

Investment rule number 1 If two investments have the same expected return and different levels of risk, the investment with the lower risk is preferred.

Investment rule number 2 If two investments have the same level of risk and different expected returns, the investment with the higher expected return is preferred.

investments The activities centering on the buying and selling of both real and financial assets.

issued shares Shares available for public purchase.

junior debt Debt issued subsequent to other (senior) debt with lower priority in terms of payment.

junk bond A speculative bond with a rating below BBB.

just in time (JIT) An inventory management system that attempts to produce only the necessary items with only the necessary quantities only at the necessary time, thereby eliminating waste and improving productivity.

legal capital The original contributions of the owners; the par value and the paid in excess of par on the common shares.

letter of comment Letter issued by the SEC that states if any information is missing from the registration filing of a company seeking to sell shares or bonds.

letter (or line) of credit A preapproved borrowing amount that works much like a credit card.

liabilities The amounts of money a company owes to others.

limited liability A type of liability in which the personal assets of the owners are separate from the company. Owners can lose only what they paid for their shares.

limited partners Those individuals in a partnership who participate only in certain aspects of the business.

line of credit A prearranged, unsecured bank loan to which a firm has access at any time up to a maximum limit.

liquidating dividend A divided issued to shareholders when the company is discontinuing operations or when a major portion of the business has been sold off.

liquidity event An event that allows angel investors or venture capitalists to cash out some or all of their ownership shares.

liquidity ratios Ratios that measure a company's ability to pay off its short-term debt obligations.

lockbox Post office box where a bank collects checks and reduces collection float by eliminating processing time.

lock-up agreement A provision that requires the original owner of a firm to maintain their shares of stock for a specific amount of time after an initial public sale, usually for a minimum of 180 days.

lump-sum payment The one-time payment of money at a future date.

M&M proposition I (with and without corporate taxes) The theoretical model that predicts capital structure to be irrelevant in a world with no corporate taxes and no financial distress costs such as bankruptcy. With taxes, however, firm value increases with an increasing debt-to-equity ratio. With financial distress costs, value first increases and then decreases beyond the optimal debt-to-equity ratio.

M&M proposition II (with and without corporate taxes) The theoretical model that predicts the weighted average cost of capital (WACC) to remain constant with an increasing debt-to-equity ratio in a world with no corporate taxes and no financial distress costs. With taxes, however, the WACC deceases with an increasing debt-to-equity ratio. With financial distress costs, the WACC first decreases and then increases.

marketable securities Financial assets that the firm plans to sell in a short period of time.

market risk premium The slope of the security market line, or the difference between the average market return and the risk-free rate; the additional reward for taking on more risk.

market value The current price of debt or equity in the capital markets, as distinguished from accounting or book value.

market value ratios Ratios that measure the performance of the firm against the perceived value of the firm from the trading value or the number of shares.

maturity date The expiration date of the bond on which the final interest payment is made as well as the principal repayment.

maturity premium The portion of the nominal interest rate that compensates the investor for the additional waiting time to receive repayment in full.

maximize return Get the most out of an investment for a given level of risk.

minimize risk Get the lowest potential for loss for a given rate of return.

modified accelerated cost recovery system (MACRS) A government-mandated accelerated depreciation system that depreciates the capital asset at an accelerated pace over time.

modified internal rate of return (MIRR) A different internal rate of return calculation that assumes the cash flows are reinvested at the firm's cost of capital.

money markets Markets for financial assets that will mature within the year.

mortgaged security A security that uses real property as collateral.

multinational firm A business that operates in more than one country.

municipal bond A bond issued by a county, city, or local government agency.

mutually exclusive project A project that precludes the choosing of another project.

National Association of Securities Dealers (NASD) Founded in 1939, a private association of most U.S. securities firms established to self-regulate and enforce market rules, provide investor education, and to resolve investor complaints for over-the-counter stocks.

National Association of Securities Dealers Automated Quotation system (NASDAQ) The world's first automated stock exchange, an electronic dealer's market that operates without a trading floor and that has multiple dealers for each stock.

nationalize The act of a local government seizing the assets of a company, usually without compensation.

negative correlation The movement of two different asset returns in different directions over time.

nepotism The hiring of relatives.

net income Accounting profits from the operations of the company after taxes.

net present value (NPV) The present value of all cash inflows minus the present value of all cash outflows.

net present value (NPV) profile of a project The graphic representation of the net present value of a project discounted at different interest rates.

net working capital Current assets minus current liabilities.

New York Stock Exchange (NYSE) One of the three well-known secondary stock markets (see also *American Stock Exchange* and *National Association of Securities Dealers Automated Quotation system*).

nominal interest rate The interest rate composed of a real interest rate plus the inflation rate.

noncumulative (dividends) The case in which, if dividends are skipped, they are forever lost to the shareholder.

nondiversifiable risk Risk that cannot be eliminated by the formation of a portfolio.

odd lot A number of shares less than a 100-share unit.

operating cash flow (OCF) The estimated cash flow generated from the basic operations of the business, or EBIT + depreciation − taxes.

operating efficiency One of the three DuPont equation components, measured by the profit margin, designed to show how well the company's sales generate net income.

operating exposure The risk of the long-run viability of a foreign business when unexpected exchange rates move against the domestic company.

operational efficiency The speed and accuracy of processing a buy or sell order at the best available price.

opportunity cost A forgone benefit of one project due to the selection of another project.

optimal capital structure The combination of debt and equity that maximizes the value of the firm.

optimal debt-to-equity ratio The point at which the marginal benefits of the tax shield of debt financing are equal to the marginal costs of the financial stress of debt financing.

optional cash purchase plans (OCPs) Plans in which a shareholder can purchase additional shares through a dividend reinvestment plan for a small fee and a small initial investment.

ordinary annuity A series of equal and regular payments in which the payments occur at the end of each period.

outstanding shares Shares that are sold and remain in the public domain.

owner of record The brokerage company that receives and transfers all distributions and communications from the stock company to the beneficiary owner.

owners' equity The residual value of the company to the owners once all liabilities have been satisfied.

par value The principal amount to be repaid at the maturity of the bond.

par value bond A bond for which the current price equals the par value of the bond.

partnership A business owned jointly by two or more individuals.

payback period The amount of time needed to recover the initial investment of a project.

payment cycle The time it takes a company to pay for its supplies.

payment date The actual day on which a declared cash dividend is paid.

pecking order hypothesis The capital structure theory that predicts that firms progress from one source of funding to another in a preferred order.

periodic interest rate The annual percentage rate divided by the number of compounding periods per year.

perpetuity An infinite series of regular and equal payments.

political risk The risk of changes in a foreign government that can affect performance.

positive correlation The movement of two different asset returns in the same direction over time.

preemptive right The provision that allows current shareholders to buy a fixed percentage of all future issues before they are offered to the general public and thus maintain their same percentage ownership in the firm.

preferred stock A stock that pays a constant dividend every period and that has priority claims over common stock.

preferred trading range The normal price at which stocks have historically traded on the NYSE, in the $20 to $40 range.

premium bond A bond for which the price is above par.

present value (PV) The value today of a cash flow in the future.

present value interest factor (PVIF) The reciprocal of the FVIF (see also *future value interest factor*).

present value interest factor of an annuity (PVIFA) The mathematical factor, $[1 - 1/(1 + r)^n]/r$, used to multiply the annuity to calculate the present value of the annuity stream.

price/earnings to growth (PEG) ratio The price to earnings ratio divided by the earnings growth rate.

primary market The market for a company's original issue of stock to the public.

prime rate The interest rate that banks charge their best customers.

principal The original loan amount borrowed.

principal-agent problem A term used in agency theory to designate the problem of motivating one party to act in the best interest of another party.

principals Owners of the business.

production cycle The time it takes a firm to produce and sell a product.

professional corporation (PC) A legal arrangement in which the owners (licensed partners) are not personally liable for the malpractice of their partners.

profit The positive (or negative) difference between an investment's ending value and its original cost.

profitability index (PI) The ratio of the present value of a project's positive cash flows to the present value of its negative cash flows.

profitability ratios Ratios that measure how effectively the company is turning sales or assets into income.

profits An accounting measure of performance during a specific period of time.

pro forma financial statements (pro formas) Forecasted accounting statements based on a set of operating and sales assumptions.

pro-rata share The pro-rated amount of their bid that bidders receive if the new issue is oversubscribed.

prospectus A document that provides potential buyers with information about the company and the impending sale of stock.

protective covenant Part of the bond indenture that spells out both required and prohibited actions of the bond issuer.

purchasing power parity The principle that predicts that the price of similar goods is the same, regardless of which currency one uses to buy the goods.

pure play Matching a project to a company with a single business focus to obtain a comparable beta.

putable bond A bond that gives the bond holder the right to sell the bond back to the company at a predetermined price prior to maturity.

quiet period (cooling-off period) The waiting period between the first filing (preliminary registration) and the approval of the sale of stock.

real assets Physical assets such as property, buildings, or commodities.

real interest rate (r^*) The reward for waiting.

record date A date on which registered stockholders are designated for receipt of dividends.

red herring A preliminary prospectus.

regular cash dividend A dividend routinely paid to shareholders, typically on a quarterly basis.

Regulation A A provision that exempts small businesses from filing with the SEC if the issue is less than $5 million.

reorder point The level of inventories at which an order should be placed.

residual claim A claim that begins after all the liabilities of the company have been satisfied.

residual dividend policy A dividend policy in which dividends are paid out of cash flow remaining from operations after cash flow has paid off debts, maintained operations, and provided cash for reinvesting.

resting the line See *clean-up period.*

return The percentage change in the gain or loss compared with the original investment.

reverse split The division of a company's stock into a lesser number of outstanding shares.

reward for waiting The real rate of interest rate paid for forgoing the use of money today.

reward-to-risk ratio See *market risk premium.*

risk A measure of the uncertainty in a set of potential outcomes when there is a chance of loss.

risk-free rate (r_f) A theoretical interest rate with zero risk of any kind.

road show A series of information sessions on a securities issue wherein the marketing syndicate invites current and potential clients to one or more major cities.

round lot 100 shares.

rule of 72 A simplified approximation to find the length of time it takes to double money whereby seventy-two is divided by the (percentage) interest rate.

S corporation A small business corporate form with less than 100 shareholders that avoids taxes at the corporate level.

safety stock Additional inventory on hand to cover delayed orders.

sales forecast The prediction of the cash inflows from future sales.

secondary markets The after-issue markets for existing or preowned shares.

secured loans Loans in which assets have been pledged against borrowed funds.

Securities and Exchange Commission (SEC) A government-authorized agency that oversees the regulations for selling financial securities.

security market line (SML) The graphical version of the capital asset pricing model showing risk (beta) on the horizontal axis and return on the vertical axis.

security of a bond See *collateral.*

semi-strong-form efficient markets Stock markets in which current prices already reflect the price history and volume of the stock as well as all available public information.

senior debt Older debt that has priority of payment over junior (younger) debt.

Separate Trading of Registered Interest and Principal (STRIPS) Zero-coupon bonds made by separating the interest and principal on U.S. government bonds.

settlement date The date when money is paid and the security transfer occurs for the transaction.

signaling hypothesis The theory that current management can signal good news information about the future stock price to both current and potential shareholders with stock splits.

silent partners Those individuals who participate in the business only as investors.

sinking fund A special fund for the retirement of debt on bonds.

slope of the security market line The market risk premium; the additional reward for taking on more risk.

Small Business Administration (SBA) See *U.S. Small Business Administration.*

sole proprietorship A business owned entirely by an individual.

solvency ratios Ratios that measure a company's ability to meet its long-term debt obligations.

special (or extra) dividend A dividend that is not guaranteed in the following period, usually one-time and non-recurring.

specialist A stock exchange dealer whose job it is to maintain an orderly market for the stock.

spot market See *spot rate.*

spot rate (spot market) The current price of an asset or the rate of currency exchange today.

spread The difference between the asking price and the bid price; in IPOs, the difference between the sale price of the stock to the public and the proceeds of the sale paid to the issuing company by the investment bank.

standard deviation The square root of the variance of the distribution of actual returns from their mean.

state bond A bond issued by an individual state government.

statement of cash flows The financial statement that displays the sources and uses of cash in three major categories: operating activities, capital spending activities, and financing activities.

statement of retained earnings An accounting document that shows the distribution of net income for the past period, based on the payment (or nonpayment) of dividends.

static theory of capital structure The capital structure theory that predicts a balance of marginal benefits and marginal costs of debt financing, assuming the assets and operations of the firm are fixed.

sticky dividends The theory that dividends are sticky downward because investors prefer a stable payout and because lower dividends may signal poor future firm performance.

stock dividend A dividend in the form of shares of stock instead of cash.

stockholders' equity See *owners' equity.*

stock option The right to buy company stock at a preset price sometime in the future.

stock repurchase plan A plan whereby a company uses the cash that would normally be used to pay a dividend to instead purchase the company's stock on the open market.

stock split The division of a company' existing shares into multiple shares with the total dollar value remaining the same.

straight-line depreciation A depreciation system in which capital assets are depreciated by the same amount each year.

straight liquidation Selling off of all assets with payment to all legal claim holders.

street name The broker listed as owner rather than the buyer.

strong-form efficient markets Stock markets in which current prices reflect the price and volume history of the stock, all publicly available information, and even all private information.

sunk costs Costs that have already been incurred and cannot be reversed.

syndicated loans Loans made by multiple banks joining together to share the income and risk.

synergy gain The increase in sales of an existing project due to the introduction of a new complementary product.

systematic risk Marketwide risk, affected by the uncertainty of future economic conditions that affect all stocks in the economy.

tax shield A tax-deductible expense such as interest that lowers taxes and, other things being constant, increases the value of the firm.

time line A linear representation of the timing of cash flows over a period of time.

time value of money (TVM) A key financial principle stating that a dollar today is worth more than a dollar tomorrow.

tombstone The advertisement of a forthcoming securities issue printed during the waiting period.

transaction costs Costs associated with various financial procedures (for example, brokerage commissions).

transaction exposure The potential loss in home currency value of future foreign currency payments.

translation exposure (accounting exposure) The risk of a negative effect on financial statements due to different countries' rules of consolidating foreign and domestic financial statements.

Treasury bill A U.S. government bond with a maturity of less than one year.

Treasury bond A U.S. government bond with a maturity of more than ten years.

Treasury note A U.S. government bond with a maturity of between two and ten years.

treasury shares See *treasury stock.*

treasury stock Shares of stock held by the company.

triangular arbitrage Making a profit without risk by exchanging three currencies.

uncertainty The absence of knowledge of the actual outcome of an event before it happens.

underwriter The financial institution that provides the process for firms to sell financial assets in the capital markets.

unsystematic risk Firm-specific risk or industry-specific risk, that is, uncertainty that is particular to a single company or single industry.

U.S. Small Business Administration (SBA) A U.S. government agency with loan programs for small businesses.

variance The statistical dispersion of the average squared difference between the actual observations and the average observation.

venture capitalist firms (funds) Groups or institutions that provide funding at higher levels than most angel investors.

weak-form efficient markets Stock markets in which current prices reflect the price history and trading volume of the stock.

weighted average cost of capital (WACC) The average of the costs of financing sources weighted by the portion of funds; the cost of capital for the firm as a whole.

well-diversified portfolio A portfolio that has essentially eliminated all unsystematic risk.

working capital accounts The current assets and current liabilities of the firm.

working capital management The process of managing the day-to-day operations of the company through its current assets and current liabilities so as to improve the flow of funds.

yield See *yield to maturity*.

yield to call The discount rate (return) for a callable premium bond.

yield curve The graphed relationship between the return rate and an asset's time to maturity.

yield to maturity (YTM) The return the bond holder receives on the bond if held to maturity.

zero-coupon bond A bond that pays no coupons over its maturity.

Index

Credits

Cover and part-opening images: Dreamstime/Alexey Bragin/ Shutterstock (top image); 350jb/Dreamstime (bottom image)

Various chapters: Wrench adjusting dollar sign icon: La Fleur Studio/Stock Illustration Source

Various chapters: "Putting Finance to Work" box imagery: Richard Tuschman/Stock Illustration Source

Chapter 1: p. 2: Tony Vita/Stock Illustration Source; p. 9: Qiun/ Shutterstock; p. 11: Eugene Ivanov/Shutterstock; p. 15 Stockbyte/Thinkstock; p. 18: Jupiterimages/Thinkstock

Chapter 2: p. 26: Kaadaa/Stock Illustration Source; p. 41: Michaeldb/Dreamstime

Chapter 3: p. 54: Choka/Dreamstime; p. 57: Yakobchuk Vasyl/ Shutterstock; p. 62: Stockbyte/Thinkstock

Chapter 4: p. 82: Steve Kropp/Stock Illustration Source; p. 99: Stockbyte/Thinkstock

Chapter 5: p. 114: Markus Gann/Shutterstock; p. 118: Sean Gladwell/Shutterstock; p. 128: Stephen F. Hayes/Stock Illustration Source

Chapter 6: p. 146: Anthonycz/Shutterstock

Chapter 7: p. 180: Dave Cutler/Stock Illustration Source; p. 186: Ocean Illustration/Veer/Corbis; p. 203: Stockbyte/Thinkstock

Chapter 8: p. 212: Paul Vismara/Stock Illustration Source; p. 233: Stockbyte/Thinkstock

Chapter 9: p. 256: United Illustrators/Fotolia; p. 260: Andrea Danti/Shutterstock; p. 265: Madartists/Dreamstime

Chapter 10: p. 296: Kiamsoon/Dreamstime; p. 301: Jean-Francois Allaux/Stock Illustration Source

Chapter 11: p. 324: Regular/Shutterstock

Chapter 12: p. 356: Rob Colvin/Stock Illustration Source; p. 361: Michael Monahan/Shutterstock

Chapter 13: p. 384: Patrimonio/Dreamstime; p. 401: Saniphoto/ Dreamstime

Chapter 14: p. 422: Svet13/Shutterstock

Chapter 15: p. 456: Creativeapril/Dreamstime; p. 460: Realrocking/ Dreamstime

Chapter 16: p. 490: Anton Balazh/Shutterstock; p. 492: Rich Wolf/ Shutterstock

Chapter 17: p. 520: Regissercom/Dreamstime; p. 532: Gibsons/ Shutterstock

Chapter 18: p. 550: Leo Kundas/Stock Illustration Source; p. 554: Lary Knox/Stock Illustration Source; p. 558: David Ridley/ Stock Illustration Source; p. 561: Olivier Le Moal/Shutterstock

Chapter 1
Financial Management
AT A GLANCE

LO1 Describe the cycle of money, the participants in the cycle, and the common objective of borrowing and lending.

The cycle of money is the movement of money from lender to borrower and back again. It is often accomplished through a financial intermediary like a bank. The common objective is to make both the lender and the borrower better off.

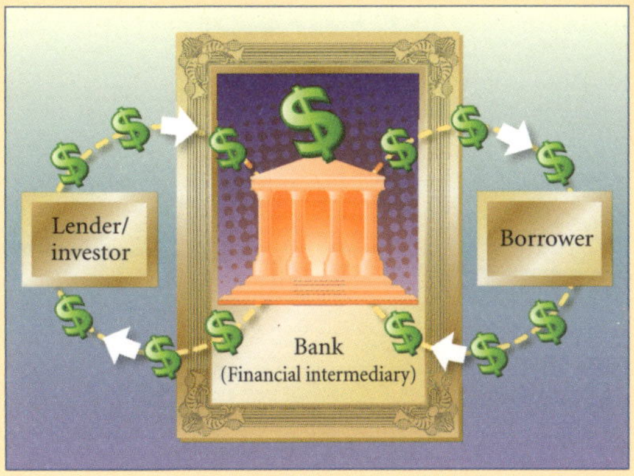

LO2 Distinguish the four main areas of finance and briefly explain the financial activities that each encompasses.

The four main areas of finance are corporate finance, investments, financial institutions and markets, and international finance. Corporate finance supports the operations of a company. Investments are the activities centered on buying and selling stocks and bonds. Financial institutions and markets are the organizations that promote the cycle of money and the buying and selling of financial assets. International finance is concerned with the multinational element of finance activities.

LO3 Explain the different ways of classifying financial markets.

There are a number of ways to classify financial markets: by type of asset traded, by maturity of assets, by owner of the assets, or by method of sale.

LO4 Discuss the three main categories of financial management.

Financial management can be subdivided into three categories: capital budgeting, capital structure, and working capital management. Capital budgeting is the process of choosing the products and services the company will produce. Capital structure is concerned with choosing the lenders the company will use to finance its operations. Working capital management involves choosing the policies that manage the day-to-day operating needs of the company.

LO5 Identify the main objective of the finance manager and how he or she might meet that objective.

The primary goal of the finance manager is to maximize the current stock price (equity value) of the firm. The finance manager works with multiple players inside and outside the firm to create and preserve the economic value of the firm's assets.

LO6 Explain how the finance manager interacts with both internal and external players.

Business activities are accomplished by a diverse set of players inside and outside the organization. The finance manager provides critical knowledge and guidance to marketing, manufacturing, human resources, supporting suppliers, and customers and interfaces with agencies like banks to meet the needs of the company.

LO7 Delineate the three main legal categories of business organizations and their respective advantages and disadvantages.

There are three main legal categories of business organizations: sole proprietorship, partnership, and corporation. The key advantage of the corporate form of business is the limited liability of the shareholders (owners). The key disadvantage is double taxation, in which profits are taxed both before and after distribution to owners. The key advantages for the sole proprietorship form of business are that the owner can make all the decisions and can keep all the profits. The disadvantage is the limited access to funding. Partnerships have more funding potential, but must share the profits and losses.

Chapter 1
Financial Management
AT A GLANCE

LO8 Illustrate agency theory and the principal-agent problem.

Companies are run by managers who may have different goals than the owners. The resolution of these potential problems is the domain of agency theory. The principal-agent problem is the conflict between the owners of the company and the managers hired by the owners to work in the owners' best interests.

LO9 Review issues in corporate governance and business ethics.

Corporate governance deals with how a company conducts its business and what controls are put in place to ensure proper procedures and ethical behavior. Although many managers and owners operate in an ethical manner, some do not. The government may add rules and regulations about the conduct of business and its officers to encourage ethical and honest behavior.

Chapter 2
Financial Statements
AT A GLANCE

LO1 Explain the foundations of the balance sheet and income statement.

There are four financial statements that report the performance of a firm: (1) the balance sheet, (2) the income statement, (3) the statement of retained earnings, and (4) the statement of cash flow. In this chapter, we examined the four financial statements and the connections between each of the four statements with particular interest in the sources and uses of cash. In finance we are generally concerned with how a company is generating cash and where the company is spending cash.

LO2 Use the cash flow identity to explain cash flow.

The cash flow identity simply states that the cash from assets is always equal to the cash to lenders and the cash to owners. Put another way, it allows a financier to reconstruct the balance sheet and income statement accounts to show where cash was generated and where cash was used during a particular time period.

LO3 Provide some context for financial reporting.

All public firms are required by law to submit annual (10-K) and quarterly (10-Q) performance reports to the U.S. Securities and Exchange Commission. Regulation fair disclosure requires that information be released to the public and not to special groups or individuals. The notes to the financial statements often provide a rich store of information about how the statements were constructed or more commentary that is relevant to the future operations of the company.

LO4 Recognize and view Internet sites that provide financial information.

The Internet has many sites that provide financial statements as well as other significant information about publicly traded firms. Not all sites are free or comprehensive. In addition, the formatting of financial data is not always consistent across different sites. Sometimes it is necessary to dig through the financial statements to get the information necessary to examine the performance of a firm.

Chapter 2
Financial Statements
AT A GLANCE

KEY EQUATIONS

accounting identity: assets ≡ liabilities + owners' equity	**2.1**
net working capital = current assets − current liabilities	**2.2**
net income = revenues − expenses	**2.3**
revenue − operating expenses = earnings before interest and taxes	**2.4**
operating cash flow = earnings before interest and taxes + depreciation − taxes	**2.5**
change in retained earnings = net income − distributed earnings	**2.6**
cash flow from assets ≡ cash flow to creditors + cash flow to owners	**2.7**

CASH FLOW IDENTITY AND COMPONENTS

● **cash flow from assets** ≡ ● cash flow to creditors + ● cash flow to owners

● cash flow from assets

cash flow from assets = operating cash flow – net capital spending – change in net working capital

operating cash flow = EBIT + depreciation – taxes

net capital spending = ending net fixed assets – beginning net fixed assets + depreciation

change in net working capital = ending net working capital – beginning net working capital

net working capital = current assets – current liabilities

● cash flow to creditors

cash flow to creditors = interest expense – net new borrowing from creditors

net new borrowing = ending long-term liabilities – beginning long-term liabilities

● cash flow to owners

cash flow to owners = dividends – net new borrowing from owners

net new borrowing from owners = change in equity

change in equity = ending common stock and paid-in-surplus – beginning common stock and paid-in-surplus

Chapter 3
The Time Value of Money (Part 1)
AT A GLANCE

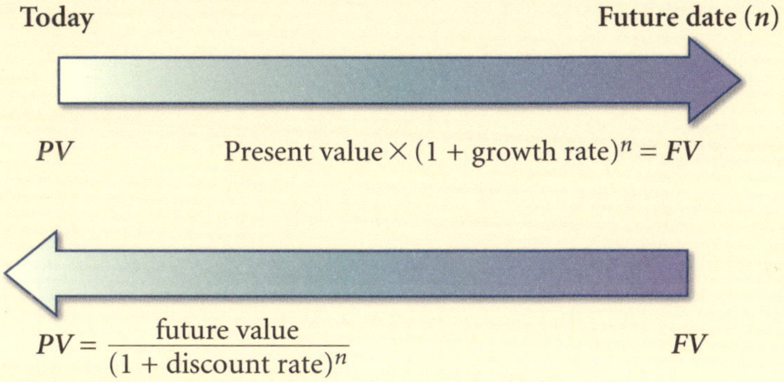

LO1 Calculate future values and understand compounding.

Future value is the value of an asset at a specific point in time in the future that is equivalent in value to a specific amount today. There is a direct relationship between the future value of an asset and the asset's present value, growth rate, and time to the future point. Future values grow faster and faster due to interest earning interest, a phenomenon called compounding of interest.

LO2 Calculate present values and understand discounting.

Present value is the value today of tomorrow's cash flow. You can determine the equivalent value of a future value in today's dollars by discounting the future value back to the present.

LO3 Calculate implied interest rates and waiting time from the time value of money equation.

The time value of money equation is robust in that it can be arranged to find each of the four different variables (future value, present value, waiting time or time to maturity, and interest rate) and thus answer a series of different questions. To find the interest rate, you need the present value, the future value, and the number of periods. To find the waiting time, you need the present value, the future value, and the interest rate.

LO4 Apply the time value of money equation using formula, calculator, and spreadsheet.

There are four ways to find solutions to time value of money problems, using the different formats of the equation, TVM keys on a calculator, a spreadsheet function, or tables. There are problems with tables due to rounding and limited values for combinations of interest rate and time.

LO5 Explain the Rule of 72, a simple estimation of doubling values.

The Rule of 72 allows you to determine how long it takes to double your money at a specific interest rate. It is a simple approximation method in which 72 is divided by the interest rate to find the number of years it takes to double your money.

Chapter 3
The Time Value of Money (Part 1)
AT A GLANCE

KEY EQUATIONS

$$FV = PV \times (1 + r)^n \qquad 3.2$$

$$PV = FV \times \frac{1}{(1 + r)^n} \qquad 3.3$$

$$r = \left(\frac{FV}{PV}\right)^{1/n} - 1 \qquad 3.4$$

$$n = \frac{\ln(FV/PV)}{\ln(1 + r)} \qquad 3.5$$

NOTATION FOR CHAPTER 3

FV	future value
FVIF	future value interest factor
n	number of time periods; waiting period
r	interest rate, growth rate, discount rate
PV	present value
PVIF	present value interest factor
TVM	time value of money

CALCULATOR KEYS

CPT	compute
FV	future value
I/Y	interest per year
N	number of periods
PMT	payment
PV	present value

EXCEL VARIABLES

Fv	future value
Nper	number of periods
Pmt	payment
Pv	present value
Rate	interest rate

Chapter 4
The Time Value of Money (Part 2)
AT A GLANCE

LO1 Compute the future value of multiple cash flows.

To obtain the future value of multiple payment streams, bring all the cash flows to the same point in time and add them together with their accumulated interest.

LO2 Determine the future value of an annuity.

An annuity is a series of equal cash payments at regular intervals across time. The future value of an annuity can be determined by multiplying the payment or deposit by the factor $[(1 + r)^n - 1]/r$, where r is the interest rate and n is the number of payments. This factor is known as the future value interest factor of an annuity (FVIFA).

LO3 Determine the present value of an annuity.

The present value of an annuity can be determined by multiplying the payment or deposit by the factor $[1 - 1/(1 + r)^n]/r$, where r is the interest rate and n the number of payments. This factor is known as the present value interest factor of an annuity (PVIFA).

LO4 Adjust the annuity formula for present value and future value for an annuity due and understand the concept of a perpetuity.

The standard PVIFA and FVIFA are for ordinary annuities. When an annuity is paid or deposited at the beginning of the period instead of the end of the period, it is an annuity due. To adjust the formulas for an annuity due, multiply the PVIFA or the FVIFA by $1 + r$.

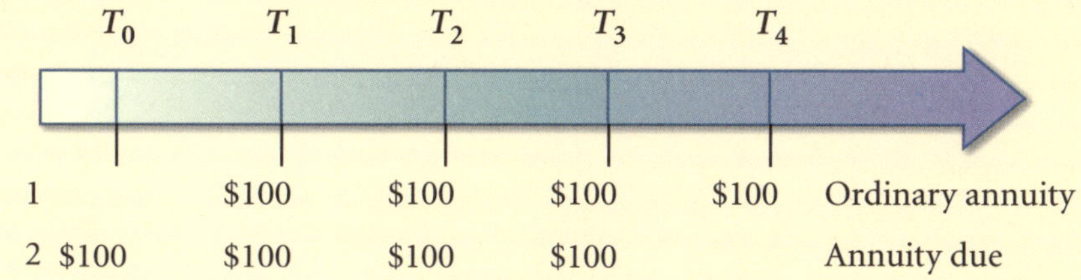

LO5 Distinguish between the different types of loan repayments: discount loans, interest-only loans, and amortized loans.

Loans can be repaid using three standard methods. A borrower can pay the entire principal and interest at the end or maturity of the loan, which is called a discount loan. The borrower can pay interest each period and the principal at maturity, which is called an interest-only loan. The borrower can make equal payments each period, paying off the interest for the period and some of the remaining principal, which is called an amortized loan.

LO6 Build and analyze amortization schedules.

To build an amortization schedule, first determine the annuity payment needed to pay off the loan. Then, each period, find the interest expense by multiplying the principal at the beginning of the period by the interest rate. Determine how much of the annuity payment is left after paying the interest and apply this amount to reduce the balance of the principal. The result becomes the ending balance of the principal for that payment period and the beginning principal balance for the start of the next period. Repeat this process for each period. The final balance should be zero following the last payment.

LO7 Calculate waiting time and interest rates for an annuity.

Rearranging the *FV* or *PV* of an annuity equation can isolate the variable n so that you can solve directly for the waiting time. You cannot isolate the variable r (interest rate), however, so you must either go through an iterative process or use a calculator or spreadsheet to solve for it.

LO8 Apply the time value of money concepts to evaluate the lottery cash flow choice.

The time value of money equations can be used to determine the implied interest rate between two lottery pay-off options of an annuity stream or a lump-sum payment. This information is not sufficient to determine the optimal choice between the two pay-off options but can provide valuable information about the implied trade-offs between the two choices.

LO9 Summarize the ten essential points about the time value of money.

The ten key points include the fact that amounts of money can be added or subtracted only if they are at the same point in time. So not all important data can be classified into the variables of present value, time, interest rate, payment, and future value.

Chapter 4
The Time Value of Money (Part 2)
AT A GLANCE

KEY EQUATIONS

$$FV = PMT \times \frac{(1+r)^n - 1}{r} \qquad \textbf{4.3}$$

$$PV = PMT \times \frac{1 - 1/(1+r)^n}{r} \qquad \textbf{4.4}$$

$$PV = \frac{PMT}{r} \qquad \textbf{4.8}$$

$$PMT = \frac{PV}{\dfrac{1 - [1/(1+r)^n]}{r}} \qquad \textbf{4.9}$$

$$n = \frac{\ln\left(\dfrac{(FV \times r)}{PMT} + 1\right)}{\ln(1+r)} \qquad \textbf{4.10}$$

NOTATION FOR CHAPTER 4

FV	future value
FVIFA	future value interest factor of an annuity
n	number of periods or number of payments
PV	present value
PVIFA	present value interest factor of an annuity
r	interest rate or discount rate
T_0	time at period zero or today or start of time period
T_n	time period n or end of time period n

CALCULATOR KEYS

BGN	beginning of period setting (for annuity due)
CPT	compute
END	end of period setting (for ordinary annuity)
FV	future value
I/Y	interest per year
N	number of periods
PMT	payment
PV	present value

SPREADSHEET VARIABLES

Fv	future value
Nper	number of periods
Pmt	payment
Pv	present value
Rate	interest rate
Type	set to 0 for ordinary annuity, set to 1 for annuity-due

Chapter 5 Interest Rates

AT A GLANCE

LO1 Discuss how financial institutions quote and compute the effective annual rate on a loan or investment.

Advertised interest rates—also called annual percentage rates (APRs)—are stated on an annual basis and are nominal interest rates. A nominal rate is one that has been adjusted for inflation when compared with the real rate of interest. Interest rates can be applied annually, semiannually, quarterly, monthly, weekly, or even daily. These rates are periodic interest rates: the APR divided by the number of compounding periods per year.

The effective annual rate (EAR) is the rate of interest actually paid or earned per year and depends on the number of compounding periods. It gives the best information on the cost of a loan or yield on an investment because it takes into account the interest earned on interest. It is the APR adjusted for compounding.

LO2 Apply the time value of money equation by accounting for the compounding periods per year.

The time value of money equation uses the periodic interest rate. To use this equation properly, it is essential to know the number of compounding periods per year. The key point is that r and n must agree in terms of periods in the equation. For example, when you use a monthly compounding period, you use the monthly periodic rate and the number of months over the life of the loan.

LO3 Set up monthly amortization tables for consumer loans and illustrate the payment changes as the compounding or annuity period changes.

When you shift from annual payments to more frequent payments, you need to calculate the interest each period, the principal reduction each period, and the ending principal balance for each period. The more frequent the payments, the lower the interest expense because you are reducing the principal at each payment.

LO4 Explain the real rate of interest and the effect of inflation on nominal interest rates.

The real rate of interest is the reward for waiting. It is the actual purchasing power increase over the investment period. Inflation, on the other hand, is the loss in purchasing power over the investment period. The nominal rate is the interest rate that provides for the increase in purchasing power by increasing the APR above the real rate by the inflation rate.

LO5 Summarize the two major premiums that differentiate interest rates: the default premium and the maturity premium.

Two premiums affect interest rates on different investments and loans. First is the default premium, which accounts for the probability that the borrower may not pay back the loan. The greater the probability the loan will not be repaid, the greater the default premium. Second is the maturity premium, which accounts for the length of the loan. The longer the borrower will take to pay back the loan, the greater the maturity premium. These two premiums account for the major differences in rates across different investments and loans.

LO6 Understand the implications of the yield curves.

Interest rates vary based on the maturity date of a bond or loan. Typically the longer a borrower takes to repay a loan the higher the interest rate. When we plot this concept on a graph with time to maturity on the x-axis and interest rates on the y-axis, we see an upward-sloping yield curve. We use the yield curve as a benchmark for the current rates in the market. Economists use the curve to predict changes in future interest rates, economic output, and growth.

LO7 Amaze your family and friends with your knowledge of interest rate history.

Interest rates can vary across different financial instruments as well as through time. Rates go up when expected inflation rises and fall when expected inflation falls. The highest interest rates were experienced in the early 1980s when inflation was at 12% to 13%. Today, inflation is 3% to 4%.

Chapter 5
Interest Rates
AT A GLANCE

KEY EQUATIONS

periodic interest rate, $r = \dfrac{APR}{m}$	**5.1**
$EAR = \left(1 + \dfrac{APR}{m}\right)^m - 1$	**5.2**
$(1 + r) = (1 + r^*) \times (1 + h)$	**5.4**
$r = r^* + h + (r^* \times h)$	**5.6**
$r = r^* + h + dp + mp$	**5.11**

NOTATION FOR CHAPTER 5

APR	annual percentage rate
APY	annual percentage yield
C/Y	compounding periods per year; also expressed as *m*
dp	default premium
EAR	effective annual rate
h	inflation
m	number of compounding periods per year (same as C/Y)
mp	maturity premium
n or nper	number of payments or number of periods
r or rate	nominal interest rate (periodic interest rate)
r^*	real rate of interest
r_f	risk-free interest rate

CALCULATOR KEYS (for some, but not all, calculators)

CPT	compute
C/Y	compounding periods per year
FV	future value
i%	periodic interest rate
I/Y	interest per year (APR rate)
N or Nper	number of payments
PMT	payment
PV	present value
P/Y	payments per year

SPREADSHEET TERMS

Fv	future value
Nper	number of payments
Pmt	payment
Pv	present value
Rate	periodic interest rate
Type	ordinary annuity or annuity-due

Chapter 6
Bonds and Bond Valuation
AT A GLANCE

LO1 Understand basic bond terminology and apply the time value of money equation in pricing bonds.

A bond is a long-term debt instrument in which a borrower agrees to pay back the loaned funds (principal) with interest on specific dates in the future. The key components of a bond are its par value, coupon rate and coupon, maturity date, and yield to maturity. Bonds are priced with a lump-sum time value of money equation for the par value and an annuity time value of money equation for the coupon payments. The discount rate in the equation is the yield to maturity of the bond. This yield is the return a bond purchaser will get over the remaining life of the bond if held to maturity and the cost to the seller of the bond. There are four steps to pricing a bond.

How to Price a Bond

1. Lay out the timing and amount of future cash flow promised.
2. Determine the appropriate discount rate for the cash flow.
3. Find the present value of the lump-sum principal and the annuity stream of coupons.
4. Add the present value of the lump-sum principal and the present value of the coupons.

LO2 Understand the difference between annual and semiannual bonds and note the key features of zero-coupon bonds.

Annual bonds pay interest once a year, whereas semiannual bonds pay interest twice a year. Most bonds are semiannual. The amount of the interest paid over the entire year is the coupon rate times the par value of the bond. The semiannual bond simply divides this annual interest into equal payments six months apart. Because the timing of the cash flow is different for these two bonds, however, the price is also different unless the bonds are selling at par value. Bonds sell at par value when the coupon rate and the yield to maturity are the same. As their name implies, zero-coupon bonds pay no coupons, but they are priced at a deep discount to their par value.

LO3 Explain the relationship between the coupon rate and the yield to maturity.

The coupon rate is the rate used to determine the coupon payment size. The yield to maturity is the discount rate for the bond's promised cash flows. When the coupon rate is less than the yield to maturity, the bond sells at a discount to its par value. When the coupon rate is greater than the yield to maturity, the bond sells at a premium above its par value. When the coupon rate and yield to maturity are the same, the bond sells for its par value.

LO4 Delineate bond ratings and why ratings affect bond prices.

Bonds are rated by agencies such as Standard and Poor's and Moody's to classify the potential for default of the bond. Bonds with the highest rating and lowest probability of default are assigned a rating of AAA. As the probability of default increases, the ratings fall. Bonds rated either Baa or BBB and above are considered investment-grade bonds. Bonds below this rating are speculative. The yield on a bond increases as its rating falls, lowering the price of the bond and thus the revenue for the issuer.

LO5 Appreciate bond history and understand the rights and obligations of buyers and sellers of bonds.

Each bond issue is detailed in its indenture, a contract that lists the specifics of the bond. Some bonds have collateral backing the bond in case of default. Some bonds—debenture bonds—have only the good reputation of the issuer backing the bond. Some companies have more than one issue; typically, the oldest issue is the senior debt, and all other debt is subordinated or junior to the oldest debt. Some bonds have sinking funds to help with retirement of the bond at maturity. Bonds have protective covenants, which are listings of permissible and nonpermissible activities that protect the interest of the bond owner.

Bonds have different features, and by altering these features you can create different types of bonds. For example, if a bond allows its coupon rate to fluctuate with the market, it is a floating rate bond. If a bond adds a feature such as the ability of the issuer to call in the bond, it is a callable bond.

Chapter 6
Bonds and Bond Valuation
AT A GLANCE

LO6 Price government bonds, notes, and bills.

Government bonds and notes are priced like most semi-annual corporate bonds: with the coupons as the annuity stream and the par value as the lump-sum payment of the principal at maturity. Treasury bills are priced on a bank discount basis. The discount on the Treasury bond can be easily converted to an annual percentage rate (APR) by finding the bond equivalent yield.

KEY EQUATIONS

$$\text{bond price} = \text{par value} \times \frac{1}{(1+r)^n} + \text{coupon} \times \frac{1 - \frac{1}{(1+r)^n}}{r} \quad \textbf{6.1}$$

$$\text{zero-coupon bond price} = \text{par value} \times \frac{1}{(1+r)^n} \quad \textbf{6.2}$$

$$\text{price} = \text{face value} \times \left[1 - \left(\text{discount rate} \times \frac{\text{days to maturity}}{360}\right)\right] \quad \textbf{6.3}$$

$$\text{discount} = \text{face value} \times \text{discount rate} \times \frac{\text{days to maturity}}{360} \quad \textbf{6.4}$$

$$BEY = \frac{365 \times \text{discount yield}}{360 - \text{days to maturity} \times \text{discount yield}} \quad \textbf{6.5}$$

NOTATION FOR CHAPTER 6

BEY	bond equivalent yield
FV	future value
PMT	ordinary annuity stream; coupon payment
r	discount rate; periodic yield
T_n	time
YTM	yield to maturity

CALCULATOR KEYS

C/Y	compounding periods per year
FV	future value; par value at maturity
I/Y	periodic yield; discount rate
N	number of coupon payments
PMT	coupon payments
PV	present value
P/Y	payments per year

SPREADSHEET TERMS

Fv	future value
Nper	number of periods
Pmt	payment stream
Pv	present value
Rate	periodic interest rate
Type	ordinary annuity or annuity-due

Chapter 7
Stocks and Stock Valuation
AT A GLANCE

LO1 Explain the basic characteristics of common stock.

Common stock is a financial asset signifying ownership in a company. Such ownership is referred to as a residual claim, meaning that the shares of earnings are due to the owner only after all debt obligations have been satisfied and preferred shareholders are paid. In addition, common stock usually carries voting rights that allow the owner of the stock to participate in the management of the company through the election of the board of directors.

LO2 Define the primary market and the secondary market.

The primary market is the market of first sale, in which companies first sell off their authorized shares to the public. The secondary markets are the after-sale markets of the existing outstanding shares, in which individual or institutional owners of stocks sell their shares to other investors. You can think of the secondary market as the "used stock" market, much as you can think of the secondary market for cars as the "used car" market.

LO3 Calculate the value of a stock given a history of dividend payments.

The value of a single share of stock is equal to its expected future cash flow, discounted at the appropriate rate. If you use the historical dividend pattern to predict the future dividend distribution, then you discount this expected dividend stream using the time value of money equations for the current stock price.

LO4 Explain the shortcomings of the dividend pricing models.

The dividend pricing model often fails to provide an accurate or even reasonable price for a stock due to (1) a poor estimate of future dividends, given the recent dividend pattern of a firm; (2) a negative growth in dividends when dividends are reduced or eliminated; and (3) absence of a dividend history. Predicting future dividends from historical dividends will inherently have some potential problems.

LO5 Calculate the price of preferred stock.

Preferred stock has a declared dividend payment based on the annual dividend rate and the stated par value of the preferred stock. Usually, there is no maturity date for preferred stock, so the value or price of the preferred stock is calculated as a perpetuity with the annual dividend as the cash flow and a discount rate appropriate for the stock.

LO6 Understand the concept of efficient markets.

Markets can exhibit efficiency in two ways—operational efficiency and informational efficiency. Operational efficiency has to do with the speed and accuracy of processing a buy or sell order at the best available price. Informational efficiency is concerned with how quickly information is reflected in the available prices for trading. There are three forms of informational efficiency: (1) weak-form, (2) semi-strong-form, and (3) strong-form. Evidence supports the semi-strong-form of efficiency, in which current prices reflect all past price history, volume history, and available public information.

Chapter 7
Stocks and Stock Valuation
AT A GLANCE

KEY EQUATIONS

$$\text{price} = \frac{\text{dividend}}{r} \quad \textbf{7.2}$$

$$\text{price}_0 = \frac{\text{Div}_0 \times (1 + g)}{r - g} \quad \textbf{7.5}$$

$$\text{price}_0 = \frac{\text{Div}_1}{r - g} \quad \textbf{7.6}$$

$$\text{price}_0 = \frac{\text{Div}_0 \times (1 + g)}{r - g} \times \left[1 - \left(\frac{1 + g}{1 + r}\right)^n\right] \quad \textbf{7.8}$$

$$r = \frac{\text{Div}_0 \times (1 + g)}{\text{price}} + g \quad \textbf{7.9}$$

$$r = \frac{\text{dividend}}{\text{price}} \quad \textbf{7.10}$$

NOTATION FOR CHAPTER 7

Div	dividend
Div_0	most recent dividend
Div_1	next dividend following most recent dividend
FV	future value
g	annual growth rate
n	number of periods; number of payments (dividends, for example)
price_0	price at time zero or current price
price_n	price at the end of period n
PV	present value
r	required rate of return

Chapter 8
Risk and Return
AT A GLANCE

LO1 Calculate profits and returns on an investment and convert holding period returns to annual returns.

Profits are the dollars gained on an investment, measured as the difference between the original cost of the investment and its ending value plus any distributions received while holding the asset. A return is the measure of the percentage of change or the ratio of the gain (or loss) to the cost of the investment. Returns are typically stated on an annual basis. To compare different investments held over different periods of time, it is necessary to convert the return that represents the entire holding period into an annualized return. Your can do a conversion with a simple interest approach or with a compound interest approach.

LO2 Define risk and explain how uncertainty relates to risk.

Uncertainty is the absence of knowledge of the actual outcome of an event before it happens. Risk is a measure of the uncertainty in a set of potential outcomes for an event in which there is a chance of some loss. Different investments have different levels of risk. We can measure and understand the acceptable level of risk for our investment choices.

LO3 Appreciate the historical returns of various investment choices.

Returns vary across time for the same type of financial assets. U.S. Treasury bills have the lowest average return and the lowest risk, whereas small-company stocks have the highest average return with the highest risk.

LO4 Calculate standard deviations and variances with historical data.

The variance of a random variable is a statistical calculation of the sum of the difference between each observation and the average observation squared and then divided by the number of observations (minus 1 to correct for degrees of freedom). The standard deviation is the square root of the variance.

LO5 Calculate expected returns and variances with conditional returns and probabilities.

When determining the expected return and the variance of the expected return, an investor is using an ex-ante view of the world (looking forward). The expected return is calculated by multiplying each potential outcome by its probability and then summing these products. The variance is the sum of the squared differences between the potential outcome and the expected outcome times the probability of the outcome. See Equations 8.8 and 8.9.

LO6 Interpret the trade-off between risk and return.

A higher expected increase in a return generally comes with an increase in risk. This reward-to-risk trade-off is a fundamental concept of finance. When it comes to risk tolerance, there are two rules to follow: (1) if two investments have the same expected return and different levels of risk, the investment with the lower risk is preferred; and (2) if two investments have the same level of risk and different expected returns, the investment with the higher expected return is preferred.

LO7 Understand when and why diversification works at minimizing risk and understand the difference between systematic and unsystematic risk.

Diversification—the spreading of investments over more than one asset—works because the high or low outcome of one asset can often be offset by the outcomes of the other asset. When assets are positively correlated, there is less diversification and less reduction in risk. When assets are negatively correlated, there is more diversification and more reduction in risk. There are two basic kinds of risks for investments: unsystematic or firm-specific risk and systematic or marketwide risk. Systematic risk cannot be avoided. Firm-specific risk can be minimized with a well-diversified portfolio of investments.

LO8 Explain beta as a measure of risk in a well-diversified portfolio.

Beta is a measure of the systematic risk of an asset. It is the covariance of the individual returns of an asset with the returns of the market.

Chapter 8
Risk and Return
AT A GLANCE

LO9 Illustrate how the security market line and the capital asset pricing model represent the two-parameter world of risk and return.

The security market line is drawn in a two-parameter world of risk and return, with the intercept being the risk-free rate. The line slopes upward as it moves along the *x*-axis, signifying that as risk increases, expected return on the asset also increases. The line illustrates a constant trade-off between adding more risk and expecting more reward.

KEY EQUATIONS

$$\text{profit} = \text{ending value} + \text{distributions} - \text{original cost} \quad \textbf{8.1}$$

$$\text{return} = \frac{\text{profit}}{\text{original cost}} \text{ or } \frac{\text{loss}}{\text{original cost}} \quad \textbf{8.2}$$

$$HPR = \frac{\text{profit}}{\text{cost}} \quad \textbf{8.3}$$

$$\text{simple annual return} = \frac{HPR}{n} \quad \textbf{8.4}$$

$$EAR = (1 + HPR)^{1/n} - 1 \quad \textbf{8.5}$$

$$\text{variance } (X) = \frac{\sum (X_i - \text{average})^2}{n - 1} = \sigma^2 \quad \textbf{8.6}$$

$$\text{standard deviation} = \sqrt{\text{variance}} = \sqrt{\sigma^2} = \sigma \quad \textbf{8.7}$$

$$\text{expected payoff} = \sum \text{payoff}_i \times \text{probability}_i \quad \textbf{8.8}$$

$$\sigma^2 = \sum (\text{payoff}_i - \text{expected payoff})^2 \times \text{probability}_i \quad \textbf{8.9}$$

$$\beta_p = \sum_{i=1}^{n} w_i \times \beta_i \quad \textbf{8.10}$$

$$E(r_i) = r_f + [E(r_m) - r_f] \times \beta_i \quad \textbf{8.11}$$

NOTATION FOR CHAPTER 8

APR	annual percentage rate
β_i	beta of an individual asset; measure of systematic risk
CAPM	capital asset pricing model
Δ	delta; change
EAR	effective annual rate
$E(r)$	expected return
$E(r_m)$	expected return on the market
HPR	holding period return
r_i	individual potential return
P_i	probability of outcome
μ	mean
n	number of years; number of observations
r	return
r_f	risk-free rate
Σ	summation sign
σ	standard deviation
σ^2	variance
SML	security market line
Std(X)	standard deviation
Var(X)	variance
w_i	weight or percentage of an individual asset in a portfolio

Chapter 9
Capital Budgeting Decision Models

AT A GLANCE

LO1 Explain capital budgeting and differentiate between short-term and long-term budgeting decisions.

In general, we can separate short-term and long-term decisions into three dimensions: length of effect, cost, and degree of information gathering prior to the decision. The longer the effect and the higher the cost associated with a decision, the greater the time and degree allotted to gathering information on choices and the more sophisticated or complex the decision model.

LO2 Explain the payback period model and its two significant weaknesses and how the discounted payback period model addresses one of the problems.

The application of each model requires estimating the future cash flow of a project in both timing and amount. The payback period simply determines how soon the future cash flow returns the initial cash outflow for the project. The discounted payback period model corrects the payback period's flaw of ignoring time value of money concepts. It discounts future cash flow and uses the present value of the future cash flows to determine how long it will take to recover the initial investment.

LO3 Understand the net present value (NPV) decision model and appreciate why it is the preferred criterion for evaluating proposed investments.

Net present value discounts all future cash flow to the present and then determines if the present value of the inflows is greater than the present value of the outflows. If two projects are being compared, the one with the highest net present value should be selected.

LO4 Calculate the most popular capital budgeting alternative to the NPV, the internal rate of return (IRR); explain how the modified internal rate of return (MIRR) model attempts to address the IRR's problems.

Internal rate of return finds the discount rate that equates the present value of the inflows with the present value of the outflows. The modified internal rate of return corrects for the implied assumption that future cash flow can be reinvested at the internal rate of return and reinvests future cash flow at the hurdle rate.

LO5 Understand the profitability index (PI) as a modification of the NPV model.

The profitability index provides a modified return rate for the NPV model. It is the ratio of the present value of the benefits of a project (future cash inflow) to the present value of the project's costs (the initial investment).

LO6 Compare and contrast the strengths and weaknesses of each decision model in a holistic way.

Each model other than the net present value has some inherent flaws as a decision model. The payback and discounted payback do not consider the cash flow after recovering the initial outflow. The internal rate of return and modified internal rate of return can lead to selecting the wrong project with mutually exclusive projects because of different discount rates for the cash flows. The profitability index implies that projects can be scaled up or down. All models help quantify project decisions with preset acceptance and rejection criteria.

Summary of Six Decision Models

	Models					
Issues	Payback Period	Discounted Payback Period	Net Present Value	Internal Rate of Return	Modified Internal Rate of Return	Profitability Index
Decision criterion	Recover investment before a set period	Recover investment before a set period	NPV is positive	IRR rate is greater than hurdle rate	MIRR rate is greater than hurdle rate	PI is greater than 1
Complexity of application	Easiest to apply	Easy to apply	Time-consuming without a calculator or spreadsheet	Time-consuming without a calculator or spreadsheet	Time-consuming without a calculator or spreadsheet	Time-consuming without a calculator or spreadsheet

Chapter 9
Capital Budgeting Decision Models
AT A GLANCE

Summary of Six Decision Models (*Continued*)

	Models					
Issues	**Payback Period**	**Discounted Payback Period**	**Net Present Value**	**Internal Rate of Return**	**Modified Internal Rate of Return**	**Profitability Index**
Time value of money	Ignored	Consistent with time value of money	Consistent with time value of money	Consistent with time value of money	Consistent with time value of money	Consistent with time value of money
Risk	Ignores cash flow after cutoff date	Ignores cash flow after cutoff date	Applies appropriate level of risk to cash flow	Risk level applied by selected hurdle rate	Risk level applied by selected hurdle rate	Applies appropriate level of risk to cash flow
Economic basis and evaluation	Too simple	Too simple	Economically sound application in risk and return. **Best decision model**	Potential for multiple IRRs and picking wrong project	Potential for multiple IRRs	Economically sound application in risk and return

KEY EQUATIONS

$$NPV = -CF_0 + \frac{CF_1}{(1+r)^1} + \frac{CF_2}{(1+r)^2} + \frac{CF_3}{(1+r)^3} + \cdots + \frac{CF_n}{(1+r)^n} \qquad \textbf{9.1}$$

$$EAA = \frac{NPV}{PVIFA} \qquad \textbf{9.2}$$

$$\text{IRR: } \$0 = CF_0 + \frac{CF_1}{(1+r)^1} + \frac{CF_2}{(1+r)^2} + \frac{CF_3}{(1+r)^3} + \cdots + \frac{CF_n}{(1+r)^n} \qquad \textbf{9.3}$$

$$\text{profitability index} = \frac{\text{present value of benefits}}{\text{present value of costs}} \qquad \textbf{9.4}$$

NOTATION FOR CHAPTER 9

CF_n	cash flow at the end of period n
EAA	equivalent annual annuity
FV	future value
IRR	internal rate of return
MIRR	modified internal rate of return
NPV	net present value
PI	profitability index
r	discount rate
Σ	summation sign

CALCULATOR KEYS

CF	cash flow
CF0	cash flow at time zero (start of project)
C01	cash flow at end of period one
C02	cash flow at end of period two
F01	number of consecutive periods with cash flow of C01
F02	number of consecutive periods with cash flow of C02
I	interest rate or discount rate for cash flow

Chapter 10
Cash Flow Estimation

AT A GLANCE

LO1 Understand the importance of cash flow and the distinction between cash flow and profits.

Profits are the accounting-measured performance of a company over a specific period of time. Because of accrual accounting, profits do not always equal cash flow for the period. In fact, profits and cash flow are rarely the same. Cash flow is the important variable for decision making.

LO2 Identify incremental cash flow.

Incremental cash flow is the increase in cash above the current cash flow that is generated by the addition of a new project. Some costs and revenues would appear on the surface to be associated with a project, but, in fact, are not used in the decision to accept or reject a project. Such is the case of sunk costs. There are also hidden costs that do need to be added to the project's overall cash flow, including opportunity costs, erosion costs, synergy gains, and working capital. Capital expenditures, depreciation, and depreciation's effect on both taxes and disposal of equipment are also part of the estimation of incremental cash flow.

LO3 Calculate depreciation and cost recovery.

Depreciation represents the expensing of a capital asset over a period of time. The cash flow occurs at the acquisition of a capital asset, but the expense is recorded in future periods. There are two common ways to allocate expenses: straight-line depreciation, in which capital assets are depreciated by the same amount each year; and the modified accelerated cost recovery system (MACRS), in which capital assets are depreciated at the maximum accelerated amount each year. The difference between the original cost and the accumulated depreciation is the book value or basis for the asset.

LO4 Understand the cash flow associated with the disposal of depreciable assets.

When an asset is sold, the difference between the book value and the selling price is a taxable event. If the selling price exceeds the book value, a tax is incurred. If the selling price is less than the book value, a tax credit is available to the firm.

LO5 Estimate incremental cash flow for capital budgeting decisions.

The estimation of incremental cash flow for a project has four basic steps:

1. Determine the initial capital investment for the project.
2. Estimate the operating cash flow generated each period by the project.
3. Determine the change in working capital, which is usually an increase at the start of the project and a reduction at the end.
4. Evaluate the proposed project using the NPV model.

To use any of the capital budgeting models, it is necessary to determine the appropriate incremental cash flow.

Chapter 11
The Cost of Capital
AT A GLANCE

LO1 Understand the different kinds of financing available to a company: debt financing, equity financing, and hybrid equity financing.

Debt financing includes capital raised through borrowing from financial institutions and other sources and through selling bonds. Equity financing includes capital raised through selling common stock to individual and institutional investors and through the use of retained earnings. Hybrid equity financing includes capital raised through selling preferred stock.

LO2 Understand the debt and equity components of the weighted average cost of capital (WACC) and explain the tax implications on debt financing and the adjustment to the WACC.

The cost of capital is the cost of each financing component used by a firm to fund its projects multiplied by that component's percentage of the total funding amount. The WACC is the cost of capital for the firm. We apply the adjusted WACC—the WACC adjusted for taxes in the debt component—to our capital budgeting decision model of net present value as the discount rate and to internal rate of return as the hurdle rate.

The cost of debt is the borrowing rate from a lender quoted as part of the loan or the yield to maturity of the company's bond. The cost of equity is the expected return of the stock given its beta, the risk-free rate, and the market risk premium. The cost of equity can also be calculated with the dividend growth model.

The interest expense paid to the lender on a loan or the coupon payments on a bond are tax-deductible expenses and reduce the overall cash outflow for a company. Dividends are not tax-deductible, so the WACC is adjusted to reflect the tax-deduction effect of interest expense.

LO3 Calculate the weights of the components using book values or market values.

The combination of funding from debt and equity affects the average cost of capital based on the percentage of funding from each source. The weight or percentage can be calculated using either the book values presented in the balance sheet accounts or the market values. The market value of debt for bonds is the current price of the bond multiplied by the number of bonds outstanding. The market value of equity is the current price of the stock multiplied by the number of shares outstanding.

LO4 Explain how the capital budgeting models use WACC.

The WACC is the discount rate in the NPV model and the hurdle rate in the IRR model. When the NPV is positive or the IRR is greater than the hurdle rate, accept the project because the project's return is sufficient to cover the weighted average cost of capital.

LO5 Determine a project's beta and its implications in capital budgeting problems.

Each project has its own level of risk, which can be estimated by finding the beta of the project and using it to determine the cost of equity in the WACC calculation. The beta accounts for the riskiness of the project in the capital budgeting problem through the WACC of the project.

LO6 Select optimal project combinations for a company's portfolio of acceptable potential projects.

When there is a constraint on the available capital for a set of projects, the selected projects should collectively have the highest NPV total. Ranking the projects by NPV and selecting the highest to lowest project until funds are exhausted does not always optimize the capital spending for the company.

Chapter 11
The Cost of Capital
AT A GLANCE

KEY EQUATIONS

$$NPV = -\text{investment} + \sum_{t=1}^{n} \frac{\text{cash flow}_t}{(1 + \text{WACC})^t} \quad \textbf{11.1}$$

$$\text{price} = \text{par value} \times \frac{1}{(1 + YTM)^n} + \text{coupon} \times \frac{1 - [1/(1 + YTM)^n]}{YTM} \quad \textbf{11.2}$$

$$\text{net price} = \frac{\text{dividend}}{R_{ps}} \quad \textbf{11.3}$$

$$R_{ps} = \frac{\text{dividend}}{\text{net price}} \quad \textbf{11.4}$$

$$R_e = E(r_i) = r_f + [E(r_m) - r_f]\beta_i \quad \textbf{11.5}$$

$$R_e = \frac{\text{Div}_0(1 + g)}{P_0} + g \quad \textbf{11.6}$$

$$R_e = \frac{\text{Div}_0(1 + g)}{P_0(1 - F)} + g \quad \textbf{11.7}$$

$$\text{after-tax cost of debt} = R_d \times (1 - T_c) \quad \textbf{11.8}$$

$$WACC_{\text{adj}} = \frac{E}{V} \times R_e + \frac{PS}{V} \times R_{ps} + \frac{D}{V} \times R_d \times (1 - T_c) \quad \textbf{11.9}$$

NOTATION FOR CHAPTER 11

β	beta
D	value of debt in dollars
Div	dividend
E	value of equity in dollars
$E(r)$	expected return
F	flotation costs as a percent of the sale value of the asset
P	price of asset
PS	value of preferred stock in dollars
R_d	cost of debt
R_e	cost of equity
r_f	risk-free rate
r_m	market return
R_{ps}	cost of preferred stock
T_c	tax rate
V	value of the firm in dollars
WACC	weighted average cost of capital
YTM	yield to maturity of a bond

Chapter 12
Forecasting and Short-Term Financial Planning
AT A GLANCE

LO1 Understand the sources and uses of cash in building a cash budget.

The cash budget estimates the future timing of cash inflow and cash outflow and projects potential shortfalls and excesses of cash. To build it, we need to estimate the sources of cash (cash inflows/receipts) and the uses of cash (cash outflows/disbursements). A cash budget usually begins with a sales forecast using both internal and external data.

New housing permits

- Counts the new housing permits filed in each county
- Classifies the permits based on the type of water system the home will use
- Historical success rate on new houses is 30%

Aging pump systems in market area

- Tracks last installation of pumps and filters in rural homes
- Target replacement period is every fifteen years
- Replacement of prior Bridge systems at 85% rate
- Replacement of other companies' systems at 10% rate

Current estimates for January sales

- Estimated Bridge systems ready for replacement in January: 105
- Estimated other companies' systems ready for replacement in January: 260
- Estimated new-home installations: 250

LO2 Explain how companies use sales forecasts to predict cash inflow.

Sales are the heart of the cash inflow of a company, and forecasting future sales helps establish anticipated cash inflow. Not all customers pay in cash, however, so it is important to determine when credit sales (accounts receivable) will turn into cash for the company. Sales forecasting can be based on the sales growth of the firm, external data from the market, or both.

LO3 Understand how production costs vary in terms of cash flow timing.

The production cost of a finished good is expensed when the item is sold, but the actual costs to produce the good often occur over a period of time. Labor costs are incurred during the production process, not at the sale. Raw materials are purchased ahead of production. Thus, the cash flow associated with production can flow out of the company at various times prior to or during the production process.

LO4 Explain possible ways to cover cash deficits and invest cash surplus.

There are four basic ways to handle cash shortfalls: savings, unsecured loans (letters of credit), secured loans (using accounts receivable or inventories), and other sources (commercial paper, trade credit, or banker's acceptance). There are also four basic ways to use cash surplus: put it in a savings account or invest it in marketable securities, repay lenders and owners (retire debt early or pay extra dividends), replace aging assets, and invest in the company, accepting positive net present value projects.

LO5 Prepare a pro forma income statement and a pro forma balance sheet.

Pro forma financial statements are future-looking statements and sheets based on the relationship between account categories in prior periods to either the sales revenues or total assets. The pro forma income statement uses projected sales as the benchmark for future expenses and net income based on the historical percentages from a previous income statement. The pro forma balance sheet uses the total assets as the benchmark for all the individual accounts, again based on a previous balance sheet.

Chapter 13
Working Capital Management
AT A GLANCE

LO1 Model the cash conversion cycle and explain its components.

Working capital management is a strategy that focuses on maintaining efficient levels of both current assets and current liabilities so that a company has greater cash inflow than outflow. The cash conversion cycle illustrates how long a company must finance its production and accounts receivables as part of the operations of the business. It is reduced by how long the company takes to pay its suppliers.

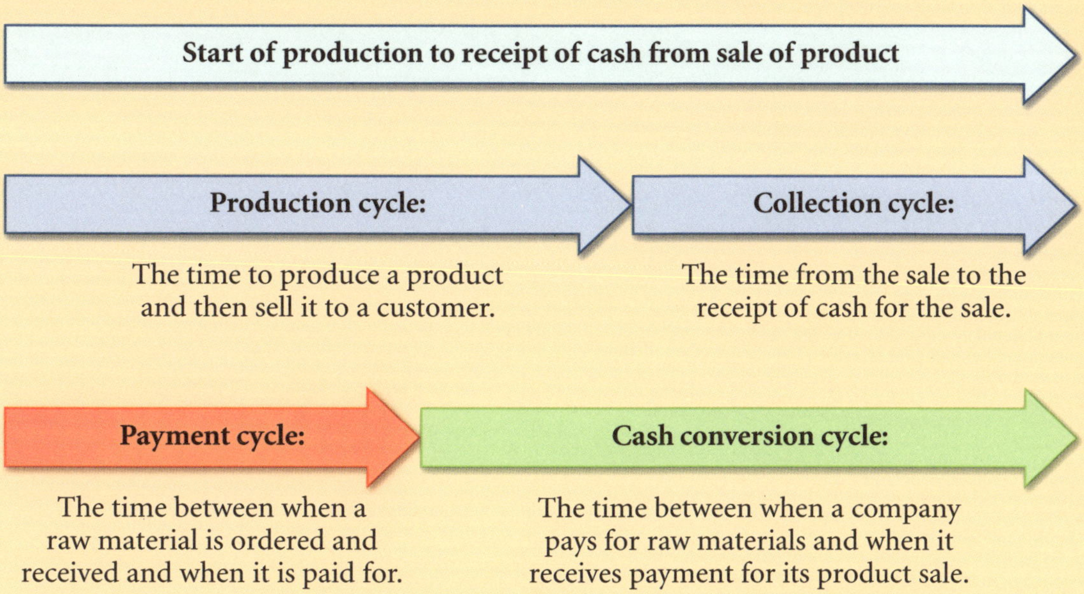

LO2 Understand why the timing of accounts receivable is important and explain the components of credit policy.

Sales do not always result in immediate cash flow to a company. Some customers pay later, and accounts receivable records these future cash payments. So, estimating when customers will pay on their accounts is important in determining the timing of future cash flow.

Credit policy is made up of three integrated components: credit terms, credit screening, and collection. Establishing who can buy on credit, setting up the credit payment parameters, and formulating a collection policy for those who fail to pay within the parameters are among the functions of the finance manager. Although the objective is to legally speed up cash inflow and slow down cash outflow, these policies and practices need to be viewed holistically with supplier and customer relationships.

LO3 Understand the float concept and its effect on cash flow and explain how to speed up receivables and slow down disbursements.

The float is the time lag between when a check is written and when the funds are available to the payee. One part of the time lag is the processing of the check to the issuer's bank. The second part of the time lag is the movement of the actual funds from the bank of the issuer to the bank of the payee. There are many different techniques to shorten the lag or lengthen the lag.

LO4 Explain inventory management techniques and calculate the economic order quantity (EOQ).

The appropriate level of inventory involves a trade-off between the carrying costs and the ordering costs. The economic order quantity model helps a finance manager find the appropriate order quantity that minimizes the total cost of holding inventory. The EOQ also helps for planning the timing of reordering inventory and the level of safety stock.

LO5 Account for working capital changes in capital budgeting decisions.

Working capital changes to support new projects are an integral part of the decision process. The timing of a buildup or drawdown of working capital accounts that support a project is part of the incremental cash flow and thus part of the decision model inputs.

Chapter 13
Working Capital Management
AT A GLANCE

KEY EQUATIONS

$$\text{cash conversion cycle} = \text{production cycle} + \text{collection cycle} - \text{payment cycle} \tag{13.1}$$

$$\text{average inventory} = \frac{\text{beginning inventory} + \text{ending inventory}}{2} \tag{13.2}$$

$$\text{inventory turnover} = \frac{\text{cost of goods sold}}{\text{average inventory}} \tag{13.3}$$

$$\text{production cycle} = \frac{365}{\text{inventory turnover}} \tag{13.4}$$

$$\text{average accounts receivable} = \frac{\text{beginning accounts receivable} + \text{ending accounts receivable}}{2} \tag{13.5}$$

$$\text{accounts receivable turnover} = \frac{\text{credit sales}}{\text{average accounts receivable}} \tag{13.6}$$

$$\text{collection cycle} = \frac{365}{\text{accounts receivable turnover rate}} \tag{13.7}$$

$$\text{average accounts payable} = \frac{\text{beginning of year accounts payable} + \text{end of year accounts payable}}{2} \tag{13.8}$$

$$\text{accounts payable turnover} = \frac{\text{cost of goods sold}}{\text{average accounts payable}} \tag{13.9}$$

$$\text{accounts payable cycle} = \frac{365}{\text{accounts payable turnover}} \tag{13.10}$$

$$\text{annual percentage rate} = \frac{\text{discount rate}}{1 - \text{discount rate}} \times \frac{365}{\text{days between payment dates}} \tag{13.11}$$

$$\text{effective annual rate} = \left(1 + \frac{\text{discount rate}}{1 - \text{discount rate}}\right)^{365/\text{days between payment dates}} - 1 \tag{13.12}$$

$$\text{total annual ordering cost} = OC \times \frac{S}{Q} \tag{13.13}$$

$$\text{total annual carrying cost} = CC \times \frac{Q}{2} \tag{13.14}$$

$$\text{total cost} = \text{ordering costs} + \text{carrying costs} \tag{13.15}$$

$$EOQ = \sqrt{\frac{2 \times S \times OC}{CC}} \tag{13.16}$$

NOTATION FOR CHAPTER 13

COGS	cost of goods sold	OC	order costs
CC	carrying costs	Q	order quantity
EOQ	economic order quantity	S	annual sales

Chapter 14
Financial Ratios and Firm Performance
AT A GLANCE

LO1 Create, understand, and interpret common-size financial statements.

The financial statements of a company are the primary sources of information that communicate the financial results of the company, both internally and externally. Every company's financial statements tell a story about the value of the business. No one financial statement tells the complete story, but used together they can help us analyze a company's performance over time and help predict future performance.

Common-size financial statements are restated financial statements in which all line items are expressed as percentages of a common base figure. This commonality allows comparison of companies of different size.

LO2 Calculate and interpret financial ratios.

Financial ratios are calculated by using information from the income statement and balance sheet. These ratios help measure and explain the performance of a company in vital areas such as liquidity, solvency, asset management, profitability, and market value.

LO3 Compare different company performances using financial ratios, historic financial ratio trends, and industry ratios.

Financial ratios are used to compare the performance of an individual company over time, against its competitors, and against firms in other industries to highlight strengths and weaknesses. However, the use of financial ratios for analysis may be just a starting point that directs the financial manager or financial analyst to the area of the company that needs more investigation in order to understand firm performance.

Chapter 14
Financial Ratios and Firm Performance
AT A GLANCE

KEY EQUATIONS

Liquidity ratios

$$\text{current ratio} = \frac{\text{current assets}}{\text{current liabilities}} \qquad \textbf{14.1}$$

$$\text{quick ratio (or acid ratio test)} = \frac{\text{current assets} - \text{inventories}}{\text{current liabilities}} \qquad \textbf{14.2}$$

$$\text{cash ratio} = \frac{\text{cash}}{\text{current liabilities}} \qquad \textbf{14.3}$$

Financial leverage ratios

$$\text{debt ratio} = \frac{\text{total assets} - \text{total equity}}{\text{total assets}} \text{ or debt ratio} = \frac{\text{total liabilities}}{\text{total assets}} \qquad \textbf{14.4}$$

$$\text{times interest earned} = \frac{\text{EBIT}}{\text{interest expense}} \qquad \textbf{14.5}$$

$$\text{cash coverage ratio} = \frac{\text{EBIT} + \text{depreciation}}{\text{interest expense}} \qquad \textbf{14.6}$$

Asset management ratios

$$\text{inventory turnover} = \frac{\text{cost of goods sold}}{\text{inventory}} \qquad \textbf{14.7}$$

$$\text{days' sales in inventory} = \frac{365}{\text{inventory turnover}} \qquad \textbf{14.8}$$

$$\text{receivables turnover} = \frac{\text{sales}}{\text{accounts receivable}} \qquad \textbf{14.9}$$

$$\text{days' sales in receivables} = \frac{365}{\text{receivables turnover}} \qquad \textbf{14.10}$$

$$\text{total asset turnover} = \frac{\text{sales}}{\text{total assets}} \qquad \textbf{14.11}$$

Profitability ratios

$$\text{profit margin} = \frac{\text{net income}}{\text{sales}} \qquad \textbf{14.12}$$

$$\text{return on assets} = \frac{\text{net income}}{\text{total assets}} \qquad \textbf{14.13}$$

$$\text{return on equity} = \frac{\text{net income}}{\text{total owners' equity}} \qquad \textbf{14.14}$$

Market value ratios

$$\text{earnings per share} = \frac{\text{net income}}{\text{number of outstanding shares}} \qquad \textbf{14.15}$$

$$\text{price to earnings ratio} = \frac{\text{price per share}}{\text{earnings per share}} \qquad \textbf{14.16}$$

$$\text{price/earnings to growth ratio} = \frac{\text{price/earnings per share}}{\text{earnings growth rate} \times 100} \qquad \textbf{14.17}$$

$$\text{market to book ratio} = \frac{\text{market value per share}}{\text{book value per share}} \qquad \textbf{14.18}$$

DuPont analysis

$$\text{return on equity} = \frac{\text{net income}}{\text{sales}} \times \frac{\text{sales}}{\text{total assets}} \times \frac{\text{total assets}}{\text{total equity}} = \frac{\text{net income}}{\text{total equity}} \qquad \textbf{14.19}$$

Chapter 15
Raising Capital
AT A GLANCE

LO1 Describe the life cycle of a business.

One classification of a business life cycle involves five phases: start-up, growth, maturity, decline, and closing. This chapter uses the life-cycle approach as a convenient way to examine the most typical sources of capital available to a business at each stage.

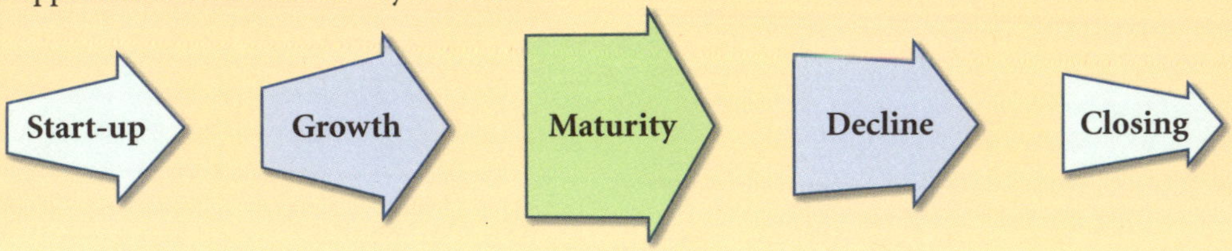

LO2 Understand the different sources of capital available to a start-up business and to a growing business.

There are five main sources of funding typically used by the start-up and growing business: personal funds, borrowed funds from family and friends, commercial bank loans, funds from business start-up programs such as the Small Business Administration, and angel financing or venture capital. Angel investors and venture capitalists loan money for new, high-risk ideas. Venture capitalists generally invest larger amounts of money from money pooled from a set of investors.

LO3 Explain the funding available to a stable or mature business.

Stable or mature businesses often need short-term financing and usually obtain it through commercial banks. Among the borrowing arrangements available are straight loans, discount loans, letter of credit or line of credit, and compensating-balance loans. For larger amounts of funding, a set of banks might coordinate a single loan, called a syndicated loan.

LO4 Explain how companies sell bonds in a capital market.

Once a business grows to a certain size and has established itself in its industry, the capital markets become a possible long-term financing source. Bonds may be issued through either private placement or public auction. The auction process is regulated by the SEC. Two of the most important documents related to bond sales are the prospectus, which provides the prospective buyer with general information about the company, and the indenture, which is the formal contract between the issuing company and the buyer.

LO5 Explain how companies sell stocks in a capital market.

The selling of common stock to the public raises funds by selling part of the company's ownership rights. The process of selling a company's stock for the first time is known as an initial public offering, and, as with the sale of bonds, is governed by the SEC. Most companies hire an investment bank to assist with the process. The investment bank becomes a partner in the process and is compensated by one of two ways. The first is through a best efforts arrangement in which the bank pledges to use its best efforts to sell shares but provides no guarantee of the amount sold. The second is through a firm commitment arrangement in which the bank guarantees a certain amount of money for the company and makes up any shortfalls.

LO6 Examine some special forms of financing: commercial paper and banker's acceptance.

One way to borrow directly from the public without going through the SEC approval process is through the issuing of commercial paper, a discounted note sold by a company to an investor with principal and interest repaid within 270 days. A banker's acceptance is a short-term credit investment created by a company and guaranteed by a bank; it is usually used for acquiring assets that self-liquidate during the normal business cycle.

LO7 Describe the options and regulations for closing a business.

Both successful and unsuccessful businesses can cease operations by liquidating assets, paying off liabilities, and distributing remaining funds to the owners. Sometimes a firm must face bankruptcy, a state of financial distress in which the company cannot pay its debts. Chapter 7 bankruptcy deals with straight liquidation of assets and distributing the proceeds to legal claimants. Chapter 11 bankruptcy involves restructuring of the company's debt and reorganization of its business affairs so that the company can remain in business.

Chapter 16
Capital Structure
AT A GLANCE

LO1 Explain why borrowing rates are different based on ability to repay loans.

Repaying a loan requires cash, and different firms generate cash more consistently and thus can meet their debt repayment consistently. The more inconsistent the cash flows, the greater the probability a firm may not have sufficient cash on hand when it is time to repay all or part of a loan. Therefore, firms that have consistent cash flow can borrow at lower rates.

LO2 Demonstrate the benefits of borrowing.

When a company borrows in the capital markets at one rate and can invest in a project that returns a higher rate, the owners of the company earn the difference between the borrowing rate and the investment rate. That is the advantage of *financial leverage*, the degree to which a firm or individual uses borrowed money to make money.

LO3 Calculate the break-even EBIT for different capital structures.

To calculate the break-even EBIT for different capital structures, set the earnings per share of each capital structure equal to each other and solve for the EBIT. For example,

$$\frac{\text{EBIT}}{400} = \frac{\text{EBIT} - \$500}{200}$$

The first capital structure has 400 shares outstanding and no debt payments. The second capital structure has 200 shares outstanding and debt requiring $500 in annual interest expense.

LO4 Explain the appropriate borrowing strategy under the pecking order hypothesis.

Under the pecking order hypothesis, a firm should use internal funds first; if external funds are required, it should borrow from the cheapest source until that source is exhausted. If more borrowing is needed, the firm progressively moves to a higher and higher cost of borrowing until it exhausts all potential funds.

LO5 Develop the arguments for the optimal capital structure in a world of no taxes and no bankruptcy and in a world of corporate taxes with no bankruptcy costs.

In a world of no taxes and no bankruptcy, the borrowing mix of a firm is irrelevant. In a world of taxes and no bankruptcy, the optimal borrowing choice is all debt. Using debt reduces the government's share of the pie to the benefit of the owners. With 100% debt, it is possible to completely eliminate the government's share.

LO6 Understand the static theory of capital structure and the trade-off between the benefits of the tax shield and the cost of bankruptcy.

In a world of taxes and bankruptcy, financial distress costs rise as more and more debt is acquired by the firm. This rising cost eventually offsets the benefits of the increasing tax shield. A firm will find its optimal capital structure—the maximum amount of debt financing—when the marginal benefits of the tax shield equal the marginal costs of financial distress.

Chapter 16
Capital Structure
AT A GLANCE

KEY EQUATIONS

$$V_E = V_L \quad \textbf{16.1}$$

$$WACC = \left(\frac{E}{V} \times R_e\right) + \left(\frac{D}{V} \times R_d \times (1 - T_c)\right) \quad \textbf{16.2}$$

$$WACC = R_a = \left(\frac{E}{V} \times R_e\right) + \left(\frac{D}{V} \times R_d\right) \quad \textbf{16.3}$$

$$R_e = R_a + (R_a - R_d) \times \frac{D}{E} \quad \textbf{16.4}$$

$$V_L = V_E + (D \times T_c) \quad \textbf{16.5}$$

NOTATION FOR CHAPTER 16

D	total amount of debt
E	total amount of equity
R_a	required return on assets
R_d	required return on debt
R_e	required return on equity
T_c	corporate tax rate
V	value of the debt and equity
V_E	value of an all-equity firm
V_L	value of a levered firm
$WACC$	weighted average cost of capital

Chapter 17
Dividends, Dividend Policy, and Stock Splits
AT A GLANCE

LO1 Understand the formal process for paying dividends and differentiate between the most common types.

Cash dividends are payments of cash to the owners of the company. As such, they are taxable as income. At one time, nearly 85% of all firms listed on the NYSE paid cash dividends on a regular basis. With the downturn in the economy in the early 2000s, that number fell to around 65% and it continued to fall with the financial meltdown of 2008. The board of directors declares the size and timing of the dividend. Payment of dividends is made to all shareholders who are listed as current owners on the date of record. The most common dividend is the quarterly cash dividend. There are also special or extra dividends that are paid infrequently and a liquidating dividend that is the final payment to a shareholder.

LO2 Explain individual preferences and issues surrounding different dividend policies.

Individuals may want a high-dividend-payout policy or a low-dividend-payout/no-dividend-payout policy. The high-dividend-payout clientele usually like the high dividends because they are used as part of their regular income. The low-dividend-payout clientele are usually trying to lower or postpone taxes on the distribution of cash dividends.

LO3 Explain how a company selects its dividend policy.

A company selects its dividend policy based on the preferences of the shareholders and the anticipated stream of cash flow available for dividends. A company will typically pick a dividend level that can be maintained into the foreseeable future so that it does not have to lower dividends in the future. A reduction in dividends is usually considered a bad signal about future earnings.

LO4 Understand stock splits and reverse splits and why companies use them.

Stock splits and reverse splits are used to move the current stock price into a preferred trading range. There is no direct increase in wealth for a shareholder, but there may be increased liquidity, and shareholders like liquid stocks.

LO5 Understand stock repurchases and dividend reinvestment programs.

Stock repurchases are another way to pay cash dividends, with the added feature that shareholders can either choose to participate in the dividend distribution by selling some of their shares or choose not to participate by holding on to all their shares. The shareholders determine what size of cash dividend they want by the number of shares they choose to sell. In a dividend reinvestment program, a shareholder's entitled cash dividend is used to buy shares in the company, typically without transaction costs. In this way, a shareholder can increase share holdings without dealing with a broker or using other standard ways to buy stock, transactions that typically have commission or other costs attached to them.

Chapter 18
International Financial Management
AT A GLANCE

LO1 Understand cultural, business, and political differences in business practices.

Multinational companies face many difficulties in the management of international business operations, including the following:

- Cultural risk can stem from cultural differences. Some issues related to cultural risk include differences in ownership structure, differences in human resource norms, the religious observations and heritage of the host country, nepotism and corrupt business practices in the host country, and protection of intellectual property rights.
- Business risk can arise from differences in business practices and the economic conditions of the host country.
- Political risk can involve changes in the government of the host country (for example, the nationalization of foreign assets as foreign governments take ownership of the local business operation).

LO2 Calculate exchange rates, cross rates, and forward rates.

Exchange rates are a function of purchasing power parity. Purchasing power parity means that the price of similar goods is the same regardless of which currency one uses to buy the goods. Cross rates are the exchange rates of two foreign currencies based on the exchange rate of those two currencies in the home or domestic currency. The forward rate is the anticipated exchange rate based on the expected inflation rates of the two currencies' home countries.

LO3 Understand transaction exposure, operating exposure, and translation exposure.

Transaction exposure is the potential loss of value when a future conversion from a foreign currency into a domestic currency takes place at a time when exchange rates have moved against the home currency. Operating exposure is the risk of loss of profit over time from a foreign operation as the foreign country's inflation rate outpaces the home country's inflation rate. Translation exposure is the potential loss on paper when financial statements from foreign operations are consolidated into domestic financial statements and different exchange rates (historical versus current) are used for different items on the financial statements.

LO4 Apply net present value to foreign projects.

The NPV capital budgeting decision model can be applied to a foreign project using either the home currency and the home discount rate or the foreign currency and the foreign discount rate. Both provide the same net present value. To convert the foreign currency into domestic currency before applying the NPV with the home discount rate, it is necessary to calculate forward exchange rates based on the expected inflation of the foreign country and the home country.

Chapter 18
International Financial Management
AT A GLANCE

KEY EQUATIONS

$$\text{direct or American rate} = \frac{\text{U.S.\$}}{1\text{ FC}} \qquad \textbf{18.1}$$

$$\frac{1}{\text{American rate}} = \text{European rate} = \frac{\text{FC}}{\$1} \qquad \textbf{18.2}$$

$$\text{direct rate foreign currency 1} \times \text{indirect rate foreign currency 2} = \text{cross rate of foreign currency 1 to foreign currency 2} \qquad \textbf{18.3}$$

$$\text{forward indirect rate} = \text{current indirect rate} \times \frac{1 + inf_f}{1 + inf_h} \qquad \textbf{18.4}$$

$$\text{forward indirect rate}_T = \text{current indirect rate} \times \left(\frac{1 + inf_f}{1 + inf_h}\right)^T \qquad \textbf{18.5}$$

$$\text{nominal rate}_h - \text{inflation rate}_h = \text{nominal rate}_f - \text{inflation rate}_f \quad \text{or}$$

$$\text{real rate}_{\text{home country}} = \text{real rate}_{\text{foreign country}} \qquad \textbf{18.6}$$

$$\text{discount rate} = \text{real rate} + \text{inflation} + \text{risk premium of project} \qquad \textbf{18.7}$$

NOTATION FOR CHAPTER 18

FC	foreign currency
inf_f	inflation in foreign country
inf_h	inflation in home country